This Book Comes With Lots of
FREE Online Resources

Nolo's award-winning website has a page dedicated just to this book. Here you can:

KEEP UP TO DATE. When there are important changes to the information in this book, we'll post updates.

GET DISCOUNTS ON NOLO PRODUCTS. Get discounts on hundreds of books, forms, and software.

READ BLOGS. Get the latest info from Nolo authors' blogs.

LISTEN TO PODCASTS. Listen to authors discuss timely issues on topics that interest you.

WATCH VIDEOS. Get a quick introduction to a legal topic with our short videos.

And that's not all.
Nolo.com contains thousands of articles on everyday legal and business issues, plus a plain-English law dictionary, all written by Nolo experts and available for free. You'll also find more useful **books, software, online apps, downloadable forms,** plus a **lawyer directory.**

NOLO
LAW for ALL

Get updates and more at
www.nolo.com/back-of-book/IMEZ.html

18th Edition

U.S. Immigration Made Easy

Ilona Bray, J.D.
Updated by Attorney Richard Link

44.99

EIGHTEENTH EDITION	JANUARY 2017
Cover Design	SUSAN PUTNEY
Production	SUSAN PUTNEY
Proofreading	ROBERT WELLS
Index	THÉRÈSE SHERE
Printing	BANG PRINTING

ISSN: 1055-9647 (print)

ISSN: 2326-0041 (epub ebook)

ISBN: 978-1-4133-2367-2 (pbk)

ISBN: 978-1-4133-2368-9 (epub book)

This book covers only United States law, unless it specifically states otherwise.

Please note

We believe accurate, plain-English legal information should help you solve many of your own legal problems. But this text is not a substitute for personalized advice from a knowledgeable lawyer. If you want the help of a trained professional—and we'll always point out situations in which we think that's a good idea—consult an attorney licensed to practice in your state.

Acknowledgments

This book was originally authored by Laurence A. Canter and Martha S. Siegel. For help in updating and revising it for recent editions, special thanks are owed to:

Richard Link, an attorney practicing in Rochester, New York, who lent his years of immigration law and editing experience to the considerable task of reviewing and updating this 18th edition. Richard went above and beyond the basics, adding useful tips and insights to make this book more comprehensive than ever.

Daniel Horne, an attorney with the firm Jackson & Hertogs, LLP, in San Francisco, California (www.jackson-hertogs.com), who provided excellent information and practice tips for recent previous editions.

Chris Pooley, an attorney practicing in Avon, Colorado, who shared his expertise and experience with H-2B visas.

Emily Doskow, an attorney in private practice and Nolo author/editor (based in Berkeley, California), for her contribution regarding international adoptions by same-sex couples.

Jimmy Go, of the law firm Go & Laster (Portland, Oregon), for his contribution regarding investor visas.

Julia Day Marquez, of the law firm Fallon, Bixby, Cheng & Lee in San Francisco, California (www.fbcl-visa.com), for her contribution regarding labor certification.

Under Nolo's roof, thanks go to the Production Department for doing the layout.

About the Authors

Ilona Bray, J.D., came to the practice of immigration law through her long interest in international human rights. Before joining Nolo as legal editor in charge of immigration, she ran a solo law practice and worked for various nonprofit immigration agencies, as an attorney at the International Institute of the East Bay (Oakland) and a Goldmark Fellow at Northwest Immigrant Rights Project (Seattle). Ms. Bray was also an intern in the legal office of Amnesty International's International Secretariat in London. Ms. Bray is a member of the American Immigration Lawyers Association (AILA). She received her law degree in 1990 from the University of Washington along with an M.A. in East Asian Studies, and her undergraduate degree from Bryn Mawr College. She has authored numerous other books for Nolo, including *Becoming a U.S. Citizen: A Guide to the Law, Exam & Interview*; *Fiancé & Marriage Visas: A Couple's Guide to U.S. Immigration*; and *Effective Fundraising for Nonprofits: Real-World Strategies That Work.*

Richard Link practices immigration law as Senior Counsel with Tully Rinckey, PLLC, in its Rochester, New York, office. He currently serves as treasurer of the Upstate New York Chapter of the American Immigration Lawyers Association. Mr. Link is a former legal editor at the national office of the American Immigration Lawyers Association (AILA) and at Thomson Reuters (West). Mr. Link received his law degree in 1990 from the University of California Davis School of Law (King Hall), where he served as senior research editor for the U.C. Davis Law Review and earned the certificate in public interest law. His undergraduate degree in Language Studies was obtained at the University of California, Santa Cruz, in 1986.

Table of Contents

Your Immigration Companion

If you're considering immigrating to the United States, or are helping someone who is, then this book was written for you. Unlike many books about immigration law, this one was written for real people, not for lawyers. We try to give you a realistic view of your immigration possibilities and how to succeed in reaching your goals.

But why is this book so thick—especially considering that the title promises it will be "easy"? Don't worry, you won't have to read the whole book. It's just that we cover a lot of ground, including some categories of visas and green cards that other books don't discuss. Also, the original law that we're trying to describe for you is not easy at all—it contains many categories of potential visas and green cards, complex criteria for who qualifies, and paperwork-intensive application procedures. All of that takes space to explain! So we start the book with an overview of your possibilities, then direct you toward one or two particular chapters that will help you understand what lies ahead if you apply.

Some people will find that they don't qualify for U.S. immigration at all, or at least not yet. Nevertheless, huge numbers of people successfully come from other countries to the U.S. every year—approximately one million receive green cards, and 30 million receive temporary visas (such as tourist, work, and student visas). With the right information and preparation you can be one of them. This book will help you:

- learn whether you match the criteria to receive either a green card (permanent residence) or a temporary (nonimmigrant) visa
- learn what difficulties you'll have to overcome
- strategize the fastest and safest way through the application process
- deal with bureaucrats and delays, and
- know when to find a lawyer.

Think of this book as your legal companion, providing practical and supportive advice and information along the way and helping you find a warm welcome in the United States.

What Doesn't This Book Cover?

You'll find loads of useful information in this book—but it's plenty thick already, and we had to leave a few topics out. In particular, removal and deportation defense are not covered here. (Definitely get a lawyer's help if you are facing immigration court proceedings.) Nor are the immigration law implications of criminal convictions covered.

Get Updates and More at This Book's Companion Page on Nolo.com

When there are important changes to the information in this book, we'll post updates online, on a page dedicated to this book

www.nolo.com/back-of-book/IMEZ.html

You'll find other useful information there, too, including author blogs, and podcasts.

Getting Started: U.S. Immigration Eligibility and Procedures

Where to Begin on Your Path Toward Immigration

f you've already tried to research how to immigrate to the United States, you may have come away more confused than enlightened. We've heard immigrants ask frustrated questions like, "Are they trying to punish me for doing things legally?" or "I can't tell whether they want to let me in or keep me out!"

The trouble is, the U.S. immigration system is a little like a mythical creature with two heads. One head is smiling and granting people the right to live or work in the United States, temporarily or permanently—especially people who:

- will pump money into the U.S. economy (such as tourists, students, and investors)
- can fill gaps in the U.S. workforce (mostly skilled workers)
- are joining up with close family members who are already U.S. citizens or permanent residents, or
- need protection from persecution or other humanitarian crises.

This creature's other head wears a frown. It is afraid that the U.S. will be overrun by huge numbers of immigrants, and so it tries to keep out anyone who:

- doesn't fit the narrow eligibility categories set forth in the U.S. immigration laws

- has a criminal record
- is a threat to U.S. ideology or national security
- has spent a long time in the U.S. illegally or committed other immigration violations
- is attempting fraud in order to immigrate, or
- will not earn enough money to stay off government assistance.

Not surprisingly, these two heads don't always work together very well. You may find that, even when you know you have a right to visit, live, or work in the U.S. and you're trying your best to fill out the applications and complete your case properly, you feel as if you're being treated like a criminal. The frowning head doesn't care. It views you as just another number and as no great loss if your application fails—or is, literally, lost in the files of thousands of other applications.

CAUTION
Have you heard people say that a U.S. citizen could simply invite a friend from overseas to live here? Those days are gone. Now, every immigrant has to find a legal category that he or she fits within, deal with demanding application forms and procedures, and pass security and other checks.

CAUTION

Almost everyone should consult an experienced immigration attorney before submitting an application. Unless your case presents no complications whatsoever, it's best to have an attorney confirm that you haven't overlooked anything. However, by preparing yourself with the information in this book, you can save money and make sure you're using a good attorney for the right services.

EXAMPLE: An American woman was engaged to a man from Mexico and figured, since she herself had been to law school, that she didn't need an attorney's help. She read that a foreign-born person who was in the U.S. on a tourist visa could get married and then apply for a green card within the United States. Unfortunately, what she didn't realize was that this possibility only works for people who decide to get married *after* entering the United States. *Applying* for a tourist visa with the idea of coming to the U.S. to get married and get a green card amounts to visa fraud and can ruin a person's chances of immigrating. Are you already confused? The U.S. immigration system doesn't always make a lot of sense. This is why an attorney's help is often needed—to get you through legal hoops that you'd never imagined existed.

A. Roadmap to U.S. Immigration

This book will cover a lot of territory— almost all of U.S. immigration law, including your basic rights, strategies, and the procedures for getting you where you need to go. Any time you cover this much ground, it helps to have a road map— particularly so you'll know which subjects or chapters you can skip entirely.

Take a look at the imaginary map below, then read the following subsections to orient yourself to the main topics on the map.

As you can see, the first stop along the way is the *Inadmissibility Gate*. This gate represents a legal problem that can stop your path to a visa or green card before you've even started. If, for example, you have committed certain crimes, been infected with certain contagious diseases, appear likely to need welfare or government assistance, have violated U.S. immigration laws, or match another description on the U.S. government's list of concerns, you are considered "inadmissible." That means you won't be allowed any type of U.S. visa or green card, except under special circumstances or with legal forgiveness called a waiver. This gate gets closed

Roadmap to U.S. Immigration

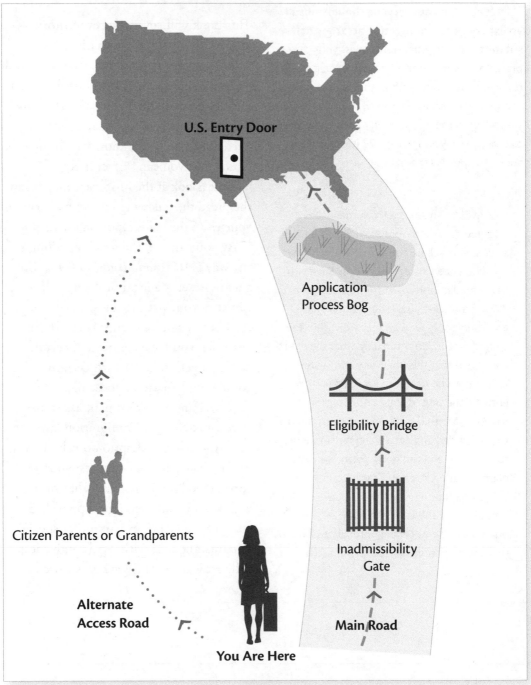

on a lot of people who lived in the U.S. illegally for more than six months, which can create either a three-year or ten-year bar to immigrating. Even if you think you haven't done anything wrong, please read Chapter 3 for more on the problem of inadmissibility.

If you get past the inadmissibility gate, the next stop along your theoretical journey is the *Eligibility Bridge*. This is where you must answer the question, "What type of visa or green card are you eligible for?" Answering this question will involve some research on your part. You might already know the answer—for example, if you've just married a U.S. citizen, it's pretty obvious that you want to apply for a green card on this basis and should read the appropriate chapter of this book (Chapter 7). Or, if your main goal is to attend college in the U.S., then you probably know that you need a student visa, and can proceed straight to the chapter covering that topic (Chapter 22).

If you don't already know you're eligible for a certain type of visa or green card, however, then start by reading Section B, below, which reviews the possibilities for spending time in the U.S. and directs you to the appropriate chapters for follow-up.

You'll see that this book covers more than just permanent green cards—we know that not everyone will either want,

or be eligible to receive, the right to live in the U.S. his or her whole life. There are many useful ways to stay in the U.S. temporarily, for example on a student or employment-based visa. And even if you don't fit into one of the usual categories, there may be an emergency or other special category that helps you.

Not many people will travel down the *Citizen Parents or Grandparents Alternate Access Road*. It's for the lucky few who, after doing a little research, realize that they are already U.S. citizens because their parents or grandparents had U.S. citizenship. Okay, we admit that this is rare. Most people would not be picking up a book on immigration if they were already U.S. citizens. Nevertheless, a few people are surprised to find that, because their parents were either born in the U.S. or became U.S. citizens later (possibly because their own parents were U.S. citizens), they are already U.S. citizens themselves—in which case they can put this book back down and go get a U.S. passport. See Chapter 2 for a full discussion of who can claim U.S. citizenship through parents.

The next stop along your journey is the *Application Process Bog*. We added this because, even after you realize that you match the eligibility requirements for a U.S. visa or green card, you can't just march into a U.S. immigration office

What You'll Need to Know

We try not to use confusing legal language in this book. However, there are a few words that will be helpful for you to know, especially if you look at other books or websites. For further definitions, see the Glossary at the back of this book.

Citizen (U.S.). A person who owes allegiance to the U.S. government, is entitled to its protection, and enjoys the highest level of rights due to members of U.S. society. A person can become a U.S. citizen through birth in the United States or its territories; through parents who are citizens; or through naturalization (after applying for citizenship and passing the citizenship exam). Citizens cannot have their status taken away except for certain extraordinary reasons.

Immigrant. Though the general public usually calls any foreign-born newcomer to the United States an immigrant, the U.S. government prefers to think of immigrants as only including those people who have attained permanent residence or a green card.

Nonimmigrant. Everyone who comes to the United States legally but with only a short-term intent to stay is considered a nonimmigrant. For instance, students and tourists are nonimmigrants.

Green card. This slang term refers to the identification card (printed in green) carried by lawful permanent residents of the United States.

Lawful permanent resident. A green card holder. This is a person who has been approved to live in the United States for an unlimited amount of time. However, the status can be taken away for certain reasons, such as having committed a crime or made one's home outside the United States. Usually after five years, a permanent resident can apply for U.S. citizenship. That number drops to three years if the immigrant has been married to and living with a U.S. citizen all that time.

Visa. A right to come to the border and apply for entry into the United States. An immigrant visa allows someone to enter the U.S. permanently; a nonimmigrant visa allows one to enter for a short-term, temporary stay. Physically, the visa usually appears as a stamp in the applicant's passport, given by a U.S. consulate overseas. Having a visa doesn't guarantee you'll actually be able to enter the U.S., because U.S. immigration officials at the border must give you the final permission to do so. But assuming you pass this inspection, your visa is your ticket in.

If you forget these words, or encounter other words that you don't understand, check the list at the back of this book.

and claim your rights on the spot. The application process involves intensive document collection, form preparation, and generally molding your life around monitoring the handling of your case until you've gotten what you want. Even if you do your part correctly, most visas and green cards take a much longer time to obtain than you would ever imagine—anywhere from a few months to several years.

Some people never make it through the bog, simply because they fail to adequately prepare their applications or to respond to government follow-up requests on time. Others get bogged down through no fault of their own because the U.S. government loses track of their application. Dealing with bureaucracy and delays is such a large concern that we've devoted a whole chapter of this book to it: Chapter 4.

And you should also read Chapter 6, on how to find and work with a high-quality immigration attorney. Attorneys are familiar with the difficulties of the application process, and the good ones will have access to inside phone numbers or email addresses to use when there's a problem. You only have one chance at getting this right, so it's often worth paying the money to hire an attorney.

If you make it this far, then the door to U.S. immigration will be opened to you.

B. The Typical Application Process

Now let's assume that you are not inadmissible and that you have what it takes to be eligible for either a permanent green card or a temporary U.S. visa. Although we'll give you more detail about the application processes later in this book, here's a preview of your main steps:

- deciding whether you'll need legal help to complete your application
- if you're applying for a permanent green card, or in some cases a temporary work visa, waiting while your U.S. family member or employer fills out what's called a "visa petition," proving either that you are the person's family member or have been offered a job; and then waiting even longer for the U.S. immigration authorities to approve the petition
- if, in the category under which you're applying, only limited numbers of visas or green cards are given out every year, waiting until the people in line ahead of you have received their visas or green cards (which can take years)
- filling out your own set of application forms, collecting documents, and submitting them to either a U.S. consulate in your home country or to the U.S. immigration authorities

- tracking your application to make sure it doesn't get lost in the system
- attending an interview at a consulate outside of the U.S. or a U.S. immigration office, at which your application is reviewed and you answer questions
- receiving either a visa for entry into the U.S. or a green card or another right to stay in the U.S. (unless you are denied, in which case, you may want to reapply), and finally
- entering the U.S. (if you're not already here), protecting your status, and working toward the next step, if any. (If you received a green card, you may want to work toward U.S. citizenship, the highest and most secure status you can receive.)

One issue that will make a big difference in how your application proceeds is whether you are currently living inside or outside the United States. The U.S. has government offices to handle U.S. immigration applications both outside the U.S. (at U.S. consulates) and within (at USCIS district offices and service centers). However, not all of these offices handle all types of immigration applications. See "Which Government Office Will Be Handling Your Immigration Application," below.

What's more, many of the people who would prefer to file their immigration applications in the United States— because they have been living here for many years, perhaps illegally—will find that they are not allowed to do so. We will discuss this at length in Chapter 3.

The short explanation is that, if you either entered the United States illegally (not with a visa or another entry document or right), overstayed a visa, or you have worked here illegally, you cannot (with a few exceptions), use the services of a USCIS immigration office. Instead, you must leave the U.S. and go to a U.S. consulate to make your visa or green card request. That creates a huge problem for people who have lived unlawfully in the United States for more than six months after January 1, 1997. See Chapter 3 for details.

C. Immigration Eligibility Self-Quiz

Since we don't know who you are, we're going make a very broad assumption: you're looking for any possible way to spend time in the United States, preferably permanently.

The following quiz will help you find out what type of visa or green card you might be eligible for and which chapter of this book to read for more information.

Question	Possible rights to a visa or green card	For more information
Are you from Canada or Mexico?	You have rights and visa possibilities that others don't.	See Chapter 5 for more on immigration possibilities for Canadians and Mexicans.
Are you engaged to marry a U.S. citizen and living overseas?	You may be eligible for a fiancé visa, allowing you to enter the United States in order to get married.	See Chapter 8 more on obtaining a fiancé visa.
Do you have any close family members (parents, husband or wife, children over 21, or brothers and sisters) who are U.S. citizens?	You may qualify for a green card if one of them is willing to petition for you.	See Chapter 7 for more information on obtaining a green card through family.
Do you have any close family members (parents, husband, or wife) who are U.S. permanent residents (green card holders)?	You may qualify for a green card if one of them is willing to petition for you.	See Chapter 7 for more information on obtaining a green card through family.
Are you a U.S. citizen who wishes to adopt a child from overseas?	You may be able to adopt an orphan or a child under age 16.	See Chapter 7 for more information on obtaining green cards for adopted children.
Do you have a job offer from a U.S. employer?	You may be able to obtain a green card, if you have the right background and qualifications, if the employer is willing to sponsor you, and in most cases, if no U.S. workers are willing or able to take the job.	See Chapter 9 for more information on getting a green card through employment.

NOTE: Some job offers may qualify you for temporary work visas; keep a lookout for these further on in this quiz.

Question	Possible rights to a visa or green card	For more information
Do you (or your spouse or parents) come from a country on the State Department's list of countries eligible to participate in the diversity visa lottery?	You can enter the visa lottery once a year. Winners who meet the educational and other qualifying criteria can apply for green cards.	See Chapter 10 for more on how the visa lottery works.
Do you have $500,000 or more to invest in the creation or expansion of a U.S. business?	You may be eligible for an investment-based green card.	See Chapter 11 for more information on obtaining an investment-based green card.
Are you a member of the clergy or a religious worker wishing to come to the U.S. to work for the same religious organization that you've already been working for over the last two years?	You may qualify for a green card as a special immigrant (or for a temporary "R" visa, described below).	See Chapter 12 for more information on obtaining a green card as a special immigrant.

Permanent Green Cards

Question	Possible rights to a visa or green card	For more information
Are you a graduate of a foreign medical school who came to the United States before January 10, 1978, and are you still living in the United States?	You may qualify for a green card as a special immigrant.	See Chapter 12 for more information on obtaining a green card as a special immigrant.
Are you a former overseas U.S. government worker or a retired employee of an international organization, and have you worked half of the last seven years in the United States?	You may qualify for a green card as a special immigrant.	See Chapter 12 for more information on obtaining a green card as a special immigrant.
Are you helping a child who is living in the U.S. and has been declared dependent on a juvenile court and eligible for long-term foster or state agency care?	The child may qualify for a green card as a special immigrant.	See Chapter 12 for more information on the child's obtaining a green card as a special immigrant.
Have you served in the U.S. armed services for a total of 12 years or more after October 15, 1978?	You may qualify for a green card as a special immigrant.	See Chapter 12 for more information on obtaining a green card as a special immigrant.
Are you fleeing a country (non-U.S.) where you have faced or fear persecution, either by the government or by someone the government can't control—and is that persecution because of your race, religion, nationality, political opinion, or membership in a particular social group?	You may (if still outside the U.S.) qualify as a refugee, which would allow you to travel to the United States and apply for a green card after one year.	See Chapter 13 for more information on obtaining refugee status from overseas.
Are you in the United States now, but fear returning to your home country because you have faced or still fear persecution, either by the government or someone the government can't control—and is that persecution because of your race, religion, nationality, political opinion, or membership in a particular social group?	You may apply for asylum within your first year in the U.S., which would allow you to stay in the United States, and apply for a green card after one year.	See Chapter 13 for more information on obtaining asylum.
Have you lived in the U.S. continuously since January 1972?	You may be eligible for a green card based on registry.	See a lawyer for help on obtaining a registry-based green card.
Have you said "no" to all of the above questions?		See an immigration attorney to reevaluate whether you qualify for any type of green card.

Permanent Green Cards

Question	Possible rights to a visa or green card	For more information
Are you interested in a short trip to the U.S. for pleasure, business, or medical care?	You may qualify for a B-1 or B-2 visitor visa.	See Chapter 15 for more information on obtaining B visas.
Has a U.S. employer offered you a job requiring highly specialized knowledge gained from a university degree or equivalent work experience?	You may qualify for an H-1B work visa (good for up to six years).	See Chapter 16 for more information on obtaining H-1B visas.
Has a U.S. employer offered you a temporary or seasonal nonagricultural job, whether skilled or unskilled?	You may qualify for an H-2B work visa (good for up to one year).	See Chapter 17 for more information on obtaining H-2B visas.
Does a U.S. company plan to offer you on-the-job training in order to help your career in your home country?	You may qualify for an H-3 visa (good for the length of the training, up to two years).	See Chapter 18 for more information on obtaining H-3 visas.
Does your company, which has offices both inside and outside the U.S., want to transfer you to the U.S. as an owner, executive, manager, or an employee with special knowledge?	You may qualify for an L-1 visa (usually good for five to seven years).	See Chapter 19 for more information on obtaining L-1 visas.
Are you a part owner or key employee of a company that trades with the U.S., and coming to the U.S. to trade or help develop or direct the company's operations?	You may qualify for an E-1 treaty trader visa (initially good for up to two years).	See Chapter 20 for more information on obtaining E-1 visas.
Are you a part owner or key employee of a U.S. company supported by investment from natives of your home country, and coming to the U.S. to work for that company?	You may qualify for an E-2 treaty investor visa (initially good for up to two years).	See Chapter 21 for more information on obtaining E-2 visas.
Have you been accepted to study at an academic or vocational school in the U.S.?	You may qualify for an F-1 (academic student) or M-1 (vocational student) visa (good for the length of your studies except that M-1s are limited to a one-year stay).	See Chapter 22 for more information on obtaining F-1 and M-1 visas.
Have you been accepted to participate in an exchange program in the U.S.?	You may qualify for a J-1 exchange visitor visa (good for the length of the program).	See Chapter 23 for more information on obtaining J-1 visas.
Has a U.S. employer offered you a job based on either your extraordinary ability in the arts, sciences, education, business, or athletics; or as a religious worker?	You may qualify for an O, P, or R visa (good for the time period necessary to accomplish an event or activity, up to three years for O and P visas, and five years in the case of R visas).	See Chapter 24 for more information on obtaining O, P, or R visas.
Have you said "no" to all of the above questions?		See an attorney to see whether you have overlooked any possibility.

Temporary Visas

Which Government Office Will Be Handling Your Immigration Application

Getting your green card or nonimmigrant visa may require dealing with more than one U.S. government agency, and maybe more than one office within that agency. The possibilities include the following:

- The **U.S. Department of State** (DOS, at www.travel.state.gov), through U.S. embassies and consulates located around the world, and its Kentucky Consular Center, which handles the diversity visa lottery and coordinates USCIS petition approval with the embassies and consulates. If you're coming from outside of the U.S., you'll be dealing primarily with a U.S. consulate—and if you're currently in the U.S., you, too, may have to travel to a consulate to complete your application. Not all U.S. consulates provide visa-processing services. To find more information about the U.S. consulate nearest to your home, either check the phone book of your country's capital city, or go to www.usembassy. gov. Note that you cannot normally apply for an immigrant visa (permanent residence) in a U.S. embassy or consulate *outside* your home country, unless the U.S. has no diplomatic relationship with the government of your homeland. You may be able to apply for *nonimmigrant* visas (such as a tourist visa) in a third country, so long as you have never overstayed your permitted time in the U.S., even by one day.

- The **National Visa Center** (NVC), a private company under contract to the DOS for the purpose of handling case files during certain intermediate parts of the green card application process. After USCIS approves a visa petition by a U.S.-based family member or company, the NVC is given the file and handles the case until it's time to forward the file to the appropriate U.S. consulate or USCIS district office.

- **U.S. Citizenship and Immigration Services** (USCIS, formerly called INS, at www.uscis.gov), an agency of the Department of Homeland Security (DHS). Even if you're living outside the United States, you may have to deal with USCIS, particularly if you're applying for a green card rather than a temporary visa. Most green card applications begin by a U.S.-based family member or company filing a visa petition with USCIS. USCIS has various types of offices that handle immigration applications, including Service Centers and Lockboxes (large processing facilities that serve a wide region, which you cannot visit in person), district offices (which interact with the public by providing forms and information and holding interviews), suboffices (like district offices, but smaller and with more limited services), Application Support Centers

Which Government Office Will Be Handling Your Immigration Application (continued)

(where you go to have fingerprints taken and, in some cases, pick up forms or turn in applications), and asylum offices (where interviews on applications for asylum are held).

- **Customs and Border Protection** (CBP at www.cbp.gov), also under DHS, responsible for patrolling the U.S. borders. This includes meeting you at an airport or other U.S. entry point when you arrive with your visa and doing a last check to make sure that your visa paperwork is in order and that you didn't obtain it through fraud or by providing false information.
- The **U.S. Department of Labor** (DOL at www.dol.gov), through its Employment and Training Administration, at www.doleta.gov. If your visa or green card application is based on a job with a U.S. employer, certain parts of the paperwork may have to be filed with and ruled on by the DOL. The DOL's role is to make sure that hiring immigrant workers doesn't make it harder for U.S. workers to get a job and that you're being paid a fair wage (one that doesn't act to bring down the wages of U.S. workers).

Although you needn't learn a lot about these various agencies, it's important to keep track of which one has your application as it makes its way through the pipeline. This is especially true if you ever change your address, because you should advise the office that actually has control of your application.

Now that you have some idea whether there's a visa or green card that you qualify for, please go on to read either Chapter 2 (if you have parents or grandparents who were U.S. citizens) or Chapter 3, concerning inadmissibility. Then proceed straight to the chapter concerning the visa or green card you're interested in.

If, after reading the detailed eligibility requirements, you confirm that you qualify, don't forget to read Chapter 4, with crucial advice on handling the paperwork and dealing with bureaucrats, and Chapter 6 on when and how to find a good lawyer.

Are You Already a U.S. Citizen?

Most people who are U.S. citizens already know it, either because they were born in the U.S. or because they successfully applied to become naturalized citizens. However, U.S. citizenship can be obtained in two additional, less well-known ways, namely:

- birth outside the U.S. to U.S. citizen parents (acquisition), or
- citizenship or naturalization of parents after the child has obtained a green card in the U.S. (derivation).

Many people born or living outside the U.S. are already U.S. citizens but don't know it. The key to acquisition of citizenship is having U.S. citizens in your direct line of ancestry. Even though you were born elsewhere and your U.S. ancestors have not lived in the U.S. for a long time, U.S. citizenship may have still been passed down the line.

Derivation of citizenship helps people who do live in the U.S., but who didn't realize that minor children with green cards can acquire citizenship automatically, without having to apply for naturalization.

TIP

You can't lose your citizenship just by living outside of the U.S. for too long. People who were born in the U.S. but have lived most of their lives in other countries sometimes believe that their long absence from the U.S. and voting or military activities elsewhere have stripped them of U.S. citizenship. That's not the case—anyone born with U.S. citizenship will retain it for life unless he or she performs some act to intentionally lose it, such as filing an oath of renunciation.

RESOURCE

This book does not describe how people with green cards can apply to become naturalized citizens. For complete information on your eligibility and the process, see *Becoming a U.S. Citizen: A Guide to the Law, Exam & Interview*, by Ilona Bray (Nolo).

What If You Were Born "Out of Wedlock" to a U.S. Citizen Father?

In many cases, your right to U.S. citizenship may depend on your relationship to a U.S. citizen father. However, if your parents weren't married at the time you were born, the laws of the time may refer to you as "illegitimate," meaning in legal terms that you have no recognized father.

As you'll see in the sections below, your right to claim citizenship may depend on your providing evidence that your father took the actions necessary to satisfy the legitimation law of your birth country. Legitimation laws require fathers to legally acknowledge their children.

A. Acquisition of Citizenship Through Birth to U.S. Citizen Parents

In many circumstances, even though a child is born outside the U.S., if at least one parent was a U.S. citizen at the time of the child's birth, he or she automatically "acquires" U.S. citizenship. When this child marries and has children, those children may also acquire U.S. citizenship at birth.

The laws governing whether or not a child born outside U.S. boundaries acquires U.S. citizenship from his or her parents have changed several times. The law that was in effect on the date of the child's birth determines whether he or she acquired U.S. citizenship from a parent or grandparent. If anyone in your direct line of ancestry might be a U.S. citizen, it is worth your time to read what the U.S. laws were on the date of your birth and theirs.

Most laws controlling the passage of U.S. citizenship from parent to child require that the parent, the child, or both have a period of living in the United States ("residence"). Sometimes the residence is required to be for a specified length of time (like five years) and sometimes it is not. When the law doesn't say exactly how long the residence period must be, you can assume that even a brief time, such as a month, might be enough. The key element is often not the amount of time but whether or not U.S. Citizenship and Immigration Services (USCIS) or the State Department believes it was a residence—in other words, that the person truly made a home here—and not a visit. If the period of stay has the character of a residence, the length of time doesn't matter.

1. Birth Prior to May 24, 1934

If you were born before 1934, the law provided that only your U.S. citizen father (not mother) could pass citizenship on to you. The rules were very simple. In order to pass on U.S. citizenship, the father must have resided in the U.S. at some time before the child's birth. The law didn't require any particular length of time or dates when the residence took place. Technically, a day or a week would be enough if it could be regarded as a residence and not just a visit. Once a child obtained U.S. citizenship at birth through a U.S. citizen father, there were no conditions to retaining it. These rules also applied to so-called illegitimate children (children born to unmarried parents), provided the U.S. citizen father had at some time legally legitimated the child (acknowledged his paternal responsibility). U.S. citizenship was then acquired at the time of legitimation, without regard to the child's age.

This law has been challenged several times as discriminatory, with some courts holding that citizenship could also be passed by the mother to the children. Congress finally addressed this issue in 1994 and amended the law, retroactively, to provide that either parent could pass his or her U.S. citizenship to children.

Consider that if you were born before May 24, 1934, and either of your parents was a U.S. citizen, that citizenship might have been passed on to you. Consider also, that if either of your parents was born before May 24, 1934, they may have acquired U.S. citizenship from either of their parents, which they then passed on to you under laws in existence at a later date. A check of the family tree may well be worth your while.

residence. If your U.S. citizenship came from only one parent, you too would have been required to reside in the U.S. for at least two years between the ages of 14 and 28 in order to keep the citizenship you got at birth. Alternately, you could retain citizenship if your noncitizen parent naturalized before you turned 18 and you began living in the U.S. permanently before age 18. Otherwise, your citizenship would be lost. If the one U.S. citizen parent was your father and your birth was illegitimate (took place while your parents weren't married), the same rules applied provided your father legally legitimated you (acknowledged paternal responsibility). Citizenship was passed on to you at the time of legitimation without regard to your age, so long as you had met the retention requirements.

2. Birth Between May 25, 1934, and January 12, 1941

If you were born between May 25, 1934, and January 12, 1941, you acquired U.S. citizenship at birth if both your parents were U.S. citizens and at least one had resided in the U.S. prior to your birth. The law at this time placed no additional conditions on retaining U.S. citizenship acquired in this way.

You could also get U.S. citizenship if only one of your parents was a U.S. citizen, as long as that parent had a prior U.S.

3. Birth Between January 13, 1941, and December 23, 1952

If you were born between January 13, 1941, and December 23, 1952, and both your parents were U.S. citizens and at least one had a prior residence in the U.S., you automatically acquired U.S. citizenship at birth, with no conditions to keeping it.

If only one parent was a U.S. citizen, that parent must have resided in the U.S. for at least ten years prior to your birth, and at least five of those years must have been after that parent reached the age of 16.

With a parent thus qualified, you then acquired U.S. citizenship at birth, but with conditions for retaining it. To keep your citizenship, you must have resided in the U.S. for at least two years between the ages of 14 and 28. Alternately, you could retain citizenship if your noncitizen parent naturalized before you turned 18 and you began living in the U.S. permanently before age 18. As a result of a U.S. Supreme Court decision, if you were born after October 9, 1952, your parent still had to fulfill the residence requirement in order to confer citizenship on you, but your own residence requirements for retaining U.S. citizenship were abolished—you need not have lived in the U.S. at all.

If your one U.S. citizen parent was your father and your birth was illegitimate (took place while your parents weren't married), the same rules applied provided you were legally legitimated (your father acknowledged paternal responsibility) prior to your 21st birthday and you were unmarried at the time of legitimation.

4. Birth Between December 24, 1952, and November 13, 1986

If at the time of your birth, both your parents were U.S. citizens and at least one had a prior residence in the U.S., you automatically acquired U.S. citizenship, with no other conditions for keeping it.

If only one parent was a U.S. citizen when you were born, that parent must have resided in the U.S. for at least ten years, and at least five of those years must have been after your parent reached the age of 14.

If your one U.S. citizen parent is your father and your birth was illegitimate (took place while your parents weren't married), the same rules apply provided you were legally legitimated (your father acknowledged paternal responsibility) prior to your 21st birthday and you were unmarried at the time of legitimation.

5. Birth Between November 14, 1986, and the Present

If at the time of your birth, both your parents were U.S. citizens and at least one had a prior residence in the U.S., you automatically acquired U.S. citizenship, with no conditions for keeping it.

If only one parent was a U.S. citizen at the time of your birth, that parent must have resided in the U.S. for at least five years and at least two of those years must have been after your parent reached the age of 14. Even with only one U.S. citizen parent, there are still no conditions to retaining your citizenship. If your one U.S. citizen parent is your father and your birth was illegitimate (took place when the parents weren't married), the same rules apply provided you were legally legitimated (your father acknowledged paternal responsibility) prior to your 18th birthday. Additionally, your father must have established paternity prior to your 18th birthday, either by acknowledgment or by court order, and must have stated, in writing, that he would support you financially until your 18th birthday.

6. Exception to Requirements for Retaining Citizenship

It is not unusual for a child born and raised outside the U.S. to have acquired U.S. citizenship at birth from parents or grandparents without knowing it. The child, ignorant of the laws and circumstances affecting his or her birthright, then proceeds to lose U.S. citizenship by failing to fulfill U.S. residency requirements.

Congress sought to address this by adding a law for people who once held U.S. citizenship but lost it by failing to fulfill the residency requirements that were in effect before 1978. Such persons can regain their citizenship by simply taking the oath of allegiance to the United States. It is not necessary that the person apply for naturalization. Contact a U.S. consulate or USCIS office for more information. The relevant statute is 8 U.S.C. § 1435(d)(1), I.N.A. § 324(d)(1).

B. Automatic Derivation of U.S. Citizenship Through Naturalized Parents

When one or both parents are or become naturalized U.S. citizens (by applying for citizenship and passing an exam), the children may, under certain circumstances, become U.S. citizens automatically. The law calls this derivation of citizenship. Becoming a U.S. citizen in this way has a special benefit because the child does not have to participate in a naturalization ceremony and can thereby avoid taking an oath renouncing allegiance to any country but the United States.

There are a number of people whose parents have been naturalized who do not realize they are U.S. citizens because they never went through a naturalization ceremony themselves. The laws on automatic naturalization of children have varied over the years. Once again, whether you achieved U.S. citizenship in this manner is determined by the laws as they were when your parents' naturalization took place.

1. Parents Naturalized Before May 24, 1934

If either parent naturalized prior to your 21st birthday and you held a green card at the time, you automatically derived U.S.

citizenship. This applied to you if you were either an illegitimate child of your U.S. citizen father (your parents weren't married when you were born) and had been legally legitimated (your father acknowledged paternal responsibility); or you were an illegitimate child of your U.S. citizen mother, whether legitimated or not. Adopted children and stepchildren did not qualify.

2. Parents Naturalized Between May 24, 1934, and January 12, 1941

If both parents became naturalized prior to your 21st birthday and you held a green card at the time, you automatically derived U.S. citizenship. This applied to you if you were an illegitimate child of your father (born when your parents weren't married) and had been legally legitimated. It also applied if you were an illegitimate child of your mother, whether legitimated or not. Adopted children did not qualify.

If only one parent became naturalized prior to your 21st birthday, you acquired U.S. citizenship automatically if you had held a green card for at least five years. The five years could have taken place before or after your parent was naturalized (as long as the years started before you turned 21), so if you hadn't held a green card for that long when the naturalization occurred, you au-tomatically became a U.S. citizen whenever you finally accumulated the five-year total.

3. Parents Naturalized Between January 13, 1941, and December 23, 1952

You derived U.S. citizenship if you held a green card and both parents were naturalized prior to your 18th birthday (or if, when one parent naturalized, the other parent was dead, or your parents were legally separated and the parent with legal custody of you naturalized). At this time, the law did not permit either so-called illegitimate (born to unmarried parents) or adopted children to derive citizenship in this manner.

4. Parents Naturalized Between December 24, 1952, and October 4, 1978

You derived U.S. citizenship if you were unmarried and both parents were naturalized prior to your 16th birthday. You must also have received a green card before your 18th birthday.

If only one parent naturalized, you could derive citizenship only if the other parent was dead, or if your parents were legally separated and the naturalized parent had custody of you. This applied to you if you were an illegitimate child of your U.S. citizen father (born while your parents weren't married) and had been legally legitimated (your father accepted paternal responsibility) or an illegitimate child of your mother, whether legitimated or not. Adopted children and stepchildren did not qualify.

5. Parents Naturalized Between October 5, 1978, and February 26, 2001

You derived U.S. citizenship if one of your parents was a U.S. citizen when you were born and never ceased to be a citizen and your other parent was naturalized prior to your 18th birthday, or the naturalization of both parents occurred before your 18th birthday. In either case, you needed to have been unmarried at the time, and have been lawfully admitted to the U.S as a permanent resident (had a green card). This applies to all children, including those who are illegitimate (born while their parents weren't married) and those who were adopted (so long as the adoption took place before you turned 18, and the naturalization(s) took place while you were living in the U.S. in the legal custody of your adoptive parent(s)). However, adopted children born prior to December 29, 1981, or after November 14, 1986, derived U.S. citizenship only if the adoption occurred prior to their 16th birthday.

Naturalization for Certain Children Living Outside the United States

Children under 18 who live outside of the U.S. in the legal and physical custody of a U.S. citizen parent can also gain citizenship through that parent. The parent must have lived in the U.S. for at least five years, at least two of which were after the age of 14, or have a U.S. citizen parent (the child's U.S. citizen grandparent) who meets this same residency requirement. In addition, children in this situation must enter the U.S. on a nonimmigrant visa (a tourist visa, for example) and submit an application to USCIS for a certificate of citizenship (the child's citizenship is not automatic in this situation).

If you plan to apply for this, get started as soon as possible—the entire process, including interview and approval of the certificate, must be completed before the child's 18th birthday. This can be difficult, with many USCIS offices backed up for years with these applications. You can file the application from abroad if you need to.

6. Parent Born in U.S. or Naturalized Between February 27, 2001, and the Present

You derived U.S. citizenship if one of your parents was born in the U.S. or if one of your parents naturalized prior to your 18th birthday while you were living in the U.S., in the legal and physical custody of that parent. You must also have had a green card (permanent residence). This law applies to both natural and adopted children.

Notice that, for the first time in the history of this law, children may derive citizenship through a parent who was born in the U.S. rather than only through a parent who later naturalizes. This has the practical effect of turning many children into citizens the instant that they obtain a green card through one U.S. citizen parent. In recognition of this instant citizenship, USCIS does not require Affidavits of Support (Form I-864) to be submitted with such children's green card applications.

C. Obtaining Proof of U.S. Citizenship

If you have acquired U.S. citizenship, at birth or derivatively after your birth as described in this chapter, you are automatically a U.S. citizen once the legal conditions have been satisfied. You don't need to apply for any document to make yourself a citizen. Nevertheless, you'll want a document proving your U.S. citizenship for certain situations, such as getting a job. If your birth took place outside the territorial U.S, and you acquired U.S. citizenship at birth from your parents or derived it through your parents' naturalization, the following types of documents will be recognized as proof of U.S. citizenship:

- U.S. passports
- certificates of citizenship, or
- certificates of consular registration of birth.

1. U.S. Passports

If you were born abroad to U.S. citizen parents, you can apply for a U.S. passport in the same way as someone born in the United States. However, you will have the added requirement of establishing your citizenship claim. Passports are available from passport offices in the U.S. (run by the U.S. Department of State) and at U.S. consulates outside the U.S., but experience shows that you have a better chance at a U.S. consulate. Wherever you apply, you will be required to present proof of your

Sample U.S. Passport

parents' U.S. citizenship and evidence that they, and you, complied with any applicable U.S. residency requirements. Review the sections on birth to a U.S. citizen for what you must prove under these circumstances. You will need to present documents such as birth or citizenship records of your parent or grandparent and work or tax records establishing U.S. residency for your parent or grandparent.

2. Certificates of Citizenship

Certificates of citizenship are issued only inside the U.S. by USCIS offices. Anyone with a claim to U.S. citizenship can apply for a certificate of citizenship. In most cases it is more difficult and takes much longer to get a certificate of citizenship than a U.S. passport. However, in situations where your U.S. citizenship was obtained automatically through the naturalization of a parent, certificate of citizenship applications are the best choice. In fact, at the time a parent is naturalized, the children can, upon the parent's request, be issued certificates of citizenship simultaneously with their naturalization certificates.

Certificates of citizenship not requested simultaneously with a parent's naturalization may be applied for later, on Form N-600 (except that a slightly different form, numbered N-600K, must be used by children living outside of the U.S. who apply for citizenship through their parents, as described in "Naturalization for Certain Children Living Outside the United States," above). The current fee for both the N-600 and the N-600K is $1,170 or zero if you are a member of the U.S. Armed Forces). Copies of these forms and detailed instructions are available on the USCIS website.

We recommend that you also prepare a cover letter explaining the basis of your claim to U.S. citizenship and describing the documents you are offering as proof. These may, depending on your basis for applying, include your parents' birth certificates, marriage certificate, and citizenship or naturalization certificates.

You should also present your own birth certificate, marriage certificates, and any divorce decrees to show legal changes in your name since birth. If you are not applying as the child of a naturalized citizen, your letter should also list whatever evidence you will be presenting to show that you have met any residency requirements as described in the section in this chapter on birth to a U.S. citizen.

The N-600 form, supporting documents, and cover letter must be submitted to the USCIS Phoenix "Lockbox," after which USCIS routes your application to one of its field offices. If you're filing Form N-600K for the child of an armed forces member stationed overseas, you must send it to the USCIS Nebraska Services Center.

You will most likely be called in for an interview on your application. In the busier USCIS offices, it can take up to a year to get a decision on an application for certificate of citizenship.

3. Certificates of Consular Registration of Birth

Certificates of consular registration of birth are issued by a U.S. consulate abroad. If your parents were U.S. citizens but were not physically in the U.S. when you were born, they may have registered your birth with a U.S. consulate to establish your right to U.S. citizenship and create an official birth record. If you're a parent who has recently given birth to a child overseas, the State Department recommends that you apply for the consular report of birth abroad as soon as possible after your child's birth. It is possible to apply, however, for children up to age 18. Your child, particularly if over age 13, can be required to appear with you when applying. There is a fee for the application.

Multiple copies can be issued at the time of registration but you might have to wait up to six months to obtain additional copies if you request them later. Therefore, parents should request at least several copies. In issuing the certificate, the consulate asks to see evidence that any residence requirements the law placed on your parents were fulfilled. The consular registration is conclusive proof of U.S. citizenship, but if your parents did not take the steps to get one when you were a child, there is no way of obtaining one now.

If your parents did not register your birth in time, you may either apply for a passport through a passport office in the U.S. or at a U.S. consulate abroad, or you may apply for a certificate of citizenship through the USCIS in the United States. You can typically get the passport much faster than the certificate of citizenship.

D. Dual Citizenship

If a child is born on U.S. soil and either or both parents are citizens of another country, it is quite possible that the child may have dual citizenship. Whether or not dual citizenship is created depends on the laws of the parents' country or countries. A child born in the U.S. is always a U.S. citizen in the eyes of the U.S. government, no matter what the laws of the parents' homelands say. (The only exception to this rule is children born of foreign diplomats.) However, if the foreign country recognizes the child as a citizen, the U.S. will recognize the non-U.S. citizenship as well.

Whenever a child is born to U.S. citizen parents but the birth takes place outside U.S. territory, again, the child may acquire dual citizenship. In this situation, the child will, depending on the laws of the country where the birth took place, usually have the nationality of the country in which he or she was actually born, in addition to U.S. citizenship through the nationality of the parents. U.S. law recognizes dual citizenship under these circumstances, and if you have acquired dual citizenship in this manner, under U.S. law you will be entitled to maintain dual status for your lifetime.

In addition, a person who becomes a U.S. citizen through naturalization can retain another country's citizenship if his or her original country allows dual citizenship. Don't go by what you've heard from friends on this one. Many countries around the world have recently changed their laws regarding dual citizenship, either to allow dual citizenship where they did not do so previously, or to restrict it where previously allowed.

If you're contemplating applying for U.S. naturalization, check with the embassy of your home country to determine whether this might impact your legal status in your country of origin.

Can You Enter or Stay in the U.S. at All?

L et's say you've found a category of visa or green card that you think you're eligible for—for example, a college has accepted you and you're hoping to get a student visa, or your mother has become a U.S. citizen and you're hoping to get a green card through her. The sad truth is that the U.S. immigration authorities still have the power to tell you "no" and deny your application if they decide that you're "inadmissible."

But what is it to be inadmissible? It means that you have a condition or characteristic that the U.S. government has decided is undesirable or would threaten the health and safety of people living in the United States. For example, if someone applying to immigrate is infected with tuberculosis, or the person once committed a violent crime, giving him or her the right to be in the United States might cause harm to U.S. citizens and residents.

The U.S. government keeps a list of the conditions and characteristics that make a person inadmissible. (See I.N.A. § 212, 8 U.S.C. § 1182.) The list includes affliction with various physical and mental disorders, commission of crimes, participation in terrorist or subversive activity, likelihood of needing welfare or other public assistance, and more. If you're found to match one of the items on this list, then you won't ordinarily be allowed to enter the United States. Or, if you've already entered, you won't be allowed to receive a green card or most other immigration benefits.

TIP
The government is stricter with green card applications than with applications for temporary visas. Although technically, your application for almost any temporary immigration benefit (such as a student visa) can be denied based on inadmissibility, in reality, inadmissibility is checked less closely when it comes to nonimmigrant applications, and certain grounds don't apply to certain visas. Also, a waiver of a ground of inadmissibility is easier to get for a nonimmigrant visa—the law doesn't attach the same requirements as it does for a green card application. (See I.N.A. § 212(d)(3), 8 U.S.C. § 1182(d)(3).)

You may be wondering how the government finds out that you're inadmissible. All green card and visa application forms ask questions designed to find out whether any grounds of inadmissibility apply in your case. Although some people obviously give false answers, those who are caught lying will have their immigration application denied for sure, and probably lose their chance to apply for any other visa or green card in the future. What's more, many of the applications—particularly those for green cards, as opposed to temporary visas— require you to supply your fingerprints or police reports as well as the results of medical examinations. If the results show that you have certain crimes on your record or communicable medical conditions, you will be found inadmissible.

Falling into one of the categories of inadmissibility doesn't mean you are absolutely barred from getting a green card or otherwise entering the United States. Some—though not all—grounds of inadmissibility may be legally excused or, in lawyer-speak, waived. But applying for a waiver is complicated, and you should consult with an attorney if you think you'll need one.

Below is a chart summarizing the grounds of inadmissibility, whether or not a waiver is available, and the special conditions you must meet in order to get a waiver. Unless otherwise indicated, the waivers described on the chart apply to people applying for green cards, not nonimmigrant visas. If you're applying for a nonimmigrant visa, you can request a waiver of many (but not all) of the grounds of inadmissibility if the consular officer recommends that you receive the waiver and USCIS approves it. (See I.N.A. § 212(d)(3), 8 U.S.C. § 1182(d)(3).) In deciding whether to recommend or approve your waiver, the officials will consider and balance three things:

- the risk of harm to society if you are allowed to enter the U.S.
- the seriousness of your criminal or immigration violation or other ground of inadmissibility, and
- your reason for wanting to come to the United States.

A. Particularly Troublesome Grounds of Inadmissibility

Below is a discussion of some of the grounds that create the most trouble for people planning to either immigrate or obtain nonimmigrant visas.

1. Likely to Become a Public Charge (Receive Government Assistance)

One of the leading reasons for green card denials is a finding that the immigrant is "likely to become a public charge" (receive welfare or need-based government assistance in the U.S.). In fact, the law requires almost all visa applicants, whether coming for a temporary or a permanent stay, to prove either that they will be self-supporting or that someone else will be responsible for supporting them.

To determine whether a person is likely to become a public charge, the government traditionally looks at the "totality of the circumstances," in other words, the whole picture. They may consider your age, health, family assets, resources, financial status, education, and skills. They may also require you to provide documentary proof of your ability to support yourself, or of other persons' promises to support you.

Summary of Grounds of Inadmissibility

Ground of Inadmissibility	Waiver Available	Conditions of Waiver
Health Problems		
Persons with communicable diseases of public health significance, in particular tuberculosis.	Yes	Waiver available to the spouse or the unmarried son or daughter or the unmarried minor lawfully adopted child of a U.S. citizen or permanent resident, or of an alien who has been issued an immigrant visa; or to an individual who has a son or daughter who is a U.S. citizen, or a permanent resident, or an alien issued an immigrant visa, upon compliance with USCIS's terms and regulations.
Persons with physical or mental disorders that threaten their own safety or the property, welfare, or safety of others.	Yes	Special conditions required by USCIS, at its discretion.
Drug abusers or addicts.	No	(But doesn't necessarily include single-use experimentation; it depends on the drug.)
Persons who fail to show that they have been vaccinated against certain vaccine-preventable diseases.	Yes	The applicant must show either that he or she subsequently received the vaccine; that the vaccine is medically inappropriate as certified by a civil surgeon; or that having the vaccine administered is contrary to the applicant's religious beliefs or moral convictions.
Criminal and Related Violations		
Persons who have committed crimes involving moral turpitude.	Yes	Waivers are not available for commission of crimes such as attempted murder or conspiracy to commit murder, or murder, torture, or drug crimes. Also, no waivers are available to persons previously admitted as permanent residents, if they have been convicted of aggravated felony since such admission or if they have fewer than seven years of lawful continuous residence before removal proceedings were initiated against them. Waivers for all other offenses are available only if the applicant is a spouse, parent, or child of a U.S. citizen or green card holder; or the only criminal activity was prostitution; or the actions occurred more than 15 years before the application for a visa or green card is filed and the alien shows that he or she is rehabilitated and is not a threat to U.S. security.

Summary of Grounds of Inadmissibility (continued)

Ground of Inadmissibility	Waiver Available	Conditions of Waiver
Persons with two or more criminal convictions.	Yes	Same as above.
Prostitutes or procurers of prostitutes.	Yes	Same as above.
Diplomats or others involved in serious criminal activity who have received immunity from prosecution.	Yes	Same as above.
Money launderers.	No	
Drug offenders.	No	Except for simple possession of less than 30 grams of marijuana. There may also be an exception for simple possession or use by juvenile offenders.
Drug traffickers.	No	
Immediate family members of drug traffickers who knowingly benefited from the illicit money within the last five years.	No	But note that the problem "washes out" after five years.
National Security and Related Violations		
Spies, governmental saboteurs, or violators of export or technology transfer laws.	No	
Persons intending to overthrow the U.S. government.	No	
Persons intending to engage in unlawful activity.	No	
Terrorists and members or representatives of foreign terrorist organizations.	No	
Persons whose entry would have adverse consequences for U.S. foreign policy, unless the applicant is an official of a foreign government, or the applicant's activities or beliefs would normally be lawful under the U.S. constitution.	No	

Summary of Grounds of Inadmissibility (continued)

Ground of Inadmissibility	Waiver Available	Conditions of Waiver
Voluntary members of totalitarian parties.	Yes	An exception is made if the membership was involuntary, or is or was when the applicant was under 16 years old, by operation of law, or for purposes of obtaining employment, food rations, or other "essentials" of living. An exception is also possible for past membership if the membership ended at least two years prior to the application (five years if the party in control of a foreign state is considered a totalitarian dictatorship). If neither applies, a waiver is available for an immigrant who is the parent, spouse, son, daughter, brother, or sister of a U.S. citizen, or a spouse, son, or daughter of a permanent resident.
Anyone having participated in genocide, torture, the persecution of any person because of race, religion, national origin, or political opinion, extrajudicial killings, or Nazi persecution.	No	
Anyone who has engaged in the recruitment or use of child soldiers.	No	
Foreign government officials who, during their service, were responsible for or directly carried out particularly severe violations of religious freedom.	No	
Economic Grounds		
Any person who, in the opinion of a USCIS or consular official, is likely to become a public charge, that is, receive public assistance or welfare in the United States. The official can consider factors such as the person's age, health, family and work history, and previous use of public benefits.	No	However, the applicant may cure the ground of inadmissibility by overcoming the reasons for it or obtaining an Affidavit of Support from a family member or friend.

Summary of Grounds of Inadmissibility (continued)

Ground of Inadmissibility	Waiver Available	Conditions of Waiver
Nonimmigrant public benefit recipients (where the individual came as a nonimmigrant and applied for benefits when he or she was not eligible or through fraud). Five-year bar to admissibility.	No	But ground of inadmissibility expires after five years.
Labor Certifications and Employment Qualifications		
Persons without approved labor certifications, if one is required in the category under which the green card application is made.	No	But see Chapter 9 for a discussion of the national interest waiver.
Graduates of unaccredited medical schools, whether inside or outside of the U.S., immigrating to the U.S. in a second or third preference category based on their profession, who have not both passed the foreign medical graduates exam and shown proficiency in English. (Physicians qualifying as special immigrants, who have been practicing medicine in the U.S. with a license since January 9, 1978, are not subject to this exclusion.)	No	
Uncertified foreign health care workers seeking entry based on clinical employment in their field (not including physicians).	Yes	But applicant may show qualifications by submitting a certificate from the Commission on Graduates of Foreign Nursing Schools or the equivalent.
Immigration Violators		
Persons who entered the U.S. without inspection by U.S. immigration authorities.	Yes	Available for certain battered women and children who came to the U.S. escaping such battery or who qualify as self-petitioners. Also available for individuals who had visa petitions or labor certifications either on file before January 14, 1998, or between that date and April 30, 2001, with proof of physical presence in the U.S. on December 21, 2000. ($1,000 penalty required for this waiver.) Does not apply to applicants outside of the U.S.

Summary of Grounds of Inadmissibility (continued)

Ground of Inadmissibility	Waiver Available	Conditions of Waiver
Persons who were deported (removed) after a hearing and seek readmission within ten years or at any time if convicted of an aggravated felony.	Yes	Advance permission to apply for admission discretionary with USCIS.
Persons who have failed to attend removal (deportation) proceedings (unless they had reasonable cause for doing so) and seek admission within five years.	Yes	Advance permission to apply for admission discretionary with USCIS.
People who have been summarily excluded from the U.S. without being admitted and again attempt to enter within five years or at any time if convicted of an aggravated felony.	Yes	Advance permission to apply for admission discretionary with USCIS.
Persons who made misrepresentations during the immigration process.	Yes	The applicant must be the spouse or child of a U.S. citizen or green card holder. A waiver will be granted if the refusal of admission would cause extreme hardship to that relative. Discretionary with USCIS.
Persons who made a false claim to U.S. citizenship.	No	
Individuals subject to a final removal (deportation) order under the Immigration and Naturalization Act § 274C (Civil Document Fraud Proceedings).	Yes	Available to permanent residents who voluntarily left the U.S., and for those applying for permanent residence as immediate relatives or based on other family petitions, if the fraud was committed solely to assist the person's spouse or child and provided that no fine was imposed as part of the previous civil proceeding.
Student visa abusers (persons who improperly obtain F-1 status to attend a public elementary school or adult education program, or transfer from a private to a public program except as permitted). Five-year bar to admissibility.	No	

Summary of Grounds of Inadmissibility (continued)

Ground of Inadmissibility	Waiver Available	Conditions of Waiver
Individuals removed more than once who seek admission within 20 years of last removal.	Yes	Discretionary with USCIS (advance permission to apply for readmission).
Individuals unlawfully present (after April 1, 1997, and after the age of 18). Presence for 180–364 days results in three-year bar to future admissibility if individual leaves the U.S. voluntarily before removal charges are brought. Presence for 365 or more days creates ten-year bar to admissibility as soon as individual leaves the U.S. for any reason.	Yes	A waiver is provided for an immigrant who has a U.S. citizen or permanent resident spouse or parent to whom refusal of the application would cause extreme hardship. There is also a complex body of law concerning when a person's presence can be considered "lawful," for example, if one has certain applications awaiting decision by USCIS or is protected by battered spouse/child provisions of the immigration laws.
Individuals unlawfully present after previous immigration violations. (Applies to persons who were in the U.S. unlawfully for an aggregate period over one year, who subsequently reenter without being properly admitted. Also applies to anyone ordered removed who subsequently attempts entry without admission.)	Yes	Women and children who are petitioning for themselves because of abuse by their U.S.-based relative and can prove that there is a connection between the abuse they suffered and their removal, departure, reentry, or attempted reentry into the United States. Anyone subject to this ground of inadmissibility can apply for a waiver and readmission after being gone from the U.S. for ten years. Admission after those ten years is discretionary with USCIS, and requires two different applications: one just for permission to reapply, and the other for a waiver of inadmissibility (showing extreme hardship to a qualifying U.S. relative).
Stowaways.	No	
Smugglers of illegal aliens.	Yes	Waivable if the applicant was smuggling in persons who were immediate family members at the time, and either is a permanent resident or is immigrating under a family-based visa petition as an immediate relative; the unmarried son or daughter of a U.S. citizen or permanent resident; or the spouse of a U.S. permanent resident.

Summary of Grounds of Inadmissibility (continued)

Ground of Inadmissibility	Waiver Available	Conditions of Waiver
Document Violations		
Persons without required current passports or visas.	No	Except certain limited circumstance waivers. Under "expedited removal" procedures, CBP may quickly exclude for five years persons who arrive without proper documents or make misrepresentations during the inspection process. No hearing is available to people subject to expedited removal, unless they can demonstrate a credible fear of persecution should they be forced to return.
Draft Evasion and Ineligibility for Citizenship		
Persons who are permanently ineligible for citizenship.	No	
Persons who are draft evaders, unless they were U.S. citizens at the time of evasion or desertion.	No	
Miscellaneous Grounds		
Practicing polygamists.	No	
Guardians accompanying excludable aliens.	No	
International child abductors. (The exclusion does not apply if the applicant is a national of a country that signed the Hague Convention on International Child Abduction.)	No	
Unlawful voters (voting in violation of any federal, state, or local law or regulation).	No	
Former U.S. citizens who renounced citizenship to avoid taxation.	No	

TIP

A few immigrants need not worry about the public charge requirement. These include:

- refugees or asylees
- people granted cancellation of removal
- Cubans or Nicaraguans applying for adjustment of status under the Nicaraguan Adjustment and Central American Relief Act of 1997 (NACARA)
- applicants for adjustment of status under the Haitian Refugee Immigration Fairness Act of 1998
- Cubans applying for adjustment under the Cuban Adjustment Act who were paroled as refugees before April 1, 1980
- Amerasian immigrants when they are first admitted to the U.S.
- "Lautenberg" parolees (certain Soviet and Indochinese parolees applying for adjustment of status)
- registry applicants (people who've lived in the U.S. since before January 1, 1972), and
- special immigrant juveniles.

a. Support Requirement for Temporary, Nonimmigrant Visa Applicants

If you plan to come to the U.S. on a temporary visa, you must be ready to prove how you are going to support yourself. If you're coming on a work-based visa, this won't normally require any extra documentation or proof—your job will usually be presumed to be enough to support you. If, however, you're coming to the U.S. on some other type of visa, chances are you won't even be allowed

to work here, in which case how you'll support yourself becomes a major issue.

For example, if you're hoping to get a tourist or a student visa, expect a major part of your application to involve proving that you have enough money—or can get it from someone else, such as a family member—to cover the costs of your entire U.S. stay.

Tourists (B-2 visa). A tourist will have to show that he or she knows how much the trip is going to cost—including hotel stays, rental cars, food, tickets, and other items—and has a way to pay for it. The more family members go with you, the more expensive the trip will be. But leaving family members at home may not be the answer. If you are the principal wage earner for your spouse and children and they are not traveling with you, you'll have to show that they will be provided for while you're away—particularly if you're planning a long trip. If it looks like your family will be going hungry while you're traveling, the official deciding your case may assume that there's more to your trip than meets the eye—perhaps that you are hoping to find employment in the United States and not go back home.

Visitors for medical care (B-2 visa). People who have arranged to come to the United States for medical care—usually specialized—are allowed to apply for a visitor visa to do so. However, showing that the care will be paid for is particularly tricky, since U.S. medical costs are extremely high. If a doctor has agreed to see you at no cost, and you can provide a letter proving this, that's a good start. But if there's a chance that the doctor will then refer you to a hospital for emergency treatment, your visa may be denied, because the consulate knows that the hospital would have to treat you for free, thus putting a strain on the U.S. health care system.

Students. If you're applying for a student visa, you must show that your education will be fully financed and all your day-to-day living expenses (including the expenses of your spouse or children if they plan to come with you) will be paid without your having to work in the United States. (And, if your family will not be coming with you, and you normally support them, the consular officer may ask you how they'll

---

Risk of Being Stopped at the Border

Even if a U.S. consular officer in your home country didn't notice that you were inadmissible to the United States, the U.S. Customs and Border Protection (CBP) inspector who meets you at the U.S. airport, border, or other entry point might. Using a power called expedited removal, the inspector can demand that you return home immediately if either of the following is true:

- The inspector thinks you are misrepresenting (lying about) practically anything connected to your request to enter the U.S., such as your purpose in coming, intent to return, prior immigration history, or use of false documents.
- You do not have the proper documentation for entry in the category you're requesting.

EXAMPLE: Boris arrives from Russia with a B-2 tourist visa. Although his visa stamp is the real thing, the border inspector discovers a ring and love letters describing wedding plans in his luggage. Upon questioning, Boris admits that he plans to marry his U.S. citizen girlfriend and apply for a green card. That makes his use of the tourist visa fraudulent, and the inspector sends him right back to Russia.

If the CBP inspector excludes you, you may not request entry again for five years, unless a special waiver is granted. If the inspector expresses an intention to find you inadmissible, you may ask to withdraw your application to enter the U.S. in order to prevent having the five-year order on your record. The CBP inspector is likely to allow this if he or she feels you cannot otherwise be admitted to the United States, so be prepared to request the opportunity to withdraw your application if it appears your only alternative is expedited removal.

be supported while you're gone.) Although some students will be permitted to work during their student years, you cannot rely on this work to prove your visa eligibility. In fact, you probably won't know until you get to the United States what type of work you'll be able to get. The permitted work will probably be low paying or a small part of your study program. That means your financing will need to come from your own resources or from family, friends, or scholarships.

Fiancés. If you're planning to come to the United States as the fiancé of a U.S. citizen (on a K-1 visa) or the spouse of a U.S. citizen who's waiting for USCIS to approve a spouse petition (on a K-3 visa), you are considered to be a nonimmigrant. (This is despite the fact that you plan to apply for a green card after arriving in the United States.) That's good news, because it means that you probably won't be asked to prove financial support in the same way someone applying for a green card through the consulate would. Your U.S. citizen fiancé (K-1) or spouse (K-3) will probably be asked to fill out an affidavit of support (Form I-134), promising to care for you financially and repay any government assistance that you receive. However, it's a short, fairly simple form, much easier than a similar one (Form I-864) that your spouse will have to fill out after you're married and applying for the green card.

b. Support Requirement for Immigrant Visa and Green Card Applicants

If you plan to apply for a green card, the U.S. immigration authorities will want to see that you'll be taken care of financially for many years to come. If you're immigrating based on employment, this is fairly easy to prove, since you'll obviously have a job. However, if you're immigrating through family, or through employment where your own relatives submitted the visa petition or own at least 5% of the petitioning company, the requirements get stiffer. Whichever family member signed your visa petition (to start your immigration process) will need to submit a lengthy document called an Affidavit of Support on Form I-864.

Form I-864 is many pages long and complicated—though fortunately, if you are the only person your petitioner is sponsoring and your petitioner can meet the sponsorship requirements based upon his or her income alone, your petitioner can use a shorter version of the form, called I-864EZ.

Note that Form I-864 is not required for most employment-based petitions or nonimmigrant visas, although some of these applicants may need to fill out a shorter, simpler Form I-134.

How much support is required? The Affidavit of Support on Form I-864 basically promises that your U.S. sponsor will pay your living expenses so that you,

2016 Poverty Guidelines

2016 HHS Poverty Guidelines for Affidavit of Support

Department of Homeland Security
U.S. Citizenship and Immigration Services

USCIS
Form I-864P
Supplement

2016 HHS Poverty Guidelines*
Minimum Income Requirements for Use in Completing Form I-864

For the 48 Contiguous States, the District of Columbia, Puerto Rico, the U.S. Virgin Islands, Guam, and the Commonwealth of the Northern Mariana Islands:

Sponsor's Household Size	100% of HHS Poverty Guidelines*	125% of HHS Poverty Guidelines*
	For sponsors on active duty in the U.S. Armed Forces who are petitioning for their spouse or child	*For all other sponsors*
2	$16,020	$20,025
3	$20,160	$25,200
4	$24,300	$30,375
5	$28,440	$35,550
6	$32,580	$40,725
7	$36,730	$45,912
8	$40,890	$51,112
	Add $4,160 for each additional person.	Add $5,200 for each additional person.

	For Alaska:			For Hawaii:	
Sponsor's Household Size	100% of HHS Poverty Guidelines*	125% of HHS Poverty Guidelines*	Sponsor's Household Size	100% of HHS Poverty Guidelines*	125% of HHS Poverty Guidelines*
	For sponsors on active duty in the U.S. Armed Forces who are petitioning for their spouse or child	*For all other sponsors*		*For sponsors on active duty in the U.S. Armed Forces who are petitioning for their spouse or child*	*For all other sponsors*
2	$20,020	$25,025	2	$18,430	$23,037
3	$25,200	$31,500	3	$23,190	$28,987
4	$30,380	$37,975	4	$27,950	$34,937
5	$35,560	$44,450	5	$32,710	$40,887
6	$40,740	$50,925	6	$37,470	$46,837
7	$45,920	$57,400	7	$42,230	$52,787
8	$51,120	$63,900	8	$47,010	$58,762
	Add $5,200 for each additional person.	Add $6,500 for each additional person.		Add $4,780 for each additional person.	Add $5,975 for each additional person.

Means - Tested Public Benefits

Federal Means-Tested Public Benefits. To date, Federal agencies administering benefit programs have determined that Federal means-tested public benefits include Food Stamps, Medicaid, Supplemental Security Income (SSI), Temporary Assistance for Needy Families (TANF), and the State Child Health Insurance Program (SCHIP).

State Means-Tested Public Benefits. Each State will determine which, if any, of its public benefits are means-tested. If a State determines that it has programs which meet this definition, it is encouraged to provide notice to the public on which programs are included. Check with the State public assistance office to determine which, if any, State assistance programs have been determined to be State means-tested public benefits.

Programs Not Included: The following Federal and State programs are not included as means-tested benefits: emergency Medicaid; short-term, non-cash emergency relief; services provided under the National School Lunch and Child Nutrition Acts; immunizations and testing and treatment for communicable diseases; student assistance under the Higher Education Act and the Public Health Service Act; certain forms of foster-care or adoption assistance under the Social Security Act; Head Start Programs; means-tested programs under the Elementary and Secondary Education Act; and Job Training Partnership Act programs.

* These poverty guidelines remain in effect for use with Form I-864, Affidavit of Support, from March 1, 2016 until new guidelines go into effect in 2017.

the immigrant, do not have to rely on government assistance. Your sponsor must show that he or she earns (or has assets worth) a certain minimum amount of money to take care of his or her own family plus you, the immigrant (plus your spouse and children if they're immigrating with you). Just how much income is needed to support a certain size family is computed every year by the federal government and published in a document called the *Poverty Guidelines* and found on USCIS Form I-864P, available at www.uscis.gov. See, for example, the *2016 Poverty Guidelines*, above. If, for example, you're marrying a U.S. citizen, and there will be two of you living in your house, then your household size is "2." Most U.S. citizen sponsors in this situation will need to show an income of $20,025 (which is 125% of the minimum income considered to be above the poverty line) in order to satisfy the *2016 Poverty Guidelines*. The numbers are slightly different if your sponsor lives in Alaska or Hawaii, and lower if you're in the military. If you have a child, then your household size is "3," and the U.S. citizen will need to show an income of $25,200 to satisfy the *2016 Poverty Guidelines*. You'll need to meet the guidelines for the year when your Affidavit of Support is filed. Don't worry if the required income levels get raised later—it won't affect you.

What if the U.S. sponsor lives overseas, too? An additional problem for sponsors required to sign Form I-864 is that they must be domiciled (which usually means "living") in the United States or a U.S. territory or possession. That means that the sponsoring relative will have to return to the United States by the time Form I-864 is submitted (which usually happens some months before your consular interview, the last step in the immigration process). And, of course, if the sponsor is giving up a job overseas, he or she will need to find a new job in the United States to replace the lost income.

There are, however, alternate ways of meeting the domicile requirement. As the U.S. State Department says on its website, "[m]any U.S. citizens and lawful permanent residents reside outside the United States on a temporary basis. 'Temporary' may cover an extended period of residence abroad. The sponsor living abroad must establish the following in order to be considered domiciled in the United States:

- He/she left the United States for a limited and not indefinite period of time,
- He/she intended to maintain a domicile in the United States, and
- He/she has evidence of continued ties to the United States."

For more information, see the State Department website at www.travel.state.gov.

If your U.S. sponsor can't be considered to have a U.S. domicile, you'll need to prove that he or she will reestablish one when you're ready to move to the United States. Be prepared to show where you will live in the U.S., where your sponsor will work, where your children have been enrolled in school, and anything else to prove that the sponsor will give up a foreign residence and intends to begin living in the United States. Your sponsor does not have to move back to the U.S. before you arrive, as long as the two of you come together.

Who can completely avoid filling out Form I-864? Even among people who would ordinarily have to fill out a Form I-864, two exceptions apply. First, if the immigrating person has already worked *legally* in the U.S. for a total of 40 "quarters" (as defined by the Social Security Administration)—about ten years—no I-864 needs to be submitted. In fact, in an interesting twist, immigrants can be credited with work done by their U.S. citizen spouse while they were married or by a U.S. citizen parent while the immigrant was under age 18. So if your U.S. citizen spouse worked 40 quarters in the U.S. during your marriage, and he or she would be the one signing your Form I-864, the support obligation is taken care of, and your spouse need not even fill out the form—but should instead fill out Form I-864W, which explains why he or she falls within an exception. Of course, it's the rare married couple who will have gone this many years (approximately ten) without applying for a green card for the immigrant. Nevertheless,

for those to whom this exception applies, it's highly useful.

The second major exception is that if the immigrant beneficiary is a child who will become a U.S. citizen immediately upon approval or entry to the U.S. for a green card (as discussed in Chapter 7), no I-864 needs to be submitted for the child, but an I-864W should be.

Others who don't need to fill out Form I-864, and should fill out an I-864W to prove it, include self-petitioning widows or widowers of U.S. citizens, and self-petitioning battered spouses or children (both explained in Chapter 7).

How long does Form I-864 bind the person who signs it? A family member who signs a Form I-864 is promising a long-term commitment. This affidavit is legally enforceable by the government for any means-tested public benefits utilized by the sponsored immigrant. In other words, if the immigrant were to use welfare or certain other forms of public assistance, the government could make the family member who signed the Affidavit of Support pay the money back. While such enforcement efforts are rare, they are not unheard of. Perhaps more importantly, the immigrant can also use the Affidavit to demand support from his or her family member. The obligation does not end until the immigrant becomes a U.S. citizen, has earned 40 work quarters, dies, or permanently leaves the United States.

CAUTION
A sponsor remains legally obligated even after a divorce. Yes, a divorced immigrant spouse could decide to sit on a couch all day and sue his or her former spouse for financial help. The sponsor may wish to have the immigrant sign a separate contract in advance agreeing not to do this, but it's not clear whether courts will enforce such a contract.

What if the family member helping you immigrate doesn't have enough money?
There are alternative ways of meeting the support requirement, even if the person who signs the immigrant visa petition (to start the process) does not have annual income (as shown on his or her tax returns) of at least 125% of poverty level for the household size being supported. If the immigrant can get a better job between tax time and submitting the Form I-864, then it's important to prove the resulting higher income using a combination of a letter from the employer (stating the sponsor's name, dates of employment, position and title, wages or salary, number of hours worked per week, prospects for long-term employment, marital status, dependents claimed, and emergency contact information) and copies of recent pay stubs, preferably up to six months' worth.

In addition, other household members may join their income to that of the main sponsor to help reach the 125% level, but only if they are living with the sponsor and they agree to be jointly liable by filing Form I-864A (Contract Between Sponsor and Household Member). And the immigrant him- or herself can add income to the mix if already living with the sponsor/petitioner in the U.S. and working legally at a job that will continue after getting the green card.

Personal assets of the sponsor or the immigrant or the sponsor's household members (such as property, bank account deposits, and personal property such as automobiles) may be used to supplement the sponsor's income. The assets must be readily convertible to cash (for example, by selling them) within one year. If using assets owned by the sponsor's household members or the immigrant, those people must submit a Form I-864A. The assets (minus any debts or liens) will be counted at only one-fifth their value for most immigrants. That changes to one third their value if the immigrant is the spouse of a U.S. citizen or the child, over age 18, of a U.S. citizen. And it changes to the full value of the assets in orphan adoption cases.

You'll also need to attach proof of these assets' ownership, location, and value, such as bank statements or title deeds.

When the person who signs the immigrant visa petition can't meet the minimum income requirement in any way, he or she is not excused from filing an I-864. That form must be filed. So, the next alternative is to find another person (a joint sponsor) who meets the 125% income requirement for his or her own household plus the immigrant and any family members getting a green card along with the immigrant. The joint sponsor may add his or her income, assets, and household members' income and assets to the sponsor's if the person is:

- willing to be jointly liable
- a U.S. legal permanent resident or citizen (not necessarily a family member)
- over 18 years old, and
- residing in the U.S.

The joint sponsor must file a separate Form I-864 Affidavit of Support (in addition to that of the primary sponsor). You can have two joint sponsors if family members will be getting a green card along with the immigrant. The two joint sponsors can combine finances to meet the minimum. They do not have to live in the same household.

What else does Form I-864 require of people who sign it? Sponsors must notify USCIS within 30 days of the sponsor's change of address, using Form I-865. Failure to do so is punishable by fines of $250 to $5,000.

If you are a sponsor and have questions about meeting the eligibility requirements, or about the scope of your legal responsibility (which may last ten or more years or until the immigrant permanently leaves the country, dies, or naturalizes), consult an immigration attorney.

How should the sponsor fill out Form I-864? You don't need to read this yet, but come back to it after reading later chapters describing your green card application

procedures. Here are some tips for the trickier questions on the form:

Part 1: Basis for filing Affidavit of Support
Here, the main sponsor writes his or her name and checks box 1.a if it's purely a family immigration case. If the sponsor is an employer/family petitioner, he or she must check box 1.b or 1.c. Nice friends or family who agree to fill in this form as joint sponsors check either box 1.d or 1.e.

Box 1.f is for situations where the immigrant's original sponsor died after the visa petition was approved and the immigrant is asking USCIS to allow the application to go forward for humanitarian reasons (called "reinstatement"). In this case, the immigrant must find another family member in the U.S. who is willing to serve as a substitute sponsor and meets the basic sponsorship requirements (age 18, domiciled in the U.S., and a U.S. citizen, permanent resident, or national). The family members who qualify to do this are the immigrant's spouse, parent, mother- or father-in-law, brother or sister, child (if at least 18 years of age), son- or daughter-in-law, sister- or brother-in-law, grandparent, grandchild, and legal guardian.

Part 2: Information on the principal immigrant
These are basic questions concerning you, the immigrant. If you haven't been assigned an A-number, or don't have a USCIS ELIS account number, that's okay—no need to write anything.

Part 3: Information on the immigrant(s) you are sponsoring

Note that there's a place to list children. You don't need to name children who were born in the United States, because the sponsor has no obligation to support them (at least not under the immigration laws, though they will be counted elsewhere within this form to test the sponsor's overall financial capacity). Notice that the form says "Do not include any relative listed on a separate visa petition." Relatives would have to be listed on a separate visa petition if they were "immediate relatives" of the petitioner, in which case each one would need his or her own Form I-864, filled out just for that person, rather than a photocopy of the mother or father's form. (For example, if a U.S. citizen father petitions for his wife and stepchildren, they are all immediate relatives, will all need separate visa petitions, and therefore will all need separate Form I-864s. But if a lawful permanent resident father petitions for his wife and stepchildren, the children are allowed to accompany the mother on her visa petition without having visa petitions separately filed for each of them, and they therefore won't need separate Form I-864s prepared on their behalf, so should all be listed on the I-864 filed for the mother.

Part 4: Information on the Sponsor

Remember that the sponsor's place of residence must be in the United States in order to be eligible as a financial sponsor. If your sponsor is living overseas and doesn't want to return to the United States until you, the immigrant, can enter as well, your sponsor must still prepare and sign this Affidavit of Support. However, a sponsor who has no income from a U.S. source will most likely have to find a joint sponsor who lives in the United States and will submit an additional affidavit.

Part 5: Sponsor's household size

This section is self-explanatory. Remember not to count anyone twice! This means if you're sponsoring your spouse, he or she is already counted in line 1—do not put the number 1 in line 3 as well.

Part 6: Sponsor's income and employment

Questions 1.a–1.d: The sponsor needs to fill in information about his or her employment here. Self-employment is fine. Be aware that if a self-employed sponsor has underreported income to the IRS in the past, the earnings shown may not be sufficient to support you. In that case, the sponsor will need to file an amended tax return and pay a penalty before the newly reported income is accepted as meeting the guidelines for sponsorship.

Question 2: Here, the sponsor is supposed to enter his or her current income. If that amount is higher than shown on the sponsor's last tax return, we suggest including supporting documentation (such as copies of pay stubs or a letter from the sponsor's employer stating the current salary). Such proof will be especially important if the raise in salary since the last tax return takes the sponsor over the *Poverty Guidelines* minimum.

Questions 3–17: This information is required from sponsors whose income is not enough by itself, but who will be using the income of members of their household to help meet the *Poverty Guidelines* minimum requirements. If the sponsor wants other people's income counted, they must be named, along with their relationship to the sponsor, and their income. The total income from the sponsor and household members goes in line 15. Unless any one of these household members is the actual immigrant and has no accompanying dependents, the person must plan to complete a separate agreement with the sponsor, using Form I-864A.

Question 20: If you don't have federal income tax returns from one or more of the past three years because you were not required to file, you'll have to attach an explanation to the form.

Part 7: Use of assets to supplement income

The sponsor needs to complete this section only if his or her income wasn't enough by itself to meet the *Poverty Guidelines* requirements. See the earlier instructions on how assets are counted, and remember to attach documents proving their existence.

Part 8: Sponsor's Contract

The sponsor's obligations are explained in this part. The sponsor must say in question 2 if he or she agreed to let someone else prepare the form, and whether the preparer is or isn't a lawyer. The preparer completes and signs part 10.

If the sponsor does not read English, check box 1.b, and have an interpreter read the form to the sponsor and verify that the sponsor understands his or her answers on the form. The interpreter will need to complete and sign part 9.

2. Having Committed Crimes or Security Violations

You're probably not a "criminal"—but you might be surprised at how a few, or seemingly minor, arrests or blotches on a person's record can ruin his or her chances of immigration. Criminal grounds are often the number one factor making temporary visa applicants inadmissible, but they affect many green card applicants, too.

Because this is such a large problem, do not be surprised or offended if, in working with an immigration attorney, the attorney asks you to have your fingerprints taken and checked against the U.S. Federal Bureau of Investigation files. The immigration authorities will eventually check the same files, so it's best to know in advance what they'll find.

Crimes. Among the many crimes that make you inadmissible are:

- any crime of moral turpitude, such as theft (which could include passing a bad check), fraud, assault, murder, rape, or arson

- virtually any drug crime more serious than simple possession of less than 30 grams of marijuana
- prostitution or procuring a prostitute, or
- any two or more criminal convictions, where the sentences for each crime, when combined, exceed five years in jail or prison.

EXAMPLE: During her green card interview, Sonya is asked why she no longer has her I-94 card. She explains that, after an argument with her husband about him spending all his time fixing up his old Chevy, she left the house and angrily lit a match to the garage, which ended up burning the whole house down. Sonya has now basically confessed to arson, which is a crime of moral turpitude. She can be denied the green card on this basis.

TIP
Kids under 18 get a break. If your case was handled in the juvenile courts, it won't result in a conviction, so you won't be inadmissible (unless you admit to a category of admissibility that doesn't require an actual conviction). Also, even if your case is handled in the adult court system, you may get help from what's called the "youthful offender exception." This exception says that a single crime of moral turpitude committed while under the age of 18 doesn't make you inadmissible if the crime itself and your release from prison occurred over five years before your immigration application. (See I.N.A. § 212(a)(2)(A)(ii)(I).)

If you've been convicted of multiple crimes involving alcohol, you may have double trouble. Even if the crime itself doesn't make you inadmissible, USCIS can, and often does, argue that multiple convictions indicate a physical or mental disorder (addiction) associated with harmful behavior—in other words, that you're inadmissible on health, rather than criminal grounds. This is most often a problem for people with convictions for DUI or DWI (driving under the influence or driving while intoxicated). Other crimes, such as assaults or domestic violence, where alcohol or drugs were contributing factors can lead to the same result.

SKIP AHEAD
See Section B, below, for information on dealing with the criminal grounds of admissibility.

Terrorism. A related area of concern is whether you are considered a security risk because you are affiliated with a terrorist or other such group. If you have any connection with any group that might conceivably be suspected of terrorism, hire a lawyer and look into this further. Under recent changes to the law within the U.S. Patriot Act, even fundraising for or supporting the humanitarian projects of a group that the U.S. government calls a terrorist organization can make you inadmissible.

3. Having Spent Too Much Time in the U.S. Unlawfully

If you have ever lived in the United States unlawfully—perhaps because you crossed the border illegally or you stayed past the expiration date on your I-94 card—you must read this section. People become inadmissible if they've been "unlawfully present" in the U.S. for 180 days (about six months) after April 1, 1997, subsequently left the U.S., and then requested admission by applying for an immigrant or non-immigrant visa from overseas.

This category of inadmissibility may not keep you out of the U.S. forever—but it will bar your reentry for a very long time. If you've spent between 180 days and 365 days (one year) in the U.S. unlawfully and then left (voluntarily, not after being placed in removal proceedings), you won't be allowed to reenter for three years. The period becomes ten years if you were unlawfully present for one year or more and then left or got deported.

If you're not in the U.S. now, but spent time in the U.S. unlawfully before you left, this could be a problem for you—though luckily, the longer you wait outside the U.S., the better, because you're already working off your three-year or ten-year bar on returning.

Even if you're in the U.S. now, however, this ground of inadmissibility may give you trouble—because you may have no choice but to leave the United States in order to finish the application for your green card. There are rare circumstances when the three- or ten-year period can be spent in the United States, such as visits pursuant to subsequently issued advance parole or a nonimmigrant waiver of inadmissibility.

The only people who can simply stay in the United States to apply for the green card are those who are eligible to use a procedure called adjustment of status. Those few people have it lucky—by not leaving the United States, they can't be barred from reentering the United States. However, the adjustment of status procedure is mainly available to people who entered the U.S. legally and continued to maintain their legal status. If you entered illegally, or under the Visa Waiver Program, or are here in unlawful status, chances are you aren't eligible to adjust status; see Section 4, below, for details.

If you aren't eligible to adjust status, your only choice is to complete your green card application through a U.S. consulate in another country. The consulate will schedule an interview for you and review your file. But at your interview, the consulate will probably tell you that you can't return to the U.S. for a full three years or ten years. There is a waiver you can apply for, but it's hard to get, as discussed in Subsection b, below.

EXAMPLE: Soo-Yun came to the U.S. from South Korea on a student visa in 2011. After she finished her studies and her permitted stay expired (in 2014), she didn't go home. She worked as a freelance computer programmer for two years. In 2016, she found an employer willing to give her a job and help her get a green card. Unfortunately, because she is not on a valid visa, and because of her unauthorized work, she cannot adjust status in the United States. Even more unfortunately, because of her two-year overstay, there is no point in her leaving to apply for the green card at a U.S. consulate overseas—they would simply tell her that because of her overstay, she must stay in Korea (or any other country outside the U.S.) for ten years before returning to the United States.

Again, this bar does not apply to someone who can stay in the U.S. and adjust status—so anyone eligible to adjust status should take advantage of this and not leave the U.S. until they get a green card. If you're not sure, consult an attorney about this complex area of the law.

a. When Your Stay May Be Lawful

If you have no choice but to apply for your green card overseas, through consular processing, it will become very important to calculate exactly how many of the days you spent in the U.S. were okay, and how many were unlawful. Any periods of your time in the United States will be considered lawful (or at least, not unlawful) for purposes of the three-year and ten-year bars if you were:

- under the age of 18

- in the U.S. prior to April 1, 1997 (only your time after that date, when the new law took effect, counts)
- in the U.S. only for short periods of time, less than six months each stay. Periods of unlawful presence are not counted in the aggregate for purposes of the three-year and ten-year bars— in other words, you have to be present for a block of time; USCIS will not add up 90 days during one stay and 90 days during another stay to find that you were unlawfully present for 180 days.
- a bona fide asylum applicant (including while your administrative or judicial review was pending), unless you were employed without authorization
- under Family Unity protection (a status that you would have applied for on Form I-817) based on being a family member of a Special Agricultural Worker
- a battered spouse or child who can show a substantial connection between the status violation or unlawful entry and the abuse
- lawfully admitted to the United States but were waiting for a USCIS decision on a valid and timely filed application for a change or extension of status (as long as you did not work without authorization), but only up to a maximum of 120 days

- awaiting a USCIS decision on a properly filed application for adjustment of status
- admitted to the U.S. as a refugee
- granted asylum
- granted withholding of deportation/removal
- granted Deferred Enforced Departure (DED)
- granted Temporary Protected Status (TPS)
- Cuban or Haitian and meet certain other criteria
- admitted for "duration of status" (D/S) (such as a student or an exchange visitor)—however, you may have begun to accrue unlawful presence if either an immigration judge found you to have violated your status and become deportable (removable), or USCIS, in the course of reviewing an application, determined that you had violated your status
- on a valid visa—assuming you were admitted until a specified date, you will begin to accrue unlawful presence only when the date on the I-94 (or any extension) has passed, the job or other basis for your visa has ended, or USCIS or an immigration judge finds that you violated your status, whichever comes first.

A couple of other rules apply mainly to people who have been in removal (Immigration Court) proceedings:

- Where the unlawful presence determination is based on a USCIS or immigration judge's finding of a status violation, the unlawful presence clock starts to run from the date determined to be when the status violation began.
- A grant of voluntary departure (V/D or V/R for voluntary return) constitutes a period of authorized stay. This includes the period between the date of the V/R order and the date by which you were told to depart. If you fail to depart by the date specified in the V/D order, the unlawful presence clock starts running.

However, there are many circumstances under which your stay is definitely unlawful. In some cases, you may be legally allowed to stay in the United States—for example, while waiting for a decision on your application for cancellation of removal or withholding of removal—but still be considered unlawfully present. People who were granted deferred action status are also considered unlawfully present. This is a complicated and evolving area of the law, so see a lawyer for a full analysis of your case.

b. Waiver of Three-Year or Ten-Year Bar

A waiver is available to an applicant who is the spouse, son, or daughter of a U.S. citizen or permanent resident, if the applicant can show that being kept out of the U.S. for three or ten years would cause the U.S. citizen extreme hardship. Note that hardship to the immigrant applicant doesn't count. Nor does hardship to the immigrant's U.S.-citizen children.

Extreme hardship usually means more hardship than is normally experienced by family separation; economic hardship is not usually sufficient to meet this requirement. These waivers are hard to get; and some U.S. consulates are more willing to grant them than others. Definitely see a lawyer for help.

c. Provisional Waiver Allows Some Applicants to Get a Predeparture Decision

Anyone who is eligible for an immigrant visa (whether based on family, employment, the diversity visa lottery, or a special immigration classification) and who qualifies for an unlawful presence waiver can apply to USCIS for a provisional waiver of inadmissibility before, not after, leaving the U.S. for their consular visa interview. If the waiver is granted, they can safely leave, knowing that if the consulate approves their immigrant visa, they can immediately return to the U.S. and become lawful permanent residents.

If denied, they can at least remain in the U.S. and explore any possible legal options—though there is a risk that USCIS might, in some cases, refer the case to ICE to institute removal proceedings.

To apply for a provisional waiver, you must:

- Be 17 years of age or older.
- Be the spouse or unmarried child of a U.S. citizen or lawful permanent resident.
- Have an approved petition (I-130 or I-360) classifying you as eligible for an immigrant visa.
- Have a pending immigrant visa case with the State Department for the approved relative petition and have paid the immigrant visa processing fee.
- Be able to demonstrate that refusal of your admission to the U.S. will cause extreme hardship to your U.S. qualifying relative, and
- Be physically present in the U.S. to file your application for a provisional unlawful presence waiver and provide biometrics.

The applicant for a provisional waiver needs to be inadmissible solely because of unlawful presence in the U.S. of 180 days or more. If the applicant is potentially inadmissible on other grounds, needing a waiver of, for example, a health condition or criminal conviction, that person will run into serious complications trying to use this provisional waiver process and may get stuck outside the United States.

The provisional waiver is filed using Form I-601A. It is also available to noncitizens in removal proceedings. As with any waiver application, it's a good idea to consult with an attorney to help you make your case.

4. Can You Get Around the Time Bars by Adjusting Status?

The rules concerning who is allowed to remain in the United States to adjust status (get a green card without having to leave for an interview at a consulate outside the U.S.) are complicated.

If you entered the U.S. properly—by being inspected by a USCIS official—and maintained your nonimmigrant status (in particular, didn't let your visa expire or do anything unauthorized), you can get your green card without leaving the United States (adjust status). However, this doesn't work for people who entered the U.S. using a visa waiver (that is, who came from one of the countries that doesn't require an advance visa to visit the U.S., and didn't in fact apply for an actual tourist or other visa)—unless they will be adjusting status as the immediate relative of a U.S. citizen.

Immediate relatives (immigrants who marry U.S. citizens or are the parent or unmarried child, under age 21, of a U.S. citizen) are allowed to adjust their status here even if they have fallen out of status or worked without authorization, as long as they did not enter without being properly inspected, or as a crewman or stowaway.

People who've been granted political asylum can also adjust status one year after their approval, under a separate provision of the law, without worrying about the usual bars on adjusting status. (See 8 C.F.R. § 209.2.)

Most everyone else, however, will be technically unable to adjust status. If, for example, you entered the United States without being inspected by a border guard or another official, entered under the Visa Waiver Program, or you have fallen out of lawful status or worked without authorization, you will not ordinarily be allowed to apply for your green card without leaving the United States first. (See I.N.A. § 245(c)(2).) A few rare exceptions exist, however, referred to as the penalty and grandfather clauses, described below.

a. The Penalty and Grandfather Clauses

If you are otherwise ineligible to get your green card by adjusting status in the U.S., your last hope might be the possibility that you were "grandfathered in," or covered under an old law (I.N.A. § 245(i)) that allowed people to pay a $1,000 penalty fee in order to adjust status.

Presently, the only people who may still adjust status by paying a penalty fee are those who either:

- had a visa petition or labor certification on file by January 14, 1998, or
- had a visa petition or labor certification on file by April 30, 2001, and can also prove that they were physically in the U.S. on December 21, 2000.

Most of the people who were eligible to immigrate under these categories have already done so, but not all. It doesn't matter who filed the visa petition or labor certification that you use as your ticket to adjust status. For example, if your U.S. citizen brother filed a visa petition on your behalf, but he died before you could get a green card, you are still allowed to use that petition as a basis to adjust status—even if you're now applying for your green card through an employer, a U.S. citizen spouse, or some other petitioner. The one catch is that the visa petition has to have been "approvable" when it was filed. In other words, if your best U.S.-citizen friend filed a visa petition on your behalf, that petition would not have been approvable, because no visa category exists allowing U.S. citizens to petition for other people based solely on friendship—so the petition wouldn't help you adjust status later.

Unmarried children younger than 17 years old and the spouses or unmarried children younger than 21 years old of legalized aliens who are qualified for and have applied for benefits under the Family Unity program can adjust status without paying the penalty fee.

b. Special Exception for Certain Employment-Based Green Card Applicants

If you are getting your green card through the first-, second-, or third-preference employment category (as a priority worker, advanced degree professional, person of exceptional ability, skilled worker, professional, or other worker) or as a special immigrant, you can have worked without authorization or fallen out of status for up to 180 days and still apply to adjust status.

This exception applies only if at the time of filing the green card application your last entry to the U.S. was legal, you have maintained continuous legal status, and you have not violated the terms of your status or other terms of admission, other than during a 180-day aggregate period.

5. Repeat Violators: The Permanent Bar

In addition to the three-year and ten-year bars described above, a separate and more serious provision punishes certain people who've entered or tried to enter the U.S. illegally. People who have either spent a total of one year's unlawful aggregate time in the U.S. or been ordered deported by an immigration judge (even after spending less than one year in the U.S.), who then leave and return or attempt to return to the United States illegally, become permanently inadmissible.

Unlike the three-year and ten-year time bars, you can accumulate a year's unlawful time through various short stays— your unlawful time doesn't have to be continuous to count against you. Like the three-year and ten-year bars, however, no unlawful time before April 1, 1997 (the date the law took effect) counts.

EXAMPLE: Sandra entered the U.S. illegally in 2005 and lived there until 2009, when she returned to Mexico. In 2009, she illegally crossed the border to the U.S., met a U.S. citizen with whom she fell in love, and got married in 2012. When she tried to apply for a green card based on her marriage, however, she was told that she was barred from applying. The reason: She had entered illegally and spent more than a year in the U.S. illegally after April 1, 1997, then left and returned by entering illegally.

You can request a waiver if you're otherwise eligible for a green card, but only after a full ten years have passed since leaving the United States. You'll also have to get USCIS's permission to reapply. See an attorney for a full analysis.

6. Having Violated Immigration Laws or Used Fraud

Although you'll have to provide a lot of documents to back up any immigration application, at times the immigration officials will have to rely on your word alone. For that reason, it's very important to them that they be able to trust your word. If you have ever been caught lying to an immigration official, using fraud, or otherwise violating the immigration laws, you are inadmissible.

EXAMPLE: Krystof's mother wins the visa lottery, and can apply for U.S. green cards for herself, her husband, and any unmarried children under the age of 21. Krystof is 20, but has secretly married. The U.S. consulate finds out, and denies him the visa. Three years later, he himself wins the visa lottery. However, his past visa fraud makes him inadmissible to the United States.

A fraud waiver is available—but, if you're applying for a green card (as opposed to a nonimmigrant visa), the waiver is available only if you have a husband, wife, or parent who is a U.S. citizen or lawful permanent resident (green card holder). That person is your "qualifying relative." Also, you must establish that your qualifying relative would suffer "extreme hardship" if you were denied admission or forced to leave the United States. (History note: Prior to the enactment of the Illegal Immigration Reform and Immigrant Responsibility Act of 1996, children could serve as qualifying relatives for parents who needed a waiver for having made misrepresentations or used false documents, but no longer.)

EXAMPLE: Graciela, a trained nurse, enters the U.S. on a tourist visa. One week later, she starts work caring for a disabled person in her home. Two months later, she finds a nursing home employer willing to sponsor her for a green card. However, because Graciela started working within 30 days of entry on a tourist visa, the law presumes that she misrepresented her intention in coming to the United States. What's more, Graciela has no qualifying relatives in the U.S., so she cannot apply for a fraud waiver.

A similar ground of inadmissibility applies to immigrants who were assessed a civil penalty for committing document fraud under Section 274C of the I.N.A (8 U.S.C. § 1324c). This is most likely to affect people who lived in the U.S. illegally and bought or sold fake green cards, Social Security cards, or other immigration-related documents. The penalty itself is usually a cease and desist order, sometimes with a money penalty of between $250 and $2,000. Document fraud means forging, counterfeiting, altering, or making any document to satisfy an immigration requirement; using, attempting to use, possessing, or receiving any such document; or using someone else's valid document.

Although a waiver is available for the document fraud ground of inadmissibility (for humanitarian purposes or to assure family unity), it's hard to get. For one thing, it's available only to applicants who have either already been approved for green cards and simply took a temporary trip out of the U.S. (and got stopped trying to come back into the country) or who are applying for family-based green cards and committed the fraud solely to assist, aid, or support their husband, wife, or child. Also, the waiver is completely unavailable if you were ordered to pay a civil fine for the document fraud. (See I.N.A. § 212(d)(12), 8 U.S.C. § 1182(d)(12).)

B. Avoiding or Reversing an Inadmissibility Finding

The U.S. immigration authorities may decide you are inadmissible any time after you have filed an application for a green card, nonimmigrant visa, or other immigration status. Typically, they won't notice the problem until you arrive for your visa or green card interview—at which time they'll often alert you to the issue, then give you more time to either prove that their suspicion that you are inadmissible is wrong, or to apply for a waiver.

Assuming your case is not denied outright, there are four ways to deal with the immigration authorities' possible denial of your application based on inadmissibility:

- In the case of physical or mental illness, you may be able to treat and cure the condition.
- You can prove that you really don't fall into the category of inadmissibility. For example, in the case of a criminal ground of inadmissibility, you may be able to go back to the criminal court and have the court set aside the criminal conviction.
- You can prove that the accusations of inadmissibility against you are a mistake and completely false.

- You can apply for a waiver of inadmissibility.

If, even after you have presented more evidence, you are found inadmissible, your application will be denied.

Some people manage to hide their inadmissibility long enough to receive a green card or visa and be admitted into the United States. However, if the problem is ever discovered, for example when they apply for U.S. citizenship, they can be deported.

In fact, in rare situations, a person who already has a green card and who leaves the U.S. can be found inadmissible upon returning. This can happen to green card holders who have either:

- given up their U.S. permanent resident status
- been outside the U.S. for 180 days (approximately six months) at a stretch
- done something illegal while outside the U.S.
- left the U.S. in the middle of removal or extradition proceedings
- committed one of the crimes that make a person inadmissible (as listed in I.N.A. § 212(a)(2)), or
- tried to enter the U.S. without going through an official inspection, or succeeded in doing so.

EXAMPLE: Maria, who is from Mexico, marries a U.S. citizen and successfully obtains a green card. Three years later however, the two of them divorce. Maria, who by now has one child, is unable to find a job that pays enough to cover child care. Also, she has no medical insurance. When her daughter becomes ill with leukemia, she drives to Mexico where she can afford to see a doctor. They stay for seven months—a long enough absence that she is once again subject to the grounds of inadmissibility. When Maria tries to return to the U.S., the border officials discover the situation and deny Maria entry on grounds that she is likely to become a public charge (receive government assistance) and is therefore inadmissible.

1. Curing the Condition That Makes You Inadmissible

If you have had a physical or mental illness that is a ground of inadmissibility and you have been cured of the condition by the time you submit your green card application, you will no longer be considered inadmissible. If the condition is not cured by the time you apply, you may still be given more time to seek a cure, or you may apply for a waiver of inadmissibility.

2. Proving That You're Not Really Inadmissible

Proving that you're not really inadmissible is mainly useful for overcoming criminal and ideological grounds of inadmissibility. Both the type of crime committed and the nature of the punishment must be examined in search of an argument for why your criminal activity doesn't really constitute a ground of inadmissibility.

For example, with some crimes, only actual convictions are grounds of inadmissibility. If you have been charged with a crime and the charges were then dropped, or if the case is still on appeal, you can argue that you weren't, in fact, convicted. Sometimes a conviction can be "vacated" if you can show it was unlawfully obtained—in essence, that you were wrongly convicted.

On the other hand, a crime that has been expunged or erased from your record (which some states allow if you, for example, successfully complete your probation and other requirements), still counts for immigration purposes. Getting a conviction expunged is still usually a good idea for many reasons, but you will need to disclose the conviction on any immigration form that asks about past convictions.

Another example involves crimes of moral turpitude. Crimes of moral turpitude are those showing dishonesty or immoral conduct. There is no set list within the laws or federal regulations of which crimes involve moral turpitude, particularly because it partly depends on the precise wording of each U.S. state's criminal laws. However, the U.S. Department of State's *Foreign Affairs Manual* does contain a list of crimes considered inside and outside the realm of "moral turpitude," at 9 FAM 40.21. Referring to this list may be useful if you're trying to determine (and persuade USCIS) whether a particular crime involved moral turpitude. That leaves some room for argument.

Crimes where the person intended to commit theft, fraud, great bodily harm, or lewd acts, or the person acted with recklessness or malice, are usually considered to fit the moral turpitude description. Committing acts that amount to a crime of moral turpitude can be a ground of inadmissibility, even if you weren't actually arrested or convicted.

Crimes with no element of moral turpitude, however, are often not considered grounds of inadmissibility.

Still other factors that may help you are the length (hopefully short) of any prison terms, how long ago the crime was committed, the number of convictions in your background, conditions of plea bargaining, and available pardons.

SEE AN EXPERT

As you can see, proving that a criminal ground of inadmissibility does not apply in your case is a complicated business. You need to have a firm grasp not only of immigration law, but the technicalities of criminal law as well. If you have a criminal problem in your past, you may be able to get a green card, but not without the help of an experienced immigration lawyer.

3. Proving That a Finding of Inadmissibility Is Factually Incorrect

You can also try to prove that the suggestion that you are inadmissible is just plain wrong. For example, if a USCIS medical examination shows that you have certain medical problems, you can present reports from other doctors stating that the first diagnosis was wrong and that you are free of the problem condition. Or, if you are accused of lying on a visa application, you can present evidence proving that you told the truth, or that your false statements were made unintentionally.

4. Applying for a Waiver

If you have no choice but to admit that the ground of inadmissibility applies to you, there's one last hope in some cases: applying for a waiver. In obtaining a waiver, you don't try to get rid of or disprove the ground of inadmissibility. Instead you ask the immigration authorities to overlook the problem and give you a green card or visa anyway. Not all grounds of inadmissibility can be waived, however. For example, people who have abused, trafficked in, or been addicted to drugs have no opportunity to apply for a waiver.

When the contents of your application clearly show that you're inadmissible, and a waiver is generally available for that ground of inadmissibility, you may submit an application for a waiver at the same time you submit the rest of your application.

In many cases, however, the issue won't come up until the final visa interview at a USCIS office or consulate. You will then be given additional time to file your waiver request. Unfortunately, having to file for a waiver at that point will slow down the process greatly—waivers can take many months to process. In many cases, the person reviewing your case does not make the final decision—it is sent to a supervisor, or even to another office. For example, if you file your waiver application with a U.S. consulate abroad, you will have to wait for the consulate to send your application to a USCIS office. The consulate cannot approve the waiver on its own.

Waiver applications are made on Form I-601 (or I-601A for the provisional waiver) and must include a filing fee ($930 for the I-601 and $630 for the I-601A plus an additional $85 for biometrics). The form and fee are just the beginning of the waiver application process, however. For USCIS to evaluate your case, it will also need to see convincing evidence that you deserve the waiver.

For example, in cases where your waiver eligibility depends on having a qualifying relative, you'd need to include a birth or marriage certificate showing that you are truly related to that person, as well as proof that your relative is a U.S. citizen or permanent resident. If the waiver requires that you show hardship to the U.S. citizen or permanent resident if you aren't allowed to immigrate to the U.S., you'd need to provide reports from doctors, psychiatrists, or others who can testify how important you are to that person (simply being emotionally close or in love is usually not enough) and discuss the difficulties (medical, psychological, educational, or other) that the person would face upon either moving to your country or being separated from you.

In a medical waiver, you'd normally need to prove that your health costs will be covered and that the nature of your condition and your personal behavior make it unlikely that you'll pass the disease to others.

SEE AN EXPERT

Many technical factors control whether your application for a waiver of inadmissibility is granted. You stand the best chance of success by hiring a good immigration lawyer. The lawyer may have some creative strategies to help you. For example, a lawyer may be able to bring you to the United States on a temporary, nonimmigrant visa (for which it's easier to obtain a waiver), giving you more time to deal with the ground of inadmissibility before applying for a green card.

Dealing With Paperwork, Government Officials, Delays, and Denials

Remember the application bog that we discussed early in the book? No matter what type of visa, green card, or other immigration status you apply for, your application process will involve a lot of paperwork—forms that you fill out, birth certificates and other documents that you collect, filing fees, and more. Then you'll have to wait while your carefully prepared application gets shuffled along with hundreds of thousands of others through a maze of government offices. You may also need to meet in person with government officials. In order to prevent any or all of your work—and your hopes—from getting mishandled, misunderstood, or lost, you're going to have to:

- set up a system for organizing your personal paperwork (see Section A, below)
- make sure that all your forms and documents are of a type that USCIS and the consulates will accept (see Section B, below)
- locate and translate some of the documents that you'll need to support your application (see Section C, below)
- protect your application before you mail it from being lost by the U.S. government (see Section D, below)
- track your application's progress and write letters or perform other follow-up in case of delays (see Section E, below)
- prepare to present yourself and your case to a government official (see

Section F, below, regarding consular interviews, Section G regarding USCIS interviews in the U.S., and Section H on how to handle interviews that go badly)

- know your options when an application is denied (see Section I, below), and
- know how to contact a U.S. Congressperson for help (see Section J, below).

This could be the most important chapter in this book for you to read and understand.

A. Getting Organized

Start by setting up a good system to keep track of all the forms and documents that you'll need during your application process. There is no feeling worse than being in front of an impatient government official while you desperately go through piles of stuff looking for that one vital slip of paper. And sometimes the government might even lose documents you send, in which case you'll be asked to provide copies of what you originally sent with your application. If you're working with an attorney, he or she will hopefully keep good copies of all materials submitted to the government. However, you'd be wise to ask for copies of everything your attorney has submitted to the relevant agency on your behalf. That way, you can keep a backup set of copies on your own.

We suggest using manila file folders and keeping them in a box or drawer. Another idea might be to keep your documents organized in a number of large envelopes and in turn place all the envelopes in an "accordion file." Label one folder or envelope Original Documents, for things like your birth certificate, marriage certificate, and USCIS or consular approval notices. Keep this file in a very safe place (such as a safe deposit box at your local bank). Be sure to remember to retrieve your originals in time to take them to your interview.

Label the other files or envelopes according to which sets of forms or documents they contain. If you're applying for a green card within the United States, for example, you might label one folder Visa Petition; another Adjustment of Status Packet; another Interview Materials (containing copies of the documents you'll want to take to your interview); and another Old Drafts/Copies. Similarly, if you're applying from a country outside of the U.S., one folder might be labeled Visa Petition, another Mailed to the NVC, another Affidavit of Support and Financial Documents, another Interview Materials, and the rest as described above.

Also keep a separate file for correspondence from USCIS or the consulate. Include your handwritten notes on any phone conversations you've had with USCIS or consular personnel. Don't forget to write the date on your notes, so you can refer to them later in further correspondence.

When you've finished filling a folder or envelope, take out some of the old drafts or items you've decided not to use and move them to the Old Drafts/Copies folder, so as not to clutter up the materials you'll take to your interview. You may want to write something like "final copy, mailed xx/xx/20xx" (you fill in the date) on the top of the copy of the application or petition document you've mailed to USCIS or the NVC.

B. How to Obtain and Prepare Immigration Application Forms

The first step in virtually every immigration application process is to fill out a government form. We haven't included copies of these forms in this book, because the government revises them frequently and you'll want to get the latest version. The forms are free and easy to obtain on your own by downloading them from the website of the relevant government agency (the most likely one being USCIS; just enter www.uscis.gov/forms to get an idea).

1. Where to Get the Forms You'll Need

The forms you'll need will come from up to three sources:

- **USCIS,** which produces the forms for any application being sent to a USCIS service center, district office, or other U.S.-based office

- the **U.S. State Department,** which produces the forms for any application being handled by a U.S. consulate in another country, or
- the **U.S. Department of Labor,** which produces the forms for certain parts of the application for an employment-based visa or green card.

TIP
The government, your immigration lawyer, and others often refer to forms not by their name or title, but by the form numbers. For example, if you apply for a family-based green card, you'll start the process with a form entitled "I-130, Petition for Alien Relative." However, this form is usually called simply the "I-130." If you don't see the number in the title, you'll probably see it at the bottom of the form.

How Nightmarish Can It Get?

Maybe you'll turn in your application and everything will go like clockwork: USCIS and consular files all in order, approval received on time. Educating yourself about the process and preparing everything carefully certainly improves your chances. But we wouldn't be doing our job if we didn't warn you about how the government bureaucracy can chew up and spit out even the best-prepared application.

Every immigration lawyer has his or her favorite horror stories. For instance, there was the client whose visa petitions were lost by USCIS—so after many months, the lawyer filed new petitions and cancelled the checks that went with the lost ones. But USCIS then found, and tried to cash, the "lost" checks—and to collect the bank charges from the client when the checks bounced.

Then there was the woman who waited over six months for USCIS to approve her

work permit—only to have it finally send her a work permit with someone else's name and photo. By the time that finally got straightened out, the work permit had expired and USCIS forced her to apply, and pay again, for a new one.

And let's not forget the woman who nearly got stuck outside the United States because USCIS refused to renew her Refugee Travel Document on the nonsensical grounds that she hadn't provided a valid address in the application. (She had, and it was the same address that USCIS had been using to correspond with her for years.)

What can you do about such absurd and Orwellian horrors? Mostly, just know in advance that they may happen to you, leave time to deal with them, and keep copies of everything.

USCIS application forms usually start with the letter "I" (such as in Form I-129 or I-130). Other USCIS forms start with "G" (general matters) or "N" (naturalization-related matters). Most USCIS forms can be downloaded from its website, at www.uscis.gov/forms.

Visiting USCIS Offices

You may, at some point, wish to visit USCIS in person, whether to ask something about its handling of your case or to pick up a form (but never to ask legal advice!). However, the agency now requires visitors to most offices to make appointments online, before they arrive. The system is called "InfoPass," and it's accessible at www.uscis.gov (click the *INFOPASS* link on the left side of the page). You'll be asked to enter information and can request an appointment date. Look for a computer with a printer—you'll need a printout of your appointment notice when you go. Also, be sure to bring photo identification and any paperwork associated with your immigration case to your appointment. You can use this same website to cancel your appointment, if necessary.

If you prefer not to deal with a computer, call 800-870-3676, and USCIS will mail you the forms. However, it usually takes a few weeks for the mailed forms to arrive. You can also pick up forms at a USCIS district office—but we advise against this. Local USCIS offices require you to make appointments before you go, and those appointments can be booked only online through the InfoPass website. If you are comfortable enough with computers to book a personal appointment, you will most likely be comfortable enough to download the relevant forms yourself from the USCIS website. Also know that some USCIS forms may be "e-filed," as described below.

State Department forms usually start with the letters "DS," for "Department of State." Immigration-related State Department forms are submitted online through the Consular Electronic Application Center (CEAC), https://ceac.state.gov.

Department of Labor forms usually start with the letters "ETA." They can be downloaded from its website at www.foreignlaborcert.doleta.gov/form.cfm. However, virtually all Department of Labor forms you will need to complete as part of a visa process (whether Labor Condition Applications for H-1B workers, Prevailing Wage Determination requests, or PERM labor certification applications) are meant to be completed and submitted online through the Department of Labor iCert Web portal at https://icert.doleta.gov. Even so, you may want to download PDF versions of these forms to your computer in advance simply to get familiar with them before submitting the online version.

2. Some Applications Can—Or Must—Be Filed Online ("e-Filing")

As of 2016, only one USCIS application form can be filled out and submitted online ("e-filed")—the I-90, Application to Replace Permanent Resident Card. Formerly, applicants could e-file other forms, but USCIS is retooling its so-called Electronic Immigration System (USCIS ELIS). In the near future, expect USCIS to be able to accommodate e-filing for more forms. USCIS offers this option for your convenience—you can still use the paper form if you want to.

The benefits of e-filing include being able to file petitions and applications from anywhere with an Internet connection, pay your fees with a credit or debit card or directly through your checking or savings account, and get immediate confirmation that USCIS received your application. E-filing also lets you avoid navigating the USCIS website to determine the USCIS address to which you must mail documents.

However, e-filing can be cumbersome. You must create an account with USCIS first—that's another user name, password, and set of security-question responses to remember! Also, USCIS's online forms programs can be frustrating—you must enter information in a particular way, and the system won't let you proceed if you don't follow the rules baked into the programming.

If you've obtained a permanent resident visa ("immigrant visa") outside the U.S., you'll have to use USCIS ELIS to pay the USCIS immigrant visa fee before you depart for the United States.

If you're outside the U.S. applying for a visa, you must file your application online through the Consular Electronic Application Center, at https://ceac.state.gov. If applying for a temporary ("nonimmigrant") visa, you use the online Form DS-160. You even submit your photos online. If you're applying for a permanent resident ("immigrant") visa, use the online Form DS-260. You can pay the application fee online, and you may be able to submit the affidavit of support and scans of supporting documents online, depending on the consulate at which you're applying. To see a sample DS-260 (showing the questions you will be asked), go to www.travel.state.gov and search for "DS-260 exemplar."

If you're an employer who needs to obtain a labor condition certification from the Department of Labor to hire a non-U.S. citizen for an "H-1B" or "E-3" job, you will have to apply online through the iCERT Visa Portal System at https://icert.doleta.gov. An exception to the electronic filing requirement is made for employers with a physical disability or lack of access to the Internet, if they obtain permission to file by paper (Form ETA-9035). The iCERT portal is also used to obtain prevailing wage determinations, and for applications to hire "H-2A" and "H-2B" temporary workers.

Employers who want to sponsor non-U.S. citizens for permanent residency and who require labor certification may, but don't need to, use the Permanent Online System at www.plc.doleta.gov.

You'll need to create separate accounts for iCERT and the Permanent Online System.

All these online filing systems allow you to save your work and come back to a form that you need to finish filling in. Also, you can authorize your attorney to access and prepare applications on your behalf. It's okay for the attorney or representative to hit the "submit" button at the end, too, as long as he or she is identified as the preparer of the form. There has been controversy about whether that's true in the case of a DS-160 "nonimmigrant" visa application, however, so if you're able to, it's better for you to hit the "submit" button on a DS-160 personally.

3. Making Sure You're Using the Most Recent Form

In small print at the top and bottom of a form, you'll see the date the form expires and the date it was issued. The expiration date is especially important, because once the government issues a new version (which it does often), you'll usually need to use the latest one. For every form you plan to submit, you should check the appropriate website just before actually mailing it. Sometimes the website will tell you a date upon which the government

will stop accepting the old version of the form. You might also learn that—as sometimes happens—no new form has been issued even though the expiration date has passed.

After you have submitted the form, you can stop worrying—you won't need to redo it even if the government issues a new form before your application has been decided.

4. Reading the Instructions That Come With the Forms

The government provides instructions for all immigration-related forms. Most are found in a separate document on the agency's website. Other times they are within the same document as the form. It's worth reading the instructions closely, because the government treats them as if they're laws you must follow. However, realize that immigration laws and procedures change quickly, while revisions of the form instructions tend to lag behind. If you see contradictory information on the government's website or a later news item, that's usually the information you should act upon.

 TIP
Save yourself time and postage. If the instructions are within the same document as the form, don't include the instruction pages submitting your application. The immigration authorities want only the part of the form you fill in, and will only throw away the instruction pages.

5. Paying the Appropriate Filing Fees

Many of the immigration forms require you to pay a fee in order to file them. (No, you can't get your money back if your case is not approved.) Don't necessarily trust the fees listed on the form instructions; they're often out of date. Even the forms in this book may be out of date by the time you read this. Current USCIS fees are displayed on the "Forms" portion of its website at www.uscis.gov/forms. (USCIS fees are based on which forms you submit, so you'll need to add up the fees yourself if you submit a combination of forms.) Alternately, you can call the USCIS National Customer Service Center line at 800-375-5283.

The State Department sets the fees for visa processing. If you're applying for an immigrant visa, the National Visa Center (NVC) will send you a fee invoice stating the amount you must pay. If applying for a nonimmigrant visa, the consulate will tell you when, where, and how much to pay. You can also see the fees on the State Department's website at travel.state.gov.

You must pay USCIS fees by personal check or money order, made out in most cases to the U.S. Department of Homeland Security. (Do not abbreviate it.) Don't send cash through the mail! Forms filed online can be paid using a credit or debit card, which can reduce any anxiety about getting the filing fee correct, and give you the immediate satisfaction of a receipt number in real time.

For some applications, you may find yourself submitting more than one petition or application at the same time. For example, in a marriage case where your spouse is here in the U.S., you can file Form I-130 (the immigrant petition filed by a U.S. spouse) and Form I-485 (the "adjustment of status" application you file for yourself) simultaneously. Or, you may file applications for your spouse and your stepchild in the same envelope. In any of these situations, resist the temptation to combine every person's filing fees into a single check.

If you submit separate, individual checks for each filing fee, then if you make a mistake on the check (for example, you forget to sign it, or you make it for the wrong amount), USCIS will reject only the filing that is affected by that check. But if you submit a single check covering all fees, you will ruin all of the filings at once if you make a mistake. It's a pain to have to write more than one check for forms and applications being submitted in the same package, but it's worth it.

6. Use a Typewriter, or Fill in the Form by Hand?

All immigration forms can be filled out using a computer. If you prefer to complete the forms by hand, this isn't the time to express your individuality with purple ink. If you can find a typewriter (maybe in an antique shop?), consider using one. If your handwriting's sloppy or hard to read, your form could get rejected, or you could cause the government to issue you documents containing incorrect information. Getting such errors corrected can be harder work than doing it right the first time.

Unless you can submit a form through an online system, after printing the form out you'll need to handwrite your signature and possibly also your answers to questions that the form didn't provide enough room to answer fully or accurately. If you hand-write anything on the forms, use black ink. Immigration agencies have been known to reject forms for use of the wrong color ink, without warning or explicit instructions about which color to use.

> **TIP**
> **Get electronic confirmation that your application arrived.** If you submit USCIS Form G-1145 with your application or petition, USCIS will send you an email and/or text message for any immigration form you send to a so-called "Lockbox" location. Although use of the G-1145 form is not mandatory, it's worth your time. You complete and affix it to the top of your application package. Then you'll receive notification that USCIS received your application, along with your all-important receipt number. This may shave days, or even weeks, off the time you would have had to wait for USCIS to mail you a hard-copy receipt. Or, if USCIS fails to mail you

the hard-copy receipt (hey, it happens), or your receipt gets lost in the mail (that happens, too), the electronic notification may provide your only evidence that USCIS received your application!

7. Inapplicable Questions

A lot of times, you will see a question on a form that just doesn't fit your situation, or one asking for information that doesn't exist. Read the instructions that come with every form to determine what the immigration agency wants you do about these questions. Most often you'll be told to write "N/A" (not applicable) rather than leave the space blank or, if the answer is "none," as in "number of children," to answer "none." (Try not to mix these two up—it irritates the government officials reading your application.) Confusingly enough, the instructions to other forms tell you the opposite: If there is no answer, just leave the space blank. If you're not sure how or whether to answer a question, seek skilled legal help. (Chapter 6 gives you information on finding a good lawyer.)

8. Telling the Truth

There will be many temptations to lie in this process—to hide a ground of inadmissibility, ignore a previous marriage, or avoid questions about previous visits to the United States, for example. But lying to the government can get you in bigger trouble than the problem you are lying about. And you've never seen anyone angrier than a government official who discovers that you've lied to him or her. Many immigration violations can be "forgiven," depending upon their context and when they occurred. However, lying on an immigration application will (almost) never be forgiven by the U.S. government, and in fact federal law requires USCIS to ban you from the U.S. forever (as in, forever) if you are deemed to have lied (including having made "material omissions") during the immigration process.

If you feel you just can't complete the form without hiding a certain piece of information—or you really don't know how to answer or explain a key question—see a lawyer. The lawyer may be able to show you how to be truthful in a way that doesn't risk having your application denied.

And even if the lawyer tells you that the application will be denied as a result of some prior violation, wouldn't you rather know that *before* wasting your time and money? Another thing to keep in mind, particularly if you are not lawfully in the U.S. at the time you submit an application: Being unlawfully present is not necessarily "dangerous" as long as you are off the government's "radar." However, submitting an application may put you very squarely on the government's radar, and perhaps leave you worse off than if you had never submitted an application. Therefore, if you ever think there is something about your past that might prevent approval of

the application, consult an attorney rather than give in to the temptation to "cover up" that issue when filing your application.

CAUTION
What if you're asked for an address and you're living in the U.S. illegally? One piece of information that frequently causes concern to immigrants living illegally in the United States is their address. Many of them wonder whether they shouldn't use a friend's address as a "mailing address." However, depending on the form and the purpose of the question, this could be interpreted as lying on an immigration form, which could disqualify your application by itself. You are expected to supply your actual address. Fortunately, USCIS has, so far, shown very little interest in using these addresses to track down people living here illegally. (However, we can't guarantee that this will continue in the future.) Many forms do allow you to include a "mailing" address (e.g., "in care of…"), but elsewhere ask you to detail your home address as of today, or perhaps over the past five years. It is important to answer those questions truthfully.

9. What's Your Name?

The easiest thing on a form should be filling out your name, right? Not in this bureaucratic morass. The immigration authorities will want not only your current name, but on certain of its forms, "other names used." Here are some important things to get straight before you start writing your name(s) in the forms to follow:

- **Current name.** When your current name is requested, it is best to insert the name you currently use for legal purposes. This will normally be the name on your bank account, driver's license, and passport. If you've always gone by a nickname (for example, your name is Richard but you always use the common nickname "Dick"), it's okay to fill in the application as "Dick," as long as you list "Richard" where the form asks for other names used. This will avoid confusion when someone compares your application form with the accompanying documents (your employer, for example, might write a letter on your behalf saying "Dick worked here…"). But there's no way to avoid a little confusion, since your birth certificate will still say Richard.

- **Legal name changes.** If you've actually done a court-ordered legal name change, include a copy of the court order, to help dispel some of the inevitable confusion. If you have changed your name without a court order (by simply beginning to use a different name and using it consistently, which is legal in many states) and you use your changed name for all legal purposes, list it as your current name.

- **Married name.** If you've just married and changed your last name as part of your marriage, use your married name. But women shouldn't feel pressured into taking on a married name. By now the U.S. immigration authorities are well aware that not all women change their names when they marry. Nor does having different last names seem to cause any confusion in the processing of your application (after all, for better and for worse, the government tends to think of you as a number, not a name).

- **Other names used.** The category for "other names used" could include nicknames. The immigration authorities will want to know about nicknames that might have made their way onto your various legal documents (or criminal record). You should also include names by which you have been commonly known, especially as an adult.

- **Previous married names.** If you have been married previously, and used a married name then, don't forget to list that name in the boxes requesting other names used.

10. Being Consistent

You will more than likely be filling out many forms in connection with your immigration application—and many of them ask for exactly the same pieces of information. If you're not consistent in filling these out, you may cause confusion. At worst, not getting your facts straight can cause the person reviewing your application to think you cannot be believed. If, for example, you live with your parents but sometimes stay with a friend and receive mail there, make up your mind which address to use and then stick to it.

C. How to Obtain Needed Documents

You would be lucky if forms were the only paperwork you had to worry about—but no, there are documents, too. For example, you often need to supply your birth and marriage certificates, school transcripts, employment records, death or divorce certificates, or the birth certificate or U.S. passport of a U.S. citizen relative who is petitioning for you.

When it's time for your visa or green card approval, you will need a passport from your own country (either to travel to the United States or to hold a stamp showing your residence status).

Within the United States, official copies of birth, death, marriage, and divorce certificates can usually be obtained from the vital records office (called the registrar's or recorder's office in some areas) of the appropriate county or locality. Even if you already have your own copy of these items, it's a good idea to request a copy from the vital records office. That's because your copy may not have been given all the official governmental stamps necessary for the immigration authorities to accept it as authentic.

You can find more details on the National Center for Health Statistics website at www.cdc.gov/nchs/w2w.htm. Or, check the blue pages of a U.S. phone book. There are also services that will order your vital records for a fee, such as www.vitalchek.com.

U.S. passports are available to U.S. citizens through the State Department; see www.passports.state.gov or the federal government pages of a U.S. phone book.

Outside of the United States, records should be obtained from official, government sources wherever possible. The sources that USCIS and the State Department consider acceptable are listed in the State Department's website, at usvisas.state.gov (click "Fees/Reciprocity" then "Visa Issuance Fee–Reciprocity Tables"). Enter the name of the country you need documents from, click the "go" button, then choose the type of document you need help with. If you are outside of the U.S. and do not have Web access, talk to your local U.S. consulate about what form of record will be acceptable, particularly if you need to document an event for which your government does not issue certificates.

1. Translating Non-English Documents

If the documents you submit are in a language other than English, you will need to provide both a copy of the original document and a certified, word-for-word translation (summaries are not acceptable). This is particularly true if you're submitting the document to a USCIS office; consulates can often deal with documents that are in the language of that country (their instructions will usually tell you if they can't).

There is no need to spend big bucks to obtain certified translations. Any trustworthy friend who is fluent in English and the language of the document can do the certified translation. Although you could do the translation yourself, or have a close relative do it, we don't recommend it. The immigration agency might think that you're translating certain words inaccurately to help your own case, and reject the document.

The translator should simply type out the translated text, then add at the bottom:

I certify that I am competent to translate from [*the language of the document*] to English and that the above [*identify the document and to whom it pertains*] is a correct and true translation to the best of my knowledge and belief.

Signed: _[*translator's full name*]_____

Address: _____

Telephone: _____

Date: _____

If you prefer, you can hire a professional translator, who should also add the same certification at the bottom of the translation.

2. Substituting for Unavailable Documents

If you cannot obtain a needed document, the immigration authorities may, under some circumstances, accept another type of evidence. For example, if your birth certificate was destroyed in a fire, you may be able to use school records or sworn statements by people who knew you to prove your date of birth.

The instructions included with various government forms usually outline the other types of evidence that will be accepted. If you substitute a new type of evidence for a missing document, you should also include a statement from the local civil authorities explaining why the original document is unavailable.

3. Creating Substitute Documents

One form of substitute document that you may need to use is a sworn declaration. For example, you might need to ask a friend or family member to prepare one affirming your date and place of birth. If so, emphasize to the person that fancy legal language is not as important as detailed facts when it comes to convincing an immigration official to accept his or her word in place of an official document.

Someone could write, for example, "I swear that Francois was born in Paris in 1962 to Mr. and Mrs. Marti." But it would be much more compelling for them to write, "I swear that I am Francois's older brother. I remember the morning that my mother brought him home from the hospital in 1962 (I was then five years old), and we grew up together in our parents' (Mr. and Mrs. Xavier Marti's) home in Paris."

The full declaration should be longer and contain more details than this example. The more details that are offered, the more likely USCIS or the consulate is to accept the declaration as the truth.

To start the declaration, the person should state his or her complete name and address, as well as country of citizenship. At the bottom of the declaration, the person should write:

I swear, under penalty of perjury, that the foregoing is true and correct to the best of my knowledge.

Signed: _____

Date: _____

If preparing sworn declarations seems like too much to accomplish, you could hire a lawyer (perhaps for this task only). Below is a sample of a full sworn declaration, written to prove that an immigrant who

is applying through marriage is no longer married to his first wife, due to her death. (Remember, when writing your own declaration, tailor it to your situation— don't follow the wording of the sample too closely—except for the sworn statement part, which should be verbatim.)

Don't Confuse a Declaration With an Affidavit

An affidavit is very similar to a declaration — it's a written statement that the author dates and signs—but it has one additional feature. Affidavits are notarized, which means that they are signed in front of someone who is authorized by the government to attest to, or certify, the authenticity of signatures. When you bring an affidavit to a notary, that person will ask for identification, such as your passport or driver's license, to make sure that you are the person whose signature is called for on the affidavit. You sign the affidavit in the presence of the notary, who makes a note of this in his or her notary book. The notary also places a stamp, or seal, on your document.

As you can see, affidavits are more formal and more trouble than simple declarations. An affidavit is not required for substitute documents such as we're describing now—but if you want to make the document look more official, and know where to find a notary, you might want to take the extra trouble. If an immigration process described in this book requires a notarized affidavit, we'll alert you.

Declaration in Support of Application of Guofeng Zheng

I, Shaoling Liu, hereby say and declare as follows:

1. I am a U.S. permanent resident, residing at 222 Rhododendron Drive, Seattle, WA 98111. My telephone number is 206-555-1212. I have been living in the United States since January 2, 2001.

2. I am originally from Mainland China, where I grew up in the same town (called Dahuo, in Suzhou province) as Guofeng Zheng.

3. I knew Guofeng's first wife, Meihua. I attended their wedding, and had dinner at their home several times. I also remember when Meihua fell ill with cancer. She was sick for many months before passing away on October 31, 2000.

4. I received the news of Meihua's death a few days later, in early November of 2000. I knew the doctor who had treated her, and he was very sad that his treatments had failed. I also attended Meihua's funeral on November 7th. Her ashes are buried in the local cemetery.

5. I am also aware that the municipal records office, where all deaths are recorded, burnt down in the year 2004. I myself had difficulty with this, when I tried to get a copy of my mother's birth certificate last year.

I swear, under penalty of perjury, that the foregoing is true and correct to the best of my knowledge.

Signed: _Shaoling Liu_

Date: _August 4, 2016_

Need a Copy of USCIS's Files on Your Case?

If you've submitted past applications to USCIS, and either lost your copies or want to see whether they added any notes to the paperwork, you can ask for a copy of your file. The procedure for doing this is to file what's called a Freedom of Information Act or FOIA request. There is no filing fee, and the first 100 pages of copies are free.

To file your request, fill out Form G-639 (available on the USCIS website) and mail or fax it to the USCIS National Records Center. Instructions and the mailing address are available with the G-639 and on USCIS's website. You can also email your FOIA request to uscis.foia@uscis.dhs.gov if you are able to scan your signature (which must be notarized or made under penalty of perjury), and attach it to the email. You don't have to use a G-639 if you prefer not to—any written request will do. Unfortunately, because FOIA requests are now processed centrally (unlike in past years), you'll probably wait several weeks at least for a reply. Track the status of your request online at https://egov.uscis.gov/foiawebstatus.

D. Before You Mail Anything

Most documents must be mailed to USCIS, the NVC, or other office, rather than delivered in person. There are three important rules to follow when mailing:

- Make copies.
- Mail your documents by a traceable method.
- Don't mail anything that you can't replace.

We'll explain the reasons for these maxims—and how to follow them.

1. Make Complete Copies

When you've at last finished filling out a packet of required immigration forms, your first instinct will be to seal them in an envelope, pop them in the mail, and forget about them for awhile. That could waste all of your hard work.

Find a photocopy machine and make copies of every page of every application, as well as any photos, documents, checks, and money orders. Carefully keep these in your records. This will help you recreate these pages and items if they're lost in the mail or in the overstuffed files of some government office. It may also help convince USCIS or the NVC to take another look for the lost items.

2. Mail by a Traceable Method

In any government agency, things get lost. The sorting of newly arrived applications seems to be a common time for them to disappear. If this happens to your application, it can become important to prove that you mailed it in the first place.

In the United States, one good option is to go to the post office and use certified mail with a return receipt for all your applications or correspondence with USCIS or the NVC. When you request a return receipt, you will prepare a little postcard that is attached to your envelope and will be signed by the person at USCIS or the NVC who physically receives your envelope. The postcard will be mailed to you, and will be your proof that the envelope was received. You can use this postcard to convince USCIS or the NVC to look for the document if it gets misplaced. Better yet, use a form of express mail, such as USPS Priority Mail Express, which includes online tracking and signature proof. This way, you will get electronic confirmation that USCIS received your mailed submission, even if the certified mail "return receipt" was sent to you. It may cost more, but considering the importance of these documents, now is not the time to save every penny.

If you're mailing something from outside of the U.S., you'll have to find the most reliable method, such as an overnight courier service like FedEx or UPS. However, courier services can't deliver to a post office box, and many USCIS addresses (in particular those of the Service Centers) are at post office boxes. You'll have to look for the Service Center's alternate address for delivery by courier, shown on the USCIS website at www.uscis.gov.

3. If You Want It Back, Don't Send It

Many immigration applications require that certain documents be attached (paper-clipping them to the form is fine). Some documents must be included in packets of forms you must file and others must be brought to interviews. Whatever you do, *don't send originals* to USCIS or the NVC.

Instead, simply photocopy any document (as long as the original is the official version), and send the copy to USCIS or the NVC. The USCIS or consular officer will have a chance to view the originals when you bring them to your interview. (Of course, if they make a special request that you mail them the original, you'll want to comply—but make copies for yourself first!) It's best to add the following text, right on the front of the copy, if there's room:

> Copies of documents submitted are exact photocopies of unaltered original documents, and I understand that I may be required to submit original documents to an immigration or consular official at a later date.
>
> Signature: _____
>
> Typed or printed name: _____
>
> Date: _____

Always make photocopies for USCIS on one-sided, 8½-by-11-inch paper. Some applicants have been known to try to create exact copies of things by cutting the image out of the full page of paper—creating, for example, a tiny photocopied green card. The government doesn't appreciate these minicopies, and will often reject them.

By the same token, the A4-size paper common outside the U.S. and 8½-by-14-inch paper (or larger) doesn't fit well into the government's files—use a photocopy machine that will change your document image to 8½-by-11 inches, if possible.

E. Dealing With Delays and Other Issues

In view of the number of people applying for visas and green cards, it's almost guaranteed that your application will take longer than you'd like it to. Many applications spend some months, or even years in processing limbo and that's without factoring in the very real possibility of government errors.

Although you can't prevent delays or other problems, you can anticipate them and be ready to deal with them when the time comes.

> CAUTION
> **Don't even think of bribing a U.S. government official.** Although there are countries where the only way to get anything

from a government official is to offer cash or other gifts, the United States is not one of them. Personnel at USCIS and the consulates may sometimes be difficult, but it's generally not because they're expecting money. In fact, most of them are proud of the fact that the United States operates strictly according to the rule of law. Offering a bribe will most likely hurt your chances of getting a green card or visa.

1. Preparing Yourself to Deal With USCIS

If USCIS is taking too long with your application or some other problem arises, your first action should be to call its National Customer Service Center at 800-375-5283. Have in front of you any receipt number assigned to your case and your Alien Registration Number ("A-number") if you've already been assigned one. (Look for the letter A followed by eight or nine digits.)

You can find your receipt number on the "notice of action" (Form I-797C) USCIS sent you. It will look something like "CSC 14-202-50007." You'll recognize it because it starts with a three-letter abbreviation—the main ones being CSC, LIN, EAC, SRC, or MSC. These abbreviations refer to the Service Center handling your application: California uses CSC (formerly WAC), Missouri (the "National Benefits Center") uses MSC or NBC, Nebraska uses LIN, Vermont uses EAC, Texas uses SRC, and the new Potomac Service Center uses YSC.

In this example, the 14 represents the fiscal year (October 1, 2013 through September 30, 2014) in which the case was received. The 202 refers to the computer workday on which the fee was collected. The 50007 represents your particular case number.

When you call USCIS Customer Service, it's a good idea to note down the date and time you're calling, the name and/or ID number of the person helping you, and the service request referral number the customer service representative gives you at the end of the call. If you need to follow up in the future, this information will make it easier.

2. When Should You Start Inquiring About Delays?

When it comes to delays, how long is too long? That is the million-dollar question. Processing times for immigration applications vary, depending on the number of people applying at a given time, the USCIS resources available during that particular time of year, and so on. If you're waiting for an initial receipt, such as one for an I-130 or I-140 visa petition that your family member or employer filed with a USCIS service center, six weeks is the longest you should wait. After that, your family member or employer should contact the bank on which the filing fee check was drawn, to determine whether the check was cashed. If not, that is a good sign the application was either lost in the mail or rejected by USCIS, and is soon to

be returned to you. However, if the filing fee check was cashed, then you now have proof that USCIS accepted your application. Here's a useful trick: After confirming that the check was cashed, try to get a photocopy of the physical check from your bank. You will find that USCIS printed the receipt number for your filing on the back of the cancelled check. Armed with that receipt number, you'll have better luck when calling USCIS at 800-375-5283 to complain.

3. USCIS Time Estimates for Application Approval

With the case receipt number you're given on the USCIS Notice of Action (Form I-797C), you can check the USCIS Case Status Online Web page to find out the last action taken on your case. Go to the USCIS website (www.uscis.gov) and click "Check Your Case Status." Enter your receipt number in the box and click the "Check Status" button.

Even without using your receipt notice, you can get an idea of how long it will take to process your application. Case processing times are found at https://egov.uscis.gov/cris/processTimesDisplayInit.do. You'll need to know which office is handling your case, because times vary among the different USCIS offices. For each type of application, USCIS will either list an estimate of the time it will take for you to get a decision (from the date of filing) or list a date. Time estimates are just that—estimates—and you can't really hold USCIS to them. They do give you a reasonably accurate idea, however. If you see a date, that means USCIS is in the process of looking at all applications filed on or before that date. If yours was filed after that date, you'll need to be patient. You'll know there's a problem only if you filed your application well before the listed date.

4. Delays Beyond USCIS Time Estimates

USCIS won't want to hear from you with more inquiries about your application until the number of processing days predicted on its website has passed. If USCIS has far exceeded the expected processing time, it's time to take further action. A possible first step, if you live close to a USCIS office, is to make an InfoPass appointment to talk with a USCIS officer in person. InfoPass appointments are made online at https://infopass.uscis.gov.

If it's too hard for you to get to a USCIS office, you can ask what's going on with your case by calling USCIS customer service or by sending an "e-request" to https://egov.uscis.gov/e-Request/Intro.do.

Certain email addresses could also come in handy. If you're wondering about an application or petition that was mailed to a USCIS "lockbox" (Chicago, Dallas, or Phoenix), contact LockboxSupport@uscis.

dhs.gov. Include the form number of your petition or application, receipt number (if you got one), and the petitioner or applicant's name and mailing address.

You can email a USCIS service center directly, but only after calling USCIS Customer Service first, and then only if 30 more days go by without any action on your case. The email addresses for the service centers are:

- California Service Center: csc-ncsc-followup@dhs.gov
- Vermont Service Center: vsc.ncscfollowup@dhs.gov
- Nebraska Service Center: NSCFollowup.NCSC@uscis.dhs.gov
- Potomac Service Center: psc.ncscfollowup@uscis.dhs.gov
- Texas Service Center: tsc.ncscfollowup@dhs.gov.

If you do not receive a response within 21 days of contacting a service center, there's one final email address to try: USCIS Headquarters Office of Service Center Operations, SCOPSSCATA@dhs.gov.

If you are still not getting results, consider contacting the USCIS Ombudsman's Office at www.dhs.gov/case-assistance. Also electronically file DHS Form 7001 (at www.dhs.gov/case-assistance—click "electronic Form DHS-7001") in order to start a formal status inquiry.

Be careful, however—although eloquent and justified outrage may eventually get USCIS's attention, never insult or threaten

Sample Receipt Notice for I-129F

Department of Homeland Security
U.S. Citizenship and Immigration Services

I-797C, Notice of Action

THE UNITED STATES OF AMERICA

RECEIPT NUMBER CSC-16-041-00000		CASE TYPE I129F PETITION FOR FIANCE(E)
RECEIVED DATE November 18, 2016	PRIORITY DATE	PETITIONER ANDERSON, CHRISTA
NOTICE DATE December 1, 2016	PAGE 1 of 1	BENEFICIARY CUEVAS, BERNARDO

ILONA BRAY RE: BERNARDO CUEVAS 950 PARKER ST. BERKELEY, CA 94710	**Notice Type:** Receipt Notice Amount received: $ 340.00

Receipt notice - If any of the above information is incorrect, call customer service immediately.

Processing time - Processing times vary by kind of case.
- You can check our current processing time for this kind of case on our website at **uscis.gov**.
- On our website you can also sign up to get free e-mail updates as we complete key processing steps on this case.
- Most of the time your case is pending the processing status will not change because we will be working on others filed earlier.
- We will notify you by mail when we make a decision on this case, or if we need something from you. If you move while this case is pending, call customer service when you move.
- Processing times can change. If you don't get a decision or update from us within our current processing time, check our website or call for an update.

If you have questions, check our website or call customer service. Please save this notice, and have it with you if you contact us about this case.

Notice to all customers with a pending I-130 petition - USCIS is now processing Form I-130, Petition for Alien Relative, as a visa number becomes available. Filing and approval of an I-130 relative petition is only the first step in helping a relative immigrate to the United States. Eligible family members must wait until there is a visa number available before they can apply for an immigrant visa or adjustment of status to a lawful permanent resident. This process will allow USCIS to concentrate resources first on cases where visas are actually available. This process should not delay the ability of one's relative to apply for an immigrant visa or adjustment of status. Refer to **www.state.gov/travel** **<http://www.state.gov/travel>** to determine current visa availability dates. For more information, please visit our website at www.uscis.gov or contact us at 1-800-375-5283.

Always remember to call customer service if you move while your case is pending. If you have a pending I-130 relative petition, also call customer service if you should decide to withdraw your petition or if you become a U.S. citizen.

Please see the additional information on the back. You will be notified separately about any other cases you filed.
IMMIGRATION & NATURALIZATION SERVICE
CALIFORNIA SERVICE CENTER
P. O. BOX 30111
LAGUNA NIGUEL CA 92607-0111
Customer Service Telephone: (800) 375-5283

Form I-797C (Rev. 08/31/04) N

a government official. This will get you nowhere and, if your letter is interpreted as a threat, may lead to a criminal prosecution as well as a quick denial.

5. Emergency Attention

If there is some reason that your application really should be given immediate attention —that is, put ahead of all the other waiting applications—you can ask USCIS to "expedite" your case. You can do this by calling the customer service number, making an InfoPass appointment, or writing a letter to the USCIS field office or service center. But limit your cries for help to true emergencies, such as:

- A family member is very ill or dying in your home country and you need permission to leave the country during your green card processing to visit them.
- You have a scheduled surgery on the same day as an important USCIS appointment.

If possible, include proof of any claimed emergency, such as a letter from a doctor. Remember, they won't change the laws to accommodate you; for example, if you are waiting in line for a family-based visa, and the government has already given out the maximum number that year, nothing you can do will convince them to give you a visa

out of next year's allotment. But if you're simply waiting for the government to act on something that it could do any time, but for being backed up with excess work, you can legitimately ask for quicker attention.

6. Dealing With Delays at the NVC

If you are seeking an immigrant visa for permanent residency in the U.S. and USCIS has approved a petition for you, your case will be sent to the National Visa Center (NVC) in Portsmouth, New Hampshire, for "preprocessing." If you run into delays or other problems at this point, you'll want to contact the NVC. There are two ways to do it.

First, try calling the NVC at 603-334-0700. Call between 7 a.m. and midnight, Eastern time, Monday through Friday (except holidays). You might have trouble getting through; keep trying.

Or, you can send your question by a form on the "Ask NVC!" webpage, https://secureforms.travel.state.gov/ask-nvc.php. Be prepared with the NVC case number (if you've received one) or else the USCIS receipt number. There's a dropdown menu that allows you to select from a list of question types. You can type comments or other questions in a box on the form. Someone at the NVC will reply to your inquiry eventually. Be patient.

TIP
Your case number is on the letter you received from the National Visa Center. It usually starts with the three-letter abbreviation for your consulate.

TIP
Even though a K-1 fiancé visa is technically a nonimmigrant visa, most consulates treat them like immigrant visa cases. Check the consulate's website for information on where to send K-1 inquiries.

7. Dealing With Delays at the Consulate

If you're applying for an immigrant visa at a U.S. consulate outside the U.S., and the NVC has told you that the case has been scheduled for an interview, your questions and concerns at this point need to be addressed to the consulate. The same is true if you are seeking a nonimmigrant visa—the case is outside the control of USCIS or the NVC, and you need to deal with the consulate directly.

Each embassy or consulate has its own contact information, usually found on its website. Email is a good way to get a response; you can also try calling the consulate. (Sometimes it's hard to find the right email on the website.)

U.S. embassies and consulates do a lot of things other than issue visas. The contact number or email address you're looking for is for the visa office or visa "section." In addition, many consulates have separate email addresses for different types of cases: immigrant visas, nonimmigrant visas, refugee cases, and so on. Make sure you're sending your email to the right address.

8. Incomplete or Lost Portions of Your Application

If USCIS or the consulate needs something to complete your application, such as further evidence of your bona fide marriage or a missing financial document, they will usually mail you a request. If you receive a request for more documentation, try to gather whatever the immigration authorities have asked for and get it in the mail as soon as possible. Don't forget to include the notification form as a cover sheet—but make a copy for yourself first. A sample of the kind of notice a Service Center might send is shown below (this sample is from a work permit application).

What should you do if you're asked for something that you know you've already sent? This is a surprisingly common occurrence. The person handling your application may have just overlooked it, or sent you a "form" letter listing everything under the sun and leaving you to sort it out. If the requested item is something inexpensive or easy to come by, don't even try arguing with USCIS or the NVC—even if you have photocopies proving that you already sent the item. Just assume it's been lost and send another one.

Lost checks or money orders are a different matter. Don't send another check or money order until you've found out what happened to the first draft. If you sent a check and haven't received information about it with your monthly bank statement, ask your bank to tell you whether your check has been cashed. If so, get the check and send USCIS a copy of both sides, so that the officials can see their own stamp and processing number. If you sent a money order and kept the receipt with the tracer number, call the company that issued the money order to find out whether it's been cashed. Ask for a copy of the cashed money order or other evidence that you can use to prove who cashed it. If you can't get a copy of the cashed money order, send a copy of your receipt and an explanation. Hopefully, they will stop bugging you for the money.

F. Attending Interviews With USCIS or Consular Officials

The final step in obtaining your visa or green card is—with very few exceptions— to attend an interview with a U.S. consular or USCIS official.

Until the date of your interview, it's quite possible that you will not have had any personal contact with any immigration official. For that reason, many applicants approach the interview with needless fear. Below, we coach you on what to expect and how to treat the interview as important— without suffering it as an ordeal.

With all the paperwork you've submitted by now (especially if you're applying for a green card, not a temporary visa), you might think the government should be able to approve your request without having to meet you face to face. However, the government views the interview as its opportunity to confirm the contents of your application after you've sworn to tell the truth (even though you represented that the answers on your application forms were true and correct when you signed them). The interview also allows the government to ask additional questions—for example, in a marriage-based green card case, to ask personal questions that will test whether your marriage is real or a sham.

1. Who Must Attend an Interview?

Almost every hopeful immigrant or visitor will need to attend an interview, whether for a temporary visa or a green card.

 SKIP AHEAD

Refugee and asylum interviews are a special case. We'll discuss what happens at these interviews in Chapter 13.

If you're applying for a family-based green card at a USCIS office, your petitioning family member will usually be required to attend the interview with you.

If you're applying for a family-based visa/green card from outside of the U.S., however, your U.S. petitioner is not usually required to attend the interview—but it's an excellent idea for the petitioner to do so, if permitted by the consulate. After all, one of the main topics of discussion will be a form your family member filled out—the Affidavit of Support—showing his or her financial situation. If your family member can confirm the contents of the affidavit in person, so much the better.

2. Preparing for Your Interview

The key to a smooth interview is preparation. Prepare all the appropriate forms and documents as described in the appropriate chapter of this book. The USCIS or consular office will send you a list with your appointment notice, but you should also prepare your own set of documents for you to refer to during the interview.

a. What to Review

In order to prepare for the oral part of the interview, your most important homework task is to review your paperwork. Look at the questions and answers on every form that you've submitted or that has been submitted for you, including by your U.S.

petitioner. Though they seem to contain only boring, dry bits of information, this information is loaded with meaning to a USCIS or consular official. The dates of your visits to different places, the financial figures, and your immigration history can all add up to a revealing picture in the official's eyes.

EXAMPLE: Leticia hates dealing with money issues, so she didn't read the Affidavit of Support that her husband filled out. And she didn't notice that her husband wrote on the form that he has "no dependents." At the interview, the officer observed, "It looks like your husband doesn't earn much. How will you be supported?" Leticia replied, "Oh, I'm sure we'll make do financially. After all, my husband's aging parents and orphan nephew all live with him and don't work and he seems to support them just fine." Leticia just created a huge problem. It's now apparent that her husband lied on his Affidavit of Support and has several dependents. He is clearly less capable of supporting Leticia than it originally appeared. As a result, the consular officer may find Leticia inadmissible as a potential public charge.

The example above shows why you and your petitioner should review all the paperwork and forms carefully to be sure both of you understand them completely. If there have been any changes or if you've noticed any errors since filling out the forms, be prepared to explain the changes and provide documents confirming the new information, if appropriate.

b. What to Wear

The interviewing officer's decision rests almost entirely on whether he or she believes that you're telling the truth. You'll come across as more sincere if you're dressed neatly, professionally, and even conservatively. Avoid T-shirts or jewelry with slogans or symbols that might make the officer wonder about your lifestyle or morals.

> EXAMPLE: Jon showed up at his interview wearing gaudy and expensive leather shoes and, around his neck, a chain with a solid gold marijuana leaf dangling from it. The officer took one look at this and went right into questioning him as to whether he had ever tried, abused, or sold drugs. When Jon wouldn't admit to anything, she referred him for another medical exam. The doctor found evidence of drug use in Jon's bloodstream, and he was denied the visa.

3. Procedures for Consular Interviews

If you're coming from a country outside of the U.S. and are interested in a temporary visa, check your consulate's website or call it to find out its appointment procedures—you may need an advance appointment, or you may simply be able to arrive and stand in line.

If you're applying for a fiancé visa or an immigrant (green card) visa, the NVC will mail you an interview notice telling you where and when to go for your visa interview.

a. Getting There Safely, on Time

If you don't live in the same city as the consulate, plan to arrive at least a few days in advance. You will need time to complete your medical exam (at a clinic designated by the consulate) and to get the test results back.

On the day of your interview, it's best to arrive early, in case there's a line. Don't be surprised if you have to wait beyond your scheduled appointment time—the consulates often schedule applicants in large groups, telling all the members of each group to show up at the same time.

 CAUTION

Beware of crime around U.S. consulates. Criminals know where the U.S. consulates are and they know that many people going for interviews are carrying large sums of money for visa fees. Take whatever precautions you think are appropriate in your country. Watch out for con artists who hang around the consulate, trying to convince people that they won't get through the front door unless they hand over some money first.

b. What the Consular Officials Will Do and Say

Here's what will happen when you arrive at the consulate for your interview. First, a clerk will check the papers and other items that you've brought, to make sure you've brought all that's needed. At this time, you might need to pay any application fees that you haven't already paid.

After these preliminaries, a consular officer will meet with you, place you under oath (have you swear to tell the truth), and review the contents of your entire application. Don't expect a cozy fireside chat in the official's office. Many consulates now conduct interviews through bulletproof glass windows that make you feel like you're in a bank or a prison.

The officer will probably start by reviewing your forms and documents. He or she may ask you questions that are identical to the ones on your forms. Since you will have reviewed these carefully, this shouldn't be a problem—but if you can't remember something, it's much better to say so than to guess at the answer.

You'll probably also have to answer other questions designed to test whether your family relationship, job offer, or other basis for going to the U.S. is the real thing. For example, if you're applying for a student visa, the consular officer will be testing to see whether your true intention is actually to look for a job and stay in the United States permanently (in which case, you don't qualify for a student visa). If you're applying for a fiancé visa or marriage-based immigrant visa, the officer may ask questions about how you and your U.S. citizen fiancé or spouse met, when you decided to get married, and other facts regarding your visits or correspondence.

If you're already married, the official may ask questions such as how many people attended the ceremony and how you've visited or corresponded with one another in recent years.

The interview can take as few as ten or 20 minutes, assuming your basis for going to the United States is obviously real, all documents are in order, and you don't fall into any of the grounds for inadmissibility. Don't panic if it lasts longer. If you find yourself getting nervous, remember to curb that understandable instinct to start babbling. Many applicants have gotten themselves into deep trouble by being unable to stop talking.

c. Delayed Approvals

Consular officers rarely deny immigrant visa applications (which lead to a green card) on the spot. (Nonimmigrant, or temporary visas, are another matter; the consulates try to give a quick "no" to vast numbers of cases.)

If there are problems that can be corrected, or if you are inadmissible but are eligible to apply for a waiver, they will normally ask you to provide additional materials. Politely ask that the officer put any requests for more materials in writing, stating exactly what is needed and why. If there are any questions having to do with your petitioner in the United States, the consular officer may send your file back to the U.S. for investigation.

Sample USCIS Rejection Notice

Department of Homeland Security
U.S. Citizenship and Immigration Services

Notice of Action

THE UNITED STATES OF AMERICA

RECEIPT NUMBER			CASE TYPE	1765
CSC-16-013-99999			APPLICATION FOR EMPLOYMENT AUTHORIZATION
RECEIPT DATE	PRIORITY DATE		APPLICANT	A99 999 999
			IVAN PLATOV
NOTICE DATE	PAGE			
October 20, 2016	1 of 1			

IVAN PLATOV
2367 BROADWAY
NEW YORK, NEW YORK 20012

Notice Type: Rejection Notice

Your Application for Employment Authorization, Form I-765, is being rejected for incorrect fee.

To establish the correct fee, you must select one eligibility category and submit the fee according to the directions on the application.

Select one eligibility category from Part 2 on the instruction sheet and write it in Item 16 on the form. Return the completed form I-765 with the correct fee as indicated on Part 5 of the instructions for processing.

Please see the additional information on the back. You will be notified separately about any other cases you filed.
IMMIGRATION & NATURALIZATION SERVICE
CALIFORNIA SERVICE CENTER
P. O. BOX 30111
LAGUNA NIGUEL CA 92607-0111
Customer Service Telephone: (949) 831 8427

Form I-797C (Rev. 09/07/93)N

EXAMPLE: A U.S. consular officer in Guatemala told Estela that he couldn't approve her immigrant visa until she brought in her "sister's tax returns." What was the problem? No such tax returns existed because the sister (who was helping sponsor Estela financially) hadn't even been working long enough to reach a tax deadline. Her lawyer in the U.S. wrote a letter explaining this, but the consulate stubbornly continued to ask for these tax returns. Because Estela didn't have the consulate's original request in writing, this led to months of arguing back and forth, with the consular officials continually changing or forgetting what it was they were looking for.

The consulate probably won't approve your visa on the spot, either. First, your name must be checked against various security databases to see whether you have a history of criminal or terrorist behavior. This can add many weeks to the approval of your application, particularly if you come from a country that the U.S. government has identified as sponsoring terrorism. Usually you have to return to the consulate later to pick up your visa—which will in some cases actually be a thick envelope stuffed full of all your supporting documents.

> CAUTION
> **Do not open the visa envelope!**
> You will give the envelope to the U.S. border officer when you arrive. The officer will examine the contents and do a last check for any problems. The border official, not the consulate, will place a stamp in your passport indicating that you are either a visa holder or a permanent resident or conditional resident.

G. Procedures for USCIS Interviews

Several months after you submit your adjustment of status packet to a USCIS Service Center, USCIS will schedule your interview at one of its local offices, hopefully near where you live. If the interview goes well—for example, your relationship to your family or employee petitioner is obviously the real deal, you don't fall into any of the grounds for inadmissibility, and your documents are in order—the interview can take as few as ten minutes.

At the end, you will be approved for unrestricted permanent residence. The exception is if you either entered on an investor visa or are applying for a marriage-based green card and you've been married for less than two years (which usually applies to anyone who entered the United States on a fiancé visa). These two categories of people receive what's called conditional residence, which is much like permanent residence except that it expires after two years. You must apply, within the three months before the expiration date, to turn your conditional residence into permanent residence.

Sample Interview Notice

Department of Homeland Security U.S. Citizenship and Immigration Services	I-797C, Notice of Action

REQUEST FOR APPLICANT TO APPEAR FOR INITIAL INTERVIEW		NOTICE DATE January 31, 2016
CASE TYPE FORM I-485, APPLICATION TO REGISTER PERMANENT RESIDENCE OR ADJUST STATUS		A# A 099 909 909
APPLICATION NUMBER 486MSC1612345678	RECEIVED DATE January 13, 2016	PRIORITY DATE January 13, 2016
		PAGE 1 of 1

HAI-ZI ZHANG
c/o ILONA BRAY
950 PARKER ST.
BERKELEY, CA 94710

You are hereby notified to appear for the interview appointment, as scheduled below, for the completion of your Application to Register Permanent Residence or Adjust Status (Form I-485) and any supporting applications or petitions. *Failure to appear for this interview and/or failure to bring the below listed items will result in the denial of your application. (8 CFR 103.2(b)(13))*

Who should come with you?

☐ **If your eligibility is based on your marriage, your husband or wife must come with you to the interview.**
☐ **If you do not speak English fluently, you should bring an interpreter.**
☐ Your attorney or authorized representative may come with you to the interview.
☐ If your eligibility is based on a parent/child relationship and the child is a minor, the petitioning parent and the child must appear for the interview.

NOTE: Every adult (over 18 years of age) who comes to the interview must bring Government-issued photo identification, such as a driver's license or ID card, in order to enter the building and to verify his/her identity at the time of the interview. You do not need to bring your children unless otherwise instructed. Please be on time, but do not arrive more than 45 minutes early. We may record or videotape your interview.

YOU MUST BRING THE FOLLOWING ITEMS WITH YOU: (Please use as a checklist to prepare for your interview)

☐ This Interview Notice and your Government issued photo identification.
☐ A completed medical examination (Form I-693) and vaccination supplement in a sealed envelope (unless already submitted).
☐ A completed Affidavit(s) of Support (Form I-864) with all required evidence, including the following, for each of your sponsors (unless already submitted):
    ☐ Federal Income Tax returns and W-2's, or certified IRS printouts, for the past 3 years;
    ☐ Letters from each current employer, verifying current rate of pay and average weekly hours, and pay stubs for the past 2 months;
    ☐ Evidence of your sponsor's and/or co-sponsor's United States Citizenship or Lawful Permanent Resident status.
☐ All documentation establishing your eligibility for Lawful Permanent Resident status.
☐ Any immigration-related documentation ever issued to you, including any Employment Authorization Document (EAD) and any Authorization for Advance Parole (Form I-512).
☐ All travel documents used to enter the United States, including Passports, Advance Parole documents (I-512) and I-94s (Arrival/Departure Document).
☐ Your Birth Certificate.
☐ Your petitioner's Birth Certificate and your petitioner's evidence of United States Citizenship or Lawful Permanent Resident Status.
☐ If you have children, bring a Birth Certificate for each of your children.
☐ If your eligibility is based on your marriage, in addition to your spouse coming to the interview with you, bring:
    ☐ A certified copy of your Marriage Document issued by the appropriate civil authority.
    ☐ Your spouse's Birth Certificate and your spouse's evidence of United States Citizenship or Lawful Permanent Resident status;
    ☐ If either you or your spouse were ever married before, all divorce decrees/death certificates for each prior marriage/former spouse;
    ☐ Birth Certificates for all children of this marriage, and custody papers for your children and for your spouse's children not living with you;
☐ Supporting evidence of your relationship, such as copies of any documentation regarding joint assets or liabilities you and your spouse may have together. This may include: tax returns, bank statements, insurance documents (car, life, health), property documents (car, house, etc.), rental agreements, utility bills, credit cards, contracts, leases, photos, correspondence and/or any other documents you feel may substantiate your relationship.
☐ Original and copy of each supporting document that you submitted with your application. Otherwise, we may keep your originals for our records.
☐ If you have ever been arrested, bring the related Police Report and the original or certified Final Court Disposition for each arrest, even if the charges have been dismissed or expunged. If no court record is available, bring a letter from the court with jurisdiction indicating this.
☐ A certified English translation for each foreign language document. The translator must certify that s/he is fluent in both languages, and that the translation in its entirety is complete and accurate.

YOU MUST APPEAR FOR THIS INTERVIEW- If an emergency, such as your own illness or a close relative's hospitalization, prevents you from appearing, call the U.S. Citizenship and Immigration Services (USCIS) National Customer Service Center at 1-800-375-5283 as soon as possible. Please be advised that rescheduling will delay processing of application/petition, and may require some steps to be repeated. It may also affect your eligibility for other immigration benefits while this application is pending.

If you have questions, please call the USCIS National Customer Service Center at 1-800-375-5283 (hearing impaired TDD service is 1-800-767-1833).

PLEASE COME TO: U.S. Citizenship and Immigration Services 630 SANSOME ST 2ND FLOOR - ADJUSTMENT OF STATUS SAN FRANCISCO CA 94111	ON: Friday, March 28, 2016 AT: 02:15 PM
3	REPRESENTATIVE COPY

Form I-797C (Rev. 01/31/05) N

The interview appointment notice will look much like the one above. Read the notice carefully—there's a chance that your local USCIS office will have added requirements that were not covered in this book.

1. Arrange for an Interpreter

USCIS doesn't provide interpreters at interviews in the United States (not even at the asylum offices). A few of their officers speak Spanish or other languages, but you can't count on getting a bilingual officer, nor can you request one. If you're not comfortable in English, you'll need to bring a friend or hire an interpreter to help.

The interpreter must be over 18 and fluent in both your language and in English. Some officers also require that the interpreter be a legal resident or citizen of the United States. (Of course, if they're here illegally, they'd be foolish to walk into a USCIS office.)

CAUTION

Paying a trained interpreter can be well worth it. Simultaneous interpretation requires language skill, fast thinking, and experience. If it's done wrong, your case could be permanently affected.

2. What the USCIS Officials Will Do and Say

In spite of the fact that hundreds of people are interviewed each day across the United States, adjustment of status interviews tend to follow a pattern. Here's what will probably happen, step by step.

1. After sitting in the waiting room with dozens of other immigrants for so long that you're sure they've forgotten you, you'll be summoned to the inner rooms of the USCIS adjustments unit.

2. You'll be brought to the USCIS officer's desk, where your identification will be checked. Just when you're seated comfortably, you, your petitioner, and your interpreter (if you've brought one) will have to stand up again, raise your right hands, and take oaths to tell the truth.

3. The officer will start by going through your written application, asking you about the facts and examining the medical and fingerprint reports for factors that might make you ineligible for a green card. As discussed earlier, this is one of the most important parts of the interview. You'll sign the application to confirm its correctness.

4. The officer will ask you and your petitioner about facts relating to your basis for immigrating. You'll get the most questions if you're applying based on marriage, in which case expect questions about where you met, when and why you decided to get married, how many people attended your wedding, or what you did on your most recent birthday or night out. You'll back up your answers with

documents that illustrate the genuine nature of your marriage, such as rental agreements and joint utility bills.

5. If there's a problem in your application that you can correct by submitting additional materials, the officer may put your case on hold and send you home with a list of additional documents to provide by mail within a specified time. For example, if your family petitioner's earnings are insufficient, the officer may suggest you find another family member to sign an I-864 Affidavit of Support. However, USCIS is showing an increasing tendency to deny applications on the spot, in which case your case could be referred to immigration court.

6. If you're applying based on marriage, and the officer suspects that your marriage is fraudulent, a whole new step could be added to the process. You might meet the Fraud Unit. There, an officer will interview you and your spouse separately—and intensively. The officer will compare the results of your two interviews.

At the end of the adjustment of status interview, the officer will tell you whether you are approved or not. Sometimes the officer will tell you that he or she is recommending you for approval but that a supervisor will need to sign off on it, in which case final approval might take several weeks. If you are approved on the spot, a stamp will be placed in your passport as evidence of your conditional or permanent residence. With this stamp, you acquire all the rights of a green card holder, including the right to work, and freedom to travel in and out of the United States. You will receive your permanent green card by mail several weeks later.

If your fingerprints have not cleared yet, your application will be approved only provisionally, pending FBI clearance. In those cases, no stamp will be placed in your passport at the interview. Instead, you should receive a written notice of approval within a month or two.

That written notice serves as your proof of U.S. residency until you receive your green card, which normally takes several weeks. If you need to travel outside the U.S. before your green card arrives, however, you must go back to the USCIS office, with your passport and the written notice of approval, and get a temporary stamp in your passport, enabling you to return after your trip. Never leave the U.S. without either your green card or a temporary passport stamp.

H. What to Do If an Interview Is Going Badly

Your chances of a smooth interview will be greatly increased by the advance preparation and organizing you're doing by using this book. Unfortunately, your efforts can't entirely guarantee a successful interview. A lot will hinge on the personality or mood of the government official.

It's important to have a balanced view of the USCIS and consular officers who will be interviewing you. They're human—and they have seen a lot of fraudulent applicants along with the worthy ones.

Certain immigration officers have been known to go out of their way to help people—for example, spending hours searching for something in a room full of old files; or fitting a person's interview into their schedule even when the person arrived two hours late. On the other hand, some officers can get downright rude or hostile. Remember that they hold much of the power—getting angry will get you nowhere fast. Remain respectful and answer honestly if you don't know or remember something. Never guess or lie.

Most USCIS officers just want to see someone who won't waste their time, has an orderly, clean case, and is legally eligible for the green card or another benefit.

CAUTION
Try to get the officer's name. USCIS and consular officers often don't tell you their name, but it may be shown on their desk. The best thing to do is politely ask the person's name at the beginning of the interview (not when things have already started to go badly, when he or she may get defensive). Then write the name down. This tidbit of information may become important later. For example, if you need to file a complaint, discuss the matter with a supervisor, or consult with an attorney, you'll have an edge if you know whom you dealt with. (An experienced attorney will know all the local USCIS officers by name and can better understand your description of what happened after learning who was involved.)

Some officers are irate no matter how the applicant behaves. You might encounter an officer who makes irrelevant accusations, acts in a discriminatory manner based on your race or gender, becomes uncontrollably angry, or persists with a line of questions or statements that is completely inappropriate. If any of these things happens, ask to see a supervisor.

If things are going badly, you don't have to let the situation go from bad to worse, ending with an on-the-spot rejection of your application. Offer to supply any information that the officer asked for, so that your case will be postponed ("pended" in USCIS lingo). When you get home, write down as many details as you can remember of the interview, while it's fresh in your mind. Then, consider consulting an attorney about your experience to learn what you can do to improve the reaction to your application.

Even if you don't speak with a lawyer, write a letter asking that a supervisor consider the interviewer's conduct when making the final review of your case. Supervisors review all cases, but they will assume the officer acted appropriately unless you tell them otherwise.

I. What to Do If an Application Is Denied

First, a word of reassurance: Neither US-CIS nor the consulates like to deny visas—particularly immigrant visas—to eligible applicants. Unless you are clearly ineligible, they may give you many chances to supplement your application and make it worthy of approval. Maybe this is the good side of a slow-moving bureaucracy—every decision takes time, even a negative one. (But don't use this as an excuse to be sloppy in putting your application together the first time.)

SEE AN EXPERT

If your visa or green card has been denied and you didn't use a lawyer, it's time to hire one. This advice is particularly important if the denial was due to something more serious than a bureaucratic mistake or a lack of documentation on your part. You'll definitely need a lawyer for the complicated procedures mentioned below, including removal proceedings and motions to reopen or reconsider. See Chapter 6 on finding a lawyer.

1. Denial of Initial Visa Petition

If the USCIS Service Center denies your initial visa petition (I-129F, I-130, or I-140), the best thing for your petitioner to do is to start over and file a new one. This is true even if a lawyer is helping.

There is an appeal process, but hardly anyone ever uses it. You'll probably spend less time starting over, and the fee is about the same. Besides, no government agency likes to admit it was wrong, so there is a tactical advantage to getting a fresh start.

The form may ask, however, whether you have ever been denied in the past; don't hide that fact, or you will hurt your chances of ever receiving a U.S. green card.

2. Denial of Visa or Green Card

If USCIS or the consulate denies you permanent residence, your response will depend on where you are—in the U.S. or in another country.

a. Denial of Green Card After Adjustment of Status Application in the U.S.

If you are applying for adjustment of status in the United States, there is technically no appeal after a denial. However, it's possible to ask USCIS to reconsider its decision (if you believe USCIS misinterpreted the law or didn't apply the law correctly to you) or to reopen proceedings to allow you to present evidence that wasn't available at the time of your interview. If you don't file a motion to reconsider or motion to reopen, and you have no other legal right to be in the United States when the application is denied (such as a pending political asylum application), you will be placed in removal proceedings in Immigration Court. There, you will have the opportunity to renew your green card application before an immigration judge. In rare circumstances, you might need to file a motion to have your case reopened or reconsidered; or you may need to file a separate suit in federal court.

CAUTION
Never ignore a notice to appear in Immigration Court. Attorneys regularly receive questions from immigrants who were scheduled for a hearing in Immigration Court and either forgot, couldn't make it, or just hoped the problem would go away. Failing to appear for a court date is the worst thing you can do to your hopes of immigrating. It will earn you an automatic order of removal (deportation), which means that DHS can pick you up and put you on a plane home anytime, with no more hearings. You'll also be hit with a ten-year mandatory prohibition on returning to the United States and further punishments if you return illegally.

b. Denial of Nonimmigrant Visa at U.S. Consulate

If you are applying for a nonimmigrant (temporary) visa through a consulate outside the United States, you have no appeal after a denial. The consulate is at least required to tell you the reason for the denial, and often the fastest thing is to fix the problem and reapply.

For example, if it appears that you have insufficient funds to support yourself while you're in the United States, you might find an additional person to fill out an Affidavit of Support on your behalf. You can reapply, but must usually wait a certain amount of time first, for example three months. Ask the consulate for details.

c. Denial of Immigrant Visa at U.S. Consulate

If you are applying for an immigrant (permanent residence) visa, the consulate will give you up to one year after the denial of your visa application to provide information aimed at reversing the denial. At the end of the year, your application will close and you must start all over again. There is no appeal from the denial or the closure.

CAUTION
Don't attempt multiple, inconsistent applications. The U.S. government keeps a record of all your applications for visas and green cards. If you come back a few years later with a new basis for immigrating, USCIS or the consulate will be happy to remind you of any past fraud or other reasons for inadmissibility. (Changing your name won't work—by the end of the application process, the U.S. immigration authorities will have your fingerprints.)

J. When All Else Fails, Call Your U.S. Congressperson

If your case turns into a true bureaucratic nightmare or a genuine miscarriage of justice, your U.S. citizen or permanent resident petitioner or employer can ask a U.S. congressperson for help. Some of them have a staff person dedicated to helping constituents who have immigration problems. A simple inquiry by a congressperson can end months of USCIS or consular stonewalling or inaction. In rare cases, the congressperson's office might be willing to put some actual pressure on USCIS or the consular office.

> **EXAMPLE:** Rodrigo, a U.S. citizen, was trying to get permission for his daughter Sandra to immigrate from Mexico. She attended her visa interview and was told to come back with more proof that she would be financially supported and not become a public charge. Although Rodrigo's income was already over the *Poverty Guidelines* levels, he found a joint sponsor, who submitted an additional Affidavit of Support for Sandra. The consulate still wasn't willing to grant the visa. Rodrigo consulted with an attorney, who wrote letters to the consulate—but got no reply. Finally his attorney wrote a letter to Rodrigo's congressperson asking for help. They submitted copies of all the relevant documents so that the congressperson would fully understand the problem. The visa was granted—with no explanation—a week after the congressperson's inquiry.

Your congressperson probably won't be surprised to hear from you. Illinois Congresswoman Janice Schakowsky reported that eight out of ten calls from her constituents were complaints about the INS (as USCIS was then called). (See "Unchecked Power of the INS Shatters American Dream," by Kim Christensen, Richard Read, Julie Sullivan, and Brent Walth, *The Oregonian*, Sunday, December 20, 2000, or more disturbingly, "*An Agent, a Green Card, and a Demand for Sex*," by Nina Bernstein, *The New York Times*, Friday, March 21, 2008.)

Don't go to your congressperson thinking he or she can do much about a visa denial. Consular officials don't care much for members of Congress trying to tell them how to do their jobs. If you decide to reapply for a visa that was denied, it certainly won't hurt to submit a letter from a congressperson pleading your case—just don't expect it to have a decisive effect.

Special Rules for Canadians and Mexicans

Many Canadian and Mexican citizens believe they are disfavored by the U.S. immigration system. Actually, the exact opposite is true, as the following special rules show.

A. Canadian Visitors and Nonimmigrants

Most Canadian citizens do not need visas to enter the U.S for a temporary stay. For the casual tourist or business visitor, this is a big benefit. With the exception of E-1 and E-2 treaty traders and investors as well as fiancé(e)s and their children (K-1 and K-2), Canadians have no need to go to a U.S. consulate and get a nonimmigrant visa.

CAUTION
Despite the benefits, you must still prove that you don't fall into one of the inadmissibility categories, which bar U.S. entry. Anyone coming into the U.S. can be examined regarding his or her health, criminal, and other history to see whether the person falls into one of the grounds of inadmissibility described in Chapter 3.

Even though a nonimmigrant visa is not usually required, Canadians still must show that they are eligible to enter the United States. For starters, you'll need to bring proof of citizenship (a valid Canadian passport) to the U.S.

port of entry. A passport by itself will be enough—and in fact is required when arriving in the U.S. by air or from outside the Western Hemisphere. A passport is also required for all land and sea entries (since June of 2009). Unlike some other nationalities, as a Canadian, your passport need not be valid beyond the duration of your planned trip to the U.S., and it need not be machine readable.

You'll also need to answer a few questions from a Customs and Border Protection (CBP) inspector at a U.S. port of entry. You might be asked to prove that you have enough money to last during the U.S. trip and that you still keep a Canadian residence to which you can return.

Canadians can visit the U.S. for up to six months at a time without a visa. An entry/exit record, called an "I-94," is not automatically generated for Canadian visitors or businesspersons entering by land as it is for people from all other countries. (An I-94 will be generated for Canadians entering in other statuses or if coming by sea or plane.) That makes it quicker to cross the border as a tourist or for business. However, you lose the advantages of the I-94 record, which include that it will show the exact date by which you're expected to depart, and serves as proof of legal entry and status when you need to to verify immigration status or employment authorization.

B. Special Work Privileges for Canadian and Mexican Visitors

Certain Canadian and Mexican professionals are granted some special work privileges.

1. Business Visits Without a Visa

The North American Free Trade Agreement (NAFTA) allows Canadian and Mexican visitors who are coming to the U.S. to do certain kinds of business or work in the U.S. to enter without work visas. There are no other countries whose citizens are granted these privileges.

In order to qualify:

- The intent of your visit must involve commercial activity.
- You must have a clear intent to continue a foreign residence.
- Your salary must come from outside the U.S.
- Your employer's principal place of business and place where it eventually accrues profits must remain in a foreign country.
- Your U.S. stay must be temporary (although the business activity may continue after you've left).
- Although you need not be a businessperson, your employment must be a necessary incident of international trade or commerce.

To take advantage of this opportunity, you must show written proof that you are engaging in one of the occupations included in the program. A letter from your employer verifying the work to be done will serve this purpose. If relevant, you should also offer evidence that you are qualified for the job, such as copies of diplomas or licenses.

These documents are presented to a U.S. immigration officer on your entry to the United States. No fee or special application is needed for Canadians. However, absent a B-1 visitor's visa issued by a U.S. embassy or consulate, Mexican nationals must obtain a valid Border Crossing Card (Form I-586) prior to arriving at the port of entry.

The types of work that Canadians and Mexicans may do in the U.S. without work visas are:

- performing research and design functions for a company located in Canada or Mexico
- supervising a crew harvesting agricultural crops (only the owner of the company qualifies)
- purchasing for a company located in Canada or Mexico
- conducting other commercial transactions for a company located in Canada or Mexico
- doing market research for a company located in Canada or Mexico
- attending trade fairs

- taking sales orders and negotiating contracts for a company located in Canada or Mexico
- transporting goods or passengers into the U.S.
- picking up goods and passengers in the U.S., only for direct transport back to Canada or Mexico
- performing normal duties as a customs broker. The goods must be exports from the U.S. to Canada or Mexico.
- servicing equipment or machinery after sales
- performing any professional services, provided no salary is paid from within the U.S.
- performing financial services for a company located in Canada
- consulting in the fields of public relations and advertising
- conducting tours that originate or have significant portions taking place in Canada, and
- performing language translation and acting as an interpreter for a company located in Canada.

In addition, you may qualify for a business visa for the same reasons people from other parts of the world do (so long as you won't be paid by a U.S. business), including to negotiate contracts, consult with business associates, litigate, participate in conventions, conferences, or seminars, and undertake independent research.

2. H-1 Visa Alternative: NAFTA TN Status

For Canadian and Mexican citizens who practice certain professional occupations and who have a job offer from a U.S. employer, there's an alternative to filing for an H-1 visa. This is called TN status. TN status lasts three years, and can be renewed in three-year increments, with no limit on renewals. You don't always have to be coming for a job—TN status can also be used by people coming for temporary training related to their profession or to conduct seminars.

At present, only the occupations listed below qualify for TN status. A bachelor's or licensure degree from a college or university is required, unless an alternative is shown in parentheses.

You must have a U.S. employer; TN status is not available for self-employment in the United States. For some professions, there are requirements in addition to a degree. These, too, are shown in parentheses. Whenever a license is required, either a federal Canadian, Mexican, or a U.S. licensing agency from any province or state is acceptable. The occupations are:

- accountant (degree or credential)
- architect (degree or license)
- computer systems analyst (with a college degree; alternatively, a postsecondary diploma, or postsecondary certificate plus three years' experience)

- dentist (professional degree or license)
- disaster relief claims adjuster (training plus a degree or three years' experience)
- economist
- engineer (degree or license)
- forester (degree or license)
- graphic designer (degree or post-secondary diploma plus three years' experience)
- hotel manager (licensure degree, or diploma or certificate plus three years' experience)
- industrial designer (degree, or certificate or diploma plus three years' experience)
- interior designer (degree, or certificate or diploma plus three years' experience)
- land surveyor (degree or license)
- landscape architect
- lawyer (degree or member of Canadian, Mexican, or U.S. bar)
- librarian
- management consultant (degree or five years' experience)
- mathematician (including statistician)
- medical professions:
  - dietitian (degree or license)
  - medical lab technologist (degree, or certificate or diploma plus three years' experience)
  - nutritionist
  - occupational therapist (degree or license)

- pharmacist (degree or license)
- physician (M.D. or license; teaching or research position only)
- physio/physical therapist (degree or license)
- psychologist (degree or license)
- recreational therapist
- registered nurse (degree or license)
- veterinarian (professional degree or license)
- range manager or conservationist
- research assistant (for colleges or universities only)
- scientific technician (degree not required if you are working with professionals in: agricultural sciences, astronomy, biology, chemistry, engineering, forestry, geology, geophysics, meteorology, or physics)
- scientist working as:
  - agronomist
  - agriculturist
  - animal breeder
  - animal scientist
  - apiculturist
  - astronomer
  - biochemist
  - biologist
  - chemist
  - dairy scientist
  - entomologist
  - epidemiologist
  - geneticist
  - geochemist
  - geologist

- geophysicist
- horticulturist
- meteorologist
- pharmacologist
- physicist
- plant breeder
- plant pathologist
- poultry scientist
- soil scientist
- zoologist
- social worker
- silviculturist
- teacher (at a college, university, or seminary only)
- technical publications writer (degree; or, alternatively, diploma or certificate plus three years' experience)
- urban planner, and
- vocational counselor.

The person seeking TN status must be coming temporarily, to engage in business activities at a professional level. A person who intends to separately apply for a green card while in the U.S. can be denied TN status, because he or she violates the requirement of intending to stay only temporarily. The person must also meet the minimum requirements for the profession or occupation in question, as set forth in Appendix 1603.D.1 to Annex 1603 of NAFTA (also found at 8 C.F.R. § 214.6(c)).

Although the basic requirements are the same for Canadians and Mexicans, the procedures are distinct.

a. TN Procedures for Canadians

There is no annual limit for Canadian TNs. If you qualify and properly apply for the visa, and are not otherwise "inadmissible" to the United States, you will get it. A Canadian professional worker may be admitted to the U.S. without advance petition approval (though you can get it if you prefer, by filing Form I-129 with USCIS) or labor certification. In order to apply, you merely go straight to any U.S. port of entry (land border crossing, U.S. airport, or U.S. preflight inspection station at a major Canadian international airport). There, a U.S. Customs and Border Protection officer will adjudicate the application, and you'll proceed directly to the United States if it's approved.

Note that you cannot apply for the TN visa unless you are actually planning on physically entering the United States that day. In other words, do not try to apply for the TN visa at a U.S. entry point in advance of the "real" trip. Although no formal application form is required, you must pay a fee (currently $50, or $56 if you're crossing the border by car).

Your spouse and unmarried minor children may accompany you, but may not work in the United States. Family members, if they are Canadian citizens, will be given "TD" status without having to make any separate application. They must bring proof of the family relationship, such as a marriage or birth certificate. If travelling with you by car, they will be charged $6 per I-94 card per person. Non-Canadian-citizen family members need to apply for a TD visa at a consulate.

If you are already lawfully present in the U.S., your U.S. employer can apply for a change of your status to TN by filing a Form I-129 petition and fee (currently $460) with the USCIS Vermont Service Center. The advantage of this process is that you can avoid a face-to-face meeting with a U.S. Customs officer in order to get the TN visa. Many U.S. Customs officers, particularly those located at a U.S./Canada land crossing or a major Canadian international airport, have a reputation for being unduly skeptical, if not confrontational, toward Canadian TN visa applicants.

You will need to supply the following documents to be given TN status:

- Canadian passport
- a job offer letter describing the proposed employment activity at a professional level, including your daily job duties, the job requirements (such as educational level or license), your salary and benefits, and how long your services will be needed (for up to three years)
- evidence of your qualifications to perform at a professional level, as demonstrated by your college degrees, licenses, memberships, or other relevant credentials that establish professional status, and

- evidence of the particular profession as one listed in Appendix 1603.D.1 to Annex 1603 of NAFTA.

When admitted, the TN professional will be given an I-94 card (if arriving by land), or an I-94 record will be created in CBP's database (if arriving by sea or air), indicating authorized status in the U.S. for up to three years. Your time may be limited if your Canadian passport has less than three years remaining before expiration, so it's a good idea to keep your passport up to date. The original period of admission can be extended in three-year increments without leaving the United States. An extension may be requested by your employer on Form I-129 and filed at the Vermont Service Center (regardless of where you live). Extensions for family members are requested simultaneously on Form I-539. An extension also may be requested by departing the U.S. prior to the first status expiration and reentering at the port of entry by presenting the above-listed documents.

b. TN Procedures for Mexicans

There is no annual cap on TNs from Mexico. If you qualify and properly apply for the visa, and are not otherwise "inadmissible" to the United States, you will get it.

If you are outside of the U.S., you can simply present yourself at a U.S. consular post to apply for TN status and an entry visa. You will need to bring a Mexican passport, proof of having filled out the online DS-160 Immigrant Visa Application, application and visa fees (currently totaling $160), plus the same types of documents as described in Subsection a, above. Your will have up to one year to first use your visa.

If you are already lawfully present in the U.S., you can apply for a change of status. The employer makes this application on Form I-129, and mails it to the USCIS Vermont Service Center.

Applicants can also obtain visas to bring their spouses and children to the U.S. (in TD status) by providing the consulate with proof of the family relationship, such as a birth or marriage certificate. Family members with TD status cannot legally work in the United States.

Upon entering the U.S., the Mexican TN professional will be given an I-94 card (if arriving by land), or an I-94 record will be created in CBP's database (if arriving by sea or air) indicating an authorized stay of up to three years. This period can be extended in three-year increments without leaving the United States.

To file for an extension, your employer must send Form I-129, together with the same types of documents used for your initial application, to the USCIS Vermont Service Center. Extensions for family members are requested simultaneously on Form I-539. If you don't mind leaving the U.S., you can also request an extension by departing before your status has expired and revisiting a U.S. consulate.

c. Advantages and Disadvantages of TN Status

The advantages of the treaty professional procedure are that you avoid potentially long delays from filing a petition in the United States. TN status is also useful for Canadians and Mexicans who have used up their six years of H-1B status, but wish to continue working in the United States. That is because there is no formal legal limit on the number of times TN status can be renewed, or the number of years one can spend working in TN status. Similarly, it's helpful for H-1B applicants who find that the annual supply of H-1B visas has run out. That is because there is no limit on the number of TN visas that may be issued in a given year. And, because the list of professions qualifying for TN status is fairly broad, it's useful for some people whose profession could never qualify them for an H-1B visa in the first place.

The main disadvantage is that professional workers using the TN instead of a standard H-1 visa must show that they intend to return to Canada or Mexico when their work in the U.S. is finished. Therefore, if you plan to apply for a green card, you should, if possible, first get a standard H-1 visa, which does not have these restrictions. (Unfortunately, not all professional TN categories qualify for an H-1B visa.)

In addition, if you have a difficult case and you are denied entry as a treaty professional, there is no avenue of appeal.

When a standard H-1 visa petition is denied, or if you apply for a TN status extension or change of status by filing an application with the USCIS Vermont Service Center, you have the ability to appeal the decision through both USCIS and, eventually, the U.S. courts.

3. Simplified Procedures for L Visas (Canadians Only)

If you are seeking a visa as an L-1 intra-company transferee, and you are a citizen of Canada, a simplified application process is available to you. Instead of going through the USCIS petition process, you can choose to take all your L-1 paperwork, along with the required fee, directly to a port of entry.

The required paperwork includes evidence of your identity and Canadian nationality (including a Canadian passport valid for at least six months beyond your intended period of stay), two copies (with original signatures on each) of a USCIS Form I-129 nonimmigrant visa petition filled out and signed by your employer, the L-1 visa application I-129 fee, and an employment letter (indicating the nature and duration of your employment and the pay being offered).

At the entry point, an immigration officer will decide on the spot whether you qualify for L-1 status (you cannot send them your paperwork in advance). Your accompanying spouse and children will be admitted on showing proof of their family relationship to you. This requires presenting a marriage certificate for your spouse and long-form birth certificates for your children.

When your status is approved, you will be given an I-94 card and admitted to the U.S. immediately. The petition is then forwarded to the appropriate service center in the U.S. and the final decision on the petition is made in about 30–60 days and mailed to you.

> **CAUTION**
> **If you're flying to the U.S., you may have to submit your paperwork to a preflight inspector before you board the plane.** In that case, plan to arrive several hours before your flight to make sure you're approved before the plane departs.

Although this method is much faster than going through normal USCIS petition procedures, if you are denied entry, your rights of appeal are limited. In addition, border inspectors are usually less experienced in deciding cases than USCIS office personnel, and therefore, may be reluctant to approve a more difficult case. When your situation is complicated, you are probably better off having your petition approved in advance at the service center and not using this alternative procedure.

4. Treaty Traders and Treaty Investors

NAFTA allows Canadians to obtain E-1 and E-2 visas. Canadians wishing to get

E-1 or E-2 status are treated exactly like persons of all other nationalities. This means that you must go to a U.S. embassy or consulate to obtain an actual visa stamp in your passport before you can enter the U.S. with an E-1 or E-2 status. Therefore, you should follow all of the procedures discussed in Chapters 20 and 21. This is the only nonimmigrant category where a visa is required of Canadians.

Although getting an E visa could previously be done in one day at a U.S. consulate in Canada, consulates are now requiring that you attend an interview on one day, then return at a later date to pick up your passport and visa.

C. Fiancés

See Chapter 8 for instructions on obtaining a K-1 fiancé visa. If you enter the U.S. with no visa, get married, and then file for a green card within the U.S., you risk a finding that you used fraud when you entered the U.S. as a supposed nonimmigrant, with the actual intent of staying permanently.

D. Simplified Procedures for Canadian Students and Exchange Visitors

Canadians entering the U.S. as F-1 students, M-1 students, or J-1 exchange visitors also have a simplified way of getting

status. First, the program that accepts you must send you an approved Certificate of Eligibility form. The Certificate of Eligibility for F-1 and M-1 students is Form SEVIS I-20. For J-1 exchange visitors, it is Form SEVIS DS-2019. These are described in Chapters 22 and 23.

Once you have a Certificate of Eligibility, you may go directly to a U.S. port of entry and present it to a U.S. immigration inspector together with proof of your Canadian citizenship (a passport) and proof that you have paid the SEVIS fee. You should also have available evidence of how you will be supported financially while in the United States. On showing these documents, you will be admitted as a student or exchange visitor. Your accompanying spouse and children will be admitted on showing proof of their family relationship to you. This requires presenting a marriage certificate for your spouse and long-form birth certificates for your children.

When you enter the U.S., you will receive an I-94 card (if arriving by land), or an I-94 record will be created in CBP's database (if arriving by sea or air) indicating your immigration status and giving the dates of the period for which you may remain in the country. Your stay will usually be for duration of status, marked "D/S" on the I-94. This means you can stay until your studies are completed. If you leave the U.S. before your status expires and want to return, you need only present the I-94 card or record (from the online database) and the Certificate of Eligibility at the port of entry and you will be admitted again.

E. F-3 Visa for Border Commuter Students

In 2002, Congress passed the Border Commuter Student Act, which created the F-3 visa. It's specifically for people commuting to the U.S. from Mexico or Canada in order to study. Students with F-3s are called "Border Commuter Students."

Before, part-time students attending school in the U.S. while they lived in Mexico or Canada were allowed to cross the border as visitors. However, the Department of Homeland Security (DHS) ended this policy for security reasons.

1. Eligibility for an F-3 Visa

To qualify for an F-3 visa, you must meet many of the same criteria as other students (discussed in Chapter 22), including that you:

- have a residence in a foreign country that you have no intention of abandoning
- are a bona fide student qualified to pursue a course of study
- seek to enter the U.S. temporarily and solely for the purpose of pursuing such a course of study
- are sufficiently knowledgeable in the English language to pursue your

studies effectively (unless the school offers a course of studies in your native tongue)
- will be able to support yourself financially during the course of study
- will be attending a DHS-approved college, university, seminary, conservatory, academic high school, elementary school, or other academic institution or a language training program, and
- the U.S. institution is located within 75 miles of the U.S. border.

Unlike the standard academic student visa (F-1), the F-3 student's course of study need not be full time, but can instead be part time. And the F-3 student has fewer options to work in the U.S. than do regular F-1 students. Border Commuter Students cannot obtain visas for family members to accompany them.

2. Application Process for an F-3 Visa

In order to apply for an F-3 visa, you must collect:

- Certificate of Eligibility, SEVIS Form I-20 (issued by the school upon accepting you for admission)
- proof of payment of the SEVIS fee ($200)
- two photos
- a bank statement or other proof of financial resources

- visa application fee of $160, and
- proof of your Canadian or Mexican citizenship plus a valid photo ID (a valid passport will work for both of these).

Mexican students must take these to the appropriate U.S. embassy or consulate. See the website of your local consulate for further instructions. Canadian students can proceed straight to the U.S. border to request the F-3 visa. Your school may also give you useful advice on this process.

At the U.S. border, the inspecting officer will stamp the first page of your I-20. The officer will also issue you an I-94 card (if arriving by land) or an I-94 record will be created in CBP's database (if arriving by sea or air) valid though the end of the semester. You must present the stamped I-20 and the I-94 record every time you cross the border to the U.S. to attend classes.

F. Preflight Inspections for Canadians

Another benefit Canadians enjoy is access to the procedure known as preflight inspection. There are U.S. immigration offices or counters located at most Canadian international airports. When Canadians fly to the U.S., they clear U.S. immigration and customs before boarding the plane. This service is considered to be a timesaving advantage.

There is a negative side to preflight inspection. In situations where a Canadian's eligibility to enter the U.S. is questionable, if the U.S. immigration inspector does not believe the Canadian traveler should be admitted, the inspector can prevent the Canadian from boarding the plane. Without preflight inspection, travelers to the U.S. can at least land on U.S. soil and are usually granted enough time in the country to stay and argue their case.

However, the law punishes those individuals who arrive without the proper documentation by making them inadmissible at the time, and, if they are given an expedited removal order, for five more years. If you are found to have made a misrepresentation to gain entry, you will become inadmissible forever. Because of this, you should be extremely cautious about presenting yourself for inspection.

G. NEXUS for Faster Entry by Canadians

Canadians can apply to enroll in the NEXUS program, which allows them to enter the U.S. faster by using dedicated vehicle lanes at the border, "Global Entry" kiosks at preclearance airports or NEXUS kiosks at other airports, and a marine telephone reporting center to report entry on their own boat.

Both Canada and the U.S. must approve your application. Any kind of immigration or criminal violation in your past will prevent you from getting a NEXUS card.

How and When to Find a Lawyer

You are not required to have a lawyer when applying for a U.S. visa or green card. If you have a straightforward case, you may be able to proceed all the way to a visa or green card without a lawyer. In fact, if you are outside of the U.S., lawyers cannot attend consular interviews with you, though they are allowed to prepare the paperwork and have follow-up communications with the consulates.

However, there are many times when a lawyer's help can make a big difference in your case and be well worth the money. Because immigration law is complicated, even a seemingly simple case can suddenly become nightmarish. In this chapter, we'll explain:

- when applicants typically should consult an attorney (Section A)
- how to find suitable counsel (Sections B, C, and D)
- how to hire, pay, and (if necessary) fire your lawyer (Sections E, F, and G), and
- how to do some legal research on your own (Section H).

CAUTION

If you are, or have ever been, in deportation (removal) proceedings, you must see a lawyer. If the proceedings aren't yet over or are on appeal, your entire immigration situation is in the power of the courts—and you are not allowed to use most of the procedures described in this book. Even if the court proceedings are over, you should ask a lawyer whether the outcome affects your current application.

A. When Do You Need a Lawyer?

The most common legal problem encountered by would-be immigrants is the claim by USCIS or the consulate that they are inadmissible for one or more of the reasons listed in Chapter 3, such as having spent time in the U.S. unlawfully, committed a crime, or previously lied to the U.S. government. If you know that any of these grounds apply to you, it makes sense to get legal help before you begin the application process.

Another important role for lawyers is helping explain your case to the immigration authorities. As you read the various chapters of this book, you'll find that the eligibility criteria for U.S. visas and green cards tend to be quite complicated. Depending on your situation, you may, for example, be trying to convince an immigration officer that you have no secret plans to stay in the U.S. permanently; are getting married for love, not for a green card; fled your country because you received verbal death threats; or are an acknowledged expert in your field. You'll be required to submit various documents to prove such things, which an attorney can help you choose and prepare. But an experienced immigration attorney will often add an item that's not required—a cover letter or memo explaining what all the evidence adds up to and making clear how your case fits within the legal requirements. Such written materials are difficult to produce if you are not experienced in immigration law. And the lawyer may also be able to argue some of these points in person—for example, at your green card interview.

Yet another circumstance that lawyers can help with is the failure of USCIS or the consulate to act on or approve your application, for reasons that have more to do with bureaucracy than law. For example, an applicant who moves from Los Angeles to San Francisco after filing a green card application might find that the application has disappeared into a bureaucratic black hole for several months. Delays at the USCIS service centers are also ridiculously common.

Lawyers don't have as much power as you—or the lawyers—might wish in such circumstances. True, the lawyer may have access to inside email inquiry lines, where they (and only they) can ask about delayed or problematic cases—but even lawyers may have trouble getting answers to such inquiries. An experienced lawyer may have contacts inside USCIS or the consulate who can give information or locate a lost file. But these lawyers can't use this privilege on an everyday basis, and long delays are truly an everyday occurrence.

The bottom line is that a lawyer in most cases has no magic words that will force the U.S. government into taking action. So, if the only help you need is with

repeatedly calling or writing to USCIS or the consulate until they come up with an answer, you'll have to decide whether it's worth it to pay a lawyer for this.

A very important time to hire a lawyer is if you are applying for something where you'll lose your rights if USCIS or a consulate doesn't act quickly. For example, a diversity visa lottery winner must get the immigration authorities to approve his or her green card before the supply has run out and before the end of that fiscal year, or his or her chance will be lost forever. Similarly, an immigrating child about to turn 21 may, in certain circumstances, lose rights or be delayed in his or her immigration process. A good lawyer will know the latest tactics for alerting USCIS or the consulates to such issues.

 SEE AN EXPERT

Don't rely on advice by USCIS information officers. Would you want the receptionist in your doctor's office to tell you whether to get brain surgery? Asking USCIS information officers for advice about your case (beyond basic procedural advice such as where to file an application and what the fees are) is equally unsafe. The people who staff USCIS phone and information services are not experts. USCIS takes no responsibility if their advice is wrong—and won't treat your application with any more sympathy. Even following the advice of officials higher up in the agency may not be safe. Always get a lawyer's opinion.

Finally, a good time to consult with an immigration lawyer is when you've researched the law and feel like you have no hope of getting a U.S. visa or green card. Before giving up, it's worth checking with a lawyer to make sure you haven't missed anything. This is particularly true if you have some urgent reason for needing to come to or stay in the United States—for example, you developed a serious illness while visiting the U.S. and might die if transported home. Some unusual (and hard-to-get) remedies, with names like "humanitarian parole" and "deferred action" may help you. However, you'll definitely need a lawyer's assistance to apply for and obtain these remedies. We don't cover them in this book.

B. Where to Get the Names of Good Immigration Lawyers

Finding a good lawyer can involve a fair amount of work. Immigration law is a specialized area; in fact, it has many subspecialities within it. So you will want to find a lawyer who specializes in immigration—you obviously don't want to consult the lawyer who wrote your best friend's will.

Whatever you do, don't just open the telephone book and pick the immigration lawyer with the biggest advertisement.

It is far better to ask a trusted person for a referral. Perhaps you know someone in the United States who is sophisticated in

practical affairs and has been through an immigration process. This person may be able to recommend his or her lawyer, or can ask that lawyer to recommend another.

Also check out Nolo's Lawyer Directory at www.nolo.com (under "Find a Lawyer," choose "Immigration" from the drop-down menu for Practice Area, and enter your zip code). This allows you to view lawyers' photos and personal profiles describing their areas of expertise and practice philosophy.

Local nonprofit organizations serving immigrants can also be excellent sources for referrals. A nonprofit organization is a charity that seeks funding from foundations and individuals to help people in need. Since they exist to serve others rather than to make a profit, they charge less and are usually staffed by people whose hearts and minds are in the right places. In the immigrant services field, examples include Northwest Immigrant Rights Project (Seattle), El Rescate (Los Angeles), the various International Institutes (nationwide), and Catholic Charities (nationwide).

For a list of U.S. government-approved nonprofits and attorneys who'll work for reduced fees, ask your local USCIS office or court or check www.justice.gov/eoir (click "Find Legal Representation" in the Action Center, then "List of Pro Bono Legal Service Providers"). You don't need to use a nonprofit from this list, but it may be safer to do so. Supposed nonprofit organizations can be unscrupulous too, or they may actually be for-profit businesses. Most nonprofits keep lists of lawyers who they know do honest immigration work for a fair price.

Yet another good resource is the American Immigration Lawyers Association (AILA)—contact them at 202-507-7600 or www.aila. org. AILA offers a lawyer referral service. Its membership is limited to lawyers who have passed a screening process, which helps keep out the less-scrupulous practitioners. But not all good immigration lawyers have joined AILA (membership is a bit pricey).

Try to get a list of a few lawyers who you've heard do good work, then meet or talk to each and choose one. If you're living in another country now, you may have to communicate with a U.S.-based lawyer primarily by email. In major cities of some countries with high levels of immigration, such as Canada and England, U.S. immigration firms have set up offices.

CAUTION
Don't contact lawyers expecting free advice. The good immigration lawyers are extremely busy and under a lot of deadline pressure. Yet many of them receive supposed "quick questions," particularly via email, from people who are not their clients and whom they've never met. It's unfair to expect a response to such contacts and also unrealistic to assume that you'll get valid advice without a full analysis of your situation.

C. How to Avoid Sleazy Lawyers

There are good and bad immigration lawyers out there. Some of the good ones are candidates for sainthood—they put in long hours dealing with a difficult bureaucracy on behalf of a clientele that typically can't pay high fees. They are also active in the community, advocating for immigrants' rights when no one else does.

The bad immigration lawyers are a nightmare—and there are more than a few of them out there. They typically try to do a high-volume business, churning out the same forms for every client regardless of their situation. Such lawyers (if they're really lawyers at all) can get clients into deep trouble by overlooking critical issues in their cases or failing to submit applications or court materials on time. But they never seem to forget to send a huge bill for their supposed help. Some signs to watch for are:

- **The lawyer approaches you in a USCIS office or another public location and tries to solicit your business.** This is not only against the lawyers' rules of professional ethics, but is also an indication that the lawyer may be incompetent—no good lawyer ever needs to find clients this way.
- **The lawyer makes big promises, such as "I guarantee I'll win your case" or "I've got a special contact who will put your application at the front of the line."** The U.S. government is in ultimate

control of your application, and any lawyer who implies that he or she has special powers is either lying or may be involved in something you don't want to be a part of.

- **The lawyer has a very fancy office and wears a lot of flashy gold jewelry.** We're all for professional appearances but a fancy office or a $2,000 outfit aren't necessarily signs of a lawyer's success at winning cases. These trappings may instead be signs that the lawyer charges high fees and counts on impressing clients with clothing rather than results.

- **The lawyer encourages you to lie on your application.** This is a tricky area. On the one hand, a good lawyer can assist you in learning what information you don't want to needlessly offer up and can help you present the truth in the best light possible. But a lawyer who coaches you to lie—for example, by telling you to pretend you lost your passport and visa when in fact you entered the United States illegally—isn't ethical. There's every chance that USCIS knows the lawyer's reputation and will scrutinize your application harder because of it.

You might think that the really bad lawyers would be out of business by now, but that isn't the case. Sad to say, neither the attorney bar associations nor the courts nor even the police take much interest in going after people who prey on immi-grants. Occasionally, nonprofits devoted to immigrants' rights will attempt to get the enforcement community interested in taking action. Unfortunately, this threat of official scrutiny isn't much of a deterrent.

TIP

If you are the victim of an unscrupulous lawyer, complain! Law enforcement won't go after lawyers who prey on immigrants until there is enough community pressure. If a lawyer, or someone pretending to be a lawyer, pulls something unethical on you, report it to the state and local bar association and the local district attorney's (DA's) office. Ask your local nonprofits if anyone else in your area is collecting such information.

D. How to Choose Among Lawyers

Once you've got your "short list" of pro-spective lawyers, you'll want to speak to each one. How much a lawyer charges is bound to be a factor in whom you choose (see Section F, below), but it shouldn't be the only factor. Here are some other im-portant considerations.

1. Familiarity With Cases Like Yours

Some immigration lawyers spend much of their time in subspecialties, such as helping people obtain asylum or employment-based visas. To learn how much experience a lawyer has in the type of visa or green card you're interested in, ask some very practical questions, such as:

- How long do you expect my case to take?
- What is the reputation of the officers at the USCIS or consular office who will handle my case?
- How many cases like mine did you handle this year?

2. Client Rapport

Your first instinct in hiring a lawyer may be to look for a shark—someone you wouldn't want to leave your child with, but who will be a tough fighter for your case. This isn't necessarily the best choice in the immigration context. Since you may need to share some highly confidential issues with your lawyer, you'll want to know that the person is discreet and thoughtful. Also, realize that a lawyer's politeness goes a long way in front of immigration officials; sharks often produce a bureaucratic backlash, whereas the lawyers with good working relations with USCIS may have doors opened to them.

3. Access to Your Lawyer

You'll want to know that you can reach your lawyer during the months that your application winds its way through the USCIS or consular bureaucracy. A lawyer's accessibility may be hard to judge at the beginning, but try listening to the lawyer's receptionist as you wait in his or her office for the first time. If you get the sense that the receptionist is rude and trying to push people off or give them flimsy excuses about why the lawyer hasn't returned their calls or won't talk to them, don't hire that lawyer.

Many immigration lawyers are sole practitioners and use an answering machine rather than a receptionist. In that case, you'll have to rely on how quickly they answer your initial calls. In your first meeting, simply ask the lawyer how quickly he or she will get back to you. If the lawyer regularly breaks promises, you'll have grounds on which to complain.

Of course, you, too, have a responsibility not to harass your lawyer with frequent calls. The lawyer should be available for legitimate questions about your case, including inquiries about approaching deadlines.

4. Explaining Services and Costs

Take a good look at any printed materials the lawyer gives you on your first visit. Are they glitzy, glossy pieces that look more like advertising than anything useful? Or are they designed to acquaint you with the process you're getting into and the lawyer's role in it? Think about this issue again before you sign the lawyer's fee agreement, described in the section immediately below. Being a good salesperson doesn't necessarily make someone a good lawyer.

E. Signing Up Your Lawyer

Many good lawyers will ask you to sign an agreement covering their services and the fees you will pay them. This is a good idea for both of you, and can help prevent misunderstandings. The contract should be written in a way you can understand; there's no law that says it has to be in confusing legal jargon. The lawyer should go over the contract with you carefully, not just push it under your nose, saying, "Sign here." Some normal contract clauses include:

- **Scope of work.** A description of exactly what the lawyer will do for you.
- **Fees.** Specification of the amount you'll pay, either as a flat fee (a lump sum you pay for a stated task, such as $2,000 for an adjustment of status application) or at an hourly rate, with a payment schedule. If you hire someone at an hourly rate, you can ask to be told as soon as the hours have hit a certain limit.

 TIP

Don't pay a big flat fee up-front. Since the lawyer already has your money, he or she will have little incentive to please you. And if you don't like the lawyer later on, chances are you won't get any of your money back. Instead, pay for a few hours' service—then if you don't like the lawyer's work, end the relationship.

- **Responsibility for expenses.** Most lawyers will ask you to cover the incidental expenses associated with the work that they do, such as phone calls, postage, and photocopying. This is fair. After all, if your case requires a one-hour phone call to the consulate in Brunei, that call shouldn't eat up the lawyer's fee. But check carefully to be sure that the lawyer charges you the actual costs of these items. Some lawyers have been known to turn a tidy profit by charging, for example, 20 cents a page for a photocopy job that really cost only three cents a page.
- **Effect of nonpayment.** Many lawyers charge interest if you fail to pay on time. This is normal and probably not worth making a big fuss about. If you have trouble paying on time, call the lawyer and ask for more time—he or she may be willing to forgo the interest if it's clear you're taking your obligation seriously.
- **Exclusion of guarantee.** The lawyer may warn you that there's no guarantee of winning your case. Though this may appear as if the lawyer is looking for an excuse to lose, it is actually a responsible way for the lawyer to protect against clients who assume they're guaranteed a win or who later accuse the lawyer of having made

Watch Out for Nonlawyers Practicing Immigration Law

Because much of immigration law involves filling in forms, people assume it's easy. They're wrong. Be careful about whom you consult with or hand your case over to. Unless the person shows you certification that he or she is a lawyer, an accredited representative, or a paralegal working under the direct supervision of a lawyer, think of them as typists. (An accredited representative is a nonlawyer who has received training from a lawyer and been recognized by USCIS as qualified to prepare USCIS applications and represent clients in court.) And this is true even though these people may go by fancy names such as "immigration consultant," "notario," or "notary public"—they do not

have a law degree. To check on whether someone is really a lawyer, ask for his or her bar number and call the state bar association.

Hiring a nonlawyer or nonaccredited representative is appropriate only if you want help with the form preparation and no more. But even seemingly minor details asked for on a form, like your date of entry to the U. S. or your address, can have legal consequences. Don't just turn your case over and let the consultant make the decisions.

If you feel you've been defrauded by an immigration consultant, you may want to sue in small claims court; see *Everybody's Guide to Small Claims Court,* by Ralph Warner (Nolo).

such promises. After all, USCIS or the consulate is the ultimate decision maker on your case.

- **Effect of changes in case.** Most lawyers will warn you that if there is something you didn't tell them about (for example, that you are still married to your first wife while trying to get a green card through your second wife) or a significant life change affects your case (for instance, you get arrested), they will charge you additional fees to cover the added work these revelations will cause. This, too, is normal; but to prevent disputes, make very sure that the contract specifies in

detail all the work that is already included. For example, a contract for a lawyer to help you with a green card application within the United States might specify that the lawyer will be responsible for "preparation of visa petition and adjustment of status packet, filing all applications with USCIS, representation at an interview, and reasonable follow-up with USCIS." If the lawyer agrees to include work on any special waivers or unusual documents (for example, waiver of inadmissibility or an extra Affidavit of Support from a joint sponsor), make sure these are mentioned in the contract.

F. Paying Your Lawyer

You may have to pay an initial consultation fee as well as a fee for the lawyer's services. The initial consultation fee can vary depending on the lawyer and your case, but usually is no less than $100. Some lawyers will treat the initial consultation fee as part payment for full services if you end up hiring them.

Some good lawyers provide free consultations. But many have found that they can't afford to spend a lot of their time this way, since many immigrants have no visa or remedy available to them, which means the lawyer gets no work after the initial consultation. Be ready to pay a reasonable fee for your initial consultation, but do not sign any contracts for further services until you're confident you've found the right lawyer. This usually means consulting with several lawyers before signing a contract with the one you like best.

Many lawyers charge flat rates for green card applications. That means you can compare prices. If the lawyer quotes an hourly rate instead, expect to pay between $150 and $350 per hour.

A higher rate doesn't necessarily mean a better lawyer. Those who charge less may be keeping their overhead low, still making their name in the business, or philosophically opposed to charging high fees. But an extremely low fee may be a sign that the person isn't really a lawyer, as covered in "Watch Out for Nonlawyers Practicing Immigration Law," above.

If the prices you are being quoted are beyond your reach but you definitely need legal help, you have a couple of options. One is to ask the lawyer to split the work with you. With this arrangement, the lawyer consults with you solely about the issue causing you difficulty, reviews a document, or performs some other key task at the hourly rate, while you do the follow-up work, such as filling out the application forms and translating or writing documents, statements, letters, or more.

Be forewarned, though, that while many lawyers will sell you advice on an hourly basis, most won't want to get into a mixed arrangement unless they are sure they won't end up cleaning up anything you might do wrong. For example, a lawyer might not agree to represent you in a USCIS interview if the lawyer wasn't hired to review your forms and documents before you submitted them to USCIS.

Another option is to look for a nonprofit organization that helps people with cases like yours. A few provide free services, while most charge reduced rates. But don't get your hopes too high. The U.S. government does not fund organizations that provide services to immigrants (except for very limited types of services), which means that most nonprofits depend on private sources of income and are chronically underfunded. The result is that many nonprofits will have long backlogs of cases and may not be able to take your case at all.

G. Firing Your Lawyer

You have the right to fire your lawyer at any time. But before you take this step, make sure that your disagreement is about something that is truly the lawyer's fault.

Many people blame their lawyer for delays that are actually caused by USCIS or the consulates. You can always consult with another lawyer regarding whether your case has been mishandled. Ask your lawyer for a complete copy of your file first—you have a right to your file at any time. If it appears that your case was mishandled, or if relations with your lawyer have deteriorated badly, firing the lawyer may be the healthiest thing for you and your immigration case.

You will have to pay the fired lawyer for any work that has already been done on your case. If you paid any money up front before the work was done, the lawyer probably was required to put it in a trust account, which is a special bank account where the money doesn't legally belong to the lawyer until he or she does the required work. When the lawyer-client relationship ends, the lawyer is permitted to withdraw enough money from the trust account to cover the work already done. If you had a flat-fee arrangement, the lawyer calculates how much he or she is due using a percentage or hourly rate, limited by the total flat-fee amount. Ask for a complete accounting of how the lawyer decided how much to keep. Don't count on getting any money back, however—flat fees are often artificially low, and it's very easy for a lawyer to show that he or she used up your fee on the work that was done.

Firing your lawyer will not affect the progress of your applications with USCIS or the consulate. However, you should send a letter to the last USCIS or consular office you heard from, directing them to send all future correspondence directly to you (or to your new lawyer).

H. Do-It-Yourself Legal Research

With or without a lawyer, you may at some point wish to look at the immigration laws yourself. If so, we applaud your self-empowerment instinct—but need to give you a few warnings. A government spokesperson once called the immigration laws a "mystery, and a mastery of obfuscation" (spokeswoman Karen Kraushaar, quoted in *The Washington Post,* April 24, 2001), and they've only gotten worse since she said that. One is tempted to think that the members of the U.S. Congress who write and amend the immigration laws deliberately made them unreadable, perhaps to confuse the rest of the representatives so they wouldn't understand what they were voting on.

The result is that researching the immigration laws is something even the experts find difficult—which means you may be wading into treacherous waters if you try it on your own. Figuring out local USCIS office procedures and policies can be even more difficult. Lawyers learn a great deal through trial and error and through the experiences of other lawyers who tried new tactics. They also learn important information from USCIS or State Department cables, memos, or other instructions, which can sometimes be found online but you have to know what you're looking for.

Does all this mean that you shouldn't ever do your own legal research? Certainly not. Some research inquiries are quite safe—for instance, if we've cited a section of the law and you want to read the exact language or see whether that section has changed, there's no magic in looking up the law and reading it. But in general, be cautious when researching, and look at several sources to confirm your findings.

Immigration laws are federal, meaning they are written by the U.S. Congress and do not vary from one state to another (though procedures and priorities for interpreting and carrying out the laws may vary among USCIS offices in different cities, states, or federal court circuits). Below we give you a rundown on the most accessible research tools. Not coincidentally, lawyers often use these tools as well.

1. The Federal Code

The federal immigration law is found in Title 8 of the United States Code. Any law library (such as the one at your local courthouse or law school) should have a complete set of the U.S. Code (traditionally abbreviated as U.S.C.). The library may also have a separate volume containing exactly the same material, but called the Immigration and Nationality Act, or I.N.A.

Unfortunately, the two sets of laws are numbered a bit differently, and not all volumes of the I.N.A. cross-reference back to the U.S. Code, and vice versa. For this reason, when code citations are mentioned in this book, we include both the U.S.C. and I.N.A. numbers. You can also access the U.S. Code via Nolo's website at www. nolo.com/legal-research. Click "Federal Law Resources," then "U.S. Code." If you already know the title (which is 8) and section, you can enter them and pull up the text immediately.

2. USCIS and State Department Regulations and Guidance

Another important source of immigration law is the Code of Federal Regulations (C.F.R.). Federal regulations are written by the agencies responsible for carrying out federal law. The regulations are meant to explain in greater detail just how the federal agency is going to carry out the law. You'll find the USCIS regulations at Title 8 of the

C.F.R.; the Department of State regulations (relevant to anyone whose application is being decided at a U.S. consulate) at Title 22 of the C.F.R.; and the Department of Labor regulations at 20 C.F.R.

If you applying to USCIS for an immigration status or benefit, the USCIS *Policy Manual* (www.uscis.gov/policymanual/HTML/ PolicyManual.html) is a great resource for understanding how USCIS will look at your case. The *Policy Manual* is replacing, piece by piece, the USCIS *Adjudicator's Field Manual*, which can be found on the USCIS website as well.

The regulations are helpful, but certainly don't have all the answers. Again, your local law library will have the C.F.R., and you can find the regulations at www.nolo.com as well.

If you are applying for a visa from outside of the U.S., you may also wish to look at the State Department's *Foreign Affairs Manual*. This is primarily meant to be an internal government document, containing instructions to the consulates on handling immigrant and nonimmigrant visa cases. However, it is available for public researching as well. Your local law library may be able to find you a copy, or see the State Department's website, at www.travel.state.gov (click the link underneath "U.S. Visas," then in the link to "Laws and Policy" section, click "Laws and Regulations," then choose "Foreign Affairs Manual, Visas 9 (FAM)").

3. Online Information

If you have Internet access, you will want to familiarize yourself with the USCIS, State Department, and Labor Department websites. The addresses are www.uscis.gov, www.travel.state.gov, and www.doleta.gov (for the Labor Department's Employment & Training Administration).

The USCIS website offers advice on various immigration benefits and applications (though the advice is so brief as to sometimes be misleading), downloads of most immigration forms, and current fees.

On the State Department website, some of the useful information is found under "U.S. Visas," including a link to the monthly *Visa Bulletin*.

The Department of Labor website, www.foreignlaborcert.doleta.gov, contains descriptions of programs for hiring foreign workers, application forms, FAQs, and more.

The Internet is full of sites put up by immigration lawyers as well as immigrants. Because the quality of these sites varies widely, we don't even attempt to review them here.

4. Court Decisions

Immigrants who have been denied visas or green cards often appeal these decisions to the federal courts. The courts' decisions in these cases are supposed to govern the future behavior of USCIS and the consulates.

However, you should hardly ever need to discuss court decisions with a USCIS or State Department official. For one thing, the officials are not likely to listen until they get a specific directive from their superiors or until the court decision is incorporated into their agency's regulations (the C.F.R.). For another thing, such discussions probably mean that your case has become complicated enough to need a lawyer. We do not attempt to teach you how to research federal court decisions here.

5. Legal Publications

Two high-quality and popular resources used by immigration lawyers are *Interpreter Releases*, a weekly update published by Thomson Reuters, and *Immigration Law and Procedure*, a multivolume, continually updated looseleaf set by Stanley Mailman and Stephen Yale-Loehr (LexisNexis).

Again, you should be able to find both at your local law library. Both are very well indexed. However, they are written for lawyers, so you'll have to wade through some technical terminology.

Internet Resources

This list summarizes the useful Internet sites that have been mentioned in this book.

- U.S. Citizenship and Immigration Services (USCIS): www.uscis.gov
- The U.S. Department of State: www.travel.state.gov
- U.S. Department of Labor, Employment & Training Administration, Office of Foreign Labor Certification: www.foreignlaborcert.doleta.gov
- U.S. consulates and embassies abroad: www.usembassy.gov.

Introduction to Permanent U.S. Residence (Green Cards)

This portion of the book introduces the topic of U.S. lawful permanent residence, otherwise known as having a green card. People all over the world have heard of green cards. It is the unofficial term for the Permanent Resident Card (Form I-551), which is, in fact, green in color.

A lot of people mistakenly believe that green cards are nothing more than work permits. While a green card does give you the right to work legally in the U.S. where and when you wish, that is just one of its features. Identifying the holder as a permanent resident of the U.S. is its main function.

Don't bother applying for a green card if actually living in the U.S. is not your goal. When you have a green card, you are required to make the U.S. your permanent home. If you don't, you risk losing your card. This does not mean your ability to travel in and out of the U.S. is limited. Freedom to travel as you choose is an important benefit of a green card. However, no matter how much you travel, your permanent home must be in the U.S., or your card will be revoked. It's wise not to spend more than six months at a time outside the United States.

All green cards issued since 1989 (except "conditional" green cards) carry expiration dates of ten years from the date of issue. This does not mean that the residency itself expires in ten years, just that the card must be replaced.

A. Categories of Green Card Applicants

There are nine categories of people who can apply for green cards. In some of the categories, you are immediately eligible for a green card, in others you must wait until one is available. We briefly describe the categories here, but refer to the appropriate chapter of this book for details.

1. Immediate Relatives

An unlimited number of green cards can be issued to immigrants who are immediate relatives of U.S. citizens. Immediate relatives are defined as:

- spouses of U.S. citizens, including recent widows and widowers
- unmarried people under the age of 21 who have at least one U.S. citizen parent
- parents of U.S. citizens, if the U.S. citizen child is age 21 or older
- stepchildren and stepparents, if the marriage creating the stepparent/ stepchild relationship took place before the child's 18th birthday, and
- parents and children related through adoption, if the adoption took place before the child reached the age of 16. All immigration rules governing natural parents and children apply to adoptive relatives but there are some additional procedures.

Immediate relatives are discussed in Chapter 7.

2. Other Relatives

Certain other family members of U.S. citizens or permanent residents are also eligible for U.S. green cards. However, only a limited number of green cards are available to these applicants. They have to wait, often many years, to get them, based on their place in the preference categories, as outlined below.

- **Family first preference.** Unmarried people, any age, who have at least one U.S. citizen parent.
- **Family second preference. 2A:** Spouses and unmarried children (under age 21) of green card holders; **2B:** Unmarried sons and daughters (who are over age 21) of green card holders.
- **Family third preference.** Married people, of any age, who have at least one U.S. citizen parent.
- **Family fourth preference.** Sisters and brothers of U.S. citizens where the citizen is over 21 years old.

Family preference categories are discussed in Chapter 7.

3. Employment-Based Green Cards

People with job skills wanted by U.S. employers are also eligible for green cards as outlined below. However, only a limited number of green cards are available to these applicants, leading in some cases to waits of several months or years, based on their place in these preference categories:

- **Employment first preference.** Priority workers, including the following three groups:
  - persons of extraordinary ability in the arts, sciences, education, business, or athletics
  - outstanding professors and researchers, and
  - managers and executives of multi-national companies.
- **Employment second preference.** Professionals with advanced degrees or exceptional ability.
- **Employment third preference.** Professionals and skilled or unskilled workers.
- **Employment fourth preference.** Religious workers, various miscellaneous categories of workers, and so-called Special Immigrants.
- **Employment fifth preference.** Individual investors willing to invest $1,000,000 in a U.S. business (or $500,000 if the business is in an economically depressed area).

These employment-based green cards are discussed in Chapter 9.

4. How the Numerical Limits Affect Your Wait for a Green Card

If a family member or employer petitions for you in a preference category—that is, a category with annual limits on the number of visas—your wait could be several years long. That's because the demand for green cards is, in most categories, far greater than the supply.

Although it's possible to estimate the likely wait in your category, this will be only an estimate. You will need to learn to track it, month by month, based on the *Visa Bulletin* published by the U.S. State Department (DOS). This system can be confusing at first.

Every government fiscal year (which starts October 1), a fresh supply of visa numbers is made available. How many depends on the numbers of people that Congress has said can get green cards in the preference categories in any one year. (For purposes of this explanation, a visa or visa number means the same thing as a green card.)

There's just one problem. Thousands of people who applied in previous years are probably still waiting for their visa. So you won't be able to make use of this fresh crop of visas right away.

Instead, the DOS has devised a system where the people who have been waiting longest have the first right to a visa. DOS keeps track of your place on the waiting list using the date that either your family member first submitted a visa petition or your employer first submitted a labor certification application, thus indicating that they'd like to help you immigrate. That date is called your Priority Date.

You will need to know your Priority Date, because the whole system of figuring out where you are in your wait for a green card depends on it. The DOS's *Visa Bulletin* gives you only one clue about the length of your wait: a list of the Priority Dates of other people who are now getting visas and green cards. By comparing your Priority Date to theirs, you'll be able to track your progress. We'll fully explain this after you are deeper into the application process.

5. Diversity Visa: Green Card Lottery

Approximately 50,000 green cards are offered each year to people from countries that in recent years have sent the fewest immigrants to the United States. The purpose of this program is to ensure a varied ethnic mix among people who immigrate to the U.S. (although applicants must also meet certain educational requirements). Therefore, green cards in this category are said to be based on ethnic diversity. The method used for choosing people who can apply for these green cards is a random selection by computer, so the program is popularly known as the green card lottery. This visa is discussed in Chapter 10.

6. Refugees and Asylees

Every year, many people seek asylum in the U.S. or try to get green cards as refugees. The two are often thought of as the same category, but there are some technical differences. A refugee receives permission to come to the U.S. in refugee status before actually arriving. Asylum is granted only after someone has physically entered the U.S., usually either as a nonimmigrant or an undocumented alien, and then submitted an application.

The qualifications for refugee status and asylum are similar. You must have either been persecuted or fear future persecution in your home country on account of your race, religion, nationality, membership in a partic-ular social group, or political opinion. If you are only fleeing poverty or general violence, you do not qualify in either category.

Both refugees and asylees can apply for green cards one year after their approval (asylees) or entry into the U.S. (refugees). (See Chapter 13 for details.)

7. Long-Term Residents and Other Special Cases

The law also allows immigration judges to grant permanent legal residence to certain people who have lived illegally in the U.S. for more than ten years, through a procedure known as cancellation of removal. They must show that their spouse or children—who are U.S. citizens— would face "exceptional and extremely unusual hardship" if the undocumented alien were forced to leave the country.

You have to be in immigration proceed-ings to seek a green card this way. If you believe that you meet this requirement, consult with a lawyer before going to the immigration authorities to turn yourself in. The number of green cards that can be given each year through cancellation of removal is limited, and it's very hard to prove "exceptional and extremely unusual hardship." We do not cover the application procedures in this book.

Another category, known as registry, allows people to adjust status if they have lived in the United States since January 1, 1972. See a lawyer if you believe you qualify for registry—we do not cover it in this book.

Individual members of Congress have, on occasion, intervened for humanitarian reasons in extraordinary cases, helping an individual obtain permanent residence even if the law would not allow it. However, this is a last resort, and you should explore all other possible options first.

CAUTION
This book does not discuss green card programs whose application deadlines have passed. For example, we do not cover the amnesty and Special Agricultural Worker (SAW) programs of the 1980s, or the so-called NACARA program—despite the fact that ongoing litiga-tion means that many of these cases are not over. For more information, consult an experienced immigration attorney.

The remaining chapters of this Part II, organized by type of green card, will give you details on your eligibility, the advantages and disadvantages of each type of green card, application procedures, and strategies for success.

B. How Many Green Cards Are Available?

There are no limits on the number of green cards that can be issued to immediate relatives of U.S. citizens. Those who qualify in any other family or employment preference-based green card category are affected by annual quotas.

Likewise, there is no limit on the number of green cards for asylees and refugees adjusting status, or for their spouses and children adjusting or joining them from overseas at the same time.

An unlimited number of green cards each year are available to persons who have held "U" visa status for three years, based on the fact that they have suffered substantial physical or mental abuse as a result of having been a victim of criminal activity and are helping the police. (See Chapter 27.) There is also no limit on the number of green cards available to the immediate family members of the U visa holder.

Green cards allocated annually to employment-based categories, including investors and Special Immigrants, number 140,000 worldwide. Approximately 480,000 green cards worldwide can be issued each year in the family categories.

Only 7% of all worldwide preference visas can be given to persons born in any one country. There are, therefore, two separate quotas: one for each country and one that is worldwide. This produces an odd result, because when you multiply the number of countries in the world by seven (the percentage allowed to each country) you get a much larger total than 100. What this means from a practical standpoint is that the 7% allotment to each country is an allowable maximum, not a guaranteed number. Applicants from a single country that has not used up its 7% green card allotment can still be prevented from getting green cards if the worldwide quota has been exhausted. As usual, there are currently waiting periods in many preference categories.

In addition to the fixed worldwide totals, 50,000 extra green cards are given each year through the ethnic diversity or lottery category. Qualifying countries and the number of green cards available to each are determined each year according to a formula. The annual limit on green cards given to nonpermanent residents in deportation (removal) proceedings through cancellation of removal is 4,000.

Getting a Green Card Through Family Members in the U.S.

I f you have close family members in the United States, they may, if they are willing, be able to help you immigrate. It depends first on what relation they are to you—the closer the relation, the more rights you have under immigration law. It also depends on whether your relatives are U.S. citizens or lawful permanent residents (green card holders). U.S. citizens can bring more distant relatives than green card holders can—their parents and brothers and sisters, for example. Also, U.S. citizens' relatives are allowed, in many cases, to immigrate faster than lawful permanent residents' relatives are. This chapter will explain who is eligible for a green card through their family members and how to apply for it.

SEE AN EXPERT

Do you need a lawyer? Many people are able to handle the application process for a family-based visa on their own, without a lawyer. However, if you have any trouble dealing with paperwork or understanding the instructions, or have any complications in your case (such as a criminal record, including that of the U.S. petitioner, particularly if he or she has committed offenses against a minor; past visa overstays in the U.S.; an abusive spouse upon whom you are relying to help you immigrate; or an immigrating child who will turn 21 soon), a lawyer is well worth the price. See Chapter 6 for tips on finding a good one.

Key Features of Family-Based Green Cards

Here are some of the advantages and disadvantages of permanent residence obtained through U.S. family members:

- Unlike with many other green cards, your educational background or work experience does not matter.
- Your spouse and unmarried children under the age of 21 are in many cases also eligible for green cards, as derivative, accompanying relatives.
- As with all green cards, yours can be taken away if you misuse it—for example, if you live outside the U.S. for too long, commit a crime, or even fail to advise the immigration authorities of your change of address.
- If you successfully keep your green card for five years (or three years if you're married to and still living with a U.S. citizen), you can apply for U.S. citizenship.

A. Are You Eligible for a Green Card Through a Relative?

You may qualify for a green card through relatives if you fall into one of the following categories:

- immediate relative of a U.S. citizen
- preference relative of a U.S. citizen or green card holder, or
- accompanying relative of someone in a preference category.

1. Immediate Relatives

These people qualify as immediate relatives:

- spouses of U.S. citizens. This includes widows and widowers of U.S. citizens if they had already started the application process at that time, or if not, if they start the application process within two years of the U.S. citizen's death.
- unmarried children of a U.S. citizen, under the age of 21, and
- parents of U.S. citizens, if the U.S. citizen child is age 21 or older. If the U.S. citizen child was abusing a parent, and then either died or lost citizenship status as a result of the abuse, the parent can file his or her own immigration petition on USCIS Form I-360. The abused parent must prove that he or she has good moral character, lives or has lived with the U.S. citizen child, and has been battered or subject to extreme cruelty by the child.

Immediate relatives may immigrate to the U.S. in unlimited numbers. They are not controlled by any annual limit or quota.

Stepparents and stepchildren qualify as immediate relatives if the marriage creating the parent/child relationship took place before the child's 18th birthday.

Same-Sex Couples Are Now Able to Obtain Green Cards Through Marriage

On June 26, 2013, the U.S. Supreme Court in *U.S. v. Windsor* struck down major portions of the federal Defense of Marriage Act (DOMA). This law once blocked individuals in same-sex marriages from receiving the federal benefits afforded to those in opposite-sex marriages, such as tax breaks and yes, immigration rights. Now, U.S. citizens and U.S. permanent residents can finally file a green card petition for their same-sex spouses.

The procedures for applying for immigration benefits for your same-sex spouse are exactly the same as described in this book. Just remember that your marriage must be legally recognized in either the state or the foreign country where the marriage was performed. And marriage is the key word:

civil unions and domestic partnerships won't count for immigration purposes.

So if you're not legally married, you will need to marry in order to obtain a green card for the foreign spouse. That might seem impossible if the foreign spouse's country does not recognize same-sex marriage or if international travel to the U.S. or another country is difficult or expensive.

A good way to get around this is to use the K-1 fiancé visa to bring your partner to the U.S. for the purpose of getting married (see Chapter 8 for information on fiancé visas). Keep in mind that this option will work only for the partners of U.S. citizens. Fiancés of U.S. permanent residents are not eligible for K-1 visas.

Parents and children related through adoption may, in some cases, qualify as immediate relatives. (See Section 2, below, for information on adopting a foreign-born child. If an adopted U.S. citizen child wants to petition for foreign-born parents to immigrate, the requirements are similar to those described below, in that the adoption must have been finalized before the child's 16th birthday, the parent must have had legal custody of the child for two years before or after the adoption, and the child must have lived with the adoptive parent for two years before or after the adoption.)

2. Adopting a Foreign-Born Child

People hoping for green cards often ask their attorneys whether they could become eligible by having a U.S. citizen adopt them. Unfortunately, this rarely works—for one thing, anyone over the age of 16 is already too old for a green card through adoption. For another thing, adopted children who are not orphaned must (if they are not from a country that's party to the Hague Convention) live in the petitioning parents' legal custody for two years before applying for the green card, which is all but impossible unless the parents live outside the United States. A third complication is that both the eligibility requirements and procedural steps are split into two. Which set applies to you depends completely on whether or not you are planning to adopt a child who is from a country that is party to the Hague Convention. The Convention, which became effective in 2008, set international standards for intercountry adoptions in order to give children greater protection from abduction, trafficking, and so forth. For the list of participating countries, go to adoption.state.gov (click "Hague Convention" then "Convention Countries").

Orphan adoptions are a bit easier in cases where the child will not be coming from a Hague Convention country. (The procedures for adopting nonorphans and orphans from Hague Convention countries are identical.) This is the reason that many U.S. citizen parents seeking to adopt look to foreign orphanages.

As a practical matter, adopting parents usually use the help of adoption agencies in the U.S., which are better versed in the procedures than many attorneys. For this reason, this book will not discuss adoption procedures at length, beyond the following introduction to the basic rules. For more information, see adoption.state.gov.

Even with an agency, expect the process to take at least six to 12 months. Although we can't provide you with a list of reputable agencies, two California-based groups that Nolo lawyers have had good experiences with are Adopt International, at 415-934-0300, www.adoptinter.org; and Adoption Connection, 415-359-2494, www.adoptionconnection.org.

Be selective in choosing an adoption agency—look for one that's been doing adoptions for many years, successfully completes a comparatively large number per year, serves the countries in which you're interested, and is happy to show you evidence that it's licensed and comes with good references. The U.S. government also provides a centralized information source, the Child Welfare Information Gateway, at www.childwelfare.gov.

a. Orphan Eligibility From Non-Hague-Convention Countries

Orphan means a child whose natural parents are either deceased, have disappeared, or have permanently and legally deserted or abandoned the child. If only one parent is absent, the child is an orphan if the other parent hasn't remarried and is incapable of providing child care that meets the standard of living in their country.

Be careful: Some parents may put a child into an orphanage temporarily, without giving up all of their parental rights, in which case the child isn't eligible to immigrate. In the case of a birth to nonmarried parents, if the law of the native country confers equal benefits to illegitimate and legitimate children, both parents must relinquish their rights.

In addition, the orphan child must be living outside the U.S. and, if not already adopted by the U.S. parents, must either be in the U.S. parents' custody or in the custody of an agent acting on their behalf in accordance with local law. You cannot file an orphan petition for a child who is present in the U.S., unless that child was paroled into the U.S. by DHS and has not been adopted in the United States. Finally, the child must be under 16 years of age when the initial visa petition (that starts the green card process) is filed.

The adopting parents themselves must also meet certain criteria. First, at least one of the parents must be a U.S. citizen; and if the other parent is not a U.S. citizen, he or she must be legally present in the United States. If an adopting parent is single, he or she must be at least 25 years of age. There are no age restrictions if the petitioner is married.

b. Orphan Immigration Procedures From Non-Hague-Convention Countries

Procedurally, the orphan adoption process begins when the U.S. citizen parents submit a visa petition to a USCIS service center. Which form they use and the precise procedures to be followed depend upon whether or not they've actually identified the child.

Parents who already have a particular child in mind would use USCIS Form I-600, accompanied by documents proving the petitioner's U.S. citizen status and qualifications to adopt, his or her marriage to the other parent, completion of a home study (by the state

International Adoption for Lesbians and Gays

Although a handful of foreign countries allow adoption by same-sex couples, it is not allowed in the most common countries for international adoptions. Most countries strongly prefer that the adopting parents be married. In fact, some won't allow adoption by single people at all. If a country requires adoptive parents to be married, then neither a same-sex couple nor a lesbian or gay individual can adopt there. Although many states in the U.S. have expanded the rights of same-sex couples to adopt, it's doubtful that such change in the U.S. will have any impact on the host country's policy.

At least one country (China) is so determined not to grant adoptions to lesbians and gays that it requires adoptive parents to sign an affidavit swearing that they are heterosexual. Apparently undeterred by signing such a form, a large number of same-sex couples have successfully adopted Chinese girls who were being raised in orphanages. As a result, if you are not heterosexual and are proceeding with a foreign adoption, you will need to keep your sexual orientation—and your relationship with your partner—hidden from the host country.

It is a judgment call whether or not you tell the agency helping you with the adoption about your sexual orientation. Many agencies operate on a wink-and-nod basis—they are fully aware of the nature of your relationship with your partner, but refer to the partner as a "roommate" in their reports to the host country and simply ignore the issue of sexual orientation.

For more about adoption and parenting for same-sex couples, check out *A Legal Guide for Lesbian & Gay Couples*, by Emily Doskow and Frederick Hertz (Nolo).

government or an approved agency) and any preadoption requirements in the state where they live, and the child's age, orphan status, legal custody status, and availability for adoption. The petition must be accompanied by an application fee (currently $775) and a fingerprinting or biometrics fee ($85) for each person who is 18 years or older who is living in the house of the adoptive parent. The parents may submit the visa petition either before or after the legal adoption is completed; and if it has been completed, they should also include the adoption certificate.

To save time, some parents can simply figure out which country they'll be adopting from, satisfy any preadoption requirements existing in the laws of the U.S. state where they live, and then start the process with a slightly different immigration form, I-600A, plus relevant documents and a $775 application fee. They would then submit Form I-600 with the remaining documents after the child has been identified, but without needing to pay the fees again. Eventually, the parents will have to meet the child in person, before or during the adoption proceedings.

After the parents have submitted the Form I-600, they will be called in for fingerprinting, and USCIS will evaluate whether they meet the various requirements. Once the petition has been approved, the procedures will follow the usual consular processing procedures described in Section E, below.

c. Nonorphan Eligibility

A nonorphan may qualify for a green card if his or her adoption was finalized before his or her 16th birthday. It doesn't matter how old the child is when the initial visa petition is filed (to start a green card application process). There is one exception to this age limit, which applies to a child between the ages of 16 and 18, if the older child is the natural sibling of a younger child you have already adopted or are adopting at the same time as the older one.

In addition to being legally adopted, the child must (if coming from a non-Hague country) have been in the legal custody of, and physically residing with, the adopting parents for at least two years before applying for a green card. It doesn't matter whether those two years were before or after the adoption took place.

As a practical matter, however, the residency requirement for children coming from non-Hague countries usually means

that at least one of the parents must live outside of the U.S. with the child for two years. USCIS doesn't offer any temporary visas allowing the child to come to the U.S. to fulfill the two-year requirement before applying for the green card. (Though in rare cases usually amounting to emergencies, it might allow something called humanitarian parole.) Most U.S. parents who don't already have a particular child in mind find it easier to locate an orphan to adopt.

Unfortunately, the combination of limited number of visas per year and the two-year residency requirement can make it impossible for a permanent resident parent or parents to be united with a newly adopted child. Here's why: The child won't be able to legally enter the U.S. until he or she has a green card. (As an "intending immigrant," the child is not going to be allowed a tourist visa.) But the child can't get a green card unless he or she has already lived in the U.S. parent's legal custody for two years. If the child had been adopted before his or her parent(s) came to the U.S., and they had lived together outside of the U.S. for two years, this would not be a problem. But if the child has recently been adopted, the family is stuck in an impossible situation. The permanent resident parent can't even choose to live outside of the U.S. for the two years, since by doing so he or she may be considered to have abandoned, or given up, his or her U.S. residence and green card.

For a nonorphan to get a green card, it is also necessary that the adopting parents meet certain requirements. They must be investigated by a U.S. state public or government-licensed private adoption agency. Such an investigation is usually part of standard adoption procedure in most U.S. states. If, however, the adoption takes place outside the U.S., or an investigation is not compulsory in the particular U.S. state where the adoption occurs, this study must now be satisfactorily completed. The age of the petitioning parent is irrelevant in filing a nonorphan petition, even if the parent is unmarried.

d. Nonorphan Immigration Procedures

If a child adopted by a U.S. citizen parent or green card holder falls into the category of nonorphan, and the child is coming from a non-Hague-Convention country, the procedures for obtaining a green card are exactly the same as those for blood-related children of parents who are U.S. citizens or green card holders. See the remainder of this chapter for further instructions. Note that for an adopted child, either a consular or U.S. filing is possible, depending on the physical location of the child when the application is submitted.

If the child is coming from a country that is party to the Hague Convention, we recommend you get an attorney's help. Below is a brief overview of the necessary procedures, which must be accomplished exactly in this order:

- **Choose an adoption service provider (ASP).** An ASP is an organization authorized to provide services in connection with a Hague adoption.
- **Commission a home study report.** This review of you, your family, your finances, and your home environment must come from an authorized Hague-adoption service provider.
- **Submit Form I-800A to USCIS.** You must file this form, titled "Application for Determination of Suitability to Adopt a Child from a Convention Country," before being matched with the child. The filing fee for Form I-800A is $775, plus $85 for biometrics, not only for the main applicant but also for each person 18 years of age or older who will be living in the household. To be eligible to file Form I-800A, you must be a U.S. citizen and habitually reside in the United States. If married, your spouse must also sign the Form I-800A and must also intend to adopt the child in question. If you are not married, you must be at least 24 years of age when you file Form I-800A, and must be at least 25 years of age when you later file Form I-800.
- **After USCIS approves your Form I-800A:** You'll need to work with the ASP to obtain a proposed adoption placement.

Moving Between the Visa Categories

During the long wait for a green card, people's life circumstances change. This may mean they move from one preference category to another, move up to immediate relative, or even lose eligibility for a green card altogether. Here's a summary of the changes that most commonly affect applicants:

- **Immediate relatives:**
  - If the spouse of a U.S. citizen divorces before being approved for a green card, he or she loses eligibility (except in cases where the U.S. citizen was abusive).
  - If the minor child of a U.S. citizen marries, she drops from immediate relative to family third preference.
  - If the unmarried child of a U.S. citizen turns 21 after the visa petition is filed, she is protected, under the Child Status Protection Act (CSPA), from changing visa categories ("aging out")—she will remain an immediate relative.
- **Family first preference relatives:** If the child of a U.S. citizen gets married, he or she drops to family third preference, but keeps the same Priority Date.
- **Family second preference relatives:**
  - If the child of a permanent resident (Category 2A) marries, he or she completely loses green card eligibility through that permanent resident.

- If a child in Category 2A turns 21 *before* his or her Priority Date is current, the child drops into category 2B and faces a longer wait (but if the child turns 21 *after* his or her Priority Date is current, he or she can retain 2A status by filing for a green card within one year, under the CSPA; the child can also subtract from his or her age the number of days it took the former INS or USCIS to make a decision on the initial visa petition).
- In cases where the petitioning spouse or parent of a second preference beneficiary becomes a U.S. citizen, the immigrant spouse or children in Category 2A become immediate relatives and the children in Category 2B move up to family first preference, keeping the same Priority Date. In some cases, however, the first preference wait may actually be longer than in the second preference category. Check the Department of State's *Visa Bulletin* to see. In those cases, the son or daughter may write to USCIS to "opt out" of the conversion.
- **Family third preference:** If the child of a U.S. citizen divorces (for real reasons, not just to get a green card), he or she moves up to family first preference and retains the same Priority Date.

- **Submit Form I-800 to USCIS.** This form, titled "Petition to Classify Convention Adoptee as an Immediate Relative," asks USCIS to recognize the child's eligibility as a Convention adoptee. There is no fee for the first Form I-800 filed for a child on the basis of an approved Form I-800A. If more than one Form I-800 is filed during the approval period for different children, the fee is $775 for the second and each subsequent Form I-800 (except that if the children were siblings before the adoption, no additional filing fee is required).
- **Adopt the child from overseas.** Alternatively, you can gain custody in order to adopt the child in the United States.
- **Obtain an immigrant visa for the child.** This will involve you and the child submitting paperwork to, and attending an interview at, a U.S. consulate in the child's home country.
- **Bring the child to the United States.**

See the USCIS instructions that come with the forms for details on where to file.

!   CAUTION
      You'll also need to follow the rules of the country you're adopting from. Not every country allows international adoptions, and those that do usually impose various requirements on the parents. For example, some countries refuse to allow single-parent adoptions, or require that adopting parents be of a certain age. You'll need to research these international requirements on your own or with the help of your adoption agency.

3. Preference Relatives

You may qualify for a green card through relatives if you fall into one of the categories below; but, depending on demand, you'll have to wait in line, possibly for many years, before claiming your green card:

- **Family first preference.** Unmarried children, any age, of a U.S. citizen.
- **Family second preference. 2A:** Spouses and unmarried children (under 21 years old) of green card holders; and **2B:** Unmarried sons and daughters of green card holders, who are at least 21 years old.
- **Family third preference.** Married children of a U.S. citizen, any age.
- **Family fourth preference.** Sisters and brothers of U.S. citizens, where the U.S. citizen is at least 21 years old.

4. Bringing Your Spouse and Children

If you are getting a green card as a preference relative and you are married or have unmarried children below the age of 21, your spouse and children can get green cards as accompanying relatives by proving their family relationship to you and filling out some applications of their own—it takes only one Form I-130 visa petition to start the process. If, however, you qualify as an immediate relative, they cannot. Ordinarily, this doesn't cause problems— for example, a U.S. citizen petitioning his or her spouse can simply file separate visa petitions for each child (on Form I-130) so that they don't have to ride on their parent's visa application.

This difference may, however, create some real problems in cases involving parents immigrating through their adult children or stepparents and stepchildren who wish to immigrate as a family (as illustrated in the examples below). This is probably one of the most difficult areas in immigration to understand. If you don't have adult children or stepchildren involved in your immigration plans, skip these examples.

EXAMPLE 1: Suppose your daughter is over age 21 and is a U.S. citizen. You are applying for a green card as an immediate relative (her mother), with your U.S.-citizen daughter acting as petitioner. Suppose also that your husband, the child's father, has died, and last year (when your child was 20) you married someone else. In that case, your spouse has a problem. He or she can't get a green card automatically as an accompanying relative, because you are an immediate relative, not a preference relative, and only preference relatives can bring accompanying relatives. But your child cannot petition for your new spouse directly, because they are not related. Any children you may have, even if they are minors, cannot be accompanying relatives

either, for the same reason. You will have to wait until you get your own green card and are living in the U.S., at which time you can petition for your spouse and children under the family second preference category (as the relative of a green card holder).

If your present marriage had taken place before your U.S. son or daughter reached the age of 18, your new husband's problem would be solved, because he would, according to immigration law, be your child's stepparent. Likewise, if your husband adopted your U.S. citizen child before the child's 16th birthday, he would qualify as an adopting parent. Stepparents and adopting parents count as immediate relatives of a U.S. citizen, and your child can petition for a stepparent or adopting parent just as if he or she were a natural parent.

Suppose instead that your spouse did not die, but is the father or mother of your U.S. citizen child. In that case, your child may file petitions for each parent at the same time, as immediate relatives, but the two filings will be completely separate.

Your U.S citizen child may also sponsor his or her brothers and sisters under the family fourth preference category. Again, however, the fact that you qualify for a green card will not help your children. There is a long wait under the quota for family fourth preference applicants, while there is no wait at all for immediate relatives. Members of the same family may be forced to immigrate on different time schedules. (On the other hand, after you get your green card, you can file a separate visa petition for your children—even if your U.S. citizen child has already filed a visa petition for them—and see which waiting period goes by the fastest.)

EXAMPLE 2: Suppose you are a permanent resident of the U.S. and just married someone who will need an immigrant visa to come to the United States. Your new spouse has a 19-year-old child from a previous marriage who wants to accompany your spouse. You didn't get married until the child was over 18, so the child is not your immediate relative stepchild.

You've been in the U.S. long enough to qualify for U.S. citizenship, and you've heard your spouse can immigrate more quickly if you get your citizenship. But does it make sense to get your citizenship before applying for your spouse?

In this situation, it's probably better for you to remain a permanent resident, so that your spouse's child can get a visa at the same time. If you file for your spouse as a citizen, the child won't be able to come along—your spouse would have to petition for the child after coming to the United States. Also, by the time you get your citizenship and your spouse gets a green card, the child may turn 21, fall into the F2B category, and face a much longer wait for a visa.

5. Marriage to a U.S. Citizen

Almost everyone knows that there are immigration advantages to marrying a U.S. citizen. It's also no secret that many who are not fortunate enough to have U.S. citizen relatives try to acquire one through a marriage of convenience.

Sham Marriages and the Law

By law, green cards are not available to people who marry only for immigration purposes. Such marriages, even though they may be legal in every other way, are regarded by immigration officials as shams. USCIS and the Department of State have been heard to assert that more than half of all the marriage applications they process are fake. It is not surprising, then, that they are especially careful about investigating marriage cases.

It is a criminal offense to file a green card application based on a sham marriage. If you attempt to qualify for a green card in this way, you will risk money penalties and a long jail sentence as well as deportation. In addition, you will almost certainly be permanently barred from getting a green card. The U.S. citizen also risks being charged a fine and/or going to jail.

RESOURCE

For a fuller discussion of all aspects of applying for a green card through marriage to a U.S. citizen or permanent resident, see *Fiancé & Marriage Visas: A Couple's Guide to U.S. Immigration,* by Ilona Bray (Nolo).

a. Two-Year Testing Period for Marriage-Based Green Cards

Because suspicions are so high regarding foreign nationals who marry U.S. citizens, they face extra hurdles in getting a green card through marriage to a U.S. citizen. If you have been married for less than two years when either your application is approved in the U.S. (you've adjusted status) or you enter the U.S. on your immigrant visa, the card will be issued only conditionally.

These conditional green cards last for two years. During the three months before your card expires, you must apply to USCIS on Form I-751 to have the condition removed and your green card made permanent. If you are still married, you and your U.S. spouse should file the I-751 together. Then, if the USCIS continues to believe your marriage was for real, not just for immigration purposes, you will receive a permanent green card.

If, however, your marriage has ended or your U.S. spouse simply refuses to cooperate, you must file for removal of the condition yourself (still using Form I-751). Under these circumstances, you can keep your green card if you show one of the following things:

- Your spouse has died, but you entered into the marriage in good faith: In other words, your marriage was not a sham.
- You are now divorced, but you originally entered into the marriage in good faith.
- Your eventual deportation will cause you extreme hardship, greater than

that suffered by most people who are deported.
- You were abused or subjected to extreme cruelty by your U.S. citizen or green card holder spouse.

A green card approved after two years of marriage is permanent, with no condition attached.

Even when you stay married for two years or more and get your permanent green card, if you divorce at a later time, your immigration benefits are still restricted. Although you can keep the green card, if you remarry within five years and petition for your next husband or wife to get a green card, USCIS will assume that your first marriage was one of convenience, unless and until you prove through convincing documentation that it was not. If you can make such a showing, you may sponsor your new spouse within five years of the first marriage. Otherwise, you have to wait until the five years has passed.

b. Marriages to Abusive U.S. Spouses

If you are the battered or abused spouse or child (unmarried, under age 21) of a U.S. citizen and he or she refuses to petition on your behalf, you can petition for yourself. (This comes from the 1994 Violence Against Women Act, or VAWA, at I.N.A. § 204(a), 8 U.S.C. § 1154.) You must be physically inside the U.S. to take advantage of this opportunity. Children between ages 21 and 25 can still petition if they can prove that the child abuse was at least one central reason for the filing delay.

You must also prove all of the following:

- that you were either battered or subjected to extreme mental cruelty by the U.S. spouse during the marriage
- that you have good moral character (note that having a prior removal order on your record is no longer a bar to establishing good moral character, thanks to amendments to VAWA passed in 2005)
- that you resided with your spouse or parent inside the U.S., or that you lived with the spouse or parent outside of the U.S. and the abuser is an employee of the U.S. government or Armed Forces, and
- if you're a spouse, that the marriage was entered into in good faith—that is, not just to get a green card.

USCIS recognizes that a wide range of behavior can constitute battery or extreme cruelty, such as threats, beatings, sexual use or exploitation, threats to deport the immigrant or turn him or her over to immigration authorities, forcible detention, or threatened or committed acts of violence against another person in order to mold the immigrant's behavior.

CAUTION

If the abuser loses his or her immigration status, you may lose your right to submit a self petition. For example, if he or she had a green card, and is removed or deported from the U.S., you are considered to have no basis to apply for residency. If you've already submitted the petition, however, you're okay. Also, an exception has been carved out for cases where the abuser loses his or her status during the two years immediately before you file your self petition for a reason that is related to or due to an incident of domestic violence. (The crime of domestic violence is a ground of removal.) The purpose of this is to make sure that you don't hesitate to call the police out of fear that you'll lose your right to self petition.

Children of the abuser can either submit their own self petition or, if their parent is self petitioning, they can gain legal status by being included on the parent's petition.

The self-petition application is done on a different form than most family petitions: USCIS Form I-360. As important as the form, however, is the collection of documents you must assemble to prove your case, including your own statement, describing the situation in detail. For some applicants, one of the toughest documents to come up with is one proving that the abuser was a U.S. citizen or lawful permanent resident (such as a copy of a U.S. passport, birth certificate, or green card). If you can't locate any such document, and if your spouse or parent obtained a green card or naturalization certificate through USCIS, it is willing to check its computer records to help you.

The completed packet must be sent to the USCIS Vermont Service Center (no fee). Also, you can, if you are married to a U.S. citizen, or are the unmarried child under age 21 of the U.S. citizen, apply to adjust status (get a green card), at the same time, using the document list in this chapter. (But you'd still send the whole packet to the Vermont Service Center.)

If you are instead married to, or the unmarried child under age 21 of, a lawful permanent resident, you must wait for a visa to become available before applying for adjustment of status. However, unlike other people in preference categories who cannot get a work permit until they apply for adjustment of status, USCIS will issue you a work permit once your I-360 is approved.

SEE AN EXPERT

Get professional help. It's worth trying to find a free or low-cost attorney at a nonprofit organization to help you with the self petition and subsequent green card application.

---

c. Marriage During Removal Proceedings

If you marry a U.S. citizen or green card holder while you are in the middle of removal (deportation) proceedings, you may still apply for a green card. However, an even stricter standard will be applied when your motives for marriage are examined. You will be required to produce clear and convincing evidence that your marriage is not a sham. Expect a very detailed marriage interview. Definitely hire an immigration attorney.

d. Widows and Widowers of U.S. Citizens

If your U.S. citizen husband or wife dies before filing a petition for you to get a green card, what happens? You may still apply by filing a petition on Form I-360. This petition must be filed no more than two years after the death of the U.S. citizen. If you remarry before you are approved for your green card, then you lose your right to it. However, if you remarry after getting a green card, it will not be taken away.

These rules apply only to the surviving spouses of U.S. citizens and their minor children. With an important new exception, spouses and other immediate relatives of green card holders may get green cards themselves only if the petitioner remains alive until the permanent residence is actually approved.

e. When a Petitioner Dies Before the Petition Is Approved

Legislation passed in 2009 has made it possible for certain people to benefit from pending immigration petitions even if the petitioner dies during the application process. This is sometimes called "automatic reinstatement." The relative must have been living in the United States at the time the petitioner died (even if he or she was traveling abroad temporarily at the exact time of death), and continue to reside in the United States on the date USCIS makes a decision on the application. The relative must also be one of the following:

- the beneficiary of a pending or approved immediate relative petition
- the beneficiary of a pending or approved family-preference visa petition, including both the principal beneficiary and any derivative beneficiaries
- a derivative beneficiary of a pending or approved employment-based visa petition
- the beneficiary of a pending or approved Form I-730, Refugee/Asylee Relative Petition
- a "T" or "U" nonimmigrant, or
- a derivative asylee (§ 208(b)(3) of the I.N.A.).

The applicant will need to find a qualified substitute financial sponsor to sign a Form I-864, Affidavit of Support.

There is no form or fee to ask for automatic reinstatement. You need to make a written request with supporting evidence of eligibility to a USCIS office. Because the law and procedure is not yet clearcut, it would be best to speak with a lawyer to determine whether you qualify and how to apply.

Even if you do not qualify for this exception, however, you may be able to demonstrate extraordinarily sympathetic circumstances to USCIS, and persuade it to grant the green card as a matter of discretion even though the petitioner died. This procedure is called humanitarian reinstatement.

B. Quick View of the Application Process

Getting a green card through a relative is a two- to four-step process. Certain parts of this process are technically the responsibility of your sponsoring relative, who is referred to as the petitioner. Other parts are meant to be done by you.

TIP

You're allowed to help the petitioner fill out the forms for you. As we give you step-by-step instructions for getting a green card, we will discuss each task according to who has the legal responsibility for carrying it out. However, even if the law presumes your relative is performing a particular task, there is nothing to stop you from helping your relative with the paperwork. In fact, we recommend that you do so. For example, you can fill out forms intended to be completed by your relative and simply ask him or her to check them over, fill in whatever is left, and sign them.

The main steps are as follows:

- Your U.S. citizen or permanent resident relative starts the process by filing what's called a visa petition (on USCIS Form I-130). If you are a widow or abused spouse or child, however, you would self-petition, by filing Form I-360. The object of the petition is to establish that you are what you say you are: namely, the qualifying relative of a qualifying sponsor.

- If you're in a preference relative category, then after USCIS approves the petition, you wait until a visa becomes available (based on your Priority Date, when your petitioner turned in the visa petition).
- Once your visa petition has been approved and a visa is available to you, you submit an application for permanent residence (an immigrant visa and green card), and attend an interview either at a U.S. consulate outside the United States or through a process called adjustment of status at a USCIS office inside the United States.
- If you applied at a U.S. consulate, you use your immigrant visa to enter the United States and claim your permanent residence status.

⊘ **CAUTION**
An approved visa petition does not by itself give you any right to be present, enter, or work in the United States. (The exception is if you are a self-petitioning abused spouse or child.) Visa petition approval is only a prerequisite to submitting the application for a green card. Your petition must be approved and your Priority Date must be current before

you are eligible for a green card. (On the other hand, if you are already living in the United States illegally and are eligible for adjustment of status, you will lose that eligibility if you leave.) Consult an attorney for a personal analysis of your case.

C. Step One: Your U.S. Relative Files the Visa Petition

To start the process of immigrating through a family member, your U.S.-based family member must submit what's called a visa petition to USCIS, on Form I-130. The visa petition asks USCIS to acknowledge that your family relationship exists and to let you go forward with green card processing. Approval of the visa petition does not mean you're guaranteed approval of your green card, however. This is only the first step in the process. Like every immigrant, you will have to file your own, extensive portion of the green card application. At that time, the U.S. immigration authorities will take a hard look at your financial situation and other factors that might make you inadmissible.

Form I-130 is available at www.uscis.gov— and it comes with extensive instructions. Aside from asking for some basic biographical information, the form takes care of some other details, like informing USCIS whether you will be continuing with your application through a U.S. consulate outside the United States or

Checklist of Forms and Documents for I-130 Visa Petition

Your family petitioner will need to assemble the following:

Forms

☐ Form I-130 (needed in all family cases except those involving widows and widowers or battered spouses).

☐ Fee for Form I-130 (currently $535; checks and money orders made out to U.S. Department of Homeland Security are accepted—do not send cash).

☐ Form I-360 (used by widows and widowers or battered spouses only, in place of Form I-130).

☐ Fee for Form I-360 (no fee for self-petitioning battered or abused spouse, parent, or child of a U.S. citizen or permanent resident, Amerasians, or special immigrant juveniles; all others pay $435).

☐ Form G-325A (needed only in marriage cases; one form is required for each spouse).

Documents

☐ Petitioner's proof of U.S. citizenship or green card status.

☐ Your long-form birth certificate, if the petition is based on a parent/child relationship.

☐ Marriage certificate, if you're applying based on marriage to a U.S. citizen or permanent resident.

☐ If either the petitioner or you has been married before, copies of all divorce and death certificates showing termination of all previous marriages.

☐ If you are applying as a battered spouse, evidence of physical abuse, such as police reports, medical or psychiatric reports, or affidavits from people familiar with the situation, such as friends, landlords, and shelter staff.

☐ If you are a father petitioning for a child, certificate showing marriage to child's mother.

☐ If you are either a father petitioning for an illegitimate child, or an illegitimate child petitioning for your father, documents proving both paternity and either legitimation or a genuine parent/child relationship.

☐ If the petition is for an adopted (nonorphan) child:

　☐ adoption decree, or child's new birth certificate showing you are the parent

　☐ evidence you and the child have lived together for at least two years, and

　☐ evidence you have had legal custody of the child for at least two years.

☐ If the petition is for a U.S. citizen's brother or sister, a copy of the parents' marriage certificate and the brother or sister's birth certificate.

☐ If you are either a stepchild petitioning for your stepparent, or a stepparent petitioning for a stepchild, the stepparent's marriage certificate as well as divorce decrees or death certificates indicating that all prior marriages of the stepparent or the natural parent were legally terminated. You must also present a stepchild's long-form birth certificate to show the names of his or her natural parents.

☐ In marriage cases, one photograph of each spouse.

☐ If you are filing a petition as a widow(er), your marriage certificate, proof that any previous marriages were legally ended, and your spouse's death certificate showing that the death occurred within the last two years.

a U.S.-based USCIS office. (If you're not sure, choose the consulate—if you change your mind later, all you need to do is notify USCIS or the National Visa Center. Doing the reverse, and transferring your case from a USCIS office to a consulate, requires filing a separate application.)

The I-130 also provides space to list your spouse and children (who may want to immigrate along with you). Be sure not to leave anyone off the list, even if that person doesn't want to immigrate now. USCIS wants to know about all your family members, and if someone who wasn't on the list decides to immigrate later, you may have trouble convincing USCIS that he or she is really a member of your family.

The checklist above provides a complete list of what should go into your visa petition.

> **CAUTION**
> **A petitioner who has been convicted of any "specified offense against a minor" is not eligible to file Form I-130.** It doesn't matter whether the immigrant is an adult or a child. See an attorney for more information or for help in requesting a waiver of this disqualification.

A few of the items on this checklist require extra explanation:

Proof of the petitioner's status. All I-130 petitions must be filed with evidence that the petitioner is either a U.S. citizen or a U.S. lawful permanent resident (green card holder). (Send copies, not originals.)

If the petitioner is a U.S. citizen by birth, a birth certificate is the best proof. Only birth certificates issued by a U.S. state government agency are acceptable. Hospital birth certificates cannot be used. When the petitioner is a U.S. citizen born outside U.S. territory, a certificate of citizenship, naturalization certificate, or U.S. consular record of birth abroad are best. An unexpired U.S. passport can also serve as proof. If the petitioner is a U.S. citizen but does not have any of these documents, read Chapter 2 to learn how to obtain them.

If the petitioner is not a U.S. citizen but is a permanent resident, his or her status can be proven with the petitioner's green card (make a copy of both sides), unexpired reentry permit, or passport with an unexpired stamp indicating admission to the U.S. as a permanent resident. (The unexpired stamp in a foreign passport is used only in the few cases where the petitioner has just been approved for a green card but is still waiting to receive the card itself. The card typically arrives by mail several months later.) When green card holders act as petitioners, USCIS will not check its own records to establish the existence of the green card. Your petitioning relative is responsible for supplying this evidence.

Married Beneficiaries Living Outside of the U.S. Can Use Fiancé (K-3) Visas

Because nonimmigrant visa applications allow short-term visits to the U.S., they are designed to be simpler than applications by people requesting the right to stay in the U.S. permanently. For this reason, it has often happened that people coming to the U.S. on a fiancé visa (a nonimmigrant visa) were able to enter the U.S. more quickly than people already married to U.S. citizens and waiting outside the U.S. to go through the entire immigrant visa/green card application process before they could enter the United States.

To address this unfairness, in December 2000, Congress created a new visa option to immigrating spouses of U.S. citizens. These spouses are now able to use a variety of the fiancé visa to enter the U.S., at which point they can wait for the approval of the Form I-130 visa petition and the chance to complete their green card application.

Like the fiancé visa, this new visa is coded with the letter K; it's called a K-3 visa. Accompanying children receive K-4 visas. (The regular fiancé visa is called K-1, and accompanying children receive K-2s.)

In reality, people rarely get K-3 visas. This is because USCIS will ignore a K-3 application if it approves the I-130 before the K-3 petition. For you, that's just as well—once your I-130 has been approved, you're ready to start your visa application process anyway. In recent years, USCIS has been approving I-130s at the same time as or before K-3 applications in almost all cases. Why then bother to apply for a K-3? Well,

there's no application fee, and it can be good insurance against the rare case in which I-130 approval might take longer than K-3 approval.

If you decide to apply for a K-3, you have to wait until you have filed the I-130.

Once USCIS sends the U.S. spouse the Form I-130 receipt (not yet the approval), the U.S. spouse can fill out and file Form I-129F, attaching a copy of the Form I-130 receipt. (You do not need to file separate I-129F petitions for each accompanying child—they are included on the fiancé petition.) There is no filing fee for Form I-129F when it is used to get a K-3/K-4 visa. (Form I-129F is also used for regular fiancés and is covered in Chapter 8. Form I-130 is covered in this chapter.)

File your Form I-129F at the USCIS Dallas Lockbox.

After the Form I-129F is approved, it is forwarded to the National Visa Center ("NVC"), which runs a check on the U.S. spouse for certain criminal convictions involving violence or sex offenses. If the U.S. spouse clears the check, the case is forwarded to the U.S. consulate abroad.

If the marriage took place outside the U.S., the fiancé visa interview should take place in the country in which the marriage took place. The procedures at the consulate are similar to those described for K-1/K-2 visas in Chapter 8.

The K-3/K-4 visas cover a two-year stay in the United States. Children who will turn 21 within those two years, however, will be issued K-4 visas that are good only until their 21st birthday. Under the Child Status Protection

Married Beneficiaries Living Outside of the U.S. Can Use Fiancé (K-3) Visas (continued)

Act, however, the Form I-130 that was filed before the child's 21st birthday will protect his or her eligibility for adjustment of status, as long as the child meets the qualifications for being a stepchild (that the marriage took place before the child turned 18).

After entering the U.S. as a K-3, you don't need to wait for approval of the Form I-130 visa petition to take the next step, submitting a green card (adjustment of status) application. The USCIS office handling your adjustment application will request your I-130 file from wherever it is then being processed.

Holders of K-3 and K-4 visas can get work authorization. Submit Form I-765 with the filing fee.

Using the K-3 visa adds an additional level of paperwork to the process of filing for permanent residence. Depending on current processing times for I-130s, however, it might help you reduce the amount of time that you are separated from your U.S. citizen petitioner.

Marriage certificate. If the basis of the petition is your marriage to a U.S. citizen or green card holder, you must establish that you are lawfully married to the petitioner. Do this by showing a valid civil marriage certificate. Church certificates are generally insufficient. You may have married in a country where marriages are not customarily recorded. Tribal areas of Africa are an example. See Chapter 4 of this book for more information, or call the nearest consulate or embassy of your home country for help with finding acceptable proof of marriage.

Proof of termination of prior marriages. If either you or your spouse has been married before, you must prove that all prior marriages were legally terminated. This requires either a divorce decree or death certificate ending every prior marriage. Where a death certificate is needed, it must be an official document issued by a government. Certificates from funeral homes are not acceptable. Divorce papers must be official court or government documents. If the death or divorce occurred in one of those few countries where such records are not kept, call the nearest consulate or embassy of your home country for advice on getting acceptable proof of death or divorce.

Birth certificates. Usually, you may verify a parent/child relationship simply by presenting the child's birth certificate. Many countries, including Canada and England, issue both short- and long-form birth certificates. Where both are available, the long form is needed because it contains the names of the parents, while the short form does not.

1. Mailing the Visa Petition

When ready, your petitioning family member must submit the visa petition. If you are filing Form I-130, it must be sent to either the USCIS Chicago or Phoenix Lockbox depending on where the petitioner lives. Check the USCIS website for the correct address by going to www.uscis. gov, clicking; I-130–Addresses The Lockbox is just a temporary processing center, however, which will route your Form I-130 petition to the appropriate USCIS Service Center (based on your petitioner's address) for further action.

If you are filing Form I-360, the USCIS Service Center that you send your petition to depends on where you live and on the reason that you qualify to use the Form I-360. Check the USCIS website for the address you should use.

USCIS regional Service Centers are not the same as USCIS local offices. For one thing, you cannot visit regional Service Centers in person—they process applications but they do not see applicants. There are several USCIS regional Service Centers spread across the United States, and other USCIS offices overseas, to serve U.S. citizen petitioners who live there.

If you are in the United States, you may be able to file your green card (adjustment of status) application (as described in Section E, below) at the same time, or concurrently, with your family member's visa petition. But you can only file concurrently under two circumstances— one, if you are an immediate relative, or two, if you're a preference relative and a visa is already available in your category, as described in Section E, below. Concurrent filing offers many advantages, including giving you the right to stay in the U.S. while the application is pending (useful if you are on a temporary visa that has expired or is due to expire soon) and the right to apply for work permits for you and your immediate family members.

 TIP
Want quick, free notification that USCIS got your application? USCIS Form G-1145 tells USCIS to send you an email and/ or text message for any immigration form being sent to the Lockbox. By downloading, completing, and affixing the form to the top of your application package, you'll be given electronic confirmation that USCIS has received your application, plus your all-important receipt number. This may save you days, or even weeks, over the time you would have had to wait for USCIS to mail you a hard-copy receipt—or even replace your receipt if USCIS fails to mail it to you or it gets lost in the mail.

2. Awaiting USCIS Approval of the Visa Petition

After filing a Form I-130 or I-360 visa petition (assuming you didn't file the petition concurrently with your green card application), you will have to wait for the petition to be approved, which can take several months or even years by itself. (See Chapter 4 for how to track the length of time USCIS is taking to decide on visa petitions, and how to track your own application online.)

Within a few weeks after mailing the petition, your family petitioner should receive a written confirmation that the papers are being processed, together with a receipt for the fees.

This notice, on Form I-797C, will also give your case file number and tell you your Priority Date. Current USCIS policy is to act more quickly on petitions whose Priority Dates are likely to become current sooner— which means that people in preference categories with long waits may literally wait years to find out whether or not their visa

Marriage Interviews After Filing I-130

The USCIS sometimes requires petition interviews in marriage cases, especially if the marriage recently took place or if there are great age or cultural differences between the spouses. Interviews are less common if the application is being filed at a U.S. consulate.

Marriage interview procedures vary with the individual personality of the examining officer, and you should be prepared to adjust to that officer's interviewing style. You and your U.S. spouse may be brought into the interviewing room separately. The interview may be videotaped. Each of you may then be questioned about your life together, how you met, what sorts of things you do as a couple, daily routines, common friends, favorite places to go, what the inside of your home looks like, and so on. These questions are intended to reveal whether or not you and your U.S. spouse

actually share a life— or whether you're committing immigration fraud. You may refuse to answer some or all questions, but doing so could result in the petition being denied.

Many couples wonder if they will be asked about the more intimate details of their relationship. USCIS policy states that the interviewers should not ask embarrassingly personal questions, but sometimes USCIS officials believe it is necessary to ask intimate questions in an attempt to uncover a fraudulent case. The best advice we can offer is be prepared for anything and cooperate as much as possible, but if you are asked questions about something you find it embarrassing to talk about, tell the interviewer that you are embarrassed by the question and explain why. The interviewer has the discretion to skip over embarrassing questions.

Sample I-130 Approval Notice

Department of Homeland Security
U.S. Citizenship and Immigration Services

I-797, Notice of Action

THE UNITED STATES OF AMERICA

RECEIPT NUMBER		CASE TYPE	I130 IMMIGRANT PETITION FOR RELATIVE, FIANCE(E), OR ORPHAN
CSC-16-047-00000			
RECEIPT DATE	PRIORITY DATE	PETITIONER	
December 15, 2016	December 14, 2016	MANCINI, ALBERTO	
NOTICE DATE	PAGE	BENEFICIARY	
April 11, 2017	1 of 1	MANCINI, TERESE	

ILONA BRAY
RE: TERESE MARIA MANCINI
   950 PARKER ST.
   BERKELEY, CA 94710

Notice Type: Approval Notice

Section: Husband or wife of
     permanent resident,
     203(a)(2)(A) INA

The above petition has been approved. We have sent the original visa petition to the **Department of State National Visa Center (NVC), 32 Rochester Avenue, Portsmouth, NH 03801-2909**. NVC processes all approved immigrant visa petitions that need consular action. It also determines which consular post is the appropriate consulate to complete visa processing. NVC will then forward the approved petition to that consulate.

The NVC will contact the person for whom you are petitioning(beneficiary) concerning further immigrant visa processing steps.

If you have any questions about visa issuance, please contact the NVC directly. However, please allow at least 90 days before calling the NVC if your beneficiary has not received correspondence from the NVC. The telephone number of the NVC is **(603) 334-0700**.

THIS FORM IS NOT A VISA NOR MAY IT BE USED IN PLACE OF A VISA.

Please see the additional information on the back. You will be notified separately about any other cases you filed.
U.S. CITIZENSHIP & IMMIGRATION SERVICES
  P.O. BOX 68005
  LEE'S SUMMIT, MO 68005
Customer Service Telephone: (800) 375-5283

Form I-797 (Rev. 01/31/05) N

petition was approved. It all works out, however (assuming the petition is approved), because your Priority Date—which is set as soon as your family petitioner files the I-130 for you—protects your place in line.

> **EXAMPLE:** Dante, who is from the Philippines, has a brother who is a U.S. citizen. The brother files a visa petition for Dante on August 1, 2012. That puts Dante in the fourth preference category. However, Dante waits a full four years —until August of 2016—for the visa petition to be approved. Although frustrating, this doesn't hurt Dante any, because his August 1, 2012, Priority Date is still years away from being current—visas are at that time only just becoming available to people who applied years before him, with Priority Dates of February 1, 1989.

If USCIS wants further information before acting on your case, it will send you a Request for Evidence (RFE), using Form I-797E. The RFE tells your family petitioner what corrections, additional pieces of information, or additional documents are expected. Your family member should make the corrections or supply the extra data and mail them back to the USCIS regional service center with the request form on top.

Once your petition is approved, USCIS will advise your family petitioner using a Notice of Action, on Form I-797 (see the sample above). If you plan to attend your visa interview at a U.S. consulate abroad, USCIS will forward the file to the National Visa Center (NVC), located in Portsmouth, New Hampshire. The NVC will then send instructions so that you may proceed with consular processing, described later in this chapter.

D. Step Two: Preference Relatives Wait for an Available Visa

If you're an immediate relative, you can skip this section. A visa is available to you as soon as you get I-130 approval. But because there are annual limits on the number of people who can receive green cards in certain categories (the preference categories), preference relatives may have to wait in line until a visa/green card becomes available. Your place in the line is tracked by a number called your Priority Date. It comes from the date on which your family petitioner filed your I-130 petition.

Let's take a closer look at how this works, by examining some sample charts from the *Visa Bulletin*, below. (They are the ones for family-based applicants; there are others for employment-based applicants.) These charts are from June 2016. To access a current *Visa Bulletin*, go to www.travel.state.gov. Click under "U.S. Visas," then look for the "Visa Bulletin" link under Law and Policy.

You'll see on the charts below that the preference categories are listed in the column on the left and the countries of origin are listed in the row across the top. The rest of the squares contain the "cutoff" dates. In other similar charts, you may see the letter "C" (for "current"), or the letter "U" (for unavailable").

The State Department publishes two different charts for family-based visa applications. If you're outside the U.S., the "Dates for Filing Family-Sponsored Visa Applications" chart lets you know how soon you can start the visa application process. The "Application Final Action Dates for Family-Sponsored Preference Cases" chart lets you know how soon you can actually receive the visa.

If you are inside the U.S. and will be adjusting status as a preference relative,

USCIS will tell you when you can apply. USCIS uses the same charts that are in the *Visa Bulletin*, and tells you which one you should look at to know when to apply. That instruction is found on the USCIS website at www.uscis.gov/visabulletininfo. It changes every month.

TIP
You can have the *Visa Bulletin* sent to you monthly, by email. This is a great way to make sure you don't forget to check how your Priority Date is advancing. Complete instructions for how to subscribe to this service can be found toward the bottom of any monthly *Visa Bulletin*.

June 2016 Application Final Action Dates for Family-Sponsored Preference Cases

Family-Sponsored	All Chargeability Areas Except Those Listed	China-mainland born	India	Mexico	Philippines
F1	15JAN09	15JAN09	15JAN09	22FEB95	22DEC04
F2A	08NOV14	08NOV14	08NOV14	01SEP14	08NOV14
F2B	22OCT09	22OCT09	22OCT09	08SEP95	01JUN05
F3	01DEC04	01DEC04	01DEC04	22OCT94	01FEB94
F4	08AUG03	01JAN03	01JAN01	15APR97	01DEC92

June 2016 Dates for Filing Family-Sponsored Visa Applications

Family-Sponsored	All Chargeability Areas Except Those Listed	China-mainland born	India	Mexico	Philippines
F1	01OCT09	01OCT09	01OCT09	01APR95	01SEP05
F2A	15OCT15	15OCT15	15OCT15	15OCT15	15OCT15
F2B	15DEC10	15DEC10	15DEC10	15MAY96	01JAN06
F3	01AUG05	01AUG05	01AUG05	01MAY95	01AUG95
F4	01MAY04	01MAY04	01MAY04	01JUN98	01APR93

Let's say you are the brother of a U.S. citizen, you're from the Philippines, and you're living there now. Let's also imagine that your brother files a petition for you to immigrate, in June 2016. To find out when it will be possible for you to apply for the visa, as you begin the process, you will need to look at the "Dates for Filing" chart in the June 2016 *Visa Bulletin*. Locate your preference category in the left column (4th Preference, on the bottom line), and your country on the top row, then find the square that corresponds to both— it's the square at the bottom right.

The Priority Date listed in that square is 01APR93 (April 1, 1993). That tells you that brothers of U.S. citizens who started this process on April 1, 1993, became eligible for green cards in the month this *Visa Bulletin* came out (June 2016). They waited over 23 years. That could mean you will have to wait just as long, starting from your June 2016 Priority Date; but your wait could be longer or shorter. It all depends on how many people are in line ahead of you and how efficient the government is in processing visas.

The waiting periods for people from the Philippines tend to be longer than from other countries, because there are so many applicants and a limit on how many can come from any one country. Most other people will wait less time. For example, if you were from Brazil and were the spouse of a lawful permanent resident, you would

look at the row for category 2A, under the first box saying "All Chargeability Areas Except Those Listed." The cutoff date there is October 15, 2015—meaning you could expect a wait of about eight months if you applied in June 2016.

These waits are frustrating, but there is truly nothing you can do to move the dates along (unless your family petitioner can become a U.S. citizen, which will often put you into a higher preference category or make you an immediate relative).

As you track these dates over the years, you'll notice they don't advance smoothly. Sometimes they get stuck on one date for months at a time, or even go backwards ("retrogress"). Other times, your square will just say "U" for unavailable, meaning no one is eligible for a green card in that category until further notice—usually when a new fiscal year begins, in October. But if you're really lucky, you may see a "C," meaning that everyone who has a visa petition on file is immediately eligible for a green card, regardless of Priority Date.

You will eventually see your own Priority Date (or a later date) on the *Visa Bulletin* Dates for Filing chart. Then you'll know you're ready for the next step in obtaining your green card.

If you have an approved petition but your Priority Date is not yet current in the Dates for Filing chart, you must wait until it is current to take the next step and file your green card application. The immigration authorities should advise you by mail a couple of months before your Priority Date finally comes up. If you do not respond to the notification within one year, the authorities can take steps to revoke your visa petition, so make sure to send any change of address, and to respond to the letter! But it's still worth tracking your Priority Date on your own, in case they forget to notify you.

! CAUTION
In the U.S. on a temporary visa? Be careful that your status does not expire before your Priority Date becomes current and you can apply for a green card. Possessing an approved visa petition does not give you any right to live in the United States. If this might become a problem, consult as soon as possible with an immigration attorney.

E. Step Three: You Submit the Visa or Green Card Application

After your visa petition has been approved and, if you are in a preference category, your Priority Date has become current, it's time for you to play a more active role in the application process: You'll need to file your application for an immigrant visa or a green card. If your spouse or children were included in the petition, they must each file their own visa or adjustment of status application.

The most important question at this point is where you file the application and attend your interview—at a USCIS office in the United States or at a U.S. consulate outside the United States? You should have already made this choice on your Form I-130, but you're allowed to change your mind, so it's worth revisiting this question.

If you're living outside of the United States now. The answer is fairly easy for people living in countries other than the U.S.— you'll file at a local U.S. consulate and attend an interview there before entering the United States. (This method is called consular processing.) If you're sure you'll use this method, skip straight to Section 2, below.

If you're living in the U.S. now. The answer is a bit more complicated for applicants already in the United States. The easiest thing for you would probably be to "adjust status" without leaving—that is, send your application to USCIS and attend your interview at a local USCIS office. If you're one of the few people legally allowed to use this option, it's a great one. Once your application is filed, your stay in the United States will be considered legal, and you can apply for permission to work. Should problems arise in your case, you will be able to wait for a decision in the United States. Also, if your application for a green card is turned down, you have greater rights of appeal inside the U.S. than you do at a U.S. consulate.

Not everyone is eligible to adjust status. First, as mentioned before, if you're a preference relative, your Priority Date must be current. Second, unless you are a VAWA self-petitioner, you can't adjust status unless you were "inspected and admitted" by a U.S. immigration officer—in other words, the last time you entered the U.S., you did so legally, with a visa or with "parole" (permission from a border officer). And third, just like someone coming into the U.S. from overseas, you must be admissible. (See Chapter 3 for grounds of inadmissibility.)

Even if you meet those basic requirements for adjusting status, you won't be able to do so (unless you're a VAWA self-petitioner) if you've ever worked in the U.S. without authorization, if you're in the U.S. with no legal status, or if you've ever fallen out of legal status (except if it wasn't your fault), unless you're an immediate relative or one of a few types of "special immigrants." Also, unless you're an immediate relative, you can't adjust status if you came to the U.S. without a visa under the Visa Waiver program. (This rule doesn't apply to visa-exempt Canadians.)

Finally, you won't be able to adjust status if you are (1) a member of a crew on a ship or plane; (2) if you're just passing through the U.S. without a visa on your way to somewhere else; (3) you've got "S" status because you're helping the police; or (4) you've engaged in certain terrorist activities.

An important, but increasingly rare, exception to adjustment of status eligibility requirements exists for people who had an approvable relative petition or labor certification application filed for them (or for their spouse or parent) before April 30, 2001. Such people, if they are admissible and a green card is immediately available to them, can adjust status by paying an extra $1,000 fee. If the petition or labor certification application was filed after January 14, 1998, they will also have to prove that they were present in the U.S. on December 21, 2000. This provision of law, known as "245(i)" adjustment, is especially helpful for people who came to the U.S. illegally and who cannot leave to get an immigrant visa because they would be subject to the ten-year reentry bar for unlawful presence if they did.

If you came to the U.S. on a K-1 visa, the only way you can adjust is on the basis of marriage to the person who petitioned for you. If the marriage never happens or doesn't work out, and you then marry someone else, you won't be allowed to adjust status on the basis of the new marriage, or on any other basis.

If you have any doubts about your ability to adjust status, consult with an immigration lawyer. The adjustment application is expensive—you don't want to spend the money to apply and have your application denied outright.

! CAUTION
You may be accused of visa fraud if you got married soon after entering the U.S. on a temporary visa. Many people misread the rules and think that they can enter the U.S. on, for example, a tourist visa, get married, and then apply for a green card in the United States. Unfortunately, this scenario often leads to accusations that you committed visa fraud—that is, pretended to be coming temporarily with the secret intent of staying permanently. For people who marry within 60 days of entering the U.S. on a temporary visa, there is a strong suspicion of visa fraud, although you will be allowed to try to show that the presumption should not be applied to you. If you marry within 30 days of entering the U.S., the government will presume fraud, and can, if it wants, deny your adjustment on that basis alone.

Whether or not you are eligible to adjust status, you may instead decide to leave the United States and apply for your green card at a U.S. consulate abroad. If the consulates are issuing visas more quickly than your local USCIS office is handling adjustment of status applications (which is possible), leaving to apply at a consulate outside of the U.S. could be a smart strategic move. However, if you have already spent six months or more in the U.S. out of legal status, or crossed the border without inspection, be sure you are not inadmissible or subject to a three-year or ten-year bar on reentering

the U.S. before you go. (See Chapter 3.) Otherwise, you could find yourself stuck outside the United States for three or ten years. Fortunately, hardship-based waivers are available for certain family members of U.S. citizens and permanent residents; get an attorney's help for this.

1. What Happens When Adjusting Status in the U.S.

The process of adjusting your status to permanent resident involves preparing a set of forms and documents (a separate set for you and each of your accompanying spouse and children), mailing these to a USCIS Lockbox, waiting for some months until you're called in to have your fingerprints taken, and then waiting a few weeks or months longer until you're called in for your final green card interview at a local USCIS office (not the one to which you sent your application). You should be approved for your green card at or soon after the interview. See Chapter 4 for information on tracking the progress of your application.

As part of your adjustment of status application, you and your family members may apply for permission to work (an Employment Authorization Document or EAD) and permission to travel while the application is pending.

CAUTION
Security checks are a likely cause of delays. As part of your adjustment of status application, the FBI runs both a fingerprint check and a name check on you, and the CIA runs a separate name check. These name checks can take months or even years, especially because many applicants have similar names. If you've been informed that your case is stalled due to security checks, get the name of a person you can keep in touch with for updates, or hire a lawyer to help with this task.

2. Paperwork to Prepare for Adjustment of Status Application

The basic form used for the U.S. adjustment of status application is Form I-485, Application for Permanent Residence. However, a handful of other forms must be prepared to accompany this main one, and you must collect various documents.

One way to get all these forms is to call the USCIS forms line at 800-870-3676 or make an InfoPass appointment to go to a local USCIS office and ask for an Adjustment of Status Packet. Or, you can obtain the forms online at www.uscis.gov (click "Forms" and select the forms you need one by one, based on the checklist below.)

The following checklist will help you assemble and keep track of the appropriate forms and documents. A complete set of the items below must also be prepared for your accompanying spouse and children.

A few of the items on this checklist need additional explanation.

Form I-485. While most of the form is self-explanatory, a few items typically raise concerns. If a particular question does not apply to you, or if the answer is "none," leave it blank. The questions on this form requiring explanation are as follows:

Part 1. This asks for general information about when and where you were born, your present address, and immigration status. If you've used a fake Social Security number or one belonging to someone else, consult a lawyer. The form also asks for an A number, that is, an eight- or nine-digit "Alien Registration Number." Normally, you will not have an A number unless you previously applied for a green card or have been in deportation proceedings (in which case you should see a lawyer).

The form also asks for your I-94 number. This is the number on the little white or green card that was tucked into your passport if you entered the U.S. by land or if you entered by air or sea before April 2013. (Green means you entered on a visa waiver. If you entered on a visa waiver, you are not eligible to adjust your status unless you are an "immediate relative" (for example, a U.S. citizen spouse). Consult with a lawyer about your options.) If you entered the U.S. by air or sea after April 2013, look up your I-94 number online at https://i94.cbp.dhs.gov.

Checklist for Adjustment of Status Application

Forms

☐ Form I-485, with filing fee (currently $1,225 for applicants ages 14 to 78 (includes biometrics fee), $750 for applicants under age 14 who are filing concurrently with a parent, as a derivative, and $1,140 for other applicants under age 14 or those age 79 or older). Checks and money orders are accepted, but do not send cash through the mail. The $1,070 includes your fingerprinting or "biometrics" fee. You'll be notified of where and when to appear. Double-check all fees at www.uscis.gov.

☐ Form I-485A (only if you'll be paying the $1,000 penalty fee and submitting I-485 Supplement A in order to adjust status).

☐ Form G-325A (if you're between ages 14 and 79).

☐ Form I-765 (optional, if you want a work permit. Your answer to Question 16 of the form should be "(c)(9)"). There is no additional fee for the Form I-765; it is included in the filing fee for Form I-485.

☐ Form I-864 Affidavit of Support (I-864, I-864EZ, I-864A, or I-864W, as appropriate), with supporting documents (including the sponsor's most recent year's federal tax returns, or transcripts, with all attachments, and proof of assets, if any are being used to prove financial ability). Accompanying spouses or children can submit a photocopy of the main form.

☐ I-131, Application for Travel Document (Advance Parole), for use if you think you'll need to travel outside the U.S. while your application is processed. There is no additional fee for the Form I-131; it is included in the filing fee for the Form I-485.

Documents

☐ Copy of your I-130 approval notice (unless you're filing the I-130 concurrently).

☐ Copy of a long-form birth certificate for you and each accompanying relative (this mainly serves as a form of identification). If the birth certificate is in another language, it must be accompanied by a full English translation.

☐ Copy of passport page with nonimmigrant visa, if any.

☐ Two photographs of you and two photographs of each accompanying relative in U.S. passport style (it's best to have a professional do these). Write your name and A-number (if you've received one from USCIS) in pencil or felt pen on the back of each photo.

☐ Sealed envelope containing medical exam report for you and for each accompanying relative (on Form I-693). (Optional, see below.)

☐ Documents showing all your arrests, convictions, and other criminal history, if you've ever been arrested. (You don't need documentation of traffic tickets unless the fine was $500 or more or the incident involved drugs or alcohol.)

☐ Evidence of any public assistance (welfare benefits) you have received or are about to receive in the United States.

☐ If your stepchild is adjusting with you, his or her application must include a copy of your marriage certificate and divorce or death evidence for previous marriages of you and your spouse.

☐ If your adopted child is adjusting with you, his or her application must include a copy of the adoption decree.

☐ If your spouse is adjusting with you, he or she should include a copy of your marriage certificate and divorce or death evidence for your previous marriages.

If you entered illegally, leave the space blank (but double-check whether you're allowed to adjust your status in the U.S.— see the discussion on eligibility to adjust, above). Under Current USCIS Status, write the type of visa you're on, such as F-1 student or H-1B worker—or if your visa has expired, write "OOS," which stands for "out of status."

Part 2. Mark Box a if you are the principal applicant or Box b if your spouse or parent is the principal applicant. Choose Box c if you entered the U.S. on a K-1 fiancé(e) or on a K-2 child of fiancé(e) visa. Do not mark any other box.

Part 3. Under Place of Last Entry into the United States, be sure to name the city through which you most recently entered— even if it was after a short trip and you'd spent time in the U.S. before. The question about whether you were "inspected" by an immigration officer simply asks whether you entered legally. The nonimmigrant visa number is the number that appears on the very top of your visa stamp. It is not the same as your visa classification.

The questions in Part 3, Section C, are meant to identify people who are inadmissible. With the exception of certain memberships in terrorist, Communist Party, or similar organizations, you will not be considered inadmissible just because you joined an organization. However, if your answer to any of the other questions is "yes,"

you may be inadmissible; see Chapter 3 for more information, or consult an attorney. Don't lie on your answers, because you will probably be found out, especially if you have engaged in criminal activity. Many grounds of inadmissibility can be legally overcome, but once a lie is detected, you could lose the legal right to correct the problem. A false answer is grounds for denying your application in itself and may result in your being permanently barred from getting a green card.

Form I-485A. This form is required only if you are doing a 245(i) adjustment (discussed above). You would be eligible only if you had a visa petition or labor certification on file before January 14, 1998, or before April 30, 2001, so long as you were in the United States on December 21, 2000. The form is self-explanatory and is intended only to determine if you are subject to the $1,000 penalty.

Form G-325A. This Biographic Information form must be filled out for you and for each accompanying relative. You need not file a G-325A for any child under the age of 14 or any adult over the age of 79. If the basis of your immigration case is marriage to a U.S. citizen, a G-325A must be completed for both you and your U.S. spouse (despite the fact that you may have already submitted one with your visa petition). This is the only type of case where full biographic data is requested on someone who is already a U.S. citizen.

Form I-864. See Chapter 3 of this book for more explanation of this form. Also pay close attention to the detailed instructions that come with the form itself.

Medical exam. You and your accompanying relatives will be required to submit medical examination reports on Form I-693. Form I-693 can be filled out only by a USCIS-approved doctor. Most USCIS-approved doctors already have the form, and it can also be downloaded from the USCIS website. To find a USCIS-approved doctor in your area, go to https://my.uscis.gov/findadoctor or call 800-375-5283 and be ready to write down the information. The fee for the exam depends on the doctor. Be prepared to pay several hundred dollars. The exam itself involves taking a medical history, blood test, and chest X-ray and administering vaccinations, if required. Pregnant women can refuse to be X-rayed until after the pregnancy. The vaccination requirement may be waived for religious, moral, or medical reasons.

Dealing With Delays in Approval of Your Work Authorization

If you want to work before your application for a green card is approved, you must file a separate application for employment authorization. To do so, fill out Form I-765 and file it together with your adjustment of status application. Be sure to keep the receipt that USCIS gives you, so you can prove that the I-765 was filed.

Legally, USCIS does not have to make a decision on your employment authorization application for up to 90 days after the notice date on the receipt it sends you. If, for some reason, you are not given a decision within 90 days, you are in theory supposed to be granted an interim employment authorization, which will last 240 days. Unfortunately, claiming this right can be extremely difficult If you haven't received your work card and it's been 75 days or more since you filed your I-765 (or since you responded to a request for evidence), contact USCIS Customer Service at 800-375-5283 and ask that a "service request" be created. That will alert the service center that it should do something about your work card, pronto. Unfortunately, there's no guarantee that it will. You may have to follow up later.

You can also make an InfoPass appointment with your local USCIS office. (Go to https://infopass.uscis.gov and follow the instructions to make an appointment.) Before doing that, though, be sure to check the status of your case online (go to www.uscis.gov, click "case status," and enter the number that's in the upper left-hand corner of the receipt for your work permit). When you go to your appointment, bring your work permit receipt and a copy of your application. The officer at the counter will contact the Service Center about your case and may be able to trigger action on the application.

Planning to Leave the U.S. Before Your Adjustment Interview?

Once your application for adjustment of status has been filed, you *must not* leave the U.S. for any reason before you have applied for and received advance permission to reenter the U.S. (Advance Parole). The only exception is for people who have held and continue to hold lawful H-1B or L-1 nonimmigrant visa status at the time of filing the adjustment of status application. Otherwise, any absence without this permission will be viewed as a termination of your application for a green card—which means that, upon return, you will be told that your green card application is dead and you have no right to enter the United States.

However, if you were out of status or unlawfully present in the U.S. for six or more months, consider consulting a lawyer before you depart the U.S., even with Advance Parole. There is a chance you could be deemed inadmissible and be stuck outside the U.S. with a three-year or ten-year bar against reentering. That risk was greatly reduced in 2012, when the Board of Immigration Appeals (BIA) ruled (*In the Matter of Arrabally and Yerrabelly*, 25 I&N Dec. 771 (BIA 2012)) that departures under Advance Parole with a pending adjustment of status application do NOT, despite previous USCIS interpretations to the contrary, trigger the unlawful presence bars.

Still, it's worth consulting a lawyer before you leave. You want to make sure you're operating on the latest interpretation of this issue before taking the risk of departing the country.

Many people simply apply for Advance Parole at the same time they apply to adjust status, just in case they might need to make an unexpected trip outside the United States. The Form I-131 used for requesting Advance Parole is fairly simple, and you need not pay any extra fee so long as you file it with the Form I-485 adjustment of status application. Or, you can wait until you're sure you have to leave, and apply at the same Service Center where you sent your adjustment of status application—but you're taking a risk this way, because USCIS may take many weeks or months to approve your Advance Parole application.

The Form I-131 will ask you about your travel plans. If filing concurrently on the basis of marriage, you don't need to have any specific plans. USCIS will recognize that you're eligible for Advance Parole without specific plans or reasons to travel.

If you're filing the I-131 separately, attach two passport-type photographs to the application. If you paid the $1,225 filing fee for the adjustment of status application, you need not pay an additional filing fee for Form I-131. Also attach a copy of the Form I-485 receipt.

If approved, you will be allowed to leave the U.S. and return again with no break in the processing of your application. If you also applied for and were granted work authorization, your evidence of authorization to travel will come in the form of a single card that gives you permission for both.

TIP
Some fiancés can skip most of the exam. If you had an exam overseas within the last year, all you need is a vaccination "Supplemental Form to I-693," also completed by a USCIS-designated doctor. The exception is if medical grounds of inadmissibility were noted during your exam or when you entered the United States.

After completion of the medical exam, and upon obtaining the test results, the doctor will give you the report in a sealed envelope. Do not open the envelope.

The main purpose of the medical exam is to verify that you are not medically inadmissible based on having a communicable disease that is deemed to have public

---

Checklist: Documents to Bring to Your Adjustment Interview

Prepare all of the following to take with you to your USCIS interview:

☐ The interview notice that USCIS sent to you—security officers at the building entrance and the receptionist will need to see it.

☐ A complete photocopy of your green card application. This is for your use—you may want to follow along as the officer asks you questions about the material you filled out on the forms, or you may find that the officer is missing something that you have a copy of.

☐ The passport that you used to enter the U.S. If you have any additional passports or travel documents, also bring those.

☐ Originals of all documents that you made copies of for submission with your application. For example, if you submitted a photocopy of an I-94, divorce decree, a birth certificate, or another official document, a USCIS officer may want to examine the originals. Similarly, your petitioner must bring original proof of U.S. citizen or green card status. Naturalized citizens ideally should bring their certificate of citizenship rather than a passport.

☐ Any documents received from USCIS or other immigration authorities. For example,

your work permit and all Advance Parole documents.

☐ Sealed envelope containing medical exam report for you and for each accompanying relative (on Form I-693) (optional; you can submit medical exam results any time up to and including the time of your interview).

☐ Any updates to the material in your application. For example, if the petitioning sponsor has a new job, bring an employer letter and pay stubs (and, if the new job pays less than the old one and puts you below the *Poverty Guidelines*, additional proof of support). If you have given birth to another child, bring the birth certificate. If you've been arrested, bring all court-certified documents related to that arrest (and be sure to consult with an attorney before the interview to make sure the arrest does not make you inadmissible).

☐ If you're applying based on marriage, evidence that it's the real thing, such as joint bank and credit card account statements, apartment leases, utility bills, love letters, wedding invitations, photos, and more.

☐ Your driver's license (or state identity card) and Social Security card (if you have one).

health significance. For those with such a disease, however, the grounds of inadmissibility can sometimes be overcome with treatment or by applying for a waiver. (See Chapter 3 for details.)

The envelope you submit to USCIS must contain results from an exam performed during the one-year period before you apply for adjustment of status. In other words, you can't give USCIS information on your health that is more than a year old. Once you've given USCIS the envelope, however, the report is good for a year. But only one year—if you submit an I-693 and a year goes by without USCIS approving your adjustment of status application, you'll have to get another exam.

Most of the time, USCIS will approve your adjustment of status application within a year, but there's no guarantee of that. If you trust USCIS to process your application quickly enough, you can submit your medical exam results with the other documents you submit when applying for adjustment of status. If you don't want to risk it, it's perfectly okay to wait until your adjustment of status interview to hand over the I-693 report in person—if you don't mind slowing down the interview for the time it takes for the USCIS officer to check the results. Or you can do it anytime in between, by mailing the report to the location specified in your most recent communication with USCIS about your application.

a. Where to Send Your Adjustment of Status Packet

As a family visa applicant, you'll need to mail your application, consisting of both forms and documents, to:

USCIS
P.O. Box 805887
Chicago, IL 60680-4120.

Or, if using Express Mail or a courier such as FedEx:

USCIS
Attn: FBAS
131 South Dearborn, 3rd Floor
Chicago, IL 60603-5517

If you're filing the I-485 concurrently with the I-130, the addresses are the same.

After filing your adjustment of status application, you will receive a receipt on Form I-797C. If USCIS requires additional evidence or information, it will send you a Request for Evidence (I-797E). You will also receive, after some weeks or months, a notice advising you where to go to have your biometrics (fingerprints) taken. These will then be used to check whether you have any history of arrests (whether by the police, FBI, DHS, or another authority). See Chapter 4 for information on how to track USCIS's progress toward your interview.

b. Your Adjustment of Status Interview

You will most likely be called in for a personal interview, which will be held at a USCIS office near you. USCIS will send you and any accompanying relatives an appointment notice, usually about two to four weeks in advance of the interview. If you have an attorney, he or she may come with you to the interview. (Even if you don't have an attorney, you could consult with or hire one at this point.)

RELATED TOPIC

See Chapter 4 for detailed information on what expect during your adjustment of status interview. If your adjustment of status application is denied, also see Chapter 4. Also, for information on how to protect your green card holder status after you're approved, see Chapter 14.

3. What Happens During Consular Processing

If you're outside the U.S., you'll be interviewed at a U.S. consulate, usually in the capital city of your country. At the beginning, consular processing involves a lot of paper being sent in various directions. First, after USCIS approves your visa petition, it will forward your file to the National Visa Center (NVC) in Portsmouth, New Hampshire. At the same time, it will send a Notice of Approval directly to your relative.

Also, either at the same time or, if you're a preference relative, when your Priority Date is close to becoming current, the NVC will send you and/or your petitioning

relative an email with instructions on how to proceed. The NVC process is done primarily online. The State Department website, www.travel.state.gov, walks you through all the steps; use it as your guide. (Search "Immigrant Visa Process" on the site.) You will need to first pay the Immigrant Visa (IV) application fee bill (currently $325) and a fee (currently $120) for reviewing the Affidavit of Support (Form I-864 or I-864EZ) or Affidavit of Support waiver (Form I-864W).

You can fill out and submit online a Form DS-261 to notify the NVC if you are using an attorney or other agent who should be kept informed of the progress of your case. You must fill out and submit the Immigrant Visa application, known as a DS-260, online. As for the Affidavit of Support, you will need to either mail it in or scan and email it to the NVC (depending on your case), along with supporting documents including the most recent year's tax returns and proof of assets, if using any to prove financial ability.

For further discussion of the requirements when filling out the Affidavit of Support, see Chapter 3. All other documents in support of your visa application must be mailed or scanned and emailed (depending on your case) to the NVC as well.

Once you respond to the NVC by submitting the requested forms and supporting documents, and it has reviewed the forms and documents for sufficiency, the

NVC will forward your file to the U.S. consulate that will be handling your case and will let you know the date, time, and place that you have been scheduled for an interview at the consulate.

You'll need to undergo a medical exam shortly before the interview. After the interview, if all goes well, you will be approved (subject to final security checks) for a visa to enter the United States.

Much of your job at this point involves convincing the consulate that you are not inadmissible for health, criminal, security, or financial reasons.

4. Forms and Documents to Prepare for Consular Processing

Preparing for the actual visa interview involves filling out one online form, collecting various documents, and undergoing a medical exam, as described next.

a. The DS-260 Online Application

The immigrant must complete and submit the DS-260 application form for an immigrant visa online, through the Consular Electronic Application Center (CEAC) at https://ceac.state.gov. You will log in to CEAC with your NVC case number and your NVC invoice ID number, both of which the NVC will send to you about six weeks after USCIS approves your petition.

The DS-260 is lengthy and asks for a lot of information that you may not have handy. But don't worry—if you can't finish it all in one sitting, the system allows you to save everything you've done so far and come back.

After submitting the Form DS-260 online, print out the confirmation page. You must bring this page to your visa interview at the U.S. consulate.

b. Supporting Documents for NVC or U.S. Consulate

The State Department's immigrant visa process website will let you know how to submit documents to the NVC. Some people can scan and email documents, others must mail them to the NVC, and others can choose either method. The first document is some version of the affidavit of support form—or forms, if you are using joint sponsors or the income of a sponsor's household member. For further discussion of the requirements when filling out the Affidavit of Support, see Chapter 3.

The checklist below provides a brief explanation of the documents you'll need to either send to the NVC or bring for your immigrant visa interview. Keep your eyes open for any special requirements that your consulate may add to this list. If you were not required to send all originals to the NVC, bring the originals and a set of copies with you to your interview. (The consular officer may want to examine the originals

Checklist: Documents for Your Consular Interview

☐ Confirmation of DS-260 receipt that you printed out after submitting the form online.

☐ Original notice of your visa petition approval (for the consulate's review).

☐ Long-form birth certificate (original, if it was not sent to the NVC, and photocopy) for you and each accompanying relative as well as for any unmarried minor children who are not immigrating with you.

☐ Marriage certificate (original, if it was not sent to the NVC, and photocopy) if you are married and bringing your spouse.

☐ If either you or your spouse has been previously married, copies of divorce and death certificates showing termination of all previous marriages (originals and photocopies).

☐ If the visa involves an adopted child, a certified copy of the adoption decree and other documentation showing the adoption qualifies the person for the visa.

☐ Documents proving the petitioner's continued employment, including a letter from the employer stating dates of employment, position and title, salary, marital status, dependents claimed, and emergency contact information; plus the last three pay stubs.

☐ Passport for you and each accompanying relative, valid for at least six months beyond the date of the interview.

☐ Police certificates from every country (except the U.S.) in which you and each accompanying relative has lived for at least six months since age 16.

☐ Fingerprints, if requested by the consulate.

☐ If you or accompanying relative served in the military forces of any country, a copy of your military records.

☐ Two color photographs of you and three color photographs of each accompanying relative.

☐ Medical exam report for you and each accompanying relative.

---

to make sure they're not fraudulent, but keep copies for your files.) Do not mail your paperwork to the consulate!

Here's some additional explanation regarding some of the items on the checklist above:

Police clearance. You personally must collect police clearance certificates from the local police authority in each country you have lived in for one year or more since your 16th birthday. Additionally, you must have a police certificate from your country

of nationality and the country you're living in currently, if you've been there for more than six months since the age of 16. You also need a police certificate from any country in which you've been arrested, no matter when. You do not need to obtain police certificates from the United States.

The State Department's immigrant visa process website contains information on how to contact the local police department to get police certificates. Some nations refuse to supply police certificates, or their certificates are not considered reliable, and so you will not be required to obtain them from those locations.

Some countries will send certificates directly to U.S. consulates but not to you personally. Before they send the certificates out, however, you must request that it be done. Usually this requires filing some type of request form, together with a set of your fingerprints.

Medical exam. Immediately before your visa interview, you and your accompanying relatives will be required to have medical examinations. Some consulates conduct the medical exams up to several days before the interview. Others schedule the medical exam and the interview on the same day. You will be told where to go and what to do in your appointment letter.

The medical examinations are conducted by private doctors. The fees depend on the doctor and country. The exam itself involves taking a medical history, blood test, and chest X-ray and receiving vaccinations, if required. Pregnant women can refuse to be X-rayed until *after* the pregnancy. The vaccination requirement may be waived for religious, moral, or medical reasons.

The main purpose of the medical exam is to verify that you are not medically inadmissible, based on having a communicable disease that is deemed to have public health significance. For those with such a disease, however, the grounds of inadmissibility can sometimes be overcome with treatment or by applying for a waiver. (See Chapter 3 for more details.) If you need a medical waiver, you will be given complete instructions by the consulate at the time of your interview, but should also consult an experienced immigration attorney.

5. Your Consular Interview

For details on what to expect during your consular visa interview, see Chapter 4. Chapter 4 also contains information on what to do if your visa is denied.

F. Step Four: Immigrant Visa Holders Enter the U.S.

If you are approved for permanent residence by a U.S. consulate overseas, the consulate will place your immigrant visa on a page in your passport. Review the visa to make sure all the information is correct. If you spot any spelling errors, contact the embassy or consulate promptly. You'll also get a sealed "visa packet" containing documents to show to border officials when you get to the United States. Don't open it.

Before you travel to the U.S., you'll have to pay one last fee: the USCIS Immigrant Fee, currently $220. (You can pay this fee after you get to the U.S., but USCIS won't send you a green card until you do.) Each member of the family traveling with you is charged the same fee. The only way to pay it is online through the USCIS Electronic Immigration System, or "ELIS." You'll need to create an ELIS account at uscis.gov/uscis-elis. Select "USCIS Immigrant Fee" and include your personal information. You'll need to have your Alien number (A-Number) and your Department of State Case ID number handy. (You got those from the consulate.) Once you're in the system, you can pay the fee for all family members in one transaction. You'll need a valid credit or debit card or U.S. bank checking account and routing numbers.

Your immigrant visa allows you to request entry to the United States at a border post, airport, or other arrival point. It's usually good for six months after you get it. You acquire the full status of green card holder only after you have been inspected and admitted into the United States. This will include being processed for the green card during "secondary inspection."

CAUTION
The clock is ticking. You must enter the U.S. before your visa expires. Check the expiration date that's printed on your visa inside your passport. The consulate usually gives you six months to make your trip, measured from the date it issues your visa. You might be given less time, however, if, for example, the results of your medical exam are in danger of getting stale.

If you are bringing any accompanying relatives, they must enter at either the same time or after you do in order to become permanent residents.

The inspection process involves a U.S. border officer opening the sealed envelope containing your visa documents and doing a last check to make sure you haven't used fraud. The border officer has "expedited removal" powers, which means he or she can turn you right around and send you home if anything appears wrong in your packet or with your answers to the officer's questions. Be polite and careful in answering.

When the officer is satisfied that everything is in order, he or she will stamp your passport to show that you're now a U.S. permanent resident (or conditional resident if you've been married less than two years and got your residence based on this marriage). This is often called an "I-551 stamp" or "ADIT" stamp. You are immediately authorized to work.

You won't receive an actual green card yet, however. Cards for you and your accompanying relatives will be ordered for you, so long as you've paid the USCIS Immigrant Fee. They will come to you by mail several weeks later at the home address you provide to U.S. Customs and Border Protection upon arriving in the United States.

G. Removing Conditional Residence in Marriage Cases

As we've already mentioned, green cards based on recent marriage to a U.S. citizen (less than two years before getting permanent residence) are issued only conditionally, meaning they will expire after two years. This is true of cards issued both to spouses and stepchildren of U.S. citizens.

To lift the condition on your conditional residence before your status expires (in other words, to go from conditional to unrestricted permanent residence), you file USCIS Form I-751. If you are still married, you and your U.S. citizen spouse file the petition jointly during the 90-day window before your card expires. The condition should be removed not only from your green card but from those of any children who came with you.

If you are divorced, or your spouse has died or refuses to join in the petition, you can file Form I-751 on your own, at any time, asking for a waiver of the joint-filing requirement.

1. Filing a Joint I-751 Petition With Your Spouse

Ideally, you and your spouse will still be happily married and living together when the time comes to file USCIS Form I-751. Nevertheless, you may file the joint petition even if you are separated or a divorce is in progress, as long as you remain legally married and your U.S. citizen spouse agrees to sign the I-751 petition.

If the two of you are living separately, however, you can expect to be called into your local USCIS office for an interview. Also, if your divorce is finalized before the joint petition has been decided on, the petition must be denied. You will have to file a new I-751 petition (plus fee) on your own, checking the appropriate box and requesting a waiver of the joint-filing requirement.

If you and your spouse are filing the petition jointly, you must file the petition 90 days or fewer before the expiration of the two-year conditional period. If you fail to meet this deadline, be prepared to show an extremely good reason why you could not file on time. Otherwise you may lose your U.S. residence and could be deported. If you and your spouse are no longer married, and you are filing the Form I-751 requesting a waiver of the joint-filing requirement, then you can file prior to the 90-day window before your status expires, or even after, through this is riskier (see an attorney).

The petition to remove the conditional status of your green card is made by filling out Form I-751, available on the USCIS website. Where stepchildren are involved, one form may be used for the entire family. It must be signed by both you and your U.S. spouse, unless, of course, you are filing on your own because your spouse has died, you are divorced, or your spouse is abusive.

Together with your form, you must also supply documents to show that your marriage was not entered into only for immigration purposes. Look for documents that prove that you and your spouse have been living together and sharing your financial and other matters, such as joint bank accounts, credit card statements, automobile and insurance policies in both names, and leases or contracts showing you rent or purchased your home in both names. It's also a good idea to submit at least two sworn affidavits from people who know both you and your U.S. spouse, explaining how it is they know that you are married. The people writing the affidavits should say how USCIS can contact them with any questions about their affidavits.

Forms and documents should be mailed together with a filing fee (currently $595 plus $85 for you and $85 for any dependent children included in the application) to either the USCIS California or Vermont Service Center, depending on where you live. Check the USCIS website for the appropriate address, fee, and P.O. box number.

Within a few weeks of mailing your petition to the Service Center, you will receive a written receipt (Form I-797) by return mail. The receipt is very important—it will be your only proof of legal status in the U.S. until your application is approved. Make a copy for your files, and use the original, together with your expired card, to prove your status to employers. Carefully note the expiration date on the receipt. It normally expires one year after USCIS received your application.

If you plan to travel in and out of the U.S. during that one year, you'll need to take your conditional green card and this receipt. Be careful not to leave the U.S. after your receipt has expired if you haven't yet received a USCIS decision. Unfortunately, USCIS may take more than a year to make its decision. If you need to take a trip outside the U.S., or if your employer is asking for proof that you're allowed to work, make an InfoPass appointment to visit your local USCIS office. USCIS can give you either a temporary I-551 stamp in your passport or an I-94 card, either of which will extend the expiration date of your conditional residence by another year.

Eventually, you will be sent an appointment notice stating when and where you must appear for biometric processing. (It's usually at a USCIS Application Support Center.) Biometric processing includes taking your photograph, signature, and index fingerprint, for use in generating your new green card. If you're between ages 14 and 79, it also includes taking your fingerprints, in order to do another criminal background check.

You will be able to check the USCIS website for current I-751 processing times, and if your application takes longer than the reported processing time, you can call the phone number on your receipt.

The Service Center has the authority to do several different things with your Form I-751. It may approve your application and send you your permanent resident card. It may send you a Request for Additional Evidence. (Always try to give USCIS the evidence it asks for, and by its deadline.) It may refer your case to your local USCIS office for an interview. Or, it may even deny your application and refer it to Immigration Court, where the immigration judge will review your application.

2. Getting a Waiver of the Requirement to File a Joint Petition

If you are unable to file a joint petition with your U.S. spouse to remove the condition on your residency, either because of divorce or because your spouse died or refuses to cooperate, you must then file for a waiver of the requirement to file the joint petition. This waiver will be granted in only three types of circumstances:

- You entered into a good-faith marriage but the marriage is legally terminated (death or divorce).
- Your deportation will cause you extreme hardship (one greater than that normally experienced by someone who is deported).

- You were battered or subjected to extreme cruelty by your U.S. spouse and the marriage was originally entered into in good faith.

Like the joint petition, an application for a waiver should ordinarily be filed before your two-year conditional residency expires, especially because you will have no legal status in the U.S. until you file the Form I-751 and receive the receipt. However, if you are forced to file late because, for example, your divorce did not become final until after the expiration date, USCIS may excuse the delay.

Waiver applications, like joint petitions, are filed on Form I-751. Where stepchildren are involved, one form may be used for the entire family, if the children received permanent residence on the same day or within 90 days of the parent. Otherwise, file a separate petition for the child and pay a separate fee.

Together with your form, you must supply documents showing that your marriage was not entered into only for immigration purposes. Proving that a marriage lasting less than two years was not a sham can be difficult. First, you might not have the cooperation of your ex-spouse. In this situation, any other proof you can present to show that you married for love and not to get a green card can help.

This is best accomplished by submitting records that you and your spouse held joint bank accounts and credit cards, had automobile and insurance policies in both names, and rented or purchased your home in both names. Sworn affidavits from people who know both you and your U.S. spouse, stating that they observed you living together during a particular period of time, are also helpful. If you had children together, this too is excellent evidence that your marriage was not a sham—include their birth certificates or your hospital records.

If you are divorced, you should also provide a copy of your divorce decree. If you have separated or if divorce proceedings have been started but aren't yet finished, you are not eligible to receive a waiver until your divorce becomes final. You can submit the I-751 without proof of divorce, but USCIS will send you a request for evidence asking you to send proof of the divorce with 87 days. If your conditional status expires and you are placed in removal proceedings before your divorce becomes final, don't panic—the immigration judge should be willing to postpone your case until the divorce proceedings are done and you can ask for a waiver. If your spouse died, provide a copy of the death certificate.

Proving extreme hardship is more difficult. Situations that might qualify include serious illness, other close family members living in the U.S., financial loss such as vested pension benefits or lost career opportunities, and serious political or economic problems in your home country. You should submit a detailed, written statement in your own words explaining the circumstances of your marriage, what you gave up to come to the U.S., and what you will lose by returning to your home country. The statement should be supported by written documentation.

If the basis of your waiver is that you were abused by your U.S. spouse, you must supply evidence such as police reports, medical or psychiatric reports, photographs, or affidavits from witnesses. If you are in divorce proceedings, court records including pleadings and depositions may be used. Your own personal written statement explaining the details of the abuse should also be submitted.

Many applications for waivers will require a personal interview before being approved. If an interview is required in your case, you will be notified by mail. The interview will be held at the USCIS local office nearest your home.

 SEE AN EXPERT
Get a lawyer if you will need to request a waiver. Due to the complexity of waiver applications, the obtuse legal criteria by which they are judged, and the severe consequences if they fail, we strongly recommend that you hire an experienced immigration lawyer to assist you in preparing the forms and documents and to accompany you to the interview.

Getting a Visa to Come Marry Your U.S. Citizen Fiancé (K-1)

If you intend to marry a U.S. citizen, your fiancé may bring you to the U.S. for the wedding, with a K-1 visa. (See I.N.A. § 214, 8 U.S.C. § 1184, 8 C.F.R. § 214.2(k).) Although it is a nonimmigrant (temporary) visa—lasting only 90 days—we have included it with the chapters on green cards because most U.S. consulates treat fiancé visas the same as immigrant (permanent resident) visas. This makes sense, because once you've obtained a K-1 visa, you're very close to being able to apply for a green card.

If you are already in the U.S., or if your fiancé lives outside of the U.S. with you, getting a K-1 visa is unnecessary. Instead, you should get married and then apply for a green card as outlined in Chapter 7.

! CAUTION
This chapter doesn't cover K-3, so-called "fiancé visas" for people who are already married. In fact, even if you're not yet married, but think you might prefer to hold your wedding in your home country, the K-3 visa is worth considering. See Chapter 7 for information on K-3 visas for married couples.

This chapter covers who is eligible for a K-1 visa and how to apply. Fiancés are fortunate in that there are no annual limits on K-1 visas, and thus no long waiting periods. The first step, fiancé visa petition approval, normally takes five to seven months. After the petition has been approved, it will take an additional two to five months (in the normal case) for the U.S. consulate to issue a visa.

Note: Although the accurate way to generally refer to both male and female fiancés is "fiancé(e)," we are using the term "fiancé" for simplicity's sake.

Key Features of Fiancé Visas

Here are some of the advantages and disadvantages of using a fiancé visa to enter the United States:

- A fiancé visa may be your only option if your U.S. citizen fiancé is unable to travel to your home country to marry you.
- Fiancé visas last for 90 days, which should, if you act reasonably quickly, give you enough time to get married and prepare your green card application. However, the fiancé visa cannot be renewed.
- Immediately upon arriving in the United States, you may apply for permission to work.
- After using a fiancé visa to go to the United States and get married, you have a choice of either returning to your home country or staying and applying for a U.S. green card.
- Your unmarried children under the age of 21 are eligible to accompany you on your fiancé visa (as K-2 visa holders).

U.S. Citizen Petitioners Must Disclose Criminal Records

In 2005, Congress became concerned that immigrating fiancés were particularly susceptible to domestic violence and abuse—particularly those whose engagements were arranged through marriage brokers (sometimes called "mail-order brides"). In response, Congress passed the International Marriage Brokers Regulation Act (IMBRA).

As a result of IMBRA, the fiancé visa petition (Form I-129F) now asks whether you and your fiancé or spouse met through an international marriage broker. If you did, the immigrant will be asked, at the visa interview, whether the broker complied with legal requirements that he or she collect information on the U.S. fiancé or spouse's criminal record and pass it to the immigrant. USCIS must also run a criminal background check on the petitioner, and forward the information, along with the approved petition, to the U.S. Department of State, which will then send these materials to the intending immigrant.

In addition, Form I-129F now asks all U.S. citizen petitioners whether they have a history of violent crime and crime relating to alcohol or controlled-substance abuse.

 SEE AN EXPERT

Do you need a lawyer? Many people are able to handle the application process for a fiancé visa on their own, without a lawyer. However, if you have any trouble dealing with paperwork or understanding the instructions, or have any complications in your case (such as a criminal record, past visa overstays in the U.S., or an immigrating child who will turn 18 soon and therefore no longer qualify as your spouse's stepchild), a lawyer is well worth the price. See Chapter 6 for tips on finding a good one.

A. Do You Qualify for a K-1 Visa?

The main eligibility criteria for getting a K-1 visa are:

- Your intended spouse is a U.S. citizen (not a permanent resident or green card holder).
- Both members of the couple are legally able to marry (single and of legal age).
- The immigrant must have a genuine intention to marry the U.S. citizen petitioner after arriving in the U.S.
- The two of you must have met and seen each other in person within the past two years.

This visa is not for use by couples who are simply considering marriage. You'll need to show proof that you truly plan to get married, such as letters to each other discussing your plans and wedding announcements to friends. One of the most convincing ways to prove this is by showing that you've actually set a date for the wedding, and made some arrangements like hiring a caterer. (But leave room for flexibility—you can't necessarily count on getting a visa in time for your planned date.)

For some couples, the requirement that they have already met is difficult or violates their religious principles. If you practice a religion in which marriages are customarily arranged by families and premarital meetings are prohibited, you can ask that a meeting requirement be waived. You'll have to show that both parties will be following all the customs of marriage and weddings that are part of the religion.

It is also possible to get a waiver of the personal meeting requirement if such a meeting would cause an extreme hardship to the U.S. citizen member of the couple. Only the most extreme situations involving medical problems are likely to be regarded as a good enough reason for the waiver to be granted. Economic problems alone are not usually acceptable.

Bringing Your Children

When you get a K-1 visa, any of your unmarried children under the age of 21 can be issued K-2 visas. This will enable them to accompany you to the U.S. They, too, will be able to apply for green cards once you get married.

> **CAUTION**
>
> **You'll need to separately apply for a green card after the marriage.** Although you must marry within the 90-day validity period of the K-1 visa, you may file for a green card—without leaving the United States—after the 90 days, as long as it is after you marry the U.S. citizen who petitioned for you. Just getting married does not, by itself, give you any legal status in the United States. To maintain your legal status beyond the 90-day period, you must submit an application for adjustment of status. Simply follow the directions for adjustment of status in Chapter 7. Because you have already gotten a K-1 visa, you are excused from the normal first step in this process (the I-130 visa petition). You will, however, be subject to the two-year conditional residency placed on green cards obtained through marriage to a U.S. citizen. This, too, is covered in Chapter 7. Read it carefully before applying for a fiancé visa.

B. Quick View of How to Apply for a K-1 Visa

Getting a K-1 visa is a four-step process:

1. Your U.S. citizen fiancé mails a visa petition on USCIS Form I-129F to the USCIS Dallas Lockbox.
2. After the petition is approved, you fill out and submit a visa application form online.
3. You collect documents, and bring them to an interview at a U.S. consulate.
4. You use your K-1 fiancé visa to enter the United States.

C. Step One: Your U.S. Citizen Fiancé Submits a Visa Petition

To start the process, your U.S. citizen fiancé will need to file what's called a fiancé visa petition. The object of the petition is to prove that:

- You have a bona fide intention of marrying a U.S. citizen within 90 days after you arrive in the United States.
- Both of you are legally able to marry.
- You have physically met each other within the past two years—or can prove that this requirement should be waived based on religion or extreme hardship to the U.S. citizen.

The Form I-129F itself is mostly self-explanatory, but here are some tips regarding certain tricky portions. Part 1 is for information about the U.S. citizen, and Part 2 is for information about the immigrant. Each of you will be asked your marital status. Check only one box, and make sure it is not the one that says "married." In Part 1, Question 14, the U.S. citizen must state whether he or she has filed petitions for other immigrant fiancés or husband/wives before. If the answer is yes, USCIS will take a closer look at their and your cases to make sure this isn't a pattern that indicates fraud.

In Part 2 (your information), Question 11 asks for an "Alien Registration Number." You won't have one unless you've previously applied for permanent, or in some cases

temporary, residency or been in deportation/removal proceedings. (See a lawyer if that's the case.) If you have a number, you must enter it here; leave the space blank if you don't. Question 12 asks for a Social Security number. You won't have one unless you've lived in the U.S.; leave the space blank if you don't.

All of the questions about past spouses are designed to make sure both of you are free to marry now.

The address where you (the immigrating fiancé) intend to live in the U.S. (Question 28) should be the same as your U.S. citizen petitioner's, or you'll raise questions. If there's a compelling reason to live apart (for example, you plan to move in together only after you marry), attach a separate document explaining that.

Question 33 asks whether you're related to your fiancé. If the two of you are blood relations, you'll have to make sure that a marriage between you is allowed in the U.S. state where you plan to marry.

For Question 34a, it's sometimes best to attach a separate statement fully explaining the details of how you met and decided to get married. This is a good opportunity to convince USCIS that your relationship is the real thing, not just a fraud to get you a green card. See the sample below.

Question 35 requires the U.S. citizen to state whether you met through an international marriage broker, and if so, to give information about the broker.

Sample Fiancé Meeting Statement—Attachment to Form I-129F

Filed by Sandra Beach on Behalf of Nigel Hollis

Question 34

I met my fiancé 18 months ago, while visiting a college friend who has settled in England. My friend Carrie had been telling me for months that she wanted to introduce me to Nigel, because of our offbeat senses of humor and shared interest in long-distance swimming. I've had bad experiences with friends trying to set me up before, so I didn't take it very seriously. But when vacation plans took me to England, I let her arrange for me and Nigel to meet over lunch at a pub.

To my amazement, we clicked right away. We had a lot to talk about—he had completed an English Channel swim a few months before, and I'm hoping to swim the Channel next year. Both of us have built our lives around swimming, which sometimes leaves little time for other things, including relationships. We compared notes on training techniques, equipment, dealing with cold water, rip tides, and more.

Our lunch lasted all afternoon and into the evening. By the end of that evening, I considered Nigel a friend and someone I could very easily fall in love with.

Nigel and I spent almost all my remaining week's vacation together. Poor Carrie joked that her plan had backfired, because I spent embarrassingly little time at her house. By the end of the week, we both knew this was headed toward a serious relationship.

Since then, Nigel and I have corresponded almost constantly by email, and call each other twice a week. During one long phone call, we decided to get married.

It was difficult deciding where we would live after marrying—Nigel has a beautiful cottage in Cornwall, and I could happily live in England. However, my mother is in poor health, and ever since my father passed away last year, she has relied on my help, so we agreed to make our home in New York.

As proof that Nigel and I are in love and plan to marry, I am attaching copies of his plane tickets to New York; photos of the two of us together; copies of our telephone bills and some of our emails; copies of catering and other contracts showing that the two of us plan to marry in July; and copies of our travel itinerary for New Zealand, where we will honeymoon.

Signed: _Sandra Beach_

Date: _August 20, 2016_

In Question 36, try to name the nearest U.S. consulate with a visa processing office in your country. (Don't worry—if you get it wrong, USCIS will figure it out.)

Part 3 collects information on the U.S. citizen petitioner. Questions 2 and 3 require the petitioner to reveal to USCIS any history of violent crime, crime relating to alcohol, or controlled substance abuse. This is for your (the immigrant's) protection—you will be told of any relevant history. The petitioner should see an attorney if there is any question about whether this section applies.

The checklist below will help your U.S. citizen petitioner prepare and assemble the various forms and documents. (Note that your U.S. citizen fiancé will now be known as your "petitioner," and you are the "beneficiary.")

1. Mailing the Fiancé Visa Petition

Once your U.S. citizen petitioner has finished the fiancé visa petition, he or she must mail it to a USCIS Lockbox in Texas. Check the USCIS website at www.uscis.gov/i-129f to get the appropriate address.

2. Awaiting Approval of the Visa Petition

Within a few weeks after mailing your petition, your fiancé should get back written confirmation that the papers are being processed, together with a receipt for the fees. This notice (on Form I-797C) will also contain your immigration file number, which is useful if the decision gets delayed.

If USCIS wants further information before acting on your case, it may send your U.S. citizen petitioner a Request for Evidence (RFE). This letter will tell the citizen what additional pieces of information or documents USCIS expects. He or she should mail the extra data or documents to USCIS by the deadline given.

Sometimes, USCIS will request a personal interview with the U.S. citizen petitioner prior to approving a fiancé petition. The purpose is to make sure a marriage will really take place after you arrive in the U.S. and to confirm that you have previously met each other. All interviews are held at USCIS local offices, to which your file will be forwarded before the interview. The USCIS local office will send the petitioner a notice of when and where to appear for the interview and instructions to bring additional documentation, if any is required.

Once your petition is approved, USCIS will send a Form I-797 Notice of Action to your U.S. citizen fiancé, indicating the approval. (See the sample notice below.) At the same time, USCIS will send a copy of your file to an office called the National Visa Center, which will assign you a case number and transfer the file to the appropriate U.S. consulate in your country.

Checklist for Fiancé Visa Petition

Forms

☐ Form I-129F, signed by the U.S. citizen petitioner, with accompanying fee (currently $535; send a check or money order, not cash). If you have children, make sure they are listed on this form, which is necessary if you want them to accompany you.

☐ Form G-325A (biographical data) filled out for you, the visa applicant.

☐ Form G-325A (biographical data) filled out for your U.S. citizen fiancé.

Documents

☐ Proof of your fiancé's U.S. citizenship, such as a copy of his or her birth certificate, U.S. passport, certificate of citizenship, naturalization certificate, or consular record of birth abroad.

☐ Proof that you and your fiancé can legally marry, such as your birth certificate to show that you are over 18 (or whatever the age of consent is in the U.S. state where you plan to marry); and if either of you has been married before, proof that all prior marriages were legally terminated, such as a divorce decree or death certificate.

☐ Proof of your intent to marry, including a statement from the U.S. citizen petitioner, describing how you met, how your relationship developed, why the two of you want to marry, and when you plan to marry. If applicable, you may also include items such as wedding announcements, catering contracts, a letter or affidavit from your pastor or justice of the peace stating that he or she has been contacted about performing your marriage ceremony.

☐ Proof that you have met in person, such as photographs of the two of you together, letters you have written to each other indicating that there has been a meeting, and copies of plane tickets, credit card receipts, and hotel receipts.

☐ If you have not met each other for religious reasons, evidence of your membership in such a religion, including a letter from an official in your religious organization verifying that you and your fiancé are members, and a detailed statement from a clergyperson explaining the religious laws concerning marriage. A letter from your parents would also be helpful.

☐ If you have not met each other because it would impose an extreme hardship on your U.S. citizen petitioner, a written statement explaining in detail why you cannot meet. If there is a medical reason why the U.S. citizen can't travel to meet you, include a letter from a medical doctor explaining the condition.

☐ If the U.S. citizen petitioner has been convicted of any of the crimes listed in the instructions to Form I-129F, certified copies of the court and police records (but get a lawyer for help with your case).

☐ One photograph of you and one photograph of your U.S. citizen fiancé, in U.S. passport style, in color. Don't submit old photos; give them ones that are less than 30 days old. Write your name in pencil or felt pen on the back of your photo.

☐ If you or your fiancé is now known by a name different than the one appearing on any document you submitted, a copy of the legal document that made the change, such as a marriage certificate, adoption decree, or court order.

Sample I-797 Notice of Action

Department of Homeland Security
U.S. Citizenship and Immigration Services

I-797, Notice of Action

THE UNITED STATES OF AMERICA

RECEIPT NUMBER		CASE TYPE I129F	
CSC-16-041-00000		PETITION FOR FIANCE(E)	

RECEIPT DATE	PRIORITY DATE	PETITIONER	
November 30, 2016		BEACH, SANDRA	

NOTICE DATE	PAGE	BENEFICIARY
April 13, 2017	1 of 1	HOLLIS, NIGEL

ILONA BRAY
RE: NIGEL IAN HOLLIS
950 PARKER ST.
BERKELEY, CA 94710

Notice Type: Approval Notice

Valid from 04/13/2017 to 08/13/2017

The above petition has been approved. We have sent the original visa petition to the Department of State National Visa Center (NVC), 32 Rochester Avenue, Portsmouth, NH 03801-2909. The INS has completed all action; further inquiries should be directed to the NVC.

The NVC now processes all approved fiance(e) petitions. The NVC processing should be complete within two to four weeks after receiving the petition from INS. The NVC will create a case record with your petition information. NVC will then send the petition to the U.S. Embassy or Consulate where your fiance(e) will be interviewed for his or her visa.

You will receive notification by mail when NVC has sent your petition to the U.S. Embassy or Consulate. The notification letter will provide you with a unique number for your case and the name and address of the U.S. Embassy or Consulate where your petition has been sent.

If it has been more than four weeks since you received this approval notice and you have not received notification from NVC that your petition has been forwarded overseas, please call NVC at (603) 334-0700. Please call between 8:00am-6:45pm Eastern Standard Time. You will need to enter the INS receipt number from this approval notice into the automated response system to receive information on your petition.

THIS FORM IS NOT A VISA NOR MAY IT BE USED IN PLACE OF A VISA.

Please see the additional information on the back. You will be notified separately about any other cases you filed.
U.S. CITIZENSHIP & IMMIGRATION SVC
CALIFORNIA SERVICE CENTER
P. O. BOX 30111
LAGUNA NIGUEL CA 92607-0111
Customer Service Telephone: (800) 375-5283

Form I-797 (Rev. 01/31/05) N

CAUTION
Don't use the approved fiancé visa petition to try to enter the United States! An approved petition does not by itself give you any immigration benefits. It is only a prerequisite to the next step, submitting your application at a U.S. consulate.

D. Step Two: You Apply at a U.S. Consulate

The consular post will send you a letter listing the documents it needs to see in order to issue you a K-1 visa, along with instructions on where to get the required medical exam and how to notify the consulate (by mail or telephone) when you are ready for an interview with a consular officer.

Each consular post has different procedures, so listen only to what your consulate tells you to do.

1. Submit Nonimmigrant Visa Application Form Online

All applicants for a K-1 visa must fill out and submit Form DS-160 online at the Consular Electronic Application Center website, https://ceac.state.gov/genniv. It's a lengthy form, but don't worry—if you can't finish it all in one sitting, you can save what you've done and come back to it. Make sure you note your Application ID number—you'll need it to get back to your form.

Even though your spouse did not have to file a separate I-129F petition for any children, you will need to file a separate DS-160 for each of them to get a K-2 visa.

2. Pay Your Fees and Schedule Your Interview

Procedures vary depending on the consular post, but often there is a way to schedule your interview and pay the application fee—also called a "machine readable visa" (MRV) fee—(currently $265) online. In any case, follow the instructions for how the consulate requires you to schedule an interview (the consulate might do this itself) and to pay. For citizens of countries that charge an extra fee to U.S. citizens seeking to go there, there may be an additional fee called a "reciprocity fee," which typically is paid the day of the interview.

A separate fee is charged for each visa application (K-1 or K-2).

CAUTION
Your approved fiancé petition has a time limit. It can be used to get a K-1 visa only within four months of the date the petition was approved. If the process is going slowly and it looks like you won't be able to get your visa within four months, it is very important that you contact the consulate and ask that it extend the validity period of your petition. Most consulates will agree to do this without a problem, unless they think you're to blame for the delay.

3. Preparing for Your Interview

See the checklist below to help you organize the documents necessary for your fiancé visa interview. This checklist shows documents that are commonly required. Your consulate may require others.

Here's some additional information regarding some of the items on the checklist below.

Police clearance. Unlike applications made in the U.S., you personally must collect police clearance certificates from each country you have lived in for one year or more since your 16th birthday. Additionally, you must have a police certificate from your home country or country of last residence, if you lived there for at least six months since the age of 16. Also, if you have ever been arrested,

---

Checklist for Fiancé Visa Interview

Forms

☐ USCIS Form I-134, Affidavit of Support, if the consulate requests it (signed by the U.S. petitioner, stating that he or she will reimburse the government if you receive public assistance or welfare).

Documents

☐ Printed confirmation page from your online DS-160 application.

☐ Originals of documents submitted in connection with the visa petition, such as your fiancé's U.S. birth certificate and proof that any previous marriages were legally ended.

☐ Documents to accompany Form I-134, such as proof of U.S. citizen's employment, copy of U.S. citizen's most recent federal tax return, and letter from U.S. citizen's bank(s) confirming the account(s).

☐ A valid passport from your home country, good for at least six months.

☐ Your original birth certificate.

☐ An original police clearance certificate, if available in your country (the instructions from the consulate will tell you).

☐ Two additional photographs of you, the immigrating fiancé (according to the consulate's photo instructions).

☐ Results of your medical examination, in an unopened envelope.

☐ Additional documents proving your relationship (to cover the time since you submitted the fiancé visa petition), such as phone bills showing calls to one another, copies of emails and other correspondence, and photos taken during recent joint vacations.

☐ Fee receipt showing that you have paid the relevant visa application fee (currently $265). The method of payment depends on the country. Check the website of the U.S. consulate where you plan to apply for your visa to learn how and where your fee can be paid in advance. Most consulates will not allow you to pay the visa fee at the time of interview.

☐ Fingerprints, if requested by the consulate.

no matter when, you'll need a certificate from the country in which the arrest took place. You do not need to obtain police certificates from the United States, or from countries where police certificates are never issued or are considered unreliable.

The State Department's website, www. travel.state.gov, contains instructions on how to obtain police certificates from every country. Otherwise, contact the local police department in your home country for instructions on how to get police certificates. To obtain police certificates from nations other than your home country, contact the nearest consulate representing that country for instructions. The U.S. consulate will tell you from which countries police certificates are not required.

Some countries will send certificates directly to U.S. consulates but not to you personally. Before they send the certificates out, however, you must request that it be done. Usually this requires filing some type of request form, together with a set of your fingerprints.

Fingerprints. A few consulates require you to submit fingerprints, though most do not. Consulates wanting fingerprints will send you instructions.

Photos. You must bring to the interview two photographs of you and two photographs of each accompanying child. They must be taken in compliance with the consulate's instructions (U.S "passport style"). Many photographers are familiar with U.S. passport style. If you're a do-it-yourself type, passport-style specifications are available on the State Department's website, www.travel.state.gov. If your religious beliefs require wearing a head covering, you should be able to keep it on for the photo. However, your full face must be visible and your head covering cannot obscure your hairline or cast shadows on your face.

Medical exam. Immediately before your visa interview, you and any accompanying children will be required to have medical examinations. Some consulates conduct the medical exams up to several days before the interview. Others schedule the medical exam and the interview on the same day. You will be told where to go and what to do in your appointment letter.

The medical examinations are conducted by private doctors. The fees depend on the doctor and country. The exam itself involves taking a medical history, blood test, and chest X-ray and administering vaccinations, if required. Pregnant women can refuse to be X-rayed until after the pregnancy. The vaccination requirement may be waived for religious, moral, or medical reasons. You also have the option to postpone your vaccinations until you're ready to apply for adjustment of status.

The main purpose of the medical exam is to verify that you are not medically inadmissible. Some medical grounds of inadmissibility can be overcome with treatment or by applying for a waiver. (See Chapter 3 for details.) If you need a medical waiver, you will be given complete instructions by the consulate at the time of your interview, but should also consult an experienced immigration attorney.

Affidavit of support. As part of overcoming the grounds of inadmissibility, you will have to show that you will not become a public charge (go on welfare) in the United States. Normally, the consulate will ask the U.S. fiancé to fill out an Affidavit of Support on Form I-134. The I-134 is simpler than the I-864 Affidavit of Support form (discussed in Chapter 3), and is not considered legally enforceable. In other words, the U.S. government is very unlikely to go after your U.S. citizen fiancé for reimbursement if you end up needing public benefits. If your U.S. citizen fiancé does not make enough money to support you, you should submit an additional I-134 from a U.S.-based family member of your U.S. citizen fiancé and hope that satisfies the consulate that you won't become a public charge.

4. Attending Your Interview

After the medical exam, you and your accompanying children will report to the consulate for the interview. Bring with you to the interview the items on the checklist

above and anything else the consulate requested. The interview process involves verification of your application's accuracy and an inspection of your documents.

 RELATED TOPIC
For details on what to expect during your consular visa interview, see Chapter 4. Also see Chapter 4 if your visa is denied.

E. Step Three: You Enter the U.S. on Your Fiancé Visa

Normally, you must use the visa to enter the U.S. within six months, though the consulate can extend this period if necessary. The inspection process involves a U.S. border officer opening the sealed envelope containing your visa documents, and doing a last check to make sure you haven't used fraud. The border officer has expedited removal powers, which means he or she can turn you right around and send you home if anything appears wrong in your packet or with your answers to the officer's questions. Be polite and careful in answering.

When the officer is satisfied that everything is in order, he or she will stamp your passport to show that you're now a K-1 visa holder, and you will be authorized to remain in the U.S. for 90 days. If you are bringing accompanying children, they must enter the U.S. at either the same time or after you do. You can apply for a work permit once you're in the U.S.—see "Employment Authorization," below.

If you're planning to apply for a green card, your most important task at this point is to get married. You can't apply for the green card until you have an official government certificate of your marriage, which sometimes takes weeks after the wedding to be prepared. For more information on applying to adjust status based on your marriage, see Chapter 7.

RESOURCE
For a fuller discussion of all aspects of applying for a fiancé visa and for your green card after you've arrived in the U.S. and gotten married, see the latest edition of *Fiancé & Marriage Visas: A Couple's Guide to U.S. Immigration*, by Ilona Bray (Nolo).

Employment Authorization

If you apply for employment authorization (a "work permit") as soon as you hit American soil, there's a chance that USCIS will act quickly enough on your application for you to start work before your permit expires. It's a slim chance, however: Your K-1 employment authorization can't last any longer than your 90-day period of stay in K-1 status, and it often takes 90 days or longer for USCIS to act on such applications.

If you need to work right away, it's better to get married as soon as possible, apply for a green card through adjustment of status right away, and include an application for a work permit with that application. Once granted, your work authorization will be good until your green card application is approved or denied. A further advantage to doing it that way is that you won't have to pay the usual $380 application fee—it's free if you apply with an adjustment of status application.

If you want to bet on USCIS being speedy and approving your work permit before your 90 K-1 days are up, complete Form I-765 (available at www.uscis.gov/i-765) and file it with USCIS, according to the instructions on the USCIS website. Answer Question 16 of the form "(a)(6)." Together with Form I-765, you must submit a copy of your I-94, and two color photos, passport style. The filing fee is $410.

Getting a Green Card
Through Employment

Every year, 140,000 green cards are made available to people whose labor or work skills are needed to fill gaps or needs in the U.S. workforce. Before you can even think about getting an employment-based green card, however, two lucky things need to happen:

- You need to receive a job offer from a U.S. employer (unless you have exceptional abilities or your work is in the national interest).
- The employer must (with a few exceptions) be willing to sponsor you for a green card—including a long process known as labor certification, which involves advertising and interviewing other people for the job you've been offered, and ultimately rejecting all of them for good reasons.

Many people would love to come to the U.S. in order to look for a job and stay permanently, but realistically, if you're from China, India, or the Philippines, employment-based green cards are mainly available to people who have advanced job skills, higher education, or extraordinary abilities. Other workers from these countries needn't give up entirely—there is a category of green card available to them—but far more ordinary workers from those countries are looking for green cards than the number of green cards available, so the wait for them can be years long. Not many employers are willing to wait this long to hire someone.

SEE AN EXPERT

Do you need a lawyer? Once you have successfully found a job, your employer will normally hire and pay for the services of a lawyer to help prepare and submit the necessary application materials. In fact, Department of Labor (DOL) rules require the employer to pay all attorneys' fees and other costs associated with a part of the process called "labor certification."

The DOL has even asked employees to sign an affidavit swearing under penalty of perjury that their employer did not require them to pay any costs relating to their labor certification.

Many large companies have experienced staff people who will take care of immigration matters for highly desirable employees. However, it is often the employee who is most interested in having the green card issued, and to some U.S. employers, the red tape of hiring a foreign employee can be an unfamiliar nuisance. If your prospective employer doesn't hire a lawyer, it's worth paying for one on your own. The lawyer's help is particularly important, because the government rules concerning the application process keep changing and are very confusing.

A. Are You Eligible for a Green Card Through Employment?

In order to qualify for a green card through employment:

- You must have an offer of full-time, permanent, U.S.-based work from an employer that is also permanently located in the United States. (See 20 C.F.R. § 656.3 for a full discussion of what types of employers qualify—for example, neither visiting diplomats nor foreign media companies can sponsor you for a green card.)

- You must have the correct background (education and work experience) for the job you've been offered.

Key Features of an Employment-Based Green Card

Here are some of the advantages and limitations of an employment-based green card:

- You must begin by working full-time for the sponsoring company when the green card is approved. You may then switch jobs or choose not to work at all, so long as your original intention wasn't to take advantage of your employer and leave as soon as you could.
- Your spouse and your unmarried children under the age of 21 may also be eligible for green cards as accompanying relatives.
- The job through which you get your green card must be for full-time work and not self-employment (with some exceptions, depending on which category of work you apply under).
- As with all green cards, yours can be taken away if you misuse it—for example, you live outside the U.S. for too long, commit crimes, or even fail to advise the immigration authorities of your change of address. However, if you successfully keep your green card for five years, you can apply for U.S. citizenship.

- There must be no qualified U.S. worker (U.S. citizen or national, green card holder, asylee, or refugee) willing or able to take the job—except in categories of green cards where labor certification is not required.

1. Which of the Five Employment Preference Categories Fits You?

Green cards through employment are divided into five preference categories. In each category, only a certain number are given out each year. Often, more people apply in a year than there are green cards available. When that happens, the people who applied latest must wait to receive their green cards as they become available.

The five employment preference categories are:

- **Employment first preference (EB-1).** Priority workers.
- **Employment second preference (EB-2).** Workers with advanced degrees or exceptional ability.
- **Employment third preference (EB-3).** Professionals, skilled workers, or unskilled workers.
- **Employment fourth preference (EB-4).** Religious workers and various miscellaneous categories of workers and other individuals; also called special immigrants.
- **Employment fifth preference (EB-5).** Individual investors willing to invest $1,000,000 in a U.S. business (or

$500,000 in a business in a rural or economically depressed area).

a. Employment First Preference (EB-1) Category

First preference, or "priority" workers, are divided into three subcategories:

- workers of extraordinary ability
- outstanding university professors or researchers, and
- transferring executives or managers of multinational companies.

Applying as a priority worker is easier than applying in most of the other employment categories, because your employer doesn't need to start out by seeking labor certification on your behalf. In fact, in the subcategory for workers of extraordinary ability, you do not even need a job offer. (People applying as professors or researchers, however, do need job offers. And transferring executives or managers must, obviously, already be employed by the company that's transferring them.)

i. EB-1: Workers of Extraordinary Ability Subcategory

You may qualify for a green card as a priority worker if you have extraordinary ability in the sciences, arts, education, business, or athletics. Your achievements must have been publicly recognized, and resulted in a period of sustained national or international acclaim. In general, if you can show that you are a widely acknowledged leader in your field, then you will be able to show that you have gained sustained acclaim.

You do not need a specific job offer in this subcategory so long as you will continue working in your field of expertise once you arrive in the United States. If, however, you have been offered a job, your employer can help with your application by filing the initial petition for you. USCIS tends to be more willing to trust, and therefore approve, "extraordinary ability" petitions submitted by an employer-sponsor. That is because USCIS can more readily imagine that you will in fact be performing these feats involving extraordinary ability if a company wants to hire you for this purpose. So if you have a choice between a "self-petition" and having an employer sign off on the petition, consider the benefits of having an employer sponsor you.

ii. EB-1: Outstanding Professors and Researchers Subcategory

You may qualify for a green card as a priority worker under the outstanding professors and researchers subcategory if you have an international reputation for being outstanding in a particular academic field. You need three years' minimum of either teaching or research experience in that field. You must also be entering the U.S. to accept a specific tenured or tenure-track teaching or research position at a university or institution of higher learning. Unlike the "extraordinary ability" category described above, you will need a specific job offer from a qualified employer in this subcategory in order to qualify.

Alternatively, you may accept a job conducting research in industry or with a research organization. The U.S. company or institution employing you should have a history of making significant achievements in research and must employ at least three other full-time research workers. Research positions must not be temporary, but rather be expected to last for an unlimited or indefinite duration.

iii. EB-1: Multinational Executives and Managers Subcategory

You may qualify for a green card as a priority worker under the multinational executives and managers subcategory if you have been employed as an executive or manager by a qualified company outside the U.S. for at least one out of the past three years. Or, if you're already in the U.S. on a temporary visa, for one of the three years before you arrived here. You must now be going to take a managerial or executive position with a U.S. branch, affiliate, or subsidiary of the same company. The U.S. office must have been in business for at least one year. (The qualifications needed are similar to those for L-1 intracompany transfer visas, discussed in Chapter 19.)

Not only do you need to meet the various qualification requirements under this subcategory, but the foreign and U.S.-based offices of your employer must either be:

- different branches of the same company
- a joint venture where the parent company owns half or has equal control and veto power
- related so that one company is a majority-controlled subsidiary of the other, or
- an affiliation in which both companies are under the control of the same person, persons, company, or group of companies.

Because your own job position, both in and out of the U.S., must be "executive" or "managerial" in nature, the exact meaning of these terms is important. A manager is defined as a person who:

- manages the organization, or a department, subdivision, function, or component of the organization
- supervises and controls the work of other supervisory, professional, or managerial employees, or manages an essential function of the organization
- has the authority to hire and fire those persons supervised, or if none are supervised, works at a senior level within the organization, and
- has the authority to make decisions concerning the day-to-day operations of the activities or function of the organization over which the manager has authority.

Note that all four of the above criteria must be met for someone's job to be considered managerial. A supervisor below the level of middle management, often called a first-line supervisor, is not normally considered a manager for green card qualifying purposes—unless the employees being supervised are professionals. The word professional here means a worker holding a university degree.

An executive is defined as a person who:
- directs the management of the organization or a major part or function of the organization
- sets the goals and policies of the organization or a part or function of the organization
- has extensive decision-making authority, and

- receives only general supervision or direction from higher-level executives, a board of directors, or the stockholders of the organization.

b. Employment Second Preference (EB-2) Category

The second preference category of green cards through employment is for:
- professionals holding advanced university degrees, and
- persons of exceptional ability in the sciences, arts, or business.

To qualify in this category, you must be coming to the U.S. specifically to work full-time in your field of expertise.

Academic Credential Evaluations

Not every country in the world operates on the same academic degree and grade level system found in the United States. If you were educated in some other country, USCIS will usually ask you to provide an academic credential evaluation from an approved consulting service to determine the U.S. equivalent of your educational level.

USCIS is not required to accept the results of an education evaluation. USCIS considers these reports "nonbinding" on its decision—but such reports can be very persuasive nonetheless. When the results are favorable, they strengthen your case. If, however, the evaluation shows that your credentials do not equal those

required for advanced degree professionals, you will not qualify in this subcategory.

A list of these accreditation services can be found at www.naces.org/members.htm.

If you were educated outside the United States, it's best to get an evaluation before USCIS asks for it. If it's favorable, include it with your petition. This strengthens your case and saves time if USCIS decides to request it later. If your evaluation is unfavorable, submit the results only if USCIS insists you do. You may also wish to consider applying in a different category, because your application in this one is likely to fail.

With limited exceptions, you must have a definite, permanent job offer from a U.S. employer. Labor certifications are normally required for this category. (For exceptions, see Subsection iii, below.) This is another preference category that is divided into subcategories.

i. EB-2: Advanced Degree Professionals Subcategory

To be a professional means, under the immigration laws, that you work in an occupation requiring, at a minimum, a baccalaureate (B.A. or B.S.) degree or its equivalent from a college or university. Therefore, to qualify as an advanced degree professional for this subcategory takes something more. Specifically, you must hold a graduate-level degree or a professional degree requiring postgraduate education, such as is standard in U.S. law or medicine.

Many people who qualify for temporary, H-1 visas in professions like nursing and engineering do not qualify for green cards in this subcategory unless they have completed postgraduate degrees.

There is, however, a substitute for having an advanced degree. You can also qualify if you have a baccalaureate degree followed by five years of work experience in a professional position. Your work experience can be either in the U.S. or abroad. The level of responsibility you exerted and knowledge you gained in that position must have increased progressively over the course of the five years, so make sure any letters you obtain documenting your employment experience also document the fact that your experience was progressively responsible over time.

ii. EB-2: Persons of Exceptional Ability Subcategory

The exceptional ability subcategory of the employment second preference covers people in the sciences, arts, and business. It's easily confused with the employment first preference priority worker subcategory for persons of extraordinary ability described above, but the requirements are slightly less strict. (However, people with jobs in education and athletics are left out of this second preference subcategory.) Typical cases might include economists, lawyers, doctors, veterinarians, physicists, market research analysts, geographers, mental health workers, and marriage and family therapists.

The main benefit of this subcategory is that you don't need to have received international acclaim in your field. Proven sustained national acclaim will meet the required standard. You must, however, still be considered significantly more accomplished than the average person in your profession.

iii. EB-2 Applicants Who Can Use a National Interest Waiver Instead of Labor Certification

If you're applying in the second preference category and your presence will benefit the U.S. in the future, you may be able to apply without having a job offer or labor certification, through what's called a national interest waiver. In order to "benefit" the U.S., you'll have to show that your work in the U.S. will have a favorable impact on its economic, employment, educational, housing, environmental, or cultural situation, or on some other important aspect of U.S. life. The impact must be *national* in scope—in other words, a public health researcher at a federal agency or a university would probably pass, while the same person coming to provide services at a local clinic would probably not.

You'll also have to show that the field in which you'll be working has "substantial intrinsic merit"—in other words, that it's a good thing in and of itself. And you'll need to demonstrate that you will prospectively and uniquely benefit the national interest to a substantially greater degree than would a similarly qualified, available U.S. worker. (Unfortunately, USCIS reinterprets this to mean that you must show that forcing you to go through the labor certification process would have an adverse impact on the U.S. national interest.)

Because the combination of the above criteria is difficult to satisfy, obtaining a national interest waiver is harder than you might expect, and you will want an experienced lawyer's help.

c. Employment Third Preference (EB-3) Category

The third preference category of green cards includes:

- professional workers
- skilled workers, and
- unskilled workers.

You'll need a permanent, full-time job offer and a labor certification under all of its subcategories. (No national interest waiver is available for the third preference.)

You may wonder what difference it makes whether you are classified as a professional worker, skilled worker, or unskilled worker. Indeed, all three categories require labor certifications and draw green cards from the same 40,000 annual allotment.

The answer is that of those 40,000 green cards available each year, only 10,000 are for unskilled workers. Accordingly, those classified as unskilled sometimes have to wait much longer for green cards than workers in the other subcategories, depending on how many other people apply. Anyone who qualifies under the EB-1 or EB-2 category with a job offer would also qualify under the EB-3 category. It's almost always advantageous to apply under EB-1 or EB-2, however, because there is either no wait for the visa or a shorter wait compared to EB-3. If you're not sure you can meet the higher standard of EB-1 or EB-2, you might want to try applying in one of those categories and in the EB-3 category at the same time—though you'll have to file two separate applications with two separate filing fees.

i. EB-3: Professional Workers (Bachelor's Degree) Subcategory

Are you a professional? Immigration law is always vague about the definition of this word, stating only that professionals include such occupations as architects, lawyers, physicians, engineers, and teachers. Aside from these examples of "professions," USCIS generally defines professional to mean a person with a university degree working in his or her field of expertise.

If you hold only a bachelor's degree and have fewer than five years of work experience, then you probably fit this category so long as the job you've been offered is one that normally requires a bachelor's degree. As long as you have the necessary degree, proving eligibility in this category is fairly simple.

ii. EB-3: Skilled Workers Subcategory

Workers engaged in occupations that normally do not require college degrees, but do need at least two years of training or experience, qualify in the subcategory of skilled workers. For example, the EB-3 category may be used for some computer and technical workers (not researchers or managers), chefs, construction first-line supervisors, stonemasons, reporters and journalists, graphic designers, and fashion designers. Relevant postsecondary training can be counted as training.

How much experience or training may be necessary for a specific job is not always clear. Your local state labor department office can tell you the exact number of years of education and experience it considers a minimum for the particular job you have been offered. Or you can look it up on the Department of Labor's O*NET OnLine website at http://onetonline.org.

iii. EB-3: Unskilled Workers Subcategory

Any job not falling into one of the subcategories already described goes into the subcategory of unskilled workers. This usually includes occupations requiring less than two years' training or experience. Housekeepers, nannies, janitors, yard workers, nurse's aides, and farm workers are among the likely applicants. Of course, your own qualifications must satisfy whatever requirements the job does normally have, or you will not succeed in getting a green card using this subcategory. For example, if you've been offered a job requiring a one-year vocational training program, you must have completed such a program before you begin working for the sponsoring employer.

d. Employment Fourth Preference (EB-4) Category

This is the fourth category of employment-based workers, also called special immigrants. One of its subcategories is religious workers, which include ministers and religious professionals. The fourth preference also includes various miscellaneous subcategories of people, from former U.S.

government workers to children dependent on the U.S. foster care system. (See Chapter 12 for a full discussion of this category.)

e. Employment Fifth Preference (EB-5) Category

This employment category is for investors willing to invest a minimum of $500,000 to $1,000,000 in a new U.S. business that will create at least ten full-time jobs for U.S. workers. The minimum amount depends on the location of the enterprise. (See Chapter 11 for a full discussion of the employment fifth preference category.)

2. Do You Have a Job Offer From a U.S. Employer?

You usually need a specific job offer from a U.S. employer in order to get a green card through employment.

TIP

Two groups of people don't need job offers. The first includes people who can qualify as workers of extraordinary ability. This is a small subgroup of the first preference *priority workers* category. The second exception is for workers with advanced degrees or exceptional ability whose work is in the national interest. Both categories are described earlier in this chapter.

The employer who offers you a job may be a company or an institution, organization, or individual located in the United States. If you yourself own a U.S. business, you cannot act as your own employer to get yourself a green card unless you are applying as an investor under the fifth preference category.

If you have an agent who books your talents for a variety of jobs, as is common in the entertainment industry, the agent may also be the source of your job offer. For an agent to act as if he or she were your employer, you must receive your salary directly from the agent.

TIP

What's the reason behind the job offer requirement? Many people are surprised to learn that they need a job offer *before* applying for a green card. The idea behind it is that you are getting a green card only because your U.S. employer could not fill the position with a U.S. worker. Put another way, the U.S. government is issuing a green card not for your benefit, but to help a U.S. company or institution.

Unless you're already working for a U.S. employer on some kind of temporary visa and that employer wants to make you permanent, finding an employer willing to offer you a job may be the hardest part of the process. Employers who might consider hiring you probably realize—or quickly will find out—that before you can start work, they must spend a lot of time, money, and effort to help get you a green card. The application process includes something called labor certification, during which the employer must prove that no qualified U.S. workers are available to take the job being offered to you. The employer will also need to assemble or produce numerous other documents, including company financial records and tax returns.

Your prospective employer should also have the patience to wait, because unless you already have a nonimmigrant work visa or some other kind of employment authorization, you cannot legally start the job until your green card application is approved. This can take anywhere from several months to several years, depending on your qualifications and nationality. However, when a potential employer badly needs your skills, it will usually cooperate with the various requirements.

3. Do You Have the Correct Background?

You must have the correct background in terms of experience, training, and education for the job you have been offered. For example, if you are a qualified nuclear scientist, but are offered a job managing a U.S. bakery, you cannot use that job offer to get a green card, because you have no background in bakery management. It is irrelevant that your native intelligence and general knowledge of business may make you quite capable of handling the bakery job. Likewise, reliability, honesty, or willingness to work hard—characteristics that are much in demand by real-world employers—will not help you in the eyes of USCIS. A match between your background and the job is the main concern.

Also, it's important that you got the experience or education before you started work with the sponsoring U.S. employer. USCIS takes the position that if the employer hired you with lesser experience or education and allowed you to acquire more experience or education later, then U.S. workers should have that same chance.

Your employer cannot, on the other hand, simply write a job offer that pulls in all your unusual qualifications, and thereby eliminate other candidates from the running.

For example, if the employer hopes to hire you as an art therapist, but claims that you must also have expertise in Renaissance art history, the DOL is likely to suspect that the employer has gone too far. In fact, unless the employer can give a good reason based on business necessity, the stated job requirements must be those normally required for the occupation and cannot exceed a measurement known as the Specific Vocational Preparation level, found in the government's O*NET Job Zones database, available online at http://onetonline. org. (See 20 C.F.R. § 656.17(h).) In line with these requirements, the employer must not have hired workers with less training or experience for jobs substantially comparable to that involved in your job opportunity. (See 20 C.F.R. § 656.17(i)(2).)

What to Tell Your Potential Employer

When you are trying to find a U.S. job, it may help if you can assure the employer that he or she is taking limited legal risks by participating in your green card application. While the employer must pay for the labor certification, it assumes absolutely no financial responsibility for you during the application process or after you enter the U.S. After you begin work, the employer must pay you the market wage for the position during the time you are actually employed.

The employer also has the right to withdraw its petition for your green card for any reason and at any time. Once you receive a green card and begin working, your employer is free to fire you at will.

Prospective employers will be asked to supply business and financial records to USCIS. Many are afraid to do this. You can reassure them by explaining that USCIS checks these records for the main purpose of proving that the business has enough money to pay your salary, not to report its findings to other federal agencies.

Employers often tag special requirements onto the job description to help the applicant get a green card—the most common being a foreign language requirement. Unfortunately, the U.S. government knows that employers will use such a requirement for the singular purpose of excluding U.S. applicants. As a result, the regulations specifically say that a language requirement cannot be included in the job description unless it is justified by business necessity. (See 20 C.F.R. § 656.17(h)(2).) The situation is not hopeless, however. An employer can show business necessity for a foreign language requirement based upon such factors as the nature of the job (a translator's job, for instance) or a demonstrable need to communicate with a large majority of the employer's customers, contractors, or employees.

4. Is Your Employer Unable to Find Qualified U.S. Workers for the Job?

Politicians in the U.S. are under a lot of pressure to show that they aren't giving away green cards to foreigners who take jobs away from U.S. citizens. To help relieve the pressure, the law requires most employers wanting to get a green card for a foreign worker to complete a process called labor certification. (Certain types of jobs, however, are considered so desperately in need of workers that labor certifications will not be required—see Section 5, below, for these "Schedule A" jobs.)

Labor certification involves proving to the U.S. Department of Labor (DOL) that there are no able, qualified U.S. workers available and willing to take the job you have been offered, in the region where the job is offered. This is not an abstract requirement.

Your prospective employer will have to advertise the job and conduct interviews. If your employer finds someone who fits the job requirements (even if the employer doesn't actually give that person the job), you won't be granted labor certification.

Even if you're better than all the other applicants, that won't be enough. If your employer finds a U.S. worker who simply meets the minimum qualifications for the job, that may push you out of the running for a green card. Also, if the U.S. worker can acquire the skills necessary to perform the job during a reasonable period of on-the-job training, that's enough to qualify him or her. (See 20 C.F.R. § 656.17(g)(2).)

If you're a college professor or a person of exceptional ability in the arts and sciences, getting a green card through employment is a little easier. It will be enough for you to show that you're *more qualified* than any suitable U.S. college and university faculty applicants, even if you're not the only one available. This difference may seem small, but since it normally takes only one minimally qualified U.S. job applicant to ruin a person's chances for a green card, it could make all the difference in the world.

Believe it or not, there are a fair number of jobs where the employer cannot find a minimally qualified U.S. worker to fill the position; that may be why the employer would be willing to help you get a green card in the first place. How much competition you have depends on what kind of job it is and where the job is located. For example, in some remote parts of the United States, employers have trouble attracting anyone to work there, while you'd probably face a lot of competition in a major city like New York or San Francisco.

Jobs that typically make successful opportunities for green card applications are those requiring workers with a college education, special knowledge, or unusual skills. Unskilled jobs that have odd working hours or other undesirable factors are also good possibilities for green card applicants.

5. Schedule A Jobs: No Formal Labor Certification Required

The U.S. Labor Department keeps track of types of jobs for which U.S. workers are in short supply. It regularly publishes a list of these jobs, called Schedule A. If the type of job you've been offered is on Schedule A, that means your employer can avoid going through the whole labor certification procedure to test the market for the availability of U.S. workers. Your employer will, however, still need to obtain a prevailing wage determination from the DOL. The employer must electronically submit DOL Form 9141, called a prevailing wage request (PWR), to the U.S. Department of Labor through its iCert Web portal at http://icert.doleta.gov.

Note that Schedule A is not a separate green card category. You still have to fit within one of the five employment preferences listed above. However, even if you'll be applying within a category that normally requires labor certification, the idea is that your employer can skip this step, because shortages of such workers are already a recognized fact.

The Schedule A list is not permanent. It changes as U.S. labor needs change. Below are the occupations presently on the Schedule A list. To check the latest version of Schedule A yourself, see 20 C.F.R. § 656.5.

a. Group I: Certain Medical Occupations

The first part of Schedule A, called Group I, covers only people in medical jobs. Those currently on the list include:

- **Physical therapists.** You must be qualified for a license in the state where you intend to practice, but you need not be licensed already.
- **Professional nurses.** This includes only registered nurses. Licensed practical nurses do not qualify. You must have either received the Commission on Graduates of Foreign Nursing Schools (CGFNS) certification or passed the National Council Licensure Examination for Registered Nurses (NCLEX-RN), which is administered by the National Council of State

Boards of Nursing. Alternatively, you qualify for Schedule A if you are licensed by the U.S. state in which you intend to practice.

b. Group II: People With Exceptional Ability in Arts or Sciences

The second part of Schedule A, called Group II, covers only people with exceptional ability in the arts or sciences. It is difficult to qualify in this category. Instead of just matching an entry on a list of jobs, you must prove that you are internationally recognized for your outstanding, well-above-standard work in the arts or sciences. You must also show that you have been practicing your science or art for at least the year prior to your application and intend to continue practicing it in the United States.

The category specifically includes college or university teachers. Other likely candidates under this category are internationally famous scientists, writers, or fine artists, such as painters and sculptors. Performing artists may also qualify if their work during the past 12 months required exceptional ability and their intended work in the United States will also require such ability.

If you try to avoid labor certification by applying under Group II, your employer must submit extensive supporting documentation proving your qualifications.

B. Quick View of the Application Process

Once you've received a suitable job offer (if you need one under your green card category), getting a green card through labor certification is a multistage process, involving these steps:

- Your employer requests what's called a prevailing wage determination (PWD) from the U.S. Department of Labor, using the Internet-based iCert system. The PWD is the Department of Labor's formal ruling as to how much money is normally paid to people in jobs like the one you've been offered. The PWD will typically expire within a year or less, so it will be important to recruit for and file the PERM labor certification soon after the PWD is issued.
- Your employer advertises and recruits for the job you've been offered and ultimately determines that there are no qualified U.S. workers available to take the job.
- Your employer files a PERM labor certification application over the Internet, using the electronic ETA Form 9089.
- You wait the several months that the DOL will take to adjudicate the PERM labor certification application. (This time frame can extend to over two years if the DOL chooses your PERM application for audit.)
- Within 180 days of the PERM labor certification approval, your employer

files a visa petition using USCIS Form I-140.
- If you're applying under a category with a backlog such that a visa is not immediately available, then after USCIS approves the petition, you wait until your Priority Date becomes current and a visa is available.
- You file a green card application using USCIS Form I-485, in connection with which you may attend an interview, either at a U.S. consulate outside of the U.S. or at a USCIS office within the United States.
- If your interview is at a consulate, you enter the U.S. with your immigrant visa, at which time you become a permanent resident.

If you qualify for an immigrant visa category that does not require labor certification, then you will not need to follow many of the steps outlined above. You or your employer will simply file the USCIS Form I-140 immigrant petition directly with USCIS. If you're already in the U.S. and eligible to adjust your status, you can likely file your I-140 petitions at the same time as a Form I-485 green card application. If you can't or don't want to file the I-140 and I-485 together, you'll need to wait until the I-140 is approved, then either file an I-485 with USCIS (if you are eligible to do so) or await instructions from the National Visa Center to prepare you for a visa interview at a U.S. embassy abroad.

! CAUTION
These application procedures were changed dramatically in 2005. In an effort to streamline the process of applying for a green card based on work, DOL issued regulations changing the application form, the recruiting requirements, and many other parts of the process. These regulations are popularly called PERM, although their official name is Labor Certification for the Permanent Employment of Aliens in the United States. Don't rely on advice from fellow immigrants who went through this process before 2005 or on written materials published before that date.

If you're married or have children below the age of 21 and you qualify for a green card through employment, your spouse and children can get green cards as accompanying relatives by providing proof of their family relationship to you. They must also, like any intending immigrant, prove that they are not inadmissible to the United States. (See Chapter 3 for details on the kinds of things that might make your relative inadmissible.)

C. Step One: The Prevailing Wage Determination

Before your employer starts the immigration application process for you, it must make sure that the salary or wages it plans to pay you are normal for the local job market. The purpose is to make sure that hiring low-cost immigrant labor doesn't weaken the wages and working conditions of U.S. workers.

To find this out, the employer must electronically submit DOL Form 9141, called a prevailing wage request (PWR), to the U.S. Department of Labor through its iCert Web portal at http://icert.doleta.gov. The DOL's prevailing wage determination (the PWD) will tell the employer how much is normally paid to people in jobs equivalent to the one you've been offered. The DOL will use its Occupational Employment Statistics (OES) program to determine the wage, or the employer can request that an alternative wage source be used.

Finding out the prevailing wage is important, because your employer must offer at least this amount in the labor certification. Even if your employer is offering a wage the DOL would find appropriate, a PERM labor certification application can be denied if the DOL learns that no PWD was issued.

D. Step Two: Employer Advertising and Recruitment

Next, your employer can begin recruiting for the job. (Actually, your employer can start recruiting before this, but must be especially careful to offer a salary that's at least as high as the prevailing wage. Otherwise, you may have to start again if the PWD reveals a wage you did not expect.)

The prevailing wage determination is valid for at least 90 days but no longer than one year. Your employer must begin recruitment while the determination is still valid, so take careful note of the PWD validity period after it's issued.

CAUTION

For you to get a green card, your employer must make a good-faith effort to find a U.S. worker. If its search uncovers one who is suited for the job and willing to accept it, the government will not approve your green card—even if you are the employer's first choice. The employer must make an honest effort at advertising and interviewing for the job. If the DOL suspects any funny business, it may insist on directly supervising additional recruitment efforts by your employer. (See 20 C.F.R. § 656.21(a).) Not only are supervised recruitment procedures expensive, due to the lengthy print advertisements which must be run in the newspapers, but they markedly increase the chance of a denial.

The necessary types of advertising depend first on whether you are applying for a professional or a nonprofessional job. Also, there are special requirements for college or university teachers selected under what's known as a competitive recruitment and selection process. (Your employer should see 20 C.F.R. § 656.18 for rules relating to professors.)

1. Recruiting Requirements for Nonprofessional Jobs

If the application is for a nonprofessional job, your employer must, at a minimum, place a job order with the State Workforce Agency (SWA) of the state in which the job is located, post a physical job notice at the worksite, and publish two newspaper advertisements. These steps must be conducted at least 30 days but no more than six months before the employer files the labor certification application.

Placing a job order with an SWA requires no fee, and minimal effort from the employer. First, the SWA will enter a description of the position, identified by the job order number, in its statewide computer bank. For 30 days, anyone throughout the state who contacts the state labor department will have an opportunity to apply for the job. The state will collect the applications and résumés and forward them to the employer.

Your employer must post a job notice at the worksite where you will be working and leave it there for ten consecutive business days, excluding weekends and federal holidays. The posting must be in a conspicuous location that other workers are likely to see, such as a break room or near the other legal notices that employers must post (such as workers' compensation notices). The notice must contain a full description of the job and identical information to what was presented in the labor certification. Also, the notice must give instructions on how to make a complaint to the Department of Labor regarding the labor certification. The employer must sign and date the notice at the end of the posting period, and then place it in its PERM compliance file.

The employer must carefully choose the newspaper in which to advertise. The government requires that the ads appear on two different Sundays in a newspaper of general circulation, which workers likely to apply for the job would be expected to read in an appropriate geographic area. If the job is located in a rural area with no Sunday paper, the employer may publish on whatever day has the widest circulation. Generally speaking, though, your employer should choose the largest newspaper in your metropolitan region. For example, if you live in a suburb some miles outside a major city like New York or Los Angeles, your employer should still choose *The New York Times* or the *Los Angeles Times*.

For exactly what information should go into the advertisements, the employer should see 20 C.F.R. § 656.17(f), which sets the requirements out quite clearly. An important point is that an ad may not state wages or terms and conditions of employment worse than those being offered to you. In other words, if the employer hopes to turn people away by announcing that the job will require

regularly taking a night shift, but the employer doesn't really plan to make you work the night shift, the government will consider that ad insufficient.

2. Recruiting Requirements for Professional Jobs

If the job you've been offered is for a professional (someone with experience and an advanced degree), then your employer must start by following the three steps required for nonprofessionals (a job order, an internal posting notice, and two print ads). However, instead of one of the Sunday advertisements ordinarily required, the employer can, if a professional journal normally would be used to advertise the job, place one advertisement in the professional journal most likely to bring responses from able, willing, qualified, and available U.S. workers.

In addition, employers recruiting for professional workers must conduct three additional steps chosen from a list published in the regulation. The list includes recruitment through: (1) job fairs; (2) the employer's website; (3) a job search website other than the employer's, which can include a Web page created by the same publisher to which the employer submitted a print ad; (4) on-campus recruiting; (5) trade or professional organizations, for example via their newsletters or trade journals; (6) private employment firms or placement agencies; (7) an employee referral program, if it includes specific incentives; (8) a notice of the job opening at a campus placement office, if the job requires a degree but no experience; (9) local and ethnic newspapers, so long as they're appropriate for the job opportunity; and (10) radio and television advertisements. (See 20 C.F.R. § 656.17(e)(ii).)

All recruiting must be completed before your employer submits any part of the actual request for labor certification.

3. Handling Job Applications

If anyone applies for the job, the employer must then review the résumés. If a candidate does not meet the minimum qualifications for the job as described in the labor certification, the employer need not interview that person. Even if a single requested qualification is missing from the résumé, that's enough reason for the employer to reject a U.S. job candidate in favor of you, if the employer wishes to do so.

However, when some acceptable résumés do turn up, the employer must interview those people within a reasonable time. (It's best to contact them within ten days of their application being submitted.) Neither you nor your attorney is permitted to attend these interviews. (20 C.F.R. § 656.10 (b)(2).)

During the interview, the employer must determine whether there are lawful grounds on which to reject the candidate. See "Lawful Grounds to Reject a Job Candidate," below.

After the interviews, the employer will hopefully still be unsatisfied and wish to employ you. If so, your employer must prepare what's called a recruitment report. (See 20 C.F.R. § 656.17(g).) The report must describe the recruitment steps undertaken, the results achieved, the number of hires, and, if applicable, the number of U.S. workers rejected, categorized by the lawful job-related reasons for such rejections. The employer must sign the report and keep it on file with all the applicants' résumés for a period of five years. The DOL may at some point audit the case and ask to see the recruitment report, all forms of recruitment, and all the résumés.

Your employer must complete all recruiting before submitting the labor certification to DOL.

E. Step Three: Your Employer Seeks Labor Certification

If, after the recruiting has been completed, your employer hasn't found a qualified, willing, available, and able U.S. worker to take the job, it can submit what's called a labor certification application to DOL. An application for labor certification can be filed only by your U.S. employer, not by you on your own. The purpose of labor certification is to satisfy the U.S. government that there are no qualified U.S. workers available

Lawful Grounds to Reject a Job Candidate

The following are the lawful, job-related reasons based on which an employer may reject U.S. applicants for an open position:

- Applicant is not a U.S. worker.
- Applicant did not have the minimum educational requirements for the position as stated in the labor certification application.
- Applicant did not have minimum experience requirements of the position as stated in the labor certification application.
- Applicant did not have the special skills required for the position.
- Applicant failed to attend a scheduled interview or respond to an interview letter.
- Applicant failed to document experience or education, when such documentation is required as a normal hiring policy.

- Applicant was offered the position, but was unavailable.
- Applicant was offered the position, but was not interested.
- Applicant refused to take a proficiency test or performed poorly on such a test, when taking the test was stated by the employer as a requirement in the labor certification application/recruitment and that the alien was required to take the exam when initially hired.
- Applicant had poor work references or failure to provide prospective references.
- Applicant was referred by an agency requiring a fee, where the employer has a policy not to pay agency fees.
- Applicant is unable to perform the stated job duties listed in the job description.

and willing to take the specific job that has been offered to you.

Employment first preference priority workers and those with occupations appearing on Schedule A do not have to go through the labor certification procedures. Their employers may move directly to the visa petition step described in Section F, below. Still, they'll have to prove that they're allowed to skip labor certification, by providing forms and documents showing that you qualify either as a priority worker or for Schedule A.

In order to apply for labor certification, your employer must complete a ten-page

form (ETA-9089), available at www. foreignlaborcert.doleta.gov. The form can be submitted either online or by mail, but DOL prefers online submissions, and this preference reveals itself in how the PERM application is handled.

To gain greater speed in processing and greater certainty in tracking the case, your employer should make every attempt to file the PERM application online, rather than through the mail. (If the PERM application is submitted online, you and your employer must make sure to sign it as soon as it receives approval, and to file the Form I-140 immigrant petition with USCIS within 180 days of this approval.) Many of the questions on the form ask for simple yes or no answers.

Your employer will not be required to submit any documentation with the ETA-9089 at the time of filing. However, your employer is expected to keep the supporting documentation on hand, in case its application is selected for audit. If your application is selected for an audit—that is, a full review by the U.S. Department of Labor—it may either be because something in your paperwork looked suspicious, or it may simply be that your application was randomly selected. The DOL has stated that its goal is to audit 10%–20% of all PERM applications submitted within a given year, so you should not be surprised (or conclude that anything was done "wrong") if your case is selected for audit.

No fee is required with the labor certification application, although a fee might be added in the future.

The Department of Labor can take several months to adjudicate your PERM application, depending upon its current workload. In the past, processing times have ranged from as little as a month to almost a year. When the current edition of this book was published, the processing time was about five months, and ten months if the case was selected for audit.

If all goes well, the labor certification will eventually be approved. Be aware, however, that an approved labor certification does

not, by itself, give you any right to live or work in the U.S. It is only a prerequisite to submitting the petition and application for a green card, and it helps hold your place in line if there's a waiting list. If the labor certification is denied, your employer has 30 days in which to request reconsideration.

F. Step Four: Your Employer Files the Visa Petition

At last, your U.S. employer can approach the U.S. immigration authorities, by filing what's called an immigrant visa petition on USCIS Form I-140. It must do so before the approved labor certification expires, that is, within 180 days of approval. During this part of the process, your employer is known as your "petitioner," and you are the "beneficiary." In a few rare cases, you yourself can file the petition (and become your own petitioner), but only if your skills are so high level that you don't need a job offer to immigrate through employment—more specifically, if you either:

- have extraordinary ability in the sciences, arts, education, business, or athletics (a subcategory of the first preference category described earlier), or
- are a professional holding an advanced degree, or have exceptional ability in the sciences, arts, or business, and you're claiming that you qualify for a national interest

Checklist of Labor Certification Documents

Below are the documents your employer must keep on hand in case of an audit after submitting Form ETA-9089.

☐ The original signed version of the certified ETA-9089 (that is, the approved labor certification).

☐ Documents justifying any unusual or restrictive job requirements, including foreign language abilities.

☐ Copies of all advertisements and other recruitment-related documents, such as notices of on-campus recruitment or contracts with a private recruiting firm. If your employer uses a website as a recruitment medium, the employer should print out dated copies of the relevant pages. If your employer uses radio or television to advertise, this can be documented with a copy of the employer's text of the employer's advertisement along with a written confirmation from the radio or TV station stating when the ad was aired.

☐ Evidence that notice was provided to the bargaining representative of the employer's employees, if any, or that the job opportunity was posted conspicuously at the employer's workplace.

☐ Recruitment report from the employer of advertising results saying why each U.S. job candidate was turned down.

☐ Any additional documents required for special cases, such as sheepherders, live-in domestics, physicians, or college and university teachers.

waiver (a subcategory of the second preference category described earlier).

Form I-140 is available at www.uscis.gov/i-140—and it comes with extensive instructions. Read them. The object of the petition is to prove that you qualify for the job as it is described in the labor certification or that you meet the requirements to file without the approved labor certification. Also, the employer must show that it has the financial ability to pay your wage.

The form also takes care of some other details, like informing USCIS whether you will be continuing with your immigrant visa application through a consulate outside of the U.S. or through a U.S.-based USCIS office. If you are already lawfully present within the United States, and qualify to do so, you will most likely want to select the option for going through a U.S.-based USCIS office.

Form I-140 also provides space to list your spouse and children. Be sure your employer doesn't leave anyone off the list, even if that person doesn't want to immigrate now. USCIS wants to know about all your family members now, and if someone who wasn't on the list decides to immigrate later, you may have trouble convincing USCIS that he or she is really a member of your family.

The following checklist will help you keep track of all the forms and documents that you and your employer will need to collect and prepare in order to file the visa petition.

Checklist of Forms and Documents for Visa Petition

Your employer will need to assemble the following:

☐ Form I-140.

☐ Fee (currently $700).

☐ Approved labor certification or evidence of qualifying as a priority worker of extraordinary ability (EB-1), or as a Schedule A worker or someone who should be granted a National Interest Waiver under the second preference category (EB-2).

☐ Evidence that your employer can actually pay the wage it's offering you. Your employer must supply such evidence as federal tax returns, annual reports, or audited financial statements. This is to show that the company's net income or net current assets are equal to or greater than the offered wage. Alternatively, you may use your W-2 forms and pay stubs generated since the PERM application was first filed, in order to demonstrate that your employer has already been paying you the required wage (which, if you think about it, is the most obvious way to demonstrate your employer's ability to pay).

☐ Evidence that you have the education necessary to perform your job, such as diplomas and transcripts from colleges or universities. Include credential evaluations if you have a foreign (non-U.S.) degree.

☐ Evidence that you have the training or experience necessary to perform your job, such as professional certificates or letters proving previous job experience.

☐ If requesting quick (premium) processing: Form I-907, with filing fee (currently $1,225).

If Applying as a Priority Worker (EB-1):

In the persons of extraordinary ability subcategory (EB-1A):

☐ Evidence that you have either received a major, internationally recognized award (like a Nobel or an Oscar), or at least three of the following:

  ☐ Evidence you have received several lesser nationally or internationally recognized prizes or awards in your field.

  ☐ Documentation of membership in associations that require outstanding achievements of their members, as recognized by national or international experts.

  ☐ Published material about you in professional or major trade publications or other major media relating to your work.

  ☐ Evidence of your participation as a judge of the work of others in your field or an allied field.

  ☐ Evidence of your original scientific, scholarly, artistic, athletic, or business-related contributions of major significance in your field.

  ☐ Evidence of your authorship (or coauthorship, though this carries less weight) of scholarly articles in professional or major trade publications or other major media.

  ☐ Evidence of the display of your work at artistic exhibitions or showcases.

  ☐ Evidence that you have performed in leading or critical roles for distinguished organizations or establishments.

Checklist of Forms and Documents for Visa Petition (continued)

☐ Evidence that you have commanded a comparatively high salary or other compensation.

☐ Evidence that you have achieved commercial success in the performing arts (box office receipts, evidence of sold-out clubs, concert halls, arenas, or stadiums, or sales data on your recordings or videos).

☐ If the above do not fit your occupation, comparable evidence.

☐ Copy of your U.S. employment contract, an employer letter, or your statement explaining how you will continue your extraordinary work in the U.S..

In the outstanding professor and researcher subcategory (EB-1B):

☐ At least two of the following:

☐ Evidence that you have received major prizes or awards for outstanding achievement in your academic field.

☐ Evidence of your membership in associations in your academic field—associations that require outstanding achievements for membership.

☐ Published material in professional publications written by others about your work. Mere citations to your work in bibliographies are not sufficient.

☐ Evidence of your participation as a judge of the work of others in the same or an allied field.

☐ Evidence of your original scientific or scholarly research contributions to the academic field.

☐ Evidence of your authorship of scholarly books or articles in scholarly journals having international circulation.

☐ Evidence that you have at least three years of teaching or research experience in your field (such as letters from former employers).

☐ If it is a university position, a letter or contract from the university stating that the U.S. position is either a tenured, tenure track, or permanent researcher position.

☐ If the employer is in private industry, evidence that it has a history of significant achievements in research, employs at least three other full-time research workers, and intends to hire you for a permanent research position.

In the multinational managers and executives subcategory (EB-1C):

☐ Notice of approval of an L-1 visa petition, if any (recommended, not required).

☐ Documents proving employment as an executive or manager with the parent company for at least one of the past three years outside of the U.S. (or, if you're already in the U.S., for one of the three years before you arrived).

☐ Documents proving that you will be working in an executive or managerial capacity, including a description of your duties.

☐ Photographs of the foreign and U.S. offices.

☐ Organizational charts for both the foreign and U.S. companies.

☐ Accountant's financial statements, including profit and loss statements, and balance sheets of both the U.S. and foreign company for the past two years.

☐ Payroll records of the foreign company for the past two years, if available.

☐ Promotional literature describing the nature of the employer's business, both U.S. and foreign.

Checklist of Forms and Documents for Visa Petition (continued)

☐ Copy of the business lease or deed for the premises of the U.S. business.

☐ Documents proving that your U.S. employer is either the same legal entity or in an affiliate or subsidiary relationship with your overseas employer, and has been doing business for at least a year, including such documents as:

    ☐ Articles of incorporation or other legal charter or business license of the foreign business.

    ☐ Articles of incorporation or other legal charter or business license of the U.S. business.

    ☐ Legal business registration certificate of the foreign business.

    ☐ Legal business registration certificate of the U.S. business.

    ☐ Tax returns of the foreign business for the past two years, if available.

    ☐ Tax returns of the U.S. business for the past two years, if available.

    ☐ If the company is publicly held, annual shareholder reports of both the U.S. and foreign companies.

    ☐ If either company is publicly held, statements from the secretary of the corporation attesting to how the companies are related.

    ☐ For private companies, copies of all outstanding stock certificates.

    ☐ For private companies, notarized affidavits from the corporations' secretaries verifying the names of the officers and directors.

    ☐ For private companies, copies of the minutes of shareholder meetings appointing the officers and directors.

    ☐ If a joint venture, copy of the joint venture agreement.

If Applying as a Second-Preference Worker (EB-2):

If you are a second-preference applicant filing your own visa petition based on a requested national interest waiver of the job offer and labor certification requirements:

☐ Written statement, support letters from colleagues and experts in your field, and other documentation explaining why an exemption from the job requirement is in the U.S. national interest.

If you are the holder of an advanced degree (EB-2A):

☐ An official academic record, showing that you have either a U.S. advanced degree or an equivalent foreign degree, or a U.S. baccalaureate (B.A.) or equivalent foreign degree together with letters from your current or former employers showing that you have at least five years of progressive postbaccalaureate experience in your specialty.

In the professional of exceptional ability in the sciences, arts, or business subcategory (EB-2B):

☐ At least three of the following:

    ☐ Evidence that you have an academic degree, diploma, certificate, or similar award from an institution of learning relating to your area of exceptional ability.

    ☐ Evidence that you have at least ten years of full-time experience in your field (letters from current or former employers).

    ☐ A license or certification to practice your profession.

    ☐ Evidence that you have commanded a comparatively high salary or other compensation.

Checklist of Forms and Documents for Visa Petition (continued)

☐ Evidence of your membership in professional associations.

☐ Evidence of your recognition for achievements and significant contributions to your industry or field. This recognition should come from your peers, governmental entities, or professional or business organizations.

☐ If none of the above types of evidence fits your occupation, submit comparable evidence of your eligibility.

If Applying as a Third-Preference Worker (EB-3):

In the professional workers subcategory (EB-3A):

☐ Evidence that you have a U.S. baccalaureate (B.A.) degree or equivalent foreign degree.

☐ Evidence that a B.A. is required for your job.

In the skilled worker subcategory (EB-3B):

☐ Evidence that you meet the educational requirements, and the minimum two years' training or experience requirements for the job.

In the unskilled worker subcategory (EB-3C):

☐ Evidence that you meet any educational, training, or experience requirements of the job.

IF YOU DID NOT SEEK A LABOR CERTIFICATION BECAUSE YOU'VE BEEN OFFERED A SCHEDULE A JOB:

☐ An original and one copy of Application for Permanent Employment Certification (Form ETA-9089), including a prevailing wage determination from the SWA. The form need not be certified, but must be signed by an authorized official of the petitioning company.

☐ Evidence of compliance with the posting/union notification requirements, including a copy of the posted notice and of any in-house postings via electronic or other media.

Group I: Medical Occupations:

☐ Evidence that notice of filing the Application for Permanent Employment Certification was provided to the bargaining representative of the employer's employees.

Physical Therapists (subcategory of Group I):
Either:

☐ Copy of a U.S. state physical therapist license, or

☐ Letter from the state physical therapy licensing agency stating that you meet all the qualifications to sit for the state exam.

Registered Nurses (subcategory of Group I):
Either:

☐ Copy of a full and unrestricted state nursing license to practice in the state where you will be employed

☐ Copy of your certificate from the Commission on Graduates of Foreign Nursing Schools (CGFNS), or

☐ Evidence that you have passed the National Council Licensure Examination for Registered Nurses (NCLEX-RN).

Group II: Exceptional Ability in the Arts or Sciences:

☐ Documentary evidence showing the widespread acclaim and international recognition accorded you by recognized experts in your field.

☐ Documentation showing that your work in your artistic or scientific field during the past year did, and your intended work in the United States will, require exceptional ability.

Checklist of Forms and Documents for Visa Petition (continued)

☐ At least two of the following:

☐ Documents proving that you have won internationally recognized prizes or awards in your field of work.

☐ Documents showing membership in selective international associations—associations that require outstanding achievement of their members, as judged by recognized international experts.

☐ Articles about your work appearing in relevant professional publications, including the title, date, and author of such published material.

☐ Documents proving that you have acted as a judge in international competitions in your field or an allied field.

☐ Evidence of your original scientific or scholarly research contributions, which were of major significance in your field.

☐ Copies of scientific or academic articles by you that have been published in international journals (including professional journals with international circulation).

☐ Documents proving that your artistic work has been exhibited in at least two different countries.

Performing artists must additionally provide:

☐ Documentary evidence that your work experience during the past 12 months did require, and your intended work in the United States will require, exceptional ability, such as:

☐ Documentation showing your current widespread acclaim and international recognition, and your receipt of internationally recognized prizes or awards for excellence.

☐ Published material by or about you, such as critical reviews or articles in major newspapers, periodicals, and/or trade journals (including the title, date, and author of such material).

☐ Documentary evidence that your earnings have been commensurate with your claimed level of ability.

☐ Playbills and star billings.

☐ Documents showing the outstanding reputation of the theaters, concert halls, night clubs, and other establishments in which you've appeared or are scheduled to appear.

☐ Documents showing the outstanding reputation of theaters or repertory companies, ballet troupes, orchestras, or other organizations in which or with which you've performed during the past year in a leading or starring capacity.

1. Submitting the Visa Petition

Your employer must submit the immigrant visa petition—Form I-140, accompanying documents, and the fee—to the USCIS Lockbox or, if you're using Premium Processing, to a USCIS regional service center that serves your employer's place of business. The USCIS website at www. uscis.gov/i-140 provides the proper address and P.O. box number.

If you are in the United States, and you have maintained valid nonimmigrant visa status, you may be able to file your green card application (Form I-485, described in Section H, below) at the same time, or concurrently, with your employer's visa petition. But you can do so only if a visa is already available in your category, as described in Section G, below. Concurrent filing offers many advantages, including giving you the right to stay in the U.S. while the application is pending (useful if your temporary visa has expired or is due to expire soon) and the right to apply for work permits for you and your immediate family members. Unfortunately, the possibility of concurrent filing is not available to everyone, as the waits for green cards in some categories have recently stretched to many months and years long.

2. Awaiting USCIS Approval of the Visa Petition

Within a few weeks after mailing the petition, your employer should receive a written confirmation that the papers are being processed, together with a receipt for the fees. This notice will also contain your case file number. If USCIS wants further information before acting on your case, it will send your employer a request for evidence (RFE). The RFE tells your employer what corrections, additional pieces of information, or additional documents are expected. Your employer should make the corrections or supply the extra data and mail them back to the USCIS regional service center with the request form on top. The approval can take several months. (See Chapter 4 for how to track the length of time USCIS is taking to decide on visa petitions and how to track your own application online.)

TIP
Faster processing—at a price. For $1,225 over and above the regular filing fees, USCIS promises "premium processing" of the visa petition, including a decision within 15 days. Currently, premium processing is available for I-140 petitions in most immigrant visa categories. You need not request premium processing at the time you first file the Form I-140, but can "upgrade" to premium processing later if your I-140 is still pending and you are getting impatient for a decision. To use the premium processing service, the employer must fill out an additional application (Form I-907) and submit the application to a special USCIS Service Center address. For complete instructions, see the USCIS website at www.uscis.gov/i-907.

The filing procedure is the same for all work-based green card petitions, but your employer must indicate which employment preference and subcategory is being requested. If you are turned down for one category, the petition will not automatically be considered for a lower category. However, your employer may always submit a new petition under a different employment preference or subcategory. For example, if you have a job offer that might fall under the skilled worker subcategory of the third preference, but you are not sure, consider filing two petitions, one as a skilled worker and another as an unskilled worker. This will save some time if the petition under the higher-level subcategory is turned down.

Once your petition is approved, USCIS will advise your employer using a Notice of Action, on Form I-797. The Notice of Action contains an important piece of information called your "Priority Date," which is used to hold your place in line for a visa if you're applying in a category where there are more applicants than visas available.

If you plan to attend your visa interview at a U.S. consulate abroad, USCIS will forward the file to the National Visa Center (NVC), located in Portsmouth, New Hampshire. The NVC will then send instructions to you so that you may proceed with consular processing, described later in this chapter.

Like the labor certification, an approved petition does not by itself give you any right to immigrate to, or live in, the United States. It is only a prerequisite to the next steps, including submitting your own application for a green card.

G. Step Five: You Might Have to Wait for an Available Visa Number

Because there are annual limits on the number of people who can receive green cards through employment, you might have to wait in line until a visa number becomes available. (You can't get a green card until you're given a visa number, regardless of whether you're coming from outside or inside the United States.) Your place in the line is tracked by your Priority Date (the date on which your employer filed your labor certification or, where formal labor certification is not required, the date your application was filed at USCIS).

Whether you will have to wait, and for how long, depends on the preference category you're in and your country of citizenship. In general, waiting periods tend to be longer for people from China, India, Mexico, and the Philippines, especially for professional and nonskilled workers. This is not because of any discrimination against those countries—it merely reflects the fact that more people from those countries apply for visas than from other countries, and there is a per-country limit. The supply of visas for those countries is regularly less than the number of people applying for them, so a waiting list forms. Persons applying in the EB-2 category, if they are not from India or China, have not experienced any wait in recent years. There is only a short wait currently for EB-3 visas for persons not from China or India, but this short wait has not always been the case, and could change at any time.

Although you can't predict how long you will wait, you can track the progress of your own Priority Date through the system, and get some sense of the rate at which it is moving. If you will be obtaining an immigrant visa at a U.S. consulate, you first need to look at the State Department's monthly *Visa Bulletin*, which lists the Priority Dates of people who are allowed to get visas that month. It's available on a recorded message at 202-663-1541, or at its website at http://travel.state.gov. (Click under "U.S. visas" and then look for the "Visa Bulletin" link in the Law and Policy section.) The State Department updates this chart around the middle of every month, but not on any exact day.

When you look at the *Visa Bulletin*, you'll see two charts. One is called "Dates for Filing of Employment-Based Visa Applications." This tells you how soon you will be allowed to file your application for a visa. The other chart, called "Application Final Action Dates for Employment-Based Preference Cases," tells you how soon the U.S. consulate can actually give you a visa.

Here's how to read a *Visa Bulletin* chart:

1. Locate your preference category in the first column. For example, if you're applying as an unskilled worker, you're in the third preference category, which is the third row down.

2. Locate your country across the top. If you don't see it listed, look in the column called "All Chargeability Areas Except Those Listed."

3. Draw lines across from your preference category and down from your country of origin. The box where your two lines cross is the one containing what's called your visa cutoff date. Sometimes, it contains a letter instead of a date. The letter "C" (for current) is good news—it means that no one needs to wait, and all applicants are immediately eligible for a visa or green card. The letter "U" (for "unavailable") is bad news—it means that all the visas have been used up for that year, and more will not become available until October (when the federal government starts its new fiscal year).

4. If, instead of a letter, your box contains a cutoff date, compare it with your Priority Date. If the cutoff date is the same as your Priority Date, or is even later, great—you can now apply for your visa, or a visa can be given to you. However, if the

June 2016 Application Final Action Date Chart for Employment-Based Visas

Employment based	All Chargeability Areas Except Those Listed	China-mainland born	El Salvador Guatemala Honduras	India	Mexico	Philippines
1st	C	C	C	C	C	C
2nd	C	01JAN10	C	01OCT04	C	C
3rd	15FEB16	01JAN10	15FEB16	22SEP04	15FEB16	01NOV08
Other Workers	15FEB16	22APR07	15FEB16	22SEP04	15FEB16	01NOV08
4th	C	C	01JAN10	C	C	C
Certain Religious Workers	C	C	01JAN10	C	C	C
5th Non-Regional Center (C5 and T5)	C	C	C	C	C	C
5th Regional Center (I5 and R5)	C	15FEB14	C	C	C	C

June 2016 Application Dates for Filing of Employment-Based Visa Applications

Employment based	All Chargeability Areas Except Those Listed	China-mainland born	India	Mexico	Philippines
1st	C	C	C	C	C
2nd	C	01JUN13	01JUL09	C	C
3rd	C	01MAY15	01JUL05	C	01JAN10
Other Workers	C	01AUG09	01JUL05	C	01JAN10
4th	C	C	C	C	C
Certain Religious Workers	C	C	C	C	C
5th Non-Regional Center (C5 and T5)	C	01MAY15	C	C	C
5th Regional Center (I5 and R5)	C	01MAY15	C	C	C

cutoff date is earlier than your Priority Date, you still have to wait—because only people who applied some time before you now have the right to apply for or receive their visa.

EXAMPLE: Parama is a citizen of India, who has been offered a job as a medical researcher in a U.S. pharmaceutical company. This puts her in the second preference visa category. Her employer files a labor certification for her in June of 2016. She immediately checks her Priority Date. As you'll see on the June 2016 chart above, the application final action cutoff date was then October 1, 2004. That means that people from India whose employers filed labor certifications for them on October 1, 2004 (or before that) were finally allowed to receive their immigrant visas in June 2016. Their wait was approximately 12 years— which suggests that Parama may wait a similar length of time.

If you have an approved immigrant visa petition but your Priority Date is not yet current in the "Dates for Filing" chart, you must wait until it is current to take the next step and file your green card (immigrant visa) application. If applying for your green card at a U.S. consulate, the National Visa Center will typically advise you by mail a couple months before your Priority Date is expected to become current (so make sure to notify them of any change of address!).

If you're adjusting status from within the U.S. based on an approved employment-based petition, USCIS won't send you any notice telling you when you can file the adjustment application. You'll have to monitor your situation monthly at www.uscis.gov/visabulletininfo.

USCIS borrows the two charts that appear in the *Visa Bulletin*, and announces which one you should look at to determine whether it's time for you to apply for adjustment. It's not always the Dates for Filing chart—USCIS may tell you to look at the Application Final Action Dates chart instead. If USCIS tells you to use the Dates for Filing chart, you'll be able to file your application sooner than if you had to use the Application Final Action Date chart, but you'll still have to wait for your Priority Date to become current according to the Application Final Action Dates chart to actually receive your green card.

The advantage to you if USCIS tells you that you can use the Dates for Filing chart is that you can submit your application for adjustment sooner, and therefore also apply sooner for U.S. work authorization, if you need it.

If you're in the United States on a temporary work visa, be careful that your status does not expire before your Priority Date becomes current and you can apply for a green card. Possessing an approved immigrant visa petition does not give you any right to live in the United States. If this looks like it might become a problem, consult as soon as possible with an immigration attorney.

H. Step Six: You Submit the Green Card Application

After your visa petition has been approved and your Priority Date has become current according to the appropriate chart, it's time for you to play a more active role in the application process: You'll need to file your application for permanent residence or a green card. (In fact, the timing works a little differently if you're in the U.S. and visa numbers are immediately available in your category. In that case, you don't have to separate the visa petition and green card application steps, because you can file the two concurrently.) If your spouse or children will be accompanying you, they must each file their own visa or adjustment applications.

The most important question at this point is where you file the application—in the United States or at a U.S. consulate in another country. You should have already made this choice on your Form I-140, but you're allowed to change your mind, so it's worth revisiting this question.

If you're living outside of the United States now. The answer is fairly easy for people living outside of the U.S. You must request visa processing at a local U.S. consulate and attend an immigrant visa interview there before entering the United States with your visa. (This method is called consular processing.)

If you're living in the U.S. now. The answer is a bit more complicated for applicants already in the United States. The easiest thing for you would probably be to adjust status without leaving—that is, file your Form I-485 adjustment of status application with USCIS and attend your interview at a local USCIS office. If you're already in the U.S. in lawful status, and eligible to use the adjustment of status procedure, it's a great option. While your Form I-485 application is awaiting a decision, your stay in the United States will be considered legal, and you can apply for permission to work. Should problems arise in your case, you will be able to wait for a decision while you live and work in the U.S., a circumstance most green card applicants prefer. Also, if your application for a green card is turned down, you have greater rights of appeal inside the U.S. than you do at a U.S. consulate.

Not everyone is eligible to adjust status. First, as mentioned before, your Priority Date must be current according to the appropriate *Visa Bulletin* chart. Second, you can't adjust status unless you were "inspected and admitted" by a U.S. immigration officer—in other words, the last time you entered the U.S., you must have done so legally, with a visa or with "parole" (permission from a border officer). And third, just like someone coming into the U.S. from overseas, you must be admissible. (See Chapter 3 for grounds of inadmissibility.)

Even if you meet those basic requirements for adjustment, you won't be able to adjust status based on an employment-based petition, if, as a general rule, you've ever worked in the U.S. without authorization, if you're in the U.S. with no legal status, or if you've ever fallen out of legal status (except if it wasn't your fault). There's an important exception for EB-1, EB-2, EB-3, and EB-4 religious workers—they can still adjust even if they have gone out of status or worked without authorization, so long as the violation did not exceed 180 days.

You can't adjust status if you came to the U.S. without a visa under the Visa Waiver program. (This rule doesn't apply to visa-exempt Canadians.)

An important, but increasingly rare, exception to adjustment of status eligibility requirements exists for people who had an approvable labor certification application filed for them (or for their spouse or parent) before April 30, 2001. Such people, if they are admissible and a green card is immediately available to them, can adjust status by paying an extra $1,000 fee. If the labor certification application was filed after January 14, 1998, they will also have to prove that they were present in the U.S. on December 21, 2000. This provision of law, known as "245(i)" adjustment, is especially helpful for people who came to the U.S. illegally and who cannot leave to get an immigrant visa because they would then be subject to the ten-year reentry bar for unlawful presence.

If you have any doubts about your ability to adjust status, consult with an immigration lawyer. The adjustment application is expensive—you don't want to spend the money to apply and have your application denied outright.

Whether or not you are eligible to adjust status, you may instead decide to leave the United States and apply for your green card at a U.S. consulate abroad. If the consulates are issuing visas more quickly than your local USCIS office is handling adjustment of status applications (which is possible), leaving to apply at a consulate in your home country could be a smart strategic move. However, if you have already spent 180 days or more in the U.S. out of legal status, or crossed the border without inspection, be sure you are not subject to the three-year or ten-year reentry bar before you go. (See Chapter 3.) Otherwise, you could find yourself stuck outside the United States for three or ten years.

1. What Happens When Adjusting Status in the U.S.

The process of adjusting your status to permanent resident involves four steps. First, you prepare a set of forms and documents—one set for you and separate sets for your accompanying spouse and for each of your accompanying children. Second, you mail those packets to USCIS. Third, you wait for some weeks or months until USCIS calls you and your family members in to have your fingerprints taken. Fourth, you wait weeks or months longer until USCIS finally either calls you and your family members in for your final green card interview at a local USCIS office or approves you without an interview.

If you are called in to your local USCIS office for an interview, you should be approved for your green card at that time or soon afterward. See Chapter 4 for information on tracking the progress of your application.

CAUTION
Remember, you may not apply to adjust status until you have an approved labor certification and your Priority Date is current according to the chart USCIS directs you to look at. You must also be eligible to adjust status in the U.S.—(see discussion above).

Dealing With Delays in Approval of Your Work Authorization

If you want to work before your application for a green card is approved, you must file a separate application for employment authorization (an "EAD"). To do so, fill out Form I-765 and file it with your Form I-485 adjustment of status application.

Legally, USCIS does not have to make a decision on your employment authorization application for up to 90 days. As discussed in Chapter 4, if more than 75 days have passed since you applied for the EAD (or since you responded to a Request for Evidence) and you haven't received your card, you can call USCIS customer service to create a "service request." Hopefully, that will cause USCIS to give your application priority attention.

As part of your adjustment of status application, you and your family members may apply for permission to work (an Employment Authorization Document or EAD). The EAD takes about 90 days to arrive by mail. It is valid in one- or two-year increments and can be extended as long as your adjustment of status is pending.

TIP
Are you here on an H-1B or L-1 visa? If so, and if your H-1B or L-1 status won't expire for a while, there's no need for you to apply for separate work permission. In fact, some lawyers specifically advise continuing to renew your H-1B status and not merely relying upon the EAD, just in case your adjustment of status application is denied (for example, because your employer goes out of business). With your H-1B or L-1 visa status still valid, you could simply switch to another employer, start a new green card application, and avoid a lot of trouble. That said, it's wise to apply for the EAD when applying for adjustment of status, as a backup. There's no extra cost for submitting the EAD application with your Form I-485, and the EAD will allow you to find other work if your H-1B or L-1 employer does not want to continue extending your visa status, or some similar complication arises.

2. Paperwork to Prepare for Adjustment of Status Application

The basic form used in the U.S. adjustment of status application is Form I-485, Application for Permanent Residence. However, a handful of other forms must be prepared to accompany this main one, and you'll need to collect various documents as well.

An easy way to get all the necessary forms is to call the USCIS forms line at 800-870-3676 and ask for the Adjustment of Status Packet. But the better and faster way is to obtain the forms online at www. uscis.gov. (Click "Forms," then select the ones you need.)

> **TIP**
> **Filing the visa petition and green card application concurrently?** To prevent confusion at the service center, it's best to label the outside of the package "I-140/I-485 concurrent filing," and explain it in a cover letter, as well.

The checklist below will help you assemble and keep track of the appropriate forms and documents. A complete set of these must also be prepared for your accompanying spouse and children.

You'll need to mail your application, consisting of both forms and documents, to a USCIS Lockbox, or if you are requesting Premium Processing, to the USCIS service center nearest the place you are living. Check for the appropriate address at www.uscis.gov/i-485-addresses.

After filing your adjustment of status application, you will receive a receipt that estimates the processing time for your application. If USCIS requires additional evidence or information, it will send you a Request for Evidence. You will also receive, after some weeks or months, a notice advising you where to go to have your fingerprints taken. These will then be used to check whether you have any history of arrests in the U.S. (whether by the police, FBI, DHS, or another authority).

3. Your Adjustment of Status Interview

Personal interviews are usually not required in applications for green cards through employment. You should simply receive an approval notice in the mail, usually several months (though sometimes years, if your priority date for some reason retrogresses) after you filed the Form I-485 application. The approval notice will inform you that your case has been approved and that your card will be sent to you by mail.

If required, the interview will be held at a USCIS office near you. You and your accompanying relatives will be sent an appointment notice, usually about two weeks in advance. If you have an attorney, he or she may come with you to the interview. Even if you don't have an attorney, you could consult with or hire one at this point, particularly if you're worried about why you've been called in for an interview.

Checklist for Adjustment of Status Application

Forms

☐ Form I-485.

☐ Filing fee: Currently $1,225 for applicants ages 14 to 78 (includes biometrics fee), $750 for applicants under age 14 who are derivatives filing concurrently with a parent, and $1,140 for applicants age 79 and over or under age 14 but not filing with a parent. The $1,070 fee includes biometrics (fingerprinting). You'll be notified of where and when to appear. Double-check all fees at www.uscis.gov/i-485.

☐ Form I-485A (only if you'll be paying an additional $1,000 penalty fee in order to adjust status).

☐ Form G-325A.

☐ Form I-765 (optional, if you want a work permit).

☐ Form I-864 (Affidavit of Support used if a relative of yours was the I-140 petitioner or owns 5% or more of the business that petitioned for you).

☐ I-131, Application for Travel Document (Advance Parole), for use if you think you'll need to travel outside the United States while your application is processed.

Documents (with language translations, as needed)

☐ Notice of approval of the visa petition—or, if you're filing the visa petition concurrently with the adjustment of status application, Form I-140 and all supporting documents as described in Section F, above.

☐ Copy of a long-form birth certificate for you and each accompanying relative.

☐ Marriage certificate if you are married and bringing your spouse.

☐ If you or your spouse was married before, copies of divorce and/or death certificates.

☐ Four photographs of you and four of each accompanying relative, in U.S. passport style (it's best to have a professional do these). Write your name and A-number (if you've received one from USCIS) in pencil or felt pen on the back of each photo. (This assumes you will submit the Forms I-765 and I-131 at this time. If not, you can subtract one photo for each form you don't submit.)

☐ Letter from the petitioning employer verifying the job is still open and the salary that will be paid.

☐ Medical exam report for you and each accompanying relative (Form I-693, filled out and signed by a USCIS-certified doctor, and presented in an unopened envelope).

☐ If you're a nurse or other health care worker, a Visa Screen certificate showing that you've met the exam and English-language requirements. (Optional at time of filing, but you must submit the certificate before the I-485 can be approved.)

When to Apply for Advance Parole

Once your Form I-485 application for adjustment of status has been filed, you must not leave the U.S. for any reason before you have applied for and received advance permission to reenter the U.S. (Advance Parole), unless you held lawful H-1B or L-1 nonimmigrant visa status at the time of filing. Any departure from the U.S. without this permission will be viewed as an abandonment of your application for a green card—which means that, upon return, you will be told that your green card application was deemed abandoned, and you may not be allowed to enter the United States.

You should apply for Advance Parole at the same time you apply to adjust status, especially because your filing fee is included in the adjustment of status fee. You can send the Form I-131 application for Advance Parole later and it will still be free, but you'll have to include a copy of the I-485 receipt notice, a copy of the biographic page of your passport, and two passport-style photographs. Your spouse should include your marriage certificate, and children must include birth certificates.

If approved, you will be allowed to leave the U.S. and return again with no break in the processing of your application.

However, if at any time you stayed in the U.S. for more than 180 days after the date you were supposed to leave, you should speak to a lawyer before you depart the U.S. even if your Advance Parole application is approved. Until recently, leaving could put you at risk of being found inadmissible due to the three-year or ten-year bars to reentry (discussed in Chapter 3). That risk was greatly reduced in 2012, when the Board of Immigration Appeals (BIA) issued a ruling called *In the Matter of Arrabally and Yerrabelly*, 25 I&N Dec. 771 (BIA 2012). The BIA said that departures under Advance Parole with a pending adjustment of status application do NOT, despite previous USCIS interpretations to the contrary, trigger the unlawful presence bars. Still, you want to make sure you're operating on the latest interpretation of this issue before taking the risk of departing the country.

RELATED TOPIC
See Chapter 4 for detailed information on what expect during your adjustment of status interview. If your adjustment of status application is denied, also see Chapter 4. And for information on how to protect your status as a green card holder after you're approved, see Chapter 14.

4. What Happens If You Chose Consular Processing

If you couldn't or chose not to obtain your green card through the adjustment of status process, then you will immigrate only after obtaining an immigrant visa from a U.S. consulate overseas. Consular processing involves a standard series of events. First, the National Visa Center (NVC) will notify you, requesting that you pay the necessary immigrant visa fee bill. After you have paid, you will need to prepare some forms and documents according to the NVC's instructions. Then you send these back to the NVC, and wait until you receive a notice scheduling you for an interview at the U.S. consulate in your home country. You will then undergo a medical exam and finally attend the interview. There, if all goes well, you will be approved (subject to final security checks) for an immigrant visa to enter the United States.

Much of your job at this point involves convincing the consulate that you are not inadmissible for health, criminal, security, or financial reasons. Luckily, since you have a job offer, proving that you can support yourself financially should not be a problem. (However, the law says that if one of your relatives was the I-140 petitioner or owns 5% or more of the business that is petitioning for you, you need to file Form I-864, an Affidavit of Support signed by that relative—see Chapter 3 for a full discussion of this affidavit. The Form I-864 usually needs to be separately sent to the NVC for review before you continue your case with the consulate.)

If you don't need to fill out an I-864 but your spouse and children will be accompanying you, you yourself will need to fill out a Form I-134 Affidavit of Support.

Checklist: Documents to Bring to Your Interview

Prepare all of the following to take with you to your USCIS interview:

☐ A complete photocopy of your green card application. This is for your use— you may want to follow along as the officer asks you questions about the material you filled out on the forms, or you may find that the officer is missing something that you have a copy of.

☐ All passports (current and expired).

☐ Driver's license or state ID card.

☐ Social Security card.

☐ Birth certificate.

☐ Marriage certificate/license (if any).

☐ Divorce/death certificates from prior marriages (if any).

☐ All IAP-66, DS-2019, and I-20 forms (if you have ever been in J-1 or F-1 status).

☐ All other original USCIS approval notices for nonimmigrant status (Forms I-797).

☐ I-94 card(s), if any.

☐ A current, original letter from your employer confirming that you are still being offered the job, and the salary you will be paid.

☐ All EADs (work permit cards) and Advance Parole documents issued to you and your family members.

☐ Documents relating to any arrests or criminal convictions—*certified* copies of final court dispositions are required.

☐ Any updates to the material in your application. For example, if your employer has changed its name, bring proof of this change. If you've been arrested, bring a full explanation (and consult with an attorney, to make sure that the arrest doesn't make you inadmissible).

The purpose is to show that you are willing and able to support your family once you're all living in the United States. If you are in the subcategory of priority workers that aren't required to have a job offer in order to get a green card, you have already submitted documents showing your intent to continue working. These documents will be enough to substitute for Form I-134.

5. NVC Processing

At the beginning, consular processing involves a lot of information being sent in various directions. First, after USCIS approves your visa petition, it will forward your file to the National Visa Center (NVC) in Portsmouth, New Hampshire. It will send you a letter or email directing you to a State Department website that will guide you through the "immigrant visa" process at the NVC.

The first thing the NVC requests is that you choose your email communication options. The NVC prefers not to communicate via postal mail; and you too should prefer email, because in this case it's quick, reliable, and secure. To start this communication, send an email to nvcinquiry@state.gov, telling it which email address or addresses to use for correspondence on your case. Also supply the name and address of your sponsoring employer, if you have one. When sending any email to the NVC, enter the NVC case number given to you within the subject line.

At this point, if you want to have someone else (an attorney or agent) receive all correspondence involved with your case, you must tell the NVC who that person is. Do so by filling out and submitting Form DS-261, Online Choice of Address and Agent at the State Department's Consular Electronic Application Center (CEAC) website, https://ceac.state.gov. The NVC recommends that this person be in the U.S. or at least have a reliable email address.

The next step is to pay the Immigrant Visa (IV) fee bill (currently $345 for employment-based immigrant visa applications). The NVC prefers that you do this online, through the CEAC website. If you can't, you'll need to mail a cashier's check or money order (not a personal check) to the NVC. Instructions are on the State Department's immigrant visa processing website, which NVC will direct you to.

a. Submitting the DS-260 Application

The application form you need to send to the NVC is called a DS-260. You fill this out and submit it online through the CEAC website at https://ceac.state.gov. Log in with your NVC case number and invoice number (which the NVC sent in its original notice to you). If you can't finish the whole form in one sitting, don't worry—you can save your work and come back to it later. Make sure to print out the confirmation page when you're done— you'll need to bring that to your interview at the U.S. consulate.

Checklist: Documents for Your Consular Interview

☐ Long-form birth certificate for you and each accompanying relative as well as for any unmarried minor children who are not immigrating with you.

☐ Marriage certificate if you are married and bringing your spouse.

☐ If either you or your spouse have been previously married, copies of divorce and death certificates showing termination of all previous marriages.

☐ Passport for you and for each accompanying relative, valid for at least six months beyond the date of the final interview.

☐ Police clearance certificates (if available).

☐ Fingerprints, if specifically requested by the consulate.

☐ If you or accompanying relative served in the military forces of any country, a copy of your military records for you and each accompanying relative.

☐ Two photographs of you and two photographs of each accompanying relative. Some consulates take the photos at the interview—you'll be told what to expect in the instructions.

☐ Letter from the petitioning employer verifying the job is still open and the salary you will be paid.

☐ Medical exam report for you and each accompanying relative.

☐ If you're a nurse, a Visa Screen certificate showing that you've met the exam and English-language requirements.

---

b. Preparing Supporting Documents

The State Department's immigrant visa process website will let you know how to submit documents to the NVC. Some people can scan and email documents, others must mail them to the NVC, and others can choose either method.

The checklist above provides a brief explanation of some of the documents you'll need to gather to send to the NVC and bring your immigrant visa interview. Keep your eyes open for any special requirements that your consulate may add to this list. If you were not required to mail all originals to the NVC, bring the originals and a set of copies with you to your interview. (The consular officer may want to examine the originals to make sure they're not fraudulent, but keep copies for your files.) Do not mail your paperwork to the consulate!

Some additional explanation regarding some of the items on the checklist follows.

Police clearance. You personally must collect police clearance certificates from your country of nationality and the country you're living in currently, if you've been there for more than six months since the age of 16. You also need a police certificate from any country in which you've been arrested, no matter when. Additionally, you must have a police certificate from each place you lived within your home country or country of last residence, if you lived there for at least six months since the age of 16. You do not need to obtain police certificates from the United States.

The State Department's immigrant visa process website contains information on how to contact the local police department to get police certificates from various countries. Some nations refuse to supply police certificates, or their certificates are not considered reliable, in which case you will not be required to obtain them from those locations.

Some countries will send certificates directly to U.S. consulates but not to you personally. Before they send the certificates out, however, you must request that it be done. Usually this requires filing some type of request form, together with a set of your fingerprints.

Fingerprints. A few consulates require you to submit fingerprints, though most do not. Consulates wanting fingerprints will send you blank fingerprint cards with instructions.

Medical exam. Before your visa interview, you and your accompanying relatives will need to schedule and undergo a medical examination. The State Department's immigrant visa processing website contains instructions on how to do this, and what to bring to your exam.

Only certain doctors can perform the medical examinations. The fees depend on the country and doctor. The exam itself involves taking a medical history, blood test, and chest X-ray and administering vaccinations, if you need them. Pregnant women can refuse to be X-rayed until after the pregnancy. The vaccination requirement may be waived for religious, moral, or medical reasons.

The main purpose of the medical exam is to verify that you are not medically inadmissible. Some medical grounds of inadmissibility can be overcome with treatment or by applying for a waiver. (See Chapter 3 for details.) If you need a medical waiver, the consulate will give you complete instructions at your interview, but you should also consult an experienced immigration attorney. After the examination, the doctor will either give you a sealed envelope with the results of the test, or send the results directly to the consulate. If you get an envelope, don't open it. Bring it to your interview along with your other documents.

TIP
Bring copies of everything you and your employer have submitted up to this point. Such copies will help you answer questions from the consular officer. They may also come in handy in case any items got lost in the transfer between the U.S. immigration offices and the U.S. consulate.

6. Your Consular Interview

Consulates hold interviews on all green card applications. The NVC will send you a notice of your interview. Read the consulate's instructions carefully for any additions or changes.

 RELATED TOPIC
For details on what to expect during your consular visa interview, see Chapter 4. For information on what to do if your visa is denied, also see Chapter 4.

I. Step Seven: Immigrant Visa Holders Enter the U.S.

After the overseas U.S. consulate has processed your application, it will place your immigrant visa on a page in your passport. Review the visa to make sure all information is correct. If there are any spelling errors, contact the embassy or consulate promptly. You'll also get a sealed "visa packet" containing documents to show to border officials when you get to the United States. Don't open it. Your immigrant visa allows you to request entry to the United States at a border post, airport, or other arrival point.

Before you travel to the U.S., you'll have to pay one last fee: the USCIS Immigrant Fee, currently $220. (You can pay this fee after you get to the U.S., but USCIS won't send you a green card until you do.) Each member of the family traveling with you is charged the same fee. The only way to pay this is online, through the USCIS Electronic Immigration System, known as ELIS. You'll need to create an ELIS account at uscis.gov/uscis-elis. (Only you can create the account—not your attorney or employer.) Select "USCIS Immigrant Fee" and include your personal information. You'll need to have your Alien number (A-Number) and Department of State Case ID number handy. (You got those from the consulate.) Once you're in the system, you can pay the fee for all family members in one transaction. You'll need a valid credit or debit card, or a U.S. bank checking account and routing numbers.

You acquire the full status of green card holder only after you have paid the USCIS Immigrant Visa Fee and been inspected and admitted into the U.S., which will include being processed for the green card during "secondary inspection." You must make that initial entry into the U.S. within six months of your interview, unless your medical examination results expire sooner than that. If you are bringing any accompanying relatives, they must enter at either the same time or after you do in order to become permanent residents.

The inspection process involves a U.S. border officer opening the sealed visa packet containing your entry documents and doing a last check to make sure you haven't used fraud. The border officer has expedited removal powers, which means he or she can turn you right around and send you home if anything appears wrong in your packet or with your answers to the officer's questions. Be polite and careful in answering.

When the officer is satisfied that everything is in order, he or she will stamp your passport to show that you're now a U.S. permanent resident and are immediately authorized to work. This stamp is often called an "I-551 stamp" or "ADIT" stamp. You won't receive an actual green card yet, however. Cards for you and your accompanying relatives will be ordered for you. They will come to you by mail several weeks later at the home address you provide to U.S. Customs and Border Protection upon arriving in the United States.

Getting a Green Card Through the Diversity Visa Lottery

The Immigration Act of 1990 created the diversity visa immigration category to benefit persons from countries that in recent years have sent the fewest numbers of immigrants to the U.S. (See I.N.A. § 203(c), 8 U.S.C. §1153(c).) You can enter the diversity visa lottery if you are a native of one of these countries and meet certain educational and other requirements. Different qualifying countries are selected each year, based on how many of their citizens immigrated to the U.S. during the previous five years, in proportion to the size of their populations.

The total number of diversity visa winners every year is 50,000 (it was formerly 55,000, but 5,000 of these are now reserved for applicants under a different program called NACARA). These 50,000 are distributed by dividing up the world into regions and allocating varying percentages of the total green cards to each region. Additionally, each qualifying country within each region is limited to no more than 7% of the available lottery green cards per year (or 3,850).

Because the method used to select winners of the diversity visa is a random drawing, it is popularly known as the *green card lottery*. However, this name is somewhat misleading, because not all winners succeed in receiving a U.S. green card. The problems are usually due to delays or because the lottery winners are found to be inadmissible to the United States. This chapter will explain who can become eligible for a green card based on the diversity visa lottery, how to apply, and how to increase your chances of success.

Key Features of the Diversity Visa

Here are some of the advantages and disadvantages of the diversity visa:

- The initial registration is free.
- The minimal requirements to qualify for this visa help people who might not fit into any other green card eligibility category.
- Winning the diversity visa lottery doesn't guarantee you a green card— you must, for example, show that you're not otherwise inadmissible to the U.S., including that you'll be able to support yourself in the United States.
- If you win, your spouse and unmarried children under the age of 21 may also get green cards as accompanying relatives.
- As with all green cards, yours can be taken away if you misuse it—for example, you live outside the U.S. for too long, commit a crime, or even fail to advise the immigration authorities of your change of address. However, if you successfully keep your green card for five years, you can apply for U.S. citizenship.

RESOURCE

The diversity visa rules and deadlines change every year, usually around September. To make sure you're getting the latest version, check the State Department website at www.travel.state.gov. (Click "Immigrate," then "Diversity Visa.")

SEE AN EXPERT

Do you need a lawyer? Entering the lottery is fairly simple and doesn't usually require a lawyer's help. USCIS strongly encourages people to complete the entry form themselves, without a "Visa Consultant," "Visa Agent," or other person who charges money to help. You may, however, need help with some of the technological parts of completing the application, which requires Internet access and digital photos. If somebody helps you, you should be there to make sure the answers to the questions are correct and to get the confirmation page and your unique confirmation number. Once you win the lottery, a lawyer's help can be well worth the investment, to make sure that government delays don't end up wasting your winning lottery ticket.

A. Are You Eligible for a Green Card Through the Lottery?

In order to enter the lottery, you must be from one of the qualifying countries and must have either a "high school" diploma (or foreign equivalent education) or a minimum of two years' experience within the last five years in a job that normally requires at least two years of training or experience. U.S. job offers are not a requirement. A "high school" education means successful completion of a formal course of elementary and secondary education comparable to completion of a 12-year course in the United States. Only formal courses of study meet the requirement, so correspondence programs or equivalency certificates (such as the General Equivalency Diploma G.E.D.) are not acceptable. Your diploma must qualify you to study at a higher level, so if you have a trade school diploma, consult with a lawyer before relying on it to qualify.

Whether the type of work you've been doing for two years qualifies will be determined based on a U.S. Department of Labor database at www.onetonline.org. Only certain specified occupations qualify you for a diversity visa.

Only the lottery winner—not his or her spouse or children—needs to meet the educational or experience requirements. However, to maximize your family's chances, a spouse or child who does meet these requirements should apply separately. (It's okay to be listed on a parent or spouse's application at the same time you file your own.) There is no minimum age to enter the lottery. However, the requirement of a high school diploma or two years' experience usually keeps out anyone under the age of 16.

! CAUTION
The lottery requirements are different from the green card requirements. Entering the lottery is just the first step. When it comes time to claim your green card, you will have to show that you are not inadmissible, which includes showing that you can support yourself financially in the U.S. or that someone there is willing to support you. It also includes showing that you haven't committed certain crimes, been involved in terrorist or subversive activities, or become afflicted with certain physical or mental defects. Also, if you are living in the United States illegally, it may be impossible for you to collect your green card anytime soon. Procedurally, you would (unless you fall into an exceptional category) have to leave the U.S. for an interview at a consulate outside of the United States. At that point, however, you could be barred from reentering the U.S. for three or ten years, depending on the length of your illegal U.S. stay. (See Chapter 3 on inadmissibility.)

There is a lottery every year, usually occurring in early fall. For example, the application period for the 2016 lottery (called "DV-2018," because 2018 is the year in which the visas will actually be given out), ran from October 4, 2016 to November 7, 2016. Applications (also called "registrations") submitted one year are not held over to the next, so if you are not selected one year you need to reapply the next year to be considered. You won't

be eligible for a diversity visa if you are a native of one of the countries from which a lot of people come to the United States. Your "native" country is the one where you were born—it doesn't matter what your citizenship is or where you live now. (But see, "Using a Family Member's Birthplace as Your Native Country," below.) For the 2016 lottery, the only countries not qualified were:

Bangladesh	India
Brazil	Jamaica
Canada	Mexico
China (mainland born, though persons born in Hong Kong SAR, Macau SAR, and Taiwan were eligible)	Nigeria
	Pakistan
	Peru
	Philippines
	South Korea
Colombia	United Kingdom (except Northern Ireland) and its dependent territories, and
Dominican Republic	
El Salvador	
Haiti	Vietnam.

If you are from a country not named on the list above, you could have applied for the lottery that took place in 2016. Most of these countries reappear on the list year after year. Winners of DV-2018 would find out by going to the Entrant Status Check website at www.dvlottery.state.gov starting May 2, 2017.

B. Quick View of the Application Process

Getting a green card through the lottery is a three-step process:

1. You register for the lottery, which simply means filling out an online application that places your name among those who may be selected through the lottery drawing system. If you've won, you can find out online within approximately eight months. (Winners are no longer personally notified.)

2. Winners can—as soon as a visa becomes available based on their registration "rank number"—proceed to filing a green card application, together with their accompanying relatives, if any.

3. If your interview was at a U.S. consulate in another country, you must enter the U.S. with your immigrant visa, at which time you become a permanent resident.

If your permanent residence cannot be approved by the end of the lottery (fiscal) year (September 30), your application becomes invalid and you lose your chance at a green card. This happens to thousands of people every year. It may not be within your control.

C. Step One: Registering for the Lottery

The rules for registering yourself in the lottery drawing change every year. For the latest, check the State Department website at http://travel.state.gov (click "Immigrate" then "Diversity Visa" for the latest announcement). There is no fee to register.

For the 2016 lottery (DV-2018) applicants were asked to fill out an application form online and to attach digital photographs meeting certain specifications. The information requested in the online form is included in "Sample Information Required in Lottery Application," below.

Failure to list your spouse and all eligible children will result in disqualification for the visa. In fact, you'll need to fill in every answer on the form, or your entry will be disqualified.

Send only one registration per person. (If you submit more than one application you'll be disqualified.) However, husbands and wives can each submit a separate application. Do not send separate registrations for children unless they qualify on their own and are willing to immigrate without you. Although unmarried children under 21 automatically qualify to immigrate with their parents, if the parents are selected, the opposite is not true. If a child is selected, the parents will not get green cards unless they are selected separately.

Using a Family Member's Birthplace as Your Native Country

To enter the lottery, an applicant must be able to claim nativity in an eligible country. Nativity in most cases is determined by the applicant's place of birth. However, if you were born in an ineligible country but your spouse was born in an eligible country, you can claim your spouse's country of birth rather than your own (so long as your spouse will be immigrating with you and you'll be entering the U.S. together).

Also, if you were born in an ineligible country, but neither of your parents was born there or resided there at the time of your birth, you may be able to claim nativity in one of your parents' countries of birth.

After you correctly register online, you will see a screen containing your name and a unique confirmation number. It's a good idea to print this confirmation screen. You will need the number to check whether you've been selected or not. If you lose your confirmation number, you can retrieve it on the DV Entrant Status Check website (described below) using the email address you registered with by entering certain personal information to confirm your identity.

CAUTION

Paying someone won't help your application. Some immigration consultants claim they can get special attention for your lottery registration if you pay them to handle it. Such claims are false. There's nothing wrong with paying a lawyer or qualified paralegal to help you complete the registration according to the instructions, but recognize that that's the only type of help you'll be getting.

Make sure to mark your calendar and check the State Department diversity visa website at www.dvlottery.state.gov as soon as it announces the winners (typically in early May), so that you can get going on your green card application if you've won.

The online DV Entrant Status Check is the only way to find out whether you've been selected—no one is going to send you a letter, email, or any other type of notice. If you get something congratulating you and asking you to send money to get the process going, you can be sure it's a scam.

Wondering about your odds of being selected? In the DV-2015 lottery, the State Department received nearly 9.4 million qualified entries. About 1.3% of those were selected.

Sample Information Required in Lottery Application

1. **Full name:** Last/family name, first name, middle name, exactly as it appears on your passport

2. **Date of birth:** Day, month, year

3. **Gender:** Male or Female

4. **City where you were born**

5. **Country where you were born:** The name of the country should be the one currently in use for the place where you were born (for example, Slovenia rather than Yugoslavia, or Kazakhstan rather than Soviet Union).

6. **Country of eligibility or chargeability for the DV program:** Normally your country of birth, unless you can use a spouse or parent's birthplace (see separate description).

7. **Entry photograph(s):** (according to photo specifications; include photos of spouse and children)

8. **Mailing address:** Address, City/Town, District/Country/Province/State, Postal Code/Zip Code, Country

9. **Country where you live today**

10. **Phone number** (optional)

11. **Email Address** (optional). (Reminder: The State Department will never send emails saying that you've been selected for the DV program. If you find out that you have been selected, the agency will use your email address only to tell you that further instructions are available on its website.)

12. **What is the highest level of education you have achieved, as of today?:** Choose either (1) Primary school only, (2) High school, no degree, (3) High school degree, (4) Vocational school, (5) Some university courses, (6) University degree, (7) Some graduate level courses, (8) Master's degree, (9) Some doctorate level courses, and (10) Doctorate degree.

13. **Marital status:** Unmarried, Married, Divorced, Widowed, Legally Separated

14. **Number of children:** Give the name, date, and place of birth of all natural children, legally adopted children, and stepchildren who are unmarried and under age 21. It doesn't matter whether you're married to the child's other parent, nor whether the child lives with you or will immigrate with you—put their names down anyway. (You don't need to mention children who are already U.S. legal permanent residents or citizens.)

15. **Spouse information:** Name, Date of Birth, Gender, City/Town of Birth, Country of Birth, Photograph. *(Note: Failure to list your spouse will result in your disqualification and refusal of all visas at the time of the visa interview.)*

16. **Children information:** Name, Date of Birth, Gender, City/Town of Birth, Country of Birth, Photograph

Dealing With the "Public Charge" Ground of Inadmissibility

Diversity lottery winners applying for a visa or adjustment of status, unlike most family-based Immigrants and some employment-based immigrants, do not need to file an I-864 Affidavit of Support form with their applications. If you, as a lottery winner, are asked to prove that you are not likely to go on public assistance or welfare in the U.S., you can submit an offer of employment from an employer in the U.S., proof of personal assets, an Affidavit of Support (Form I-134) submitted by a relative or friend residing in the U.S., or some other type of proof. (Although the Form I-134 is usually reserved for use with temporary visas, and the Form I-864 Affidavit of Support is usually used with applications for green cards, the DV lottery visa uses the Form I-134.) If you're submitting an Affidavit of Support (Form I-134) and

family members are immigrating through your DV winning, make sure to list them on the Form I-134 as accompanying you. Your sponsor on the Form I-134 will need to attach documents to show that the information contained in the form is true. These should include, where applicable: a copy of the most recent federal income taxes (with W-2s) showing the income of the person signing the Form I-134; a statement from the bank with details about accounts including the date opened, the total amount deposited for the past year, and the present balance; and a letter from the employer verifying current employment, job title, salary, and whether the position is permanent. Also attach a copy of the document that shows the immigration status of the person signing the Form I-134.

D. Step Two: Your Application for Permanent Residence

If your name has been drawn in the lottery, you must act quickly to apply for your green card. This is because the State Department selects more people than it has visas for, just to make sure all the visas get used up. (Lots of people who are selected end up not qualifying to get a visa.) Only 50,000 visas are available each year, but for the DV-2015 year, for example, approximately 125,514 applicants were selected.

The DV Entrant Status Check gives instructions to people selected in the lottery. You must respond to these instructions to get your case going. After you respond, the case will go to the State Department's Kentucky Consular Center (KCC) for processing, if you are overseas. If you are in the U.S. and will be adjusting your status to permanent legal resident, you will start the adjustment application process with USCIS at the appropriate time (see below).

One important piece of information you'll receive upon selection is your case number, which is also called your rank number. You are allowed to submit your application for a visa or adjustment of status according to when a visa becomes available in your regional category according to your rank number, so the lower the rank number, the better.

Visas start to become available on the first day of each fiscal year (October 1). To see if your rank number has been reached, check the current Department of State *Visa Bulletin* by going to www.travel.state.gov, and clicking under "U.S. Visas" then "Visa Bulletin" in the Law and Policy section. The State Department publishes diversity visa rankings 50 to 60 days the future. If you're adjusting status, USCIS will accept applications from persons whose rank number is below any future cutoff listed in the *Visa Bulletin*. Take advantage of this opportunity, because it can save you crucial weeks of processing time. You'll have to wait for your rank to become "current," however, to actually receive approval.

If your spouse or children will be accompanying you from overseas, they must each file their own visa applications. You can bring a spouse you married after you entered the lottery, or a child born after you entered the lottery—just make sure to list the person on the visa or adjustment application.

A big part of the green card application is proving that you are not inadmissible to the United States. Review Chapter 3 regarding the grounds of inadmissibility.

One of the most problematic inadmissibility issues for lottery visa applicants is the possibility of becoming a public charge (receiving government assistance in the U.S.). See "Dealing With the 'Public Charge' Ground of Inadmissibility," above.

The first question for anyone selected in the diversity lottery is whether to apply for U.S. permanent residency at a USCIS office in the United States or at a U.S. consulate outside of the United States.

If you're living outside of the United States now. The answer is fairly easy for people currently living outside of the U.S. You'll file at a local U.S. consulate and attend an interview there before entering the United States. (This method is called consular processing.)

If you're living in the U.S. now. The answer is a bit more complicated for applicants already in the United States. Ordinarily, the most convenient choice would probably be for you to adjust status without leaving—that is, send your application to USCIS and attend your interview at a local USCIS office. Once your application is filed, your stay in the United States will be considered legal, and you can apply for permission to work. Should problems arise in your case, you'll be able to wait for a decision in the U.S., a circumstance most green card applicants prefer. Also, if your application for a green card is turned down, you have greater rights of appeal inside the U.S. than you do at a U.S. consulate.

Not everyone is eligible to adjust status. First, the diversity green card must be immediately available to you. Second, you can't adjust status unless you were "inspected and admitted" by a U.S. immigration officer—in other words, the last time you entered the U.S., you did so legally, with a visa or with "parole" (permission from a border officer). And third, just like someone coming into the U.S. from overseas, you must be admissible. (See Chapter 3 for grounds of inadmissibility.)

Even if you meet those basic requirements for adjustment, you won't be able to adjust status if you've ever worked in the U.S. without authorization, if you're in the U.S. with no legal status, or if you've ever fallen out of legal status (except if it wasn't your fault). Also, you can't adjust status if you came to the U.S. without a visa under the Visa Waiver program. (This rule doesn't apply to visa-exempt Canadians.)

An important, but increasingly rare, exception to adjustment of status eligibility requirements exists for people who had an approvable relative petition or labor certification application filed for them (or for their spouse or parent) before April 30, 2001. Such people, if they are admissible and a green card is immediately available to them, can

adjust status by paying an extra $1,000 fee. If the petition or labor certification application was filed after January 14, 1998, they will also have to prove that they were present in the U.S. on December 21, 2000. This provision of law, known as "245(i)" adjustment, is especially helpful for people who came to the U.S. illegally and who cannot leave to get an immigrant visa because they would then be subject to the ten-year reentry bar for unlawful presence.

If you have any doubts about your ability to adjust status, consult with an immigration lawyer. The adjustment application is expensive—you don't want to spend the money to apply and have your application denied outright.

Even if you are eligible to adjust status, you may instead decide to leave the United States and apply for your green card at a U.S. consulate abroad. If the consulates are issuing visas more quickly than your local USCIS office is handling adjustment of status applications, leaving to apply at a consulate outside of the U.S. could be a smart strategic move. Remember, time is all-important in a lottery-based green card application. However, if you have already spent 180 days or more in the U.S. out of legal status, or crossed the border without inspection, see an attorney to be sure you are not inadmissible or subject to a three-year or ten-year waiting period, before you go. (See Chapter 3.) Otherwise, you could find yourself stuck outside the United States for three or ten years, though it may be possible for you to apply for a "provisional waiver" before you go.

The need for speed. Let's look a little closer at why it's so important to submit your green card application in an office that's not too slow or backed up. If your immigrant visa isn't issued before the end of the fiscal year for which you were selected, your registration becomes void and you lose your chance for the green card. The deadline is the end of the fiscal year *for*, and not *in*, the year you were picked. The government fiscal years begin on October 1 and end on September 30. This means that if you were selected after the registration period that took place between October and November of 2014, and found out you'd won in May 2015, your deadline for receiving an approval of either your immigrant visa (if you're processing outside of the U.S.) or your adjustment of status (if you're processing in the U.S.) would be September 30, 2016.

Although that gives you just over a year to apply, attend your interview, and receive an approval, that's actually less time than it sounds like. In fact, it's the typical processing time in many consular and USCIS offices, so if one small thing goes wrong, you could be out of the running. You must, therefore, file as soon as you possibly can to be sure the processing is completed in time.

Another reason for speed is that the U.S. government selects many more people than there are green cards available. It assumes some of these people either will not qualify or will change their minds about immigrating. If the assumption is wrong and everyone selected does mail in applications, the green cards will be given on a first-come, first-served basis. It is, therefore, possible that even though you win the lottery, that year's green card allotment will be used up before your own interview is scheduled, so you will not get a green card.

If you have any children who will turn 21 soon, you have yet another reason to want the process to go quickly. Once the child turns 21, he or she technically loses eligibility for the diversity visa. Fortunately, children have some protection under a law called the Child Status Protection Act (CSPA). This law allows you to subtract from the child's actual age the number of days that passed between the first day people were allowed to register for the program that year and the date your registration was selected. See a lawyer for the details and a personal analysis.

CAUTION
Only a U.S. consulate or embassy in your home country is required to accept your lottery green card application. You can ask a consulate located elsewhere to accept your application, but it has the option to say "no," and, in fact, will turn down most such requests.

1. Adjusting Status in the United States

The process of adjusting your status to permanent resident on the basis of being selected in the diversity lottery involves paying a fee, preparing a set of forms and documents (a separate set for you, your spouse, and each of your accompanying children), mailing these to the USCIS Chicago lockbox, waiting for some weeks until you're called in to have your fingerprints taken, and then waiting a few weeks or months longer until you're called in for your final green card interview at a local USCIS office. You should be approved for your green card at or soon after the interview. See Chapter 4 for information on tracking the progress of your application.

Your spouse and children listed on the diversity lottery application, and any spouse or child you acquired after you entered the lottery, can adjust with you if they are in the U.S. with you and are eligible to adjust.

If your spouse or children still live overseas, however, you must complete your adjustment of status before they can get their immigrant visas. After you've adjusted, it's up to you to request that USCIS notify the U.S. embassy or consulate where your family intends to apply. Give the embassy or consulate an address where your family members can be contacted to schedule an interview. The embassy or consulate will provide all further instructions.

As part of your adjustment of status application, you and your family members in the U.S. may apply for permission to work (an Employment Authorization Document or EAD). You may also apply for permission to travel while your application for adjustment of status is pending (using Form I-131).

 CAUTION

Security checks are the most likely cause of delays. If you're between 14 and 79 years old, as part of your adjustment of status application, USCIS will have the FBI run both a fingerprint check and a name check on you, and will search for your name in the Interagency Border Inspection System (IBIS) database to detect crimes, fraud schemes, and any other illegal activities with which you may have been involved. These name checks can take several months or even. longer if yours is a common name. The FBI fingerprint check and the IBIS name check must be complete before USCIS can approve your application, but if the FBI name check hasn't been resolved within six months and your application is otherwise approvable, USCIS should not wait any longer to approve it. If you've been informed that your I-485 application stalled due to security checks, try to check in with the local USCIS district office regularly via InfoPass appointments, or hire a lawyer to help.

Checklist of Documents to Bring to USCIS Adjustment of Status Interview

☐ A complete photocopy of your green card application. This is for your use— you may want to follow along as the officer asks you questions about the material you filled out on the forms, or you may find that the officer is missing something that you have a copy of.

☐ All passport(s) you and every one of your family members have ever used to enter the U.S. If you or any of your family members have additional passports or travel documents, also bring those.

☐ Originals of all documents that you made copies of for submission with your application. For example, if you submitted a photocopy of a birth certificate or other official document, a USCIS officer may want to examine the original.

☐ Any documents received from USCIS or other immigration authorities. For example, your EAD (work permit) and your Advance Parole document, if you received one.

☐ Any updates to the material in your application. For example, if you have given birth to another child, bring the birth certificate. If you've been arrested, bring a full explanation (and consult with an attorney, to make sure that the arrest doesn't make you inadmissible).

☐ Driver's license (or state identity card) and Social Security card if you have these.

When you submit your application for adjustment of status, write in BIG, BOLD LETTERS in the margins of the Form I-485: "DV LOTTERY CASE; PLEASE COMPLETE I-485 PROCESSING BY SEPTEMBER 30, 20xx." Fill in the appropriate year. We also recommend that you make this notation on the outside of your envelope. This lets USCIS know that it might be necessary for your application to be taken out of line, in order for you to be interviewed and approved before the end of the fiscal year.

a. The Diversity Visa Fee

The first step in adjusting your status as a diversity lottery winner is to pay a nonrefundable diversity visa fee to the State Department, currently $330. This fee is separate from any others you will pay to USCIS as part of your adjustment application.

You must pay a separate diversity visa fee for each member of your immediate family who plans to adjust status with you. If your family members are still overseas and will join you after you adjust, do not pay the diversity fee for them at this time. They will pay it as part of their immigrant visa processing.

Checklist for Adjustment of Status Application

Forms

☐ Form I-485.

☐ Form I-485A (only if you'll be paying the $1,000 penalty fee in order to adjust status).

☐ Form G-325A , if between ages 14 and 79.

☐ Form I-765 (optional, if you want a work permit).

☐ I-131, Application for Travel Document (Advance Parole), if you might travel outside the U.S. during application processing.

Documents

☐ Copy of the official notice that your lottery registration was selected.

☐ Copy of your receipt from paying the diversity visa lottery processing fee.

☐ Copy of passport page with nonimmigrant visa (if applicable).

☐ Copy of passport page with admission (entry) or parole stamp (if applicable).

☐ Proof of education. The lottery green card program requires applicants to have either a "high school" diploma or foreign equivalent, or job skills needing at least two years of experience or training to learn. Appropriate evidence would be either a copy of your high school diploma or proof of job skill training, such as a vocational school certificate, and proof of at least two years of skilled employment verified by letters from past employers.

☐ Copy of a long-form birth certificate for you and each accompanying relative. If this is in another language, it must be accompanied by a full English translation.

☐ Marriage certificate if you are married and bringing your spouse.

☐ If you or your spouse was married before, copies of divorce and death certificates.

☐ Copy of I-94 arrival/departure record for you and each accompanying relative.

☐ Two color photographs of you and two of each accompanying relative in U.S. passport style. (Have a professional do these.) Write your name and A-number (if you've received one from USCIS) in pencil or felt pen on the back of each photo.

☐ Certified copies of court records, if you've ever been arrested.

☐ Sealed envelope containing medical exam report for you and for each accompanying relative (on Form I-693) (optional; you can submit medical exam results any time up to and including the time of your interview). There will be a fee for the exam. The fee is from $50 to $150 per exam. The doctor will take your medical history, do a blood test and chest X-ray, and give vaccinations if needed. Pregnant women may refuse to be X-rayed until after the baby's birth.

☐ If you need to request a waiver of inadmissibility on Form I-601, include this as well.

Fees

☐ Filing fee. Currently $1,225 for applicants ages 14 to 78 (includes biometrics fee), $750 for applicants under age 14 who are derivatives filing concurrently with a parent, and $1,140 for applicants over age 79 or under age 14 but not filing with a parent. The fee covers the work permit (Form I-765), travel document (Advance Parole, Form I-131), and fingerprinting (biometrics). USCIS will send receipts and a letter scheduling you for fingerprinting. In addition, if you're in the U.S. illegally, but allowed to adjust status under old laws, you must pay a $1,000 penalty fee, described above. Checks and money orders are accepted, made out to "U.S. Department of Homeland Security." Don't mail cash. Double-check all fees at www.uscis.gov.

The State Department's visa website, www.travel.state.gov, provides instructions for paying the fee. For the DV-2017 lottery year, applicants were required to send a cashier's check or postal money order for $330 to a State Department P.O. box in St. Louis. Certain information had to be provided with payment, including the DV case number, the person's name and address, and the number of persons for whom payment was being made. The State Department requests that you enclose a self-addressed, stamped envelope as well, so it can mail a receipt back to you. You'll need to bring that receipt to your interview, so hold on to it.

You must pay the diversity visa fee before processing of your case can continue.

b. Paperwork to Prepare for Adjustment of Status Application

The basic form used in the U.S. adjustment of status application is Form I-485, Application to Register Permanent Residence or Adjust Status. However, a handful of other forms must be prepared to accompany this main one.

One way to get all these forms is to call the USCIS forms line at 800-870-3676 and ask for the Adjustment of Status Packet. Or, you can obtain the forms online at www.uscis.gov (click "Forms," then select the forms you need one by one, based on the checklist above).

The checklist above will help you assemble and keep track of the appropriate forms and documents. A complete set of these must also be prepared for your accompanying spouse and children if they are adjusting status with you.

TIP

Tips for filling out Form I-485: You'll notice on the first page of the form, under "Part 2. Application Type," it asks you to choose the basis upon which you're applying for a green card. Mark Box h (other basis of eligibility) and write in "Diversity Lottery Winner." Leave the other boxes in Part 2 blank. Form I-485 also asks for an "A number." Normally, you will not have an A number unless you previously applied for a green card or have been in deportation proceedings (in which case you should see a lawyer). It also asks for your "I-94 number." The I-94 is a record of your last arrival into the U.S., with an indication of when you must leave by. (If you're Canadian and came as a visitor by car, you weren't given an I-94.) If you last entered by air or sea after April 30, 2013, you can find your I-94 number online at https://i94.cbp.dhs.gov. If you last entered before that date, or entered by land, your I-94 number is on the little white or green card that was tucked into your passport when you arrived. (Green means you entered on a visa waiver, and cannot adjust status.) If USCIS granted an extension of stay or change of status since the last time you entered, it provided you with a new I-94.

Dealing With Delays in Approval of Your Work Authorization

If you want to work before your application for a green card is approved, you must file a separate application for employment authorization. To do so, fill out Form I-765 and file it together with your adjustment of status application (with no added fee).

Legally, USCIS does not have to make a decision on your employment authorization application for up to 90 days. If, for some reason, you are not given a decision within 90 days, in theory you have the right to an interim employment authorization that will last 240 days. Unfortunately, claiming this right can be extremely difficult.

What you can do if your work permit is not issued within 75 days is call USCIS customer service and ask to create a "service request." This will alert the office processing the I-765 that it needs to issue your work permit soon.

If you are lawfully present in the United States, and have been notified that you won the diversity visa lottery and verified that your rank number is current and a visa (green card) is available, you'll need to mail your application, consisting of both forms and documents, to USCIS, P.O. Box 805887, Chicago, IL 60680-4120. If you're using express mail or a courier service, send the application to USCIS, Attn: FBAS, 131 South Dearborn - 3rd Floor, Chicago, IL 60603-5517.

After filing your I-485 adjustment of status application, you will receive a receipt that estimates the processing time for your application. A more accurate processing time, however, can be found on the USCIS website. Go to www.uscis.gov, click "Check Your Case Status," find the link for "Check Processing Times," and select the USCIS office (likely a "Field Office") where your I-485 is being processed. You also can use your receipt number to check your "case status" online, and can sign up to receive automatic email updates about your case.

If USCIS requires additional evidence or information, it will send you a Request for Evidence (RFE). You will also receive, after some weeks or months, a notice advising you where to go to have your fingerprints taken. These will then be used to check whether you have any history of arrests (whether by the police, FBI, DHS, or other authority).

c. Your Adjustment of Status Interview

You will be called in for a personal interview, which will be held at a USCIS office near you. USCIS will send you and your accompanying relatives an appointment notice two or more weeks in advance of the interview. If you have an attorney, he or she may come with you to the interview. (Even if you don't have an attorney, you could consult with or hire one at this point.)

Read This If You Plan to Leave the U.S. Before Your Adjustment Interview

Once your application for adjustment of status has been filed, you must not leave the U.S. for any reason before you have applied for and received advance permission to reenter the U.S. (Advance Parole). The only exception is if you held lawful H-1B or L-1 nonimmigrant visa status at the time you filed the I-485 application.

Any absence without this permission will be viewed as an abandonment of your application for a green card—which means that, upon return, you may be told by U.S. Customs and Border Protection (CBP) that your green card application is cancelled and you have no right to enter the United States.

It's best to simply apply for Advance Parole at the same time you apply to adjust status, just in case. Or, you can wait until you're sure you have to leave, and apply at the same service center where you sent your adjustment of status application—but you're taking a risk this way, because USCIS may take several months to approve your Advance Parole application.

Your application for Advance Parole should include Form I-131, together with the filing fee, two passport-type photographs, and a copy of your adjustment of status filing receipt (only if you've already sent in that application).

If approved, you will be allowed to leave the U.S. and return again with no break in the processing of your application. If you applied for and were granted work authorization as well, your evidence of authorization to travel will come in the form of a single card that gives you permission for both.

RELATED TOPIC

See Chapter 4 for detailed information on what to expect during your adjustment of status interview. If your adjustment of status application is denied, also see Chapter 4. And for information on how to protect your status as a green card holder after you're approved, see Chapter 14.

2. Consular Processing

If you are not currently residing in the United States, or would rather not obtain your green card through the adjustment of status process, then your most likely option is immigrant visa processing through a U.S. consulate in your home country. Consular processing requires you to prepare some forms and documents according to instructions, pay fees, undergo a medical exam, prepare documents for an interview at the U.S. consulate, and finally attend the interview. There, if all goes well, you will be approved (subject to final security checks) for a visa to enter the United States.

Much of your job at this point involves convincing the consulate that you are not inadmissible for health, criminal, security, or financial reasons. You will be asked to undergo a medical exam and provide evidence that you have no criminal record.

a. The Consular Application Form

The application form you (and each family member coming with you) need to send to the Kentucky Consular Center (KCC) is called a DS-260. You fill this out and submit it online through the CEAC website, https://ceac.state.gov. Log in to CEAC with the DV case number that was given to you when you won the lottery. If you can't finish the whole form in one sitting, don't worry—you can save your work and come back later. Make sure to print the confirmation page when done—you'll need to bring it to your consular interview. The KCC will review the information on your DS-260 and let you know if there are any problems. The KCC may request that you go back to CEAC to update information on your DS-260.

> **TIP**
>
> **Need to contact the KCC?** Be ready with your name and case number, exactly as they appear in the DV Entrant Status Check. Write your case number clearly in the upper right-hand corner of all correspondence sent to the KCC, or in the subject line of your email. The KCC telephone number is 606-526-7500 (7:30 a.m. until 4:00 p.m. EST), and the email address is KCCDV@state.gov.

b. Supporting Documents

The State Department's diversity visa process website will let you know which documents to bring to your interview at the consulate. (Do not send documents to the KCC.) The checklist below provides a brief explanation of some of the documents you'll need.

Keep your eyes open for any special requirements that your consulate may add to this list.

Some additional explanation regarding some of the items on the checklist follows:

Proof of education. The lottery green card program requires applicants to have either a high school diploma or the foreign equivalent or job skills needing at least two years of experience or training to learn. Appropriate evidence would be either a copy of your diploma or proof of at least two years of skilled employment within the past five years verified by letters from past employers. A specific job offer in the U.S. is not required.

Police clearance. You personally must collect police clearance certificates from each country or place you have lived in for one year or more since your 16th birthday. Additionally, you must have a police certificate from every place in your country of nationality, if you lived there for at least six months since the age of 16. You do not need to obtain police certificates from the

United States. If you've ever been arrested at any time in your life, you'll need to obtain a police certificate from the country in which the arrest took place.

The State Department's diversity visa process website links you to information on how to contact the local police department to get police certificates from various countries. Some nations refuse to supply police certificates, or their certificates are not considered reliable. You will not be required to obtain them from those locations.

Some countries will send certificates directly to U.S. consulates but not to you personally. Before they send the certificates out, however, you must request that it be done. Usually this requires filing some type of request form, together with a set of your fingerprints.

Fingerprints. A few consulates require you to submit fingerprints, though most do not. Consulates wanting fingerprints will send you blank fingerprint cards with instructions.

Photos. You and each accompanying relative must bring two passport-style photographs to the consulate. Many photographers are familiar with U.S. passport style. If you are a do-it-yourself type, passport-style specifications are available on the State Department's website, www.travel.state.gov. If your religious beliefs require wearing a head covering, you should be able to keep it on for the photo. However, your full face must be visible and your head covering cannot obscure your hairline or cast shadows on your face.

Medical exam. Before your visa interview, you and your accompanying relatives will need to schedule and undergo a medical examination. The State Department's diversity visa website contains instructions on how to do this, and what to bring to your exam.

Only certain doctors can perform the examination. The fees depend on the country and the doctor. The exam itself involves taking a medical history, blood test, and chest X-ray and administering vaccinations, if you need them. Pregnant women can refuse to be X-rayed until after the pregnancy. The vaccination requirement may be waived for religious, moral, or medical reasons.

The main purpose of the medical exam is to verify that you are not medically inadmissible. Some medical grounds of inadmissibility can be overcome with treatment or by applying for a waiver. (See Chapter 3 for details.) If you need a medical waiver, the consulate will give you complete instructions at your interview, but you should also consult an experienced immigration attorney.

After the examination, the doctor will either give you a sealed envelope with the results of the test, or send the results directly to the consulate. If you get an envelope, don't open it. Bring it to your interview along with your other documents.

Checklist of Documents and Forms for Consular Interview

☐ Appointment information printed from the Entrant Status Check on the E-DV website.

☐ DS-260 confirmation page.

☐ Passport(s) valid for six months beyond the intended date of entry into the U.S. for you and each family member applying for a visa.

☐ Original documents or certified copies of all supporting documents, and one photocopy of each document. Those documents include:

    ☐ Proof that your education or training meets the requirements for the diversity visa.

    ☐ Long-form birth certificate for you and each accompanying relative as well as of any unmarried minor children who are not immigrating with you.

☐ Marriage certificate if you are married and bringing your spouse.

☐ If either you or your spouse has been previously married, copies of divorce and death certificates showing termination of all previous marriages.

☐ Police certificates.

☐ Fingerprints, if specifically requested by the consulate.

☐ If you or accompanying relatives served in the military forces of any country, a copy of your military records.

☐ Two color photographs of you and two photographs of each accompanying relative, in U.S. passport style.

☐ Medical exam report for you and each accompanying relative (unless the physician sent it directly to the consulate).

c. Paying the Fee

Before the interview at the consulate, you must pay the Diversity Visa Lottery fee. Currently the fee is $330 per person. This fee is nonrefundable, whether a visa is issued or not.

How you pay this fee depends on the procedures at the U.S. embassy or consulate where you're applying. It will give you instructions. You will most likely be asked to pay in advance, but some consulates collect fees at the interview.

d. Your Consular Interview

Consulates hold interviews on all green card applications. A written notice of your interview appointment will be sent to you a few weeks before the appointment date. The appointment notice will tell you what to bring to your interview, including your photographs, passports, and so on. See the checklist, above for the items usually requested, but also read the consular list carefully for any additions or changes. If you can't make it to your scheduled interview, contact the consulate as soon as possible to reschedule. Avoid delaying too much, however, because you're in a race against other lottery winners and a fiscal year deadline.

RELATED TOPIC

For details on what to expect during your consular visa interview, see Chapter 4. And for information on what to do if your visa is denied, see Chapter 4 as well.

E. Step Three: Immigrant Visa Holders Enter the U.S.

If you processed your application through a U.S. consulate overseas, your immigrant visa will be placed on a page in your passport. Review the visa to make sure all the information is correct. If you see any spelling errors, contact the embassy or consulate promptly. You'll also get a sealed "visa packet" containing documents to show to border officials when you get to the United States. Don't open it.

Your immigrant visa allows you to request entry to the U.S. at a border post, airport, or other arrival point. Before you can get a green card, however, you have to pay one last fee: the USCIS Immigrant Fee, currently $220. Each member of the family traveling with you will be charged the same fee.

The only way to pay this fee is online, through the USCIS Electronic Immigration System, known as ELIS. You'll need to create an ELIS account at uscis.gov/uscis-elis. Select "USCIS Immigrant Fee" and include your personal information. Have your Alien number (A-Number) and Department of State Case ID numbers handy. (You got those from the consulate.) Once you're in, you can pay the fee for all family members in one transaction. You'll need a valid credit or debit card, or U.S. bank checking account and routing numbers.

You acquire the full status of green card holder only after being inspected and admitted into the U.S., which will include being processed for the green card during "secondary inspection." If you are bringing accompanying relatives, they must enter at either the same time or after you do in order to become permanent residents.

CAUTION

The clock is ticking. You must enter the U.S. before your visa expires. Check the date printed on your visa, inside your passport. The consulate usually gives you six months to make the trip, measured from the date it issues the visa. You might be given less time, however, if, for example, the results of your medical exam are in danger of getting stale.

The inspection process involves a U.S. border officer opening the sealed visa packet containing your entry documents and doing a last check to make sure you haven't used fraud. The border officer has expedited removal powers, which means he or she can turn you right around and send you home if anything appears wrong in your packet or with your answers to the officer's questions. Be polite and careful in answering.

Once satisfied that everything is in order, the officer will stamp your passport to show that you're now a U.S. permanent resident and are immediately authorized to work.

This stamp is often called an "I-551 stamp" or "ADIT" stamp. You won't receive an actual green card yet, however. Cards for you and your accompanying relatives will be ordered for you, as long as you've paid the USCIS Immigrant Fee. They will come to you by mail several weeks later at the home address you provide to U.S. Customs and Border Protection upon arriving in the United States.

SKIP AHEAD
Ready for information on how to protect your status as a green card holder? See Chapter 14.

Getting a Green Card as an Investor

Like many countries, the U.S. provides an avenue for entry to wealthy people who will pump money into its economy. (See I.N.A. § 203(b)(5), 8 U.S.C. § 1153(b)(5).) However, it's not like buying a ticket to get in. Applicants for a green card through investment (Employment Fifth Preference or EB-5) must not only invest between $500,000 and $1 million in a U.S. business, they must take an active role in that business (though they don't need to control it). This chapter will discuss who is eligible for a green card through investment and how to apply.

Green cards for investors are limited to 10,000 per year, with 3,000 of those reserved for persons investing in rural areas or areas of high unemployment. Like other visa categories, the EB-5 category has a per-country quota of 7% (700 of the 10,000). The 10,000-visa quota includes not only the investor, but spouses and children seeking green cards along with the investor. If the State Department believes that the quota (either per country or the 10,000 visa total) will be exceeded for the year, it will establish a waiting list based on your Priority Date (the day you filed the first portion of your application). This happened for the first time ever in September 2014 with EB-5 visas for Chinese nationals, who had met their per-country limit.

USCIS can easily reject applications in the EB-5 category, partly because the eligibility requirements are narrow, and partly because evidentiary requirements are strict due to the category's history of fraud and misuse. In fact, some lawyers encourage their clients to use their wealth to fit themselves into another category with a greater chance of success. For example, by investing in a company outside the United States that has a U.S. affiliate, the person might qualify to immigrate as a transferring executive or manager (priority worker, in category EB-1).

SEE AN EXPERT

Do you need a lawyer? If you can afford an investment-based green card, you can afford the services of a high-quality immigration lawyer. The EB-5 category is one of the single most difficult categories under which to establish eligibility, and certainly the most expensive. It's well worth the investment to gain legal advice before taking any significant steps toward using this strategy. If you try the application once on your own and fail, you may damage your chances of success in the future. What's more, because you are expected to make the investment first, and apply for the green card later, you could waste a lot of money.

Because you're investing a substantial amount of money, you should get input from financial, tax, accounting, investment, and other business professionals. An immigration lawyer is not necessarily qualified to advise you on the business aspects of the investment. Many companies offer a full range of services to potential EB-5 investors, including advice on which regional centers to invest in.

Key Features of an Investment-Based Green Card

Here are some of the advantages and limitations of an investment-based green card:

- As long as you have money to invest and can demonstrate that you are in the process of investing it in a for-profit business, you yourself do not need to have any particular business training or experience. Nor does it matter which country you come from, although the immigration authorities are more suspicious about fraud with applicants from certain countries.
- Your green card will initially be only conditional—that is, it will expire in two years, after which you will need to apply to renew it and make it permanent.
- You can choose to invest your money in a business anywhere in the U.S., so long as you maintain your investment long enough for the green card to become permanent and are actively engaged with the company you invest in.

- After your green card becomes permanent, you can work for another company or not work at all.
- You must actually live in the United States—you may not use the green card only for work and travel purposes.
- Your spouse and unmarried children under the age of 21 can get green cards as accompanying relatives.
- As with all green cards, yours can be taken away if you misuse it—for example, you live outside the U.S. for too long, commit a crime, or even fail to advise the immigration authorities of your change of address. However, if you keep your green card for five years and live in the U.S. continuously during that time (yes, your two years as a conditional resident count), you can apply for U.S. citizenship.

A. Are You Eligible for a Green Card Through Investment?

Green cards through investment are available to anyone who invests a minimum of $1 million in creating a new U.S. business or restructuring or expanding one that already exists. It doesn't matter where you got the money—gifts and inheritances, for example, are fine—so long as you obtained it lawfully. The business must employ at least ten full-time workers, produce a service or product, and benefit the U.S. economy. Full-time employment is defined as requiring at least 35 hours of service per week.

The investor, his or her spouse, and their children may not be counted among the ten employees. Other family members may be counted, however. The ten workers don't necessarily have to be U.S. citizens, but they must have more than a temporary (nonimmigrant) visa—green card holders, and any other foreign nationals who have the legal right to indefinitely live and work in the United States, can all be counted. Independent contractors do not count toward the ten employees. (See 8 C.F.R. § 204.6(e).)

The required dollar amount of the investment may be reduced to $500,000 if the business is located in a rural area or in an urban area with an unemployment rate certified by the state government to be at least 150% of the national average. Rural areas are defined as any location not part of an official metropolitan statistical area or not within the outer boundaries of any city having a population of 20,000 or more. State governments will identify the parts of the particular state that are high in unemployment, and will notify USCIS of which locations qualify. Even if you know that the area of your intended investment has extremely high unemployment, it will not qualify for the lesser dollar amount unless the state government has specifically designated it as a high-unemployment area for the purpose of green cards through investment.

Also, the investor must be actively engaged in the company, either in a managerial or a policy-forming role. (See 8 C.F.R. § 204.6(j)(5).) Passive investments, such as land speculation, do not ordinarily qualify you for a green card in this category—except under the regional center program described next.

Under the EB-5 regional center program (currently set to expire on December 9, 2016, though this program is regularly extended), 3,000 EB-5 visas are set aside for immigrants who invest in "designated regional centers." Regional centers are designated (and sometimes preapproved as qualifying investment vehicles) by USCIS, but run privately, and work to promote economic growth through increased export sales, improved regional productivity, creation of new jobs, and increased domestic capital investment. Investors in regional centers need not prove that they themselves provided new jobs for ten U.S. workers, only that as a result of the investor's contribution, the regional center created ten or more jobs, directly or indirectly, or increased regional productivity.

The overwhelming majority of EB-5 green cards are obtained by investment in regional centers, for two reasons. First, most regional centers operate in rural or high-unemployment areas that allow for a $500,000 investment rather than $1 million, and second, they allow a wealthy investor to make a cash investment without creating or managing a new enterprise. The key for regional center investors, however, is to make sure that the regional center is well-managed—the fact that USCIS has designated the center as an investment vehicle does not guarantee that the regional center will succeed long enough to allow the investor to become an unconditional permanent resident. And don't forget that this program will have ended on December 9, 2016 unless Congress voted to renew it.

USCIS also has the authority to require a greater amount of investment than $1 million. This may occur when the investor chooses to locate the business in an area of low unemployment. At present, USCIS has adopted the policy of not raising dollar investment requirements on this basis.

The investment must be an equity investment (ownership share), rather than an unsecured loan. Also, you must place your investment at risk of partial or total loss if the business does badly. However, the entire investment does not have to be made in cash. Cash equivalents, such as certificates of deposits, securitized loans, and promissory notes, can count in the total. So can the value of equipment, inventory, or other tangible property. (See 8 C.F.R. § 204.6(e).) Borrowed funds may be used as long as the investor is personally liable in the event of a default, and the loan is adequately secured (and not by assets of the business being purchased). This means that mortgages on the business assets disqualify the amount borrowed from being calculated into the total investment figure.

A number of investors may join together in creating or expanding a U.S. business and each may qualify for a green card through the single company. However, the individual investment of each person must still be for the minimum qualifying amount, and each investor must be separately responsible for the creation of ten new jobs. For example, if five people each invest $1 million in a new business that will employ at least 50 U.S. workers, all five investors qualify for green cards. But what if other investors also put money into that same business? The five hypothetical investors may still be credited with creating all 50 jobs, as long as the other investors are not seeking green cards through the investment.

The investment must be made in a "new" commercial enterprise. To do this you can either create an original business, you can buy a business that was established after November 29, 1990, or you can buy a business and restructure or reorganize it so that a new business entity is formed.

There are two exceptions to the rule that the investment must be in a "new" commercial enterprise. The first exception is that you can buy an existing business and expand it. To qualify by expanding an existing business, you must increase either the number of employees or the net worth of the business by at least 40%. You must also make the full required investment ($1 million or $500,000 depending on location) and you must still show that you created at least ten full-time jobs for U.S. workers.

The second exception to the "new" commercial enterprise rule is that you can buy a troubled business and save it from going under. To do so, you must show that the business has been around for at least two years and has had an annual loss of 20% of the company's net worth at some point over the 24 months prior to the purchase. You must still invest the full required amount, but you are not required to show that you created ten jobs. Rather, you must show that for two years from the date of purchase, you employed at least as many people as were employed at the time of the investment.

TIP
You can file your application before you have made the full required investment. (Investing all this money can take a long time.) But you'll need to show that you are actively in the process of investing. This means that you have placed enough capital at risk in the investment to convince USCIS that you are committed to the business. There is no established amount that must be invested before filing the case, unfortunately. You must use your judgment when weighing whether USCIS will believe that you are committed to the investment.

1. Two-Year Testing Period for Investor-Based Green Cards

A green card for an investor is first issued only conditionally. The conditional green card is granted for two years. When the two years are over, the investor will have to file a request with USCIS to remove

the condition and make his or her U.S. residence "permanent."

In deciding whether the condition should be removed, USCIS will investigate whether the full investment has actually been completed, whether ten full-time U.S. workers have been hired, whether the business is still operating, whether the investor has taken an active role in running the business, and whether the investor still maintains an investment stake in the business.

When any of the required factors cannot be established to the satisfaction of USCIS, or if the petition for removal of the condition is not filed within the final 90 days of the two-year conditional period, the investor will lose his or her green card and be subject to removal from the U.S. (deportation). If, on the other hand, USCIS is satisfied that the investment still meets all requirements, USCIS will remove the condition and issue a permanent green card.

2. Bringing Your Spouse and Children

If you are married or have unmarried children below the age of 21 and you acquire a green card through investment, your spouse and children can get green cards as accompanying relatives by providing proof of their family relationship to you and submitting other required paperwork and documents. Their green cards will also be issued conditionally and will become permanent when yours does.

3. Inadmissibility

If you have ever committed a crime, been involved in a terrorist organization, lied on an immigration application, lied to an immigration officer, suffered particular physical or mental illness as specified by USCIS, or are otherwise inadmissible, you may be unable to receive a green card unless you can qualify for what is known as a "waiver of inadmissibility." (See Chapter 3 to find out exactly who is inadmissible and how you can overcome these problems.) Your family members will also have to show that they are not inadmissible.

B. Quick View of the Application Process

Getting a green card through investment is a three- to five-step process. Unlike many other types of green card applications, you perform all the steps on your own, without needing someone in the U.S. to file a petition on your behalf. The steps include:

1. You mail or eFile what's called a visa petition to USCIS to show that you either have made or are in the process of making a qualifying business investment in the United States.
2. If the State Department has established a waiting list because demand for EB-5 visas exceeds the quota, you wait until your Priority Date is current and a visa is available to you.
3. Once your Priority Date is current, you and your accompanying relatives submit your applications for green cards, either at a U.S. consulate outside the United States, or possibly at a USCIS office within the United States (an option mainly available to people who are already legally in the United States).
4. If your interview was held at a U.S. consulate in another country, you enter the U.S. with your immigrant visa, at which time you become a permanent resident.
5. You must apply to remove the conditions to your conditional resident status during the 90-day period prior to your second anniversary as a conditional resident.

C. Step One: You File a Visa Petition

To begin your immigration process, you must file what's called a visa petition on Form I-526. The purpose of this form is to show that you're actively making an investment in a qualified U.S. business. Form I-526 is available at www.uscis.gov/i-526—and it comes with extensive instructions about what documentation to include with your form.

The I-526 form also takes care of some other details, like informing USCIS whether you will be continuing with your application through a consulate outside of the U.S. or through a U.S.-based USCIS office. (If you're not sure, choose the consulate—if you change your mind later, all you need to do is ask the National Visa Center (NVC) to transfer your file to USCIS. Doing the reverse, transferring your case from a USCIS office to a consulate outside of the U.S., requires filing a separate application.)

The following checklist will help you keep track of all the forms and documents that go into your initial visa petition.

If you are in the process of starting up the business, you may be unable to produce all of the items on the checklist. In that case, at a minimum you will have to present evidence that you have sufficient funds to invest, such as bank statements or lines of credit sufficient to purchase the business, and a written contract legally committing you to make the investment. You must also include a detailed written explanation of the nature of the business, containing statements of how much will be invested, where the funds for investment will come from, how the funds will be used, and a list of the specific job openings you expect to have over the first two years of the business, including job title, job

---

Checklist of Forms and Documents for Visa Petition

☐ Form I-526.

☐ Application fee (currently $3,675; checks or money orders are accepted, but not cash).

☐ Evidence that you have invested or are in the process of making an investment, such as:

  ☐ Accountant's financial statements, including profit and loss statements and balance sheets of the company for past two years.

  ☐ Bank wire transfer memos showing amount of money sent to the U.S. from abroad.

  ☐ Letters from banks or bank statements indicating average account balance of the business.

  ☐ Evidence of deposits of funds in the business's bank account.

  ☐ Comprehensive business plan with cash-flow projections for next three years.

  ☐ Contracts for purchase and bills of sale for purchase of capital goods and inventory.

☐ Lease agreements for business premises, contracts to purchase, deeds for business real estate, or construction contracts and blueprints for building the business premises.

☐ Evidence that investment funds were obtained lawfully, including:

  ☐ Foreign business registration records, if your funds come from a business you own.

  ☐ Securities statements, if the funds came from trading, bonds, or stocks.

  ☐ Tax returns for you and your business filed anywhere in the world within the past five years.

  ☐ Financial statement for your business.

  ☐ Personal and business bank statements for previous 12 months.

  ☐ Letters from members of the business community confirming your occupation and your successes.

Checklist of Forms and Documents for Visa Petition (continued)

☐ Certified copies of all pending civil or criminal actions and proceedings, or any private civil actions involving money judgments against you within the past 15 years.

☐ Evidence that you've invested in a lawful, for-profit, active business entity in the U.S., or else invested enough in an existing business to make its net worth or number of employees go up by at least 40%, such as:

  ☐ Articles of incorporation, partnership agreement, or other legal charter or business license of the company, together with a notarized affidavit from an official of the company certifying who owns the business and in what percentages.

  ☐ Copies of all outstanding stock certificates, if the business is a corporation.

  ☐ Evidence of payment for equity (match wire transfer value to stock ledger share value).

☐ Notarized affidavit from the secretary of the corporation, or, if the business is not a corporation, from the official record keeper of the business, stating the names of each owner and percentages of the company owned.

☐ Credit agreements with suppliers.

☐ Evidence that you transferred capital resulting in a 40% or higher gain in number of employees or net worth.

☐ Payroll records of the company for the past two years, if available.

☐ If applicable, evidence certifying that the business is located in a rural or high-unemployment area, such as a letter from your state government.

---

description, salary, and when these jobs will become available. Finally, you should submit a comprehensive business plan supporting all of these documents.

1. Sending the Visa Petition

Mail your completed I-526 with supporting documents and fee to the USCIS "Dallas Lockbox" located at the following address: USCIS, P.O. Box 660168, Dallas, TX 75266. Or, if you're using FedEx or similar overnight courier, mail to USCIS, ATTN: I-526, 2501 S. State Highway 121 Business, Suite 400, Lewisville, TX 75067.

2. Awaiting USCIS Approval of the Visa Petition

Within a few weeks after submitting the petition, you should receive a written confirmation that the application is being processed, together with a receipt for the fees. This notice will also give your immigration case file number.

If USCIS wants further information before acting on your case, it will return all petition papers, forms, and documents to you, together with another form known as an I-797E Request for Evidence. The I-797E tells you what corrections, additional pieces of information, or additional documents are expected. You should make the corrections or supply the extra data and mail the whole package back to the regional service center, with a copy of the I-797E on top.

After filing Form I-526, you will have to wait for the petition to be approved, which can take several months by itself. (See Chapter 4 for how to track the length of time USCIS is taking to decide on visa petitions and how to track your own application online.)

Once your petition is approved, a Notice of Action Form I-797 will be sent to you, indicating the approval. If you plan to apply for your green card at a U.S. consulate abroad, USCIS will forward the file to the National Visa Center (NVC) located in Portsmouth, New Hampshire. The NVC will then send instructions to you so that you may proceed with the next step, described later in this chapter.

Alternatively, if you are legally present in the U.S., and wish to apply for your green card within the U.S., you can file for "adjustment of status" using Form I-485. (See Step Three, below.)

An approved petition does not by itself give you any right to immigrate to, or live in, the United States. It is only a prerequisite to the next step, submitting your own application for a green card.

D. Step Two: You Await an Available Visa Number

Because there are annual limits on the number of people who can receive green cards through investment, it's possible (especially if you are from China) that you will have to wait in line until you can apply for a visa or green card. Of course, this isn't a physical line you must stand in, but a kind of waiting list run by the U.S. State Department, which will determine when you can move to the next stage. Your place in the line is marked by a number called your Priority Date, which is determined by the date on which you filed your I-526 visa petition.

If you will be getting an immigrant visa from a U.S. consulate, you can see whether you must wait to apply for the visa by consulting the State Department's *Visa Bulletin*. It's available on a recorded message at 202-663-1541, or at the State Department's website at http://travel.state.gov (click under "U.S. visas" then look for the "Visa Bulletin" link in the Law and Policy section.)

The State Department updates the *Visa Bulletin* around the middle of every month, but not on any particular day. As described in Chapter 10, the *Visa Bulletin* contains two charts relating to employment-based visa applications. One is called "Dates for Filing of Employment-Based Visa Applications" and the other is called "Application Final Action Dates for Employment-Based Preference Cases." In the Dates for Filing chart, find the row for the 5th preference, and look at the column for your country. (If you don't see your country, you're in the column for "All Chargeability Areas Except Those Listed.")

If you see a "C," that's good. That means the category is current for you, and there's no wait to apply. If you see a date that's on or after your Priority Date, that's good too. That means you're free to apply for your visa or adjust status. If you see a date that's before your Priority Date, however, it means you can't apply yet. You have to keep checking each month's *Visa Bulletin* until you see a "C" or a date that's on or after your Priority Date.

If you are inside the U.S. and will be adjusting status, USCIS will tell you when you can apply. USCIS uses the same charts that are in the *Visa Bulletin*, and tells you which one to look at to see when to apply. That instruction is found on the USCIS website at www.uscis.gov/visabulletininfo. It changes monthly.

E. Step Three: You Apply for an Immigrant Visa or Green Card

Once your visa petition has been approved, and assuming your Priority Date is current

according to the appropriate chart, you can apply for an immigrant visa or green card. If your spouse or children will be accompanying you, they must each file their own applications. A big part of any application for permanent residence is proving that you are not inadmissible to the United States. Review Chapter 3 regarding the grounds of inadmissibility.

The most important question at this point in the process is where you file the application—in the United States or at a consulate outside of the United States? You should have already made this choice on your Form I-526, but you're allowed to change your mind, so it's worth revisiting the question.

If you're living outside of the U.S. now. The answer is fairly easy for people living outside of the United States. You'll file at a local U.S. consulate and attend an interview there before entering the United States. (This method is called consular processing.)

If you're living in the U.S. now. The answer is a bit more complicated for applicants already in the United States. Ordinarily, the most convenient choice would probably be for you to adjust status without leaving—that is, send your application to USCIS and attend your interview at a local USCIS office. Once your application is filed, your stay in the United States will be considered legal, and you can apply for permission to work. Should problems arise in your case, you'll be able to wait for a decision in the U.S., a circumstance most green card applicants prefer. Also, if your application for a green card is turned down, you have greater rights of appeal inside the U.S. than you do at a U.S. consulate.

One catch is that you are allowed to adjust status only if you're already in the U.S. legally, that is, on a valid, unexpired visa or other form of permission (with a few exceptions). You might, for example, already be on a temporary visa such as a treaty investor (E-2) visa. If, however, you're living in the United States with no legal status, or have worked without authorization, or you entered legally without a visa under the Visa Waiver program, you are barred from filing your green card application inside the United States. See Chapter 10 on adjustment of employment-based applicants for more information on adjustment eligibility.

Whether or not you are eligible to adjust status, you may instead decide to leave the United States and apply for your green card at a U.S. consulate abroad. If the consulates are issuing visas more quickly than your local USCIS office is handling adjustment of status applications (which is possible), leaving to apply at a consulate outside of the U.S. could be a smart strategic move. However, if you have already spent 180 days or more in

the U.S. out of legal status, or crossed the border without inspection, be sure you are not inadmissible or subject to a three-year or ten-year waiting period before you go. (See Chapter 3.) Otherwise, you could find yourself stuck outside the U.S. for three or ten years.

1. Adjusting Status in the U.S.

The process of adjusting your status to permanent resident involves preparing a set of forms and documents (a separate set for you, your spouse, and each of your accompanying children), mailing these to USCIS, waiting for some weeks until you're called in to have your fingerprints taken, and then waiting a few weeks or months longer until you're called in for your final green card interview at a local USCIS office (not the one to which you sent your application). You should be approved for your green card at, or soon after, the interview. In some cases, the interview is waived, in which case you'll get a letter in the mail telling you you've been approved. See Chapter 4 for information on tracking the progress of your application.

As part of your adjustment of status application, you and your family members may apply for permission to work (an Employment Authorization Document, or EAD). The EAD takes about 90 days to get. It is valid in one- or two-year increments and can be extended as many times as you need until your adjustment of status application is decided.

 CAUTION
Security checks are a likely cause of delays. If you're between 14 and 79 years old: As part of your adjustment of status application, USCIS will have the FBI run both a fingerprint check and a name check on you, and will search for your name in the Interagency Border Inspection System (IBIS) database to detect any crimes, fraud schemes, or other illegal activities with which you may have been involved. These name checks can take several months, or even longer if yours is a common name. The FBI fingerprint check and the IBIS name check must be complete before USCIS can approve your application, but if the FBI name check hasn't been resolved within six months and your application is otherwise approvable, USCIS should not wait any longer to approve it. If you've been informed that your case is stalled due to security checks, get the name of a person you can keep in touch with for updates, or hire a lawyer to help with this task.

a. Paperwork to Prepare for Adjustment of Status Application

The basic form used in the U.S. adjustment of status application is Form I-485, Application for Permanent Residence. However, a handful of other forms and documents must be prepared to accompany this main one.

An easy way to get all these forms is to call the USCIS forms line at 800-870-3676 and ask for the Adjustment of Status Packet. Or, you can obtain the forms online at www.uscis.gov/forms. (Select the forms you need one by one based on the checklist below.)

The checklist below will help you assemble and keep track of the appropriate forms and documents. A complete set of the items on the checklist must also be prepared for your accompanying spouse and children.

TIP
Tip for filling out Form I-485: You'll notice that on the first page of the form, under "Part 2. Application Type," it asks you to choose the basis upon which you're applying for a green card. Mark Box a if you're the investor, Box b if you're a spouse or child.

On the checklist shown below, the Medical Examination Report could use extra explanation:

You must submit a Medical Examination Report for each applicant. This is done on Form I-693, which a USCIS-authorized physician or medical clinic will give you. To find a doctor who can do your medical exam, call the USCIS National Customer Service Center at 800-375-5283 or use the online USCIS Civil Surgeons Locator at https://my.uscis.gov/findadoctor. You'll have to pay the doctor's fee for the exam. The exam itself involves taking a medical history, blood test, and chest X-ray, and administering vaccinations if needed or recommended for you. Pregnant women may refuse to be X-rayed until after the baby is born.

After completion of the medical exam, and upon obtaining the test results, the doctor will give you the results in a sealed envelope. Do not open the envelope. USCIS expects the envelope to be delivered unopened, so as to prevent tampering.

b. Mailing the Adjustment Packet

After you have finished preparing the adjustment of status paperwork, you must mail it to USCIS. (Do so by certified mail, return receipt requested or via courier, and keep a complete copy of everything you send in.) At the time this book went to print, investor visa adjustments are to be mailed to one of two USCIS "Lockboxes," depending upon one's residence at time of filing. Applicants in the Western U.S. will file at the Phoenix Lockbox, at: USCIS, P.O. Box 21281, Phoenix, AZ 85036. For Express Mail and courier deliveries (e.g., FedEx), use this address: USCIS, Attn: AOS, 1820 E. Skyharbor Circle S, Suite 100, Phoenix, AZ 85034. Applicants in the Eastern U.S. will file at the Dallas Lockbox, at: USCIS, P.O. Box 660867, Dallas, TX 75266. For Express Mail and courier deliveries (e.g., FedEx), use this address: USCIS, Attn: AOS, 2501 S. State Hwy, 121 Business, Suite 400, Lewisville, TX 75067. Double-check the USCIS website www.uscis.gov/i-485-addresses for the correct address.

Generally, after filing your green card application, you will receive notice of your fingerprint appointment within 90 days. To find out the typical processing time for your local office, go to www.uscis.gov, click "Check Your Case Status," find the link for "Check Processing Times," and select the USCIS office (likely a Field Office) where your I-485 is being processed. USCIS might ask you to come in for an interview as part of the process. The interview notice will tell you whether any further documentation is needed.

Dealing With Delays in Approval of Your Work Authorization

If you want to work before your application for a green card is approved, you must file a separate application for employment authorization. To do so, fill out Form I-765 and file it together with your adjustment of status application. If you do it this way there is no filing fee.

Legally, USCIS does not have to make a decision on your employment authorization application for up to 90 days from the date on your receipt notice. If, for some reason, you are not given a decision within 75 days, you can call USCIS Customer Service and ask it to create a "service request." This will let the office handling your case know that it needs to do something about your work card soon.

Checklist for Adjustment of Status Application

Forms

☐ Form I-485, with filing fee (currently $1,225 for applicants ages 14 to 78 (includes biometrics fee), $750 for derivative applicants under age 14 who are filing concurrently with a parent, and $1,140 for applicants under age 14 who are not filing with a parent). Checks and money orders are accepted, but don't send cash through the mail.

☐ Form I-485A (only if you'll be paying the $1,000 penalty fee in order to adjust status).

☐ Form G-325A.

☐ Form I-765 (optional, if you want a work permit). On I-765 Question 16, answer the question "(c)(9)."

☐ I-131, Application for Travel Document (Advance Parole), for use if you think you'll need to travel outside the United States while your application is processed.

Documents (Remember, all foreign-language documents must be accompanied by an English translation with translator's certification.)

☐ Copy of your I-526 approval notice.

☐ Copy of a long-form birth certificate for you and each accompanying relative.

☐ Marriage certificate if you are married and bringing your spouse.

☐ If either you or your spouse have been previously married, copies of divorce and death certificates showing termination of all previous marriages.

☐ Copy of I-94 card (Arrival/Departure record) for you and each accompanying relative, if you were given a physical card instead of being entered into a database.

☐ Four photographs of you and four of each accompanying relative, in U.S. passport style (it's best to have a professional do these). Write your name and A number (if you've received one from USCIS) in pencil or felt pen on the back of each photo. (This assumes you will submit the Forms I-765 and I-131 at this time. If not, you can subtract one photo for each form you don't submit.)

☐ Medical exam report for you and each accompanying relative (Form I-693, filled out and signed by a USCIS-certified doctor, and presented in an unopened envelope).

c. Your Adjustment of Status Interview

You may be called in for a personal interview, which will be held at a USCIS office near you. However, personal interviews are often waived in green-card-through-investment applications. If USCIS requires you to attend an interview, it will send you and your accompanying relatives an appointment notice, usually about two weeks in advance of the interview. If you have an attorney, he or she may come with you to the interview. (Even if you don't have an attorney, you could consult with or hire one at this point.)

If everything is in order, your application will be approved at the conclusion of the interview or soon after. Your passport will be stamped to show that you have been admitted to the U.S. as a conditional resident, and your green card will be ordered.

The green card will come to you in the mail several weeks after the interview. It will show a two-year expiration date. (See Section G, below, "Converting Your Conditional Residence Into Permanent Residence," for how to become a permanent resident after two years.)

If you need to travel outside the U.S. before your green card arrives, however, you must go back to the USCIS office with your passport and the written notice of approval. A temporary stamp will be placed in your passport, enabling you to return after your trip. Never leave the U.S. without either your green card or a temporary stamp in your passport.

Read This If You Plan to Leave the U.S. Before Your Adjustment Interview

Once your application for adjustment of status has been filed, you must not leave the U.S. for any reason before your approval without first applying for and receiving advance permission to reenter the U.S. (Advance Parole).

Any absence without this permission will be viewed as a termination of your application for a green card—which means that, upon return, you will be told that your green card application is abandoned and you may not be able to enter the United States.

There is an exception to this rule for people with valid H-1B or L-1 visas. They may travel internationally without abandoning their adjustment of status application.

Your application for Advance Parole is made on Form I-131, which you file at the same time as your I-485. If you do it this way, there is no additional filing fee. You'll have to explain why you need to leave the country and where you plan to go.

If approved, you will be allowed to leave the U.S. and return again with no break in the processing of your application. However, if you were out of status for 180 days or more, speak to a lawyer before you depart the U.S. even on the basis of Advance Parole. Until recently, to do so would risk subjecting you to a three-year or ten-year bar to reentry. That risk was greatly reduced in 2012, when the Board of Immigration Appeals (BIA) issued a ruling called *Matter of Arrabally and Yerrabelly*, 25 I&N Dec. 771 (BIA 2012). The BIA said that departures under Advance Parole with a pending adjustment of status application do NOT, despite previous USCIS interpretations to the contrary, trigger the unlawful presence bars.

If you applied for and were granted work authorization as well, your evidence of authorization to travel will come in the form of a single card that gives you permission for both.

Checklist of Documents to Bring to Your Adjustment Interview

Prepare all of the following to take with you to your USCIS interview:

☐ The interview notice that USCIS sent to you—security officers at the building entrance and the receptionist will need to see it.

☐ A complete photocopy of your green card application. This is for your use—you may want to follow along as the officer asks you questions about the material you filled out on the forms, or you may find that the officer is missing something that you have a copy of.

☐ All passports (current and expired).

☐ Driver's license or state ID card.

☐ Social Security card.

☐ Advance parole document(s) and EAD card(s) (work permits).

☐ Birth certificate.

☐ Marriage certificate/license (if any).

☐ Divorce/death certificates from prior marriages (if any).

☐ All IAP-66, DS-2019, and I-20 forms (only if you have ever been in J-1 or F-1 visa status).

☐ All other original USCIS approval notices for nonimmigrant status (Forms I-797).

☐ I-94 card(s), if you were given them.

☐ Documents relating to any arrests or criminal convictions—certified copies of final court dispositions.

☐ Any updates to the material in your application. For example, if you have given birth to another child, bring the birth certificate. If you've been arrested, bring a full explanation (and consult with an attorney, to make sure that the arrest doesn't make you inadmissible).

☐ Any other documents requested in the interview notice.

RELATED TOPIC

See Chapter 4 for details on what to expect during your adjustment of status interview. If your adjustment of status application is denied, also see Chapter 4. For information on how to protect your status as a green card holder after you're approved, see Chapter 14.

2. Consular Processing

If you opt out of the adjustment of status process, or if you are not qualified for it, then you will be required to obtain an immigrant visa at a U.S. consulate overseas before you can immigrate. This process is known as "consular immigrant visa processing."

Consular processing requires you to prepare some forms and documents according to instructions, pay fees, undergo a medical exam, get police certificates, prepare additional documents for the interview, and finally, attend the interview at the consulate. There, if all goes well, you will be approved (subject to final security checks) for an immigrant visa to enter the United States.

Much of your job at this point involves convincing the consulate that you are not inadmissible for health, criminal, security, or financial reasons.

TIP

The NVC has people specially trained in handling I-526 investor cases. If you have a question about an approved I-526 that has been sent to the NVC, you can email the EB-5 Investor Assistance Desk at NVCeb-5@state. gov. Don't send your documents to this email address, however, except for documents proving your relationship to a spouse or child who is immigrating with you.

a. National Visa Center Processing

At the beginning, consular processing involves a lot of information being sent in various directions. First, after USCIS approves your visa petition, it will forward your file to the National Visa Center (NVC) in Portsmouth, New Hampshire. It will send you a letter or email directing you to a State Department website that will guide you through the "immigrant visa" process at the NVC.

The first thing NVC requests is that you choose your email communication options. The NVC wants to communicate with you by email rather than by mailing you letters. You, too, should prefer email, because it's a quicker, more reliable, and more secure way of communicating with the NVC. To establish this communication, send an email to nvcinquiry@state.gov telling it which email address or addresses to send correspondence to. Always include the NVC case number it gave you in your email subject line.

At this point, if you want to have someone else (an attorney or agent) receive all correspondence involved with your case, you must tell the NVC who that person is by submitting Form DS-261, Online Choice of Address and Agent. The NVC recommends that this person be in the U.S., or at least have a reliable email address. Fill out Form DS-261 and submit it online, at the State Department's Consular Electronic Application Center (CEAC) website, https://ceac.state.gov.

The next step is to pay the Immigrant Visa (IV) fee bill (currently $345 for EB-5 immigrant visa applications). The NVC prefers that you do this online through the CEAC website. If you can't, mail a cashier's check or money order (not a personal check) to the NVC. Instructions are given on the State Department's immigrant visa processing website, to which the NVC will direct you.

The application form you need to send to the NVC is called a DS-260. Fill this out and submit it through the CEAC website, https://ceac.state.gov. To log in to CEAC, use your NVC case number and invoice number (which the NVC sent in its original notice to you).

If you can't finish the whole form in one sitting, don't worry—you can save your work and come back to it later. Make sure to print the confirmation page when you're done. You'll need to bring it to your interview at the consulate.

b. Supporting Documents

The State Department's immigrant visa process website will let you know how to submit documents to the NVC. Some people can scan and email documents, others must mail them to the NVC, and others can choose either method.

The checklist below provides a brief explanation of some of the documents you'll need to gather to send to the NVC and bring to your immigrant visa interview. Keep your eyes open for any special requirements that your consulate may add to this list. If you were not required to mail all originals to the NVC, bring the originals and a set of copies with you to your interview (the consular officer may want to examine the originals to make sure they're not fraudulent, but keep copies for your files). Do not mail your paperwork to the consulate!

Here is some additional explanation regarding some of the items on the checklist.

Checklist of Documents for Your Consular Interview

- ☐ DS-260 receipt that you printed out after submitting the form online.
- ☐ Copy of I-526 approval notice from USCIS (it should have been sent directly to the consulate, but bring a copy just in case).
- ☐ Long-form birth certificate for you and for each accompanying relative as well as for any unmarried minor children who are *not* immigrating with you.
- ☐ Marriage certificate if you are married and bringing your spouse.
- ☐ If either you or your spouse have been previously married, copies of divorce and death certificates showing termination of all previous marriages.
- ☐ Passport for you and for each accompanying relative, valid for at least six months beyond the date of the final interview.

- ☐ Required police certificates.
- ☐ Fingerprints, if specifically requested by the consulate.
- ☐ If you or accompanying relative served in the military forces of any country, a copy of your military records.
- ☐ Passport-type photographs, two of you and two of each accompanying relative. Some consulates now take the photos at the interview. This will be clear from the instructions.
- ☐ Medical exam report for you and for each accompanying relative.
- ☐ Any additional documents requested in the interview notice.

Police clearance. You personally must collect police clearance certificates from each country you have lived in for one year or more since your 16th birthday. Additionally, you must have a police certificate from every place in your home country or country of last residence, if you lived there for at least six months since the age of 16. You do not need to obtain police certificates from the United States.

The State Department's immigrant visa process website contains information on how to contact the local police department to get police certificates from various countries. Some countries refuse to supply police certificates, or their certificates are not considered reliable, and so you will not be required to obtain them from those locations.

Some countries will send certificates directly to U.S. consulates but not to you personally. Before they send the certificates out, however, you must request that it be done. Usually this requires filing some type of request form, together with a set of your fingerprints.

Photos. You and each accompanying relative must bring two passport-style photographs to your interview. Many photographers are familiar with U.S. passport style. If you are a do-it-yourself type, passport-style specifications are available on the State Department's website, www.travel.state.gov. If your religious beliefs require wearing a head covering, you should be able to keep it on for the photo. However, your eyes and face must still be visible, and your head covering cannot obscure your hairline or cast shadows on your face.

Fingerprints. A few consulates require you to submit fingerprints, though most do not. Consulates wanting fingerprints will send you blank fingerprint cards with instructions.

Medical exam. Before your visa interview, you and your accompanying relatives will need to schedule and undergo a medical examination. The State Department's immigrant visa processing website contains instructions on how to do this, and what to bring to your exam.

Only certain doctors can perform the examination. The fees depend on the country and doctor.

The exam itself involves taking a medical history, blood test, and chest X-ray and administering vaccinations, if you need them. Pregnant women can refuse to be X-rayed until after the pregnancy. The vaccination requirement may be waived for religious, moral, or medical reasons.

The main purpose of the medical exam is to verify that you are not medically inadmissible. Some medical grounds of inadmissibility can be overcome with treatment or by applying for a waiver. (See Chapter 3 for details.) If you need a medical waiver, you will be given complete instructions by the consulate at the time of your interview, but you should also consult an experienced immigration attorney.

After the examination, the doctor will either give you a sealed envelope with the results of the test, or send the results directly to the consulate. If you get an envelope, don't open it. Bring it to your interview along with your other documents.

c. Your Consular Interview

Consulates hold interviews on all green card applications. The NVC will send you a notice of your interview date. Review the State Department's immigrant visa website for instructions on what to bring to the interview and how to prepare for it. Make sure you read instructions from the consulate carefully for any additions or changes.

 RELATED TOPIC
For details on what to expect during your consular visa interview, see Chapter 4. And for information on what to do if your visa is denied, see Chapter 4 as well.

F. Step Four: Immigrant Visa Holders Enter the U.S.

If you processed your application through a U.S. consulate overseas, your immigrant visa will be placed on a page in your passport. Review the visa to make sure all the information is correct. If you see any spelling errors, contact the embassy or consulate promptly. You'll also get a sealed "visa packet" containing documents to show to border officials when you get to the United States. Don't open it!

Your immigrant visa allows you to request entry to the United States at a border post, airport, or other arrival point. Before you can receive a green card, however, you have to pay one last fee: the USCIS Immigrant Fee, currently $220. Each member of the family traveling with you will be charged the same fee. The only way to pay this fee is through the online USCIS Electronic Immigration System, known as ELIS. You'll need to create an ELIS account at uscis.gov/uscis-elis. Select "USCIS Immigrant Fee" and include your personal information. Have your Alien number (A-Number) and Department of State Case ID number handy. (You got these from the consulate.) Once you're in, you can pay the fee for all family members in one transaction. You'll need a valid credit or debit card, or U.S. bank checking account and routing numbers.

USCIS suggests that you pay the Immigrant Fee before departing for the United States. You don't have to, but USCIS won't give you a green card until you do. It doesn't make much sense to wait, because you're going to want your green card as soon as possible.

The inspection process involves a U.S. border officer opening the sealed visa packet containing your entry documents, and doing a last check to make sure you haven't used fraud. The border officer has expedited removal powers, which means he or she can turn you right around and send you home if anything appears wrong in your packet or with your answers to the officer's questions. Be polite and careful in answering.

> CAUTION
> **The clock is ticking.** You must enter the U.S. before your visa expires. Check the date printed on your visa inside your passport. The consulate usually gives you six months to make the trip, measured from the date it issues the visa. You might be given less time, however, if, for example, the results of your medical exam are in danger of getting stale.

When the officer is satisfied that everything is in order, he or she will stamp your passport to show that you're now a U.S. permanent resident and are immediately authorized to work. This stamp is often called an "I-551 stamp" or "ADIT stamp." You won't receive an actual green card yet, however.

Green cards for you and your accompanying relatives will be ordered for you (as long as you've paid the Immigrant Fee), and will come by mail several weeks later, to the address you provided upon arrival. The cards will show a two-year expiration date. (See Section G, below, for how to become a permanent resident after two years.)

G. Step Five: Converting Your Conditional Residence Into Permanent Residence

As we've stated, green cards through investment are first issued conditionally, for two years. After the two years are up, in order to make the green cards permanent, you must then go through a procedure to remove the conditions from your residence. Give your full attention to this part of the process—an astonishing number of these applications are denied. Often it's because the regional center in which the conditional green card holder invested was not able to come through on its promises.

File the items on the checklist below with the USCIS Service Center with jurisdiction over the area where your company or regional center is located. You must file this application during the 90-day period prior to the expiration of your conditional resident status. Your spouse and children should be included on the form.

Failure to submit the I-829 and documentation within the 90-day window period will cause USCIS to terminate your resident status, and it may start removal (deportation) proceedings against you and your family members. If you miss the deadline you can still file the removal petition for "good cause and extenuating circumstances" up to the time USCIS commences removal proceedings. After your case arrives

---

Checklist for Removal of Conditions on Residence

- ☐ USCIS Form I-829, with filing fee (currently $3,750; plus $85 for biometrics).
- ☐ Additional biometrics fee for each dependent (spouse or child) included in your application ($85).
- ☐ Copies of your and your family members' green cards.
- ☐ Evidence that you actually established the commercial enterprise (such as federal income tax returns).
- ☐ Evidence that you actively invested the required capital (such as articles of incorporation, a business license, and financial statements).
- ☐ Evidence that you have substantially met and maintained the capital investment requirement throughout your conditional residence (such as bank statements, invoices, receipts, contracts, tax returns, etc.).
- ☐ Evidence of the number of full-time employees when you made the investment, and at the time you're filing the I-829. Evidence can include payroll records, tax documents, and Forms I-9.
- ☐ Documentation showing the results of all arrests, charges, pleas, trials, alternative sentencing programs, etc., if any, since becoming a conditional permanent resident.

---

at the Immigration Court, the judge may terminate proceedings and restore permanent resident status, but only if USCIS agrees to this.

After USCIS receives your I-829 application, it will send you a receipt notice. Guard this notice carefully—it is also proof that your status has been extended for the months that USCIS will take to approve your permanent residence. If you need to travel internationally, you'll need to take both this notice and your expired green card to your local USCIS office (after scheduling an appointment on the InfoPass system). USCIS will give you what's called an I-551 stamp in your passport allowing you to travel and return. If the extension expires before you've gotten an answer from USCIS, go to your local USCIS office with your passport for a stamp further extending your status.

During this time period, you will also be sent an appointment notice stating when and where you must appear for biometric processing. (It's usually at a USCIS Application Support Center.) Biometric processing includes taking your photograph, signature, and index fingerprint, for use in generating your new green card. If you're between ages 14 and 79, it also includes taking your fingerprints, in order to do another criminal background check.

USCIS may or may not interview you in connection with the I-829 filing. If your accompanying documentation makes it clear you have fulfilled the requirements for the green card, you should be approved without an interview.

If USCIS requires an interview, it will be held at a local USCIS office near where your commercial enterprise is located. If you fail to appear for the interview, USCIS regulations specify that USCIS should put you, the petitioner-entrepreneur, into removal proceedings. (If that happens, you can still write USCIS and request that the interview be rescheduled or waived. If it is rescheduled or waived, your conditional resident status is restored. Otherwise, the petition has to be considered in Immigration Court as discussed above.)

Upon approval of your request to remove the conditions on your residence, your U.S. residency will become permanent. A new green card will be sent to you, with a ten-year expiration date.

SKIP AHEAD
Ready for information on how to protect your status as a green card holder after you're approved? See Chapter 14.

Getting a Green Card as a Special Immigrant

This chapter covers six categories of so-called special immigrants. The name is somewhat misleading—it actually refers to the employment fourth preference category, which encompasses religious workers, foreign medical graduates, employees of the U.S. consulate in Hong Kong, former foreign U.S. government workers, retired employees of international organizations, juveniles declared dependent on a U.S. juvenile court, and more. (There are other categories of special immigrants that we don't cover in this book because they apply to so few people, such as former employees of the Panama Canal Zone and international broadcasting employees.)

Ten thousand green cards are available each year for all special immigrant categories taken together. No more than 5,000 of that total can go to nonclergy religious workers.

A. Do You Qualify for a Green Card as a Special Immigrant?

Occasionally, laws are passed making green cards available to people in special situations. Special immigrant green cards are available to the following people:

- workers for recognized religious organizations
- foreign medical graduates who have been in the U.S. a long time

- foreign workers who are or were formerly longtime employees of the U.S. government abroad
- retired officers or employees of certain international organizations who have lived in the U.S. for a certain time
- foreign nationals who have been declared dependent on juvenile courts in the United States ("special immigrant juveniles")
- persons who served honorably for 12 years on active U.S. military duty after October 15, 1978
- Panama Canal Zone workers (a little-used category that is not discussed further in this chapter)
- Iraqi and Afghan translators/interpreters (a little-used category that is not discussed further in this chapter)
- Iraqis who have assisted the United States (a little-used category that is not discussed further in this chapter)
- NATO civilian employees and their families (a little-used category that is not discussed further in this chapter), and
- persons coming to work as broadcasters for the International Broadcasting Bureau of the Broadcasting Board of Governors, or for its grantee (a little-used category that is not discussed further in this chapter).

Key Features of a Special-Immigrant-Based Green Card

If you qualify for this type of green card, here are some of its advantages and limitations:

- Although not many green cards are available in this category, the eligibility criteria are so narrowly defined that if you fit them, you have a good chance of getting a green card.
- You must actually plan to live in the United States—you must not use the green card only for work and travel purposes.
- Your spouse and unmarried children under the age of 21 can get green cards as accompanying relatives.
- As with all green cards, yours can be taken away if you misuse it—for example, you live outside the U.S. for too long, commit a crime, or even fail to advise the immigration authorities of your change of address. However, if you successfully keep your green card for five years, you can apply for U.S. citizenship.

SEE AN EXPERT

Do you need a lawyer? If you think you might fit into one of the more obscure categories that we don't cover in this chapter, you'll probably want to seek an immigration lawyer's help. In any case, a lawyer can help you prove that you fit into the category you're seeking and navigate the often difficult bureaucratic requirements.

1. Religious Workers

There are two subcategories of special immigrant religious workers: ministers and other religious workers. Minister is defined as a person authorized by a recognized religious denomination to conduct religious activities. This includes not only ministers, priests, and rabbis, but also salaried Buddhist monks, commissioned officers of the Salvation Army, practitioners and nurses of the Christian Science Church, and ordained deacons. Usually, to be considered a minister, you must have formal recognition from the religion in question, such as a license, a certificate of ordination, or another qualification to conduct religious worship.

The subcategory of "other religious workers" covers people who are in a "religious vocation" or "religious occupation" and are authorized to perform normal religious duties, but are not considered part of the clergy. This includes anyone performing a traditional religious function, such as liturgical workers, religious instructors, religious counselors, cantors, catechists, workers in religious hospitals or religious health care facilities, missionaries, religious translators, or religious broadcasters. It does not cover workers involved in purely nonreligious functions such as janitors, maintenance workers, clerical staff, fundraisers, or even singers. It also does not cover volunteers. USCIS requires that religious workers be working in a traditionally permanent salaried position within the denomination and be assigned only religious duties.

To qualify for a green card in either of the two religious subcategories, you must have been a member for at least the past two years of a recognized religion that has a bona fide nonprofit organization in the United States. During those two years, you must have been employed continuously (though not necessarily full time) by that same religious group. Your sole purpose in coming to the U.S. must be to work as a minister of that religion (and your denomination must need additional ministers), or, at the request of the organization, to work in some other capacity related to the religion's activities in the United States. Spouses and children (unmarried, under age 21) may apply with you.

This provision of the law has been the subject of some controversy and there have been efforts in Congress to eliminate it as a way of getting permanent residence. The nonminister religious worker classification within the law is currently set to expire in December 2016. By the time you read this, it may have been reauthorized, as it has been many times—or maybe Congress will have dropped the ball this time.

2. Foreign Medical Graduates

If you are a graduate of a foreign medical school who came to the U.S. before January 10, 1978, on either an H or J visa, you qualify as a special immigrant if you can meet all of the following conditions:

- You were permanently licensed to practice medicine in some U.S. state on or before January 9, 1978.
- You were physically in the U.S. and practicing medicine on January 9, 1978.
- You have lived continuously in the U.S. and practiced medicine since January 9, 1978.
- If you came to the U.S. on a J-1 visa and were subject to the two-year home residency requirement, you got a waiver of the home residency requirement, or you have a "no objection letter" from your home government.

3. International U.S. Government Workers

If you have been employed abroad by the U.S. government for at least 15 years, you may apply for a green card as a special immigrant. Your spouse and children may apply with you. To qualify, you must have the recommendation of the principal officer-in-charge of the U.S. government foreign office in which you were employed. The U.S. Secretary of State must also approve the recommendation. In addition, certain employees of the American Institute in Taiwan can qualify under this category. The director of the Institute must recommend you.

4. Retired Employees of International Organizations

If you are a retired employee of an international organization, you qualify for a green card under the following conditions:

- You have resided in the U.S. for at least 15 years prior to your retirement, on a G-4 or N visa.
- You lived and were physically present in the U.S. for at least half of the seven years immediately before applying for a green card.
- You apply to receive a green card within six months after your retirement.

If you are the unmarried child of an officer, employee, former officer, or former employee of an international organization, you qualify for a green card if all of the following are true:

- You have a G-4 or N visa.
- You lived and were physically present in the U.S. for at least half of the seven-year period before applying for a green card.
- You lived in the U.S. for at least a total of seven years while you were between the ages of five and 21.
- You apply for a green card before your 25th birthday.

If you are the spouse of an officer or employee in this special immigrant class, you qualify for a green card as an accompanying relative. However, if you were married to a qualifying officer or employee who has died, you can still get a green card if you lived in the U.S. for at least 15 years on a G-4 or N visa before the death of your spouse, you have lived in the U.S. for at least one half of the seven years before your application, and you apply within six months after your spouse's death.

5. Persons Declared Dependent on a Juvenile Court

A foreign national child can qualify for a green card as a special immigrant juvenile if:

- He or she is under age 21 and unmarried (and remains both under 21 and unmarried up to the time the green card application is filed, meaning you should act quickly in the case of a child who is nearing age 21).
- He or she has been declared dependent on a juvenile court located in the U.S. and that court either says the child is eligible for long-term foster care or has committed the child to the care of a state agency, due to abuse, neglect, or abandonment.
- The child is separated from at least one parent (doesn't need to be both) due to abuse, neglect, abandonment, or a similar basis found under state law.

- The court has determined that it is in the minor's best interest to remain in the United States.

(See I.N.A. § 203(b)(4), 8 U.S.C. § 1153(b)(4); I.N.A. § 101(a)(27), 8 U.S.C. § 1101; 8 C.F.R. § 204.11.)

Special immigrant juvenile status requires the consent of the DHS in the form of an approved I-360 petition from USCIS. If a child crosses the border without an adult and is put in the care of the Office of Refugee Resettlement within the Department of Health and Human Services (HHS), HHS must agree to let the juvenile court enter the necessary order, unless the court is not going to determine or alter custody.

> **CAUTION**
> **People who get their permanent residency as a special immigrant juvenile may not petition for their natural or prior adoptive parents to immigrate to the United States.** This is because the U.S. offers this special green card to juvenile immigrants with the understanding that the children need to get away from their homeland parents—so it would make little sense for them to be reunited with those parents.

6. Servicepeople With 12 Years' Duty

If you have served a total of 12 years of active duty with the U.S. armed services after October 12, 1978, you may qualify for special immigrant status. You need to have enlisted outside the U.S. under the terms of a treaty between the U.S. and your country. If you've served six years and have reenlisted for another six, you also qualify.

7. Your Spouse and Children

If you are married or have children below the age of 21 and you get a green card as a special immigrant (except as a special immigrant juvenile), your spouse and children can get green cards as accompanying relatives simply by providing proof of their family relationship to you. In a few special immigrant categories, they must additionally prove other factors, such as how long they lived with you.

> **CAUTION**
> **Anyone can be refused a green card based on inadmissibility.** If you have ever been arrested for a crime, lied on an immigration application, lied to an immigration officer, or you suffer from a particular physical or mental illness, you may be inadmissible and therefore ineligible for a green card. In some cases, a waiver of inadmissibility may be available. (See Chapter 3.)

B. Quick View of the Application Process

Unlike with many other types of green card applications, you perform all the steps on your own, without needing someone in the U.S. to file a petition on your behalf. The steps include:

1. You mail what's called a visa petition (Form I-360) to a USCIS regional Service Center or Lockbox proving that you fit one of the special immigrant categories.

2. If the number of petitions is greater than the number of available EB-4 visas when you apply, you wait until you are allowed to apply for an immigrant visa or green card. (Fortunately, there is rarely a wait in this category.)

3. After your petition has been approved, and if your Priority Date is current, you and your accompanying relatives submit your applications for permanent residence, either at a U.S. consulate outside the United States, or possibly at a USCIS office within the United States (an option mainly available to people who are already legally in the United States).

4. If your interview was held at a U.S. consulate in another country, you enter the U.S. with your immigrant visa, at which time you become a permanent resident.

TIP
Certain types of special immigrants can combine some of these steps. Children of international organization employees, as well as special immigrant juveniles, are allowed to file their visa petition concurrently with their green card application (assuming there is

no wait to apply). This exception attempts to protect them from becoming too old to qualify for the green card. Religious workers and others, however, cannot file concurrently.

C. Step One: You File the Visa Petition

To begin your immigration process, you must file what's called a visa petition on Form I-360. Its purpose is to show that you meet the eligibility criteria for your special immigrant category. You'll normally have to supply supporting documents.

Form I-360 is available at www.uscis. gov/i-360—and it comes with extensive instructions about what documentation to include with it. The form also takes care of some other details, like informing USCIS whether you will be continuing with your application through a consulate outside of the U.S. or through a U.S.-based USCIS office. If you're not sure, choose the consulate. If you change your mind later, all you need to do is ask the NVC to transfer your case file to USCIS. Doing the reverse, transferring your case from a USCIS office to a consulate, requires filing a separate application, using USCIS Form I-824.

The checklist below will help you keep track of all the forms and documents that go into your initial visa petition.

Checklist of Forms and Documents for Visa Petition

☐ Form I-360.

☐ Application fee (currently $435, but free to special immigrant juveniles, and Iraqi or Afghan nationals who worked for the U.S. government; checks or money orders are accepted, but not cash).

Religious Workers:

☐ Diplomas and certificates showing your academic and professional qualifications (the minimum requirement is a bachelor's degree (B.A.); if you're a minister, include proof of your ordination).

☐ Detailed letter from the U.S. religious organization, fully describing the operation of the organization both in and out of the U.S., including the number of followers in both your home country and the United States.

☐ If you are a minister, the letter above should also describe why your services are needed, including details regarding the current number of ministers, the congregation size, your duties, and what has been done before to meet the need.

☐ Letter from the U.S. organization giving details of your U.S. job offer, including title, duties, qualifications, and your salary and other compensation.

☐ Written verification that you have been a member of and worked (for pay) for that same organization for at least two years.

☐ Evidence that the religious organization in the U.S. is eligible for tax-exempt (§ 501(c)(3)) status under the Internal Revenue Code.

☐ Evidence that the organization is able to pay you.

Foreign Medical Graduates:

☐ A copy of your original I-94 card (even if it has expired) or your passport with a visa stamp showing you were admitted to the U.S. with a J or H visa prior to January 9, 1978.

☐ Copy of your medical license issued by any U.S. state prior to January 9, 1978, or a letter from the medical board of a state verifying you were licensed.

☐ Evidence that you have been employed as a physician since January 9, 1978, such as a letter from your employer, or your personal income tax returns, including W-2 forms, for all years from 1977 to the present.

☐ Evidence of your continuous residence in the U.S. since entry. Proof of this can include your personal income tax returns for each year, your children's school records, your utility bills, bank records, letters from employers, and the like.

☐ If you had a J-1 visa, a copy of your Certificate of Eligibility (DS-2019 or IAP-66) and, if it indicated you were subject to the foreign residence requirement, a "no objection" letter from the embassy of your home country.

U.S. Government Workers Abroad:

☐ Verification of at least 15 years of U.S. government employment outside the U.S. or with the American Institute in Taiwan (for example, copies of your personal tax returns or a letter of verification from the U.S. government agency that employed you).

☐ Letter of recommendation for a green card from the principal officer-in-charge of the agency where you worked.

☐ Letter of recommendation from the U.S. Secretary of State. The agency you worked for should be able to assist you in getting this.

Checklist of Forms and Documents for Visa Petition (continued)

Retired Employees of International Organizations:

☐ Evidence you have lived in the U.S. on a G-4 or N visa for the past 15 years, such as copies of passports, I-94 cards, or U.S. tax returns; or if these are not available, a detailed letter from the international organization in the U.S. stating your periods of employment and visa status.

☐ Evidence that you lived in the U.S. for at least half of the seven-year period prior to filing for a green card. Copies of your passport and I-94 cards during the past seven years would again be the best proof. You need to make a complete copy of your passport to show your entries and departures. If unavailable, other acceptable proofs of your physical presence in the U.S. are a letter from your employer stating the number of days you worked in the U.S. and bank statements showing regular deposits and withdrawals during this time.

☐ A letter from the U.S. employer or other written verification of your retirement date (which must have occurred within the six months before submitting this application).

Children of International Organization Retirees:

☐ Letter from the international organization in the U.S. employing your parent, verifying his or her position and period of employment.

☐ Your long-form birth certificate showing the names of your parents.

☐ Evidence that you have been physically present in the U.S. for at least half of the seven-year period immediately before applying for a green card. A complete copy of your passport and all I-94 cards issued is usually sufficient.

☐ If your passport and I-94 cards are unavailable or do not show your entries and departures for at least the past seven years, other evidence of your presence in the U.S. for one half of the past seven years, such as letters from employers stating the number of days you worked in the U.S. or school records.

Special Immigrant Juveniles:

☐ Copy of a juvenile court decree declaring the child's dependency on the court or placing the juvenile under the custody of a guardian or state agency or department.

☐ The court order should also state that the child is eligible for guardianship or long-term foster care due to abuse, neglect, or abandonment.

☐ If it is not specifically stated in the court decree, and the court will not amend the decree to include it, a letter from the juvenile court judge stating the following:

   ☐ That the child is eligible for guardianship or long-term foster care.

   ☐ That it would not be in the child's best interest to return him or her to the home country.

☐ Proof of the child's age, such as a birth certificate, passport, or foreign document (such as a cedula or cartilla).

Servicepeople:

☐ Certified proof of your active duty status for 12 years, or of six years' duty plus reenlistment.

☐ Your birth certificate showing that you are a native of a country that has a treaty with the U.S. covering military service.

1. Submitting the Visa Petition

Where you'll submit or send your visa petition depends on what subcategory of special immigrant you are applying under. Go to the USCIS website (www.uscis.gov /i-360-addresses) to get the exact address and P.O. box number of the service center or Lockbox that is right for you.

2. Awaiting Approval of the Visa Petition

Within a few weeks after sending the petition, you should receive a written confirmation that the papers are being processed, together with a receipt for the fees. This notice will also contain your immigration case file ("receipt") number.

If USCIS wants further information before acting on your case, it will return all petition papers, forms, and documents to you, together with an I-797E Request for Evidence. This will tell you what corrections, additional pieces of information, or additional documents USCIS expects. You should make the corrections or supply the extra data and mail the whole package back to the regional service center, with a copy of the I-797E Request for Evidence on top.

After filing Form I-360, you will have to wait for the petition to be approved, which can take several months by itself. (See Chapter 4 for how to track the length of time USCIS is taking to decide on visa

petitions, and how to track your own application online.)

Once your petition is approved, a Notice of Action (on Form I-797) will be sent to you, indicating the approval. If you plan to apply for an immigrant visa at a U.S. consulate abroad, USCIS will forward the file to the National Visa Center (NVC) in Portsmouth, New Hampshire. The NVC will then send instructions to you so that you may proceed with the next step, described later in this chapter.

An approved petition does not by itself give you any right to immigrate to or live in the United States. It is only a prerequisite to the next step, submitting your own application for a permanent residence.

D. Step Two: You Await an Available Visa Number

Because there are annual limits on the number of people who can receive green cards as special immigrants, it's possible— depending on which country you're from— that you will have to wait in line until you are allowed to file your application for an immigrant visa or green card. Your place in the line is tracked by your Priority Date. It comes from the date on which you filed your I-360 visa petition.

Special immigrants, since they are considered "employment-based" seekers of permanent residence, check their ability to

	June 2016 Priority Dates for Employment-Based Visas Chart				
Employment- Based	**All Chargeability Areas Except Those Listed**	**China-mainland born**	**India**	**Mexico**	**Philippines**
1st	C	C	C	C	C
2nd	C	01JUN13	01JUL09	C	C
3rd	C	01MAY15	01JUL05	C	01JAN10
Other Workers	C	01AUG09	01JUL05	C	01JAN10
4th	C	C	C	C	C
Certain Religious Workers	C	C	C	C	C
5th Non-Regional Center (C5 and T5)	C	01MAY15	C	C	C
5th Non-Regional Center (I5 and R5)	C	01MAY15	C	C	C

apply for and receive permanent residence the same way as other employment-based immigrants. That process is described in Chapter 9.

Above is a filing date chart from the State Department's *Visa Bulletin*. The filing date chart will let you know whether you are currently able to apply for an immigrant visa at a U.S. consulate, and USCIS may tell you to use the filing date chart if you're adjusting status from within the United States. Notice that there are separate rows for "4th" and "Certain Religious Workers." If you're applying as a special immigrant religious worker, look at that row rather than the "4th" row. If you see a "C" in the column for your country, there is no wait to apply for a visa or green card.

E. Step Three: You Apply for Permanent Residence

Once your visa petition has been approved, and your Priority Date has become current according to the appropriate *Visa Bulletin* chart, you can apply for permanent residence. If you are in a category where your spouse or children can accompany you, they must each file their own applications. A big part of the application is proving that you are not inadmissible to the United States. Review Chapter 3 regarding the grounds of inadmissibility. Note, however, that special immigrant juveniles are exempted from many of the grounds of inadmissibility, including those regarding the likelihood of becoming a public charge, and the need for a proper immigrant visa or labor certification. (See I.N.A. § 245(h)(2), 8 U.S.C. § 1255(h)(2).)

The most important question at this point is where you file the application—in the United States or at a U.S. consulate in another country. You should have already made this choice on your Form I-360, but you're allowed to change your mind, so it's worth revisiting the question.

If you're living outside of the U.S. now. The answer is fairly easy for people living outside of the United States—you'll file at a local U.S. consulate and attend an interview there before entering the United States. (This method is called consular processing.)

If you're living in the U.S. now. The answer is a bit more complicated. Ordinarily, the most convenient choice would be for you to adjust status without leaving the U.S.— that is, file your application with USCIS and attend your interview at a local USCIS office. Once your application is filed, your stay in the United States will be considered legal, and you can apply for permission to work. Should problems arise in your case, you'll be able to wait for a decision in the U.S., a circumstance most green card applicants prefer. Also, if your application for a green card is turned down, you have greater rights of appeal inside the U.S. than you do at a U.S. consulate.

Not everyone is eligible to adjust status. First your Priority Date must be current according to the appropriate *Visa Bulletin* chart. Second, you can't adjust status unless you were "inspected and admitted" by a U.S. immigration officer—in other words, the last time you entered the U.S., you did so legally, with a visa or with "parole" (permission from a border officer). And third, just like someone coming into the U.S. from overseas, you must be admissible. (See Chapter 3 for grounds of inadmissibility.)

Even if you meet those basic requirements for adjustment, you won't be able to adjust status based on an EB-4 petition if, as a general rule, you've ever worked in the U.S. without authorization, you're in the U.S. with no legal status, or you've ever fallen out of legal status (except if wasn't your fault). There's an important exception for EB-4 religious workers, however—they can still adjust even if they have gone out of status or worked without authorization, so long as the violation did not exceed 180 days.

You can't adjust status if you came to the U.S. without a visa under the Visa Waiver program. (This rule doesn't apply to visa-exempt Canadians.)

An important, but increasingly rare, exception to adjustment of status eligibility requirements exists for people who had an approvable labor certification application filed for them (or for their spouse or parent) before April 30, 2001. Such people, if they are admissible and a green card is immediately available to them, can adjust status by paying an extra $1,000 fee. If the labor certification application was filed after January 14, 1998, they will also have to prove that they were present in the U.S. on December 21, 2000. This provision of law, known as "245(i)" adjustment, is especially helpful for people who came to the U.S. illegally and who cannot leave to get an immigrant visa because they would then be subject to the ten-year reentry bar for unlawful presence.

If you have any doubts about your ability to adjust status, consult with an immigration lawyer. The adjustment application is expensive—you don't want to spend the money to apply and have your application denied because you were not eligible.

TIP
Special immigrant juveniles, foreign medical graduates, unmarried sons or daughters of international organization officers, and servicepeople will be able to adjust status. The law exempts them from various grounds of inadmissibility, including the requirement that they have entered with a proper immigrant visa. In addition, special immigrant juveniles are deemed to have been "paroled" into the United States (a legal form of entry and one that causes them not to accrue unlawful status). (See I.N.A. § 245(a),(h), 8 U.S.C. § 1255(a),(h).)

Whether or not you're eligible to adjust status, you may instead decide to leave the United States and apply for your green card at a U.S. consulate abroad. If the consulates are issuing visas more quickly than your local USCIS office is handling adjustment of status applications (which is common), leaving to apply at a U.S. consulate in another country could be a smart strategic move. However, if you have already spent 180 days or more in the U.S. out of legal status, or crossed the border without inspection, be sure you are not inadmissible or subject to a three-year or ten-year reentry bar before you go. (See Chapter 3.) Otherwise, you could find yourself stuck outside the U.S. for three or ten years.

1. Adjusting Status in the U.S.

The process of adjusting your status to permanent resident involves preparing a set of forms and documents (a separate set for you, your spouse, and each of your accompanying children), mailing these to USCIS, waiting for some weeks until you're called in to have your biometrics (fingerprints) taken, and then waiting a few weeks or months longer until you're called in for your final green card interview at a local USCIS office (not the one to which you sent your application). You should be approved for your green card at or soon after the interview. Nowadays, the interview is often waived for EB-4 applicants, in which case you'll get a letter in the mail telling you you've been approved. See Chapter 4 for information on tracking the progress of your application.

Checklist for Adjustment of Status Application

Forms

☐ Form I-485.

☐ Form I-485A (only if you'll be paying the $1,000 penalty fee in order to adjust status).

☐ Form G-325A.

☐ Form I-765 (optional, if you want a work permit). On I-765 Question 16, answer "(c)(9)."

☐ I-131, Application for Travel Document (Advance Parole), for use if you think you'll need to travel outside the United States while your application is processed.

Documents (Remember, all foreign-language documents must be accompanied by an English translation with translator's certification.)

☐ Copy of your I-360 approval notice (unless you're filing the I-360 concurrently).

☐ Evidence of your eligibility for the category under which you are filing.

☐ Copy of a long-form birth certificate for you and each accompanying relative.

☐ Marriage certificate, if you are married and bringing your spouse.

☐ If either you or your spouse has been previously married, copies of divorce and death certificates showing termination of all previous marriages.

☐ Copy of I-94 card (if you received one, rather than the usual recent practice of entering your I-94 information into a database, accessible online).

☐ Four photographs of you and four of each accompanying relative, in U.S. passport style (it's best to have a professional do these). Write your name and A number (if you've received one from USCIS) in pencil or felt pen on the back of each photo. (This assumes you will submit the Forms I-765 and I-131 at this time. If not, you can subtract two photos for each form you don't submit.)

☐ Medical exam report for you and for each accompanying relative (Form I-693, filled out and signed by a USCIS-certified doctor and presented in an unopened envelope). The fee depends on the doctor. The exam itself involves taking a medical history, blood test, and chest X-ray and administering vaccinations if applicable and/or recommended for you. Pregnant women may refuse to be X-rayed until after the baby is born.

Fees

☐ Filing fee is currently $1,225 for applicants ages 14 to 78 (includes biometrics fee), $750 for applicants under age 14 who are derivatives filing concurrently with a parent, and $1,140 for applicants age 79 and older or applicants under age 14 filing alone. In addition, if you are in the U.S. illegally, but are allowed to adjust status under old laws, you must pay a $1,000 penalty fee. Checks and money orders are accepted, but we advise against sending cash through the mail. Double-check all fees on the instructions for Form I-485 or I-485A.

In the unlikely event that USCIS indicated that you could apply for adjustment of status before a green card could actually be given to you, you will have to wait until the green card can be released. You can track your wait by checking the "Application Final Action Dates for Employment-Based Visa Applications" chart in the *Visa Bulletin*.

As part of your adjustment of status application, you and your family members may apply for permission to work (an Employment Authorization Document or EAD).

> ! **CAUTION**
> **Security checks are a likely cause of delays.** If you're between 14 and 79 years old, as part of your adjustment of status application, USCIS will have the FBI run both a fingerprint check and a name check on you, and will search for your name in the Interagency Border Inspection System (IBIS) database to detect crimes, fraud schemes, and any other illegal activities with which you may have been involved. These name checks can take several months, or even longer if yours is a common name. The FBI fingerprint check and the IBIS name check must be complete before USCIS can approve your application, but if the FBI name check hasn't been resolved within six months and your application is otherwise approvable, USCIS should not wait any longer to approve it. If you've been informed that your case is stalled due to security checks, get the name of a person you can keep in touch with for updates or hire a lawyer to help with this task.

a. Paperwork to Prepare for Adjustment of Status Application

The basic form used in the U.S. adjustment of status application is Form I-485, Application for Permanent Residence. However, a handful of other forms and documents must be prepared to accompany this main one.

One way to get all these forms is to call the USCIS forms line at 800-870-3676 and ask for the Adjustment of Status Packet. Or, you can obtain the forms online at www.uscis.gov/forms. (Select the forms you need one by one based on the checklist above.)

The checklist will help you assemble and keep track of the appropriate forms and documents. A complete set of the items on this list must also be prepared for your accompanying spouse and children.

> 💡 **TIP**
> **Tip for filling out Form I-485:** You'll notice on the first page of the form, under "Part 2. Application Type," it asks you to choose the basis upon which you're applying for a green card. Mark Box a if you're the primary applicant; Box b if you're a spouse or child.

On the checklist below, the Medical Examination Report could use extra explanation:

You must submit a Medical Examination Report for each applicant. This is done on Form I-693, which a USCIS-authorized physician or medical clinic will give you.

To find a doctor who can do your medical exam, call the USCIS National Customer Service Center at 800-375-5283 or find one online using the USCIS Civil Surgeons Locator at https://my.uscis.gov/findadoctor.

Dealing With Delays in Approval of Your Work Authorization

If you don't already have work authorization and you want to work before your application for a green card is approved, you must file a separate application for employment authorization. To do so, fill out Form I-765 and file it together with your adjustment of status application. (Answer Question 16 of the form "(c)(9).") If you do it this way, there is no additional filing fee.

Legally, USCIS does not have to make a decision on your employment authorization application for up to 90 days. If for some reason you are not given a decision within 75 days, you can call USCIS Customer Service and ask that it send a "service request" to the service center handling your case. This should let the service center know that it should take action on your application right away.

You'll have to pay the doctor's fee for the exam. The exam itself involves taking a medical history, blood test, and chest X-ray and administering vaccinations if applicable and/or recommended for you. Pregnant women may refuse to be X-rayed until after the baby is born.

After completion of the medical exam, and upon obtaining the test results, the doctor will give you the results in a sealed envelope. Do not open the envelope, or USCIS will suspect tampering and reject it.

b. Mailing the Adjustment Packet

After you have finished preparing the adjustment of status paperwork, you must mail it to a USCIS Lockbox serving your geographic region. Addresses are on the USCIS website, www.uscis.gov/i-485/addresses. Submit your application by U.S. certified mail, return receipt requested, or by a courier such as FedEx, and keep a complete copy of everything you send in.

Generally, after filing your green card application, you will not hear anything from USCIS for several weeks. Then you should receive notices of your fingerprint (biometrics) and interview appointments. The interview notice will also tell you what documentation you should bring.

c. Your Adjustment of Status Interview

You may be called in for a personal interview, which will be held at a USCIS office near you. However, personal interviews are often waived in special immigrant applications. If USCIS requires you to attend an interview, it will send you and your accompanying relatives an appointment notice, usually about two weeks in advance of the interview. If you have an attorney, he or she may come with you to the interview. (Even if you don't have an attorney, you could consult with or hire one at this point.)

RELATED TOPIC

See Chapter 4 for detailed information on what expect during your adjustment of status interview. If your adjustment of status application is denied, also see Chapter 4.

If everything is in order, your application will be approved at the conclusion of the adjustment of status interview or soon after. Your passport will be stamped to show that you have been admitted to the U.S. as a permanent resident, and your green card will be ordered. The green card will come to you in the mail several weeks after the interview. If you need to travel outside the U.S. before your green card arrives, however, you must schedule an InfoPass appointment at https://infopass. uscis.gov and go back to the USCIS office with your passport and the written notice of approval. A temporary stamp will be placed in your passport, enabling you to return after your trip. Never leave the U.S. without either your green card or a temporary stamp in your passport.

SKIP AHEAD

Ready for information on how to protect and renew your green card status after you're approved? See Chapter 14.

Checklist: Documents to Bring to Your Adjustment Interview

Prepare all of the following to take with you to your USCIS interview:

☐ The interview notice that USCIS sent to you—security officers at the building entrance and the receptionist will need to see it.

☐ A complete photocopy of your green card application. This is for your use— you may want to follow along as the officer asks you questions about the material you filled out on the forms, or you may find that the officer is missing something that you have a copy of.

☐ All passports (current and expired).

☐ Driver's license or state ID card.

☐ Social Security card.

☐ Advance parole document(s) and EAD card(s) (work permits).

☐ Birth certificate(s).

☐ Marriage certificate/license (if any).

☐ Divorce/death certificates from prior marriages (if any).

☐ All IAP-66, DS-2019, I-20 forms (only if you have ever been in J-1 or F-1 status).

☐ All other original USCIS approval notices for nonimmigrant status (Forms I-797).

☐ I-94 card(s), if you have them.

☐ Documents relating to any arrests or criminal convictions—certified copies of final court dispositions are required.

☐ Any updates to the material in your application. For example, if you have given birth to another child, bring its birth certificate. If you've been arrested, bring a full explanation (and consult with an attorney, to make sure that the arrest doesn't make you inadmissible).

Read This If You Plan to Leave the U.S. Before Your Adjustment Interview

Once your application for adjustment of status has been filed, you must not leave the U.S. for any reason before you have applied for and received advance permission to reenter the U.S. (Advance Parole). Any absence without this permission will be viewed as an abandonment of your application for a green card—which means that, upon return, you may not be allowed to enter the United States.

You should apply for Advance Parole at the same time that you apply for adjustment of status, because the filing fee is included in the adjustment of status fee. There is no additional filing fee for extensions beyond the initial one-year document. The form you need is the I-131. You'll have to explain why you need to leave the country and where you're planning on going.

If approved, you will be allowed to leave the U.S. and return again with no break in the processing of your application. However, if you have been out of status for 180 days or more, talk to a lawyer before you depart the U.S.— even if your Advance Parole is approved. Until recently, any departures would risk subjecting you to the three- or ten-year bars to reentry.

That risk was greatly reduced in 2012, when the Board of Immigration Appeals (BIA) issued a ruling called *Matter of Arrabally and Yerrabelly*, 25 I&N Dec. 771 (BIA 2012). The BIA said that departures under Advance Parole with a pending adjustment of status application do NOT, despite previous USCIS interpretations to the contrary, trigger the unlawful presence bars.

If you applied for and are granted work authorization as well, your evidence of authorization to travel will come in the form of a single card that gives you permission for both.

2. Consular Processing

If you have opted for consular immigrant visa processing instead of adjustment of status (described above), you will follow a different set of filing procedures. Consular processing requires you to pay fees, prepare some forms and documents according to instructions, send these to the National Visa Center (NVC), prepare additional documents for the visa interview at the consulate, and finally attend the interview. There, if all goes well, you will be approved (subject to final security checks) for a visa to enter the United States.

Much of your job at this point involves convincing the consulate that you are not inadmissible for health, criminal, security, or financial reasons. You will be asked to undergo a medical exam and possibly provide evidence that you have no criminal record.

a. National Visa Center Processing

At the beginning, consular processing involves a lot of information being sent in various directions. First, after USCIS approves your visa petition, it will forward your file to the NVC in Portsmouth, New Hampshire. After your date for filing has arrived, the NVC will send you a letter or email directing you to a State Department website that will guide you through the "immigrant visa" process at the NVC.

The first thing the NVC requests is that you choose your email communication options. The NVC wants to communicate with you by email, not postal mail. You too should prefer email, because it's a quicker, more reliable, and more secure way of communicating with the NVC. To establish this communication with the NVC, send an email to nvcinquiry@ state.gov telling it which email address or addresses it should send correspondence to. You must also give it the name and address of the sponsoring employer, if you have one. Include your NVC case number in the subject line.

At this point, if you want someone else (an attorney or agent) to receive all correspondence involved with your case, you must tell the NVC who that person is by submitting Form DS-261, Online Choice of Address and Agent. The NVC recommends that this person be in the U.S., or at least have a reliable email address. Fill out Form DS-261 and submit it online, at the State Department's

Consular Electronic Application Center (CEAC) website, https://ceac.state.gov.

The next step is to pay the Immigrant Visa (IV) fee bill (currently $205 for EB-4 immigrant visa applications). The NVC prefers that you do this through the CEAC website. If you can't, mail a cashier's check or money order (not a personal check) to the NVC. Instructions are on the State Department's immigrant visa processing website to which the NVC directs you.

i. The Application Form

The application form you need to send to the NVC is called a DS-260. You fill this out online and submit through the CEAC website, https://ceac.state.gov. Log in to CEAC with the NVC case number and invoice number that the NVC sent in its original notice to you. If you can't finish the whole form in one sitting, don't worry— you can save your work and come back to it later. Make sure to print the confirmation page when you're done—you'll need to bring it to your interview at the consulate.

ii. Supporting Documents

The State Department's immigrant visa process website will let you know how to submit documents to the NVC. Some people can scan and email documents, others must mail them to the NVC, and others can choose either method. The checklist above provides a brief explanation of some of the documents you'll need to gather to send to the NVC and bring to your immigrant visa interview.

Keep your eyes open for any special requirements that your consulate may add to this list. If you were not required to mail all originals to the NVC, bring the originals and a set of copies with you to your interview. (The consular officer may want to examine the originals to make sure they're not fraudulent, but keep copies for your files.) Do not mail your paperwork to the consulate!

Following is some additional information regarding items on the checklist.

Police clearance. You personally must collect police clearance certificates from each country or place you have ever been arrested in. Even if you have not been arrested, you need to get a police certificate from each country you have lived in for one year or more since your 16th birthday. Additionally, you must have a police certificate from your home country or country of last residence, if you lived there for at least six months since the age of 16. You do not need to obtain police certificates from the United States.

The State Department's immigrant visa process website contains information on how to contact the local police department to get police certificates in various countries. Some nations refuse to supply police certificates, or their certificates are not considered reliable, so you will not be required to obtain them from those locations.

Some countries will send certificates directly to U.S. consulates but not to you personally. Before they send the certificates out, however, you must request that it be done. Usually this requires filing some type of request form, together with a set of your fingerprints.

Photos. You and each accompanying relative must bring two passport-style photographs to your interview. Many photographers are familiar with U.S. passport style. If you are a do-it-yourself type, passport-style specifications are available on the State Department's website, www.travel.state.gov.

If your religious beliefs require wearing a head covering, you should be able to keep it on for the photo. However, your full face must be visible and your head covering cannot obscure your hairline or cast shadows on your face.

Fingerprints. A few consulates require you to submit fingerprints, though most do not. Consulates wanting fingerprints will send you blank fingerprint cards with instructions.

Medical exam. Before your visa interview, you and your accompanying relatives will need to schedule and undergo a medical examination. The State Department's immigrant visa processing website contains instructions on how to do this, and on what to bring to your exam.

Only certain doctors can perform the examination. The fees depend on the country and doctor. The exam itself involves taking a medical history, blood test, and chest X-ray and administering vaccinations, if you need any. Pregnant women can refuse to be X-rayed until after the pregnancy. The vaccination requirement may be waived for religious, moral, or medical reasons.

The main purpose of the medical exam is to verify that you are not medically inadmissible. Some medical grounds of inadmissibility can be overcome with treatment or by applying for a waiver. (See Chapter 3 for details.) If you need a medical waiver, the consulate will give you complete instructions at your interview, but you should also consult an experienced immigration attorney. After the examination, the doctor will either give you a sealed envelope with the results of the test, or send the results directly to the consulate. If you get an envelope, don't open it. Bring it to your interview along with your other documents.

b. Your Consular Interview

Consulates hold interviews on all green card applications. The NVC will send you a notice of your interview date. Review the State Department's immigrant visa website for instructions on what to bring to the interview and how to prepare for it. Read instructions from the consulate carefully, for any additions or changes.

c. You Might Have to Wait for Your Visa

If you filed your visa application before the "application final action date" in the *Visa Bulletin*, you will have to wait until that date before getting your immigrant visa. There's not likely to be much of a wait, since the NVC and consulate probably waited to schedule your interview until close to the time a visa was actually available to you.

F. Step Four: Immigrant Visa Holders Enter the U.S.

After processing your application, the consulate will place your immigrant visa on a page in your passport. Review the visa to make sure all information is correct. If you spot spelling errors, contact the embassy or consulate promptly. You'll also get a sealed "visa packet" containing documents to show to border officials when you get to the United States. Don't open it.

Your immigrant visa allows you to request entry to the United States at a border post, airport, or other arrival point. Before you travel to the U.S., you have to pay one last fee: the USCIS Immigrant Fee, currently $220. (You can pay this fee after you get to the U.S., but USCIS won't send you a green card until you do.) Each member of the family traveling with you is charged the same fee. The only way to pay it is through the online USCIS Electronic Immigration System, or "ELIS." You'll need to create an ELIS account at https:// myaccount.uscis.dhs.gov. Select "USCIS Immigrant Fee" and include your personal

Checklist of Documents for Your Consular Interview

☐ Confirmation of DS-260 receipt that you printed out after submitting the form online.

☐ Notice of approval of your visa petition.

☐ Long-form birth certificate for you and each accompanying relative as well as of any unmarried minor children who are not immigrating with you.

☐ Marriage certificate, if you are married and bringing your spouse.

☐ If either you or your spouse has been previously married, copies of divorce and death certificates showing termination of all previous marriages.

☐ Passport for you and each accompanying relative, valid for at least six months beyond the date of the interview.

☐ Required police certificates.

☐ Fingerprints, if specifically requested by the consulate.

☐ If you or accompanying relative served in the military forces of any country, a copy of your military records.

☐ Two photographs of you and two photographs of each accompanying relative. Some consulates now take the photos at the interview. This will be clear from the instructions.

☐ Medical exam report for you and for each accompanying relative.

information. You'll need your Alien number (A-Number) and Department of State Case ID number handy. (You got those from the consulate.) Once you're in the system, you can pay the fee for all family members in one transaction. You'll need a valid credit or debit card, or U.S. bank checking account and routing numbers.

The inspection process involves a U.S. border officer opening the sealed envelope containing your visa documents, and doing a last check to make sure you haven't used fraud. The border officer has expedited removal powers, which means he or she can turn you right around and send you home if anything appears wrong in your packet or with your answers to the officer's questions. Be polite and careful in answering.

CAUTION

The clock is ticking. You must enter the U.S. before your visa expires. Check the date printed on your visa inside your passport. The consulate usually gives you six months to make the trip, measured from the date it issues the visa. You might be given less time, however, if, for example, the results of your medical exam are in danger of getting stale

Dealing With the "Public Charge" Ground of Inadmissibility

As an EB-4 special immigrant, you do not need to file the I-864 Affidavit of Support form required of many other immigrants, in which a U.S. sponsor promises to back you up financially. However, EB-4 special immigrants (except for juveniles) are still subject to the "public charge" ground of inadmissibility. To prove that you are not likely to go on public assistance or welfare in the U.S., you can submit an offer of employment from an employer in the U.S., proof of personal assets, an Affidavit of Support (Form I-134) prepared by a relative or friend residing in the U.S., or other proof.

Your sponsor on the I-134 will need to attach documents showing that the information given in the form is true. These should include, where applicable:

- a copy of the most recent federal income taxes (with W-2s) showing the income of the person signing the Form I-134
- a statement from the bank with details about accounts including the date opened, the total amount deposited for the past year, and the present balance, and
- a letter from the employer verifying current employment, job title, salary, and whether the position is permanent.

Also attach a copy of the document that shows the immigration status of the person signing the Form I-134.

Before agreeing to sign an Affidavit of Support on your behalf, your family member or friend will want to know the legal extent of the financial obligations that come with it. Section 6 of the form describes those obligations.

When the officer is satisfied that everything is in order, he or she will stamp your passport to show that you're now a U.S. permanent resident and are immediately authorized to work. This stamp is often called an "I-551 stamp" or "ADIT stamp." You won't receive an actual green card yet, however. You will be processed for your green card by U.S. Customs and Border Protection after being placed in "secondary inspection."

Green cards for you and your accompanying relatives will be ordered for you if you have paid the USCIS Immigrant Fee, and will come by mail several weeks later, to the address you provided upon arrival.

SKIP AHEAD
Ready for information on how to protect and renew your green card after you get it? See Chapter 14.

Getting a Green Card as an Asylee or Refugee

For some immigrants, getting out of their home country and finding safe haven in a country like the United States is literally a matter of life and death. The immigration laws offer help to such people, although the door is not as open as you might wish. This chapter covers the process for gaining admission to the U.S. as a refugee, and the process for persons already in the U.S. (or at the border) to seek asylum and the right to stay in the United States. Refugees and persons granted asylum (and their immediate family) can apply for a green card to gain all the rights of permanent residence in the U.S., including eventual citizenship.

SEE AN EXPERT

Do you need a lawyer? Yes! This chapter will give you an outline of how to apply for refugee or asylee status. However, given the risks you'll face if your application is denied, and that preparing an asylum application is more like writing a book than filling out a form, it's worth trying to get additional help. An experienced lawyer can show you how to highlight the important parts of your story in a way that turns your case into a winner. Within the U.S., a number of organizations offer free or low-cost help to refugees and asylees. See, for example, the searchable directory on www.asylumlaw.org (registration required).

CAUTION

Any inadmissible person may be denied U.S. entry or status. If you have ever committed a serious crime, been involved in a terrorist group, lied on an immigration application, lied to an immigration officer, or suffered one of a few specific physical or mental illnesses, you may be inadmissible. That can cause a denial of your initial application, and is even more likely to cause a denial of your application for permanent resident status after being given refugee status or asylum. However, most grounds of inadmissibility can be waived (forgiven) for refugees and asylees, except those grounds concerning the commission of serious crimes, persecution of others, or participation in subversive or terrorist activities such that you are considered a possible threat to U.S. security. (Unlike the normal waiver of inadmissibility, this waiver does not require you to have a family member who is already a permanent resident or U.S. citizen.)

A. Do You Qualify as a Refugee or an Asylee?

People who are fleeing persecution in their home country may be granted either refugee or asylum status—which allows them to stay in the U.S. until it's safe to return to their home country. If, after a year, conditions are no safer, both refugees and asylees can apply for a U.S. green card (permanent residence).

To qualify as a refugee or an asylee, you must have experienced persecution in the past or have a well-founded fear of persecution in the future in your home country. Persecution is defined generally as a serious threat to your life or freedom. It needs to be a nationwide threat—you won't be thought to have a well-founded fear of persecution if you could avoid the problem simply by relocating to another part of the country. The fact that you are suffering economically is not considered a reason for granting refugee or asylee status. Nor is it enough if someone has a grudge against you, or has committed crimes against you for random or personal reasons.

The main difference between asylees and refugees is where they start their application process. People physically outside the U.S. must apply for refugee status. Even if you have been designated as a refugee by the United Nations High Commissioner for Refugees (UNHCR), you will still need to apply separately to the U.S. government, which will make its own decision about whether to accept you. The U.S. government gives out only a limited number of refugee visas each year. (The number is set by the U.S. president.) Refugees must ordinarily be outside their country of origin, but the U.S. president can authorize USCIS to process some individuals in their home countries.

You cannot apply for asylum until you have reached U.S. soil. Asylees do not need financial sponsors to be granted asylum. There is no annual limit on the number of people granted asylum.

CAUTION
If you file an asylum application that USCIS decides is frivolous (has no basis), you will be permanently ineligible for any benefits under U.S. immigration law. That means that you will never be given any U.S. visa or green card, even if you were to marry a U.S. citizen, get a U.S. job offer, or the like. Don't worry that your application will be deemed frivolous if it is denied for any reason—USCIS will find your application frivolous only if you had no business even considering asylum as an option.

Beyond these differences, the qualifying requirements for refugees and asylees are the same.

CAUTION
Avoid leaving the United States after submitting your asylum application. If you absolutely must travel before getting a decision on your asylum application, apply for permission to return to the U.S. on USCIS Form I-131. Whatever you do, do not go back to the country from which you are claiming a fear of persecution.

1. Persecution or Well-Founded Fear of Persecution

To establish eligibility for asylum or refugee status, you must prove you are either the victim of past persecution or you fear future persecution. In the case of past persecution, you must prove that you were persecuted in your home country or last country of residence. The persecution must have been based on at least one of five grounds: your race, religion, nationality, political opinion, or membership in a particular social group.

Proving this connection between the persecution and one of these five grounds is one of the most difficult parts of an application for asylee or refugee status—and it got more difficult in 2005, when the REAL ID Act added a requirement that one of the five grounds was or will be a "central reason" for your persecution.

Although the law does not specifically list types of persecution, it does specify that refugees and asylees can include people who have undergone or fear a "coercive population control program" (such as forced abortion or sterilization—this was directed primarily at mainland China).

Persecution may also in some cases be based on your gender, including cultural practices such as female genital cutting or forced marriage. Domestic violence, honor killing, and trafficking (sexual or labor) are increasingly recognized as bases for asylee status, particularly in cases where the police and government compound the problem by failing to protect the women or prosecute the perpetrators and where the victim was prevented from leaving the abusive situation. For more on these developing areas of the law, see the website of the Center for Gender & Refugee Studies, based at Hastings College of the Law, at http://cgrs.uchastings.edu.

The persecution doesn't need to come from your country's government or other authorities only. Refugee law also recognizes persecution by groups that the government is unable to control, such as guerrillas, warring tribes, or organized vigilantes. Again, however, the persecution must have some political or social basis—a member of a criminal network who comes after you just because you haven't paid him off is not persecuting you according to refugee law.

If you have not actually suffered persecution in the past, you can still qualify for asylum or refugee status if you have a genuine fear of future persecution in your home country or last country of residence. For example, if you were the secretary of a student dissident group, and undercover agents sent you death threats, or killed the treasurer and president of your group, you could probably show a reasonable fear of persecution. You do not have to prove that you are likely to be singled out for persecution from the members of a generally persecuted group. You need only show a pattern or practice, whereby groups of persons who are similar to you are being persecuted. Then, you must show that you either belong to or would be identified with the persecuted group.

2. Evidence Showing Persecution

One of the most difficult parts of an asylum applicant's case can be proving that your story is true. In the past, it was enough to present convincing and consistent testimony, supported by newspaper articles, reports from human rights organizations, and other general evidence of the conditions in your country. As of 2005, however, the decision maker in your case may additionally require you to present "corroborating evidence" of your own claim, unless you "do not have the evidence and cannot reasonably obtain the evidence"—and it will be up to the decision maker to decide whether or not that is the case. (See REAL ID Act of 2005 § 101.)

In addition, the 2005 legal changes allow the decision maker to decide whether you look like you're telling the truth based on your demeanor, candor, inherent plausibility, and the consistency of your written and oral statements. In a worst-case scenario, the fact that you wrote one address on your asylum application and then remembered the address differently during your interview could be held against you. If the decision maker thinks you're lying, your case will, of course, be denied.

Cultural differences can make it difficult for some people to convince the judge that they're telling the truth. For example, in some cultures it is not polite to look someone like the judge in the eye—while in the United States, failing to look someone directly in the eye is considered a sign of dishonesty. Victims of torture or trauma may also find it difficult to make eye contact or openly discuss—or even sometimes remember—the details of their persecution. (If you work with a lawyer, he or she will help you practice telling your story and may help arrange a psychiatrist's report to help explain how your difficulties were caused by your persecution.)

3. No Firm Resettlement in Another Country and Unavailability of Safe Haven Elsewhere

Though you may clearly be fleeing persecution, you generally cannot come to the U.S. as a refugee or an asylee if you have already been granted or offered a permanent status in another country. You may prefer coming to the U.S., but that makes no difference. The availability of permanent status in another country is known as "firm resettlement."

If you've lived in another country before coming to the U.S., however, you can still qualify for refugee or asylum status in the U.S. if you entered the other country while fleeing persecution, stayed there only as long as was necessary to arrange your continued travel, and did not establish significant ties to that country. In addition, if your rights there with respect to living conditions, employment, holding of property, and travel were significantly less than those of actual citizens or full residents, you may still apply for refugee status or asylum in the United States.

4. No Record of Crimes or Persecuting Others

Some people are legally prohibited from becoming refugees or asylees in the United States. (This is based on I.N.A. § 101(a)(42), 8 U.S.C. § 1101(a)(42); I.N.A. § 241(b)(3), 8 U.S.C. § 1231(b)(3); and certain of the grounds of inadmissibility at I.N.A. § 212 and described in Chapter 3.) These laws bar anyone who has been:

- **Convicted of a "particularly serious crime," and is therefore a danger to the community of the United States.** There is no list of particularly serious crimes—the decision is made case by case. However, all "aggravated felonies" are considered particularly serious crimes. Because of the immigration laws' strict definitions of aggravated felonies, some crimes that may have been called misdemeanors when committed will be looked upon as aggravated felonies.
- **Convicted of a serious nonpolitical crime in a country outside the United States.** Applicants whose crimes were nonserious or political in nature may still qualify for refugee or asylee status.
- **Involved in terrorist activity.** The definition of a terrorist includes having been involved in such illegal activities as assassination; violent attacks upon an internationally protected person; hijacking or sabotaging a means of transport; using explosives, firearms, or other devices to endanger others or cause substantial damage to property; seizing, detaining, and threatening to kill, injure, or continue to detain people in order to compel a governmental organization or someone else to act; and more. It also includes giving food, money, or other material support to a terrorist organization (with possible exceptions if a person did so under duress, for example at gunpoint).
- **Involved in the persecution of others.** This can include ordering, inciting, assisting, or otherwise participating in genocide, torture, extrajudicial killings, or other abuses.
- **Responsible, while serving as a foreign government official, for particularly severe violations of religious freedom.** This includes arbitrary prohibitions or punishment for freely worshiping, preaching, praying, changing religions, and more.

5. No Improvement of Circumstances in Your Home Country

If you prove that you've been persecuted in the past, you are assumed to have a well-founded fear of persecution in the future. However, if USCIS sees that circumstances in your home country have fundamentally changed since you filed your application, it may decide that you don't actually have a well-founded fear anymore, and deny you asylum or refugee status. For example, USCIS could argue that because the civil war in your country has ended and peace accords have been signed, you have nothing more to fear from either side of the conflict. It could make a similar argument if something has changed in your personal circumstances—if, for example, you were once persecuted because you were thought to be the illegitimate daughter of a high-ranking political figure, but your country's newspapers have since reported that DNA tests showed that someone else was your father.

Still, asylum is sometimes granted even after an improvement in country conditions, for humanitarian reasons.

6. One-Year Time Limit for Asylum Application

You must file an asylum application within one year after you arrive in the U.S. to be eligible for asylum. USCIS won't count your application as having been "filed" until it reaches their office—so don't wait until a whole year is up to put it in the mail! If you mail the application within a year but USCIS receives it past the deadline, you'll have to show by "clear and convincing documentary evidence" that you mailed the application before the one-year deadline.

There are a few exceptions. You can apply for asylum after one year if you can show either changed circumstances that have a major effect on your eligibility for asylum or extraordinary circumstances explaining why your application wasn't filed on time. Changed circumstances can include changes in conditions in your country; for example if you're a member of an ethnic or religious group that a new government has begun targeting. Extraordinary circumstances can include events or factors beyond your control that caused the late filing, such as a medical problem.

If you have maintained legal status in the U.S.—for example, you came with a work or student visa—you can apply for asylum past the one-year deadline. Once your legal status expires, however, you must apply within a "reasonable time" after that—don't wait a whole year!

7. Asylum (and Related Remedies) as a Defense to Deportation

Asylum is also a defense to deportation. You need to prove the same exact things to qualify, but instead of USCIS, an immigration judge decides whether you should be given asylum rather than deported.

If you're in removal (deportation) proceedings before an immigration judge, even if you don't qualify for asylum, you may qualify for a remedy called withholding of removal. It is harder to get than asylum—if you didn't experience persecution in the past, you have to show that you'd be "more likely than not" to face persecution if returned to your country. Nevertheless, withholding of removal is useful in cases where, for example, you missed the one-year deadline for applying for asylum, or you've committed minor crimes that make you ineligible for asylum but not ineligible for withholding.

Withholding of removal isn't the best of remedies—it essentially means that although you won't be granted asylum or the right to later get a green card, you won't be removed from the U.S. and you'll be allowed to work while you're here. However, if you leave the U.S. on your own, you won't be permitted to return, because you'll have an order of removal in your file.

Another related defense to deportation, for those who can show that it is more likely than not that they would be tortured if returned to their home country, is available under an international treaty called the U.N. Convention Against Torture. While you don't have to show that the persecution you experienced or fear is on account of one of the five protected grounds—race, religion, nationality, membership in a particular social group, or political opinion—these cases are not often granted, because it's hard to prove that you're more likely than not to face torture. Like withholding, however, it's helpful for people who missed the one-year asylum filing deadline or have committed crimes. Even serious crimes won't bar you from Torture Convention relief, though you may be kept in detention if you appear to be a danger to the United States.

If you're in removal proceedings and need to ask for asylum, withholding of removal, or relief under the Convention Against Torture, it's well worth your money to hire a lawyer to argue your case. You will file an I-589 form with the court to request these remedies; all three are covered by the same form.

You'll need to give the original asylum application and all supporting documents to the judge, and a copy of everything to the government lawyer. The judge may require you to give the court another copy to pass along to the State Department. In addition, you have to send a copy of the first three pages of the I-589 to the USCIS Nebraska Service Center. There is no filing fee.

USCIS will send you a receipt in the mail, and later will notify you where and when to go for fingerprinting. You'll get a confirmation document after you've been fingerprinted, which you must give to the judge before your request for asylum, withholding, or Convention Against Torture relief can be heard.

8. Numerical Limits on Refugees

Refugees (but not asylees) have an annual quota set each year by the U.S. president. The quota may vary by country.

The president also decides how the total will be divided among the various regions of the world, such as Latin America, Southeast Asia, Eastern Europe, and Africa. Recently, the annual quota has gone down to 70,000. However, even after setting the quota, the U.S. government makes no guarantees that it will allow this many people in. (In fiscal year 2015, for example, the government admitted 69,933 refugees.) Applications are approved on a first-come, first-served basis. It is not unusual for qualified refugees to end up on a waiting list.

The refugee quota cannot be accurately forecast, because the number of slots available each year changes. Some countries get many refugee numbers in a given year while others receive practically none. Refugee applications can take from several months to a year or more for approval.

9. Financial Sponsorship—Refugees

Your refugee application will not be approved unless you can show that you have a way to pay for your transportation to the U.S. and a means of support once you arrive. (This rule doesn't apply to asylum applicants, who are already in the U.S.) This is usually done by finding a financial sponsor, such as relatives already in the U.S., or a private charitable group, such as a church or refugee assistance organization. Occasionally, the U.S. government itself allocates money for refugee assistance.

10. Alternate Refugee Entrance as a Parolee

If you qualify for refugee status but the quota has been exhausted for the year, you may be permitted to come to the U.S. as a parolee without a visa. Parolees are permitted to work and live indefinitely in the U.S., but their futures are less certain than those of refugees. Parolee status can be revoked at any time and does not lead to a green card. A parolee may apply for asylum after arriving in the U.S., but there is no guarantee it will be granted.

A request for parole status must be made in writing to the USCIS central office in Washington, DC. Such applications are most likely to be approved if you will be joining family already in the U.S. or if you cannot remain temporarily in the country where you filed your refugee application. There is no special form to file in requesting parole status. The USCIS office that handles your refugee application can help you with the procedures.

11. Bringing Your Spouse and Children

If you are married or have children under the age of 21 and you get either refugee or asylee status, your spouse and children can also be granted refugee or asylee status by providing proof of their family relationship to you. Accompanying relative status allows your family to live and work in the United States.

If you're a refugee traveling with your family, or an asylee whose family is already in the U.S. with you, simply including your family members' names and information on your application will be enough to get them granted refugee or asylee status along with you. (Unfortunately, if your case is denied, this will also get them deported with you.)

If you are traveling separately from your spouse and children when you are granted refugee status, or they are outside the U.S. when you are granted asylum, you will need to submit a separate application to a USCIS Service Center asking that they be allowed to join you—and to do so within two years of your obtaining your

status. This is done on Form I-730. See the USCIS website at www.uscis.gov for the form and more information.

B. How to Apply for Refugee Status

USCIS will not grant your refugee status until you have first been found eligible for a refugee interview by the U.S. Refugee Admissions Program (USRAP). The USRAP's first priority is refugees who have been identified and referred to the program by the United Nations High Commissioner for Refugees (UNHCR), a U.S. embassy, or a designated nongovernmental organization (NGO). USRAP itself also identifies groups of special humanitarian concern, giving them second priority. Finally, USRAP tries to reunite families—spouses, unmarried children under 21, and parents of current or former refugees or asylees.

If you think you might be eligible for refugee status, contact the nearest UNHCR office or U.S. consulate. If you have relatives in the U.S., they should contact the nearest refugee resettlement agency for advice and help in preparing the necessary forms in support of your application.

If you receive a referral from the USRAP, a U.S. State Department-funded Resettlement Service Center (RSC) will help you fill out a refugee application. There is no fee to apply for refugee status and the information you provide will not be shared with your home country.

You will be interviewed abroad by a specially trained USCIS officer, who will determine whether you are eligible for refugee resettlement. The interview is friendly—the officer wants to hear your story and see if you qualify for resettlement to the United States. Specifically, the officer needs to determine whether you meet the definition of a refugee; whether you are a priority refugee (according to the USRAP priorities discussed above); whether you firmly resettled in some other country after leaving your home country; and whether there might be any problems that would prevent you from being admitted to the United States.

The officer will rely heavily on what you tell him or her, and decide whether you're being truthful about everything you say. The officer will also review any documents you have to support your application. The conditions in your home country will be factored in, as well.

If the interview goes well, the RSC will initiate background security checks and arrange medical examinations so that you can be approved to enter the United States.

Normally the process of resettling someone in the U.S. as a refugee takes six to 12 months. In urgent situations, the U.S. State Department's Bureau of Population, Refugees, and Migration can speed the process so that a person can be relocated in eight to ten weeks.

1. Submitting an Appeal When Refugee Status Is Denied

When a USCIS office outside of the U.S denies a refugee application, there is no formal appeal available, although you are free to reapply as often as you like. When your application is denied, the reasons will be explained. The most common reason is failure to show that you either have been subject to persecution or have a reasonable fear of being persecuted if you remain in your home country. Sometimes, presenting more evidence of an unclear fact can bring about a better result.

Although there's no right to have a court review the denial, you can submit a Request for Review of your case to USCIS. (Someone else can submit the Request for you if you give up your right to keep your case private. You might want to think about hiring a lawyer at this time.) USCIS doesn't have to take a second look at your case, but it usually will. You can make the request only once. There is no filing fee.

You need to submit the Request for Review within 90 days of the date of the denial notice. The address you send it to depends on your location. Find the address at www. uscis.gov (follow the links Humanitarian,

Refugee, Request for Review Tip Sheet, and Request for Review Filing Locations).

The Request must be in English, and any supporting documents should be translated into English. You must include a detailed explanation of why the officer who interviewed you was wrong to deny your case, or give USCIS new information that would cause the agency to change its mind. Include your RSC case number on every page and give USCIS a complete return address so it can respond.

You will receive a written decision from USCIS regarding your Request. USCIS may grant your case or say that you are still denied. It's also possible that USCIS will want to interview you again, or ask you to provide additional evidence in writing before it makes a final decision.

2. Entering the U.S. After Refugee Status Is Granted

On entering the U.S. as a refugee, you will be met at the border by an officer of Customs and Border Protection (CBP), who will give you a refugee admission stamp in your passport.

After you arrive, you will be eligible for medical and cash assistance. You are eligible to work right away, although you'll have to wait for the actual Employment Authorization Document (EAD) card to be mailed to you. (The refugee resettlement agency responsible for helping you will apply for your EAD.) In the meantime, you can give an employer your "I-94" number and a copy of your I-94 record, which you can print from https://i94.cbp.dhs.gov.

Normally, you are granted refugee status for one year, after which you can apply for a green card.

C. How to Apply for Asylum

If you are physically present in the U.S. in either legal or undocumented status, and you are otherwise qualified, you may apply for asylum. If you are not presently in removal proceedings, you must submit your application by mail to a USCIS regional service center. You will then be called in for an interview, and you will receive a decision in writing a few weeks later. (See Section 2, below.)

If your case is denied, unless you are in valid status at the time, you will end up in removal proceedings. This means that you will be "referred" to an immigration judge. If you are already in removal proceedings, your application must be filed with the court and immigration judge presiding over your case, and you should seek a lawyer's help. (See Section A7, above.)

If you have no status in the U.S. that allows you to work, earning money to afford a lawyer will be difficult. You cannot apply for work authorization until either your asylum request has been approved or your application has been pending for five months (150 days) without a decision.

1. Step One: Preparing and Submitting Your Asylum Application

Your application for asylum will consist of Form I-589 and documents, as indicated on the checklist below. You must file the application by mail. You need to include the original and one copy of your signed Form I-589, the original and one copy of any supplementary sheets and supplementary statements, and two copies of any additional supporting documents you choose to submit. There is no filing fee. The proper regional service center address for filing asylum cases is given on the USCIS website at www.uscis.gov/i-589.

The regional service center will initially review your application to determine whether any legal prohibition prevents your application being approved, such as a serious criminal conviction or an indication that you have persecuted others. (If that is the case, your application will be denied quickly and you may be placed in deportation (removal) proceedings.)

Assuming you pass that hurdle, you will later receive an appointment to have your fingerprints taken. These will be used to check your police and immigration record.

a. Filling Out Form I-589

Be sure to answer all questions on Form I-589 as fully as possible. USCIS or an immigration judge will closely review your answers for inconsistencies and will be doubtful about new information that arises during an interview or hearing unless you can show good reasons why such information was not initially included in your written application. If there isn't enough space to answer a question on the form, write "see attached sheet." Then prepare your own statement—as lengthy as you want.

The statement should be in your own words and be reasonably detailed (though not so detailed that you'll get confused in retelling it at your interview). For example, USCIS will not be convinced if you say only "I was persecuted by the government and am afraid to go back." But an applicant who explains that "I was tortured by the local security forces after I joined the union and am terrified that if I go back they'll kill me in the same way they killed many other union members" has a much better chance. (And this is only the beginning—this applicant, for example, should include a history of his union involvement, a description of the torture, and an account of what happened to other union members.)

The following discussion of how to answer particular questions on the I-589 covers the version that expires 12/31/2016; if and when the form is updated, the question numbering may change.

i. Part A. I.

Questions 1 and 2. Question 1 asks for your Alien Registration Number or "A #."

Normally, you will not have an A number unless you have previously applied for a green card, were paroled into the U.S., or are already in removal (deportation) proceedings. And you won't have a Social Security number unless you've been in the U.S. with the right to work, and applied for one. If you do not have these numbers, leave the questions blank.

Questions 3–12. These questions are self-explanatory.

Question 13. This question asks for your nationality. You are stateless if your nationality has been taken away from you and you have no legal right to live in any country. The fact that you might be arrested if you return to your home country does not make you stateless.

Questions 14–16. Be sure that this information is consistent with your asylum claim; if you are claiming persecution based on your religion, race, or nationality, this section should reflect that fact.

Question 17. Check Box a, b, or c to indicate whether you have ever been before an immigration judge; and if you have, consult a lawyer immediately.

Question 18. Box b asks for your I-94 number, which is the number on the white entry card you received if you entered the U.S. legally, at a land border, or if you entered before May 2013 at an airport or seaport. (If your entry card is colored green, that means that you entered the U.S. on the Visa Waiver Program; in which case, the Asylum Office does

Asylum Application Checklist

Forms (original and one copy)

☐ Form I-589. (No fee.)

Documents (two copies)

☐ Copies of personal identification (such as a passport or birth certificate) for you and each accompanying relative.

☐ Copies of all immigration documents, such as I-94 cards if you have them.

☐ Copy of long-form birth certificate for you and each accompanying relative.

☐ Copy of marriage certificate if your spouse is included in your application.

☐ If either you or your spouse have ever been married, copies of divorce and death certificates showing termination of all previous marriages.

☐ Personal sworn affidavit describing in detail your reasons for seeking political asylum.

☐ Newspaper articles describing the conditions of persecution in your home country.

☐ Affidavits from knowledgeable people describing the conditions of persecution in your home country.

☐ Written human rights reports about your country supplied by organizations, such as Amnesty International or Human Rights Watch, or the U.S. State Department's *Country Reports on Human Rights Practices.*

☐ Color passport photos—one of you, one of your spouse, and one of each of your children, with the person's name (and A number, if any) written in pencil or felt pen on the back.

Requesting Asylum at a U.S. Border, an Airport, or Another Entry Point

If you can get a U.S. visa, such as a tourist visa, you can apply for asylum when you arrive, by telling the inspections officer that you fear returning to your country and wish to apply for asylum. However, it's best not to mention this unless the officer is acting like he or she doesn't plan to let you into the U.S. anyway. If you start the application process now, you'll have very little time in which to find a lawyer or prepare.

In fact, someone requesting entry to the U.S. can be quickly found inadmissible and deported for five years. This can happen if an inspector believes that you are making a misrepresentation (committing fraud), or misrepresented the truth when you got your visa, or if you do not have the proper travel or visa documents at the time you request entry. This quick deportation procedure is known as "expedited removal." It can be applied to everyone except people entering the United States under the Visa Waiver Program (according to a 1999 decision by the Board of Immigration Appeals).

There is an exception to the expedited removal process for people who fear persecution and request asylum.

So, even if you do not have the proper documents or you have made a misrepresentation, you could still be allowed to enter the U.S. if you make clear that your reason is to apply for asylum and you can show that you'd be likely to win asylum.

After you have said you want to apply for asylum, you'll immediately be given a "credible fear" interview by an asylum officer. The purpose of this interview is to make sure you have a significant possibility of winning your case. Most importantly, the officer will want to be sure that your request is based on a fear of persecution as described earlier in this section. This interview is supposed to be scheduled quickly, within one or two days, but it has been taking longer.

If the officer isn't convinced of your fear, you must request a hearing before an immigration judge or you will be deported for five years. The judge must hold the hearing within seven days in person or by telephone.

If the judge finds that you have a credible fear of persecution, you'll be scheduled for a full hearing, and should seek an attorney. This proceeding will progress much like a normal asylum proceeding as described in this chapter (except that it will be in court, which we don't cover). Most asylum applicants are held in detention at this point, although you can and should request release, called parole. You're most likely to be granted parole if you can verify your identity, have family or other contacts in the area, and can post a bond (money that you give up if you don't show up for future hearings) and can show you'll be financially supported until a decision is made on your case. If you fail the credible fear test before the immigration judge, you will be deported from the United States.

not have the authority to consider your application and will refer you directly to an immigration judge for a hearing. See an attorney for help.) If you were not given an I-94 card when you entered legally, you still have an I-94 number—find it online at https://i94.cbp.dhs.gov.

Questions 19–24. Self-explanatory.

ii. Part A. II.

This section asks for information about your husband or wife, and children. Mention all of them, whether or not they are applying for asylum. Be aware that you must be legally married to your current spouse for him or her to be granted asylum under your application. Your children will be given asylum along with you if they were unmarried and under 21 years old at the time that USCIS receives your asylum application.

iii. Part A. III.

If your prior address was in a third country (not your home country) for an extended period of time, you will need to show that you were not firmly resettled—that is, you were not granted permanent residence or otherwise entitled to substantial benefits and privileges in that country.

iv. Part B.

Question 1. This question asks what basis you are seeking asylum on—that is, why your persecutor was motivated to single you out. In the top part of Question 1, you can check more than one box. If the first four boxes (race, religion, nationality, political opinion) don't seem to fit—for

example, you're disabled or HIV positive, a female subject to female genital cutting, or a member of a nonpolitical club—your best choice may be "particular social group." Try to avoid checking nothing but the Torture Convention box—this means that you won't actually be applying for political asylum, but only to be spared from removal (deportation) for awhile.

For Questions A and B, your answer should be "yes" to at least B, and preferably A and B, otherwise you don't qualify for asylum. Instead of trying to fit your answer into the spaces on the form, it is best to put down "See my attached affidavit" and write your entire response on a separate sheet of paper (with your name at the top to avoid the possibility of part of your answer getting misplaced).

Question B is intended to find out what you think will happen to you if you return to your home country. Be as specific as you can, explaining how you will be arrested, tried by the military, tortured, sentenced to jail, put to death, or whatever consequence you might suffer. You should also write "See my attached affidavit and supporting documentation" (and then give more details in your affidavit).

Question 2. This question asks whether you or your family members have been accused, charged, arrested, detained, interrogated, convicted, sentenced, or imprisoned in any country. Your answer to this question can help your case if the action against you was a violation of your human rights, for example if you were arrested and beaten for taking part in a lawful, nonviolent protest march. However, your answer can hurt your case if it shows that you are a criminal and the government was merely taking appropriate, lawful action against you.

Questions 3A and 3B. These questions ask about your and your family's involvement in organizations and groups, such as political parties, guerrilla groups, labor unions, and paramilitary organizations. It is very helpful to your claim if you can identify some group to which you belong. To succeed in your claim for asylum, you must have been persecuted for a reason— and that reason must be your connection with some identifiable group. However, if you identify yourself with a group that is known to commit acts of terrorism or persecute others, then your asylum application will likely be denied.

If your persecution wasn't because of your race, religion, nationality, or political opinion, you must define a "particular social group" of which you are a member. Describe the group as specifically as possible, such as "women who refuse to wear the veil," "people who are descendants of the former ruling family," "people with olive-colored skin," or "people who live on the poor side of town." It should be a group whose history of experiencing discrimination or persecution you can explain and document. Defining a "particular social group" is the key to

many asylum cases. A good lawyer will be be familiar with the enormous amount of law that USCIS and the courts have developed around this issue.

Question 4. This question asks whether you fear being tortured in your home country. The answer may be based on what happened to you in the past or what is happening to persons who are in similar circumstances to yours. Answering "yes" is obviously required if you are asking for relief under the Convention Against Torture. For an asylum case, answering "yes" will help, but answering "no" will not hurt your case if you can show you're afraid of other types of serious harm if returned to your country.

v. Part C.

Questions 1 and 2. These questions request information about any prior asylum applications and whether you were firmly resettled in another country before coming to the United States. If you answer "yes" to either of these questions, consult with an asylum expert or attorney before filing your Form I-589.

Questions 3–6. If you answer "yes," consult with an asylum expert or attorney before filing your Form I-589, as one or more of your family members may be ineligible for asylum.

With regard to Question 5, see the discussion of the time limits that apply to application for asylum, above. If you answer "yes" to this question, you may be ineligible for asylum; but consult with an asylum expert or attorney to see if you fall under one of the exceptions discussed above.

vi. Parts D and E.

These sections request your signature and information about the person who prepared the application. Keep in mind that a person who files a fraudulent application may be subject to criminal penalties and barred from getting any applications or benefits approved by USCIS and will probably be deported. There are also criminal penalties for failure to disclose one's role in helping to prepare and/or submit an application which contains false information. Finally, USCIS may use the information on the application to deport you, if you are not granted asylum.

vii. Parts F and G.

Leave these blank when you submit your application.

b. Creating and Collecting Documents to Accompany Form I-589

It is common for asylum applicants to have fled their home countries hurriedly, without time to gather many personal documents. Frequently, asylees also have been denied passports. Therefore, USCIS does not insist upon any specific documentation to support asylum applications. Some type of personal identification should be provided, however. If you entered the U.S. legally, you should present copies of your I-94 card (if you have one), visa, and passport.

Applying for a Work Permit If 150 Days Go by With No Decision

If, after submitting your asylum application, you receive no decision on your case within five months (and you weren't the cause of any delays), you're in luck—you can apply for a work permit if you need one. USCIS tries to make sure you don't wait this long, but in recent years it's been taking several years to give people a decision on their asylum application. You should, therefore, keep track of the days since you filed your application.

If you are able to apply for a work permit, fill out Form I-765 according to the instructions that come with the form. There will be no fee for your first work permit. Answer Question 16 "(c)(8)."

With your I-765 form, you'll need to enclose evidence that your asylum application was filed with USCIS (its receipt notice is best). Also, send a copy of the front and back of your I-94 card (if you have one), a copy of some kind of government-issued photo ID, and two photos (the usual passport style). On the back of the photos, write your name and A number (if you have one) in pencil or felt pen.

Send your work permit application to the USCIS Service Center indicated in the instructions or on the USCIS website (www.uscis.gov/i-765).

For each accompanying relative (spouse or unmarried children under age 21), provide copies of documents showing their family relationship to you. You may prove a parent/child relationship by presenting the child's long-form birth certificate. Many countries issue both short- and long-form birth certificates. Where both are available, the long form is needed, because it contains the names of the parents while the short form does not. If you are accompanied by your spouse, you must prove that you are lawfully married. This is best shown by a civil marriage certificate. If any of these documents are unavailable, the USCIS office may, at its discretion, accept other kinds of proof, including notarized affidavits from you or other people familiar with your family situation.

Additionally, you must provide documents to support your claim of persecution by the government of your home country. The burden is on you to prove your eligibility. One document proving fear of persecution is your own sworn statement explaining your persecution or fear of persecution. The statement should be in your own words and need not be in any special form—though at the end, above your signature, it's best to add the words "I swear that the foregoing is true and correct to the best of my knowledge." Additional documents may include:

- newspaper articles describing the type of persecution you would encounter if you returned to your home country
- affidavits from other people, preferably experts or people in positions of authority, who know you personally or have personally experienced similar persecution in your home country, and
- written human rights reports about your country supplied by organizations such as Amnesty International or Human Rights Watch, or the U.S. State Department's *Country Reports on Human Rights Practices*.

If the persecution is based on your membership in any type of group, including a particular social group, you must not only supply evidence that the group is experiencing persecution, but also offer proof that you are a member of that group.

2. Step Two: Attending Your Asylum Interview

Assuming your application is not summarily denied by the Service Center, you will be asked to come to an asylum office for a personal interview. Asylum interviews are conducted at only a few locations, so you may be required to travel for the interview. You will receive notice of the time of your interview in the mail. Some applications for asylum are sent by USCIS for review to the U.S. Department of State, which makes a recommendation on the application.

You can't choose the asylum officer who will interview you. However, if you're a woman, and your persecution involved experiences that you would feel uncomfortable describing in front of a man, you can ask to be interviewed by a female officer.

Expect the interview to last about a half hour. If you don't speak English, you must bring an interpreter with you.

> **CAUTION**
> **Paying a trained interpreter can be well worth it.** Simultaneous interpretation requires language skill, fast thinking, and experience. If it's done wrong, your case could be permanently affected. For instance, we know of a case where a man nearly lost his case for asylum because of the interpreter. His written application told of the murder of his parents by Guatemalan security forces. But at the interview, the interpreter kept translating "padres" (the Spanish word for "parents") as "father." That led the interviewer to think that the man couldn't get his story straight—had one parent died, or two? Fortunately the lawyer spoke Spanish and helped clear matters up, but that won't always be the case.

The officer will start by asking you to raise your right hand and swear to tell the truth. Then he or she will go over some of the basic information in your application.

Eventually, the officer will ask you to describe the persecution that you experienced or the basis of your fear of persecution. Some officers may ask you a general question and invite you to talk at length, others may ask more specific questions based on the statement you submitted with your application. These officers are highly trained regarding the conditions in your country and will also be asking questions to test whether you match their other knowledge about the country or its citizens, or whether you are who you say you are. For example, if you claim to be from a certain religious minority, the officer might ask you to describe in detail certain rituals done within that religion.

You will sign the I-589 form you submitted, which means you swear that everything in it is true.

The asylum officer will not tell you whether you are approved for asylum at the interview.

You'll likely have to return to the Asylum Office to get your decision, a few weeks after the interview. A clerk at the front desk will tell you the decision on your application in person and give you a written document confirming it.

It may take USCIS longer to give you a decision if you were interviewed at a district office (rather than an asylum office), are currently in valid immigration status, or if your case needs to be reviewed by USCIS Asylum Division Headquarters staff. In any of these circumstances, you will likely receive the decision by mail.

3. If Your Asylum Is Approved

Once you've been granted asylum, whether by the USCIS Asylum Office or by an immigration judge, you'll be given a small card, called an I-94, that proves your status and should be kept with your passport. (Make a copy for your records, too, and keep it in a safe place.) With your I-94, you can obtain a Social Security number and driver's license, which is more than enough to show an employer that you have a right to work.

If you wish, however, you can also apply for an employment authorization card, by mailing Form I-765. You'll find the form and instructions on the USCIS website at www.uscis.gov/i-765. Answer Question 16 with "(a)(5)." There is no fee for your first work permit, but a $380 fee for renewals.

TIP

Protect your asylee status. Although there is no limit on how long you can stay in the United States as an asylee, your rights can be taken away, for example if conditions in your home country get better or you commit a crime. Plan to submit an application for a green card as soon as you can (exactly one year from your asylum approval date). And don't travel outside the United States without first getting a "refugee travel document" (which you apply for on Form I-131; the form and instructions are at www.uscis. gov/i-131). And whatever you do, don't travel to your home country—USCIS may see that as a sign that you don't really fear returning there and deny you reentry to the U.S. after your trip, or later deny your application for a green card. (If your spouse or children got asylum based on your application, however, they can ordinarily travel to your home country without fear of being barred from returning to the U.S. But be cautious, particularly if, in your application, you claimed that they were targets as well.)

Did you leave a husband, wife, or child (unmarried, under age 21) in your home country when you fled to the United States? If so, that person may now be eligible to join you as a fellow asylee. This works only if you were married, or were the child's parent, before leaving your country. In other words, you can't now get married or adopt a child and apply to bring them here. To apply, fill out a separate Form I-730 for each person coming—it's available at www.uscis.gov/i-730. Also be aware that your family members can be denied entry if they've committed serious nonpolitical crimes, been affiliated with terrorism, or otherwise violated other provisions of the immigration laws at I.N.A. § 208(b)(2), or 8 U.S.C. § 1158.

4. If Your Asylum Application Is Denied

If, after your interview, the officer expects to deny your asylum application, but you are currently in some other legal immigration status, he or she may send you a written notice by mail warning you and explaining the reasons. In that case, you have an opportunity to send the asylum officer additional materials or a personal statement to try to overcome his or her doubts.

More often, you'll simply receive your denial when you go to pick up your decision. Although the Asylum Office calls this a "referral" to Immigration Court, in reality it's the equivalent of receiving a denial from the Asylum Office. You will be given what's called a Notice to Appear (NTA), which is the start of a removal proceeding. In Immigration Court, your application may be considered again by an immigration judge. You can (and should) hire an immigration lawyer, who will help you fully prepare additional written materials and present your story orally before the judge.

If your application is then turned down by the immigration judge, you may file an appeal with the Board of Immigration Appeals, in Washington, DC. If that appeal is unsuccessful, you may have your case reviewed in a U.S. Circuit Court of Appeals. You should not attempt such appeals without the assistance of an experienced immigration lawyer, because you are in serious danger of being deported.

D. How to Get a Green Card as a Refugee or an Asylee

Refugees who get their status before entering the U.S. are entitled to apply for green cards one year or more after arriving in the United States. Asylees are also eligible to apply for green cards one year or more after their asylee status is granted. You will not receive a notice to apply. You will have to keep track on your own of when you are eligible to apply, then assemble and submit your application for what's called "adjustment of status."

It's worth applying for your green card as soon as you can. For one thing, DHS has the authority to revoke (cancel) your asylum status if a change in your home country conditions makes it no longer dangerous for you to return there. The procedures for revoking asylum status are complicated, however, and not often used.

> TIP
> **The sooner you get your green card, the sooner you can apply for U.S. citizenship.** Since citizenship is the most secure status the U.S. can offer, it's worth applying as soon as you're eligible.

Special Green Card Procedures for Certain People Who Got Asylum Through a Spouse or Parent

A USCIS policy announced in 2008 affects refugees and asylees who obtained their status as derivatives (through a spouse or parent), but who no longer qualify for derivative status. Examples of this include children who obtained status through a parent's application but who are now over 21 years old, a spouse who is no longer married to the principal asylum applicant, and spouses or children where the principal refugee/asylee has been found to no longer meet the definition of a refugee. (Your best bet if your life situation has changed and you have any questions about your continuing eligibility is to talk to an attorney.)

In such cases, USCIS requires the derivative applicant to file what's called a "nunc pro tunc" asylum application (on the same Form I-589 that is used to apply for asylum) before filing the adjustment of status application. The Form I-589 is then granted nunc pro tunc, that is, back to the date of the first grant of refugee/asylee status.

If you fail to file a nunc pro tunc asylum application before submitting the I-485 application for adjustment of status, your I-485 will be denied (and the fees will not be refunded), but you will remain in valid refugee/asylee status and may refile the I-485 after successfully filing your nunc pro tunc asylum application.

Nunc pro tunc asylum applications are not subject to the same requirements of a regular asylum application. You don't need to show that you've been persecuted or that you have a well-founded fear of persecution. USCIS is mainly interested in confirming your relationship to the principal asylee and collecting biographic information about you.

You'll need to submit your nunc pro tunc application to the same USCIS Service Center address used for submitting asylum applications. Be sure you write "NUNC PRO TUNC APPLICATION" in bold letters so that your application is not treated as a regular asylum application, and attach proof of your prior grant of asylum.

The process of applying for your green card—that is, adjusting your status to permanent resident—involves preparing a set of forms and documents (a separate set for you and each of your accompanying spouse and children), mailing these to a USCIS Lockbox, and waiting for some weeks until you're called in to have your fingerprints taken. See Chapter 4 for information on tracking the progress of your application.

As noted earlier, the Social Security number that you obtained with your asylee I-94, along with your driver's license, is more than enough to show employers that you have the right to work.

You must be "admissible" to the U.S. to get a green card as an asylee or refugee, although not all the grounds of inadmissibility discussed in Chapter 3 apply to you. Most important, you do not have to worry about being inadmissible as a "public charge" or for having come to the U.S. without proper entry documents. All other grounds of inadmissibility (except the security-related and terrorist grounds mentioned above) can be "waived" (forgiven) by USCIS. The asylum officer will tell you whether you need to prepare a waiver application (on Form I-602). Often the officer will grant a waiver as part of approving a green card, without requiring an I-602.

If your green card can be approved without an interview, you will receive your green card in the mail. It will be backdated one year from the approval. So, for example, if your case was approved on July 15, 2013, your card will show that your permanent residence began on July 15, 2012. (That will help you when it's time to apply for U.S. citizenship.) If USCIS cannot tell from your application whether your permanent residence should be approved, it will schedule you for an interview at a local USCIS office.

CAUTION

Security checks are a likely cause of delays. If you're between 14 and 79 years old, as part of your adjustment of status application, USCIS will have the FBI run both a fingerprint check and a name check on you, and will search for your name in the Interagency Border Inspection System (IBIS) database to detect crimes, fraud schemes, and other illegal activities with which you may have been involved. These name checks can take several months, or even longer if yours is a common name. The FBI fingerprint check and the IBIS name check must be complete before USCIS can approve your application, but if the FBI name check hasn't been resolved within six months and your application is otherwise approvable, USCIS should not wait any longer to approve it. If you've been informed that your case is stalled due to security checks, get the name of a person you can keep in touch with for updates, or hire a lawyer to help with this task.

1. Step One: Preparing Your Adjustment of Status Application

The basic form used in the U.S. adjustment of status application is Form I-485, Application to Register Permanent Residence or Adjust Status. However, a handful of other forms as well as documents must be prepared to accompany this main one.

One way to get all these forms is to call the USCIS forms line at 800-870-3676 and ask for the Adjustment of Status Packet (but throw out the Form I-864 Affidavit of Support—as an asylee, you won't need it).

Checklist for Adjustment of Status Application

Forms

☐ Form I-485.

☐ Form G-325A (but you need not file a G-325A for any child under the age of 14).

☐ Form I-765 (optional, if you need a work permit or "EAD").

☐ I-131, Application for Travel Document, for use if you think you'll need to travel outside the United States while your application is processed. *Do not travel to the country from which you gained asylum or refugee status, or you will lose your right to this status.*

Documents

☐ Copy of your I-94 card (if any), showing approval of your asylum or refugee status; alternately, asylees can submit their approval letters and refugees can submit a copy of their work EADs.

☐ If you were granted asylum by an immigration judge, a copy of the judge's order.

☐ Copy of the I-94 card you received at your last entry to the U.S. (This may be your original I-94 card, from before you were granted asylum, or it may be an I-94 issued to you when you returned from traveling outside the U.S. using a refugee travel document that you got after being granted asylum.)

☐ Copy of a long-form birth certificate for you and each accompanying relative. If this is in another language, it must be accompanied by a full English translation.

☐ Evidence that you've been physically present in the U.S. for one year. USCIS asks that you submit only a few of these documents. Choose ones that cover broad periods of time, such as a letter of employment, a lease, school enrollment records, or similar documentation.

☐ Proof of any absences from the U.S. since you have been granted asylum or entered as a refugee, for example, photocopies of pages in a refugee travel document or passport. (These absences subtract from your one year, so do the math and make sure you don't submit your adjustment of status application early.)

☐ A medical exam report done by a USCIS-approved doctor (with exception for some refugees and recently arrived children or spouses of asylees; see below) on Form I-693, in a sealed envelope.

☐ Marriage certificate, if you are married and bringing your spouse.

☐ If either you or your spouse has been previously married, copies of divorce and death certificates showing termination of all previous marriages.

☐ Four photographs of you and two photographs of each accompanying relative in U.S. passport style (it's best to have a professional do these). Write your name and A number in pencil or felt pen on the back of each photo. (This assumes you will submit the Forms I-765 and I-131 at this time. If not, you can subtract one photo for each form you don't submit.)

Fee

☐ Filing fee for Form I-485 (asylees only, not refugees). Currently $1,225 for applicants ages 14 to 78 (includes biometrics fee), $1,140 for applicants age 79 and over or under age 14 and not filing with a parent, and $750 for derivative applicants under age 14 who are filing concurrently with a parent. Checks and money orders are accepted, but we advise against sending cash through the mail. Double-check all fees at www.uscis.gov/i-485. Or, rather than sending the filing fee, you can request that USCIS accept your application with no fee by filing USCIS Form I-912 with proof that you qualify for a fee waiver because you don't have enough money. For more information, see www.uscis.gov/i-912.

Or, you can obtain the forms online at www.uscis.gov. (On the home page, click, "Green Card," then "Apply" then "Green Card Through Refugee or Asylee Status," and look for the links to forms on the right side of the page.)

The checklist above will help you assemble and keep track of the forms and documents. A complete set must also be prepared for your spouse and children if they're in the U.S. and were also granted asylum or refugee status at least a year ago.

Form I-485: This is the main form you'll fill out, and needs a bit more explanation.

Part 1. Part 1 asks for general information about when and where you were born, your present address, and your immigration status ("refugee" or "asylee"). It also asks for an A number. Everyone who enters the U.S. as a refugee or has applied for asylum is given an eight- or nine-digit A number.

Part 2. Mark Box d if you're an asylee. Mark Box h if you're a refugee, and copy the explanation in their example on a separate sheet of paper that you attach to the form, since there won't be enough room to write it all in the space provided.

Part 3. The questions in Sections A through C are self-explanatory. If you didn't use a visa to enter the U.S., write "N/A" for the related questions. The questions in Section C are meant to identify people who are inadmissible. With the exception of certain memberships in the Communist Party or terrorist organizations, you will not be deemed inadmissible simply because you joined an organization. However, if your answer to any of the other questions is "yes," you may be inadmissible and need a waiver. (See Chapter 3, which is intended to help you identify and overcome such obstacles.)

Medical exam. You and your accompanying relatives will be required to submit medical examination reports. You must get a medical exam done by a USCIS-authorized physician or medical clinic. To find a list of approved physicians in your area, go to https://my.uscis.gov/findadoctor or call 800-375-5283 and write down the doctors' names and contact information by hand (quickly!).

The fees depend on the doctor. The exam itself involves taking a medical history, blood test, and chest X-ray and administering vaccinations, if required. Pregnant women can refuse to be X-rayed until after the pregnancy. The vaccination requirement may be waived for religious, moral, or medical reasons.

TIP

Some refugees and derivative asylees can skip most of the medical exam. If you are a refugee, or the child or spouse of an asylee who entered the U.S. after the primary asylum applicant was approved, and you had an exam overseas, here's a way to save money: By applying no more than one year after arriving in the U.S. (as a refugee) or within one year of completing your required one year of U.S. physical presence (as a derivative asylee) all you need is a vaccination Supplemental Form to I-693, also completed by a USCIS-designated doctor. The exception is if medical grounds of inadmissibility were noted when you entered the United States.

After completion of the medical exam, and upon obtaining the test results, the doctor will give you the report in a sealed envelope. Do not open the envelope! Turn it into USCIS just as it is, sealed.

The main purpose of the medical exam is to verify that you are not medically inadmissible. Some medical grounds of inadmissibility can be overcome with treatment or by applying for a waiver. (See Chapter 3 for details.)

As a refugee or asylum applicant, you'll need to mail your application, consisting of both forms and documents, to either the Phoenix or the Dallas Lockbox, depending on the state in which you live. Check www.uscis.gov/i-485-addresses for the appropriate address.

After filing your adjustment of status application, you will receive a receipt notice. If USCIS requires additional evidence or information, it will send you a Request for Evidence form (I-797E). You will also receive, after some weeks, a notice advising you where to go to have your fingerprints taken. These will then be used to check whether you have any history of arrests (whether by the police, FBI, DHS, or other authority).

Read This If You Plan to Leave the U.S. Before Your Adjustment Interview

While waiting for a decision on your adjustment of status application, you're allowed to travel outside the U.S. using your refugee/asylee travel document. We recommend that you do NOT use the passport of your home country, because the U.S. immigration authorities may view this as inconsistent with your refugee/asylee status, and refuse to let you return.

---

2. Step Two: Attending Your Adjustment of Status Interview

You may be called in for a personal interview, which will be held at a USCIS office near you. USCIS will send you and your accompanying relatives an appointment notice, at least two weeks in advance of the interview. If you have an attorney, he or she may come with you to the interview. (Even if you don't have an attorney, you could consult with or hire one at this point.)

Be prepared to explain at your interview why you still fear returning to the country from which you fled. If you no longer fear returning there, you do not qualify for your asylee or refugee status and, therefore, do not qualify for the green card. If any dramatic changes have occurred to supposedly improve conditions in your

Checklist of Documents to Bring to Your Adjustment Interview

☐ The interview notice that USCIS sent to you—security officers at the building entrance and the receptionist will need to see it.

☐ A complete photocopy of your green card application. This is for your use—you may want to follow along as the officer asks you questions about the material you filled out on the forms, or you may find that the officer is missing something that you have a copy of.

☐ Photo identification or passport for you and every one of your family members. (It's best to bring all of your passports or Refugee Travel Documents.)

☐ Originals of all documents that you made copies of for submission with your application. For example, if you submitted a photocopy of a birth certificate or another official document, a USCIS officer may want to examine the original.

☐ Any documents received from USCIS or other immigration authorities. For example, if you left the country on Advance Parole, bring this permit.

☐ Any updates to the material in your application. For example, if you have given birth to another child, bring the birth certificate. If you've been arrested, bring certified court documents and a full explanation (and, most importantly, consult with an attorney to make sure that the arrest doesn't make you inadmissible and removable).

country—such as a regime change or peace treaty—you'll have some extra explaining to do. If possible, supply supporting documents under such circumstances. If you don't already have an attorney, this would be a good time to hire one.

The checklist on this page will help you prepare for your interview. Prepare all these items for yourself and your family members.

 RELATED TOPIC

See Chapter 4 for detailed information on what expect during your adjustment of status interview—and what to do if your adjustment of status application is denied. Also, for information on how to protect your status as a green card holder after you're approved, see Chapter 14.

CAUTION

Even after you get your green card, try not to return to your home country. Family emergencies are usually an acceptable reason to go, but making casual trips may cause the immigration authorities to reexamine your asylum application. They may decide that you are not really afraid to return there, and that your asylum application was therefore fraudulent—which could lead to cancellation of your green card.

After Your Approval for a Green Card

f you're reading this after becoming a permanent or conditional resident, congratulations! But don't stop reading. This chapter will give you some important tips on how to protect and enjoy your new status.

A. How to Prove You're a U.S. Resident

Whether you came through a consulate outside the U.S. or applied for adjustment of status in the U.S., you won't get an actual green card right away. Until the card arrives, a temporary stamp in your passport will serve as evidence of your permanent resident status (or, for newly married or investor applicants, your conditional resident status). This stamp, in blue ink, is often called an "I-551 stamp" or "ADIT stamp." You can show this stamp to employers or use it to travel in and out of the United States.

You may have to wait several weeks or months for the actual green card. If you're over the age of 18, the law requires you to carry your green card or other evidence of your status at all times. But keep a photocopy of it in a safe place, in case it's lost or stolen—this will make it much easier to get a replacement card from USCIS.

If you applied to adjust status at a USCIS office in the States and were not approved in person, you'll receive a letter from USCIS. Unfortunately, this letter is rather unclear at first sight.

Many immigrants who receive it don't understand what it means, and a few have tossed it in the trash. This letter, however, is the official notice of approval for residency. A sample is shown below. When you receive it, make a copy for your records and take it with your passport to your local USCIS office, where your passport will be stamped to show that you're a resident.

CAUTION
Don't let your ADIT stamp expire. The temporary stamp in your passport may expire before you get your green card. This doesn't mean you've lost your legal right to live in the United States, but it can be very inconvenient if you're working or you're traveling abroad. If you see that the stamp is about to expire, make an InfoPass appointment at https://infopass.uscis.gov, to go to your local USCIS office for another stamp. They probably won't be able to tell you when your card will arrive, since the card is being manufactured in a USCIS factory elsewhere, but they can give you a form with which to make an inquiry.

B. Traveling Abroad

There's no question about it—travel outside the United States is one of your rights as a conditional or permanent resident. But don't stay away too long. As the term "resident" suggests, you are expected to reside—that is, make your home—in the United States. If you make your home outside the United States, you could lose your green card.

Sample Notice of Action

Department of Homeland Security
U.S. Citizenship and Immigration Services

I-797, Notice of Action

THE UNITED STATES OF AMERICA

RECEIPT NUMBER		CASE TYPE	I485 APPLICATION TO ADJUST TO PERMANENT RESIDENT STATUS
MSC16-010-33333			
RECEIPT DATE	PRIORITY DATE	PETITIONER	
October 12, 2016			A096 944-222 BOONMEE, LAWAN
NOTICE DATE	PAGE	BENEFICIARY	
January 23, 2017	1 of 1		

ILONA BRAY
950 PARKER STREET
BERKELEY, CA 94710

Notice Type: Approval Notice

Section: Adjustment as direct
beneficiary of immigrant
petition
COA: CR6

The above petition has been approved. We have sent the original visa petition to the Department of State National Visa Center (NVC), 32 Rochester Avenue, Portsmouth, NH 03801-2909. The INS has completed all action; further inquiries should be directed to the NVC.

The NVC now processes all approved fiance(e) petitions. The NVC processing should be complete within two to four weeks after receiving the petition from INS. The NVC will create a case record with your petition information. NVC will then send the petition to the U.S. Embassy or Consulate where your fiance(e) will be interviewed for his or her visa.

You will receive notification by mail when NVC has sent your petition to the U.S. Embassy or Consulate. The notification letter will provide you with a unique number for your case and the name and address of the U.S. Embassy or Consulate where your petition has been sent.

If it has been more than four weeks since you received this approval notice and you have not received notification from NVC that your petition has been forwarded overseas, please call NVC at (603) 334-0700. Please call between 8:00am-6:45pm Eastern Standard Time. You will need to enter the INS receipt number from this approval notice into the automated response system to receive information on your petition.

THIS FORM IS NOT A VISA NOR MAY IT BE USED IN PLACE OF A VISA.

Please see the additional information on the back. You will be notified separately about any other cases you filed.
U.S. CITIZENSHIP & IMMIGRATION SVC
CALIFORNIA SERVICE CENTER
P. O. BOX 30111
LAGUNA NIGUEL CA 92607-0111
Customer Service Telephone: (800) 375-5283

Form I-797 (Rev. 01/31/05) N

Applying for a Social Security Number

With your U.S. residency, you are eligible for a Social Security number. This is a number given to all people legally living and working in the United States, to identify them and allow them to pay into a system of retirement insurance. You may have already applied for a Social Security number if you received a work permit before getting your green card. If not, now is the time to apply. You'll need this number before you start work—your new employer will ask for it in order to file taxes on your behalf.

To apply for your number, visit your local Social Security office. You can find it in your phone book within the federal government pages (usually blue) or on the Social Security Administration's website at www.ssa.gov.

U.S. border officers have the power to decide whether returning green card holders are living outside the country. The officer will ask when you left the United States, what you were doing while you were away, and where you make your home. Being away for longer than six months will definitely raise suspicion; being away for more than a year guarantees that you will have to attend an Immigration Court hearing before you can reclaim your U.S. residency and green card.

Before deciding whether you have abandoned your residency, the U.S. border officer will look at other factors besides the length of time you were away. The officer may note whether you:

- pay U.S. taxes
- own a home or apartment or have a long-term lease in the United States
- were employed in the foreign country
- took your family to the foreign country
- are returning to the U.S. with a one-way ticket or a round-trip ticket back to the foreign country, and
- maintained other ties with the United States.

If you're coming back after a trip of several months, you can make your entry to the United States easier by bringing copies of documents that show that your home base is still in the United States. These documents could include your U.S. tax returns, home lease, evidence of employment, or other relevant documents.

Many immigrants mistakenly believe that to keep your green card, all you need to do is enter the U.S. at least once a year. The fact is that if you ever leave with the intention of making some other country your permanent home, you give up your U.S. residency when you go.

 TIP

Get permission before leaving. If you know in advance that you're going to have to spend more than a year outside the United States, you can apply for a reentry permit. Use

Form I-131, Application for Travel Document, available at your local USCIS district office or on the USCIS website at www.uscis.gov/i-131. Check Box 1.a in Part 2 for reentry permits. You will have to explain to USCIS the purpose of your trip and how much time you've already spent outside the United States. Make sure to submit this form before you leave the United States. Follow the mailing instructions at www.uscis.gov/i-131. (Reentry permits cannot be applied for online.) The fee is currently $660 for people between ages 14 and 79. For those older or younger, the fee is $575 (because "biometrics"—fingerprinting and other proof of identification—are not required). Reentry permits cannot be renewed and can be applied for only inside the United States. Therefore, if you need a second reentry permit, you must return briefly and apply for it.

If you stay outside the U.S. for more than one year and do not get a reentry permit before leaving, then in order to come back again, you must apply at a U.S. consulate abroad for a special immigrant visa as a returning resident. To get this visa, you will have to convince the consular officer that your absence from the U.S. has been temporary and you never planned to abandon your U.S. residence. You will have to show evidence that you were kept away longer than one year due to unforeseen circumstances. Such evidence might be a letter from a doctor showing that you or a family member had a medical problem. If you do not have a very good reason for failing to return within one year, there is a strong chance you will lose your green card.

The Commuter Exception

Green card holders who commute to work in the U.S. from Canada or Mexico on a daily or seasonal basis may keep their cards even while actually living outside the country. If you know at the time of applying for your immigrant visa that you're going to be working in the U.S. but living in Canada or Mexico, you should ask the consulate for a commuter green card. After your visa approval and first entry into the U.S., you must also tell the Customs and Border Protection (CBP) officer you want a commuter green card. That way, when CBP orders your green card, it will arrive with a notation that you are a commuter, and it will be easier to cross the border every day.

If you want to switch from a regular green card to a commuter green card, you need to file Form I-90, which is an application for a new green card. Include evidence of your employment and residence. The filing fee is currently $450. You can file the I-90 online if you wish—instructions are at www.uscis.gov/file-online—but you must send supporting documents by mail. In Part 2 of the form, check box 2.h1. USCIS will not mail the new green card to you—you must let USCIS know in the box at 2.h1.1 where you will be crossing the border. You'll pick up your commuter green card there.

To keep commuter status, you'll have to remain employed in the U.S., and prove that to CBP periodically.

If you have a commuter green card but are moving to the U.S. and want a regular green card (especially important if you're planning to apply for U.S. citizenship), you must use the same form, the I-90, with filing fee. In Part 2, check box 2.h2. Include evidence of your U.S. residence, and turn in your commuter green card.

C. Your Immigrating Family Members' Rights

If children immigrated with you, their legal status will pretty much match yours. If you received conditional, rather than permanent residency, so did they—and they will also have to apply for permanent residency 90 days before the second anniversary of the date they won conditional residency.

If you got a green card through marriage to a U.S. citizen, some special rules apply. If your spouse was a permanent resident when you were approved, then you, as well as your children, must wait five years before applying for U.S. citizenship. However, if your spouse was a U.S. citizen when you were approved and you're still living together three years after your approval, you can apply for citizenship after these three years—and when you're approved, your children under 18 become citizens automatically (as long as they are living in the U.S. citizen parent's custody).

This right comes from the Child Citizenship Act of 2000. To prove their citizenship, your children will automatically receive a certificate of citizenship from USCIS by mail, within about six weeks of entering the United States. Children who are over 18 when they become permanent residents will have to wait five years before applying for citizenship (despite the fact that you, their parent, need wait only three years).

D. Losing Your Permanent Resident Status

You can lose your U.S. permanent resident status by violating the law (committing a crime) or by violating the terms of your residency, such as by staying out of the United States and living abroad for too long, as explained above in Section B. If you are in the United States, such a violation could make you removable (formerly called deportable), in which case USCIS might start Immigration Court proceedings against you and eventually send you away. If you attempt to return to the United States, you could be found inadmissible and kept out.

RELATED TOPIC
For more on inadmissibility, see the discussion in Chapter 3 and I.N.A. § 101(a)(13)(C), 8 U.S.C. § 1101(a)(13)(c). The grounds of inadmissibility overlap with the grounds of removability or deportability, but they are set out separately in the immigration laws, and there are some significant differences. See I.N.A. § 237(a), or 8 U.S.C. § 1227(a) for more on removability.

A full discussion of removability is beyond the scope of this book. In brief, you become removable if you:

- fail to advise USCIS of your changes of address within ten days of moving
- are involved in document fraud or alien smuggling
- go on welfare or government assistance (become a public charge) within the first five years of entry, if it's because of a reason that existed before you came to the United States (see I.N.A. § 237(a)(5), 8 U.S.C. § 1227(a)(5))
- fail to comply with a condition of your green card (such as failing to follow a course of treatment to cure an illness you had when you were approved for residency)
- commit a certain type of crime, including domestic violence, or
- violate the immigration laws (for example, participate in a sham marriage or help smuggle other aliens into the United States).

You probably aren't planning on a crime spree as soon as you get your green card, but the message to take from the criminal grounds of removability is that you have to be extra careful. Your U.S. citizen friends might not worry too much about engaging in certain illegal activities, such as shooting a gun at the sky on the Fourth of July or sharing a marijuana cigarette at a party. But if you are caught participating in these same activities, you could lose your green card and be removed from the United States.

Men 18–25 Must Register for the Military Draft

Lawful U.S. resident males (green card holders) who are over 18 and under 26 years are required to register for military service, otherwise known as the Selective Service. It's possible, if you were living in the U.S. and then adjusted status, that you were automatically registered when you applied for a driver's license or some other government benefit. You can check at www.sss.gov. If you haven't registered yourself or been automatically registered, you must go to www.sss.gov and register online, or mail a registration form to Selective Service System, P.O. Box 94739, Palatine, IL 60094-4739. The form can be found online at www.sss.gov or at most U.S. post offices. USCIS won't remove you if you don't register, but it will hold up your eventual citizenship application.

E. How to Renew or Replace Your Green Card

This section is about the green card itself —the little laminated card that shows you're a resident. If something happens to the card—if it expires or gets lost—you don't ordinarily lose your status.

The only exception is that when the cards of conditional (not permanent) residents expire, their status expires along with it, as discussed in the chapters concerning conditional residents. However, the law requires you to have a valid green card in your possession. And, it's not a bad thing to have on hand in case you travel, get a new job, or get picked up by an overeager immigration officer who thinks you "look" illegal.

1. Renewing Expiring Green Cards

If you are a permanent resident (not a conditional resident), your status does not expire—but your green card *does* expire, every ten years. When the expiration date on your green card is six months away, you will need to apply to renew it. Also, children who are permanent residents must apply for a replacement green card when they reach their 14th birthday (within 30 days). If the existing card will not expire before the child's 16th birthday, you need not pay an application fee—though you must still pay the biometrics fee. (See 8 C.F.R. § 264.5.)

Use Form I-90, available at your local USCIS office, by mail after calling 800-870-3676, or on the USCIS website at www.uscis.gov/i-90. You can also submit this form electronically through the USCIS website at www.uscis.gov/file-online. If you mail a paper application, USCIS will process it through its electronic system and create an online account for you. You can monitor the progress of your application through your online account. (USCIS will send you instructions for how to do this.) Don't worry—you'll still get notices in the mail. Instructions are not included in this book, but Form I-90 comes with a fairly complete set of instructions.

Alternately, if you are ready and eligible to apply for U.S. citizenship, you can submit the citizenship application instead of renewing the green card. (If a USCIS officer tries to tell you that you need an unexpired green card in order to apply for citizenship, don't accept it as true. Ask for a supervisor's help.) It might take you over a year to get your citizenship, but USCIS doesn't mind if you carry around an expired green card in this circumstance. If you need to change jobs or travel, however, you will probably want to renew the green card, to prove to the rest of the world that you are still a permanent resident.

2. Replacing Lost or Stolen Green Cards

If your green card is lost, stolen, accidentally dropped into a blender, or otherwise destroyed, you will need to apply for a new one. Like renewal, this is done using Form I-90 (see instructions in Section 1, above, on how to file the form).

You Can Be Removed for Not Telling USCIS You've Changed Your Address

In 2002, the Immigration and Naturalization Service (INS, now called USCIS) shocked immigrants and their advocates by starting to enforce little-known provisions of the immigration law that make it a crime for immigrants not to submit immediate notifications whenever they change their address. The potential punishments include fines, imprisonment, or removal. While the immigration authorities largely ignored these legal provisions in the past, their post-September 11 security focus changed this. Unfortunately, a number of innocents may be caught in the trap.

As a green card holder, you must take steps to protect yourself. Within ten days of your move, advise USCIS online or by mail using Form AR-11. Note that you can't just send one notification per family—every member of your household needs to have a separate form submitted for him or her, by mail or online.

It is easiest to change your address online. at www.uscis.gov/ar-11 (click the link for online filing). The question about your "last address" refers only to your last address in the United States, not your last address in any other country. The address you supply should be where you actually live, not a P.O. box or work address. There is no fee for submitting Form AR-11 or changing your address online.

In addition, if you have any applications on file that are waiting for a USCIS decision—for example, if you've applied for citizenship—you need to separately file a change of address at whichever USCIS office is handling your application. Check with that office for its procedures—a letter may be enough.

What if more than ten days have already passed and you've only just discovered your responsibility to file Form AR-11? Most attorneys advise that you tell USCIS of your address change now, to show USCIS you made an attempt to comply and to assure that USCIS has your current address. USCIS can forgive a failure to notify if that failure wasn't willful (intentional).

As with everything you send to USCIS, if you choose to mail your AR-11, realize that there's a chance it will get lost. Be sure to make a photocopy of your Form AR-11 and any notifications you send to other USCIS offices. Then mail everything by courier or certified mail with a return receipt. The return receipt or courier tracking system is particularly important because USCIS won't send you any separate acknowledgment that it has received your Form AR-11. Put your copies and the return receipt in a safe place in case you ever need to prove to USCIS that you complied with the law.

TIP

Report all stolen green cards to the police. Green cards are a hot item, and there is always a possibility that yours will be stolen and sold. If this happens, be sure to file a police report. You may not get your card back, but when you apply for a replacement card, the report will help convince USCIS that you didn't sell your own card.

3. Correcting USCIS Errors on Your Green Card

When you receive your green card, take a close look at it—USCIS occasionally makes errors, such as your name or birth date. It's worth taking the time to correct these. Fortunately, USCIS has agreed that people should not be charged a fee for correcting the USCIS's own mistakes.

This procedure also requires filling out a Form I-90. In addition, you must send your actual green card (the one containing the incorrect information) along with documentation to prove the mistake. For example, if your name was spelled wrong, send a copy of your birth certificate or passport.

If USCIS decides that the mistake was your fault, perhaps because you filled out an application wrong, it will charge you a filing fee and fingerprint (called biometrics) fee.

4. Dealing With Green Cards That Never Arrive

Your green card is being produced in a seemingly busy factory, and waits of three to six or more months are not uncommon. If yours is very late, call USCIS Customer Service or make an InfoPass appointment to visit your local USCIS office.

F. Green Cards and U.S. Citizenship

Green card holders can, after a certain time, apply for U.S. citizenship. Except in rare cases, no one can become a U.S. citizen without first receiving a green card.

It is frequently said that green cards give all the benefits of U.S. citizenship except the rights to vote and hold public office. The differences between the two are actually greater. The most important distinction is that if you violate certain laws or abandon your U.S. residence, you can lose your green card. U.S. citizenship cannot be taken away, unless you acquired it fraudulently or voluntarily give it up. Another important difference is that U.S. citizenship allows you to petition for more of your family members to immigrate than a green card does, and their immigration will be faster.

The time period you have to wait before applying for U.S. citizenship ranges between three and five years—three years for people married to U.S. citizens, five years for everyone else. However, asylees can actually apply four years after their approval for permanent residence, because their one year as an asylee counts, and refugees can apply five years after entry to the U.S., no matter when they became permanent residents. In all cases you can file the application three months before you've completed the required three, four, or five years—USCIS figures it will take at least three months to decide on your application, by which time you will have qualified.

You must also meet other eligibility criteria before applying for citizenship. You'll have to have behaved in a way that shows your good moral character while you had your green card, and you must have lived in the U.S. for most of that time.

TIP

For complete instructions on how to apply for U.S. citizenship, see *Becoming a U.S. Citizen: A Guide to the Law, Exam & Interview*, by Ilona Bray (Nolo).

G. Green Cards and U.S. Taxes

Once you get a green card, you automatically become a U.S. tax resident. U.S. tax residents must file a tax return and declare their entire incomes to the U.S. government, even if part or all of that income has been earned from investments or business activities carried on outside U.S. borders. This does not necessarily mean that the U.S. government will tax all of your worldwide income. International treaties often regulate whether or not you must pay U.S. taxes on income earned elsewhere. However, green card holders have to at least report all income they have earned worldwide.

You may believe that the number of days you spend in the U.S. each year has some effect on whether or not you are a U.S. tax resident. This is true for people who have nonimmigrant (temporary) visas. It is not true for green card holders. If you have a green card, your worldwide income must be reported to the U.S. government, even if you remain outside the U.S. for an entire year.

As a green card holder, you must file a U.S. federal tax return each year by April 15th. You are eligible for most all of the deductions and credits allowed to U.S. citizens. Also, to avoid double taxation, you may claim a foreign tax credit for income tax you've paid or owe to a foreign country. Failure to follow U.S. tax laws may be considered a crime. If you are found guilty of a tax crime, your green card can be revoked and you may be removed from the United States.

To find out exactly how to follow U.S. tax laws, consult an accountant, a tax attorney, or the nearest office of the U.S. Internal Revenue Service (or see its website at www.irs.gov).

Introduction to Nonimmigrant (Temporary) Visas

There are many kinds of non-immigrant (temporary) visas. Each is issued for a different purpose and each is known by a letter-number combination as well as a name. You may be familiar with the more popular types of nonimmigrant visas, such as B-2 visitors, E-2 investors, or F-1 students. All of these fall into the general nonimmigrant group.

When you get a nonimmigrant visa, the U.S. government assumes you will perform a specific activity while you are in the United States. You are therefore given a specialized visa authorizing that activity—and only that activity—for a specific, limited time.

How is a nonimmigrant visa different from a green card? The most basic difference is that all green cards are permanent while all nonimmigrant visas are temporary. If you hold a green card, you are considered a permanent resident of the United States. Your green card can be taken away only if you violate certain laws or regulations. The exact opposite is true of nonimmigrant visas—they're very easy for the government to take away from you. For example, if you travel to the U.S. on a nonimmigrant visa and the border authorities think you do not plan to go home after your stay is over, the visa will be taken away. After you've held a green card for a certain length of time, you can become a U.S. citizen; a nonimmigrant visa, however, will never lead to U.S. citizenship.

> **CAUTION**
>
> **Never lie to get a visa.** People who use fraudulent documents, make misrepresentations, or attempt entry to the U.S. without proper documentation, can be refused entry at the U.S. border or airport, removed from the U.S. and prevented from returning for five years or more. Accordingly, it is extremely important to understand the requirements of the visa classification you are requesting and not make any misrepresentations of your intent or qualifications for that particular visa.

A. Types of Nonimmigrant Visas

Nonimmigrant visas differ from each other in the kinds of privileges they offer, as well as how long they last. Here is a summary list of the various nonimmigrant visas available:

A-1. Ambassadors, public ministers, or career diplomats, and their spouses and children

A-2. Other accredited officials or employees of foreign governments and their spouses and children

A-3. Personal attendants, servants, or employees of A-1 and A-2 visa holders, and their spouses and children

B-1. Business visitors. (Also GB for temporary business visitors to Guam; and WB, for business visitors from countries participating in the Visa Waiver Program.)

B-2. Visitors for pleasure or medical treatment. (Also, WV tourists from countries participating in the Visa Waiver Program. See Chapter 15 for a description of this program and the countries included.)

C-1. Foreign travelers in immediate and continuous transit through the U.S.

C-2. Foreign travelers going directly to and from the United Nations Headquarters District

CW-1. Workers in the Commonwealth of the Northern Mariana Islands

CW-2. Spouses and children of CW-1 workers

D-1. Crewmen who need to land temporarily in the U.S. and who will depart aboard the same ship or plane on which they arrived

D-2. Crew members who need to land temporarily in the U.S. and who will depart aboard a different ship or plane than the one on which they arrived

E-1. Treaty traders working for a U.S. company and their spouses and children

E-2. Treaty investors working for a U.S. company and their spouses and children

E-3. Nationals of Australia working in a specialty occupation that requires a bachelor's degree or higher education, and their spouses and children

F-1. Academic or language students

F-2. Spouses and children of F-1 visa holders

F-3. Citizens or residents of Mexico or Canada commuting to the U.S. as academic or language students

G-1. Designated principal resident representatives of foreign governments coming to the U.S. to work for an international organization, their spouses and children, and their staff members

G-2. Other accredited representatives of foreign governments coming to the U.S. to work for an international organization, and their spouses and children

G-3. Representatives of foreign governments and their spouses and children who would ordinarily qualify for G-1 or G-2 visas except that their governments are not members of an international organization

G-4. Officers or employees of international organizations and their spouses and children

G-5. Attendants, servants, and personal employees of G-1 through G-4 visa holders and their spouses and children

H-1B. Persons working in specialty occupations requiring at least a bachelor's degree or its equivalent in on-the-job experience and distinguished fashion models

H-1C. Registered nurses working in areas where health professionals are in short supply

H-2A. Temporary agricultural workers coming to the U.S. to fill positions for which a temporary shortage of U.S.

workers has been recognized by the U.S. Department of Agriculture

H-2B. Temporary workers of various kinds coming to the U.S. to perform temporary jobs for which there is a shortage of available qualified U.S. workers

H-3. Temporary trainees

H-4. Spouses and children of H-1, H-2, or H-3 visa holders

I. Bona fide representatives of the foreign press coming to the U.S. to work solely in that capacity and their spouses and children

J-1. Exchange visitors coming to the U.S. to study, work, or train as part of an exchange program officially recognized by the U.S. Information Agency

J-2. Spouses and children of J-1 visa holders

K-1. Fiancé(e)s of U.S. citizens coming to the U.S. for the purpose of getting married

K-2. Minor, unmarried children of K-1 visa holders

K-3. Spouses of U.S. citizens who have filed both a fiancé visa petition and a separate application to enter the U.S.

K-4. Minor, unmarried children of K-3 visa holders

L-1. Intracompany transferees who work in positions as managers, executives, or persons with specialized knowledge

L-2. Spouses and children of L-1 visa holders

M-1. Vocational or other nonacademic students, other than language students

M-2. Spouses and children of M-1 visa holders

M-3. Citizens or residents of Mexico or Canada commuting to the U.S. to attend a vocational program

N-8. Parents of certain special immigrants

N-9. Children of certain special immigrants

NATO-1, NATO-2, NATO-3, NATO-4, and NATO-5. Associates coming to the U.S. under applicable provisions of the NATO Treaty and their spouses and children

NATO-6. Members of civilian components accompanying military forces on missions authorized under the NATO Treaty and their spouses and children

NATO-7. Attendants, servants, or personal employees of NATO-1 through NATO-6 visa holders and their spouses and children

O-1. Persons of extraordinary ability in the sciences, arts, education, business, or athletics

O-2. Essential support staff of O-1 visa holders

O-3. Spouses and children of O-1 and O-2 visa holders

P-1. Internationally recognized athletes and entertainers and their essential support staff

P-2. Entertainers coming to perform in the U.S. through a government-recognized exchange program

P-3. Artists and entertainers coming to the U.S. in a group for the purpose of presenting culturally unique performances

P-4. Spouses and children of P-1, P-2, and P-3 visa holders

Q-1. Exchange visitors coming to the U.S. to participate in international cultural exchange programs

Q-2. Participants in the Irish Peace Process Cultural and Training Program (Walsh visas)

Q-3. Spouses and children of Q-1 visa holders

R-1. Ministers and other workers of recognized religions

R-2. Spouses and children of R-1 visa holders

S-1. People coming to the U.S. to supply critical information to federal or state authorities where it has been determined that their presence in the U.S. is essential to the success of a criminal investigation or prosecution

S-5 or S-6. People coming to the U.S. to provide critical information to federal authorities or a court, who will be in danger as a result of providing such information and are eligible to receive a reward for the information

S-7. Spouses and children of S visa holders

T. Women and children who are in the United States because they are victims of trafficking, who are cooperating with law enforcement, and who fear extreme hardship (such as retribution) if returned home

T-2, T-3. Spouses and children of victims of trafficking

TD. Spouses or children of TN visa holders

TN. NAFTA professionals from Canada or Mexico

U. Victims of criminal abuse in the U.S., who are cooperating with law enforcement

U-2, U-3. Spouses and children of U-1 visa holders

V. Spouses and minor unmarried children of lawful permanent residents who have been waiting three or more years to get a green card and whose initial visa petition was submitted to the INS before December 21, 2000.

You can probably see that some of these visas will apply to larger groups of people than others. In this book, we have covered in detail those nonimmigrant visas utilized by the greatest majority of people. If you wish information on some of the lesser-used nonimmigrant visas, contact your USCIS local office or U.S. consulate, or see an attorney.

B. Difference Between a Visa and a Status

A nonimmigrant visa is something you can see and touch. It is a stamp placed on a page in your passport. Your nonimmigrant visa gives you certain privileges, most importantly the right to request entry to the United States. Visas are entry documents. There are, however, other privileges that come with visas, such as permission to work, study, or invest in the United States. Different privileges are attached to different visas.

A visa stamp cannot be issued inside the United States. It can be obtained only at a U.S. embassy or consulate in another country. But some people who are already in the U.S. gain immigration privileges without getting the matching visa first, by applying for a change of status. For example, you could enter on a tourist visa and apply for a change to H-1B status.

Status is the name given to the particular privileges you receive once you're in the United States. For example, if you're in student status, you have the privilege of attending school here. Again, different groups of privileges go with different types of statuses and visas. However, the ability to enter the U.S. is not part of the status. Only an actual, physical visa can be used to enter the U.S., so if you apply for a particular status and then leave the U.S., you'll have to visit a U.S. consulate and apply for a visa before you return.

C. Heightened Security Measures

Owing to the September 11, 2001, terrorist acts on the United States, everyone applying for a visa to the U.S. can expect delays due to background and security checks. Nearly every applicant is now required to appear for a personal visa interview, resulting in long waits at the consulates. Same-day visa processing is virtually a thing of the past. The waits are made even longer by the U.S.

consulates' practice regarding suspicious cases—these are being forwarded to the U.S. Federal Bureau of Investigation (FBI), thus adding weeks or even months to the decision-making process.

D. Getting Your Visa at a Consulate Outside Your Home Country

Some people may wish to obtain a nonimmigrant visa at a U.S. consulate other than one in their home country. This is called third-country national, or TCN, processing. Not all U.S. embassies and consulates allow TCN processing, and even those that do sometimes suspend that service from time to time. If you're applying for an E visa, TCN processing is almost never allowed.

TCN processing is prohibited if you have been unlawfully present in the U.S. under a prior visa status. Even if you overstayed your status by just one day, your visa will be automatically canceled, you will not be eligible for TCN processing, and you will have to return to your home country to apply for a new visa.

If you were admitted to the U.S. on an A, F, G, or J visa for duration of status (indicated as "D/S" on your Form I-94) and you remain in the U.S. beyond the time for which your status was conferred, you may still be eligible for TCN processing. You will be barred only if USCIS (or the former INS) or an immigration judge has determined that you were unlawfully present. Six or more months of unlawful presence acquired after April 1, 1997, is also a ground of inadmissibility if you leave the United States. (See Chapter 3 for details.)

E. At the Border

Even after obtaining a nonimmigrant visa, you aren't guaranteed entry into the United States. When you arrive at a U.S. airport, seaport, or land border post, you must present your visa, along with any supporting paperwork such as your proof of financial support or school acceptance. The person who reviews these materials will be part of a different arm of the U.S. government than you've dealt with before—it's called Customs and Border Protection, or CBP. The CBP inspector will examine your paperwork, possibly search your luggage, and ask questions to make sure you deserved the visa in the first place.

A CBP inspector has the power to deport someone requesting admission to the U.S. if either of the following apply:

- The inspector believes you are making a misrepresentation about practically anything connected to your entering the U.S., such as your purpose in coming, intent to leave, or prior immigration history.
- You do not have the proper documentation to support your entry to the U.S. in the category you are requesting.

If the inspector decides not to let you in (called "expedited removal"), you may not request entry again for five years, unless you were entering under the Visa Waiver Program or the immigration authorities grant a special waiver. For this reason, it is extremely important to understand the terms of your requested status and to not make any misrepresentations.

If you are about to be found inadmissible, you can ask to withdraw your application to enter the U.S. to prevent having the five-year bar on your record. The CBP may allow you to do so in some cases. You can also ask to see a judge if you fear you'd be persecuted after returning to your home country and deserve asylum (see Chapter 13).

Assuming you don't have such problems, your passport will be stamped and an I-94 record will be created, as described in Section F4, below. You may also be fingerprinted and photographed.

F. Time Limits on Nonimmigrant Visas

Just as nonimmigrant visas vary in purpose, they also vary as to how long they last—that is, for how long you can use them to enter the United States. When you arrive, the border official will give you a separate expiration date for your status, that is, how long you can stay.

To fully understand the limits on your rights to enter and then stay in the U.S., you'll need to look at:

- the expiration date of your petition or certificate of eligibility, if one is required
- the expiration date of your visa
- the number of entries permitted on your visa
- the date on your I-94 arrival/departure record
- the expiration date of your passport (rules are different for Canadians—see Chapter 5), and
- the expiration date of your status.

1. Expiration Date of Your Visa Petition or Certificate of Eligibility

Most visas can be obtained by applying directly to your local U.S. consulate. However, to get an H, L, O, P, or Q work visa, or to get a U visa, you must first have a petition approved by USCIS. And F student visas, M student visas, and J exchange visitor visas require that you first obtain certificates of eligibility from a U.S. school or employer. Such petitions and certificates of eligibility will indicate the desired starting and expiration dates of the visa.

When you enter the U.S. with one of these visas, you should also bring the certificate of eligibility or Notice of Approval for the petition. The CBP officer who admits you into the country will then know from the petition or certificate of eligibility, not the visa in your passport, how long you are permitted to stay. The

officer will create an I-94 record in a CBP database, and give you an I-94 card if you are coming through a land border. This will show the date by which you must leave.

2. Expiration Date of Your Visa

A visa serves two purposes: It allows you to request entry to the U.S., and it gives you the right to engage in certain activities once you have arrived. Permissible activities vary with the type of visa. The expiration date on your visa does not show how long you can stay in the U.S. once you arrive (see the I-94 for that date), but it does indicate how long you have the right to enter or reenter the U.S. with visa privileges.

Nonimmigrant visas can be issued for any length of time up to a certain maximum allowed by law, depending on the type of visa. Visitor's visas, for example, can last up to ten years. (Remember, this means only that you have entry privileges for ten years, not that you can stay for that long.) Many other nonimmigrant visas can be issued for up to five years.

Citizens of some countries can't get visas issued for the maximum period usually allowed by law. The shorter time limitation is based on the nationality of the applicant, not the location of the consulate that issues the visa.

Remember that the visa controls only how long you have the right to enter the U.S., not how long you can stay. Even nationals of those countries who receive visas of shorter duration can have petitions or certificates of eligibility approved for the maximum length of stay. Then, when they do make an entry, they may stay for the full length of time indicated on the approved petition or certificate of eligibility—even if it's beyond the expiration date of their visa—and that date will be recorded on the I-94.

If your visa expires before your petition or certificate of eligibility, you can renew your visa at a U.S. consulate the next time you travel outside of the United States. You can also choose to stay in the U.S. without traveling for the full term of your petition or certificate of eligibility. Then the fact that your visa may expire doesn't really matter.

3. Number of U.S. Entries Permitted on the Visa

Most visas are the multiple-entry type. This means that until the visa expires, you may use it to go in and out of the U.S. an unlimited number of times. Some visas are the single-entry type. If you hold such a visa, you may use it to enter the U.S. only once. When you leave, you can't return again with that same visa, even if time still remains before its expiration date.

4. Departure Date on Your I-94 Record

When you enter the U.S. on a nonimmigrant visa through a land border, a Customs and Border Protection (CBP) officer will give you a small white card called an I-94 card (except if you're a Canadian coming as a tourist). This is your arrival/departure record. If you enter by air or sea, you won't get a card, but an I-94 record will be created in a CBP database.

We have already mentioned that the required departure date you get will come from either the immigration laws or the date on your petition or certificate of eligibility, if you have one. It is this date and not the expiration date of the visa that controls how long you can stay.

U.S. government regulations state that when you enter the U.S., you should be admitted for the full amount of time remaining on your petition, if you have one. Normally, this is also the expiration date of your visa. In practice, the departure date on your I-94, the final date on your petition, and the expiration date of your visa will usually all be the same.

Occasionally, however, a CBP inspector will, on the I-94, give you a shorter stay than the dates on your petition indicate. Although this is technically improper, it is best not to argue with the inspector. In such cases, if the date on your I-94 is about to pass and you still wish to remain in the U.S., you can apply for an extension. Directions on how to apply for extensions are in the specific chapters on the various types of visas.

In rare cases, your status might expire on a date that wasn't shown in your I-94. Students are the best example. Their I-94 might say "D/S," which stands for duration of status and means that they can stay for as long as they are actively pursuing the academic program for which they entered the United States. After graduation, however, students are expected to leave within a short time.

5. Expiration Date of Your Passport

You can't get into the U.S. without a valid passport. There are some limited exceptions to this rule for Mexicans with border crossing cards and Canadians (described in Chapter 5). Remember that visas are stamped inside your passport. When you are ready to receive the visa stamp, make sure you have a passport that is not expired or about to expire. You will not normally be admitted to the U.S. with an expired passport, even if the visa inside is still current.

The general rule is that your passport must be valid for at least six months past the date you're allowed to stay. Most countries, however, have an agreement with the U.S. exempting their citizens from this rule. Even if you are from such a country, your passport needs to be valid at least through the date you're allowed to stay.

There is a simple solution to the problem of an expired or expiring passport. If your passport contains a visa that is still in effect but the passport itself is expiring or has already expired, you should apply for a new passport but keep the old one with the current visa stamp. When entering the U.S., show both the new passport and the old one containing the valid visa. Then your visa will be honored for its full term.

Limited Travel When Your Visa Has Expired

If you have an expired visa in your passport but time left on your authorized period of stay, you can still do some traveling on a limited basis. Specifically, you are permitted to go to Canada or Mexico, or, if you're an F student or J exchange visitor, to an island adjacent to the U.S. (most of the Caribbean islands) as well, for up to 30 days, and return to the U.S. without getting a new visa. You must be in possession of a valid admission stamp or paper Form I-94.

However, there are limitations on this privilege. For one thing, you cannot apply for a new visa while you're away, because this will set a new security check into motion and the State Department doesn't want to risk people entering the U.S. while security checks are pending. For another thing, you are not allowed to use this procedure if you're from a country that the U.S. government has identified as supporting terrorism. As of this book's printing, those countries included Syria, Sudan, and Iran.

This limited travel law (known as "automatic revalidation" of your visa) is also very useful to Mexican nationals in the U.S. on work and study visas. This is because they are often hampered in simply visiting their homes by the fact that many types of visas to Mexican nationals are issued for only six months at a time.

6. Changing or Extending Your Status

If you are presently in the U.S. in valid nonimmigrant status, but want to switch to another nonimmigrant category, you may be able to change your status without leaving the United States. You cannot change your status if you entered under the Visa Waiver Program, or if you are in C, D, or K status. No one in the U.S. can change to K-3 or K-4 status from any other status.

You may also be able to extend your current status in the U.S. beyond the time that was originally given to you on your I-94. Extension is not possible if you entered under the Visa Waiver Program or if you are in C, D, K-1, or K-2 status.

USCIS Form I-539 is the one you'd normally use to change or extend status, although in some situations, a petitioner would need to file Form I-129 to qualify you for the new or extended status. You must request a change or extension of status while still in status—if your I-94 has expired, you will likely need to go back home to get a visa. See a lawyer if your I-94 has expired.

You will not receive an updated visa if your status is changed or extended. For example, you could go from F-1 student status to H-1B specialty worker status. Your new status will be written on an I-94 card you receive when your request for change of status is approved. Your period of authorized stay will be extended to the time allowed in the new status category.

G. Effect of Nonimmigrant Visas on Green Cards

Many people ask, "How does getting a nonimmigrant visa affect my ability to get a green card?" The answer is that usually, there is no effect at all. From a strictly legal standpoint, getting a nonimmigrant visa will not help you to get a green card, nor will it hurt you.

If you must have a nonimmigrant visa so you can go to the U.S. right away, but are definitely planning to apply for a green card later, you should probably not begin the process of applying for a green card (for example, by having a relative or an employer file a visa petition on your behalf) until you have less need to travel. When you can wait for the green card to come through without too much inconvenience, only then should you start applying for one. That's because you may be blocked from entering for your temporary stay if you appear to have an "immigrant intent"—that is, you plan to stay in the United States permanently.

There are certain nonimmigrant visa categories that allow you to apply for a green card without worrying about immigrant intent. By law, immigrant intent is not a factor for consideration in H-1A, H-1B, L, O, and P visa applications. And, in fact, getting one of these visas can help you develop ties to a U.S. employer that might then agree to sponsor you for a green card.

H. Nonimmigrant Visas and U.S. Taxes

Though nonimmigrants are, by definition, not permanent residents of the U.S., it is possible to become a tax resident simply by spending a certain amount of time in the U.S. each year. If you become a tax resident, your entire worldwide income must be reported to the U.S. government. It doesn't matter if a portion or all of that income was earned from investments or business activities carried on outside the United States. The income still must be reported.

Becoming a tax resident does not necessarily mean that the U.S. government will actually tax all of your worldwide income. International treaties control whether or not you must pay U.S. taxes on income earned elsewhere. However, if you stay in the U.S. long enough to become a tax resident, you will have to at least report all income you have earned worldwide—a paperwork burden, if nothing else.

At what point do you become a tax resident? If you have been in the U.S. for a weighted total of 183 days during the previous three years, you are a tax resident unless you spent fewer than 30 days in the U.S. in the current tax year.

For determining the weighted total number of days, each day in the current tax year counts as one, each day in the previous year counts as only one-third of a day, and each day in the second previous year counts as only one-sixth of a day. This latter rule does not apply to students, professional athletes, certain foreign government employees, and certain teachers.

You also may avoid being a tax resident if you spent fewer than 183 days of the current tax year in the U.S., you maintain a tax home in another country, and you have a closer connection to that country than to the United States.

There are other exceptions to these rules. A tax treaty between the U.S. and your home country may also alter these rules. If you are unsure of your situation, consult with a tax accountant or lawyer.

If you do become a tax resident, you must file a U.S. federal tax return each year by April 15. The good news is, if you've been working for a U.S. employer that's been withholding taxes from your paycheck, you may be due a refund. But failure to follow U.S. tax laws may be considered a criminal offense and can make it more difficult for you to stay in the U.S. or ultimately obtain permanent residency. To find out exactly how to comply with U.S. tax laws, consult a tax professional or the nearest office of the Internal Revenue Service (IRS) or visit its website at www.irs.gov.

Getting a Business or Tourist (B-1 or B-2) Visa

Millions of people come to the United States as tourist (B-2) or business (B-1) visitors every year. (See I.N.A § 101(a)(15)(B), 8 U.S.C. § 1101(a)(15)(B); 8 C.F.R. § 214.) The U.S. naturally wants to keep its doors open to these visitors who will enjoy the country's scenic and cultural pleasures and engage in business and other exchanges with people in the United States.

As with every visa, however, some tension surrounds its distribution. No one wants to see this visa used by people intending to do harm in the United States or to stay and never leave. As a result, U.S. consulates around the world deny a surprising number of visitor visas—in many cases to people who just weren't prepared for the rigors of the application process. B visa refusal rates vary by country. For example, in fiscal year 2015, the State Department reported that the approximate B visa refusal rate for China was 10%; for India, 24%; for Indonesia, 9%; for Bangladesh, 60%; for Pakistan, 40%; for Nigeria, 33%; for Russia, 10%, for the Philippines, 28%; for Turkey, 14%; and for the Ukraine, 34%.

This chapter explains who is eligible for a temporary visa for business or pleasure, and how to maximize the odds of success when you apply. Most consulates can approve and issue visitors' visas within days, although security measures can delay their final decision by weeks or months.

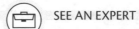 **SEE AN EXPERT**

Do you need a lawyer? Applying for a visitor visa is fairly simple and doesn't usually require a lawyer's help. If, however, you've had trouble getting visas in the past, have ever overstayed a visa, or are from a country thought to sponsor terrorism, a lawyer's help can be well worth the investment.

Key Features of the Visitor Visa

Here are some of the advantages and disadvantages of the visitor visa:

- The application process is reasonably quick and straightforward.
- Visitor visas are most often issued as "B-1/B-2," allowing you to engage in certain business activities and tourist activities under the terms of a single visa.
- B-1/B-2 visitor visas are often multiple entry, meaning you can use them for many trips to the United States.
- Although you may make many trips to the U.S. on your visitor visa, the length of each visit is normally limited to between 30 days and six months. After that, you must leave the U.S. or apply for an extension of your stay.
- Although if you're from certain countries you might not need a visa at all, getting one allows you to stay longer and gain rights to extend or change your status once in the United States.
- You may not accept a job in the U.S. or operate a business on a B-1 or B-2 visitor visa.

A. Do You Qualify for a Visitor Visa?

You qualify for a B-1 visa if you are coming to the U.S. as a visitor for a temporary business trip. You qualify for a B-2 visa if you are visiting the U.S. temporarily, either as a tourist or for medical treatment. Often, these two visas are issued together in combination so you have all the options under both. However, you must demonstrate to both the U.S. consulate that issues the visa and the U.S. Customs and Border Protection (CBP) officer at the airport or border your intent to return to your home country after your visit is over. Usually, you must demonstrate that you have a job and permanent address overseas to which you will return.

A B-1 visa allows you to be in the U.S. for business purposes, such as making investments, buying goods, attending seminars, or performing other temporary work-related activities for an employer located outside the United States. You may not, however, be employed or operate your own company. You may not be paid by a source inside the United States. It is sometimes difficult to draw the line between permissible business activities and illegal employment on a B-1 visa.

Unlike the B-1 visitor, the B-2 tourist may not engage in business-related activities at all. A condition of being admitted on a B-2 visa is that you are visiting solely for purposes of pleasure or medical treatment.

If you enter the U.S. with a B visa, your intention must be to come only as a temporary visitor. Tourists are usually given stays of up to six months and business visitors may stay as necessary up to a maximum of one year. The date your permitted stay will expire will be shown on your Form I-94 Arrival/Departure Record. If you arrive by air or sea, CBP will enter your I-94 record into a database, which you can access at https://i94.cbp.dhs.gov. If you arrive at a land border a CBP officer will put a little white I-94 card into your passport. Theoretically, you may leave the U.S. at the end of your stay, return the next day, and be readmitted for another stay. Alternatively, before your permitted stay has expired, you can apply for an extension of stay without leaving. (See Section C, below.)

If your travel history shows that you are spending most of your time in the U.S., CBP will assume you have the intent to be more than just a temporary visitor. On this basis, you can be denied entry altogether, even though you do have a valid visa. Some people, thinking that they have found a loophole in the system, try to live in the U.S. permanently on a visitor's visa by merely taking brief trips outside the country every time their permitted stay expires. Do not expect this tactic to work for very long. However, those who want to have vacation homes in the U.S. and live in them for about six months each year may do so legally.

1. Exception to the Visitor's Visa Requirement: The Visa Waiver Program

If you're planning to come to the U.S. for tourism or business, are willing to leave within 90 days, haven't been denied past visas or violated their terms, and come from a country that does not have a history of illegal immigration to the U.S., you may be able to avoid formally applying for a visa before your trip. A so-called visa waiver is available to people from the countries currently participating in the Visa Waiver Program (VWP), including: Andorra, Austria, Australia, Belgium, Brunei, Chile, Czech Republic, Denmark, Estonia, Finland, France, Germany, Greece, Hungary, Iceland, Ireland, Italy, Japan, Latvia, Liechtenstein, Lithuania, Luxembourg, Malta, Monaco, the Netherlands, New Zealand, Norway, Portugal, San Marino, Singapore, Slovakia, Slovenia, South Korea, Spain, Sweden, Switzerland, Taiwan, and the United Kingdom. (Foreign media representatives, however, cannot use a visa waiver, as the purpose of their stay is not considered business. They must obtain a nonimmigrant media visa.)

Each visitor who enters under the VWP must arrive with a transportation ticket to leave the United States. They must also present what's called a machine readable passport (MRP), that is, one with two lines of scannable characters at the bottom of the biographical information page. The passport must be good for at least six months past the date of entry. Entry under the VWP is permitted on land through Canada or Mexico, but qualifying visitors must show evidence at the border of sufficient funds to live in the U.S. without working.

Visa Exemption for Canadians and Bermudians

If you're a citizen of Canada or Bermuda, you don't need a B-1 or B-2 visa to enter the United States. You can just show your passport at the border and explain that you're coming as a visitor for business or pleasure. You're not entering under the Visa Waiver Program—rather, you're what's called "visa exempt."

VWP travelers must obtain authorization through the Electronic System for Travel Authorization (ESTA) prior to traveling to the United States. Do so at https://esta.cbp.dhs.gov/esta. You'll need to pay a $14 fee.

The application asks for biographic information, information about your passport and travel arrangements, and questions relevant to security. The system is supposed to give an immediate automated response for most people, but in some cases it may take up to 72 hours. For that reason, DHS recommends that travelers submit the information at least 72 hours before travel. Before boarding an airline, the carrier will electronically verify that you have an approved travel authorization on file. Every passenger using the Visa Waiver Program must have ESTA authorization, even infants traveling without their own tickets.

If you are not approved for travel by ESTA, you will not be able to use the Visa Waiver Program, but might still be able to obtain a standard tourist visa.

When you enter the U.S. under the Visa Waiver Program, you will not be allowed to extend your stay, to change your status to another nonimmigrant classification, or to apply for a green card without first leaving the country. (The only exception is for persons who marry a U.S. citizen or are the unmarried children or parents of a U.S. citizen.)

Participation in the VWP is optional, not a requirement. People from visa waiver countries can still get standard visitor's visas, but should be prepared to explain to the U.S. consulate why using the Visa Waiver Program would not be sufficient. You will have more flexibility and rights once you enter the U.S. if you come with a visa.

For more information, see the State Department website at www.travel.state. gov (click "Tourism & Visit," then "Visa Waiver Program").

B. How to Apply for a Visitor Visa

The exact steps to applying for a B visa depend on the U.S. embassy or consulate where you're applying. You'll most likely need to:

- prepare and submit an application
- gather some personal documents
- pay the required fee, and
- meet with an official at a U.S. embassy or consulate.

For additional information on these application procedures, consult the website of the U.S. embassy or consulate where you're applying, and see the State Department website at www.travel.state.gov (click "Tourism & Visit" and then "Visitor Visa").

1. Step One: Preparing and Submitting Your Application

Your visa application will consist of a government form and, if the consulate requires them, some documents that you collect yourself. The form, called a DS-160, can be completed only online. You will bring the supporting documents with you to your visa interview.

To access the DS-160, go to the State Department's Consular Electronic Application Center (CEAC) website, at https://ceac.state.gov. You must fill out the form in English. If a question is marked "optional," you can leave the answer space blank. Answer with "Does Not Apply" if the question does not fit your situation. You'll find that most questions require some answer—the system will not allow you to submit an application if you don't answer a mandatory question. You electronically sign your DS-160 by clicking the "Sign Application" button at the end of the form.

Can't Fill Out Form DS-160 Yourself?

An applicant who is illiterate or unable to complete the application can have someone else fill the form out for him or her, as long as that helper is identified on the "Sign and Submit" page of the application.

However, the person who's getting the visa should click the "Sign Application" button him- or herself. Attorneys (or anyone else) should not click that button for an applicant, except if the applicant is under the age of 16 or physically incapable of completing the application. In that case a parent or guardian may fill out the application and click the "Sign Application" button. If the applicant has no parent or legal guardian, any person having legal custody of, or a legitimate interest in, the applicant may do it.

The DS-160 asks for a lot of information. It will help if you have the following documents nearby:

- Your passport.
- Your travel itinerary, if you have already made travel arrangements.
- Your résumé or curriculum vitae. You may be required to provide information about your current and previous education and work history.

Consult your travel records (or your memory!) before starting the application. You'll need to provide the dates of your last five visits or trips to the United States, if you have previously been there. You may also be asked for your international travel history for the past five years.

 TIP
No need to complete the DS-160 in one sitting. It's a lengthy form. Fortunately, you can save your work and return to it later. When you begin a new DS-160, you will be issued a unique application identification (ID) number after selecting and answering a security question. You must have your application ID to return to your application. The information you enter in your DS-160 is saved every time you click the "Next" button at the bottom of a page. However, an application is saved on CEAC for only 30 days. If you want to access your application after 30 days, you must save it by selecting the "Save Application to File" button. Then, click the "Save" button on the File Download window.

You must also upload a U.S. passport-style photo to CEAC as part of your application. Information on how to provide a suitable photo is provided on the State Department's website at www.travel.state.gov. (Follow the links to "Tourism & Visit or Business," "Visitor Visa," and then "Photograph Requirements.") If you have trouble getting the system to accept your photo, ask someone who's good with computers for help. As a last resort, you can bring a photo to your interview at the U.S. consulate.

After you've submitted the DS-160 online, print and keep the barcode confirmation page. You'll need to bring it to your consular interview.

2. Step Two: Scheduling Interview at U.S. Embassy or Consulate

After your DS-160 has been accepted, it's up to you to schedule an interview at a U.S. embassy or consulate. While interviews are generally not required for applicants under 14 years old or over 80 years old, consular officers have the discretion to require an interview of any applicant, regardless of age.

Although, technically, the law allows you to apply for a B visa at any U.S. consulate you choose, from a practical standpoint, your case will be given greatest consideration at the consulate in your home country. Applying in some other country creates suspicion about your motives for choosing their consulate. (Often, when an applicant is having trouble at a home consulate, he or she will seek a more lenient office in some other country.) Nevertheless, if you can demonstrate that you otherwise had business outside your home country, and it was more convenient therefore to apply in a so-called "third country," then applying outside your home country will not necessarily be held against you.

If you have ever been present in the U.S. unlawfully, you must apply in your home country. Even if you overstayed your status in the U.S. by just one day, you must return to your home country and apply for the visa from that consulate. There is an exception: If you were admitted to the U.S. for the duration of your status (indicated by a "D/S" on your I-94 form) and you remained in the U.S. beyond that time or purpose for which your status was conferred, you may still be able to apply in a third country. In that situation, you will be barred from third-country national processing only if an immigration judge or USCIS official officially determines that you were unlawfully present. You may find that your success in applying as a third-country national depends on your country, the consulate, and the relative seriousness of your offense.

All consulates insist on advance appointments. No walk-in applications are allowed. Since procedures for scheduling interviews at the consulates vary, telephone or check the consulate's website in advance to find out about local policies. For information on consulates, go to www.usembassy.gov.

3. Step Three: Pay the Application Fee

Most consulates require you to pay the visa application fee, currently $160 for B visas, before your interview. The consulate will give you instructions on how and when to make payment.

4. Step Four: Gather Supporting Documents

The consulate will likely tell you to come to the interview with documents that support your eligibility for a B visa. You'll definitely need to bring your passport, the DS-160 confirmation page, your fee payment receipt (if advance payment was required), and a photo if you weren't able to upload one successfully to CEAC, or perhaps even if you were. In addition, consulates like to see:

- Documents showing the purpose of your trip, such as an itinerary and hotel arrangements
- Documents assuring that you'll leave the U.S. on time and return to your home country, such as ownership of real estate, relationships with close family members staying behind, and proof that a job will be waiting for you upon your return.
- Proof of ability to cover your expenses, such as:
  - Letter from a friend or relative inviting you to visit, stating you are welcome to stay with him or her.
  - Bank statements.
  - Personal financial statements.
  - Evidence of your current sources of income.
- If you are coming to the U.S. on business, a letter from your foreign employer describing your job and telling what you will be doing for the employer during your U.S. trip. The letter should explain that you will be paid only from sources outside the U.S. and state when you will be expected to return from your trip. If you'll be attending a trade show or similar business event, bring promotional materials, flyers, and proof that you are registered for it.
- If coming to the U.S. for medical treatment, a statement by your doctor containing your diagnosis and the reason why you must visit the U.S. for treatment, as well as a letter from the doctor or facility from which you'll receive treatment in the U.S., saying how long your treatment will last and listing the expected costs, as well as your own proof of financial resources to cover the trip and your medical expenses.

A letter of invitation or Affidavit of Support from U.S. family or friends is not needed to apply for a B visa. You can bring those things to your interview, but the consulate won't really care. The consular officer will be more concerned about your residence and ties to your home country.

5. Step Five: Attend Interview at the Embassy or Consulate

The last step in your process will be attending an interview with a consular officer. During the interview, the officer will examine your Form DS-160 application for accuracy. He or she will ask you questions about your ties to your home country and the state of your financial resources. The officer will surely ask you how long you intend to remain in the United States. Any answer suggesting uncertainty about plans to return or an interest in applying for a green card is likely to result in a denial of your B visa. The typical interview lasts only a few minutes, and the officer is under intense pressure to make a quick decision on your case.

At some point in the application process, usually at the interview, you will need to have ink-free, digital fingerprint scans taken. Based on these fingerprints, the consular officer will initiate various security checks to make sure you haven't been involved in criminal or terrorist activity. Because the U.S. is doing more comprehensive security checks than in the past, you are unlikely to receive a decision on your visa the same day as the interview. Security checks can add days, weeks, or (more rarely) months to the processing time.

C. Visa Issuance and Entry Into the U.S.

Some people, after their visa is approved, must pay an additional visa issuance fee—it depends on whether your country charges U.S. citizens a similar fee. (Most countries don't.)

The consulate will tell you how it's going to return your passport to you. Usually one must pick it up in person, but some consulates mail it. The visa will be affixed to a page in your passport.

Border Crossing Cards for Mexicans

Citizens of Mexico can receive Border Crossing Cards (BCC) that are combined with their B-1/B-2 visa. The B1/B2-BCC may be in the form of a card (most frequently) or a "Lincoln Foil" stamped into the passport (if you apply at certain U.S. consulates in Mexico). The BCC was once called a "Laser Visa"—if you have an unexpired one, it's still good for U.S. entry. Although you need an unexpired Mexican passport in order to get a BCC, you can use the BCC to enter the U.S. by land with an expired passport as long as you stay within the border zone (25 miles in Texas and California, 55 miles in New Mexico, and 75 miles in Arizona).

While there is a definite difference between B-1 and B-2 visas, the two are frequently issued together as a "B-1/B-2" visa. This visa typically allows its holders to make visitor trips to the U.S. for the next ten years.

On entering the U.S. with your new B visa, an I-94 Arrival/Departure record will be created (if you enter by air or sea), and if you enter at a land border, you will be given an I-94 card. It will contain the dates of your authorized stay. You are normally permitted to remain in the U.S. for six months. Each time you exit and reenter the U.S., you will get a new I-94 with a new period of authorized stay. If you weren't given an I-94 card, check your I-94 record at https://i94.cbp.dhs.gov.

! CAUTION

Even with a valid visitor visa, entry at the U.S. border can be unpleasant for some. Expect the immigration officials who greet you to question you closely about the purpose of your stay, your means of support, and your plans to depart on time. For security reasons, you may be searched. See Chapter 3 for more on these officials' ability to prevent you from entering.

D. Extensions of Stay

Assuming you can show that you're not just trying to stay in the U.S. indefinitely and your total stay will not exceed one year, USCIS may, in rare instances, grant you an extension of your B-1 or B-2 visitor stay. (Extensions are not available to people who entered on the Visa Waiver Program, except for outright emergencies—visit your local USCIS office in such a case.) Six additional months is the longest extension possible under the law, but asking for the full amount will create suspicion as to your intentions.

Checklist for Extension Application

Forms

☐ USCIS Form I-539, with application fee, currently $290. If you have a spouse or children coming with you, also complete the I-539 supplement (they don't need separate Forms I-539).

Documents

☐ Copy of your I-94, if you have one.

☐ A copy of your valid, unexpired passport.

☐ A description of your means of financial support while in the U.S., with bank or financial records if you have them.

☐ A written statement by you, explaining the reason you need to stay longer, why that extended stay will be temporary, what arrangements you've made to leave the U.S., and how you're dealing with your house and your job back in your home country.

☐ Proof of the relationship between you and accompanying family members, such as a child's long-form birth certificate or your marriage certificate.

☐ If you are a business visitor, a letter from your foreign employer explaining why you need the extension of stay.

You must submit your request for an extension before the date on your I-94 has passed, but USCIS recommends submitting it 45 days before that. (Rules are different for Canadians. See Chapter 5.)

To apply for an extension of stay, mail the items on the checklist above according to the instructions at www.uscis.gov/i-539-addresses. (To access the form and its instructions, and get the exact USCIS address, go to the USCIS website at www.uscis.gov/i-539 or call 800-870-3676.)

If USCIS wants further information before acting on your request, it will issue a Request for Evidence (RFE). The RFE will tell you what additional pieces of information or documents are expected before a decision can be reached, and by what deadline (usually 30 days) such materials must be provided. Supply the extra data and mail the whole package back to the USCIS regional service center. RFEs for ELIS users are handled online.

Assuming you filed your application on time, you will be permitted to remain in the U.S. past the date of your authorized stay (as shown on your I-94) while you are waiting for USCIS's decision. Unfortunately, the USCIS Service Centers can take longer than six months to make a decision on requests for an extension of stay. Even if it takes 12 months for USCIS to issue a decision, the extension will be for only as long as you requested—and as mentioned earlier, any request for an extension longer than six months is likely to be denied. Therefore, you should plan to leave the U.S. by the extended date

that you requested, even if you have not received the decision on your request by that date. On the other hand, because you are lawfully present in the United States for as long as the application remains pending, you will have effectively been "granted" the extension by the time you return back home, even if the application is subsequently denied after your departure.

If your application is filed at a USCIS Service Center that is processing requests in less than six months, you will receive a Notice of Action on Form I-797, indicating the approval with the new date on a tear-off card that's meant to serve as a new I-94 card.

If your application for an extension of stay is denied, you will be sent a written notice explaining the reasons for the negative decision. This written decision will be sent to the U.S. address listed on your Form I-539, meaning that you may not receive the decision if it arrives after you have left. The most common reason for denial is that USCIS feels you are merely trying to prolong your U.S. stay indefinitely. When your application is denied, you will normally be given a period of 30 days to leave the U.S. voluntarily. Failure to leave within that time may result in removal proceedings and deportation. Of course, if you have already left the United States by the time the denial is issued, then it no longer matters.

Getting a Temporary Specialty Worker (H-1B) Visa

H-1B temporary visas are made available to workers in occupations requiring highly specialized knowledge and to distinguished fashion models. (See I.N.A. § 101(a)(15)(H), 8 U.S.C. § 1101(a) (15)(H).) This visa is commonly used by workers in computer and other high-tech industries, but it's also available to people in other specialized fields, from accountants to attorneys to librarians to dietitians and other scientific or medical workers.

There's no limit, or "cap," on the number of H-1B visa petitions that can be approved for persons who will work for an institution of higher education (or a nonprofit affiliated with one), a nonprofit research organization, or a government research organization. Nor is there any limit on the number of H-1B petitions that can be approved for people who have already been counted against any year's cap on the number of visas, such as those extending previous H-1B visas.

Other applicants compete for one of only 85,000 H-1B visas that become newly available each fiscal year. (Fiscal years start October 1.)

Once that limit is reached in a given year—and it almost always is—no more H-1B visas can be approved until the start of the next fiscal year. Also, not all of the 85,000 total are freely available.

Within that number, 20,000 are reserved for people with a minimum Master's-level degree from a U.S. academic institution. And not all of the remaining 65,000 visas are available to everyone—a certain number are earmarked for Chile and Singapore, which have both signed trade agreements with the U.S. allocating H-1Bs to citizens of those countries.

Key Features of the H-1B Visa

Here are some of the advantages and disadvantages of the H-1B visa:

- You can work legally in the U.S. for your H-1B sponsor, up to a maximum of six years (plus any extensions, as described in this chapter).
- Visas are available for your accompanying spouse and minor children. Your spouse can apply for work authorization, but your minor children's H-4 status does not allow them to work.
- You may travel in and out of the U.S. or remain here continuously until your H-1B status expires.
- If your employer dismisses you before your authorized stay expires, the employer must pay for the trip back to your home country. This is true even if the cause of the firing was your own fault. This liability does not apply if you quit the job—only if you are fired.

SEE AN EXPERT
Do you need a lawyer? You can't apply for an H-1B without having an employer first—and it's in your employer's interest to hire a lawyer to help. Because more people try to get H-1B visas every year than there are visas available, a lawyer can help make sure that your application gets done right the first time, and gets filed before the visas run out.

A. Do You Qualify for an H-1B Visa or Status?

To qualify for an H-1B visa, you must first have a job offer from a U.S. employer for duties to be performed in the United States. In addition, the requirements for getting an H-1B visa include that:

- You are coming to (or remaining in) the U.S. to perform services in a specialty occupation with a college degree or its equivalent in work experience, or to be a distinguished fashion model.
- You have a job offer from a U.S. employer for work to be performed in the U.S., and you have been offered at least the prevailing wage that is paid in the same geographic area for that type of job (or the actual wage paid to similar workers at that employer—whichever is the higher of the two wages).

- You have the correct background to qualify for the job you have been offered.
- Your employer has filed a Labor Condition Application (LCA) with the Department of Labor (DOL).

Your job itself must also meet certain criteria, including at least one of the following:

- A bachelor's degree or higher degree (or the equivalent) is the minimum requirement for entry into the position.
- The degree requirement is common to the industry in parallel positions among similar organizations, or the duties of the position are so complex that it can be performed only by a person with a degree.
- The employer normally requires a degree or its equivalent for the position.
- The nature of the specific duties is so specialized and complex that knowledge required to perform the duties is usually associated with a bachelor's or higher degree.

To qualify for H-1B, unless you are a fashion model, you need at least a bachelor's degree or substantial on-the-job experience that is the equivalent of a bachelor's degree. If you're qualifying through a bachelor's degree, it's preferable if it's not in a liberal arts or general business subject area, which USCIS tends to view as insufficiently specialized.

If you don't have a bachelor's degree but will be attempting to qualify through work experience, USCIS usually wants to see three years of specialized training and/or work experience for every year of college that you would have attended. Therefore, if you have not attended any universities, you must typically show 12 years of professional experience.

You must be intending to perform services in a so-called specialty occupation. If a license to practice your particular occupation is required by the U.S. state in which you will be working, then, in addition to your educational credentials, you must also have the appropriate license.

Fashion models need not meet the specialty occupation requirements. Instead, they must show that they are nationally or internationally recognized for their achievements, and will be employed in a position requiring someone of distinguished merit and ability. They must be renowned, leading, or well known.

 RESOURCE

For more information on H-1B visas for fashion models, see the USCIS regulations at 8 C.F.R. § 214.2(h)(4)(vii). Because this is such a specialized area, this chapter does not provide details on applying as a fashion model, but the regulations do a good job of spelling out the documentary and other requirements.

B-1 in Lieu of H-1B

The State Department recognizes that some people who qualify for H-1B visas could also be classified as B-1 business visitors, based on their intended activities in the United States. If you're eligible for an H-1B but are having trouble getting H-1B petition approval, or simply don't want to go through the time and expense, the "B-1 in lieu of H-1B" visa is worth considering. (Not all consulates are receptive to this concept, however.) The main consideration is that you will not receive any salary or other payment from a U.S. source other than an expense allowance or other reimbursement for incidental expenses. If you are granted a B-1 in lieu of H-1B, the consulate is approving business activities that push the boundaries of what would otherwise be permissible on a B visa. Your visa will be a B-1 (or B-1/B-2) with its short period of authorized stay (six months to a year). It's possible that no notation will be made on the visa saying that it is in lieu of an H-1B.

To get an H-1B visa, not only do your job qualifications have to meet the standards mentioned above, but you need to have the correct type of background for the job you are offered. If your academic and professional credentials are strong, but they do not match the job, then you are not eligible for an H-1B visa.

H-1B visas are only rarely given to prominent businesspeople without college degrees, even though these people may have substantial on-the-job experience. (O-1 visas may be available to this group. See Chapter 24.) H-1B visas are likewise not given to athletes and entertainers, who should consider instead O or P visas (discussed in Chapter 24). Professional nurses are rarely eligible for H-1B visas, because most nursing jobs require a two-year degree rather than a four-year bachelor's degree.

> **TIP**
> **Unlike many other nonimmigrant visas, you don't have to prove that you plan to return home at the end of your U.S. stay.** In fact, you can (if you are separately eligible) have family members or employers submit applications for you to get a permanent green card at the same time that you're pursuing your H-1B visa—which would be the kiss of death for most other temporary visa applications. It's a different story, however, if you aren't eligible for a green card now but openly admit that you have no intention of leaving the U.S. after your visa expires—then your visa will be denied.

1. Job Criteria

Specialty occupations include, but are not limited to, accountants, architects, engineers, artists, dietitians, chiropractors, librarians, computer systems analysts, physical therapists, chemists, pharmacists,

medical technologists, hotel managers (large hotels), and upper-level business managers.

Some occupations requiring licenses do not usually fall into the H-1B category because college degrees are not normally needed. Such occupations include many types of medical technicians, real estate agents, plumbers, and electricians. Unless at least a four-year bachelor's degree is required, people in such occupations are limited to the more restrictive H-2B visa described in Chapter 17 or must try to qualify directly for a green card.

Limitations on Qualifying Physicians

Although physicians can qualify for H-1B visas, they must have a medical license issued by the state where they will practice medicine. To get licensed, a foreign medical graduate must pass all steps of the USMLE (the U.S. Medical Licensure Exam), obtain certification by the Educational Commission on Foreign Medical Graduates (ECFMG), and complete a U.S. residency program. Specifically, physicians who are not licensed can only work at a teaching or research job in a public or nonprofit private educational or research institution or agency. Jobs that primarily involve patient care will not qualify this group for H-1B visas (although some patient care is allowed if necessary within the teaching or research context). See 8 C.F.R. § 214.2(h)(4)(viii).

2. Job Offer From a U.S. Employer for Work Performed Inside the U.S.

To get an H-1B visa or status, you need a specific job offer from a qualified employer for work to be performed inside the United States. The employer will act as your petitioner in getting your H-1B (and you become the beneficiary).

Many people are surprised to learn that they require an employment offer before applying for a work visa. The idea behind it is that you are being granted an H-1B visa only because your services have been recognized as essential to a U.S. enterprise. Put another way, the U.S. government is issuing the visa not for your benefit, but to help the U.S. economy.

In theory, the petitioner may be a company or an individual. In practice, getting sponsored by an individual is very difficult. Increasingly, USCIS is applying increased scrutiny to very small companies (those with fewer than 25 employees). Whether or not you can form your own corporation and have that corporation act as your sponsoring employer is not completely clear under the law, but published policy memoranda make this strategy virtually impossible.

The employer must also be offering you at least the prevailing wage that is paid for your type of job in that geographic area. The U.S. Department of Labor's National Prevailing Wage Center publishes periodic surveys of salaries and can provide you with prevailing wage information. If your employer elects to rely on its own or a different survey, however, it will be required to identify the source of the information.

3. Specialty Occupation

The job offered can't be for just any type of work. The position must really require the skills of a highly educated person. For example, you may be a certified public accountant holding an advanced college degree. Public accounting clearly qualifies as a professional occupation. However, if you are offered a job as a bookkeeper, you will not get an H-1B visa, because it doesn't take a highly educated accountant to carry out standard bookkeeping tasks.

4. Correct Background

You must have the correct background for the job you have been offered. For example, if you are a qualified nuclear scientist, but are offered a position managing a U.S. automobile factory, you will not be granted an H-1B visa, because you have no background in automobile factory management. If, however, the job you are offered requires a background in nuclear science, then you would be eligible for the H-1B visa.

It is irrelevant that your native intelligence and general knowledge of business may make you quite capable of handling the automobile factory job. Likewise, reliability or willingness to work hard, characteristics difficult to find and much in demand by real-world employers, are not a USCIS consideration.

5. Approved Attestation

A business cannot sponsor you for an H-1B petition unless it first files an attestation, or promise, also known as a Labor Condition Application (LCA), with the U.S. Department of Labor (DOL). The attestation is a document similar to a sworn declaration or written oath. It must include a number of statements ensuring that both U.S. and foreign workers are being treated fairly. These are discussed below in Section C.

The Road to a Green Card

Having an H-1B visa gives you no legal advantage in applying for a green card. Realistically, however, it is probably easier to get an employer to sponsor you for an H-1B visa than a green card, and coming to the U.S. first with an H-1B gives you the opportunity to decide whether you really want to live in the U.S. permanently. Once you are in the U.S. with a work permit, it is also usually easier to find an employer willing to sponsor you for a green card—or to convince your current employer to do so.

6. Bringing Your Spouse and Children

When you qualify for an H-1B visa, your spouse and your unmarried children under age 21 can apply for H-4 visas by providing proof of their family relationship to you. H-4 visas authorize your family members to stay with you in the U.S. and to study in the U.S., and allow your spouse (but not your children) to work in the United States. Like you, however, your family members will have to prove that they are not inadmissible to the United States. (See Chapter 3.)

B. Quick View of the H-1B Visa Application Process

The process of getting an H-1B visa has two or three stages:

- Your U.S. employer files a Labor Condition Application (LCA) with the U.S. Department of Labor through the iCert Web portal (http://icert.doleta.gov), and posts notice of the filing at the workplace.
- After approval of the LCA, your U.S. employer files a petition on USCIS Form I-129. If you're already in the U.S. in a lawful status—and one that allows you to change status—this petition can simultaneously ask that your status be changed to H-1B worker, in which case, if the

petition is approved, the process will successfully end here.

- If you're outside the U.S., then after the petition is approved, you submit your own application for an H-1B visa to a U.S. consulate (unless you're from Canada or Bermuda, in which case you can skip this step).

- You use either your visa or (if you're from Canada or Bermuda) the notice of your approved visa petition to enter the U.S. and claim your H-1B status.

TIP

Nothing stops you from helping with the employer's tasks during this application process. For example, you can fill out forms intended to be completed by your employer and simply ask the employer to check them over and sign them. The less your U.S. employer is inconvenienced, the more likely it will be willing to act as sponsor for your visa. You'll likely find, however, that your employer has hired a lawyer to help it through the H-1B application process.

C. Step One: Your Employer Files an LCA

No employer can sponsor you for an H-1B unless it first files a Labor Condition Application with the DOL. The LCA can be submitted up to six months before you plan to start work. An LCA is similar to a sworn declaration or a written oath. It must include the following information and statements:

- the job title for which H-1B workers are needed

- a statement of the number of foreign workers to be hired in that job

- a statement of the wages to be paid the foreign worker, what the prevailing wage is for that job, and where the employer obtained the prevailing wage information

- a written promise that foreign nationals will be paid 100% of the prevailing market wage for the position (or the employer's actual wage, whichever is higher) and will receive the same benefits as the U.S. coworkers

- a statement that there are no strikes, lockouts, or work stoppages in progress involving the jobs to be filled by H-1B workers, and

- a statement that the employer has given notice of the filing of H-1B attestations to either the labor union representing the type of employee involved, or, if no union exists, that the employer has posted notice of filing in at least two conspicuous locations at the place of employment for a period of ten days.

Fortunately, the prevailing wage rules recognize that academic institutions can't always match salaries in private industry. Therefore, if you're applying for a job at an institution of higher education or an affiliated or related nonprofit, at a nonprofit research organization, or at a governmental research organization, your employer will need only show that it will pay the prevailing wage as compared to similar institutions.

The law frowns on employers who rely too heavily on H-1B workers, however. Employers who are "H-1B dependent," or who have committed certain labor-related violations in the last five years, will have to make additional statements on the attestation form (except in cases where they're paying the worker more than $60,000 or the worker has a Master's degree or higher). H-1B dependent means that their workforce includes either:

- 25 or fewer full-time employees and eight or more H-1B employees
- 26 to 50 full-time employees and 13 or more H-1B employees, or
- 51 or more full-time employees and at least 15% H-1B employees.

The additional attestations that such H-1B-dependent employers must make include that:

- The H-1B worker will not displace U.S. workers.
- If the employer places the employee with another employer or worksite, the original employer will first make

certain that no U.S. workers will be displaced there.

- The employer has made good-faith efforts to recruit U.S. workers for the job, at the prevailing wage.

A separate LCA must be filed for each type of job the company wishes to fill with H-1B workers.

Filing the LCA is a very simple matter. Form ETA-9035E is submitted through the iCert portal at https://icert.doleta.gov. The iCert system requires you to create your own account.

The form has all necessary statements already written out, with blanks to be filled in with the appropriate occupations, numbers of workers, and salaries. The DOL will accept for filing all complete attestations; however, anyone, including other employees at the petitioning company, can file a complaint against it. The primary objective here is to require employers to pay H-1B workers at least the prevailing wage or average (weighted average) salary for that type of job in the particular geographic area.

When the attestation is accepted, your employer will print the LCA and sign it. The LCA must be posted at the workplace and kept in a file for public inspection, along with supporting documentation. A copy of the certified LCA must also be submitted to USCIS as a supporting document to the H-1B petition.

D. Step Two: Your Employer Files a Petition

Your employer needs to submit a petition to USCIS, on Form I-129. The object of the petition is to prove three things:

- that you personally qualify for H-1B status
- that your future job is of a high enough level to warrant someone with your advanced skills, and
- that you have the correct background and skills to match the job requirements.

> ⚲ **TIP**
>
> **U.S. immigration law prevents employers from passing business expenses off onto H-1B employees.** USCIS interprets this to mean that employers are required to pay all filing fees for H-1Bs, including any surcharge fee to pay for premium processing. In addition, employers must pay attorney's fees associated with filing the LCA and I-129. If your employer makes you pay these fees (directly or through a reduction of your salary), then the employer could be subject to back pay awards and fines if audited by the Department of Labor.

Because the new batch of "cap-subject" H-1B visas does not become available until October 1 every year, you can't start work until October 1 if you're subject to the cap. USCIS allows the H-1B petition to be filed six months in advance of that date—on April 1. All employers must be prepared to file their cap-subject H-1B petitions by April 1 every year, because there is usually fierce competition for H-1B visas, which are processed on a first-come, first-served basis. In years that USCIS anticipates a flood of applications on April 1 (which is most years), it conducts a "lottery" to select which applications received in early April it will process. (See "The Petition Selection Lottery," below.)

1. Simultaneous Change of Status If You're Already in the U.S.

If you're already in the U.S. in lawful status, such as on a student or other temporary visa, the petition can be used to ask your status be immediately changed to H-1B worker. (Part 2, Question 4, of Form I-129 offers choices addressing this issue.) You can't, however, take advantage of this option if you entered the U.S. on a visa waiver, or using a C (alien in transit), TWOV (alien in transit without a visa), D (crewman), or any K (fiancé) visa. Certain J-1 (exchange visitor) visa holders are prohibited from changing status, as well. M-1 (vocational student) visa holders can change to H-1B only if the training received as a vocational student in the U.S. did not provide the qualifications for the H-1B job. To change status to H-1B, you must have:

- entered the U.S. legally
- never worked in the U.S. illegally, and
- not passed the expiration date on your I-94.

There is another problem that comes up only in U.S. filings. It is the issue of what is called "preconceived intent." To approve a change of status, USCIS must believe that at the time you originally entered the U.S. as a visitor or with some other nonimmigrant visa, you did not intend to apply for a different status. If USCIS thinks you had a preconceived plan to use one visa to enter the U.S. with an eye to applying for a different status after getting there, it may deny your application. (You can get around the preconceived intent issue by leaving the U.S. and applying for your H-1B visa at a U.S. consulate in another country.)

Your spouse and children, if they are also in the U.S. with you, can't change their status by being mentioned on your Form I-129, but must submit separate Forms I-539. They can submit these either at the same time your employer submits Form I-129, or afterward. (If they submit them afterward, however, they will need to include either a copy of the USCIS receipt notice indicating that your petition is pending, or a copy of the petition approval notice.)

TIP
Your eligibility to apply in the U.S. has nothing to do with your overall eligibility for an H-1B visa. Many applicants who are barred from filing in the U.S., but otherwise qualify for H-1B status, may still apply successfully for an H-1B visa at a U.S. consulate in another country.

If you decide to apply for a change of status within the U.S., realize that you still don't have the H-1B visa that you'll need if you ever leave the U.S.—a change of status only gives you H-1B status. Visas are never given inside the United States. They are issued exclusively by U.S. consulates in other countries. If you file in the U.S. and you are successful, you will get to remain in the U.S. with H-1B privileges until the status expires. But should you leave the country for any reason before that time, you will have to apply for an H-1B visa at a U.S. consulate before returning to the United States. Moreover, the fact that your H-1B status has been approved in the U.S. does not guarantee that the consulate will also approve your visa. For these reasons, some people simply file through a consulate.

2. Assembling the Petition

The checklist below will help you and your employer assemble the necessary items for the petition. Make sure everything is filed in *duplicate* (two copies). USCIS needs to forward a copy of your petition to the U.S. State Department so that you can more easily be issued the H1-B visa when (or if) you apply at the U.S. consulate.

A few items on this checklist require some extra explanation.

Form I-129 and H Supplement. The basic form for the visa petition is USCIS Form I-129 and its H Supplement. The I-129 form

Checklist for H-1B Visa Petition

- ☐ Form I-129, H Supplement, and H-1B Data Collection and Filing Fee Exemption Supplement.

- ☐ Base filing fee: $460.

- ☐ Additional fee of either $750 or $1,500, depending on employer's answers to the questions on the H-1B Data Collection and Filing Fee Exemption Supplement form.

- ☐ Fraud prevention and detection fee (currently $500).

- ☐ Possible filing surcharge. If your petitioning employer has more than 50 employees, and over half its workforce is in H or L visa status, be prepared to pay a further surcharge of $4,000. If the petitioning employer does not have more than 50 employees, or less than half of its workforce is in H or L visa status, it should include a written statement to this effect with the petition.

- ☐ If you will be applying in the United States and your family members are with you and need a change of status, Form I-539 with accompanying fee (currently $290) and copies of your family members' I-94s or other proof of lawful immigration status and of their relationship to you, the primary beneficiary (such as marriage and birth certificates). One Form I-539 and fee will cover your spouse and all your children. Your family members should fill out this form, not your employer.

- ☐ If you're in the U.S., a copy of your I-94 or other proof of your current lawful, unexpired immigration status.

- ☐ Copy of the biographic page of your passport.

- ☐ Copy of employer's certified attestation Form ETA-9035 or ETA-9035E.

- ☐ Proof of employer's ability to pay your salary, such as annual report, tax returns, and accounting statements.

- ☐ A letter signed by your employer, describing the terms of your employment, including job duties, hours, and salary. It is acceptable that the employment be "at will" and not of any particular duration.

- ☐ Evidence that your job will be in a "specialty occupation."

- ☐ Evidence that you have the required degree, such as your college and university diplomas (and if they're from a foreign university, evidence that they're equivalent to U.S. degrees). If you attended a school but did not graduate, the transcript is required. If you attended any relevant training courses, include a copy of the certificate of completion. If you attended a college or university outside the U.S., you may need a professional evaluator's opinion that the degree is equivalent to a U.S. bachelor's.

- ☐ If you do not have a degree, evidence that your combined education and experience is equivalent to a degree.

- ☐ If the job requires a license or another permit to practice in the U.S. state where you'll be located, a copy of your license or permit.

- ☐ If your intended job is as a physician, proof that you have passed the appropriate exams and met state licensing requirements.

If requesting quick (premium) processing:

- ☐ Form I-907, with $1,225 filing fee.

is used for many different nonimmigrant visas. In addition to the basic part of the form that applies to all types of visas, it comes with several supplements for each specific nonimmigrant category. Simply use the supplement that applies to you.

Proof of specialty occupation. Sometimes, as with positions for physicians, accountants, and similarly recognized professions, the highly specialized nature of the work is common knowledge. In such cases, the employer's letter will serve to prove both the existence and the level of the job. Where it is not evident that the position is a specialty occupation, additional documents are required. Your employer should write out and submit a detailed description of all job functions, with an explanation of how advanced knowledge and education are essential to their performance. If it remains unclear that the job requires a high-level employee, your employer might need to get written affidavits from experts, such as educators in the field or other employers in similar businesses, stating that jobs of this kind are normally held by highly qualified and degreed individuals.

Proof of employer's ability to pay your salary. Your employer must be able to prove its existence and financial viability. If the employer is large and well known, it is usually enough to state the annual gross receipts or income in the letter it submits describing the job opportunity and duties. If the employer is very small, USCIS may request documents to verify the existence and financial solvency of the employer's business. In that case, USCIS will specifically advise your employer of the documents it wishes to see, including tax returns, audited financial statements, copies of contracts or invoices with customers, quarterly payroll records, and the like.

Publicly held companies do not have to produce tax returns, accounting records, or bank statements. For them, the most recently published annual report filed with the SEC will be sufficient to prove the ability to pay wages. Again, the larger the company, the less evidence USCIS demands of its ability to pay additional salaries.

Special documents for physicians. Graduates of medical schools outside the U.S. or Canada may not get H-1B visas as practicing physicians unless they have passed the USMLE licensing exam or an equivalent exam and satisfy the state licensing requirements if they will provide direct patient care services. State licensure, however, is not required of foreign medical graduates who come to the U.S. to work solely in teaching or research positions at a public or nonprofit institution. In those cases, any patient care activities must be incidental to the teaching or research functions.

Therefore, in addition to all other documents required from members of the professions, the petitioning employer must submit a certificate showing you have passed the USMLE, your ECFMG certificate, and your state license. In the alternative, your employer can show that you will be employed as either a teacher or researcher and that any patient care will be undertaken only as part of the teaching or research. This written statement does not have to be in any special form but simply in the petitioner's own words.

3. Mailing the Petition

After assembling the petition, your U.S. employer must mail it to either the California Service Center (CSC) or the Vermont Service Center (VSC), whichever has jurisdiction over the employer's place of business. (As you might imagine, the CSC accepts applications from companies with worksites in the Western United States, and VSC accepts applications from employers located in the East.) If you'll be coming from outside the U.S., your employer must send a second copy of the full application and supporting documents. (Even if you're changing status from within the U.S., it's a good idea for the employer to send a second copy, since you can't predict whether or when you might need to go abroad and then apply for an H-1B visa with which to return.)

The instructions to the I-129, available on the USCIS website at www.uscis. gov/i-129, contain the filing addresses.

Due to competition for the limited number of "cap-subject" H-1B petitions that become annually available on October 1, your employer must be prepared to file the petition as soon as USCIS allows it. The earliest your employer can file is six months in advance—on April 1. (See Section 4, below.) Petitions not subject to the cap can be filed at any time, and you can begin the H-1B job as soon as your visa is processed or change of status approved.

4. The Petition Selection Lottery for "Cap-Subject" H-1Bs

In most years, USCIS expects to receive many more "cap-subject" H-1B petitions than the law allows it to approve. In fiscal year 2017, for example, (for H-1B visas and jobs that can start October 1, 2016), USCIS reportedly received about 236,000 H-1B petitions during the filing period that began April 1, 2016. Because only 85,000 petitions could be approved, USCIS conducted a computer-generated random selection process ("lottery") to select enough petitions to meet the 65,000 general-category cap and the 20,000 cap under the advanced degree exemption. Usually, all petitions received in the first five business days in April are entered in the lottery, to avoid unfairness to potential victims of a slow mail service.

Academic Credential Evaluations

Not every country in the world operates on the same academic degree and grade level systems found in the United States. If you were educated in some other country, USCIS may ask for an academic credential evaluation from an approved consulting service to determine the U.S. equivalent of your educational level.

Evaluations from accredited credential evaluation services are not binding on USCIS. When the results are favorable (showing you have the equivalent of the educational level required by your U.S. employer) the evaluation strengthens your case.

We recommend always obtaining a credential evaluation where non-U.S. education is a factor. We also advise getting the evaluation before USCIS asks for it. If it's favorable, include it with your petition. If not, and your credentials are less than what your employer has asked for, do not submit the results unless USCIS insists. Discuss this with your employer, who may ask for less education in the job description.

Before sending your academic documents to an evaluation service, you might call ahead to discuss your prospects. If your prospects are truly bleak, you may decide not to order the evaluation and save the service charge (typically upwards of $100).

Several qualified credential evaluation services are recognized by USCIS, among them International Education Research Foundation, www.ierf.org; and Educational Credential Evaluators, Inc., www.ece.org.

Credential evaluation companies will usually evaluate only formal education, not job experience. Some U.S. universities offer evaluations of foreign academic credentials and will recognize work experience as having an academic equivalent. Therefore, if you lack formal education but can show many years of experience, you are better off trying to get an evaluation from a U.S. college or university. When sending your credentials to a U.S. university, include documents showing your complete academic background as well as all relevant career achievements. Letters of recommendation from former employers are good proof of work experience. Also submit evidence of any special accomplishments, such as awards or published articles. USCIS can be influenced, but is not bound by, academic evaluations from U.S. colleges and universities.

USCIS conducts a lottery to select 20,000 advanced degree H-1B petitions first. All advanced degree petitions not selected then became part of the lottery for the 65,000 limit. USCIS will reject and return any petition not selected in the lottery and return the filing fee checks, unless the petition is found to be a duplicate filing.

5. Awaiting a Decision on the Petition

If your cap-subject petition is selected in the lottery, or if you're not subject to the cap, your employer will receive a written confirmation that the papers are being processed, as well as a receipt for the fee. This notice will also give your immigration file number.

If USCIS wants further information before acting on your case, it will send your employer a form known as a Request for Evidence on Form I-797E. Your employer should supply the extra data requested and mail it to the service center.

H-1B petitions are normally approved within two to five months. Timing can vary over the course of the year, so check the posted processing times for USCIS to understand when your petition is likely to be decided. See Chapter 4 for a discussion of how to monitor your case. After a period of time, a Form I-797 Notice of

Action will be sent to your employer, showing the petition was approved. If you plan to submit your visa application at a U.S. consulate abroad, USCIS will notify the Kentucky Consular Center, which will electronically notify the consulate and send your file there. Only the employer receives communications from USCIS about the petition, because technically it is the employer who is seeking the visa or change of status on your behalf.

 TIP

Faster processing—at a price. For $1,225 over and above the regular filing fees, USCIS promises "premium processing" of the petition, including action on your case within 15 calendar days. To use this service, the employer must fill out an additional application (Form I-907) and submit the application to a special USCIS service center address. For complete instructions, see the USCIS website at www.uscis.gov/i-907. USCIS is not obliged to provide better service for people who opt for premium processing, That is, your case is no more likely to be approved simply because you requested premium processing. However, petitioners can expect better communication options if something goes wrong (such as a typographical error on the approval notice or issues in responding to a Request for Evidence). You should strongly consider paying for premium processing if you can afford it.

Be aware that an approved petition does not by itself give you any immigration privileges (unless it was approved with a grant of change or extension of status). It is only a prerequisite to the next step, submitting your application for an H-1B visa.

E. Step Three: Applicants Outside the U.S. Apply for Visa

After the H-1B visa petition filed by your employer has been approved, USCIS will send a Form I-797B, Notice of Action, with which you can apply for a visa at a U.S. consulate—normally in your home country. Also, you'll have to wait until the consulate's computer system reflects that your visa petition was approved. Check with your local U.S. consulate regarding its application procedures. Many insist on advance appointments. Just getting an appointment can take several weeks, so plan ahead.

You'll need to go online to submit the main form for this process, the Non-immigrant Visa Application (Form DS-160). You can submit your photos digitally at the same time. For instructions, see the State Department website at https://ceac.state. gov/genniv.

TIP

If you're visa exempt, you can skip this step. Citizens of Canada and Bermuda need not apply to a U.S. consulate. Instead, they can proceed directly to the United States with Form I-797B and supporting documents to request entry. (See 8 C.F.R. § 212.1.)

CAUTION

Have you been, or are you now, working or living illegally in the United States? If so, see Chapter 3 regarding whether or not you can still get an H-1B visa from a U.S. consulate. You may have become inadmissible or subject to a three-year or ten-year bar on reentry.

The checklist shown below will help you prepare your consular application.

As part of your application, the consulate will require you and your family members to pay an application fee and attend an interview. You may have to pay an additional fee for visa issuance if you're from a country that charges similar fees for visas to U.S. citizens who wish to work there.

RELATED TOPIC

See Chapter 4 for what to expect during consular interviews, and what to do if your application is denied.

Applying at a Consulate That's Not in Your Home Country

The law allows most people to apply for an H-1B visa at any U.S. consulate they choose—with one exception. If you have ever overstayed the amount of time you were authorized to be in the U.S. as shown on your I-94, your visa will be automatically cancelled and you cannot apply as a third-country national (at a consulate outside your home country). Even if you overstayed your status in the U.S. by just one day, you must return to your home country and apply for the visa from that consulate. There is an exception. If you were admitted to the U.S. for the duration of your status (indicated by a "D/S" on your I-94 form and most common with student visas) and you remained in the U.S. beyond that time for which your status was conferred, you will be barred from third-country national processing only if an immigration judge or USCIS (or former INS) officer has determined that you were unlawfully present. You may find that your success in applying as a third-country national will depend on your country, the consulate, and the relative seriousness of your offense. Being unlawfully present is also a ground of inadmissibility if the period of unlawful presence is 180 days or more. (See Chapter 3.)

Even if you are eligible for third-country national processing, your case will be given the greatest consideration at the consulate in your home country. Applying in some other country creates suspicion in the minds of the consular officers there about your motives for choosing their consulate. Often, when an applicant expects trouble at a home consulate, he or she will seek a more lenient consular office in some other country. This practice of consulate shopping is frowned upon by officials in the system. Unless you have a very good reason for being elsewhere (such as a temporary job assignment in some other nation), it is often smarter to file your visa application in your home country.

H-1B Visa Application Checklist

- ☐ Form DS-160, Nonimmigrant Visa Application (can be completed only at https://ceac.state.gov/genniv).
- ☐ Original Form I-797 notice showing approval of the H-1B petition.
- ☐ Copy of the I-129 visa petition, certified Labor Condition Application, and support materials that were used to obtain the H-1B visa petition approval.
- ☐ Valid passport for you and each accompanying relative.
- ☐ Your original diploma.
- ☐ If requested by the consulate or if you were unable to upload one with your DS-160 application, one U.S. passport-type photo of you and one of each accompanying relative. (This is best done by a professional photographer; the consulate can give you a list.)
- ☐ If your spouse and children will be accompanying you, original documents verifying their family relationship to you, such as marriage and birth certificates.
- ☐ Fee receipt showing that you have paid the relevant machine-readable visa (MRV) application fee (currently $190). The financial institution at which you must pay will vary from country to country. Check the website of the U.S. consulate where you plan to apply for your visa to learn how to pay the fee in advance. Most consulates will not allow you to pay the application fee at the time of interview.
- ☐ Visa reciprocity fee. You may have to pay an additional visa issuance fee if you're from a country that charges similar fees for visas to U.S. citizens who wish to work there.

Watch Out for Expedited Removal

The law empowers a CBP inspector at the U.S. airport or border to summarily (without allowing judicial review) bar entry to someone requesting admission to the U.S. if either of the following is true:

- The inspector thinks you are lying about practically anything connected with entering the U.S., including your purpose in coming, intent to return, and prior immigration history. This includes the use or suspected use of false documents.
- You do not have the proper documentation to support your entry to the U.S. in the category you are requesting.

If the inspector excludes you, you cannot be readmitted to the U.S. for five years, unless USCIS grants a special waiver. For this reason it is extremely important to understand the terms of your requested status, and to not make any misrepresentations. If you are found to be inadmissible, you may ask the CBP inspector to withdraw your application to enter the U.S. in order to prevent having the five-year deportation order on your record. The CBP will often allow this if they feel you cannot otherwise be admitted to the United States, so be prepared to request the opportunity to withdraw your application if it appears your only alternative is expedited removal.

F. Step Four: H-1B Visa Holders Enter the U.S.

You have until the expiration date on your H-1B visa to enter the United States. The border officer will examine your paperwork, ask you some questions, and if all is in order, approve you for entry. He or she will stamp your passport and create an I-94 Arrival/Departure record for you (if you enter by air or sea). If you enter at a land border, you will be given a small white I-94 card. Your I-94 shows how long you can stay. Normally, you are permitted to remain up to the expiration date on your H-1B petition. (However, if your passport will expire before the petition's expiration date, some CBP officers will issue the I-94 until only the date of the passport's expiration.) Each time you exit and reenter the U.S., you will get a new I-94 authorizing your stay up to the final date indicated on the petition.

G. Extending Your U.S. Stay

H-1B status can be extended for three years at a time, for up to a maximum of six years. Although an extension is usually easier to get than the initial H-1B visa, it is not automatic. USCIS has the right to reconsider your qualifications based on any changes in the facts or law, and your employer must maintain a valid attestation for your position. As always, however, good cases that are well prepared will be successful.

There are two ways to extend your H-1B status beyond the six-year maximum period that otherwise applies. Both ways are available only if you have started the process of getting your green card.

The first way is if you started your green card process by filing a permanent labor certification application more than a year before you reached your six-year maximum, in which case you can extend your H-1B status for a year at a time as long as you are pursuing a green card. The second is if you have received approval of your employer's I-140 petition to qualify you for a green card but a green card is not yet available to you. If this is the case, you qualify for three-year extensions of H-1B status until the green card becomes available or is denied.

Extension procedures are identical to the procedures followed in getting the initial visa. You should include the full set of filing forms and supporting documents that you used for the original case. However, your employer is not required to pay the $500 antifraud fee if you are extending the H-1B visa. Also, your employer is not required to pay the $750 or $1,500 employer retraining fund fee if you are filing the second extension for work with that employer.

In order to travel internationally after your H-1B extension is approved, you will need to arrange for a new consular appointment, to get a new visa. You can travel on the old H-1B visa only during its period of validity. However, U.S. immigration officials are lenient in one important way. You can use the original H-1B visa in your passport during its full validity period even if you change employers and get a new I-797 approval notice for the new employer. In this case, when you enter the U.S., you show the new original approval notice together with the original H-1B visa in your passport (with the old employer's name written on it). U.S. immigration officials will admit you to work with the new employer.

Working While Your Extension Petition Is Pending

If you file your petition for an extension of H-1B status before your authorized stay expires, you are automatically permitted to continue working for up to 240 days while you are waiting for a decision. If, however, your authorized stay expires after you have filed for an extension but before you receive an approval, and more than 240 days go by without getting a decision on your extension petition, your work authorization ceases and you must stop working. You will not be able to continue working until your extension is finally approved.

If you're getting close to the 240-day limit and haven't gotten your extension yet, email scopsscata@dhs.gov and ask to prioritize your case.

TIP
Ask your employer to prepare a PERM labor certification application by the end of your fourth year of H-1B status. The labor certification should ideally be filed by the end of your fifth year if you wish to maximize your chances of extending your H-1B status beyond the six-year maximum period. Failing that, an approved I-140 immigrant petition may allow you to extend your H-1B status beyond the sixth year. This is true even if the labor certification that underlay the immigrant petition was filed after the end of your fifth year of H-1B status.

H. Your Rights as an H-1B Worker

Once you've got H-1B status, the law offers you various forms of protection. For example, your employer is required to begin paying you, as a new H-1B employee, within 30 days of your entry into the United States. If you are already in the U.S., your employer must pay you within 60 days of your approval as an H-1B worker. The employer is also prohibited from "benching" you, that is, putting you on involuntary, unpaid leave. This prohibition holds true even if the employer has insufficient work for you or you lack a permit or license. Employees must be paid for any time spent in nonproductive status due to a decision by the employer.

If you want to leave your H-1B job for another one, the law allows you to do that, as long as you entered the U.S. lawfully, have never worked without permission, still have time left in H-1B status, and the new employer is willing to file an H-1B petition for you. The new employer should check box "e" (change of employer) in question 2 of Part 2 of the I-129. You won't have to wait for petition approval—you can start as soon as the new employer files the petition. You'll lose your H-1B status if the petition is ultimately denied, however.

What if you get fired from or otherwise lose your old H-1B job unexpectedly, before the new employer petitions for you? You lose H-1B status as soon as you're not working at the old H-1B job, which typically means you have to go back home to get a new H-1B.

However, USCIS tends to be forgiving if only a few days or weeks go by while the new employer applies for an LCA and gets ready to file the new H-1B petition, and you otherwise act as quickly as possible.

You'll need to explain to USCIS what happened and ask it to excuse your time out of status when filing the new petition. By law, USCIS is not required to give you a break, but there is little harm in proceeding this way. The worst that could happen (assuming you didn't do anything to make yourself inadmissible since entering the U.S.) is that you will be told to make a trip back to your country to pick up the visa.

TIP

Employers are prohibited from trying to keep hold of H-1B employees by forcing them to pay a penalty if they leave the job prior to a certain date. On the other hand, if the employer is simply trying to recover reasonable costs expended in the course of obtaining the H-1B visa petition approval, such "liquidated damages" provisions may be enforced. In short, make sure you know your rights as an H-1B employee. If you ever feel that you are being treated unfairly, consider hiring an immigration attorney who is experienced in H-1B visa matters.

Getting a Temporary Nonagricultural Worker (H-2B) Visa

The H-2B visa was created to allow people to come to the U.S. temporarily to fill nonagricultural jobs for which U.S. workers are in short supply. A total of 66,000 H-2B visa petitions may be approved during the government year (fiscal year), which ends on September 30. (See I.N.A. § 101(a)(15)(H), 8 U.S.C. § 1101(a)(15)(H).) Recent law effectively divided the fiscal year in two, however, so that no more than 33,000 visas can be passed out during the first six months. Although the 66,000 total doesn't include H-2B workers in the U.S. and seeking to extend status, or accompanying spouses and children, lately the annual quota has not been enough to meet the demand. This chapter will explain who is eligible for an H-2B visa and how to apply.

Key Features of the H-2B Visa

Here are some of the advantages and disadvantages of the H-2B visa:

- You can work legally in the U.S. in H-2B status for short periods of time.
- Visas may be available for your accompanying spouse and minor children, but it may not be worth the risk of including them (as described in this chapter) and they may not work, unless they qualify for a work visa in their own right.
- You may travel in and out of the U.S. or remain here continuously until your H-2B status expires.

SEE AN EXPERT

Do you need a lawyer? You can't apply for an H-2B without having an employer first—and it's in your employer's interest to hire a lawyer to help. Because more people have recently been trying to get H-2B visas than there are visas available, a lawyer can help make sure that your application gets it done right the first time, and gets it filed before the visas run out.

A. Do You Qualify for an H-2B Visa?

H-2B visas are aimed at skilled and unskilled workers, as compared to H-1B visas, which are intended for college-educated workers. There are numerous requirements for obtaining an H-2B visa:

- You must either come from a participating country or qualify for an exception. The list of current H-2B participating countries can be found on the USCIS website (at www.uscis.gov, follow the links to Working in the U.S., Temporary Workers, and H-2B Non-Agricultural Workers) and is determined by the following factors:
  - The country's cooperation with respect to issuance of travel documents for citizens, subjects, nationals, and residents of that country who are subject to a final order of removal from the United States
  - The number of final and unexecuted U.S. orders of removal against

citizens, subjects, nationals, and residents of that country

- The number of U.S. orders of removal executed against citizens, subjects, nationals, and residents of that country, and

- Such other factors as may serve the U.S. interest.

To qualify for an exception, a person from a nonparticipating country may show that he or she is the beneficiary of an approved H-2B petition and that approval would serve the U.S. interest. Factors that USCIS considers in deciding whether to grant an exception include: (1) a worker with the required skills is not available from among foreign workers from a participating country; (2) the person has been previously admitted to the United States in H-2B status; (3) the lack of potential for abuse, fraud, or other harm to the integrity of the H-2B visa program; and (4) other factors as may serve the U.S. interest.

- You must have a job offer from a U.S. employer to perform work that is temporary, meaning seasonal, one-time, peak load, or intermittent.

- You must have the correct background to qualify for the job you have been offered.

- There must be no qualified U.S. workers willing or able to take the job. A temporary labor certification is required.

- You must intend to return home when your visa expires.

H-2B Participating Countries

At the time this book went to print, the H-2B participating countries included Andorra, Argentina, Australia, Austria, Barbados, Belgium, Belize, Brazil, Brunei, Bulgaria, Canada, Chile, Colombia, Costa Rica, Croatia, Czech Republic, Denmark, Dominican Republic, Ecuador, El Salvador, Estonia, Ethiopia, Fiji, Finland, France, Germany, Greece, Grenada, Guatemala, Haiti, Honduras, Hungary, Iceland, Ireland, Israel, Italy, Jamaica, Japan, Kiribati, Latvia, Liechtenstein, Lithuania, Luxembourg, Macedonia, Madagascar, Malta, Mexico, Montenegro, Nauru, the Netherlands, New Zealand, Nicaragua, Norway, Panama, Papua New Guinea, Peru, Philippines, Poland, Portugal, Romania, Samoa, San Marino, Serbia, Singapore, Slovakia, Slovenia, Solomon Islands, South Africa, South Korea, Spain, Switzerland, Sweden, Taiwan, Thailand, Timor-Leste, Tonga, Turkey, Tuvalu, Ukraine, United Kingdom, Uruguay, and Vanuatu. If you're not from one of these countries, you can get an H-2B visa only if USCIS determines that it is in the U.S. interest to give you one.

The term temporary refers to the employer's need for the duties performed by the position. There must be a specific

---

Temporary Agricultural Worker: H-2A Visas

Under the 1986 amendments to the U.S. immigration laws, temporary agricultural workers are now treated differently from all other types of temporary workers. Agricultural workers are now issued H-2A visas while all other temporary workers receive H-2B visas.

The rules for getting temporary agricultural worker visas are extremely complex and beyond the scope of this book. The basic requirements are that before a non-U.S. agricultural worker may be granted an H-2A visa, the prospective employer must attempt to find U.S. agricultural workers. The employer must search for U.S. workers not just in the employer's own immediate geographical area, but throughout the entire adjacent region of the country. The employer must do this by undertaking a multistate recruitment effort.

Moreover, H-2A visas will not, as a practical matter, be issued to foreign workers who are already in the U.S. illegally. Due to the great amount of effort involved in obtaining H-2A visas, they will be attractive mostly to employers who urgently need to bring in a large crew of foreign laborers at one time to work on a particular harvest. From a practical standpoint, the employer may either have to travel abroad or use the services of a foreign labor contractor to find these crews of temporary foreign workers. H-2A visas are not often practical for bringing one temporary agricultural worker at a time to the United States, unless the employer knows of a worker that it wants very badly.

---

beginning and end to the employer's need for your services. Seasonal laborers, workers on short-term business projects, and those who come to the U.S. as trainers of other workers commonly get H-2B visas. A job can be deemed temporary if it is a one-time occurrence, meets a seasonal or peak-load need, or fulfills an intermittent but not regular need of the employer.

H-2B visas are also frequently used for entertainers who cannot meet the criteria for O or P visas. H-2B visas enable such entertainers to come to the U.S. for specific bookings. These bookings are considered temporary positions.

Other jobs that have met the criteria include athletes, camp counselors, craft-persons, horse trainers, and home attendants for terminally ill patients. Although we've just given you some examples of jobs that meet the USCIS's definition of temporary, be aware that most jobs do not.

1. Job Offer From a U.S. Employer

You need a specific job offer from a U.S. employer to get an H-2B visa. The employer will have to act as the petitioner in getting your H-2B visa. Many people are surprised to learn that they require an employment offer before applying for a work visa. The idea behind it is that you are being granted an H-2B visa because your services are essential to a U.S. company. Put another way, the U.S. government issues the visa to help your U.S. employer, not for your benefit.

The petitioner may be a company or an individual. Generally, you cannot act as your own employer. An agent who books your talents for a variety of jobs can be the source of the job offer if the salary is paid to you directly by the agent and not by the individual places where you perform. This is a common arrangement for entertainers.

The job you are offered can't be just any position. First, it must be one that meets the legal definition of temporary. To be considered temporary, the period of the employer's need for services must be nine months or less.

Second, the employer's need must be either one-time, seasonal, based on a peak-load need, or based on an intermittent need. An example of a one-time need would be a specific project, such as building a housing development. Seasonal needs are fairly self-explanatory—workers at a ski resort would be a good example. Peak-load needs often occur around tourist or holiday seasons, when employers bring in extra workers whom they let go afterwards. Intermittent needs are

ones where the employer needs workers occasionally for short periods, but not for long enough to justify hiring someone permanently. Professional minor-league baseball players are a common example of employees who do seasonal work. (Major-league players will usually qualify for O visas. See Chapter 24.)

2. Correct Background

You must have the correct background and abilities for the job you have been offered. For example, if you are a qualified insurance salesman but are offered a job that requires experience supervising a catering project, you will not be granted an H-2B visa for that job if you have no background in catering. It is irrelevant that your native intelligence and general knowledge of business may make you quite capable of handling the catering job. Likewise, reliability or willingness to work hard, characteristics difficult to find and much sought after by real-world employers, are not a USCIS consideration. If you lack the required background in the job offered, the petition will fail.

H-2B visas can be issued to unskilled as well as skilled workers. If your job offer happens to be for employment as an unskilled worker, there are, by definition no specific background qualifications for you to meet. Under these circumstances, your natural abilities may be a consideration,

Entertainment Industry Workers: Special Considerations

Entertainment industry workers, both the performers and the many workers it takes to make a movie or to stage a live performance, often need temporary U.S. work visas.

H-1B visas are not available to entertainers or athletes. The better-known ones will qualify for O or P visas. (See Chapter 24.) An individual entertainment industry worker who is not well known, not part of a well-known group, or not part of an international production team is limited to an H-2B visa.

The challenge is both the temporariness of the job and the availability of similarly qualified U.S. workers. The definition of temporariness is narrow: If, for example, a Las Vegas nightclub wants to book an act for only one week, USCIS will still say that the job is not temporary because nightclubs are always employing acts to perform there. (The job is not temporary even if the booking is.) On the other hand, jobs for performers on tour are considered temporary, as are jobs for workers on motion pictures. That is because tours and motion picture productions always end.

Even if the job is clearly temporary, your U.S. employer must still get a clearance from the Department of Labor (DOL) acknowledging that no U.S. workers are available to fill the job. All H-2B applications for entertainment industry workers are filed with the Certifying Officer at the Office of Foreign Labor Certification's Chicago National Processing Center (CNPC). The CNPC will determine the prevailing wage that must be paid to the worker. The employer must

place a "job order" with the State Workforce Agency (SWA) serving the area of intended employment. Then the employer must contact the appropriate U.S. entertainment industry union to see if the union can find a U.S. worker to fill the position or has some other objection to a non-U.S. worker taking the job. Since there are many competent U.S. entertainment industry workers looking for employment, getting union approval on an H-2B case may be difficult.

The availability of competing U.S. workers is not a problem in several situations. H-2B visas are readily available to all performing and nonperforming members of lesser-known troupes coming to the U.S. on tour. Moreover, U.S. entertainment industry unions are usually reluctant to break up performing units. Therefore, an entire touring group, from performers to technicians and stage hands, can all get H-2B visas.

The offer of employment must be from a U.S. employer. The workers cannot be self-employed nor can they be working in the U.S. for a foreign company. Individual performers, therefore, normally have to get their H-2B visas through a central booking agent. This is acceptable, provided the booking agent acts as the employer in every respect, including being responsible for paying the salary.

Foreign entertainment industry working units, such as film companies, that wish to get H-2B visas will need to do one of two things to supply themselves with the required U.S. employer. They can be sponsored for visas by an

Entertainment Industry Workers: Special Considerations (continued)

established U.S. company that will act as the employer of each individual foreign employee. Alternatively, the foreign group may form its own U.S. corporation and have it act as the employer. U.S. corporations are set up by state governments in the U.S. state where the business will be headquartered. Forming a U.S. corporation is extremely simple and in most states can be accomplished in a matter of days. Information on how to form a U.S. corporation is available from the office of the secretary of state located in each state capital and from Nolo's *Incorporate Your Business: A Legal Guide to Forming a Corporation in Your State*, by Anthony Mancuso.

but you do not need to be concerned about having the correct background.

3. No Qualified U.S. Workers

To obtain an H-2B visa, there must be no qualified U.S. workers available to take the particular job. Your prospective employer must successfully complete a temporary labor certification to prove the unavailability of U.S. workers and that employment of H-2B workers will not adversely affect the wages and/or working conditions of similarly employed U.S. workers. (Wages are often the key to the H-2B visa—employers can almost always recruit a qualified U.S. worker if they offer high enough wages.) This condition may or may not be hard to meet, depending on the type of job. Where the jobs are meant for skilled and unskilled workers rather than professionals, the competition factor can be a problem. Many employers do go begging, however, for want of either qualified or willing U.S. applicants, especially for temporary positions.

4. Intent to Return to Your Home Country

H-2B visas are meant to be temporary. At the time of applying, you must intend to return home when the visa expires. If you have it in mind to take up permanent residence in the U.S., you are legally ineligible for an H-2B visa. You must have bona fide nonimmigrant intent to qualify for H-2B classification. Bona fide nonimmigrant intent means you maintain a permanent residence abroad that you have no intention of abandoning and you do not intend to remain in the U.S. beyond the authorized period of stay.

The U.S. government knows it is difficult to read minds. Expect to be asked for evidence showing that when you go to the United States on an H-2B visa, you are leaving behind possessions, property, or family members as incentive for your eventual return. Don't quit your job, sell your car, and move out of your place all at once!

5. Bringing Your Spouse and Children

When you qualify for an H-2B visa, your spouse and unmarried children under age 21 can, in theory, apply for H-4 visas by providing proof of their family relationship to you. Like you, your family members would have to show that they are not inadmissible (see Chapter 3). An H-4 visa would authorize your accompanying relatives to stay with you in the U.S., but not to work here.

In practice, however, applying for H-4 visas for your family may not be a good idea. If the consular officer sees you uprooting your entire family for a temporary, seasonal job that's supposed to last for less than a year, he or she may suspect that you don't really intend to leave the United States. You'll need to show ties to your home country such as a job, property, or a lease, and family—and family is the most important of these. In addition, showing an unabandoned foreign residence is much harder if your family isn't living there. Leaving a spouse and children behind can, in some cases, be the key to establishing the bona fide, nonimmigrant intent required for obtaining an H-2B visa. (That can sometimes be a problem for young, single people.)

6. Limitations on Your Period of Stay

As an H-2B nonimmigrant, you will be subject to a three-year limitation on the aggregate (total) period of your H-2B stay. Upon departure from the United States for three months, you become eligible for another three years of H-2B status.

Seasonal workers who do not reside continuously in the United States are exempt from the three-year limitation.

Time spent outside the United States during the validity period of an approved H-2B petition counts toward the three-year limitation unless it is "interruptive" of your stay. If you have accumulated fewer than 18 months of H-2B stay, a departure from the United States must be for at least 45 days to be considered "interruptive." If you have accumulated more than 18 months of H-2B stay, a departure from the United States must be at least two months long to be considered interruptive. (See 8 C.F.R. § 214.2(h)(13)(v).)

The way in which H-2B nonimmigrants deal with these time limitations tends to fall into one of two patterns. Some H-2B nonimmigrants return to their home countries during the off season each year, thereby establishing a track record of bona fide nonimmigrant intent—in other words, showing the immigration authorities that they can be counted on to return home when their stay is over. Other H-2B nonimmigrants either obtain extensions of stay or switch employers in order to remain in the United States continuously for the entire three-year period. Although this is legal, H-2B nonimmigrants who remain in the United States for the entire three-year period may have more difficulty in establishing bona fide nonimmigrant intent if they apply for new H-2B visas after finally departing the United States and spending the required three months outside it.

B. Possibilities for a Green Card From H-2B Status

Being in the U.S. on an H-2B visa gives you no advantage in applying for a U.S. green card. In fact, it will almost certainly prove to be a drawback. That is because H-2B visas, like most nonimmigrant visas, are intended only for those who plan to return home once their jobs or other activities in the U.S. are completed. However, if you apply for a green card, you are in effect making a statement that you never intend to leave the United States. Therefore, USCIS may allow you to keep H-2B status while pursuing a green card, but only if you can convince USCIS that you did not intend to get a green card when you originally applied for the H-2B visa and that you will return home if you are unable to secure a green card before your H-2B visa expires. Doing this can be difficult. If you do not succeed, your H-2B status can be taken away.

It is also important to understand that even if you argue successfully and keep your H-2B status, the visa and the petition each carry a maximum duration of nine months and will probably expire before you get a green card. Once you have taken certain steps toward applying for a green card, you will be absolutely barred from receiving an extension of your H-2B status. Should you, for any reason, lose your H-2B status, it may affect your green card application.

Another problem comes up if it is your current H-2B sponsoring employer who also wants to sponsor you for a green card. USCIS regulations provide that if you have an approved permanent labor certification sponsored by the same employer who petitioned for your H-2B visa, and for the same job that you are doing while in H-2B status, then no H-2B extension will be granted. In general, to apply for a green card through employment and retain an H-2B visa, even until its expiration date, you must have a different sponsoring employer for the green card than you had for the H-2B visa.

If what you really want is a green card, apply for it directly and disregard H-2B visas. Although the green card is harder to get and may take several years, in the long run, you will be happier with the results. Also, relatively few jobs qualify as temporary for H-2B visa purposes and you may actually have a better chance of getting a green card through a given job than an H-2B visa.

C. Quick View of the H-2B Visa Application Process

Once you have been offered a job, getting an H-2B visa is a multistep process, which involves getting approval from at least two and sometimes three government agencies, depending on whether you're applying from within the U.S. or from another country. The process includes the following:

- Your U.S. employer requests what's called a "prevailing wage determination" (PWD) by filing Form ETA-9141 with the U.S. Department of Labor (DOL).
- Your U.S. employer files an application for what's called temporary labor certification (Form ETA-9142B) with the U.S. Department of Labor (DOL), and simultaneously places a job order with a State Workforce Agency.
- Your U.S. employer goes through a process of recruiting any available U.S. workers for the job.
- Your U.S. employer files what's called a nonimmigrant visa petition on USCIS Form I-129. If you're already in the U.S. in lawful status, this petition can simultaneously ask that your status be changed to H-2B worker, in which case the process will successfully end here.
- If you're outside the U.S., then after the visa petition is approved, you submit an application for an H-2B visa to a U.S. consulate, possibly in a group with your fellow workers (unless you're from Canada or Bermuda, in which case you can skip this step).

Emergency Filing Procedures

If an employer needs employees to start work sooner than the 75 days that processing of the temporary labor certification application normally takes, it can make an "emergency" filing, requesting a quicker DOL determination. The request is included with the temporary labor certification application.

The request must explain why there is "good and substantial cause" for quicker processing. Examples of valid reasons include a substantial loss of U.S. workers due to acts of God or a similar unforeseeable manmade catastrophic event (such as an oil spill or controlled flooding) that's wholly outside the employer's control, unforeseeable changes in market conditions, and pandemic health issues. Your employer will not succeed in arguing that there's an emergency merely because the annual limit on the number of H-1B visas that can be given out will soon be reached.

If your employer makes an emergency filing, it can request a prevailing wage determination at the same time as it files the application for temporary labor certification (rather than before). It does not have to comply with the job order deadlines.

- Finally, you use either your visa or (if you're from Canada or Bermuda) the notice of your approved visa petition to enter the U.S. and claim your H-2B status.

D. Step One: Your Employer Applies for PWD

Before your employer starts the immigration application process for you, it must make sure that the salary or wages it plans to pay you are normal for the local job market. The purpose is to make sure that hiring low-cost immigrant labor doesn't weaken the wages and working conditions of U.S. workers.

To find this out, the employer must electronically submit a DOL Form ETA-9141, called a prevailing wage request (PWR), to the U.S. Department of Labor through its iCert Web portal at http://icert.doleta.gov. The ETA 9141 will include a job description, description of the qualifications required for the job, dates of the employer's temporary need, and your work schedule.

The DOL's response—called a Prevailing Wage Determination (PWD)—will tell the employer how much is normally paid to people in jobs equivalent to the one you've been offered. Finding out the prevailing wage is important, because your employer must offer at least this amount in the temporary labor certification. Even if your employer is offering a wage the DOL

would find appropriate, a temporary labor certification application can be denied if the DOL learns that no PWD was issued.

TIP

A new, preliminary step may soon be added to the H-2B application process. USCIS has announced that it will require employers to file a request for H-2B registration with the Chicago NPC. As of the date this book was published, however, this rule had not yet come into effect. The request will need to be filed between 120 and 150 days before the employer wants the employee to start work, except in emergency situations. To be registered, the employer must establish that its need for nonagricultural services or labor is truly temporary. Registrations will be good for three years.

E. Step Two: Your Employer Places a Job Order

As part of its job-advertising duties, your U.S. employer must send a "job order" to a "State Workforce Agency" (SWA). A job order is an advertisement containing certain required information about the job's duties and compensation, and the necessary skills, training, or experience needed to do the job. An SWA is the government agency within each state in charge of employment. All SWAs publish advertisements for jobs open to the public (job orders).

There is no USCIS or DOL form to submit a job order. Each SWA has its own way of collecting job orders. Your employer will send the job order information to the SWA serving the job location, and will let the SWA know that it's being sent in connection with an H-2B application. This must be done between 75 and 90 days before the job is supposed to start, unless the employer has an emergency need for workers (see Section F1, below).

A copy of the job order must be sent to the DOL with the application for temporary labor certification (step three, below). If the DOL accepts the job order, the SWA will add it to its "job bank" for the public to access. In addition, DOL will add the job to its Electronic Job Registry. The SWA and DOL keep the job order active until 21 days before the job is supposed to start.

1. Handling Applications From U.S. Workers

If your employer receives applications from any U.S. workers and there is any possibility the applicants are qualified, the employer must interview the applicants as soon as possible. If an application clearly establishes that the applicant is unqualified, the employer is not required to interview the applicant.

After the interviews, if the employer is unsatisfied and still wishes to employ you, the employer must prepare a report stating why the U.S. job candidates were not suitable. Once an interview has been held, the employer is no longer limited to rejecting candidates only because they do not meet the job description as stated in the ad. Poor work habits, lack of job stability, questionable character, and similar business considerations, if legitimate, are also satisfactory reasons. In addition, it sometimes comes out in an interview that the prospective worker's qualifications are not what they appeared to be on the résumé. This provides still another reason to turn down the U.S. candidate.

The DOL does not consider the fact that you may be more qualified than any other candidate to be a valid reason for rejecting a U.S. worker. Being the most qualified is not enough. You must be the only one who is qualified. The employer cannot be forced to hire a U.S. worker who happens to apply for the job as a result of the required advertising, but if a qualified U.S. worker does turn up and your prospective employer cannot find a solid business reason to reject him or her, the temporary labor certification application filed on your behalf will fail.

If, however, any qualified U.S. workers apply for the job opportunity, the employer must promptly offer them employment for your labor certification to be approved. If the labor certification is for multiple workers, it may be partially certified for the number of alien workers requested minus the number of U.S. workers that accepted offers of employment.

2. Recruitment Report

The last step in the recruitment process—after all other recruitment steps have been completed—is for your employer to prepare "results of recruitment." This consists of a list of all the applicants for the position, including their contact information. It must also include the name of each recruitment activity (such as the name of the newspaper in which the ads appeared) or source. For each applicant, the employer must explain why the applicant was not hired. If the employer could not reach an applicant, then it needs to have sent the applicant a letter by certified mail asking him or her to contact the employer for an interview, and must include copies of those certified letters in the results of recruitment as well.

The initial recruitment report must be submitted to the DOL by the date specified in the Notice of Acceptance. The employer is required to continue to update the recruitment report if necessary (such as if more applications arrive). At the end of the recruitment period, the employer must prepare and sign a final recruitment report reflecting the activities and results of the full recruitment period.

3. The Employer's Obligation to Retain Documents

Employers are required to retain all recruitment documentation and documentation establishing their temporary need for three years, including résumés or applications of U.S. workers and job offers or reasons for rejecting any unqualified U.S. workers.

DOL may audit the employer and request all recruitment documentation and documentation establishing temporary need such as payroll records with the number of hours worked and wages paid for each worker in the occupation, name of each worker in the occupation, documentation of whether each worker is permanent or temporary, and documentation of whether each worker is a U.S. worker or foreign worker.

F. Step Three: Your Employer Applies for Temporary Labor Certification

At the same your employer submits its job order to the SWA, it must send an application for temporary labor certification to the DOL on ETA Form 9142B.

 CAUTION
H-2B visas run out by the end of the year. Only 66,000 H-2B visas are available annually; 33,000 on October 1 and 33,000 on April 1. (They split the total visa allocation into two pools to be sure that some visas are available for winter seasons and some for summer seasons.) The visas for both pools may be used up very quickly, so it's best to try to file your case as early as possible.

1. Filling Out and Assembling the Temporary Labor Certification Application

Although most of ETA Form 9142B is fairly straightforward, a few of the questions require extra attention.

In Section F, the employer is asked to describe the job being offered. This question should be answered with as much detail as possible. Daily duties, typical projects, supervisory responsibilities, the kinds and use of any machinery or equipment, and foreign language skills needed should all be thoroughly explained. If there are special job conditions, such as the requirement to live in the employer's home, or unusual physical demands, these too must be described. The employer should not fail to put down any activity the job requires, no matter how obvious it may seem. It is possible to use a detailed job description to eliminate U.S. candidates if the candidates are unable to perform the job as described.

While the employer should do its best to describe the position and its demands fully, the employer should not invent aspects of the job that don't exist or seem excessive for the industry. For example, suppose the job opening is for a trainer of bakery managers, but in the job description the employer states that all applicants must have a background in nuclear science. This sort of illogical requirement makes it clear to the reviewer that the job description is not legitimate, but deliberately made up to discourage U.S. workers from applying.

When the job description lacks real-world credibility, the ETA 9142B will be rejected or sent back and the employer will be asked to justify the more unusual demands. If the reviewer cannot be convinced that the job description reflects the employer's true needs, the temporary labor certification will be denied.

The employer should also guard against describing the job in a way that seems more appropriate for two separate workers instead of one. For example, if the job is that of summer resort restaurant manager and the job description requires the applicant not only to manage the restaurant but to do the cooking as well, the reviewer might decide the combination of duties discourages U.S. workers because managers may not want to cook and cooks may not want to manage. Once again, this will result in denial of the temporary labor certifications.

Section B Questions 5 and 6 ask for the exact dates of the employer's temporary need for you to work in the United States. H-2B status will not be approved for more than nine months at a time. The petition will be approved only through the dates requested on the temporary labor certification. Remember, the dates you ask for are the dates you will get, so the employer should get a prevailing wage determination, and file the ETA 9142 as soon as possible before needing you, to allow some lead time for visa processing.

Temporary Labor Certification Checklist

☐ Form ETA 9142B.

☐ A copy of the job order sent to the SWA.

☐ Copy of signed and dated Appendix B to ETA Form 9142B (containing certifications by the employer).

☐ If the prevailing wage determination (PWD) case number was not entered into section G.3 of the Form 9142B, a copy of the valid ETA Form 9141 containing the PWD.

☐ If there wasn't enough room for it in section B.9 of the 9142B, a statement of temporary need (by the job contractor and employer if a job contractor is filing).

☐ If the employer is using special procedures applicable to entertainers, tree planters, and so forth, other documentation required under those special procedures (such as itineraries).

☐ If applicable, copy of the MSPA Farm Labor Contractor Certificate for the employer and/or agent.

☐ If applicable, copy of agent agreement demonstrating authority to represent employer or job contractor.

☐ Copies of all agreements that the employer and, if applicable, attorney or agent have with any agent or recruiter with whom it engages or plans to engage in international recruitment.

☐ Document containing the identity and location of all persons and entities hired by or working for the foreign labor recruiter or agent, and any of the agents or employees of those persons and entities, to recruit prospective foreign workers.

☐ For emergency filings, a statement of good cause, and if there wasn't time to get a PWD, an original ETA 9141.

Section Fb asks for the minimum experience and education the job requires. The answer to this question should describe the demands of the job, not the personal qualifications of the potential H-2B visa recipient. For example, you may have a degree from a technical school representing two years of automotive mechanic's training, but if the position you have been offered is for a live-in housekeeper for the summer, being an automotive mechanic usually has nothing to do with being a housekeeper and therefore should not be mentioned in the answer to this question. It is the job offer that the employer must describe, not you.

When counting up how many years of relevant experience you have to offer, you may not include experience gained from working for your petitioning employer. You must be prepared to prove that you met the minimum experience and education requirements as stated in Section Fb of the ETA 9142B before you started working for the petitioner, even if you have been employed there for some time.

As with salary levels, the DOL also has specific guidelines on what the minimum number of years of experience and education should be for a certain kind of job. The state employment agency office can tell your employer exactly the number of years of education and experience it considers a normal minimum for the particular job you have been offered. This number comes from a Web-based database

Foreign Language Requirements

According to the DOL, foreign language capability is not a valid requirement for most jobs, except perhaps the occupations of foreign language teacher or translator. By foreign language capability, we mean the ability to speak English plus at least one other language. Many temporary labor certification job descriptions contain a foreign language requirement because petitioning employers know it is a good way to decrease the chances that qualified U.S. workers will apply for the job.

If your employer wants a foreign language capability in the job description, the employer must prove this need is real by preparing and submitting a signed statement explaining the business reasons why. The statement does not have to be in any particular form but it should answer obvious questions like: What is it about the employer's business that makes knowledge of a foreign language necessary? Why does this position require knowledge of a foreign language if someone else in the company already speaks that language? Why couldn't the company simply hire a translator as a separate employee or use a translator on a part-time basis when the need arises? The employer must show that the need for the employee to speak a foreign language is very great and that no alternative arrangement will be an adequate substitute.

A good example of how to approach this problem is an employer who owns a restaurant in a resort and is trying to justify a foreign language requirement for a seasonal waiter. Here, the employer can explain that a large percentage of the restaurant's customers speak the particular foreign language in question and expect to be addressed in that language when they come in to eat. If the restaurant's clientele demand it, it is reasonable that all employees of this restaurant who have contact with the public be able to speak the language of the customers.

The DOL doesn't like foreign language requirements, because it is well aware that most people who apply for temporary labor certification have the ability to speak a language other than English. The DOL regards this as a poor excuse to keep a U.S. worker from taking a job. Therefore, it is usually best not to include a language requirement, especially if the temporary labor certification is likely to be approved anyway. If, however, the occupation being certified is relatively unskilled, as in the case of the seasonal waiter, a language requirement supported by strong documents showing a real business need may mean the difference between success and failure of the temporary labor certification.

called O*NET (www.onetonline.org). The number of years of experience and education it lists for each job is the total allowable years of both experience and education.

Suppose the employer genuinely feels the company needs a person with more total years of education and experience than the O*NET database indicates. Then a letter from the employer should be submitted with the ETA 9142B form, giving the reason additional years of background are justified. The DOL will normally respect the employer's judgment if it seems reasonable. This letter does not have to be in any special form. A simple explanation in your employer's own words will do.

When a certain number of months appears in the box after question 4a of Section 4b, the employer is also asked to specify, in question 4b, which occupation it wants the experience to be in. If the experience is required in another relevant field, this requirement should be stated in the box after question 5, "Special Requirements." That box also should contain any special knowledge or skills required, such as foreign language ability, familiarity with certain types of machinery, or special physical capabilities (the strength to do heavy lifting, for example). Later, you will have to prove in some way that you can perform the job duties listed in Section Fa, but you will not have to show an exact number of years of education or on-the-job experience as you will for the qualifications listed in Section Fb.

Part H of the form is now left blank, because recruitment happens after the form is filed.

Your employer must submit the ETA 9142B via the iCert portal (preferably) or by mail to the national processing center of the DOL (in Chicago) for a decision. Several documents must accompany the Form 9142B. We've provided a checklist above.

2. The Temporary Labor Certification Decision

Within seven business days from when the employer's application for temporary labor certification is received by the Chicago NPC, a notice will be sent to the employer. If the certifying officer (CO) reviewing the application determines that the application or job order is incomplete, contains errors or inaccuracies, or does not meet the relevant regulatory requirements, the CO will issue a Notice of Deficiency. This notice will set forth all reasons why the application failed to meet the acceptance criteria, and will give the employer ten business days to submit the required modifications or to request administrative review.

If, on the other hand, the application meets the criteria, the CO will issue a Notice of Acceptance. This notice will include instructions for the employer related to the recruitment of U.S. workers, the submission of the required recruitment report (see Step Four below), and any other actions required for approval and certification of the employer's H-2B application.

If the DOL thinks the temporary labor certification is unsatisfactory, it will deny it and send the employer a written decision explaining the reasons. The most common reason for denial is that the job is not temporary in nature. A denial may be appealed to the DOL's Board of Alien Labor Certification Appeals (BALCA). To succeed on appeal, the employer will have to convince BALCA that the national processing center was wrong.

G. Step Four: Your Employer Conducts Recruitment

Your employer will have to satisfy the U.S. government that the wage offered to you does not undercut the wages of similarly employed U.S. workers and that there are no qualified U.S. workers available to take the job you've been offered.

The government requires your employer to recruit U.S. workers for your job before it hires you, to see whether there are any takers. The job order is just one part of that recruitment. Your employer also must:

- Place a print advertisement (containing specified information) on two separate days, one of which must be a Sunday (unless no Sunday edition exists), in a newspaper of general circulation serving the area of intended employment and appropriate to the occupation and workers likely to apply for the job opportunity.

- Contact former U.S. employees employed in the occupation and at the place of employment during the previous year, including workers laid off within 120 days before the date of need (except those U.S. workers dismissed for cause or who abandoned the worksite), to inform them of the job opportunity and ask whether they are interested in returning.

- Provide a copy of the application for temporary employment certification and the job order to the bargaining representative, where workers are unionized.

- If there is no union or bargaining representative, then (1) post the job opportunity in at least two conspicuous locations for at least 15 consecutive business days at the place(s) of anticipated employment, or (2) post the notice by a means that provides reasonable notification to all employees in the occupation and area of intended employment, such as the company's intranet.

- Conduct any additional recruitment activities as directed by the CO.

Recruitment begins only after an employer's application for temporary employment certification is accepted for processing by the certifying officer and a Notice of Acceptance (NOA) is issued.

The employer must conduct recruitment for 14 calendar days after the NOA is issued. If the job opportunity must be posted, however, it must stay posted for a minimum of 15 business days. Also, you're not safe until 21 days before your job is supposed to start. Until then, the employer must consider all U.S. applicants, and must offer employment to each U.S. worker who is qualified and who will be available to do the job.

H. Step Five: The DOL Certifies the Temporary Labor Application

After the employer submits its recruitment report and if the application for temporary labor certification meets all regulatory requirements and criteria for certification, the certifying officer will approve the application. The employer will receive an original certified ETA Form 9142B and a Final Determination letter.

I. Step Six: Your Employer Submits an H-2B Visa Petition

After receiving a decision on the temporary labor certification, your employer can shift focus to filing a visa petition with USCIS, on Form I-129. The object of the petition is to prove all of the following:

- The job is temporary or seasonal in nature.

- No qualified U.S. workers are available for the job.
- You have the correct background, skills, and abilities to match the job requirements.
- Your U.S. employer has the financial ability to pay your salary.

Like the temporary labor certification, an approved petition does not by itself give you any immigration privileges (unless it is for an extension of your stay). It is only a prerequisite to the next step, submitting your application for a nonimmigrant visa.

The employer may request approval for unnamed workers if they are outside the United States. However, any workers within the U.S. must be named on the petition. The employer must specify the countries of citizenship of the H-2B workers it plans to hire, whether the workers are named or not, in the H Classification Supplement to Form I-129, Section 2, Question 4. The countries must be participating countries or the employer must request an exception, providing the evidence required by questions 5.a through 6.b.

1. Simultaneous Change of Status If You're Already in the U.S.

If you're already in the U.S. in lawful status, such as on a student or other temporary visa, the I-129 petition can be used to request that the USCIS immediately change your status to H-2B worker. (Part 2,

Question 4, of Form I-129 offers choices addressing this issue.) However, you can't take advantage of this option if you entered the U.S. on a visa waiver, or if you entered using a C (alien in transit), TWOV (alien in transit without a visa), D (crewman), K-1 (fiancé), K-2 (dependent of a fiancé), J-1 (exchange visitor), or M-1 (vocational student) visa. You must have:

- entered the U.S. legally
- never worked in U.S. illegally, and
- not passed the expiration date on your I-94.

There is another problem that comes up only in U.S. filings. It is the issue of what is called "preconceived intent." To approve a change of status, USCIS must believe that at the time you originally entered the U.S. as a visitor or with some other nonimmigrant visa, you did not intend to apply for a different status. If USCIS thinks you had a preconceived plan to use one visa to enter the U.S. with an eye to applying for a different status after getting there, it may deny your application. (You can get around the preconceived intent issue by leaving the U.S. and applying for your H-2B visa at a U.S. consulate in another country.)

Your spouse and children, if they are also in the U.S. with you, can't change their status by being mentioned on your Form I-129, but must submit separate Forms I-539. They can submit these either at the same time as your employer submits Form I-129, or afterward. (If

they submit them afterward, however, they will need to include either a copy of the USCIS receipt notice indicating that your petition is pending, or a copy of the petition approval notice.)

> **TIP**
>
> **Your eligibility to apply in the U.S. has nothing to do with overall eligibility for an H-2B visa.** Many applicants who are barred from filing in the U.S. but otherwise qualify for H-2B status may still apply successfully for an H-2B visa at a U.S. consulate in another country.

If you apply for a change of status within the U.S., you will receive only H-2B status, not the H-2B visa. The H-2B visa is a physical stamp in your passport that you will need if you ever want to re-enter the United States. Visas are never given inside the United States. They are issued exclusively by U.S. consulates in other countries. If you file in the U.S. and you are successful, you may remain in the U.S. with H-2B privileges until the status expires. But should you leave the country for any reason before that time, you will have to apply for the visa itself at a U.S. consulate before returning to the United States—unless, that is, you are traveling to Mexico or Canada for fewer than 30 days. In that case, you may apply for readmission to the United States with your unexpired I-94. Nationals of countries that are on the U.S. Department of State list of state sponsors of terrorism and aliens who apply for

H-2B Visa Petition Checklist

☐ Form I-129 and H Supplement.

☐ Filing fee (currently $460).

☐ Antifraud fee (currently $500).

☐ Form I-907, with $1,225 filing fee if requesting quick ("premium") processing.

☐ Original, temporary labor certification form, certified ETA 9142B.

☐ Signed copy of Appendix B to ETA Form 9142B.

☐ If you'll be applying in the U.S. and your family members are with you and need a change of status, Form I-539 with accompanying fee (currently $290) and copies of your family members' I-94 or other proof of lawful immigration status and of their relationship to you (marriage, birth certificates). One Form I-539 and fee will cover your spouse and all your unmarried children under 21. Your family members should fill out and sign this form, not your employer.

☐ If you're in the U.S., a copy of your I-94 or other proof of your current lawful, unexpired immigration status. (Canadian visitors usually won't have an I-94.)

☐ A photocopy of the biographic information page of your passport and that of any family members traveling with you, showing the date of issuance and date of expiration.

☐ If you're in the U.S., it's wise to supply evidence of your ties to your home country, strong enough to motivate your eventual return. Include any deeds verifying ownership of a house or other real property, written statements from you explaining that close relatives are staying behind, or a letter from a company in your home country showing that you have a job waiting when you return from the United States together with an explanation of why the foreign employer is willing to keep the position open for you.

☐ Copy of documents submitted in connection with the temporary labor certification application.

☐ Detailed written statement from the employer explaining why the position is temporary or seasonal. If the need is seasonal or intermittent, the statement should explain whether it is expected to occur again. If the job is temporary because it's tied to a specific project of the employer and will end upon its completion, attach a copy of the employer's contract for that project.

☐ Proof that you have the minimum education and experience called for in the advertisements and job description. If special requirements were added, you must prove you have those skills or abilities as well.

☐ If your employer asked for a specific type or amount of education, all your diplomas and transcripts. If you were educated outside the U.S., USCIS may request a credential evaluation.

☐ Proof of employer's ability to pay your salary, such as annual report, tax returns, and accounting statements.

☐ If your job is as an entertainer touring the U.S., a copy of the touring route schedule, including cities and dates of performance.

Academic Credential Evaluations

Not every country in the world operates on the same academic degree and grade level systems found in the United States. If you were educated in some other country, USCIS may ask for an academic credential evaluation from an approved consulting service to determine the U.S. equivalent of your educational level.

Evaluations from accredited credential evaluation services are not binding on USCIS. When the results are favorable (showing you have the equivalent of the educational level required by your U.S. employer) the evaluation strengthens your case.

We recommend obtaining a credential evaluation in every case where non-U.S. education is a factor. We also advise getting the evaluation before USCIS asks for it. If it's favorable, include it with your petition. If not, and your credentials are less than what your employer has asked for, do not submit the results unless USCIS insists. Discuss this with your employer, who may ask for less education in the job description. Also note that if the credential evaluation shows that you have the educational equivalent of a U.S. university bachelor's degree or more, you may be eligible for an H-1B visa and should consider applying for that instead. (See Chapter 16.)

Before sending an evaluation service your academic documents, you might call ahead to discuss your prospects. If your prospects are truly bleak, you may decide not to order the evaluation and save the service charge (typically upwards of $100).

Several qualified credential evaluation services are recognized by USCIS, among them International Education Research Foundation, www.ierf.org, and Educational Credential Evaluators, Inc., www.ece.org.

Credential evaluation companies will evaluate only formal education, usually not job experience. Some U.S. universities offer evaluations of foreign academic credentials and will recognize work experience as having an academic equivalent. Therefore, if you lack formal education but can show many years of experience, you are better off trying to get an evaluation from a U.S. college or university. When sending your credentials to a U.S. university, include documents showing your complete academic background, as well as all relevant career achievements. Letters of recommendation from former employers are good proof of work experience. Also submit evidence of any special accomplishments, such as awards or published articles. USCIS can be influenced, but is not bound by, academic evaluations from U.S. colleges and universities.

visas in Mexico, Canada, or adjacent islands are ineligible for automatic visa revalidation. Countries on the list of state-sponsored terrorism as of August 2016 were Iran, Sudan, and Syria. Moreover, the fact that your H-2B status has been approved in the U.S. does not guarantee that the consulate will also approve your visa. Therefore, if you have a choice of whether to file a change of status in the U.S. or apply through a U.S. consulate in your home country, you'll have to decide which is better for you, balancing the convenience of staying in the U.S. now versus the certainty of being allowed to return if you leave the United States before your H-2B status has expired.

2. Assembling the Visa Petition

The checklist below will help you and your employer assemble the necessary items for the visa petition.

A couple of items on this checklist require some extra explanation.

Form I-129 and H Supplement. The basic form for the visa petition is immigration Form I-129 and its H Supplement. The Form I-129 is used for many different non-immigrant visas. In addition to the basic part of the form that applies to all types of visas, it comes with several supplements for each specific nonimmigrant category. Simply use the supplement that applies to you—the H Supplement.

The employer may choose to list more than one foreign employee on a single I-129 petition. This is done if the employer has more than one opening to be filled for the same type of job. If more than one employee is to be included, Attachment-1, which is also part of Form I-129, should be completed for each additional employee.

Proof of your job qualifications. Evidence of your job experience should include letters or notarized affidavits from previous employers. These do not have to be in any special form but simply in your former employer's own words. The letters should clearly indicate what your position was with the company, your specific job duties, and the length of time you were employed. If letters from previous employers are unavailable, you may be able to prove your work experience with your personal tax returns or by affidavits from former coworkers. Proof of special knowledge or skills can be supplied through notarized affidavits, either from you or someone else who can swear you have the special ability (such as skill to use a particular machine or speak a foreign language) required. These, too, need not be in any special form.

3. Mailing the Visa Petition

After assembling the visa petition, your U.S. employer must mail it to the regional service center that has jurisdiction over the employer's place of business. Addresses are at www.uscis.gov/i-129. If you'll be coming from outside the U.S., your employer must send duplicate versions of the form.

H-2B Visa Application Checklist

☐ Form DS-160, Nonimmigrant Visa Application (an online form, which can be completed only at https://ceac.state. gov/genniv).

☐ Original I-797 notice showing approval of the H-2B petition, if available.

☐ Valid passport for you and each accompanying relative.

☐ If requested by the consulate or if you were unable to upload one with your DS-160 application, one U.S. passport-type photo of you and one of each accompanying relative. (This is best taken by a professional photographer; the consulate can give you a list.)

☐ If your spouse and children will be accompanying you, original documents verifying their family relationship to you, such as marriage and birth certificates.

☐ Original documents showing that you meet the qualifications for the job, including your diploma and experience letters.

☐ Documents establishing your intent to leave the U.S. when your status expires, such as deeds verifying ownership of a house or other real property, written statements from you explaining that close relatives are staying behind, or letters from a company showing that you have a job waiting when you return from the United States, together with an explanation of why the foreign employer is willing to keep the position open for you.

☐ Fee receipt showing that you have paid the relevant machine-readable visa (MRV) application fee (currently $190). The financial institution at which you must pay depends on the country. Check the website of the U.S. consulate where you plan to apply for your visa to learn how to pay the fee. Most consulates will not allow you to pay the visa fee at the time of interview.

☐ Visa reciprocity fee. You may have to pay an additional visa issuance fee if you're from a country that charges similar fees for visas to U.S. citizens who wish to work there.

4. Awaiting a Decision on the Visa Petition

Within a few weeks after mailing in the petition, your employer should get back a written confirmation that the papers are being processed, together with a receipt for the fee. This notice will also contain your immigration file number. If USCIS wants further information before acting on your case, it will send your employer a form known as a Request for Evidence on Form I-797E. Your employer should supply the extra data requested and mail it back to the service center.

As of June 2016, USCIS was making decisions on H-2B applications in about one month. If the decision is favorable, a Form I-797 Notice of Action will be sent to your employer, showing the petition was approved. If you plan to submit your visa application at a U.S. consulate abroad,

Applying at a Consulate That's Not in Your Home Country

The law allows most people to apply for an H-2B visa at any U.S. consulate they choose—with one exception. If you have ever been present in the U.S. unlawfully, your visa will be automatically cancelled and you cannot apply as a third-country national (at a consulate outside your home country). Even if you overstayed your status in the U.S. by just one day, you must return to your home country and apply for the visa from that consulate. There is an exception. If you were admitted to the U.S. for the duration of your status (indicated by a "D/S" on your I-94—common with student visas) and you remained in the U.S. beyond that time for which your status was conferred, you will be barred from third-country national processing only if an immigration judge or USCIS (or, formerly INS) officer has determined that you were unlawfully present. You may find that your success in applying as a third-country national will depend on your country, the consulate, and the relative seriousness of your offense. Being unlawfully present is also a ground of inadmissibility if the period of unlawful presence is 180 days or more. (See Chapter 3.)

Even if you are eligible for third-country national processing, your case will be given the greatest consideration at the consulate in your home country. Applying in some other country creates suspicion in the minds of the consular officers there about your motives for choosing their consulate. Often, when an applicant expects trouble at a home consulate, he or she will seek a more lenient consular office in some other country. This practice of consulate shopping is frowned upon by officials in the system. Unless you have a very good reason for being elsewhere (such as a temporary job assignment in some other nation), it is often smarter to file your visa application in your home country.

USCIS will also notify the Kentucky Consular Center (KCC), which will electronically notify the U.S. consulate in your home country and send your file there. Only the employer receives communications from USCIS about the petition, because it is the employer who is seeking the visa on your behalf.

TIP

Faster processing—at a price. For $1,225 over and above the regular filing fees, USCIS promises premium processing of the visa petition, including action on the case within 15 days. To use this service, the employer must fill out an additional application (Form I-907) and submit the application to a special USCIS service center address. For complete instructions, see the USCIS website at www.uscis.gov/i-907.

Be aware that an approved petition does not, if you are overseas, give you any immigration privileges. It is only a prerequisite to the next step, submitting your application for an H-2B visa.

J. Step Seven: Applicants Outside the U.S. Apply to a U.S. Consulate

After the H-2B visa petition filed by your employer has been approved, the appropriate U.S. consulate will be notified electronically by the KCC, as mentioned above. Check with your local U.S. consulate regarding its application procedures. Many insist on advance appointments. Just getting an appointment can take several weeks, so plan ahead.

> **TIP**
> **If you're visa exempt, you may be able to skip this step.** Citizens of Canada and Bermuda need not apply to a U.S. consulate. Instead, they can proceed directly to the U.S. with Form I-797B and supporting documents to request entry. (See 8 C.F.R. § 212.1.)

> **CAUTION**
> **Have you been, or are you now, working or living illegally in the United States?** If so, see Chapter 3 regarding whether you can still get an H-2B visa from a U.S. consulate. You may have become inadmissible or subject to a three-year or ten-year bar on reentry.

The checklist above will help you prepare your consular application. You'll need to go online to submit the main form for this process, the Nonimmigrant Visa Application (Form DS-160). You can submit your photos digitally at the same time. For instructions, see the State Department website at https://ceac.state.gov/genniv.

As part of your application, the consulate will require you (and your family members if they are coming to the U.S. with you) to attend an interview. During the interview, a consular officer will examine the data in your application for accuracy, especially regarding facts about your own qualifications. Evidence of ties to your home country will also be checked. During the interview, you will surely be asked how long you intend to remain in the United States. Any answer indicating that you are unsure about plans to return or have an interest in applying for a green card is likely to result in a denial of your H-2B visa.

> **RELATED TOPIC**
> **See Chapter 4 for what else to expect during consular interviews, and what to do if your application is denied.**

K. Step Eight: You Enter the U.S. With Your H-2B Visa

You have until the expiration date on your H-2B visa to enter the United States. The border officer will examine your paperwork, ask you some questions, and if all is in order, approve you for entry. He or she will stamp your passport, and your I-94 shows how long you can stay. You are permitted to remain in the U.S. for ten days after the expiration date on your H-2B approval notice. (However, if your passport will expire before the petition's expiration date, some CBP officers will issue the I-94 until only the date of the passport expiration.) Each time you exit and reenter the U.S., you will get a new I-94 authorizing your stay up to the final date indicated on the petition or for the validity period of the approved petition plus ten days.

L. Extending Your U.S. Stay

H-2B visas may be extended for up to a total of three years. Extensions are not automatic, nor are they easier to get than the original visa. Extensions are more difficult to obtain if you are attempting to stay at the same job, because DOL is less likely to believe that the job is truly temporary. It is easier to extend H-2B status by switching to a new employer whose need for your services begins when your prior job concludes. For example, you could work a winter/spring season with a ski resort and then change employers and extend your status by starting work with a company that needs summer workers, such as lifeguards. If you depart the United

States for three months, you are eligible for another three years of H-2B status.

To extend your H-2B visa, the temporary labor certification, petition, and visa stamp will all have to be updated. As with the original application, you can file either at USCIS in the U.S. or at a U.S. consulate abroad.

1. Step One: Temporary Labor Certification

The process for getting an extension of the temporary labor certification is identical in every respect with the one used to obtain the original temporary labor certification.

2. Step Two: Extension Petition

Petition extension procedures are nearly identical to the procedures followed in getting the initial visa petition approval. Fully document your application so that your case is not delayed if USCIS cannot locate your previous file. Submit the new Temporary Labor Certification and the Notice of Action indicating the approval that your employer received on the original petition. All your personal U.S. income tax returns and W-2 forms for the time period you have already been working in the U.S. on an H-2B visa are required as well. Once USCIS has these documents, it will notify the employer if any further data are needed.

Working While Your Extension Petition Is Pending

In the unlikely event that your employer files a petition to extend your H-2B status for the same job, you are automatically permitted to continue working for up to 240 days while you are waiting for a decision. However, since the H-2B category is temporary and is based on an established temporary period of need, it is very unlikely that the employment will qualify for the automatic 240-day extension of work authorization. An extension would, after all, require the employer to establish that its period of need has changed, yet is still temporary and still meets all the H-2B requirements such as not exceeding nine months. If your authorized stay expires after you have filed for an extension but before you receive an approval, and more than 240 days go by without getting a decision on your extension petition for the same job opportunity with the same employer, your work authorization ceases and you must stop working.

3. Step Three: Visa Revalidation

If you must leave the U.S. after your extension has been approved, you must get a new visa stamp issued at a consulate in order to return. The exception is if you are traveling to Mexico or Canada for fewer than 30 days. In that case, you may apply for readmission to the United States with your unexpired I-94 document. Bring along all the documents you supplied for your U.S. extension.

Watch Out for Expedited Removal

The law empowers a Customs and Border Protection (CBP) inspector at the U.S. airport or border to summarily (without allowing judicial review) bar entry to someone requesting admission to the U.S. if either of the following is true:

- The inspector thinks you are lying about practically anything connected with entering the U.S., including your purpose in coming, intent to return, and prior immigration history. This includes the use or suspected use of false documents.
- You do not have the proper documentation to support your entry to the U.S. in the category you are requesting.

If the inspector excludes you, you cannot be readmitted to the U.S. for five years, unless USCIS grants a special waiver. For this reason it is extremely important to understand the terms of your requested status, and to not make any misrepresentations. If you are found to be inadmissible, you may ask the CBP inspector to withdraw your application to enter the U.S. in order to prevent having the five-year deportation order on your record. The CBP may allow this in some exceptional cases.

Getting a Temporary Trainee (H-3) Visa

The H-3 visa is useful for a limited group of people—those who have been invited to participate in a training program in the United States. The training may be offered by a U.S. branch of their own company or by an unrelated U.S. company. However, the training must be unavailable in the worker's home country. There are no limits on the number of people who can be granted H-3 visas each year.

The USCIS regulations recognize some specific types of trainees as potentially H-3 eligible. These include medical interns or residents who are attending a medical school abroad, if the student will engage in employment as an extern during his or her medical school vacation, and licensed nurses who need a brief period of training that is unavailable in their native country. (See 8 C.F.R § 214.2(h)(7).) The H-3 is not, however, available to physicians wanting to receive graduate medical education or training.

The H-3 visa can also be used by 50 special education exchange visitors per year—that is, people coming to the U.S. for a special education training program educating children who have physical, emotional, or mental disabilities. (See 8 C.F.R. § 214.2(h)(7)(iv).) The requirements for this group are slightly different than for other trainees.

SEE AN EXPERT

Do you need a lawyer? You can't apply for an H-3 visa without having an employer first—and it's in your employer's interest to hire a lawyer to help. A lawyer can help make sure that your application gets done right the first time (including by writing a complete cover letter explaining why you qualify) and gets decided on before the training program begins.

A. Do You Qualify for an H-3 Visa?

You qualify for an H-3 visa if you are coming to the U.S. for on-the-job training to be provided by a U.S. company. Productive employment in the U.S. can be only a minor part of the total program. The purpose of the training should be to further your career in your home country. Similar training opportunities must be unavailable there.

CAUTION

Very few training programs meet USCIS's strict rules. In fact, it's often cheaper and easier to apply for a B-1 business visitor visa, especially if the training program lasts for less than six months (the maximum stay on a B-1 visa). Even if you do qualify, you should explore the quicker, less expensive, and more convenient option of the B-1 visa. Some consulates will approve a so-called "B-1 in lieu of H-3" visa (and mark the visa as such) if you clearly qualify for H-3 and you're clearly an employee of a non-U.S. company. See Chapter 15 for how to get a B-1 visa.

Key Features of the H-3 Visa

Here are some of the advantages and disadvantages of the H-3 visa:

- You can participate in a training program offered by a U.S. company and work legally in the U.S. for the company that is training you, so long as that work is incidental to the training program.
- You are restricted to working only for the employer who admitted you to the training program and acted as sponsor for your H-3 visa.
- Your visa can be approved for the length of time needed to complete the training program, although no more than two years are normally permitted. Extensions of one year at a time may be allowed, but only if the original training has not yet been completed, and only within the overall two-year maximum.
- The visa doesn't allow any grace period for travel, so ideally the trainer should build this time into the program description.
- You and your family can travel in and out of the U.S. or remain in the U.S. continuously while your H-3 visa is valid.
- Visas are available for your accompanying spouse and minor children (unmarried and under age 21).
- Your spouse and children may not accept employment in the United States. Children are expected to attend school, and adults can attend school part time under the terms of the H-4 visa.
- If you stay in H-3 status for the full two years (or 18 months if you're participating in a special education program), then you cannot get any more time in H or L visa status until you have been outside the U.S. for six months. Other changes of status are allowed, but must be requested before your H-3 visa has expired.

You must also possess the necessary background and experience to complete the U.S. training program successfully. Obviously, however, this should be the first time you'll receive this particular type of training. And, as with many nonimmigrant visas, you are eligible for an H-3 visa only if you intend to return to your home country when the visa expires.

Training programs supporting H-3 visas exist most often in two situations. A multinational company with branches in various countries might train employees in its U.S. branches before sending them to work elsewhere. Or, a U.S. company may wish to establish a beneficial business relationship with a foreign company. A good way to do this is by bringing in some of the foreign company's personnel and teaching them about the U.S. business. These people then develop personal ties with the U.S. company.

1. Your Invitation to a Training Program

You need a specific offer to participate in a job training program from a U.S. company or U.S. government agency. The job training slot you are invited to fill can't be in just any occupation. It must be one that will further your career abroad. Many types of occupations qualify, however. For example, you could be coming for training in agriculture, commerce, communications, finance, government, industry, or virtually any other field. (However, physicians are ineligible to use this category.)

The training program must be formal in structure with a curriculum, books, and study materials. (We'll discuss how to prove this further along in this chapter.)

2. Training Is Unavailable in Your Home Country

One of the more difficult requirements for getting an H-3 visa is that the training you will receive in the U.S. must be unavailable to you in your home country. This does not mean that the training cannot exist there, but only that you, personally, do not have access to it.

3. Any Productive Employment Is Incidental

Although you can work in the U.S. while on your H-3 visa, the employment must be merely incidental and necessary to the training activities. If the employment aspect takes up so much time that the company could justify hiring a full-time U.S. worker to perform these duties, your H-3 visa will be denied. As a rule, any productive employment must have a training aspect. You will not qualify for an H-3 visa if this is not clear.

4. You Have the Correct Background

You must have the correct background for the training position you are offered. For example, for a training position as an intern with a U.S. law firm, intended to further your career as an international lawyer, you would have to show that you have a law degree.

5. You Intend to Return to Your Home Country

H-3 visas are meant to be temporary. At the time of applying, you must intend to return home when the visa expires. If you have it in mind to take up permanent residence in the U.S., you are ineligible for an H-3 visa. The U.S. government knows it is difficult to read minds. Expect to be asked for evidence showing that when you complete your training, you will go back home and use it there.

If you are training for work that doesn't exist in your home country, you'll have trouble. For example, if you will be in a training program for offshore oil drilling and you come from a country that is landlocked and has no oil, no one will believe you plan to take the skills learned in the U.S. back home.

You will also be asked for evidence that you are leaving behind possessions, property, or family members as incentives for your eventual return.

6. Bringing Your Relatives

When you qualify for an H-3 visa, your spouse and unmarried children under age 21 can get H-4 visas by providing proof of their family relationship to you. H-4 visas authorize your family members to stay with you in the U.S., but not to work there. They may, however, study at U.S. schools.

B. Quick View of the H-3 Visa Application Process

Once you have been offered a training position by a U.S. company, getting an H-3 visa is a one- to three-step process:

- The U.S. company where you will be trained files what's called a visa

petition on USCIS Form I-129. If you're already in the U.S. in lawful status, this petition can simultaneously ask that your status be changed to H-3 worker, in which case, the process should successfully end here.

- If you're outside the U.S., then after the visa petition is approved, you schedule an interview at a U.S. consulate for visa issuance (unless you're from Canada or Bermuda, in which case you can skip this step).

- You use either your visa or (if you're from Canada or Bermuda) the notice of your approved visa petition to enter the U.S. and claim your H-3 status.

> **TIP**
> **Nothing stops you from helping with the employer's tasks during this application process.** For example, you can fill out forms intended to be completed by your employer and simply ask the employer to check them over and sign them. The less your U.S. employer is inconvenienced, the more likely it will be willing to act as sponsor for your visa.

C. Step One: Your Employer Submits an H-3 Visa Petition

The process starts when your U.S. employer/trainer sends a visa petition to USCIS on Form I-129. The object of the petition is to prove four things, including that:

- A qualifying formal training position has been offered to you by a U.S. company.
- You have the correct background for the training.
- The training is unavailable to you in your home country.
- The training will further your career in your home country.

1. Simultaneous Change of Status If You're Already in the U.S.

If you're already in the U.S. in lawful status, such as on a student or other temporary visa, the petition can be used to ask that your status be immediately changed to H-3 temporary trainee. (Part 2, Question 4, of Form I-129 offers choices addressing this issue.) You can't, however, take advantage of this option if you entered the U.S. on a visa waiver or if you entered using a C (alien in transit), TWOV (alien in transit without a visa), D (crewman), or any K (fiancé) visa. Certain J-1 (exchange visitor) visa holders are prohibited from changing status as well. M-1 (vocational student) visa holders can change to H-3 only if the training received as a vocational student in the U.S. did not provide the

---

Applying for a Green Card From H-3 Status

Being in the U.S. on an H-3 visa gives you no advantage in getting a green card, and, in fact, may prove to be a drawback. That is because H-3 visas, like most nonimmigrant visas, are intended only for those who plan to return home once their training or other activities in the U.S. are completed.

If you apply for a green card, you are in effect making a statement that you never intend to leave the U.S. In fact, if your method of applying for a green card is through employment, as discussed in Chapter 9, you are making it appear that you're really utilizing the H-3 visa to establish a career in the U.S. and so are no longer qualified for H-3 status. Therefore, although you are permitted to apply for the green card, it may create an obstacle to extending your H-3 status.

If you are denied extension of your H-3 status, it will not normally affect your green card application. You will simply risk being without your nonimmigrant visa until you get your green card. However, if you are out of status for either 180 days or 12 months, or you work without authorization, you may not be able to get your green card. Read Chapter 3 regarding inadmissibility and bars to adjustment of status before you overstay 180 days or depart the United States.

If what you really want is a green card, apply for it directly and disregard H-3 visas. Although it may be more difficult to get a green card, which could take several years, in the long run you will be happier with the results—not to mention the fact that you will be obeying the law by not trying to hide your true intentions.

qualifications for participation in the H-3 training program. Also, if you have already been in the U.S. for 18 months under any H or L status, you may not seek a change to H-3 status until you've lived outside the U.S. for six months.

Other than these restrictions, you're allowed to change status if you:

- entered the U.S. legally
- have never worked in the U.S. illegally or otherwise violated the terms of your visa, and
- the expiration date on your I-94 hasn't passed.

There is another problem that comes up only in U.S. filings. It is the issue of what is called "preconceived intent." To approve a change of status, USCIS must believe that at the time you originally entered the U.S. as a visitor or with some other nonimmigrant visa, you did not intend to apply for a different status. If USCIS thinks you had a preconceived plan to use one visa to enter the U.S. with an eye toward applying for a different status after getting here, it may deny your application. (You can get around the preconceived intent issue by leaving the U.S. and applying for your H-3 visa at a U.S. consulate in another country.)

Here's a little insider information. USCIS uses the "30/60 rule" to judge preconceived intent. If you enter the U.S. on one type of visa and within 30 days you seek to change visas or apply for a green

card, then USCIS will presume that you had preconceived intent to violate your visa. If you wait 60 days to change visas or apply for a green card, USCIS may still decide that you had preconceived intent—but not necessarily. If you wait for more than 60 days to try to change your status, then you are less likely to have problems.

Your spouse and children, if they are also in the U.S. with you, can't change their status by being mentioned on your Form I-129, but must submit a separate Form I-539. (If they all share a status, they'll only need to file one Form I-539.) They can submit it either at the same time as your employer submits Form I-129, or afterward. (If they submit it afterward, however, they will need to include either a copy of the USCIS receipt notice indicating that your petition is pending or a copy of the petition approval notice.)

TIP
Your eligibility to apply from within the U.S. has nothing to do with your overall eligibility for an H-3 visa. Many applicants who are barred from filing in the U.S., but otherwise qualify for H-3 status, may still apply successfully for an H-3 visa at a U.S. consulate in another country.

If you decide to apply for a change of status within the U.S., you will receive only H-3 status, not the H-3 visa. The H-3 visa is a physical stamp in your passport that you will need if you ever want to reenter the United States. Visas are never given inside the United States. They are issued exclusively by U.S. consulates in other countries.

If you file in the U.S. and you are successful, you will get to remain in the U.S. with H-3 privileges until the status expires. But should you leave the country for any reason before that time, you will have to apply for the visa itself at a U.S. consulate before returning to the United States. Moreover, the fact that your H-3 status has been approved in the U.S. does not guarantee that the consulate will also approve your visa.

2. Preparing the Visa Petition

The checklist below will help you and your employer assemble the necessary items for the visa petition.

A few items on this checklist require the following explanation.

Form I-129 and H Supplement. The basic form for the visa petition is immigration Form I-129 and its H Supplement. The I-129 form is used for many different nonimmigrant visas. In addition to the basic part of the form that applies to all types of visas, it comes with several supplements for each specific nonimmigrant category. Simply use the supplement that applies to you.

The employer may choose to list more than one foreign trainee on a single I-129

petition. This is done if the employer has more than one opening to be filled for the same type of training position. If more than one trainee is to be included, Attachment-1, which is also part of Form I-129, should be completed for each additional person.

For purposes of Part 5, Question 11, of the Form I-129, note that the dates of intended training should not exceed a total of two years, which is the maximum period of time for which an H-3 petition may be approved. The maximum reduces to 18 months if you are applying for a training program in special education of disabled children.

Section 3 of the H Supplement requires a written explanation of why the employer is willing to incur the cost of training you. There should be some logical way in which your training will financially benefit the U.S. employer, such as to help it with business abroad after you return to your home country.

Describing the training program. It is not enough for the employer to simply write a few sentences like, "The training will cover these subjects." A good application for an H-3 visa will contain several carefully prepared documents, typically including a profile of the petitioning company (with photo of the premises), an overview of the type and purpose of the training, a description of the skills and educational background of the people providing the training, a day-by-day or week-by-week schedule of training activities, an account of the number of hours that will be spent in the classroom versus performing on-the-job training or productive employment that's incidental and necessary to the training (experts say that USCIS won't approve the petition unless a minimum of 15% of the trainee's time will be spent in the classroom), a description of what exactly the trainee will be doing and how progress will be evaluated, samples of the actual training materials (such as a syllabus and training manual), and any other relevant details.

Showing that training is unavailable in your home country. Your employer/trainer must prove that you cannot receive the same training in your home country. This is best shown by letters or affidavits from authorities in your home country who are leaders of industry, officials in government, or administrators in universities. The letters should give the names and positions of the writers. In such a letter, it should be stated that the writer is acquainted with the training program you intend to pursue in the U.S. and that similar training is not available in your home country. It may take a lot of effort to get these statements, but without them, your H-3 visa stands little chance of approval.

Showing how training will further your career. Ideally, the H-3 training program will be related to your current occupation at home. In that case, your U.S. employer can show the nature of your present job with a letter from your foreign employer explaining how the training will further your career in your home country—without overtraining you.

If you are not now employed in the occupation for which you hope to get U.S. training, it would be helpful to have a letter from a company in your homeland offering you a job based on the completion of your training in the United States. If you can't get a letter containing a specific job offer for the future, you will have to present evidence that jobs in the field for which you are training are available. Your U.S. employer must then submit a general statement from a leader in the industry for which you will be trained or an official of the government department of labor in your home country, confirming that there is a demand for persons with the type of training you will receive.

Proving you are qualified for the training program. If the nature of the training you will receive requires special background for entering the program, the employer must submit evidence showing that you have that background. For example, if the training is at a professional level, such as internships for lawyers or engineers, your employer must submit evidence that you are already qualified to practice law or engineering at home. The employer should also submit copies of your diplomas, and

H-3 Visa Petition Checklist

☐ Form I-129, including H Supplement.

☐ Filing fee: $460.

☐ If you will be applying in the U.S. and your family members are with you and need a change of status, Form I-539, the fee (currently $370), and copies of your family members' I-94s or other proof of lawful immigration status and of their relationship to you (such as marriage and birth certificates). One Form I-539 and fee covers your spouse and all your children. Family members should fill out and sign this form, not your employer.

☐ If you're in the U.S., a copy of your I-94 or other proof of your current lawful, unexpired immigration status (except Canadian visitors, who are not expected to have I-94s).

☐ If you're in the U.S., we recommend that you supply evidence that ties to your home country are strong enough to motivate your eventual return. Proof of ties to your home country can include deeds for a house or other real property, your written statements explaining that close relatives are staying behind, or a letter from a company in your home country showing that you have a job waiting when you return.

☐ If you're outside the U.S., a copy of your passport.

All trainees except special education visitors:

☐ Detailed written statement from the employer containing a company profile and photo and describing the training program, including the overall schedule and number of hours per week in classroom study, on-the-job training, productive employment, and unsupervised work or study. Also, include a description of the curriculum, with names of any textbooks and the subjects to be covered, what "homework" and other tasks you'll be expected to complete, what skills you'll acquire, how your progress will be evaluated, and the names and qualifications of the trainers.

☐ Additional explanation from the employer regarding why it is willing to incur the cost of your training without getting much, if any, productive work out of you in return.

☐ A summary of your prior relevant training and experience, such as diplomas and letters from past employers. Nurses must provide proof that they have a full and unrestricted nursing license to work in the country where they obtained a nursing education, or that their education took place in the U.S. or Canada.

☐ Explanation of why you need the training, the absence of similar training in your country, and how the training will benefit you in your career in your home country.

Special education visitors only:

☐ A description of the structured training program, professionally trained staff, facilities, and how you'll participate in the program.

☐ Evidence that any custodial care of children will be incidental to the training program.

☐ Evidence that you are almost done getting a B.A. degree in special education, or already have a B.A., or have extensive prior training in teaching children with disabilities.

If requesting quick (premium) processing:

☐ Form I-907, with $1,225 filing fee.

if you have previous professional work experience, letters from your foreign employers describing the nature and length of your previous employment.

3. Mailing the Visa Petition

After assembling the visa petition, your U.S. employer must mail it to either the California Service Center or the Vermont Service Center, whichever has jurisdiction over the employer's place of business. If you'll be coming from outside the U.S., your employer must send duplicate versions of the form (two signed originals; copies are not acceptable). The USCIS website at www.uscis.gov/i-129/addresses, contains the filing addresses.

4. Awaiting a Decision on the Visa Petition

Within a few weeks after mailing in the petition, your employer should get back a written confirmation that the papers are being processed, together with a receipt for the fee. This notice will also contain your immigration file number. If USCIS wants further information before acting on your case, it will send your employer a Request for Evidence (RFE) on Form I-797E. Your employer should supply the extra data requested within the specified time.

H-3 petitions are normally approved within two to three months. (Check current processing times online at www.uscis.gov; follow the links to Check Your Case Status and Check Processing Times.) When this happens, a Form I-797, Notice of Action, will be sent to your employer, showing the petition was approved. If you plan to submit your visa application at a U.S. consulate abroad, USCIS will notify the the Kentucky Consular Center, which will electronically notify the consulate and send your file there.

TIP
Faster processing—at a price. For $1,225 over and above the regular filing fees, USCIS promises premium processing of the visa petition, including a decision on the case within 15 days. To use this service, the employer must fill out an additional application (Form I-907) and submit it to a special USCIS service center address. For complete instructions, see the USCIS website at www.uscis.gov/i-907.

Be aware that an approved petition does not, if you are overseas, give you any immigration privileges. It is only a prerequisite to the next step, submitting your application for an H-3 visa.

D. Step Two: Applicants Outside the U.S. Apply to a U.S. Consulate

After the H-3 visa petition filed by your employer has been approved, USCIS will send you a Form I-797B, with which you can apply for a visa at a U.S. consulate—normally in your home country. (Some consulates will insist upon waiting for formal notification directly from USCIS, but most will accept an original Form I-797B from you.)

Check with your local U.S. consulate regarding its application procedures. All consulates require advance appointments. Just getting an appointment can take several weeks, so plan ahead.

TIP

If you're visa exempt, you may be able to skip this step. Citizens of Canada and Bermuda need not apply to a U.S. consulate. Instead, they can proceed directly to the U.S. with Form I-797B and supporting documents to request entry. (See 8 C.F.R. § 212.1.)

CAUTION

Have you been, or are you now, working or living illegally in the United States? If so, see Chapter 3 regarding whether you can still get an H-3 visa from a U.S. consulate. You may have become inadmissible or subject to a three-year or ten-year bar on reentry.

The checklist below will help you prepare your consular application. You'll need to go online to submit the main form for this process, the Nonimmigrant Visa Application (Form DS-160). You can submit your photos digitally at the same time. For instructions,

see the State Department website at https://ceac.state.gov/genniv.

As part of your application, the consulate will require you and your family members to pay an application fee and attend an interview. During the interview, a consular officer will examine the data in your application for accuracy. Evidence of ties to your home country will also be checked. During the interview, you will surely be asked how long you intend to remain in the United States. Any answer indicating that you are unsure about plans to return or have an interest in applying for a green card is likely to result in a denial of your H-3 visa.

RELATED TOPIC

See Chapter 4 for what else to expect during consular interviews, and what to do if your application is denied.

E. Step Three: H-3 Visa Holders Enter the U.S.

You have until the expiration date on your H-3 visa to enter the United States. The U.S. border officer will examine your paperwork, ask you some questions, and, if all is in order, approve you for entry. He or she will stamp your passport and create an I-94 Arrival/Departure record for you (if you enter by air or sea). If you enter at a land border, the border officer will give you a small white card called an I-94.

Applying at a Consulate That's Not in Your Home Country

The law allows most people to apply for an H-3 visa at any U.S. consulate they choose—with one exception. If you have ever been present in the U.S. unlawfully (for example, overstayed a visa), your visa will be automatically cancelled and you cannot apply as a third-country national (at a consulate outside your home country). Even if you overstayed your status in the U.S. by just one day, you must return to your home country and apply for the visa from that consulate. There is an exception. If you were admitted to the U.S. for the duration of your status (indicated by "D/S" on your I-94 and most common with student visas) and you remained in the U.S. beyond the time for which your status was conferred, you will be barred from third-country national processing only if an immigration judge or USCIS (or formerly INS) officer has determined that you were unlawfully present. You may find that your success in applying as a third-country national will depend on your country, the consulate, and the relative seriousness of your offense. Being unlawfully present is also a ground of inadmissibility if the period of unlawful presence is 180 days or more. (See Chapter 3.)

Even if you are eligible for third-country national processing, your case will be given the greatest consideration at the consulate in your home country. Applying in some other country creates suspicion in the minds of the consular officers there about your motives for choosing their consulate. Often, when an applicant expects trouble at a home consulate, he or she will seek a more lenient consular office in some other country. This practice of consulate shopping is frowned upon by officials in the system. Unless you have a very good reason for being elsewhere (such as a temporary job assignment in some other nation), it is often smarter to file your visa application in your home country.

Your I-94 shows how long you can stay. Normally, you are permitted to remain up to the expiration date on your H-3 petition. (However, if your passport will expire before the petition's expiration date, some CBP officers will stamp the I-94 with the same expiration date as the passport has.) Each time you exit and reenter the U.S., you will get a new I-94 authorizing your stay up to the final date indicated on the petition.

F. Extending Your U.S. Stay

H-3 visas can be extended only if your original permitted stay was less than two years, to bring your stay up to a total of two years' time spent in H-3 status. (Again, the total limit reduces to 18 months for special education exchange visitors.) An extension is usually easier to get than the original petition approval. However, USCIS has the right to

H-3 Visa Application Checklist

☐ Form DS-160, Nonimmigrant Visa Application. (This is an online form, and can be completed only at https://ceac.state.gov/genniv.)

☐ Original Form I-797 notice of approval of the H-3 petition.

☐ Copy of the I-129 visa petition and support materials that were used to obtain the H-3 visa petition approval.

☐ Valid passport for you and each accompanying relative.

☐ If requested by the consulate or if you were unable to upload one with your DS-160 application, one U.S. passport-type photo of you and one of each accompanying relative. (This is best done by a professional photographer; the consulate can give you a list.)

☐ If your spouse and children will be accompanying you, documents verifying their family relationship to you, such as original marriage and birth certificates.

☐ Documents establishing your intent to leave the U.S. when your status expires, such as deeds verifying ownership of a house or other real property, written statements from you explaining that close relatives are staying behind, or letters from a company showing that you have a job waiting when you return from the United States.

☐ Fee receipt showing that you have paid the relevant machine-readable visa (MRV) application fee (currently $190). The financial institution at which you must pay depends on the country. Check the website of the U.S. consulate where you plan to apply for your visa to learn how to pay the fee. Most consulates will not allow you to pay the visa fee at the time of interview.

☐ Visa reciprocity fee. You may have to pay a visa issuance fee (known as a "reciprocity fee") if you're from a country that charges similar fees for visas to U.S. citizens.

---

reconsider your qualifications based on any changes in the facts or law. When the original application for an H-3 visa was weak, it is not unusual for an extension request to be turned down. As always, however, good cases that are well prepared will generally be successful.

To extend your H-3 visa, the petition, I-94, and visa stamp will each have to be updated. As with the original application, you can file either in the U.S. or at a consulate.

1. H-3 Extension Petition

Your employer will need to file another I-129 petition, fully documented in the same manner as the first petition. It should also include:

- a letter from the employer requesting your status be extended, with an explanation of why the training has not yet been completed

- a copy of your U.S. income tax returns for the previous year, including W-2 forms (being sure that no employment other than that for your H-3 employer is reflected in your tax documents)

- a copy of your I-94 card (if you have one),
- a copy of the first Notice of Action I-797.

If you have a spouse and children with you in the U.S. and would like to apply without leaving for a consulate in another country, they will need to submit Form I-539, as described in Section C, above.

Working While Your Extension Petition Is Pending

If you file your petition for an extension of H-3 status before your authorized stay expires, you are automatically permitted to continue in the training program for up to 240 days while you are waiting for a decision. If, however, your authorized stay expires after you have filed for an extension but before you receive an approval, and more than 240 days go by without getting a decision on your extension petition, your authorization to be in the training program ceases.

Watch Out for Expedited Removal

The law empowers a Customs and Border Protection (CBP) inspector at the U.S. airport or border to summarily (without allowing judicial review) bar entry to someone requesting admission to the U.S. if either of the following is true:

- The inspector thinks you are lying about practically anything connected with entering the U.S., including your purpose in coming, intent to return, and prior immigration history. This includes the use or suspected use of false documents.
- You do not have the proper documentation to support your entry to the U.S. in the category you are requesting.

If the inspector excludes you, you cannot be readmitted to the U.S. for five years, unless USCIS grants a special waiver. For this reason, it is extremely important to understand the terms of your requested status and to not make any misrepresentations. If you are found to be inadmissible, you may ask the CBP inspector to withdraw your application to enter the U.S. in order to prevent having the five-year deportation order on your record. The CBP may allow this in some exceptional cases.

2. H-3 Visa Revalidation

If you must leave the U.S. after your extension has been approved, you must get a new visa stamp issued at a consulate before you return. (Years ago, you could have your visa revalidated by applying to the U.S. State Department, but no longer.)

Reread Section D, above. The procedures for consular extensions are identical.

> ⚠ **CAUTION**
>
> Once your two-year (or 18-month) stay is over, you cannot use another H visa, or an L visa, until you have left the U.S. and stayed outside for six months.

Getting an Intracompany Transferee (L-1) Visa

The L-1 visa allows managers, executives, or especially knowledgeable employees who work outside the U.S. for a company that has an affiliated entity inside the U.S. to come to the U.S. and perform services for that entity. There are no limits on how many people can get L-1 visas every year.

SEE AN EXPERT
Do you need a lawyer? You can't apply for an L-1 visa without having an employer first—and it's in your employer's interest to hire a lawyer to help. A lawyer can help make sure that your application gets done right the first time and deal with all the bureaucratic hurdles.

A. Do You Qualify for an L-1 Visa?

You qualify for an L-1 visa if you have been employed outside the U.S. for at least one continuous year out of the past three years, and you are transferred to the U.S. to work as a manager, an executive, or a specialized-knowledge worker.

The U.S. company to which you are transferring must be a parent, branch, a subsidiary, an affiliate, or a joint venture partner of your non-U.S. employer. The non-U.S. company must remain in operation while you have the L-1 visa. "Non-U.S. company" means that it is physically located outside the United

Key Features of the L-1 Visa

Here are some of the advantages and disadvantages of the L-1 visa:

- You can work legally in the U.S. for your L-1 sponsor for up to three years on your first visa. You may then apply for extensions of two years at a time, up to a maximum of seven years if you're a manager or executive, or five years if you're a person with specialized knowledge. Previous time spent in H visa status counts toward the five or seven years, unfortunately.
- You may work only for the U.S. employer who acted as your visa sponsor, and it must be a parent, branch, or a subsidiary, an affiliate, or a joint venture partner of the company that currently employs you outside the United States.
- Visas are available for your accompanying spouse and minor children, and your spouse may apply for employment authorization in the United States.
- You may travel in and out of the U.S. or remain here continuously until your L-1 status expires.
- If you have an L-1 visa, and you want to apply for a U.S. green card through employment, you can do so. Executives and managers likely qualify for an EB-1 green card. (See Chapter 9.)
- The L-1 visa is "dual intent," which means that you can get the visa even if you are also seeking a green card.

States. Such a company may be a foreign division of a U.S.-based business or it may have originated in a country outside the United States. Either one fits the definition of a non-U.S. company. You should show that you can expect to go back to work for the non-U.S. company upon your return. If your foreign employer closes, the U.S. employer must have a related foreign company to which you could theoretically be transferred.

If you're coming to the U.S. to establish a new office (generally any office open less than year), your employer must show that it has bought or leased sufficient space to house the new office, and that the new U.S. office will support an executive or managerial position within one year of the petition approval.

To get an L-1 visa, it is not necessary that either your non-U.S. or prospective U.S. employer be operating in a particular business structure. Many legal forms of doing business are acceptable, including, but not restricted to, corporations, limited corporations, partnerships, joint ventures, and sole proprietorships. The employer may also be a nonprofit or religious organization.

Although you are generally expected to work full time in the U.S., you can work somewhat less if you dedicate a significant portion of your time to the job on a regular and systematic basis.

1. Manager, Executive, or Person With Specialized Knowledge

To be eligible for an L-1 visa, the job you hold with the non-U.S. company must be that of a manager, an executive, or a person with specialized knowledge. Managers and executives receive L-1A visas and people with special knowledge receive L-1B visas. You must have worked in one or the other of those positions for a total of at least one year out of the past three years. That year must have been spent outside the United States. For immigration purposes, the definitions of "manager," "executive," and "specialized knowledge" are more restricted than their everyday meanings.

a. Managers

A manager is defined as a person who has all of the following characteristics:

- He or she manages the entire organization or a department, subdivision, function, or component of the organization.
- He or she supervises and controls the work of other supervisory, professional, or managerial employees or manages an essential function, department, or subdivision of the organization.
- He or she has the authority to hire and fire or recommend these and other personnel decisions regarding the employees being supervised. If no employees are supervised, the

manager must work at a senior level within the organization or function.

- He or she has the authority to make decisions concerning the day-to-day operations of the portion of the organization under his or her management.

First-line supervisors are lower management personnel who directly oversee nonmanagement workers. A first-line supervisor is not normally considered a manager unless the employees supervised are professionals. The word "professionals" here means workers holding a university degree in a field related to their occupation.

A manager coming to work for a U.S. office that has been in operation for at least one year also likely qualifies for a green card as an EB-1 priority worker. See Chapter 9 for details.

b. Executives

An executive is defined as a person whose primary role includes that:

- He or she directs the management of the organization or a major function or component of it.
- He or she sets the goals or policies of the organization or a part or function of it.
- He or she has extensive discretionary decision-making authority.
- He or she receives only general supervision or direction from higher-level executives, a board of directors, or the stockholders of the organization.

An executive coming to work for a U.S. office that has been in operation for at least one year also likely qualifies for a green card as an EB-1 priority worker. Again, see Chapter 9 for details.

c. Persons With Specialized Knowledge

The term "specialized knowledge" refers to an understanding of the employer company, its products, services, research, equipment, techniques, management or other interests and its application in international markets, or advanced knowledge of the company's processes and procedures. USCIS and consular officers will be looking for knowledge that is not held commonly throughout the industry, but is truly specialized. They will also be looking to see that such knowledge is not readily available in the United States.

2. Parent, Branch, Subsidiary, Affiliate, or Joint Venture Partner

L-1 visas are available only to employees of companies outside the U.S. that have related U.S. parents, branches, subsidiaries, affiliates, or joint venture partners. There is also a special category for international accounting firms. For visa purposes, these terms have specific definitions.

a. Parent

A parent is a non-U.S. company that owns more than 50% of your U.S. employer.

b. Branches

Branches are simply different operating locations of the same company. The clearest example of this is a single international corporation that has branch offices in many countries.

c. Subsidiaries

In a subsidiary relationship, the U.S. company owns a controlling percentage of the foreign company, that is, 50% or more.

d. Affiliates

Affiliate business relationships are more difficult to demonstrate than those of branches or subsidiaries because there is no direct ownership between the two companies. Instead, they share the fact that both are controlled by a common third entity, either a company, group of companies, individual, or group of people.

There are two methods of ownership that will support an L-1 visa based on an affiliate relationship. The first is for one common person or business entity to own at least 50% of the non-U.S. company and 50% of the U.S. company. If no single entity owns at least 50% of both companies, the second possibility is for each owner of the non-U.S. company to also own the U.S. company, and in the same percentages. For example, if five different people each own 20% of the stock of the non-U.S. company, then the same five people must each own 20% of the U.S. company for an affiliate relationship to exist.

e. Joint Venture Partners

A joint venture exists when there is no common ownership between the two companies, but they have jointly undertaken a common business operation or project. To qualify for L-1 purposes, each company must have veto power over decisions, take an equal share of the profits, and bear the losses on an equal basis.

In a situation where both the U.S. and non-U.S. companies are in the corporate or limited form and the majority of the stock of both is publicly held, unless they are simply branches of the same company that wish to transfer employees between them, the joint venture relationship is the only one that is practical for L-1 qualifying purposes. The ownership of a publicly held company is too vast and diverse to prove any of the other types of qualifying business relationships.

f. International Accounting Firms

L-1 visas are available to employees and partners of international accounting firms. In the case of big accounting firms, the interests between one country and another are not usually close enough to qualify as affiliates under normal L-1 visa rules. Nevertheless, the law considers the managers of such companies qualified to support L-1 visa petitions for their employees. The firm must be part of an international accounting organization with an internationally recognized name. Ultimately, this option applies to only a limited number of very large and prominent firms.

3. Blanket L-1 Visas: Privileges for Large Companies

Large U.S. companies (other than nonprofits) that are parents, branches, subsidiaries, or affiliates of non-U.S. companies may obtain what is known as a "blanket L-1 status." This status enables qualified U.S. companies that require frequent transferring of non-U.S. employees to their related U.S. companies to do so easily. Instead of submitting individual petitions for each transferee, the company itself gets a general approval for transferring employees. This eliminates much of the time and paperwork involved in each individual case. However, an individual must still submit a visa petition to the visa officer at the interview at the U.S. consulate using a simplified USCIS visa petition on Form I-129S. If a non-U.S. company has more than one U.S. branch, subsidiary, or affiliate, it need obtain only one blanket L-1 petition for all of its related U.S. companies.

It is the company itself and not the individual employee that qualifies for blanket L-1 status. Also, although the U.S. company must be a parent, branch, subsidiary, or affiliate of a non-U.S. company to qualify, it is the U.S. company that petitions for and receives the blanket L-1 status.

Initially, a blanket L-1 petition can be approved for only three years. However, if the company continues to qualify, at the end of three years it can obtain an indefinite renewal.

The definitions for manager and executives under blanket L-1 visas are the same as for those who apply for individual L-1 visas. However, the specialized knowledge category differs from the one for individual L-1 applicants. For the blanket visa, they must not only have specialized knowledge but must work in a professional capacity, as well.

If a company has the need and meets the following requirements, it should obtain a blanket L-1 petition:

- The petitioning U.S. company to which employees may be transferred must be a parent, branch, or subsidiary, or an affiliate of a company outside the United States. (Note that a joint venture partnership is not a qualifying business relationship for blanket L-1 status purposes.)
- Both the U.S. company and its related non-U.S. company must be engaged in actual commercial trade or rendering of services.
- The U.S. company must have been engaged in business for at least one year.
- The U.S. company must have a total of at least three branches, subsidiaries,

Academic Credential Evaluations

If you are applying for a blanket L-1 visa at a U.S. consulate as a specialized knowledge professional, you may need to show that you hold at least a bachelor's degree. Evidence that you are personally eligible as a specialized knowledge professional should include copies of diplomas and transcripts from the colleges and universities you attended. However, not every country operates on the same academic degree and grade level systems found in the United States. If you were educated outside the U.S., USCIS or the U.S. consulate may ask for an academic credential evaluation from an approved U.S. consulting service to determine the U.S. equivalent of your educational level.

When the results of a credential evaluation are favorable, they strengthen your case. If, however, the evaluation shows that your credentials do not equal at least a U.S. bachelor's degree, do not submit the evaluation with your application; your status as a "professional" may be called into question.

We recommend obtaining a credential evaluation in every case where non-U.S. education is a factor. In addition, we advise getting the evaluation before USCIS or the consulate has the opportunity to ask for it. When the evaluation is favorable, include it with your application—it saves time if USCIS or the consulate decides to request it later.

Before sending a credential evaluation service your academic documents, you may want to call in advance to discuss your prospects over the telephone. Usually, you can get some idea of the likelihood for receiving good results. If your prospects are truly bleak, you may decide not to order the evaluation and to save the service charge, which is typically upwards of $100.

There are several qualified credential evaluation services recognized by USCIS, listed at the website of the National Association of Credential Evaluation Services (www.naces.org). Some of these NACES organizations will evaluate only formal education, not job experience. However, others have contacts with experts (typically university professors) who can consider employment experience in addition to academics.

When sending your credentials to a U.S. university, include documents showing your complete academic background, as well as letters from former employers verifying your work experience. Evidence of any special accomplishments, such as awards or published articles, should also be submitted.

Be warned, however, that these evaluations are merely advisory in nature. While USCIS or the U.S. consulate may take the evaluations into consideration, they are not obliged to do so.

or affiliates, although all three need not be located in the United States.

The company and any related U.S. companies must either have:

- successfully obtained L-1 visas for at least ten of its employees during the past 12 months
- combined U.S. annual sales of at least $25 million, or
- a total of at least 1,000 employees actually working in the United States.

4. Specialized Knowledge Professionals Under Blanket L-1 Visas

This category is only for employees of companies with blanket L-1 status. It is a more stringent substitute for the specialized knowledge category available to individual L-1 applicants. USCIS's regulations require that an individual have specialized knowledge, as defined above, and that he or she further be a member of the professions as that term is defined in immigration law. The law specifically lists architects, engineers, lawyers, physicians, surgeons, and teachers in elementary and secondary schools, colleges, academies, or seminaries.

The term "profession," however, has been more liberally interpreted in other contexts. It may also include any occupation that requires theoretical and practical knowledge to perform the occupation in such fields as architecture, physical and social sciences, business specialties, and the arts. For these occupations, professional status requires completion of a university education reflected by at least a bachelor's degree in a specific occupational specialty, as long as that degree is the minimum requirement for entry to that occupation.

Under these criteria, the following occupations have also been found to be professional: accountant, computer systems analyst, physical therapist, chemist, pharmacist, medical technologist, hotel manager, fashion designer, commercial airline pilot of 747s or other large aircraft, and upper-level business managers.

Other occupations may also be considered professional, as long as they meet the criteria discussed above.

5. Bringing Your Immediate Relatives

When you qualify for an L-1 visa, your spouse and unmarried children under age 21 can get L-2 visas by providing proof of their family relationship to you. L-2 visas authorize your accompanying relatives to stay with you in the U.S., but only your spouse will be permitted to apply for employment authorization (a work permit).

To take advantage of the right to work, after arriving in the U.S, your spouse should apply for a work permit. This is done on Form I-765. In filling out the form, your spouse should write "spouse of L nonimmigrant" in Question 15 and (a)(18) in Question 16.

Your spouse will need to mail this form, together with proof of your visa status, a copy of his or her I-94 card (if he or she has one), the filing fee (currently $380), and two photos, to the appropriate USCIS service center for your geographic region. For the address and other information, call USCIS Information at 800-375-5283 or see the USCIS website (www.uscis.gov/i-765).

B. Possibilities for a Green Card From L-1 Status

If you qualify for, or currently have, an L-1 visa as a manager or an executive, you are probably eligible for a green card through employment. (See Chapter 9.) EB-1 applicants do not have to go through the rigorous procedures of labor certification, which is usually the first step required for those seeking green cards through employment.

L-1B visa holders may also apply for a green card in any of the family- or employment-based categories available to them. If you are seeking a green card on the basis of the employment that got you the L-1B visa, the likely categories are EB-2 or EB-3. (See Chapter 9.) These categories do require labor certification (unless you qualify for an EB-2 "national interest waiver"). The purpose of the labor certification procedure is to show that there are no U.S. workers available to take the permanent U.S. job that has been offered to you.

C. Quick View of the L-1 Visa Application Process

Once you have been offered a job transfer to the U.S., getting an L-1 visa as an individual is a one- to three-step process:

- The U.S. company to which you will be transferred files what's called a visa petition on USCIS Form I-129. If you're already in the U.S. in lawful status, this petition can simultaneously ask that your status be changed to L-1 transferee, in which case the process will successfully end here.
- If you're outside the U.S., then after the visa petition is approved, you submit your own application for an L-1 visa to a U.S. consulate (unless you're from Canada or Bermuda, in which case you can skip this step).
- You use either your visa or (if you're from Canada or Bermuda) the notice of your approved visa petition to enter the U.S. and claim your L-1 status. If you're a Canadian citizen, you may submit the visa petition directly to U.S. Customs at a Class A port of entry along the U.S./Canada border or preflight inspection when you enter the United States. The U.S. Customs inspector will then make the decision on whether to allow you entry. (See Chapter 5 for more on special rules for Canadians.)

> **TIP**
> **Nothing stops you from helping with the employer's tasks during this application process.** For example, you can fill out forms intended to be completed by your employer and simply ask the employer to check them over and sign them. The less your U.S. employer is inconvenienced, the more it may be willing to act as sponsor for your visa.

D. Step One: Your U.S. Employer Files a Visa Petition

The process starts when your U.S. employer sends a visa petition to USCIS. Your employer can choose to either submit an individual L-1 visa petition (Form I-129), just for you, or a blanket petition (Form I-129S), if it expects to transfer a number of employees on an ongoing basis. The object of the individual L-1 petition is to prove three things:

- that you have been employed outside the U.S. for at least one of the past three years with a related employer
- that the company you worked for outside the U.S. has a parent, branch, subsidiary, affiliate, or joint venture partner company in the U.S., and
- that the U.S. entity requires your services to work as a manager, executive, or specialized knowledge employee.

If your non-U.S. employer wants to transfer you to the U.S. and regularly transfers others, ask whether the company already has an approved blanket petition. If so, applicants outside of the U.S. who need an actual visa should ask their potential U.S. employer to fill out and send him or her a completed Form I-129S (original plus two copies) and also to send one copy of the earlier approval notice (Form I-797) of the blanket L-1 petition. The applicant will include these documents with his or her visa application at a U.S. consulate overseas (as described in Section E, below).

For applicants already in the U.S., the employer will need to submit Form I-129 asking for a change of status, as described in Section 1, below.

If the U.S. company transfers many employees to the U.S. but has not obtained a blanket L-1 visa, you might suggest that it look into getting one.

1. Simultaneous Change of Status If You're Already Legally in the U.S.

If you're already in the U.S. in lawful status, such as on a student or other temporary visa, the petition can be used to ask that your status be immediately changed to L-1 transferee. (Part 2, Question 4, of Form I-129 offers choices addressing this issue.) However, you can't take advantage of this option if you entered the U.S. on a visa waiver or if you entered using a C (alien in transit), TWOV (alien in transit without a visa), D (crewman), or any K (fiancé) visa. Certain J-1 (exchange visitor) visa holders are prohibited from changing status as well.

Other than these restrictions, you're allowed to change status if you:

- entered the U.S. legally
- have never worked in the U.S. illegally, and
- the expiration date on your I-94 hasn't passed.

There is another problem that comes up only in U.S. filings. It is the issue of what is called "preconceived intent." To approve a change of status, USCIS must believe that at the time you originally entered the U.S., as a visitor or with some other nonimmigrant visa, you did not intend to apply for a different status. If USCIS thinks you had a preconceived plan to use one visa to enter the U.S. with an eye to applying for a different status after getting there, it may deny your application. (You can get around the preconceived intent issue by leaving the U.S. and applying for your L-1 visa at a U.S. consulate in another country.)

Your spouse and children, if they are also in the U.S. with you, can't change their status by being mentioned on your Form I-129, but must submit a separate Form I-539 (one for the whole family). They can submit this either at the same time as your employer submits Form I 129, or afterward. (If they submit Form I-539 afterward, however, they will need to include either a copy of the USCIS receipt notice indicating that your petition is pending, or a copy of the petition approval notice.)

TIP

Your eligibility to apply in the U.S. has nothing to do with overall eligibility for an L-1 visa. Many applicants who are barred from filing in the U.S., but otherwise qualify for L-1 status, may still apply successfully for an L-1 visa at a U.S. consulate in another country.

If you decide to apply for a change of status within the U.S., realize that you still won't have the L-1 visa that you'll need if you ever leave the United States. A change of status only gives you L-1 status with the right to stay in the U.S.; it does not give you the right to reenter. Visas are never given inside the United States. They are issued exclusively by U.S. consulates in other countries. If you file in the U.S. and you are successful, you will get to remain in the U.S. with L-1 privileges until the status expires. But should you leave the country for any reason before that time, you will have to apply for the visa itself at a U.S. consulate before returning to the United States. Moreover, the fact that your L-1 status has been approved in the U.S. does not guarantee that the consulate will also approve your visa. For this reason, many people choose to leave the U.S. and apply through a consulate.

2. Preparing the Visa Petition

The checklist below will help you and your employer assemble the necessary items for the visa petition.

L-1 Visa Petition (Not Under Blanket) Checklist

☐ Form I-129, with L Supplement.

☐ Filing fee: $460.

☐ Possible filing surcharge. If your petitioning employer has more than 50 employees, and over half its workforce is in H or L visa status, be prepared to pay a further surcharge of $4,500. If the petitioning employer does not have more than 50 employees, or less than half of its workforce is in H or L visa status, it should include a written statement to this effect with the petition.

☐ Fraud Prevention and Detection Fee: $500 (separate check or money order).

☐ Evidence of a qualifying relationship between the U.S. and foreign company, such as:

　☐ Articles of incorporation or other legal charter or business license of the non-U.S. company.

　☐ Articles of incorporation or other legal charter or business license of the U.S. company.

　☐ Legal business registration certificate of the non-U.S. company.

　☐ Legal business registration certificate of the U.S. company.

　☐ Tax returns of the non-U.S. company for the past two years.

　☐ Tax returns of the U.S. company for the past two years, if available.

　☐ Copies of all outstanding stock certificates, if the business is a corporation.

　☐ Stock ledger showing all share issuances.

　☐ Notarized affidavit from the secretary of the corporation, or, if the business is not a corporation, from the official record keeper of the business, stating the names of each owner and percentages of the company owned.

☐ If the business relationship is a joint venture, a copy of the written joint venture agreement.

☐ Annual shareholder reports of the U.S. and non-U.S. companies, if publicly held.

☐ Accountant's financial statements, including profit and loss statements and balance sheets of the non-U.S. company, for the past two years.

☐ Accountant's financial statements, including profit and loss statements and balance sheets of the U.S. company for the past two years, if available.

☐ If more than half the stock of either the U.S. or non-U.S. company is publicly held, statements from the secretary of the corporation describing how the companies are related.

☐ If you will be coming to the U.S. to open a new office:

　☐ Evidence that you have office space, such as a signed lease agreement, mortgages, or other proof of real estate purchase, or business plan, marketing materials, or other descriptions of the business connecting its activity with the space acquired.

　☐ Evidence that your overseas employment was in a managerial, executive, or specialized knowledge capacity, such as organization charts showing your position; patents or other evidence of the company's technology, products, or services that are based on your work; performance reviews; loans/financing on behalf of the company; organizational job descriptions for your position and those positions that reported above and/or below you, if applicable; and a résumé describing your job accomplishments.

L-1 Visa Petition (Not Under Blanket) Checklist (continued)

- ☐ Evidence that your company has the ability to pay you and start the business in the U.S., including evidence of the size of the U.S. investment, the organizational structure of the foreign and U.S. businesses, and the size and financial condition of the foreign business.

- ☐ If you will have an L-1 managerial or executive role, evidence that the U.S. business will be able to support such a position within a year.

- ☐ If your company is applying to extend your L-1A visa after the initial one year for a new office: Evidence that the new office is fully functioning and can support you as an executive or manager, such as purchase orders, contracts, or other evidence of commercial activity; payroll records for employees hired; bank statements; financial reporting documents showing monthly income; continued venture capital or other third-party investment contribution based on achieved milestones; media coverage of the business; position descriptions providing the roles and responsibilities of all current employees; or other evidence clearly demonstrating how you are relieved of nonqualifying duties.

- ☐ If you will be applying in the U.S. and your family members are with you and need a change of status, Form I-539 with accompanying fee (currently $290) and copies of your family members' I-94s or other proof of lawful immigration status and of their relationship to you (such as marriage and birth certificates). One Form I-539 and fee will cover your spouse and all your children. This form is meant to be filled out and signed by your family members, not by your employer.

- ☐ If you're in the U.S., a copy of your I-94 or other proof of your current lawful, unexpired immigration status (Canadians who are just visiting are not expected to have I-94 cards).

- ☐ If you're outside the U.S., a copy of your passport.

- ☐ Documents proving one year of employment outside the U.S. during the last three years, such as copies of your wage statements and your personal income tax return filed in your home country for the most recent year. If tax returns are unavailable, submit a notarized statement from the bookkeeping department or accountant of your non-U.S. employer, with a statement explaining the situation.

- ☐ Documents proving employment outside of U.S. as an executive, a manager, or a person with specialized knowledge, including organization charts for both the domestic and foreign employer.

- ☐ A statement describing your proposed job's necessary qualifications, duties, salary, and dates of employment.

- ☐ Evidence that the proposed employment will be in an executive, a managerial, or a specialized knowledge capacity.

If requesting quick (premium) processing:

- ☐ Form I-907, with $1,225 filing fee.
- ☐ Form I-129S, with L Supplement.
- ☐ Copy of approval notice for the blanket petition.
- ☐ Filing fee: $460.
- ☐ If the L-1 worker won't need a visa, Fraud Prevention and Detection Fee: $500 (separate check or money order). An L worker who needs a visa will be asked to pay the $500 fee at the consulate.

L-1 Visa Petition (Under Blanket) Checklist

☐ Possible filing surcharge. If your petitioning employer has more than 50 employees, has over half its workforce in H or L visa status, and is required to pay the $500 fraud prevention and detection fee (see above), a further surcharge of $4,500. An L worker who needs a visa will be asked to pay the $4,500 fee at the consulate. If the L worker is Canadian and does not need a visa, he or she will have to pay the fee at the time of admission, or the employer will be contacted to pay the fee at that time. If the petitioning employer does not have more than 50 employees, or less than half of its workforce is in H or L visa status, it should include a written statement to that effect with the petition.

☐ Letter from employer detailing the dates of employment, job duties, qualifications, and salary.

☐ If you are qualifying on the basis of specialized knowledge, a copy of your U.S. degree or foreign equivalent degree (with equivalency report if necessary), or evidence establishing that the combination of your education and experience is the equivalent of a U.S. degree.

☐ Documents showing that the U.S. company is actively engaged in commercial trade or services, has been in business for at least one year, and has three or more domestic or foreign branches, subsidiaries, or affiliates. (Many of the documents you've already assembled to prove the qualifying relationship between the U.S. and foreign company will serve to prove this as well.)

☐ One of the following:

  ☐ Company income tax returns, audited accountant's financial statements, or the annual shareholders' report showing combined annual sales for all of the related U.S. employer companies totaling at least $25 million.

  ☐ Copies of the Notice of Action Forms I-797 showing at least ten L-1 approvals during the past year.

  ☐ The most recent quarterly state unemployment tax return and federal employment tax return Form 940 showing at least 1,000 employees for all of the related U.S. employer business locations.

If requesting quick (premium) processing:

☐ Form I-907, with $1,225 filing fee.

A few items on this checklist require the following explanation.

Form I-129 and L Supplement. The basic form for the visa petition is immigration Form I-129 and its L Supplement. The I-129 form is used for many different non-immigrant visas. In addition to the basic part of the form that applies to all types of visas, it comes with several supplements for each specific nonimmigrant category. Simply use the supplement that applies to you. If your employer wants the ability to file petitions for employees under the blanket procedures, it will file Form I-129 for permission to do this. If it then petitions for you under the blanket procedures, it will file Form I-129S for you, instead of Form I-129 and the L Supplement.

Proof that you are a manager, an executive, or a person with specialized knowledge. Your U.S. employer must submit evidence that your employment abroad fits the USCIS definition of manager, executive, or person with specialized knowledge, and that your employment in the U.S. will be one of these types. To prove this, submit detailed statements from both the U.S. and non-U.S. employers explaining your dates of employment, qualifications, salary, and specific duties as well as (if you're a supervisor) the number and kind of employees you supervise. Organizational charts are helpful to show managerial duties. If the petition is based on specialized knowledge, the statements should also describe the nature of the specialized knowledge and how it will be used in your U.S. job. The statements should also include a description of the job you'll be doing in the U.S., including the duties, and evidence that the position is executive, managerial, or requires specialized knowledge. These statements may be in your employer's own words and do not have to be in any special form. The type of position you held in the overseas company does not have to match the type of position you will hold in the United States. That is, a person who was a manager overseas can qualify as an L-1B specialized knowledge worker, or a person who was a specialized knowledge worker in the company overseas can qualify for an L-1A visa as an executive.

Proof that the U.S. and non-U.S. companies are engaged in trade or the rendering of services. For a blanket petition, the petitioning U.S. employer should submit as many documents as possible to show that both the U.S. and non-U.S. companies are financially healthy and presently engaged in trade or the rendering of services. Such documents could include:

- copies of the articles of incorporation or other legal charters
- any business registration certificates

- company tax returns for the past two years
- company annual reports or financial statements for the past two years, including balance sheets and profit/loss statements
- payroll records for the past two years
- letters of reference from chambers of commerce
- promotional literature describing the nature of the company
- letters from banks indicating average account balances, and
- copies of leases or deeds for business premises.

3. Mailing the Visa Petition

After assembling an I-129 visa petition, your U.S. employer must mail it to either the California Service Center or the Vermont Service Center, whichever has jurisdiction over the employer's place of business. The correct filing addresses are at www.uscis.gov/i-129-addresses. If you'll be coming from outside the U.S., your employer must send duplicate versions of the form (two signed originals; copies are not acceptable).

An I-129S petition for entry under an approved blanket petition is given to the consulate when you apply for your visa. If you don't need a visa (if, for example, you're changing status within the U.S.), you file the I-129S at the Service Center that approved the blanket petition. If you're Canadian, you can present the I-129S at the border when you're ready to enter the United States.

4. Awaiting a Decision on the Visa Petition

Within a few weeks after mailing in the petition, your employer should get back a written confirmation that the papers are being processed, together with a receipt for the fee. This notice will also contain your immigration file number. If USCIS wants further information before acting on your case, it will send your employer a Request for Evidence (RFE) on Form I-797E. Your employer should supply the extra data requested within the specified time.

L-1 petitions are normally approved within six weeks. Check current processing times online at www.uscis.gov (follow the links to "Check Your Case Status" and "Check Processing Times"). When this happens, a Form I-797 Notice of Action will be sent to your employer, showing the petition was approved. If you plan to submit your visa application at a U.S. consulate abroad, USCIS will notify the Kentucky Consular Center, which will electronically notify the consulate and send your file there. Only the employer receives communications from USCIS about the petition, because technically it is the employer who is seeking the visa on your behalf.

Applying at a Consulate That's Not in Your Home Country

The law allows most people to apply for an L-1 visa at any U.S. consulate they choose—with one exception. If you have ever been present in the U.S. unlawfully, your visa will be automatically cancelled and you cannot apply as a third-country national (at a consulate outside your home country). Even if you overstayed your status in the U.S. by just one day, you must return to your home country and apply for the visa from that consulate. There is an exception. If you were admitted to the U.S. for the duration of your status (indicated by "D/S" on your I-94 and most common with student visas) and you remained in the U.S. beyond the time for which your status was conferred, you will be barred from third-country national processing only if an immigration judge or USCIS (or formerly INS) officer has determined that you were unlawfully present. You may find that your success in applying as a third-country

national will depend on your country, the consulate, and the relative seriousness of your offense. Being unlawfully present is also a ground of inadmissibility if the period of unlawful presence is 180 days or more. (See Chapter 3.)

Even if you are eligible for third-country national processing, your case will be given the greatest consideration at the consulate in your home country. Applying in some other country creates suspicion in the minds of the consular officers there about your motives for choosing their consulate. Often, when an applicant expects trouble at a home consulate, he or she will seek a more lenient consular office in some other country. This practice of consulate shopping is frowned upon by officials in the system. Unless you have a very good reason for being elsewhere (such as a temporary job assignment in some other nation), it is often smarter to file your visa application in your home country.

TIP

Faster processing—at a price. For $1,225 over and above the regular filing fees, USCIS promises premium processing of the visa petition, including a decision on the case within 15 days. Currently, premium processing is available for I-129 petitions in most immigrant visa categories. You need not request premium

processing at the time you first file the Form I-129, but can upgrade to it later if your I-129 is still pending and you are getting impatient for a decision. To use this service, the employer must fill out an additional application (Form I-907) and submit it to a special USCIS service center address. For complete instructions, see the USCIS website at www.uscis.gov/i-907.

Be aware that an approved petition does not, if you are overseas, give you any immigration privileges. It is only a prerequisite to the next step, submitting your application for an L-1 visa.

E. Step Two: Applicants Outside the U.S. Apply to a U.S. Consulate

After the individual L-1 visa petition filed by your employer has been approved, USCIS will send a Form I-797B Notice of Action, with which you can apply for a visa at a U.S. consulate—normally in your home country. If your U.S. employer has already been approved for L-1 blanket status, the U.S. company should send you the Form I-129S in triplicate along with a copy of the blanket L-1 approval on Form I-797.

Check with your local U.S. consulate regarding its application procedures. All consulates insist on advance appointments. Just getting an appointment can take several weeks, so plan ahead.

> **TIP**
>
> **If you're visa exempt, you may be able to skip this step.** Citizens of Canada and Bermuda need not apply to a U.S. consulate. Instead, they can proceed directly to the U.S. with Form I-797B and supporting documents to request entry. (See 8 C.F.R. § 212.1.) In fact, Canadian citizens alone can simply present their petition paperwork to a U.S. Customs officer located at any of Canada's major international airports, or at major Canadian land crossings. This can be quite convenient if approved; the process can be done in minutes, prior to a plane departure. (See Chapter 5 for more on special rules for Canadians.) Of course, this procedure can also carry hazards. If the U.S. Customs officer finds a defect in the L-1 petition, you may not be allowed on the plane, or (if at a land crossing) to drive into the United States. You'll have to decide whether to risk applying in person rather than waiting for USCIS's decision on an I-129 petition.

> **CAUTION**
>
> **Have you been, or are you now, working or living illegally in the United States?** If so, see Chapter 3 regarding whether you can still get an L-1 visa from a U.S. consulate. You may have become inadmissible or subject to a three-year or ten-year bar on reentry.

The checklist below will help you prepare your consular application. You'll need to go online to submit the main form for this process, the Nonimmigrant Visa Application (Form DS-160). You can submit your photos digitally at the same time. For instructions, see the State Department website at https://ceac.state.gov/genniv.

As part of your application, the consulate will require you and your family members to pay an application fee and attend an interview. During the interview, a

L-1 Visa Application Checklist

☐ Form DS-160, Nonimmigrant Visa Application (must be prepared and submitted online, at https://ceac.state.gov/genniv).

☐ Notice showing approval of the L-1 petition (Form I-797).

☐ Valid passport for you and each accompanying relative.

☐ If requested by the consulate or if you were unable to upload one with your DS-160 application, one U.S. passport-style photo of you and one of each accompanying relative. (This is best done by a professional photographer; the consulate can give you a list.)

☐ If your spouse and children will be accompanying you, original documents verifying their family relationship to you, such as marriage and birth certificates.

☐ Fee receipt showing that you have paid the relevant machine-readable visa (MRV) application fee (currently $190). The financial institution at which you must pay depends on the country. Check the website of the U.S. consulate where you plan to apply for your visa to learn how to pay the fee. Most consulates will not allow you to pay the visa fee at the time of interview.

☐ Visa reciprocity fee. You may have to pay this visa issuance fee if you're from a country that charges similar fees for visas to U.S. citizens who wish to work there.

Additional documents required if applying under a blanket petition:

☐ Your Form I-129S.

☐ $500 fraud prevention and detection fee, and if applicable, the $4,500 border security fee.

☐ Documents proving that you were employed outside of the U.S. by the non-U.S. company for at least one of the past three years, such as copies of your wage statements and your personal income tax return filed in your home country for the most recent year. If tax returns are unavailable, submit a notarized statement from the bookkeeping department or accountant of your non-U.S. employer, with a statement explaining the situation.

☐ Documents proving employment outside of the U.S. as an executive, a manager, or a person with specialized knowledge (see detailed suggestions for types of documents under Section D2, above).

☐ Documents showing that your employment in the U.S. will be as an executive, a manager, or a person with specialized knowledge, such as a detailed statement from both the U.S. and non-U.S. employers explaining your specific duties as well as the number and kind of employees you will supervise (if applicable); and, if your application is based on specialized knowledge, how that knowledge will be used in your U.S. job.

☐ If applying as a specialized knowledge worker, documents showing you meet the definition of a professional, such as copies of diplomas and transcripts from the colleges and universities you attended. If you attended a school but did not graduate, submit the transcript. If you were educated outside of the U.S., you need to supply a credential evaluation from an approved evaluation service as explained in "Academic Credential Evaluations," above.

☐ If you're applying to come to the U.S. to start a new office, documentation that office space has been acquired.

consular officer will examine the data in your application for accuracy. See Chapter 4 for what else to expect during consular interviews and what to do if your application is denied.

F. Step Three: L-1 Visa Holders Enter the U.S.

You have until the expiration date on your L-1 visa to enter the United States. The U.S. Customs and Border Protection (CBP) officer will examine your paperwork, ask you some questions, and if all is in order, approve you for entry. He or she will stamp your passport and create an I-94 Arrival/Departure record for you (if you enter by air or sea). If you enter at a land border, you will be given a small white I-94 card. Your I-94 shows how long you can stay.

Normally, you are permitted to remain up to the expiration date on your Form I-797 visa petition approval notice or, if using an L-1 visa issued for a blanket L petition, on your Certificate of Eligibility Form I-129S. Persons coming to start a new office are limited to one year.

If you are coming to the U.S. on a blanket L-1 visa, the U.S. consulate will stamp and issue you three copies of Form I-129S, as well as a copy of the Notice of Action indicating approval of the blanket L-1 petition. You must bring these copies of Form I-129S if you are seeking admission on a blanket L visa, so that U.S.

CBP officers can endorse the form and give you two endorsed copies. Each time you exit and reenter the U.S., you will need to present the endorsed I-129S. (Your L-2 family members should carry a copy too, if they ever enter without you.) You will get a new I-94 authorizing your stay up to the final date indicated on the I-797 or I-129S.

> CAUTION
> **Watch out for confusion about exactly how long someone entering the U.S. on a blanket L visa is allowed to stay after each entry.** (The State Department and CBP have had different interpretations of the law on this point.) If your I-94 says you can stay past the validity date endorsed on your I-129S, to be safe you should get your employer to petition USCIS to extend your blanket L status or return home to get a new blanket L visa with an extended I-129S validity date.

G. Extending Your U.S. Stay

L-1 visa status can be extended for two years at a time, but you may not hold an L-1 visa for longer than a total of seven years if you are an L-1A manager or executive, or five years if you're an L-1B specialized knowledge professional. Although an extension is usually easier to get than the L-1 visa itself, it is not automatic. USCIS has the right to reconsider your qualifications based on any changes in the facts or law. As always, however, good cases that are well prepared will usually be successful.

To extend your L-1 visa stay in the United States, you need only file an I-129 extension petition with USCIS. Approval will allow you to continue residing and working in the United States. However, if you have plans to travel internationally, then the petition and visa stamp will both have to be updated. Like the original application procedures, you can file either in the U.S. or at a consulate.

Your period of authorized stay, which is based on the validity period of your I-129 or I-129S, will not necessarily match the validity period of your visa, which is based on "reciprocity"—the amount of time U.S. citizens in a similar situation are given by your home country. If you're entering under a blanket L-1, you can be given up to three years on each entry limited by the end date on the I-129S; your passport won't expire, and you won't exceed the maximum time allowable in L status.

If your L-1 visa obtained under a blanket application lasts longer than your authorized period of stay as shown on the initial I-129S, your employer can file a new I-129 and I-129S seeking an extension, if you are planning to remain in the United States.

If you're a blanket L visa holder who wants to travel outside the U.S. and return to your job after the I-129S expires, unfortunately you can't just get the consulate or CBP to extend your I-129S until your visa expires. Currently, your employer would have to file a new petition and you would have to obtain a new visa at the consulate, with all the time and expense that implies.

Working While Your Extension Petition Is Pending

If you file your petition for an extension of L-1 status before your authorized stay expires, you are automatically permitted to continue working under the same terms of your L visa, for up to eight months (240 days) while you are waiting for a decision. If, however, your authorized stay expires after you have filed for an extension but before you receive an approval, and more than eight months (240 days) go by without getting a decision on your extension petition, you must stop working.

1. L-1 Extension Petition

Your employer must start your extension application by filing another Form I-129 and/or I-129S visa petition, in much the same way as before. The best practice is to fully document an extension application as well as the initial request, since USCIS will probably not have the original file and papers on site, and it could cause a long delay if they have to request the old file to decide the extension request. In addition to the same documents you filed with the first petition, you must submit your I-94. You should also submit a copy of the first Notice of Action I-797 (approval notice), or I-129S (if you entered under a blanket L), a letter from your employer stating why your extension is required, and a copy of your two most recent pay stubs.

2. L-1 Visa Revalidation

If you must leave the U.S. after your L-1 extension of status has been approved, but after your first L-1 visa has expired, you must get a new L-1 visa stamp issued at a consulate in order to return. Read Section E, above. The procedures for consular extensions are identical.

3. Blanket L-1 Extensions

This section briefly describes how a company can apply for an extension of its blanket L-1 status. (This is not an explanation of how an individual may extend his or her own L-1 visa if the person arrived in the U.S. under a company's blanket L-1 visa. Extensions for individuals who obtained visas under the blanket program are handled in the same manner as explained above, except that a Certificate of Eligibility Form I-129S must also be submitted.)

Watch Out for Expedited Removal

The Immigration and Nationality Act empowers a Customs and Border Protection (CBP) inspector at the U.S. airport or border to summarily (without allowing judicial review) bar entry to someone requesting admission to the U.S. if either of the following is true:

- The inspector thinks you are lying about practically anything connected with entering the U.S., including your purpose in coming, intent to return, and prior immigration history. This includes the use or suspected use of false documents.
- You do not have the proper documentation to support your entry to the U.S. in the category you are requesting.

If the inspector excludes you, you cannot be readmitted to the U.S. for five years, unless USCIS grants a special waiver. For this reason, it is extremely important to understand the terms of your requested status and to not make any misrepresentations. If you are found to be inadmissible, you may ask the CBP inspector to withdraw your application to enter the U.S. in order to prevent having the five-year deportation order on your record. The CBP is likely to allow this if they feel you cannot otherwise be admitted to the United States, so be prepared to request the opportunity to withdraw your application if it appears your only alternative is expedited removal.

A company holding an approved blanket L-1 petition will have to extend that petition only one time. After the initial three-year approval period, the blanket L-1 visa petition can be extended with indefinite validity.

The company must begin by filing a new Form I-129 and L Supplement. The only documents required are:

- a copy of the previous Notice of Action, Form I-797, and
- a written list of the names of all transferees admitted under the blanket L-1 petition for the previous three years. For each person, include the position held, name of the specific company where the person worked, the date of initial admission, and the date of final departure.

If the company doesn't file this extension petition, or if the petition gets denied, the company will have to use the individual process for three years before seeking blanket approval again.

CAUTION

Once you've spent your maximum amount of time on an L-1 visa, you probably won't be able to return to the U.S. for a while. L-1 periods of stay are limited to either five years (for the L-1B specialized knowledge workers) or seven years (for multinational managers or executives). The rules say that you have to spend one full year outside the United States before returning with another H or L visa. (See 8 C.F.R. § 214.2(l)(12).)

Getting a Treaty Trader (E-1) Visa

The United States has entered into trade treaties with several countries and established the E-1 visa to help citizens of those countries to more easily engage in international trading activities. (See I.N.A. § 101(a)(15)(E), 8 U.S.C. § 1101(a)(l5)(E); 8 C.F.R. § 214.2(e); 22 C.F.R. § 41.51.) If you are a businessperson from one of these countries, and you plan to either engage in substantial trade with the U.S. or work for an enterprise that does substantial trade with the U.S., then an E-1 visa may be the one for you.

Some people call this visa the next best thing to permanent residence, because it allows the E-1 visa holder to be self-employed, and because it can be renewed indefinitely. There is no limit on the number of E-1 visas that can be issued every year.

 SEE AN EXPERT
Do you need a lawyer? Simply figuring out whether you're eligible for a treaty trader visa can be difficult, and the procedural requirements are as complicated as most other U.S. visas. Hiring a lawyer might be a wise business expenditure.

A. Do You Qualify for an E-1 Visa?

To qualify for an E-1 visa:
- You must be from a qualifying country.
- You must work for a qualifying business.
- You must be either a 50% (or greater) owner or key employee.
- Most of your company's trade must be with the United States.

Key Features of the E-1 Visa

Here are some of the advantages and disadvantages of the E-1 visa:
- You can work legally in the U.S. for a U.S. company if more than 50% of its business is with your home country, and your country has entered a trade treaty with the United States.
- You are restricted to working only for the U.S. employer or a self-owned business that acted as your visa sponsor.
- Your initial visa may extend up to two years, with unlimited possible two-year extensions.
- Visas are available for your accompanying spouse and minor children, but your children may not accept employment in the United States.
- Your spouse may accept U.S. employment.
- You may travel in and out of the U.S. or remain here continuously until your E-1 status expires.

1. Citizen of a Treaty Country

E-1 visas are available to citizens of selected countries that have trade treaties with the United States. Those countries with treaties currently in effect are:

Argentina	Korea (South)
Australia	Kosovo
Austria	Latvia
Belgium	Liberia
Bolivia	Luxembourg
Bosnia and	Macedonia
Herzegovina	Mexico
Brunei	Montenegro
Canada	The Netherlands
Chile	Norway
Colombia	Oman
Costa Rica	Pakistan
Croatia	Paraguay
Denmark	Philippines
Estonia	Poland
Ethiopia	Serbia
Finland	Singapore
France	Slovenia
Germany	Spain
Greece	Suriname
Honduras	Sweden
Iran	Switzerland
Ireland	Taiwan
Israel	Thailand
Italy	Togo
Japan	Turkey
Jordan	United Kingdom.

Because treaty provisions are subject to change, be sure your country has one in force before proceeding with your application. The complete list is kept at Volume 9 of the *Foreign Affairs Manual* (*FAM*), § 402.9-10. (You can find the *FAM* on the U.S. State Department website at https://fam.state.gov.)

2. Company Owned by Citizens of a Qualifying Country

At least 50% of the business with which you're associated must be owned by citizens of your treaty country. (See 9 FAM § 402.9-4(B).) The company may be owned by you or by others. If the company is owned in part or in whole by others, and some or all of them already live in the U.S., those people may need to have E-1 visas themselves before the company can act as an E-1 sponsor for you. Specifically:

- at least 50% of the company must be owned by citizens of a single trade treaty country, and
- the owners from the single trade treaty country must either live outside the U.S. and be classifiable for E-1 status or live inside the U.S. with E-1 visas.

This second condition can be a little confusing. Some examples may help to make it clearer.

EXAMPLE 1: The company is owned 100% by one person. The owner is a citizen of a trade treaty country and lives outside the U.S. in his home country. He would qualify for E-1 status if he sought to enter the United States.

In this case the owner does not need to already have an E-1 visa for the company to support your E-1 visa application. He has already fulfilled the alternative condition by living outside the U.S. and being eligible for such status.

EXAMPLE 2: The company is owned in equal shares by two people. Each owner is a citizen of the same trade treaty country. One owner lives in the U.S. on a green card. The other still lives in his home country and is classifiable as an E-1.

In this case, neither owner needs an E-1 visa for the company to support your E-1 application, because 50% of the owners have fulfilled the qualifying conditions. If, however, we changed this example so that both owners lived in the U.S., at least one of them would need an E-1 visa to fulfill the required conditions. (Green card holders do not qualify as treaty investors for E-1 purposes.)

EXAMPLE 3: The company is owned in equal shares by 100 people. Thirty owners are citizens of a particular trade treaty country but live in the United States. Thirty other owners are citizens of the same trade treaty country and they are living in their home country, but are eligible as E-1 visa holders. The remaining 40 owners are U.S. citizens.

In this situation, if the company is to act as an E-1 sponsor for others, 20 of the 30 owners who are citizens of the trade treaty country but live in the U.S. must hold E-1 visas. Remember that only 50 of the owners need to be citizens of the treaty country. Of those 50, each must either live outside the U.S. and be classifiable as E-1s, or live in the U.S. on an E-1 visa. In our example, 30 live outside the United States. Therefore, only 20 of the trade treaty country citizens living inside the U.S. need have E-1 visas to make up the necessary 50% total of qualifying owners.

Additionally, USCIS regulations allow a different test in the case of publicly traded corporations in which it is difficult to determine the nationality of each shareholder. In the situation where a corporation's stock is traded exclusively in the country of incorporation, it may be presumed to have the nationality of the country where the stocks are exchanged.

3. You Must Be Either a Supervisor or Manager or a Key Employee

E-1 visas may be issued to people who are executives, supervisors, supervisory role executives, or persons whose skills are essential to the enterprise.

a. Executives and Supervisors

The main duties of your position must be executive or supervisory and give you ultimate control and responsibility for the operation of at least a major part of the enterprise. The immigration authorities will apply the following standards to determine whether a given position fits the bill:

- An "executive" position normally gives the employee great authority in determining the policy and direction of the enterprise.
- A "supervisory" position normally entails responsibility for supervising a major portion of an enterprise's operations and does not usually involve direct supervision of low-level employees.
- Your skills, experience, salary, and title should be on a par with executive or supervisory positions. The position should carry overall authority and responsibility in the context of the enterprise, such as discretionary decision making, policy setting, direction and management of business operations, and supervision of other professional and supervisory personnel.

b. Essential Employees

If you're not an executive or supervisor, you may still get an E-1 visa if you are an employee with special qualifications that make your services essential to the efficient operation of the enterprise. Your skills do not have to be unique or one of a kind, but they should be indispensable to the success of the investment. USCIS evaluates employees' skills on a case-by-case basis. However, if your skills are commonplace or readily available in the U.S. labor market, showing that you are essential will be difficult.

The immigration authorities will consider the following to determine whether a nonexecutive, nonsupervisory person should be classified as an E-1 employee because his or her skills are essential:

- the degree of expertise in the area of operations involved
- the degree of experience and training with the enterprise
- whether U.S. workers possess the individual's skills or aptitude
- the length of time required to train an individual to perform the job duties of the position
- the relationship of the individual's skills and talents to the overall operations of the entity, and
- the salary the special qualifications can command.

Knowledge of a foreign language and/or culture will not by itself constitute the degree of essentiality required.

4. More Than 50% of the Company's Trade Must Be Between the U.S. and Your Home Country

More than 50% of the company's trade must be between the U.S. and the treaty nation citizen's home country. For example, if you are from the U.K. and are in the business of importing English antiques to the U.S., more than 50% of your inventory, as measured by its cash value, must have been imported directly from the United Kingdom. If some other company does the importing and your business simply buys the British goods once they reach the U.S., you will not qualify for the visa because your company is not directly engaged in trade with the United Kingdom.

The law is liberal in its definition of what constitutes trade. The most straightforward example is the import or export of a tangible product, but exchange of monies or services can also qualify. For example, the transfer of technology through scientifically knowledgeable employees or the rendering of services have been recognized as trade. Activities other than the sale of goods that have been officially recognized by the U.S. Department of State as trade for E-1 purposes include international banking, insurance, transportation, communications, data processing, advertising, accounting, design and engineering, management consulting, tourism, technology and its transfer, and some news-gathering activities.

5. Substantial Trade

A company must be carrying on a substantial amount of trade between the U.S. and the home country in order for the company to successfully support your E-1 application. The term "substantial" is not defined in the law by a strict numerical measure. In fact it is not specifically defined at all, though USCIS regulations state that there must be a "continuous flow" of trade items between the two countries.

What is considered substantial depends on the type of business. For example, a business that imports heavy machinery may not have to show a huge number of sales, but will have to show a greater dollar volume of business than a business importing candy bars to meet the requirement of substantial trade.

There are three general tests—dollars, volume, and frequency—that can normally be relied on to measure substantiality. The company must be able to meet the minimum standards of all three.

a. Dollar Amount of Trade

The dollar amount (not the retail value) of the inventory, services, or other commodities purchased from or sold to the treaty country should exceed $200,000 per year. However, some consulates require the sales or purchases to equal or exceed as much as $500,000, while others may accept as little as $50,000. A specific sum is not written into the law. The individual

Possibilities for a Green Card From E-1 Status

If you have an E-1 visa, you can file to get a green card, but being in the U.S. on an E-1 visa gives you no advantage in doing so, and in fact may prove to be a drawback. To begin with, there is no immigrant visa category in which E-1 owners of companies engaged in international trade fit. The U.S. employment-based immigration system is mainly set up for employees working for employers, not for employers looking to sponsor themselves. There is the EB-5 category for immigrant investors, but the high capital requirements and complex rules governing that immigrant category make it all but impossible for most investors to qualify. Therefore, it is more likely that people who enter in E-1 status will immigrate only after being sponsored as an employee by some other company. Alternatively, they may perhaps immigrate through other visa categories, such as the diversity visa lottery or family-based immigration. Furthermore, E-1 visas, like most nonimmigrant visas, are intended only for people who plan on leaving the U.S. once their temporary jobs or other activities there are completed.

If you do find a way to qualify for a green card, and are sponsored for one, you are in effect making a statement that you never intend to leave the United States. Therefore, the U.S. government may allow you to keep E-1 status while pursuing a green card, but only if you can convince it that you did not intend to get a green card when you originally applied for the E-1 visa and that you will leave the U.S. if you are unable to secure a green card before your E-1 visa expires.

Proving these things can be tricky. If you do not succeed, your E-1 visa may be taken away. Should this happen, it may affect your green card application, since being out of status or working without authorization may be a bar to getting a green card in the U.S. or, if you overstay your visa period, may subject you to a waiting period of three or ten years if you depart the U.S. and apply for a visa. (See Chapter 3.)

---

consular officer has the authority to require varying amounts in different cases. However, experience shows that anything under the $200,000 mark is a weak case.

b. Volume

If the company sells products, to satisfy the volume test, its import or export trade must be enough to create full-time business in the United States. If the company sells services, the volume should be large enough to support the E-1 visa holder and at least one other worker. Some businesses do not meet the volume test when they are first starting up, but grow to the required size as time goes on. Purchasing a growing business may be one way to fulfill the volume requirement immediately.

c. Frequency

The company must import to or export from the U.S. with sufficient frequency to maintain a full inventory at all times. One shipment is not enough. Importation or exportation must be ongoing.

> **CAUTION**
> **These three measures have been partly derived from our own experience and not the immigration laws.** It is possible for an E-1 visa to be approved with a smaller amount of trade than we have described in our three tests. With E-1 visas, a great deal is left to the judgment of the USCIS or consular officer evaluating the application.

6. Intent to Leave the U.S.

E-1 visas are meant to be temporary. At the time of your application, you must intend to depart the U.S. when your business there is completed. As previously mentioned, you are not required to maintain a foreign residence abroad.

The U.S. government knows it is difficult to read minds. Expect to be asked for evidence showing that when you go to the U.S. on an E-1 visa, you eventually plan to leave. In many nonimmigrant categories, you are asked to show proof that you will keep a house or an apartment outside the U.S., indicating that you eventually intend to go back to your home country. You do not need to keep a home outside the U.S. to qualify for an E-1 visa—but it would help. You will certainly be asked to show that you have some family members, possessions, or property elsewhere in the world as an incentive for your eventual departure from the United States.

7. Bringing Your Spouse and Children

When you qualify for an E-1 visa, your spouse and unmarried children under age 21 can also get E-1 visas by providing proof of their family relationship to you. Your spouse will also be permitted to work in the United States.

To take advantage of the right to work, your spouse must, after arriving in the U.S., apply for a work permit. This is done on USCIS Form I-765 (available on the USCIS website at www.uscis.gov/i-765). In filling out the form, your spouse should write "spouse of E nonimmigrant" in Question 15, and (a)(17) in Question 16.

Your spouse will need to mail this form, together with proof of your visa status, a copy of your marriage certificate, a copy of his or her I-94 card, the filing fee (currently $410), and two passport-style photos, to the appropriate USCIS service center for your geographic region. For the address and other information, call USCIS Information at 800-375-5283 or see the USCIS website (www.uscis.gov/i-765-addresses).

B. Quick View of the E-1 Visa Application Process

Once you have opened a qualifying company engaged in trade between your home country and the United States, or been offered a job as a key employee of a qualifying company owned by others from your country, getting an E-1 visa is a one- or two-step process, depending on whether you are applying from inside the U.S. or at a U.S. consulate outside the United States:

- If you're outside the U.S., you file an application at a U.S. consulate there. If you are already in the U.S. legally in some other type of nonimmigrant status, you can, under some circumstances, apply for a change to E-1 status at a USCIS office inside the United States. (However, if you were admitted without a visa, such as under the Visa Waiver Program, you may not change your status in the United States.)
- You use your visa to enter the U.S. and claim your E-1 status.

C. How to Apply From Outside the U.S.

Applicants outside the U.S. must apply for an E-1 visa at a U.S. consulate in their home country. The exact steps to take to apply for an E-1 visa depend on the U.S. embassy or consulate where you're applying. You will most likely need to:

- prepare and submit an online application
- schedule an interview at a U.S. embassy or consulate
- gather documents and fill out another form
- pay the required fee, and
- meet with an official at the U.S. embassy or consulate.

For additional information on these procedures, consult the website of the U.S. embassy or consulate where you're applying, and see the State Department website at www.travel.state.gov (click "Employment" and then "Treaty Trader and Investor Visa").

 CAUTION
Have you been, or are you now, working or living illegally in the United States? If so, see Chapter 3 regarding whether you can still get a visa from a U.S. consulate. You may have become inadmissible or subject to a three-year or ten-year bar on reentry.

1. Preparing and Submitting Your Application Form

Your visa application process starts with a government form called a DS-160, which can be completed only online. To access the DS-160, go to the State Department's Consular Electronic Application Center (CEAC) website, at https://ceac.state.gov. The form must be filled out in English. If a question is marked "optional," you can leave the answer space blank. You can answer with "Does Not Apply" if the question does not fit your situation. Most questions require some answer—the system will not allow you to submit an application if you don't answer a mandatory question. Electronically sign your DS-160 by clicking the "Sign Application" button at the end of the form.

The DS-160 asks for a lot of information. It will help if you have the following documents nearby:

- your passport
- your travel itinerary, if you have already made travel arrangements, and
- your résumé or curriculum vitae (in order to provide information about your current and previous education and work history).

Consult your travel records (or your memory!) before starting the application. You'll need to provide the dates of your last five visits or trips to the U.S., if you have previously been there. You may also be asked for your international travel history for the past five years.

You must also upload a U.S. passport-style photo to CEAC with your application. Information on how to provide a suitable photo is provided on the State Department's website at www.travel.state.gov. (Follow the links to "Employment," "Treaty Trader and Investor Visa," "Photograph Requirements.") If you have trouble getting the system to accept your photo, ask someone who's good with computers for help. As a last resort you can just bring a photo to your consular interview.

After you've submitted the DS-160 online, print and keep the barcode confirmation page. You'll need to bring it to your interview at the U.S. consulate.

TIP

You don't need to finish Form DS-160 in one sitting. The system allows you to save your work and return to it later. When you begin the DS-160, you will be issued a unique application identification (ID) number after selecting and answering a security question. You must have your application ID in order to return to your application. The information you entered in your DS-160 is saved every time you click the "Next" button at the bottom of a page. However, an application is saved on CEAC for only 30 days. If you will want to access your application after 30 days, save it by selecting the "Save Application to File" button. Then, click the "Save" button on the File Download window.

Applying at a Consulate Outside of Your Home Country

The law allows most people to apply for visas at any U.S. consulate they choose. You'll find, however, that most consulates around the world will not allow you to apply for an E-1 visa unless you are a resident of the district they service. The consulate in your home country is the one that's best able to determine whether your business qualifies under that country's treaty, so that's where you're expected to apply.

2. Schedule an Interview at a U.S. Embassy or Consulate

After your DS-160 has been accepted, it's up to you to schedule an interview at a U.S. embassy or consulate. While interviews are generally not required for applicants under 14 years old or over 80 years old, consular officers have the discretion to require an interview of any applicant, regardless of age.

All consulates insist on advance appointments. No walk-ins are allowed. Since procedures for scheduling interviews at the consulates vary, telephone or check the consulate's website in advance to find out about local policies. For information on consulates, go to www.usembassy.gov.

3. Pay the Application Fee

Most consulates require you to pay the visa application fee, currently $205 for E-1 visas, before your interview. The consulate will give you instructions on how and when to make payment.

4. Gather Supporting Documents

The consulate will tell you to come to the interview with documents that support your eligibility for an E-1 visa. You'll definitely need to bring your passport, the DS-160 confirmation page, your fee payment receipt (if advance payment was required), and a photo if you weren't able to upload one successfully to CEAC, or perhaps even if you were.

You'll have to prepare another government form—the DS-156E—at this point. You can find it at www.travel.gov (click under "US Visas," then "All Forms" under the "Forms and Fees" section.) Fill it out online, print it, sign it, and bring it to your interview. If you're getting an E-1 visa as an employee, you'll need to have someone who has signing authority for the company (a "responsible officer") sign the form instead of you.

The exact documentation you'll be asked to bring depends on you and the business. Generally, consulates like to see the evidence discussed below.

a. Proof of the Nationality of the Qualifying Business Owners

You must show that the qualifying business is owned by citizens of one of the trade treaty countries. If you are not the owner yourself, you will need to show that both you and those who do own the company are citizens of the same treaty country, usually by showing copies of their passports.

Also provide documents showing where each of the owners is living currently. Affidavits from each of these owners stating their places of residence will serve this purpose. If any are living in the U.S., copies of their passports and I-94s are also needed to demonstrate that they hold valid

E-1 visas. Remember, if the owners of the company live in the U.S., at least 50% must also hold E-1 visas for the business to support your own E-1 application.

You will need to prove that you or other nationals of your country own at least 50% of the qualifying business. If the qualifying business is a corporation, you should submit copies of all stock certificates, together with a notarized affidavit from the secretary of the corporation listing the name of each shareholder and the number of shares each owns. The affidavit must account for all the shares issued to date. Remember that at least 50% must be owned by nationals of your treaty country.

If the qualifying business is not incorporated, instead of copies of stock certificates, you will need to present legal papers proving the existence and ownership of the company. These may be partnership agreements, business registration certificates, or business licenses, together with a notarized affidavit from an official of the company certifying who owns the business and in what percentages.

b. Proof That You Are a Key Employee

If you are not the majority owner of the company, you must submit evidence that your job in the U.S. will fit the USCIS definition of an executive, a supervisor, or an essential employee. To prove this, present detailed statements from the sponsoring business explaining your specific duties as well as the number and kind of employees you will supervise. If the application is based on your special position as an employee, the statements should also describe the nature of the essential knowledge or experience, how it will be used, and why it is essential in your U.S. job. These required statements may be in your employer's own words and do not have to be in any special form.

c. Proof of the Existence of an Active Business

You should submit documents to show that your E-1 visa application is based on a real, ongoing business. Such evidence should include:

- articles of incorporation or other business charter of the qualifying company
- bank statements for the qualifying company
- credit agreements with suppliers
- letters of credit issued
- leases or deeds for business premises and warehouse space
- payroll reports
- tax returns filed in the past two years, if any, including payroll tax returns, and
- promotional literature or advertising.

If the business is newly formed, there will be no tax returns yet. You should then submit a detailed business plan including financial projections for the next five years.

d. Proof That a Majority of the Company's Trade Is Between the U.S. and Your Home Country

More than 50% of the company's total trade must consist of commerce between your treaty home country and the United States. This is best shown by presenting copies of all import or export documents from the previous 12 months, including purchase or sale orders, bills of lading and customs entry documents, contracts with suppliers outside of the U.S, and a balance sheet from the qualifying company showing the total amount of inventory for the same period. Comparison of the balance sheet with the import or export documents will show the percentage of the company's trade devoted to commerce between the U.S. and the trade treaty country. The dollar amount of the imports or exports between the U.S. and your home country must total more than 50% of the entire inventory.

e. Proof That the Trade Is Substantial

The qualifying company's trade between the U.S. and your home treaty country must be substantial, meeting the three tests previously described: dollar, volume, and frequency. The same documents presented to prove that the majority of the company's trade is between the U.S. and your home treaty country will also serve to show that the trade is substantial.

5. Attending Your Consular Interview

The last step in the process will be to attend an interview with a consular officer. The officer will examine the data in your DS-160 application form and documents for accuracy, especially regarding facts about the substantiality of the business and the nationality of the owners. Evidence of ties to your home country will also be checked. During the interview, you will surely be asked how long you intend to remain in the United States. Any answer indicating that you are unsure about plans to return or have an interest in applying for a green card is likely to result in a denial of your visa. (See Chapter 4 for what else to expect during consular interviews, and what to do if your application is denied.)

At some point in the application process, most likely at the interview, you will need to have ink-free, digital fingerprint scans taken. The consular officer will then initiate various security checks to make sure you haven't been involved in criminal or terrorist activity. Because the U.S. is doing more comprehensive security checks than in the past, you are unlikely to receive a decision on your visa the same day as the interview. Security checks can add days, weeks, or (more rarely) months to the processing time.

6. Visa Issuance and Entry into the United States

Some people, after their visa is approved, must pay an additional visa issuance fee—it depends on whether your country charges U.S. citizens a similar fee. (Most countries don't.)

The consulate will tell you how it plans to return your passport to you. Most applicants pick it up in person, but some consulates mail it back. The visa will be affixed to a page in the passport.

You have until the expiration date that appears on your E-1 visa to enter the United States. When you get to the U.S., the border officer will examine your paperwork, ask you some questions, and if all is in order, approve you for entry. The officer will create an I-94 Arrival/Departure record (if you enter by air or sea), and if you enter at a land border, will put an I-94 card in your passport.

Your I-94 contains the dates showing your authorized stay. You will likely be permitted to remain in the U.S. for two years. Each time you exit and reenter the U.S., you will get a new I-94 with a new period of authorized stay. If you do not wish to leave the U.S. after that time, you can apply for extensions of stay, which are issued in two-year increments for as long as you maintain your E-1 status qualifications. (See Section E, below.)

D. How to Apply If You're in the U.S.

If you are physically present in the U.S., you may apply for E-1 status without leaving the country on the following conditions:

- You entered the U.S. legally and not on a visa waiver.
- You have never worked illegally.
- The date on your I-94 has not passed.
- You are admissible and none of the bars to changing status apply to you (see Chapter 3).

If you were admitted as a visitor without a visa under the Visa Waiver Program, you may not apply from within the United States. Similarly, you can't take advantage of this option if you entered the U.S. using a C (alien in transit), TWOV (alien in transit without a visa), D (crewman), or any K (fiancé) visa. Certain J-1 (exchange visitor) visa holders are prohibited from changing status as well.

TIP

Your eligibility to apply in the U.S. has nothing to do with your overall eligibility for an E-1 visa. Many applicants who are barred from filing in the U.S. but otherwise qualify for E-1 status may still apply successfully for an E-1 visa at a U.S. consulate in their home country.

There is another problem that comes up only in U.S. filings. It is the issue of what is called preconceived intent. To approve a change of status, USCIS must believe that at the time you originally entered the U.S. as a visitor or with some other nonimmigrant visa, you did not intend to apply for a different status. If USCIS thinks you had a preconceived plan to use one visa to enter the U.S. with an eye to applying for a different status after getting there, it may deny your application. (You can get around the preconceived intent issue by leaving the U.S. and applying for your E-1 visa at a U.S. consulate in another country.)

In technical terms, what you will be applying for in the U.S. is a change of status. To do so, you'll need to file an application with USCIS on Form I-129 (Petition for a Nonimmigrant Worker), with accompanying documents to prove your eligibility. If your spouse and children will be accompanying you, they must file for their change of status on a different form, called Form I-539.

If you decide to apply for a change of status within the U.S., you should realize that you still don't have the E-1 visa that you'll need if you ever leave the U.S.—a change of status only gives you E-1 status. Visas are never given inside the United States. They are issued exclusively by U.S. consulates in other countries. If you file in the U.S. and you are successful, you will get to remain in the U.S. with E-1 privileges until the status expires. But should you leave the country for any reason before that time, you will have to apply for the visa itself at a U.S. consulate before returning to the United States. Moreover, the fact that your E-1 status has been approved in the U.S. does not guarantee that the consulate will also approve your visa. You'll have to present a whole new application, and they will evaluate it with little or no consideration for the previous USCIS decision. For this reason, many people find it easier to leave the U.S. and apply at a U.S. consulate from the start.

1. Preparing the Change of Status Application

The checklist below will help you prepare the documents and forms for your change of status application.

For further explanation of some of the key items on this checklist, see Section C1, above.

Although it is not a requirement, one additional item that you may wish to add to the paperwork package is a cover letter. Cover letters act as a summary and index to the forms and documents, and are often used by immigration attorneys or U.S. companies that process many visas for their employees. Cover letters begin with a statement summarizing the facts of the case and explaining why the particular applicant is eligible for the visa.

This statement is followed by a list of the forms and documents submitted. If it is carefully written, a cover letter can make the case clearer and easier to process for the consular or USCIS officer evaluating it. This is particularly important in an E-1 visa case where the documentation by itself may require explanation. Cover letters must be individually tailored to each case, so if you don't think you can write a good one, just leave it out and submit only your forms and documents; or hire an attorney to help.

2. Mailing the Change of Status Petition

After assembling the I-129 petition, you must mail it to the USCIS California Service Center. The USCIS website instructions for Form I-129 will give you the exact address. USCIS Service Centers are not the same as USCIS local offices—for one thing, you cannot visit regional Service Centers in person.

3. Awaiting a Decision on the Change of Status Petition

Within a few weeks after mailing in the petition, you should get back a written confirmation that the papers are being processed, together with a receipt for the fee. This notice will also contain your immigration file number. If USCIS wants further information before acting on your case, it will send you a form known as a Request for Evidence (RFE). Supply the extra data requested and mail it back to the service center.

I-129 petitions for E-1 status normally take two to three months to review. (Check current processing times at www.uscis.gov. Follow the links to "Check Your Case Status" and "Check Processing Times.") If you're successful, USCIS will send you a Form I-797 Notice of Action, showing that the change of status has been approved. An I-94 card showing your authorized period of stay will be attached to the bottom of the form.

 TIP

Faster processing—at a price. For $1,225 over and above the regular filing fees, USCIS promises premium processing of the visa petition, including a decision within 15 days. Currently, premium processing is available for I-129 petitions in most immigrant visa categories. You need not request premium processing at the time you first file the Form I-129, but can "upgrade" to premium processing later if your I-129 is still pending and you are getting impatient for a decision. To use this service, the employer must fill out an additional application (Form I-907) and submit it to a special USCIS service center address. For complete instructions, see the USCIS website at www.uscis.gov/i-907.

E-1 Change of Status Checklist

☐ Form I-129, with E-1/E-2 Classification Supplement (signed and submitted by you, if you're self-employed, or by your employer).

☐ Filing fee: $460.

☐ If your family members are with you and need a change of status, Form I-539 with accompanying fee (currently $370) and copies of your family members' I-94s or other proof of lawful immigration status and of their relationship to you (such as marriage and birth certificates). One Form I-539 and fee will cover your spouse and all your children. This form is meant to be filled out and signed by your family members, not by your employer.

☐ If either you or your spouse have ever been married before, copies of divorce and death certificates showing termination of all previous marriages.

☐ A copy of your I-94 or other proof of your current lawful, unexpired immigration status (except Canadian visitors, who are not expected to have I-94s).

☐ Proof of the nationality of the qualifying business owners.

☐ Proof that you are a key employee.

☐ Proof of the existence of an active business.

☐ Proof that a majority of the company's trade is between the U.S. and your home country.

☐ Proof that the trade is substantial.

☐ Documents establishing your intent to leave the U.S. when your status expires, such as deeds verifying ownership of a house or other real property, written statements from you explaining that close relatives are staying behind, or letters from a company showing that you have a job waiting when you return from the United States.

☐ Cover letter (optional).

If requesting quick (premium) processing:

☐ Form I-907, with $1,225 filing fee.

E. Extending Your U.S. Stay

E-1 visas can be renewed for up to five years at a time and E-1 status stays can be extended for two years at a time (depending on your home country). When you enter the U.S. with an E-1 visa, your authorized stay as indicated on your I-94 is limited to two years at a time. If you have a five-year visa, this means your I-94 may expire before your visa does. Do not think it is okay to overstay the I-94! Even if your E-1 visa has not expired, make sure you take at least one international trip every two years, to avoid staying past the date on your I-94.

Although an extension is usually easier to get than the E-1 visa itself, it is not automatic. USCIS or the consulate has the right to reconsider your qualifications based on any changes in the facts or law. When the original application for an E-1 visa or status was weak, it is not unusual for an extension request to be turned down.

Working While Your Extension Application Is Pending

If you file your application for an extension of E-1 status before your authorized stay expires, you are automatically permitted to continue working for up to 240 days while you are waiting for a decision. If, however, your authorized stay expires after you have filed for an extension, but before you receive an approval, and more than 240 days go by without getting a decision on your extension application, your work authorization ends and you must stop working.

If you have received E-1 status in the U.S. but never applied for a visa, it's best to stay in the U.S. to apply for an extension of your status (in case the consulate disagrees with USCIS's original decision approving your E-1 status). However, if you have an E-1 visa that is still valid but your I-94 is about to expire, it is generally better to leave the U.S. and return again instead of trying to extend your status in the United States. When you return to the U.S. on your valid E-1 visa, you will automatically receive a new I-94 and a new one- or two-year period of authorized stay. By leaving and reentering, no extension application will be needed and there will be no reevaluation of your qualifications. This method works only until your visa expires, of course. At some point, you'll have to return to your home consulate and get a new visa.

The general procedures for an E-1 extension from within the U.S. are the same as those described in Section D, above. The forms, documents, and fees are identical.

CAUTION

The fact that you were issued one E-1 visa does not mean you will be issued a second one. And even if you are issued a second one, that does not mean you will be issued a third one. Each and every time you apply for a new E-1 visa, the visa officer is going to evaluate your company's growth and your profitability. If you have not grown sufficiently to hire U.S. workers, or if you have not turned a significant profit, you are likely to have your E-1 visa renewal application denied, even if you had no problem getting the first E-1 visa. Many people have found to their dismay that their E-1 visa renewal applications were denied just at the point they were starting to reach profitability. Make sure you demonstrate profitability before you reapply for your second (or third, etc.) E-1 visa. Otherwise, you will want to seek alternative visa options.

Watch Out for Expedited Removal

The law empowers a Customs and Border Protection (CBP) inspector at the U.S. airport or border to summarily (without allowing judicial review) bar entry to someone requesting admission to the U.S. if either of the following is true:

- The inspector thinks you are lying about practically anything connected with entering the U.S., including your purpose in coming, intent to return, and prior immigration history. This includes the use or suspected use of false documents.
- You do not have the proper documentation to support your entry to the U.S. in the category you are requesting.

If the inspector excludes you, you cannot be readmitted to the U.S. for five years, unless USCIS grants a special waiver. For this reason it is extremely important to understand the terms of your requested status, and to not make any misrepresentations. If you are found to be inadmissible, you may ask the CBP inspector to withdraw your application to enter the U.S. in order to prevent having the five-year deportation order on your record. The CBP may allow this in some exceptional cases.

F. Visa Revalidation

If you leave the U.S. with an expired E-1 visa stamp, you must have a new visa issued at a consulate before returning (even if you've extended your E-1 status with USCIS). Reread procedures for consular filing in Section C, above. The procedures for consular visa extensions are identical. It's possible, however, that your consulate will waive the interview requirement if you're renewing the visa within a year of its expiration.

If you are outside the U.S. with a valid (unexpired) visa, you need only reenter and a new I-94 authorizing your stay for one or two years will be created for you.

Getting a Treaty Investor (E-2) Visa

An E-2 visa allows businesspeople from certain countries to work in the U.S. for a business in which people from their country have invested. (See I.N.A. § 101(a)(15)(E), 8 U.S.C. § 1101(a)(l5)(E); 8 C.F.R. § 214.2(e); 22 C.F.R. § 41.51.) Like the E-1 visa, some people call the E-2 the next best thing to permanent residence, because of the possibility of self-employment and the unlimited number of extensions. There are no limits on the number of E-2 visas that can be issued each year.

CAUTION

Do not confuse E-2 treaty investor visas with green cards through investment, discussed in Chapter 11. The E-2 visa is a completely different type of visa with completely different requirements. For one thing, it's a nonimmigrant visa. All nonimmigrant visas are temporary, while green cards are permanent. Moreover, a green card through investment requires a dollar investment of $500,000 or more, while an E-2 visa has no dollar minimum. Do not think the E-2 visa will do anything in itself to help you immigrate permanently. There are a great many E-2 nonimmigrant visa holders who are not able to leverage their business into a means for immigration sponsorship. On the other hand, the E-2 visa is renewable indefinitely, at least in theory, so this may be all you require. Again, see Chapter 11 to compare.

Key Features of the E-2 Visa

Here are some of the advantages and disadvantages of the E-2 visa:

- You can work legally in the U.S. for a U.S. business in which a substantial cash investment has been made by you or other citizens of your home country, so long as your country has a trade treaty with the U.S.
- You may travel in and out of the U.S. or remain here continuously until your visa and status expire.
- You are restricted to working only for the employer or self-owned business that acted as your E-2 visa sponsor.
- Your initial visa may last up to five years (depending on what country you're coming from), with unlimited possible five-year extensions.
- Each time you enter the U.S., you will be admitted for two years.
- Visas are available for your accompanying spouse and minor children, but your children cannot work here.
- Your spouse will be permitted to accept employment in the U.S.

A. Do You Qualify for an E-2 Visa?

There are six requirements for getting an E-2 visa:

- You must be a citizen of a country that has an investor treaty with the United States.

- You must be coming to work in the U.S. for a company you own or one that is at least 50% owned by other nationals of your home country.
- You must be either the owner or a key employee of the U.S. business.
- You or the company must have made a substantial investment in the U.S. business.
- The U.S. company must be an active, for-profit business.
- You must intend to leave the U.S. when your business in the U.S. is completed.

1. Countries That Have Treaties With the U.S.

E-2 visas are available to citizens of only selected countries that have investor treaties with the United States. Legal residence is not enough. With the exception of E-2 applicants from the U.K., you need not be presently residing in your country of citizenship in order to qualify for an E-2 visa. When you are a citizen of more than one nation, you may qualify for an E-2 visa if at least one of them has an investor treaty with the United States.

Those countries with investor treaties currently in effect are:

Albania
Argentina
Armenia
Australia
Austria
Azerbaijan
Bahrain
Bangladesh
Belgium
Bolivia
Bosnia and Herzegovina
Bulgaria
Cameroon
Canada
Chile
Colombia
Congo (Brazzaville)
Congo (Democratic Republic of, Kinshasa)
Costa Rica
Croatia
Czech Republic
Denmark
Ecuador
Egypt
Estonia
Ethiopia
Finland
France
Georgia
Germany
Grenada
Honduras
Iran
Ireland
Italy
Jamaica
Japan
Jordan
Kazakhstan
Korea (South)
Kosovo
Kyrgyzstan
Latvia
Liberia
Lithuania
Luxembourg
Macedonia
Mexico
Moldova
Mongolia
Montenegro
Morocco
Netherlands, The
Norway
Oman
Pakistan
Panama
Paraguay
Philippines
Poland
Romania
Serbia
Senegal
Singapore
Slovak Republic
Slovenia
Spain
Sri Lanka
Suriname
Sweden
Switzerland
Taiwan
Thailand
Togo
Trinidad and Tobago
Tunisia
Turkey
Ukraine
United Kingdom.

Because treaty provisions are subject to change, be sure your country has one in force before proceeding with your application. The complete list is kept at Volume 9 of the *Foreign Affairs Manual* (*FAM*), § 402.9-10. (You can find the *Foreign Affairs Manual* on the U.S. State Department website at https://fam.state.gov.)

2. Whether Your Company Is Owned by Citizens of a Qualifying Country

To get an E-2 visa, you must be coming to the U.S. to work for a business that is at least 50% owned by citizens of your treaty country. The company may be owned by you or others. If the company is owned in part or in whole by others, and some or all of them already live in the U.S., those people may need to have E-2 visas themselves before the company can act as an E-2 sponsor for you. Specifically:

- At least 50% of the company must be owned by citizens of a single investor treaty country.
- The owners from the single investor treaty country must either (a) live outside the U.S. and be eligible for treaty investor status, or (b) live inside the U.S. with E-2 or other nonimmigrant visa status.

This second condition can be a little confusing. Some examples may help to make it clearer.

EXAMPLE 1: The company is owned 100% by one person (not you). The owner is a citizen of an investor treaty country and lives outside the U.S. in his or her home country.

In this case, the owner does not need an E-2 visa for the company to support your E-2 visa application, but must be able to satisfy the criteria for an E-2 visa if he or she were to apply. In other words, the owner cannot be a U.S. citizen or lawful permanent resident.

EXAMPLE 2: The company is owned in equal shares by two people (neither of them you). Each owner is a citizen of the same investor treaty country. One owner lives in the U.S. on a green card. The other still lives in his home country.

In this case, the owner living abroad must be classifiable for E-2 status. If, however, we changed this example so that both owners lived in the U.S., the owner who is a green card holder would not qualify as a treaty investor, so his or her shares would not count toward the 50% ownership requirement. In this case, the second owner would need to be in E status, or some other nonimmigrant visa status.

EXAMPLE 3: The company is owned in equal shares by 100 people. Thirty owners are citizens of a particular investor treaty country but live in the United States. Thirty other owners are citizens of the same investor treaty country and they are living in their home country. The remaining 40 owners are U.S. citizens.

In this situation, if the company is to act as an E-2 visa sponsor for others, 20 of the 30 owners who are citizens of the investor treaty country but live in the U.S. must hold E-2 visas. Remember that only 50 of the owners need to be citizens of the treaty country. Of those 50, each must either live outside the U.S. and be classifiable for E-2 status or live in the U.S. on an E-2 or other nonimmigrant visa. In our example, 30 live outside the United States. Therefore, only 20 of the investor treaty country citizens living inside the U.S. need to have E-2 visas to make up the necessary 50% total of qualifying owners.

USCIS allows a different test in the case of publicly traded corporations in which it is difficult to determine the nationality of each shareholder. If a corporation's stock is traded exclusively in the country of incorporation, it may be presumed to have the nationality of the country where the stocks are exchanged.

3. You Must Be a 50% Owner or a Supervisor, an Executive, or a Key Employee

E-2 visas may be issued only to the principal owners or key employees of the qualifying business, provided all have the same treaty nationality. To qualify as a principal owner, you must:

- own at least 50% of—and exercise voting control within—the company and

- develop and direct the business.

To qualify as a key employee, you must be considered either:

- an executive or a supervisor, or
- a person whose skills are essential to the enterprise.

a. Definition of Executives and Supervisors

For E-2 classification purposes, your executive or supervisory position must give you ultimate control and responsibility for the operation of at least a major part of the enterprise. (See 22 C.F.R. § 41.51(b)(12).) The immigration authorities will apply the following standards to determine whether a given position fits the bill:

- An "executive" position normally gives the employee great authority in determining policy and direction of the enterprise.
- A "supervisory" position normally entails responsibility for supervising a major portion of an enterprise's operations and does not usually involve direct supervision of low-level employees.
- Your skills, experience, salary, and title should be on a par with executive or supervisory positions, and the position should carry overall authority and responsibility in the context of the enterprise, such as discretionary decision making, policy setting, direction and management of business operations, and supervision of other professional and supervisory personnel.

b. Essential Employees

By requiring that employees who are not executives or supervisors be essential, the immigration authorities intend to favor specialists over ordinary skilled workers. The employee's skills do not have to be unique or one of a kind but they should be indispensable to the success of the investment. USCIS evaluates employees' skills on a case-by-case basis. However, if the skills possessed by the employee are commonplace or readily available in the U.S. labor market, USCIS might not believe that the employee is essential.

Specifically, the immigration authorities will consider the following to determine whether an individual who is neither an executive or a supervisor and who is not at least a 50% owner, should be classified as an E-2 employee because of the essentiality of his or her skills:

- the degree of expertise in the area of operations involved
- the degree of experience and training with the enterprise
- whether U.S. workers possess the individual's skills or aptitude
- the length of the applicant's specific experience or training
- the length of time required to train someone else to perform the job duties of the position
- the relationship of the individual's skills and talents to the overall operations of the entity, and

- the salary the special qualifications can command.

(See 22 C.F.R. § 41.51(b)(13).)

Knowledge of a foreign language and/ or culture will not by itself constitute the degree of essentiality required.

4. The Investment Must Be Substantial

You or your company must be in the process of investing a substantial amount in the U.S. business in order to successfully support an E-2 visa application. To "invest" means putting capital or assets at risk with the goal of generating a profit (you can't invest in a nonprofit enterprise). (See 22 C.F.R. § 41.51(b)(7).) It's okay if the money was gifted or loaned to you.

The term "substantial" is not defined in the law by any strict numerical measure. What is considered substantial depends on the type of business. For example, an automobile manufacturer will have to show a greater dollar amount of investment than a retail toy store in order to meet the requirement of substantial investment. The lower the cost of the business, the higher the percentage of funds you'll need to invest in order to qualify.

The State Department advises its consular officers to consider the following in regards to whether the investment is substantial:

- its substantiality in a proportional sense, that is, compared with the amount it would take to buy or create the same sort of business

- whether the investment is enough to ensure your commitment to the successful operation of the enterprise, and
- whether the investment is of a magnitude to support the likelihood that you will successfully develop and direct the enterprise.

(See 9 FAM § 402.9-6(D).)

TIP

Visa officers often have a general figure in mind as to what they consider a "substantial" investment. This is despite the fact that there is no legal "minimum" investment amount required. You may be able to conclusively prove that a mere $10,000 will allow you to profitably establish a lemonade stand in the United States. However, the visa officer is unlikely to consider such an investment substantial. Thus, the investment must not only be substantial enough to establish and sustain the enterprise, but also must be a significant sum in its own right. Investment amounts below $100,000, no matter what the size or purpose of the business, are likely to receive increased scrutiny from visa officers. That doesn't mean they are impossible, but the risk of denial will increase. Be prepared to demonstrate through a detailed business plan how the business is likely to rapidly grow over time and to offer a comparative study demonstrating that similar businesses in your proposed U.S. location have been able to grow from similar capital investments.

5. The Enterprise Must Not Produce Marginal Profits

The immigration authorities want to make sure you're not just establishing a minor operation to generate nothing more than a living for the owners and therefore get you an E-2 visa, so they require that the enterprise not be "marginal." (See 9 FAM § 402.9-6(E).) That is, your business must be able to make a significant economic contribution to the community, either right away or at least within five years of when you start.

6. It Must Be a Bona Fide, Active Business

The investment must be in a for-profit business that is actively engaged in trade or the rendering of services and one that meets the applicable legal requirements for doing business in the state or region. (See 22 C.F.R. § 41.51(b)(8).) Investment in holding companies, stocks, bonds, and real property will not support an E-2 visa application, since they are not considered "active" investments. (See 9 FAM § 402.9-6(C).)

The test is whether the business requires active supervisory or executive oversight on a day-to-day basis. Clearly, retail, wholesale, and manufacturing operations require such supervision, while stock purchases and land speculation do not. There are some types of investments, especially in real estate, where the line between a qualifying and nonqualifying business investment is difficult to draw. For example, if you purchase and rent out a single home or duplex, this is not the type of investment that will support an E-2 visa application, even if the dollar amount is adequate. If you purchase and rent out an eight- or ten-unit apartment building, that is probably a marginal case. As the number of rental units becomes greater, the need for daily management increases, and the case for an E-2 visa becomes stronger.

> **TIP**
>
> **Be prepared for extra scrutiny if you base your investment on the purchase of real property.** While you may be able to demonstrate that the nature of the business will require day-to-day management, consular officers are wary of real estate speculators trying to "buy" an E-2 visa for the purchase price of their property. This is true no matter how wealthy the investor, and no matter how expensive the property—so-called "passive" investments will not yield an E-2 visa.

7. Your Intent to Leave the U.S.

E-2 visas are meant to be temporary. At the time of your application, you must intend to depart the U.S. when your business there is completed. As previously mentioned, you are not required to maintain a foreign residence abroad.

The U.S. government knows it is difficult to read minds. Expect to be asked for evidence showing that when you go to the U.S. on an E-2 visa, you eventually plan to leave. In many nonimmigrant categories, you are asked to show proof that you will keep a house or an apartment outside the U.S., indicating that you eventually intend to go back to your home country. You do not need to keep a home outside the U.S. to qualify for an E-2 visa—but it would help. You will certainly be asked to show that you have some family members, possessions, or property elsewhere in the world as an incentive for your eventual departure from the United States.

8. Bringing Your Spouse and Children

When you qualify for an E-2 visa, your spouse and unmarried children under age 21 can also get E-2 visas by providing proof of their family relationship to you. Your spouse, but not your children, will be permitted to apply for employment authorization in the United States.

To take advantage of the right to work, your spouse should, after arriving in the United States, apply for a work permit. This is done on USCIS Form I-765 (available on the USCIS website at www.uscis.gov/i-765). In filling out the form, your spouse should write "spouse of E nonimmigrant" in Question 15, and (a)(17) in Question 16.

Your spouse will need to mail this form, together with proof of your visa status, a copy of his or her I-94, the filing fee (currently $410), and two passport-style photos, to the appropriate USCIS service center for your geographic region. For the address and other information, call USCIS Information at 800-375-5283 or see the USCIS website (www.uscis.gov/i-765-addresses).

B. Quick View of the E-2 Visa Application Process

Once you have opened a qualifying company engaged in trade between your home country and the United States, or been offered a job as a key employee of a qualifying company owned by others from your country, getting an E-2 visa is a one- or two-step process, depending on whether you are applying from inside the U.S. or at a U.S. consulate outside the United States:

- If you're outside the U.S., you file an application at a U.S. consulate there. If you are already in the U.S. legally in some other type of nonimmigrant status, you can, under some circumstances, apply for a change to E-2 status at a USCIS office inside the United States. (However, if you were admitted without a visa, such as under the Visa Waiver Program, you may not change your status in the United States.)
- You use your visa to enter the U.S. and claim your E-2 status.

TIP

Nothing stops you from helping with your U.S. employer's tasks during this application process. For example, you can fill out forms intended to be completed by your employer and simply ask the employer to check them over and sign them. The less your U.S. employer is inconvenienced, the more it may be willing to act as sponsor for your visa.

C. How to Apply From Outside the U.S.

Applicants outside the U.S. must apply for an E-2 visa at a U.S. consulate in their home country. (Even you, Canadians!) The exact steps to take to apply for an E-2 visa depend on the U.S. embassy or consulate where you're applying. You will probably need to:

- prepare and submit an online application
- schedule an interview at a U.S. embassy or consulate
- gather some documents and (if you're not the principal investor) fill out another form
- pay the required fee, and
- meet with an official at a U.S. embassy or consulate.

Some consulates require that all application steps, including fee payment and document submission, be complete and pass a review before going any further.

Also, consulates in certain countries that send a lot of treaty investors and their employees to the U.S. have a process that requires or allows companies, as a preliminary step, to register as E-2 enterprises. The company sends all the required proof of E-2 eligibility (except for information that relates to an employee applicant) to the consulate first. If the company is registered, subsequent applications by employees will be easier, since they will need only to focus on the individual's eligibility for the E-2 visa.

For additional information on these application procedures, consult the website of the U.S. embassy or consulate where you're applying, and see the State Department website at www.travel.state.gov (click "Employment" and then "Treaty Trader and Investor Visa").

> ! CAUTION
> **Have you been, or are you now, working or living illegally in the United States?** If so, see Chapter 3 regarding whether you can still get a visa from a U.S. consulate. You may have become inadmissible or subject to a three-year or ten-year bar on reentry.

1. Preparing and Submitting Your Application Form

Your visa application process starts with a government form called a DS-160. It can be completed only online; go to the State Department's Consular Electronic Application Center (CEAC) website, at https://ceac.state.gov. The form must be filled out in English.

If a question is marked "optional," you can leave the answer space blank. You can answer with "Does Not Apply" if the question does not match your situation. Most questions require some answer—the system will not allow you to submit the application if you don't answer a mandatory question. Electronically sign your DS-160 by clicking the "Sign Application" button at the end of the form.

Because the DS-160 asks for a lot of information, it will help to have the following documents nearby:

- your passport
- your travel itinerary, if you have already made travel arrangements, and
- your résumé or curriculum vitae (in case you're required to provide information about your current and previous education and work history).

Consult your travel records (or your memory!) before starting the application. You'll need to provide the dates of your last five visits or trips to the U.S., if you have previously been there. You may also be asked for your international travel history for the past five years.

TIP

No need to finish Form DS-160 in one sitting. You can save your work and return to it later. When you begin the DS-160, you will be issued a unique application identification (ID) number after selecting and answering a security question. Keep track of your application ID, so that you can return to your application. The information you entered in your DS-160 is saved every time you click the "Next" button at the bottom of a page. However, an application is saved on CEAC for only 30 days. If you will want to access your application after 30 days, you must save it by selecting the "Save Application to File" button. Then, click the "Save" button on the File Download window.

You must also, as part of your application, upload a U.S. passport-style photo to CEAC. Information on how to provide a suitable photo is on the State Department's website, www.travel.state.gov. (Follow the links to "Employment," "Treaty Trader and Investor Visa," and "Photograph Requirements.") If you have trouble getting the system to accept your photo, ask someone who's good with computers for help. As a last resort, just bring a photo to your consular interview.

After you've submitted the DS-160 online, print and keep the barcode confirmation page. You'll need to bring it to your interview at the U.S. consulate.

2. Schedule an Interview at a U.S. Embassy or Consulate

After your DS-160 has been accepted, it's up to you to schedule an interview at a U.S. embassy or consulate. While interviews are generally not required for applicants under 14 years old or over 80 years old, consular officers have the discretion to require an interview of any applicant, regardless of age.

All consulates insist on advance appointments. No walk-ins are allowed. Since procedures for scheduling interviews at the consulates vary, telephone or check the consulate's website in advance to find out about local policies. For information on consulates, go to www.usembassy.gov.

Applying at a Consulate Outside of Your Home Country

The law allows most people to apply for visas at any U.S. consulate they choose. You'll find, however, that most consulates around the world will not allow you to apply for an E-2 visa unless you are a resident of the district it services. The consulate in your home country is the one best able to determine whether your business investment qualifies under that country's treaty, so that's where you're expected to apply.

3. Pay the Application Fee

Most consulates require you to pay the visa application fee, currently $205 for E-2 visas, before your interview. The consulate will give you instructions on how and when to make payment.

4. Gather Supporting Documents

If you did not already submit them, the consulate will tell you to come to the interview with documents that support your eligibility for an E-2 visa. You'll definitely need to bring your passport, the DS-160 confirmation page, your fee payment receipt (if advance payment was required), and a photo, if you weren't able to upload one successfully to CEAC, or perhaps even if you were.

If you're an E-2 executive, manager, or essential employee, you'll have to prepare another government form—the DS-156E—at this point. (Principal investors can skip this.) Access this form on the State Department website (at www.travel. gov, click "US Visas," then "All Forms" under the "Forms and Fees" section.) Fill it out online, print it, sign it, and bring it to your interview. If you're getting an E-2 visa as an employee, you'll need to have someone who has signing authority for the company (a "responsible officer") sign the form instead of you.

The exact documentation you'll be asked to bring depends on you and the business. Most consulates like to see the evidence discussed below.

a. Proof of the Nationality of the Qualifying Business Owners

You must show that the qualifying business is owned by citizens of one of the investment treaty countries. If you are not the owner yourself, you will need to show that both you and those who do own the company are citizens of the same treaty country, usually by showing copies of their passports.

Also, provide documents showing where each of the owners is living currently. Affidavits from each of these owners stating their places of residence will serve this purpose. If any are living in the U.S., also submit copies of their passports and I-94s, to demonstrate that they hold valid E-2 visas. Remember, if the owners of the company live in the U.S., at least 50% must also hold E-2 visas for the business to support your own E-2 application.

You will need to prove that you or other nationals of your country own at least 50% of the qualifying business. If the business is a corporation, submit copies of all stock certificates and a notarized affidavit from the secretary of the corporation listing the name of each shareholder and the number of shares each owns. The affidavit must account for all the shares issued to date.

Possibilities for a Green Card From E-2 Status

If you have an E-2 visa, you can file to get a green card, but being in the U.S. on an E-2 visa gives you no advantage in doing so, and in fact may prove to be a drawback. To begin with, there is no practically viable immigrant visa category by which E-2 owners of companies engaged in international trade can qualify. The U.S. employment-based immigration system is primarily set up for employees working for employers, not for employers looking to sponsor themselves. There is the EB-5 category for immigrant investors, but the high capital requirements and complex rules governing that immigrant category make it all but impossible for most investors to qualify. Therefore, it is more likely that people who enter in E-2 status will immigrate only after being sponsored as an employee by some other company. Alternatively, they may perhaps immigrate through other visa categories, such as the diversity visa lottery or family-based immigration. Furthermore, E-2 visas, like most nonimmigrant visas, are intended only for people who plan on leaving the U.S. once their temporary jobs or other activities there are completed.

If you do find a way to qualify for a green card, and opt for sponsorship, you are in effect making a statement that you never intend to leave the United States. Therefore, the U.S. government may allow you to keep E-2 status while pursuing a green card, but only if you can convince it that you did not intend to get a green card when you originally applied for the E-2 visa and that you will leave the U.S. if you are unable to secure a green card before your E-2 visa expires. Proving these things can be tricky. If you do not succeed, your E-2 visa may be taken away. Should this happen, it may affect your green card application, since being out of status or working without authorization may be a bar to getting a green card in the United States. In some instances, if you overstay your visa period, you may create a waiting period of three or ten years if you depart the U.S. and apply for a visa. (See Chapter 3.)

Remember, at least 50% must be owned by nationals of your treaty country.

If the qualifying business is not incorporated, instead of copies of stock certificates, you will need to present legal papers proving the existence and ownership of the company. These may be partnership agreements, business registration certificates, or business licenses, together with a notarized affidavit from an official of the company certifying who owns the business and in what percentages.

b. Proof That You Are a Key Employee

If you are not the majority owner of the company, you must submit evidence that your job in the U.S. will fit the USCIS definition of supervisor, executive, essential employee, or person with predominantly supervisory job duties. To prove this, detailed statements from the sponsoring business explaining your specific duties, as well as the number and kind of employees you will supervise, must be presented. If the application is based on your essentiality as an employee, the statements should also describe the nature of the essential knowledge or experience, how it will be used, and why it is essential in your U.S. job. These required statements may be in your employer's own words and do not have to be in any special form.

c. Proof of the Existence of an Active Business

You'll need to submit documents to show that your E-2 visa application is based on a real, ongoing business. Such evidence should include:

- articles of incorporation or other business charter of the qualifying company
- bank statements for the qualifying company
- credit agreements with suppliers
- letters of credit issued

- leases or deeds for business premises and warehouse space
- accounts payable reports
- invoices and accounts receivable
- payroll reports
- tax returns filed in the past two years, if any, including payroll tax returns, and
- promotional literature or advertising.

If the business is newly formed, there will be no tax returns yet. You should then submit a detailed business plan including financial projections for the next five years.

d. Documents Showing That the Business Is Not a Marginal Income Producer

You'll need to prove that the business already generates, or will eventually generate, high enough revenues to support you and your family above a marginal income level. If the U.S. business is already operating, payroll records showing that you employ U.S. workers will help serve the purpose, as will bank statements and the last two years' tax returns. Also include accountants' financial statements for the business, including balance sheets.

If the business is a start-up, include a copy of your business plan, including financial analyses of projected revenues. If you don't have a business plan, your first task will be to create one. To support the plan, use documents such as market surveys, written summaries of trade association statistics, or written reports from qualified business consultants. Be sure that the documents indicate how many U.S. workers will be employed by the business, and highlight any other ways in which the business will make an economic contribution to the community.

e. Documents Showing That the Investment Is Substantial

The business investment made in the U.S. qualifying company must be a genuine investment, and it must be substantial. To show that you truly have invested, or are actively in the process of investing, include:

- proof that you have irrevocably committed the funds, for example proof that you've already paid them for purchase of the business, or that you've placed them in escrow pending issuance of the visa. (Simply showing that you have money in a bank account will not be enough.)
- proof that the assets or funds invested are in your name and you have control over them. You'll need to name the source of these funds (for example, a loan, sale of assets, or bank account), then provide documents tracing the flow of funds from their source to the business (for example, canceled checks deposited in the business checking account) and from

the business to the actual investment (for example, canceled checks showing purchase of buildings, land, or equipment). Include any loan and mortgage documents and note whether the loan is secured by the business.

- proof that the investment is at risk, that is, subject to personal loss if the business fails. The documents showing the source of—and your control and commitment of—the funds should ordinarily serve this purpose.

Documents to prove that the investment is substantial may include:

- those indicating the purchase price of the business or, for a new business, the expenses necessary to make the business operational
- bank wire transfer memos showing money sent to the U.S. from abroad
- contracts and bills of sale for purchase of capital goods and inventory
- leases, deeds, or contracts for purchase of business premises
- construction contracts and blueprints for building business premises
- payroll records, and
- comprehensive business plans with cash flow projections for the next five years, showing how the enterprise will support more than you (and your family) by then.

5. Attending Your Consular Interview

The last step in your process will be to attend an interview with a U.S. consular officer. During the interview, the officer will examine the data in your DS-160 application form and your supporting documents for accuracy, especially regarding facts about the substantiality of the business and the nationality of the owners. Evidence of ties to your home country will also be checked. During the interview, you will surely be asked how long you intend to remain in the United States. Any answer indicating that you are unsure about plans to return or have an interest in applying for a green card is likely to result in a denial of your visa. See Chapter 4 for what else to expect during consular interviews and what to do if your application is denied.

At some point in the application process, usually at the interview, you will need to have ink-free, digital fingerprint scans taken. Based on these, the consular officer will initiate various security checks to make sure you haven't been involved in criminal or terrorist activity. Because the U.S. is doing more comprehensive security checks than in the past, you are unlikely to receive a decision on your visa the same day as the interview. Security checks can add days, weeks, or (more rarely) months to the processing time.

6. Visa Issuance and Entry Into the United States

Some people, after their visa is approved, must pay an additional visa issuance fee—depending on whether your country charges U.S. citizens a similar fee. (Most countries don't.)

The consulate will tell you exactly how it's going to return your passport to you. Most applicants pick it up in person, but sometimes the consulate mails it. The visa will be affixed to a page in your passport.

You have until the expiration date that appears on your E-2 visa to enter the United States. When you get to the U.S., the border officer will examine your paperwork, ask you some questions, and if all is in order, approve you for entry. The officer will create an I-94 Arrival/ Departure record (if you enter by air or sea) or if you enter at a land border, will put an I-94 card in your passport. Your I-94 contains the dates of your authorized U.S. stay.

You will most likely be permitted to remain in the U.S. for two years. Each time you exit and reenter the U.S., you will get a new I-94 with a new period of authorized stay. If you do not wish to leave the U.S. after that time, you can apply for an extension of stay. These are approved in two-year increments for as long as you maintain your E-2 status qualifications. (See Section E, below.)

D. How to Apply If You're in the U.S.

If you are physically present in the U.S., you may apply for E-2 status without leaving the country on the following conditions:

- You entered the U.S. legally and not on a visa waiver.
- You have never worked illegally.
- The date on your I-94 has not passed.
- You are admissible and none of the bars to changing status apply to you (see Chapter 3).

If you were admitted as a visitor without a visa under the Visa Waiver Program, you may not apply from within the United States. Similarly, you can't take advantage of this option if you entered the U.S. using a C (alien in transit), TWOV (alien in transit without a visa), D (crewman), or any K (fiancé) visa. Certain J-1 (exchange visitor), visa holders are prohibited from changing status as well.

TIP

Your eligibility to apply in the U.S. has nothing to do with your overall eligibility for an E-2 visa. Many applicants who are barred from filing in the U.S. but otherwise qualify for E-2 status may still apply successfully for an E-2 visa at a U.S. consulate in their home country.

There is another problem that comes up only in U.S. filings. It is the issue of what is called preconceived intent. To approve a change of status, USCIS must believe that at the time you originally entered the U.S. as a visitor or with some other nonimmigrant visa, you did not intend to apply for a different status. If USCIS thinks you had a preconceived plan to use one visa to enter the U.S. with an eye to applying for a different status after getting there, it may deny your application. (You can get around the preconceived intent issue by leaving the U.S. and applying for your E-2 visa at a U.S. consulate in another country.)

In technical terms, what you will be applying for in the U.S. is a change of status. To do so, you'll need to file an application with USCIS on Form I-129 (Petition for a Nonimmigrant Worker), with accompanying documents to prove your eligibility. If your spouse and children will be accompanying you, they must file for their change of status on a different form, called Form I-539.

If you decide to apply for a change of status within the U.S., realize that you still don't have the E-2 visa that you'll need if you ever leave the U.S.—a change of status gives you only E-2 status. Visas are never given inside the United States. They are issued exclusively by U.S. consulates in other countries. If you file in the U.S. and you are successful, you will get to remain in the U.S. with E-2 privileges until the status expires. But should you leave the country for any reason before that time, you will have to apply for the visa itself at a U.S. consulate before returning to the United States. Moreover, the fact that your E-2 status has been approved in the U.S. does not guarantee that the consulate will also approve your visa. You'll have to present a whole new application, and they will evaluate it with little or no consideration for the previous USCIS decision. For this reason, many people find it easier to leave the U.S. and apply at a U.S. consulate from the start.

1. Preparing the Change of Status Application

The checklist below will help you prepare the documents and forms for your change of status application.

For further explanation of some of the key items on this checklist, see Section C1, above.

Although it is not a requirement, one additional item that you may wish to add to the paperwork package is a cover letter. Cover letters act as a summary and index to the forms and documents, and are often used by immigration attorneys or U.S. companies that process many visas for their employees. Cover letters begin with a statement summarizing the facts of the case and explaining why the particular applicant is eligible for the visa. This statement is followed by a list of the

forms and documents being submitted. If it is carefully written, a cover letter can make the case clearer and easier to process for the USCIS officer evaluating it. This is particularly important in an E-2 visa case, where the documentation by itself may require explanation, and you probably won't get a chance to meet personally with a USCIS officer. Cover letters must be individually tailored to each case, so if you don't think you can write a good one, just leave it out and submit only your forms and documents; or hire an attorney to help.

2. Mailing the Change of Status Petition

After assembling the I-129 petition, mail it to the USCIS California Service Center. The USCIS website instructions for Form I-129 will give you the exact address (at www.uscis.gov/i-129). USCIS regional Service Centers are not the same as USCIS local offices. For one thing, you cannot visit regional Service Centers in person.

3. Awaiting a Decision on the Change of Status Petition

Within a few weeks after mailing in the petition, you or your employer should get back a written confirmation that the papers are being processed, together with

E-2 Change of Status Checklist

- ☐ Form I-129, with E-1/E-2 Classification Supplement.
- ☐ Filing fee: $460.
- ☐ If your family members are with you and need a change of status, Form I-539 with accompanying fee (currently $370) and copies of your family members' I-94s or other proof of lawful immigration status and of their relationship to you (such as marriage and birth certificates). One Form I-539 and fee will cover your spouse and all your children.
- ☐ If either you or your spouse have ever been married before, copies of divorce and death certificates showing termination of all previous marriages.
- ☐ A copy of your I-94 or other proof of your current lawful, unexpired immigration status (except that Canadians who are just visiting are not expected to have I-94s).
- ☐ Proof of the nationality of the qualifying business owners.
- ☐ Proof that you are the principal investor, or an executive, manager, or key employee.
- ☐ Proof that the investment is or will be substantial.
- ☐ Proof that the business will produce greater-than-marginal profits.
- ☐ Proof of the existence of a bona fide, active business.
- ☐ Documents establishing your intent to leave the U.S. when your status expires, such as deeds verifying ownership of a house or other real property, written statements from you explaining that close relatives are staying behind, or letters from a company showing that you have a job waiting when you return from the United States.
- ☐ Cover letter (optional).

If requesting quick (premium) processing:

- ☐ Form I-907, with $1,225 filing fee.

a receipt for the fee. This notice will also contain your immigration file number.

If USCIS wants further information before acting on your case, it will send you a form known as a Request for Evidence (RFE). Supply the extra data requested and mail it back to the Service Center.

I-129 petitions for E-2 status normally take USCIS two to three months to review.

(Check current processing times online at www.uscis.gov. Follow the links to "Check Your Case Status" and "Check Processing Times.") If you're successful, USCIS will send you a Form I-797 Notice of Action, showing the change of status has been approved. A new I-94 card showing your authorized period of stay will be attached to the bottom of the form.

Watch Out for Expedited Removal

The law empowers a Customs and Border Protection (CBP) inspector at the U.S. airport or border to summarily (without allowing judicial review) bar entry to someone requesting admission to the U.S. if either of the following is true:

- The inspector thinks you are lying about practically anything connected with entering the U.S., including your purpose in coming, intent to return, and prior immigration history. This includes the use or suspected use of false documents.
- You do not have the proper documentation to support your entry to the U.S. in the category you are requesting.

If the inspector excludes you, you cannot be readmitted to the U.S. for five years, unless USCIS grants a special waiver. For this reason it is extremely important to understand the terms of your requested status, and to not make any misrepresentations. If you are found to be inadmissible, you may ask the CBP inspector to withdraw your application to enter the U.S. in order to prevent having the five-year deportation order on your record. The CBP may allow this in some exceptional cases.

TIP

Faster processing—at a price. For $1,225 over and above the regular filing fees, USCIS promises "premium processing" of the visa petition, including a decision on your case within 15 days. To use this service, the employer must fill out an additional application (Form I-907) and submit it to a special USCIS service center address. For complete instructions, see the USCIS website at www.uscis.gov/i-907.

USCIS is not obliged to provide better service to applicants who opt for premium processing. That is, your case is no more likely to be approved simply because premium processing is requested. However, petitioners can expect better communication options if something goes wrong (such as a typographical error on the approval notice or issues in responding to a Request for Evidence). You should strongly consider paying for premium processing if possible.

E. Extending Your U.S. Stay

E-2 visas can be extended for up to five years at a time (depending on your home country) and E-2 status stays can be extended for two years at a time. When you enter the U.S. with an E-2 visa, your authorized stay as indicated on your I-94, will be limited to two years. If you have a five-year visa, this means your I-94 may expire before your visa does. Do not think it is okay to overstay the I-94! Even if your E-2 visa has not expired, make sure you take at least one international trip every two years, to avoid staying past the date on your I-94.

Although an extension is usually easier to get than the E-2 visa itself, it is not automatic. USCIS or the consulate has the right to reconsider your qualifications based on any changes in the facts or law. When the original application for an E-2 visa or status was weak, it is not unusual for an extension request to be turned down. As always, however, good cases that are well prepared will usually be successful.

If you have received E-2 status in the U.S. but never applied for a visa, it's best to stay in the U.S. to apply for an extension of your status (in case the consulate disagrees with USCIS's original decision approving your E-2 status). However, if you have an E-2 visa that is still valid but your I-94 is about to expire, it is generally better to leave the U.S. and return again instead of trying to extend your status in the United States. When you return to the U.S. on your valid E-2 visa, you will automatically receive a new I-94 and a new one- or two-year period of authorized stay. By leaving and reentering, no extension application will be needed and there will be no reevaluation of your qualifications. This method works only until your visa expires, of course. At some point, you'll have to return to your home consulate and get a new visa.

The general procedures for an E-2 extension from within the U.S. are the same as those described in Section D, above. The forms, documents, and fees are identical.

F. Revalidating Your Visa

If you leave the U.S. with an expired E-2 visa stamp, you must have a new visa issued at a consulate before returning (even if you've extended your E-2 status with USCIS). Reread procedures for the application for consular filing in Section C, above. The procedures for consular visa extensions are identical. It's possible, however, that your consulate will waive the interview requirement, if you're renewing the visa within a year of its expiration.

If you are outside the U.S. with a valid visa, you need only reenter and a new I-94 authorizing your stay for one or two years will be created for you.

TIP
The fact that you got the first E-2 visa does not mean you'll get a second one. And even if you get a second E-2 visa, that does not mean you will be issued a third one. Each and every time you apply for a new E-2 visa, the visa officer will evaluate your company's growth and profitability. If you have not grown sufficiently to hire U.S. workers, or if you have not turned over a significant profit, you are likely to have your E-2 visa renewal application denied, even if you had no problem getting the first E-2 visa. Many people have found to their dismay that their E-2 visa renewal applications were denied just at the point they were starting to reach profitability. Make sure you demonstrate profitability before you reapply for your second (or third, etc.) E-2 visa.

Working While Your Extension Application Is Pending

If you file your application for an extension of E-2 status before your authorized stay expires, you are automatically permitted to continue working for up to 240 days while you are waiting for a decision. If, however, your authorized stay expires after you have filed for an extension but before you receive an approval, and more than 240 days go by without getting a decision on your extension application, your work authorization ends and you must stop working.

Getting a Student (F-1 or M-1) Visa

Whether you want to enter a short cooking course or get a Ph.D. in philosophy, a student visa may allow you to do so. In any given year, approximately 500,000 people will come to the U.S. to study. There is no limit on the number of people who can receive student visas. We'll actually cover two types of student visas in this chapter, the M-1 visa for vocational students and the F-1 visa for academic students. (See I.N.A. § 101(a)(15)(F), 8 C.F.R. § 214(f); I.N.A. § 101(a)(15)(M), 8 C.F.R. § 214(m).)

Not everyone planning to study in the U.S. needs a student visa. Tourists who are taking a class or two for recreational purposes can do so without violating their tourist visa status. All other persons in nonimmigrant status (except C transit and D crewmen) can attend school in the U.S. full time or part time, so long as they abide by the rules of their status. Green card holders can, of course, go to school wherever and whenever they want.

Spouses and children, if they have status in the U.S. through you, can go to school too, but if your status expires, they won't be able to stay in the U.S. to finish classes. In most cases, children lose their derivative status at the age of 21 and must apply for a change of status to F-1 or M-1 if they wish to remain in the U.S. to continue their course of study.

Key Features of the M-1 Student Visa

Here are some of the advantages and disadvantages of the M-1, vocational student, visa:

- The application process is reasonably quick and straightforward.
- You may come to the U.S. as a full-time vocational or nonacademic student enrolled in a program leading to a degree or certificate.
- You can transfer from one school to another, but only if you apply for and receive permission from USCIS to do so. Once you are six months into the program of studies, you are prohibited from transferring except under truly exceptional circumstances.
- You are never permitted to change your course of study.

- You may not work during your studies.
- You may get permission to work for up to six months after your studies are done. The job must be considered practical training for your field of study.
- You may travel in and out of the U.S. or remain there until the completion of your studies, up to a maximum of one year. If you have not completed your program in a year or by the time your school projected, whichever is less, you must apply for an extension.
- The maximum extension allowed is three years from the original start date.
- Visas are available for accompanying relatives, although relatives may not accept employment in the United States.

Key Features of the F-1 Student Visa

Here are some of the advantages and disadvantages of the F-1, academic student, visa:

- Once you've been accepted by a U.S. school, the application process is reasonably quick and straightforward.
- You may come to the U.S. as a full-time academic or language student enrolled in a program leading to a degree or certificate.
- You may not obtain an F visa to study at a public elementary school or a publicly funded adult education program. Nor may you obtain an F visa to study at a public secondary school unless you prepay the full cost of such program, for a maximum of one year.
- You can transfer from one school to another or switch academic programs by going through a simple procedure to notify USCIS.
- You may work legally in a part-time job on campus. Also, you may get special permission to work off campus if it is economically urgent or if the job provides practical training for your field of study.
- You may travel in and out of the U.S. or remain there until the completion of your studies.
- After college graduation, you may stay in the U.S. and receive training through work experience for up to 12 months, or 24 months if you have a "STEM" degree.
- Visas are available for accompanying relatives, but relatives may not accept employment in the United States.

 SEE AN EXPERT

Do you need a lawyer? Applying for a student visa is fairly simple and doesn't usually require a lawyer's help. Most schools provide you a great deal of help and advice with the application process, often through the services of a foreign student adviser or designated school official (DSO). If, however, you've had trouble getting visas in the past, have ever overstayed a visa, or are from a country thought to sponsor terrorism, a lawyer's help can be well worth the investment.

A. Do You Qualify for a Student (M-1 or F-1) Visa?

To qualify for an M-1 or F-1 student visa, you first must have been accepted at a school approved by the U.S. government. You must be also coming to the U.S. as a bona fide student pursuing a full course of study. Your intended school program must lead to an objective such as a degree, diploma, or certificate.

You must also already be accepted by the school of your choice and have enough money to study full time without working. You must be able to speak, read, and write English well enough to understand the course work or, alternatively, the school can offer special tutoring or instruction in your native tongue to help overcome any language barriers.

In addition to your academic and financial qualifications, you must prove that you intend to return to your home country when your program of studies is over.

At every government-approved school, there is a person on the staff known as the designated school official (DSO). The DSO is recognized by USCIS and the consulates as having primary responsibility for dealing with foreign students.

![icon] CAUTION
An interest in certain subjects may bar you from entry. If you're planning to study a subject with international security implications, such as biochemistry, nuclear physics, or missile telemetry, and you're from a country on the U.S. government's list of supporters of terrorism, you may not be allowed a student visa.

1. Acceptance at a Government-Approved School

Student visas are issued only to students who will attend U.S. schools that have received prior approval from USCIS for enrollment of foreign students. Virtually all public and accredited private colleges, universities, and vocational schools have been approved. To become approved, the school must take the initiative and file a formal application with USCIS. If you do not plan to attend a public school or a fully accredited college or university, before you apply for either an F-1 or M-1 visa you should check with the school you have selected to be sure it has been approved by USCIS to accept foreign students.

Coming to the U.S. to Look for a School

As a prospective student, you can come to the U.S. as a tourist for the purpose of locating a school you want to attend. If you do this, however, be sure to tell the consular officer at your B-2 visa interview that this is your intent so that he or she can make the appropriate annotation in your passport (usually "Prospective Student—school not yet selected").

Otherwise, if you later request a change of status from a visitor visa to a student visa, USCIS will presume that you committed fraud by applying for a visitor visa when you intended to come to the U.S. to study. USCIS will then refuse your application to convert to student status. Therefore, if you enter the U.S. on a B-2 visa and do not have the annotation indicating that you are a prospective student, you will need to leave the U.S. before your authorized stay expires, so that you can apply for a student visa from your home country.

Once the school has accepted you, it will issue you a certificate (SEVIS Form I-20), which you can use to continue with your immigration application.

2. Bona Fide Student

Although it should go without saying, your intentions in coming to the U.S. must truly be to study. The U.S. government is on the lookout for people who use a student visa as a means to gain entry to the U.S. for other purposes. This visa has come under particular scrutiny since the terrorist attacks of September 11, 2001, because some of the terrorists were on student visas. In addition,

the U.S. immigration authorities are always concerned with preventing people from entering the U.S. who have no intention of leaving at the end of their authorized stay. See Section 7, below, for more on proving your intentions to leave on time.

3. Full Course of Study

What is a full course of study? The good news is, you don't have to stay in school during normal school vacations. Also, on-campus employment under the terms of a scholarship, a fellowship, or an assistantship can be considered part of your full course of study. Other than the general rules,

---

You Can't Use a Student Visa to Attend a Public School for Free

In the 1990s, Congress decided that the U.S. should not pay to educate people from other countries. It amended the immigration laws to provide that no student visa will be issued to a person wishing to attend a public elementary school (kindergarten through eighth grade) or a publicly funded adult education program. The rules are slightly different for high schools. You can attend a maximum of one year of public high school (ninth through 12th grade), but you will have to pay the local school district for the entire cost of your education for the year.

The cost of the year in a U.S. high school depends on the local school district—you'll have to contact the district directly. Expect

to be charged several thousand dollars. Some school districts are not able to calculate their costs. If you plan to attend school in one of these districts, you won't be allowed a visa.

There's nothing to stop you from attending a private elementary or high school—except maybe the tuition, which can be as high as U.S. college tuition. You should also know that some immigrants are allowed to attend public schools, such as those accompanying their parents on another visa, as well as undocumented children (whose rights are protected by the Supreme Court's decision in *Plyler v. Doe*, 457 U.S. 202 (1982)). The reasoning is that they have no option to attend school in their home country.

however, the time requirements of full-time enrollment vary depending on the type of program you're enrolled in.

Undergraduate college or university programs. If you are an undergraduate at a U.S. college or university, you must be enrolled in at least 12 semester or quarter hours of instruction per term. An exception to this is if you are in your last term and need fewer than 12 semester hours to graduate.

Postgraduate college or university programs. If you are a graduate student, full-time studies are whatever the designated school official says they are. For example, a graduate student may be working on a dissertation and taking no classes at all, but still be considered a full-time student, if the designated school official approves.

Programs of specialized college-level schools. When your course of studies is at a specialized school offering recognized college-level degrees or certificates in language, liberal arts, fine arts, or other nonvocational programs, you must be attending at least 12 hours of class per week. This means 12 hours by the clock, not 12 semester hours.

Any other language, liberal arts, fine arts, or other nonvocational training program. You must attend at least 18 clock hours a week if the dominant part of the course of study is classroom instruction, or at least 22 clock hours a week if the dominant part of the course of study consists of laboratory work.

High school, middle school, and primary school programs. These students must attend the minimum number of class hours per week that the school requires for normal progress toward graduation. However, the school may recommend a lesser load for a foreign student with a limited understanding of English.

Technical, vocational, or other non-academic programs. To be classified as a full-time student in a technical, a vocational, or another type of nonacademic program, you must attend at least 18 clock hours per week, if the courses consist mostly of classroom study. If the courses are made up primarily of laboratory work, 22 clock hours per week is the minimum.

> **CAUTION**
>
> **F-1 students: Watch out for online or other nonclassroom credits.** You're limited to taking one online class or three credits per session, term, semester, trimester, or quarter. This also includes closed circuit, cable, microwave, or audio conferencing and other long-distance classes that don't require your physical attendance. What's more, if you're in a language study program, you can't count any online or distance education classes toward your full course of study requirement.

4. Program Leading to the Attainment of a Specific Educational or Vocational Objective

In order to qualify for a student visa, you must be enrolled in a program that leads to the attainment of a specific educational or vocational objective. For example, a diploma or certificate would be an obvious goal. Nevertheless, you could come to the U.S. to take a semester of college courses as your "objective," so long as your study is full time during that one semester. You must also maintain a full-time course load, as described above.

5. Knowledge of English

To qualify for a student visa, you must know the English language well enough to pursue your studies effectively. Most U.S. colleges and universities will not admit students whose native language is not English until they first pass an English proficiency test such as the TOEFL. Tests can be arranged in your home country. Your chosen school in the U.S. will tell you if such a test is required and how to go about taking it.

Usually, consular officials let each school decide for itself who is and is not qualified to study there. Still, during the consular interview at which your visa is approved or denied, the official will be listening closely to your ability to understand and communicate in English. Occasionally, even when a school is willing to admit you without a strong knowledge of English, the U.S. consulate may refuse to issue a student visa because it thinks your English is not good enough. You may still be able to satisfy the consulate if the school you plan to attend is willing to supply English

language tutoring or, alternatively, offers a course of studies in your native tongue.

Permission to Take a Reduced Load

When you are unable to carry a full-time course load due to health problems or academic issues, you may be permitted to keep your student status even though you are not going to school full-time, as long as you first get permission from your DSO. However, your course load cannot be reduced to fewer than six semester or quarter hours, or half the clock hours required for a full course of study. A reduced course load to less than half-time is acceptable only for defined medical reasons or for your final school term if the school determines that fewer courses are needed to complete your course of study.

No special USCIS application is necessary to take a reduced load. However, USCIS has the right to challenge your status at a later date. Therefore, get a written statement from your DSO explaining that he or she believes it is medically or academically necessary for you to reduce your course load, and giving the reasons why.

6. Adequate Financial Resources

You must show that you have enough money to complete your entire course of studies without working. At the time you apply for a student visa, you must have enough cash on hand to cover all first-year expenses. In addition, you must be able to show a reliable source of money available to pay for subsequent years. This is normally accomplished by having your parents or other close relatives promise in writing to finance your education, and submit proof of their ability to do so.

7. Intent to Return to Your Home Country

Student visas are meant to be temporary. At the time of applying, you must intend to return home when your studies are completed. If you have it in mind to take up permanent residence in the U.S., you are legally ineligible for a student visa. The U.S. government knows it is difficult to read minds. Therefore, you may be asked for evidence that you will be leaving behind possessions, property, or family members as an incentive for your eventual return. It is also helpful if you can show that you have a job waiting at home after graduation. Of course, if you're young and just starting college, you may not have many such ties. The important thing to emphasize is that it's also too early in your life to have formed a firm intent to leave your home country and settle in the United States.

If you are studying to prepare yourself for an occupation in which no jobs are available in your home country, be advised that the immigration authorities have traditionally been skeptical of such applications. The State Department has, however, instructed visa officers at U.S. consulates to give equal consideration to all F-1 visa applications regardless of whether the area of study was likely to provide an employment opportunity in the visa applicant's home country. However, there is no way to determine whether this bias in favor of "professional" education has left all visa officers' considerations.

8. Bringing Your Spouse and Children

When you qualify for an F-1 or M-1 visa, your spouse and unmarried children under age 21 can get F-2 or M-2 visas. Your school will have to issue separate SEVIS Forms I-20 for them. They'll also need to show the U.S. consulate proof of their family relationship to you (such as marriage and birth certificates) and that you have sufficient financial resources to support them in the U.S. so that they will have no need to work. F-2 and M-2 visas authorize your accompanying relatives to stay with you in the U.S., but not to accept employment.

Family members may also enroll in elementary or secondary school (kindergarten through 12th grade), or in any avocational or recreational studies. They may not, however, enroll full time in a degree-granting course of postsecondary study without obtaining their own visa.

B. How Long the Student Visa Will Last

Most visas come with a fairly automatic length of time you're allowed to stay in the United States. With a student visa, however, it's a bit more complicated. The first thing to understand is that the expiration date on any nonimmigrant visa, including a student visa, merely indicates how long you have the right to request entry to the United States. It doesn't tell how long you may stay in the U.S. once you arrive.

Both F-1 and M-1 entry visas are typically issued for the estimated length of time it will take to complete your proposed program of studies. Consulates will use their judgment in deciding the expiration date of the visa.

More importantly, however, when you enter the U.S. using a valid student visa, an I-94 Arrival/Departure record will be created for you (if you enter by air or sea). If you enter at a land border, you will be given a small white I-94 card. With all other types of nonimmigrant visas, a border officer would normally enter an expiration date on the I-94 record as you enter the country, to tell you how long you can stay. But with a student I-94, particularly for an F-1 student, it's more likely that the border officer will note D/S, for "duration of status." This means that you may remain in the U.S. in student status for as long as it takes to complete your educational objectives, provided you finish within what USCIS and your school consider a reasonable period of time. The following specific rules control the time you may spend in the U.S. as a student:

- F-1 and M-1 students, and their accompanying family members, can arrive in the United States up to 30 days before the start of classes.

- Once you arrive in the U.S., you may remain in student status without requesting an extension, for up to your projected completion date as indicated on the paperwork from your school (Form SEVIS I-20A-B for F students; Form SEVIS I-20M-N for M students), plus a 60-day (F-1) or 30-day (M-1) grace period. (This is conditioned on your remaining enrolled in an approved program of studies, maintaining your full-time student status, and not becoming inadmissible or deportable.) If you receive the school's permission to withdraw from your studies, your grace period will be 15 days.

- If your student status expires because your maximum stay (as indicated on your I-20A-B or I-20M-N) is up, you can apply to your designated school official for an extension of stay. To receive an extension, you will have to show that you are still enrolled

Possibilities for a Green Card From Student Status

If you have an F-1 or M-1 visa, you are not barred from filing for a green card, but being in the U.S. on a student visa gives you no direct advantage in doing so. Earning a degree may, however, help you indirectly, especially if you happen to be studying in a field where there is a shortage of qualified U.S. workers. (A key element in getting most green cards through employment is proving that there are not enough U.S. workers available to fill a position for which you are qualified.) College graduates also have a number of other advantages in applying for a green card through employment. (See Chapter 9 for details.)

Keep in mind, however, that student visas, like all nonimmigrant visas, are meant to be temporary. They are intended only for people who plan on returning home once their studies in the U.S. are completed. Therefore, if you decide to apply for a green card before your studies are finished, the U.S. government will allow you to maintain student status while pursuing a green card, but only if you are able to convince it of two things: First, that you did not intend to get a green card when you originally applied for the F-1 or M-1 visa, and second, that you will return home if you are unable to secure a green card before your student status expires. Proving these things can be difficult.

If you do not succeed, your student visa may be taken away. If this happens, it will not directly affect your green card application. You will simply risk being without a nonimmigrant visa until you get your green card—meaning you'll have to return home in the interim.

If you instead choose to stay out of status for even six or 12 months and then depart the U.S., it may result in a three-year or ten-year bar to returning to the United States. However, current USCIS interpretations state that a student who goes out of status does not begin to accumulate time toward these six- or 12-month unlawful-stay periods until a USCIS official or an immigration judge makes a ruling that the person is out of status. This means that if you stop attending school for some reason, you will not begin to accrue time toward the overstay bars unless you come to the government's attention. This could happen, for example, if you request reinstatement of student status and the USCIS denies it. Then you would begin to accrue unlawful time as of the date of the USCIS's decision, and could face a three-year or ten-year bar to returning to the United States. (See Chapter 3 for a discussion of how being out of status can affect your ability to get a green card.) Consult a lawyer for more information.

Applying at a Consulate That's Not in Your Home Country

The law allows most people to apply for an F-1 visa at any U.S. consulate they choose—with one exception. If you have ever been present in the U.S. unlawfully, your visa will be automatically cancelled and you cannot apply as a third-country national (at a consulate outside your home country). Even if you overstayed your status in the U.S. by just one day, you must return to your home country and apply for the visa from that consulate. There is an exception. If you were admitted to the U.S. for the duration of your status (indicated by "D/S" on your I-94) and you remained in the U.S. beyond the time for which your status was conferred, you will be barred from third-country national processing only if an immigration judge or USCIS (or INS, formerly) officer has determined that you were unlawfully present. You may find that your success in applying as a third-country national will depend on your country, the

consulate, and the relative seriousness of your offense. Being unlawfully present is also a ground of inadmissibility if the period of unlawful presence is 180 days or more. (See Chapter 3.)

Even if you are eligible for third-country national processing, your case will be given the greatest consideration at the consulate in your home country. Applying in some other country creates suspicion in the minds of the consular officers there about your motives for choosing their consulate. Often, when an applicant expects trouble at a home consulate, he or she will seek a more lenient consular office in some other country. This practice of consulate shopping is frowned upon by officials in the system. Unless you have a very good reason for being elsewhere (such as a temporary job assignment in some other nation), it is often smarter to file your visa application in your home country.

in an approved program, that you are still eligible for nonimmigrant student status, and that there is a good reason why it is taking you extra time to complete your studies. You must do so within 30 days of the I-20 expiration date. If that date passes, you are out of status and will have to return home and get a new visa.

C. Quick View of the Student Visa Application Process

Getting either an F-1 or M-1 visa is a two- to three-step process:

- You apply to schools, and once you're accepted, your school fills out and sends you a form known as a Certificate of Eligibility (SEVIS I-20). You will use this certificate in preparing your application for a student visa.

- You apply for either a student visa (if you're currently in another country) or for a change to student status (if you're in the U.S., eligible to change status from another visa, and would prefer this to leaving and applying at a consulate).

- If you're outside the U.S., you use your student visa to enter and claim your student status.

(If you are Canadian, your application procedures will be different from those of other applicants. See Chapter 5.)

D. Step One: Your School Issues a SEVIS I-20

You can't start the visa application process until you have been admitted to a USCIS-approved school. This book does not discuss how to find the right U.S. school or program, nor how to get accepted to it. You'll need to get started well in advance. If you're applying to academic programs, start contacting schools at least a year before you plan to start your studies. Most students submit between five and ten applications to a mix of schools, including some that they know they have a good chance of being admitted to.

Some good resources to consult about schools and admissions processes include www.studyusa.com (publisher of *Study in the USA* magazine), www.princetonreview.com (the Princeton Review, a test preparation company with an admissions services division), and http://studyinthestates.dhs.gov (the Department of Homeland Security's website on studying in the U.S.).

Also, most U.S. consulates have a library where you can look at materials about schools in the United States. Some U.S. colleges actually recruit in other countries. If you're in high school but your school can't tell you about local college fairs or recruiting activities, contact the nearest American School (a school that caters to U.S. students in other countries or those learning English), which is usually a popular destination for recruiters.

Once a school has accepted you and you've indicated that you will attend (usually by paying a deposit), the school will send you a Certificate of Eligibility form (SEVIS I-120), more commonly called an I-20. At the same time, the school will be required to notify the U.S. consulate in your home country.

F-1 students will get what's called a SEVIS I-20A-B and M-1 students will get a SEVIS I-20M-N. The school should not charge you any money for issuing the I-20. It's a fairly simple document, simply stating to the U.S. government that you have submitted all the right paperwork and financial documents, the school has evaluated your application and it meets its standards, and you have been accepted for enrollment in a full course of study. When you receive the form, review it carefully, and advise the school if it contains any errors. Then you will need to sign the form.

E. Step Two for Applicants Outside the U.S.: Applying at a U.S. Consulate

Anyone with a Certificate of Eligibility (SEVIS I-20) from a U.S. school indicating acceptance by the school into a full-time program can apply for an F-1 or M-1 visa at a U.S. consulate in his or her home country. You must be physically present in order to apply there.

The exact steps to take to apply for a student visa depend on the U.S. embassy or consulate where you're applying. You will most likely need to:

- prepare and submit an online application
- schedule and interview at a U.S. embassy or consulate
- gather some personal documents
- pay the required fees, and
- meet with an official at the U.S. embassy or consulate.

For additional information on these procedures, consult the website of the U.S. embassy or consulate where you're applying, and see the State Department website at www.travel.state.gov (click "Study & Exchange" and then "Student Visa").

Embassies and consulates are able to issue your student visa up to 120 days before the course of study begins. There's no reason to wait until then to submit your application, however. Given the lengthy delays in visa processing caused by background checks, it is to your advantage to submit your application as early as possible, giving the consulate extra time for the security clearances.

> **CAUTION**
> **Have you been, or are you now, working or living illegally in the United States?** If so, see Chapter 3 regarding whether you can still get an F or M visa from a U.S. consulate. You may have become inadmissible or subject to a three-year or ten-year bar on reentry.

1. Preparing and Submitting Your Visa Application

Your visa application will consist of a government form and some documents that you collect yourself. The form, called a DS-160, can be completed only online. You will bring the supporting documents with you to your visa interview.

Access the DS-160 at the State Department's Consular Electronic Application Center (CEAC) website, https://ceac.state.gov. If a question is marked "optional," you can leave the answer space blank. You can answer a question with "Does Not Apply" if it does not match your situation. Most questions require some answer—the system will not allow you to submit an application if you don't answer a mandatory question. Electronically sign your DS-160 by clicking the "Sign Application" button at the end of the form.

Because the DS-160 asks for a lot of information, it will help to have the following documents nearby:

- your passport
- your travel itinerary, if you have already made travel arrangements, and
- your résumé or curriculum vitae (in case you are required to provide information about your current and previous education and work history).

Consult your travel records (or your memory!) before starting the application. You'll need to provide the dates of your last five visits or trips to the U.S., if you have previously been there. You may also be asked for your international travel history for the past five years.

 TIP

You don't need to finish the DS-160 in one sitting. You can save your work and return to it later. When you begin a new DS-160, you will be issued a unique application identification (ID) number after selecting and answering a security question. You will need this ID number in order to return to your application. The information you enter in your DS-160 is saved every time you click the "Next" button at the bottom of a page. However, CEAC saves

applications for only 30 days. If you will want to access your application after 30 days, you must save it by selecting the "Save Application to File" button. Then, click the "Save" button on the File Download window.

You must also, as part of your application, upload a U.S. passport-style photo to CEAC. Information on how to provide a suitable photo is on the State Department's website, www.travel.state.gov. (Follow the links to "Study & Exchange," "Student Visas," and "Photograph Requirements.") If you have trouble getting the system to accept your photo, ask someone who's good with computers for help. As a last resort, you can just bring a photo to your consular interview.

After you've submitted the DS-160 online, print and keep the barcode confirmation page. You'll need to bring that to your interview at the U.S. consulate.

2. Schedule an Interview at a U.S. Embassy or Consulate

After your DS-160 has been accepted, it's up to you to schedule an interview at a U.S. embassy or consulate. While interviews are generally not required for applicants under 14 years old or over 80 years old, consular officers have the discretion to require an interview of any applicant, regardless of age.

The waiting time for an interview appointment varies from country to country. Check the Department of State's website at www.travel.state.gov for the current wait time at your consulate (click under "U.S. Visas," then enter the city where your consulate is located in the "Plan Ahead" section).

3. Pay the Visa Application Fee

Most consulates require you to pay the visa application fee, currently $160 for F and M visas, before your interview. The consulate will give you instructions on how and when to make payment.

4. Pay the SEVIS Fee

Before your appointment, you'll need to pay a fee (currently $200) to support the U.S. student-tracking database called SEVIS. Your school may take care of processing this payment for you. If not, you'll need to do it yourself, either online or by mail.

To submit the form online, go to www.FMJfee.com, complete the online Form I-901, and pay with a credit card. To submit the form by mail, download it from the Immigration and Customs Enforcement (ICE) website at www.ice. gov/sevis/i901 and mail it, together with your check or money order drawn on a U.S. bank and payable in U.S. currency, to the address indicated on the form. SEVIS will not mail you a receipt for the paid fee. You'll have to print payment confirmation from the FMJFEE website (www.fmjfee. com). Click on the "Check I-901 Status/

Print Payment Confirmation" button. After entering your SEVIS ID, last name, and date of birth you will be able to print your payment confirmation. You'll need it for the interview at the consulate.

Don't wait too long to pay the SEVIS fee. Although you can't pay it before getting an I-20, and it doesn't have to be paid before you schedule your interview, it must be paid by the time of the actual interview. You can't get a visa or enter the U.S. without paying it.

5. Gather Supporting Documents

The consulate will likely tell you to come to the interview with documents that support your eligibility for an F visa. You'll definitely need to bring your passport, the DS-160 confirmation page, your fee payment confirmation (if advance payment was required), the I-20A-B or I-20M-N, and a photo if you weren't able to upload one successfully to CEAC, or perhaps even if you were. In addition, consulates like to see:

Evidence of academic qualifications. If you will be attending a U.S. college or university, some consular officers will require you to prove that you are academically qualified to pursue the program, even though the school itself has already accepted you. Therefore, you should present evidence of all of your previous education, in the form of official transcripts and diplomas from schools you attended. Also, submit standardized test results, if your school required such tests. If these documents are not available, submit detailed letters by officials of the schools you previously attended, describing the extent and nature of your education.

Evidence of intent to return. You will need documents establishing your intent to leave the U.S. when your studies are completed. The consulate will want to see evidence of ties to some other country so strong that you will be highly motivated to return there. Proof of such ties can include deeds verifying ownership of a house or other real property, written statements from you explaining that close relatives live there, or letters from a company showing that you have a job waiting when you return from the United States.

Evidence of sufficient funds. Most important, you must submit documents showing that you presently have sufficient funds available to cover all tuition and living costs for your first year of study. The SEVIS I-20 gives the school's estimate of what your total annual expenses will be. Specifically, you must show you have that much money presently available. You must also document that you have a source of funds to cover your expenses in future years without having to work.

The best evidence of your ability to pay educational expenses is a letter from a bank, or a bank statement, either in the U.S. or abroad, showing an account in your name with a balance of at least the amount of money it will take to pay for your first year of education.

Alternatively, you can submit a written guarantee of support signed by an immediate relative, preferably a parent, together with your relative's bank statements. Unless your relative can show enough assets to prove he or she can support you without additional income, you should also show that your relative is presently employed. You can document this by submitting a letter from the employer verifying your relative's work situation.

Although the guarantee of support may be in the form of a simple written statement in your relative's own words, we suggest you use Form I-134, called an Affidavit of Support, especially if the person who will support you lives in the United States. A copy of this form is on the USCIS website at www.uscis.gov/i-134. The questions on Form I-134 are self-explanatory. Be aware that the form was designed to be filled out by someone living in the United States. Since it is quite likely that the person who will support you is living outside the U.S., any questions that apply to U.S. residents should be answered "N/A."

Additional documents for flight trainees. If you're applying for an F or M visa for U.S. flight training, you will be required to submit written information and documents specifying the following:

- your reason for the training (be specific)
- current employer and your position
- who is paying for the training (name and relationship)
- your most recent flight certifications and ratings
- information on what kind of aircraft the training is for (document must be signed by a school official in the United States)
- certified take-off weight of the aircraft type (document must be signed by a school official in the U.S.), and
- current rank or title if you are presently working as an active pilot.

6. Attending Your Consular Interview

Most consulates will require an interview before issuing a student visa. During the interview, a consular officer will examine the forms and documents for accuracy. The consular officer will verify your I-20 record electronically through the SEVIS system. Your visa will not be issued if you are not entered into the SEVIS database, even if you have an approved I-20. Your documents proving your ability to finance your education will be carefully checked, as will evidence of ties to your home country.

During the interview you will surely be asked how long you intend to remain in the United States. Any answer indicating uncertainty about plans to return home or an interest in applying for a green card is likely to result in a denial of your student visa.

Because of security requirements, you are unlikely to be approved for your visa on the same day as your interview. At some point in the application process, most likely at the interview, you will need to have ink-free, digital fingerprint scans taken. Based on these, the consular officer will initiate various security checks to make sure you haven't been involved in criminal or terrorist activity. This can add weeks or months to the processing of your visa, particularly if you come from a country that the U.S. suspects of supporting terrorism. To get your visa, you may have to pay a visa issuance fee (known as a "reciprocity fee") if you're from a country that charges similar fees for visas to U.S. citizens.

F. Step Two for Some Applicants Inside the U.S.: Applying to USCIS for a Change of Status

If you are physically present in the U.S., you may apply for a change to F-1 or M-1 status without leaving the country on the following conditions:

- You have been accepted as a student by a U.S. government-approved school and the school has given you a Certificate of Eligibility, Form SEVIS I-20, and has entered you into the SEVIS database.

- You entered the U.S. legally and not under the Visa Waiver Program, or using a C (alien in transit), TWOV (alien in transit without a visa), D (crewman), any K (fiancé), or S (informant) visa. Certain J-1 (exchange visitor) visa holders cannot change to F-1.
- You have never worked in the U.S. illegally.
- The date on your I-94 has not passed.
- You are not inadmissible.

TIP

Eligibility to apply while you're in the U.S. has nothing to do with your overall eligibility for an F-1 or M-1 visa. Applicants who are barred from filing in the U.S. but otherwise qualify for student status can sometimes apply successfully for an F-1 or M-1 visa at a U.S. consulate in their home country.

Overall, USCIS offices do not favor change of status applications. In general, to approve a change of status, USCIS must believe that at the time you originally entered the U.S. you truly intended to fulfill the terms of your visa, and were not just using the visa as a way to get into the U.S. so that you could apply for a different type of status.

Because it can be more difficult to get a student visa than a tourist visa, USCIS *presumes* that any request to change status from B-2 to a student visa indicates a

fraudulent use of the B-2 visa at the time of entry to the U.S. and will, therefore, always deny the request for change of status, with two exceptions.

The first exception is if you made it clear when you applied for the B-2 visa that you were entering the U.S. to look for a school to enroll in. The second exception is if you made it clear when you applied for the B-2 visa that you already were accepted as a student in a U.S. school and that you wanted to enter the U.S. more than 30 days before the start of your course in order to be a tourist. Most tourists in the U.S. will not fall into either of these exceptions and will need to leave the U.S. and apply for the visa at a U.S. consulate in another country. But understand the pitfalls involved in departing the U.S. (discussed in Chapter 3, especially if you have lived here unlawfully) before making your decision.

If you decide to apply for a change of status within the U.S., realize that you still don't have the F-1 or M-1 visa that you'll need if you ever leave the U.S. and want to return—a change of status gives you only F-1 or M-1 status. Visas are never given inside the United States. They are issued exclusively by U.S. consulates in other countries. If you file in the U.S. and you are successful, you will get to remain in the U.S. with F-1 or M-1 student privileges until the status expires. But should you leave the country for any reason before that time, you will have to apply for the visa itself at a U.S. consulate before returning to the United States. Moreover, the fact that your student status has been approved in the U.S. does not guarantee that the consulate will also approve your visa. For these reasons, many applicants choose to leave the U.S. and apply for their student visa through a consulate.

1. Preparing Your Change of Status Application

Before submitting your application, you'll need to pay a fee (currently $200) to support the U.S. student-tracking database called SEVIS. Your school may take care of processing this fee payment for you. If not, you'll need to do it yourself, either online or by mail. To submit the form online, go to www.FMJfee.com. There is an option now to pay by Western Union, which will allow speedy processing. To submit the form by mail, download it from the Immigration and Customs Enforcement (ICE) website at www.ice.gov/sevis/i901, and mail it, together with your check or money order drawn on a U.S. bank and payable in U.S. currency, to the address indicated on the form. For more information on these requirements, see www.ice.gov/sevis/i901. SEVIS will not mail you a receipt for the paid fee. You'll have to print payment confirmation from the FMJFEE website (www.fmjfee.com). Click on the "Check I-901 Status/Print Payment Confirmation"

button. After entering your SEVIS ID, last name, and date of birth you will be able to print your payment confirmation. You'll need it for the adjustment interview.

The checklist below will help you assemble the necessary items for the change of status application.

For additional explanation of some of the items on this checklist, see Section E5, above.

2. Submitting the Change of Status Application

After assembling the change of status application, you can mail it to the USCIS Lockbox in Texas. USCIS Lockboxes are not the same as USCIS local offices; for one thing, you cannot visit them in person. The addresses for mailing (regular mail and express mail) are on the instructions to the I-539. See www.uscis.gov/i-539.

3. Awaiting a Decision on the Change of Status Application

Within a few weeks after mailing in the I-539 petition, you should get back a written confirmation that the papers are being processed, together with a receipt for the fee. This notice will also contain your immigration file number.

If USCIS wants further information before acting on your case, it will send you a form known as a Request for Evidence

Checklist for Student Change of Status Application

☐ Form I-539, Application to Extend/ Change Nonimmigrant Status, with accompanying fee (currently $370; pay by check or money order, not cash). One Form I-539 and fee will cover you, your spouse, and all your children, if they are in the U.S. with you and in the same visa status or are accompanying beneficiaries of your current visa status. But be sure to complete the I-539 Supplement for your spouse and children.

☐ Photocopy of Form SEVIS I-20, filled out by your school and signed by you.

☐ The confirmation page showing that you paid the SEVIS fee (currently $200).

☐ Copies of proof of your family members' relationship to you, such as marriage and birth certificates.

☐ A copy of your Form I-94 (and those of your spouse and children, if they're applying with you) or other proof of your current lawful, unexpired immigration status (except Canadians just visiting the U.S., who are not expected to have I-94s).

☐ If either you or your spouse has ever been married before, copies of divorce and death certificates showing termination of all previous marriages.

☐ Copies of transcripts, diplomas, and results of any standardized tests required by the school you'll be attending, showing your previous education and your qualifications to pursue your chosen course of study.

☐ Copies of documents showing reasons that you'll return to your home country, such as ownership of real estate, relationships with close family members staying behind, and proof that a job will be waiting for you on your return.

☐ Proof of sufficient funds, such as:

  ☐ Form I-134, Affidavit of Support, from a U.S. friend or relative, or letter from a friend or relative promising support.

  ☐ Bank statements.

  ☐ Personal financial statements.

  ☐ Evidence of your current sources of income.

(RFE). You should supply the extra data requested and mail it back to USCIS.

Until recently, foreign students could submit applications for student status and begin school before receiving USCIS's approval. Now, applicants must wait for USCIS's decision before starting school. Check the USCIS website for current processing times to determine how long you may expect to wait for a decision.

(At www.uscis.gov, follow the links to "Check Your Case Status" and "USCIS Processing Times.")

When your application has been approved, USCIS will notify you using a Form I-797 Notice of Action. A new I-94 card will be attached to the bottom of the form. You will also be issued an I-20 Student ID.

G. Step Three: Student Visa Holders Enter the U.S.

For F-1 students coming from abroad, on your first entry to the U.S., you will not be able to enter more than 30 days before your program start date. For M-1 students, you can enter the U.S. up to 45 days before the start of school. When you arrive in the U.S. with your new F-1 or M-1 visa, the border officer will examine your paperwork, ask you some questions, and if all is in order, approve you for entry. An I-94 Arrival/Departure record will be created for you (if you enter by air or sea). If you enter at a land border, you will be given a small white I-94 card. Your I-94 shows how long you can stay, either until a specific date or for the duration of your student status ("D/S"). Also shown will be the name of the school you have been authorized to attend.

Each time you exit and reenter the U.S., you will get a new I-94 card authorizing your stay and indicating the time limit. When you have stayed in the U.S. on an M-1 visa for a year (or whatever time you were given) and you wish to remain longer, you may apply for one two-year extension of your I-20 to your DSO. F-1 students may apply for extensions of stay indefinitely, as long as they continue to maintain their eligibility for the status and their DSO grants an extension to complete studies.

Watch Out for Expedited Removal

The law empowers a Customs and Border Protection (CBP) inspector at the U.S. airport or border to summarily (without allowing judicial review) bar entry to someone requesting admission to the U.S. if either of the following is true:

- The inspector thinks you are lying about practically anything connected with entering the U.S., including your purpose in coming, intent to return home, and prior immigration history. This includes the use or suspected use of false documents.
- You do not have the proper documentation to support your entry to the U.S. in the category you are requesting.

If the inspector excludes you, you cannot be readmitted to the U.S. for five years, unless USCIS grants a special waiver. For this reason it is extremely important to understand the terms of your requested status and to not say anything that could be taken as a lie. If you are found to be inadmissible, you may ask the CBP inspector to withdraw your application to enter the U.S. in order to prevent having the five-year deportation order on your record. The CBP may allow this in some exceptional cases.

H. Extending Your Student Stay

Student visas and student statuses can be extended to allow necessary continuation of your studies. F-1 students can extend their permitted stay up to the revised estimated completion date of their academic program. M-1 students can, after one year, extend their permitted stay for a maximum of two more years.

Your authorized stay as indicated on your Form I-20 may last longer than the expiration date of the entry visa stamped in your passport, or it may expire before your visa expires. Therefore, depending on your situation, you may need to extend your I-20 date, your visa, or both. Statuses as written on the Forms I-20 can be extended only by your DSO in the United States. Student visas can be extended only at consulates (but you can wait until your next trip outside the U.S.).

Extensions are not automatic. Your DSO or the consular officers have the right to reconsider your qualifications based on any changes in the facts or law. If you seem not to be making progress toward your academic or vocational objectives, your extension request may be turned down. As always, however, good cases that are well prepared will ordinarily be successful.

If you need to extend the duration of your status as shown on the I-20 ID student copy, contact your DSO, who is responsible for making the extension and forwarding the information and paperwork to USCIS. Be sure, however, to request your extension before the end date on your I-20. If you are unable to complete your educational program before that date and you don't request an extension by then, you are out of status and must apply for reinstatement or leave the United States.

I. Traveling Outside the U.S. While You're a Student

As long as your student visa is valid and hasn't expired, you may travel outside the U.S. for up to five months and then return to resume your studies. (Make sure, however, that you haven't done anything to make yourself inadmissible, as discussed in Chapter 3.) Your passport must be valid at the time you reenter, and people from certain countries must have passports that are valid for at least six months after the time of reentry.

As a general rule, once your visa expires, you'll need to get a new one to reenter the U.S. if you leave for any reason. That means reapplying at a U.S. consulate using the same procedures discussed earlier in this chapter. An expired visa might never be a problem for some students, since student visas are typically issued for the expected length of your course of study.

If your visa does expire before you graduate, you might not necessarily have to get a new one if you want to travel. You can take short trips to Canada, Mexico,

Schools' Responsibilities to Track International Students

Schools must make various reports to USCIS concerning international students. When a school issues an I-20 to a student, it will be required to notify the U.S. consulate in the student's home country. When that consulate approves the student's visa, it will be required to notify USCIS.

During the student's time at school, the school will have to keep USCIS up to date on the student's status and whereabouts through a database called SEVIS. The information and documents that schools must routinely make available to USCIS for each international student include:

- name, date, and place of birth and country of citizenship
- current address
- visa classification, date of visa issuance or classification granted
- in-school status (full-time or part-time)
- date when studies began
- degree program and field of study
- whether the student has been certified for practical training and the dates of such certification
- date that studies were terminated, and the reason, if known
- written application for admission, transcripts or other course records, proof of financial responsibility, and other documents that the school evaluated in admitting the student
- number of credits completed per semester
- photocopy of Form I-20 ID, and
- record of any academic disciplinary actions due to criminal convictions.

On top of maintaining this database, the school must actually report news of each international student to USCIS each semester, no later than 30 days after the deadline for class registration. The information the schools must report includes: whether each student has enrolled, identification of any student who has dropped below a full course of study without authorization, and each student's current address.

In addition, the school has 21 days in which to report various changes in your situation. This means that you must report all of these to the school as soon as possible—you have only ten days in the case of address changes. These changes include: your failure to maintain student status or complete your educational program, a change in your address or name, your early graduation prior to the program end date on your form I-20, or any disciplinary action the school has taken against you.

F-1 Graduates Who Apply for H-1B: The "Cap Gap"

- Certain F-1 graduates who have found an employer to file an H-1B petition for them formerly faced a problem: They couldn't start their H-1B job until October 1, but they graduated in May and therefore fell out of status. This period of time is called the "cap gap," because it's caused by the the law having placed a cap on the number of new H-1B petitions that can be approved (in all but a few categories of jobs) every year, which results in most of H-1B approvals being issued with an October 1 start date for the job. (See Chapter 16 regarding H-1B visas.)

- To solve the cap gap problem, USCIS allows students with a pending H-1B petition to remain in F-1 status until their H-1B job starts in October. If the petition is not successful for any reason, you will have the usual 60-day grace period before leaving the U.S. (and you cannot work during that time). You won't get the 60-day grace period, however, if the petition denial is due to a status violation, misrepresentation, or fraud, or if the petition is revoked after approval due to a status violation, misrepresentation, or fraud. In such a case, you'll have to leave the U.S. immediately.

- To get proof of continuing F-1 status during a "cap gap," in April you must bring evidence of a timely filed H-1B petition (indicating a request for change of status rather than for consular processing) to your DSO. This evidence would be a copy of the petition and FedEx, UPS, or USPS Express/certified mail receipt. The DSO will issue a preliminary cap-gap I-20 showing an extension until June 1.

If the H-1B petition is selected in the "lottery" (see Chapter 16), you will return to your DSO with a copy of your employer's Form I-797 indicating that the petition was filed and accepted. The DSO will then issue a new cap-gap I-20, indicating the continued extension of F-1 status through September 30.

If you've been given a cap-gap extension, you can travel and reenter the U.S. during the gap if you have a valid employment authorization document (EAD). Don't travel if your change of status to H-1B hasn't been approved yet, however, because leaving the U.S. will be seen as an abandonment of your change of status application. If you don't have an EAD or if you must leave while your application to change to H-1B is pending, you can always pick up the H-1B visa at the consulate in your home country. That could create serious timing problems for you, though. It's best to talk with an immigration lawyer before you leave the United States.

or (if you're in F status) certain Caribbean islands and return to the U.S. even if your visa has expired, as long as you have a valid I-20 and a valid, unexpired I-94 (which usually just means that you're still in student status). It's best if you don't apply for a new visa on such a trip, because if you do, you can't take advantage of this so-called "automatic visa revalidation," and you might get stuck outside the U.S. for longer than you want to be.

Make sure you travel with your I-20 and I-94 so you can show them when you return. The CBP officer will be checking the SEVIS database as well. If there's a problem with your student status records, the CBP officer will let you in, but will give you a Form I-515A and notify your school. The I-515A tells you how to correct the problem, and gives you 30 days to do so. If the Student and Exchange Visitor Program (SEVP) doesn't hear from you in 30 days, it will send you and your school a Notice of Intent to Terminate. You'll have 14 days to comply. If you don't, SEVP will terminate your student status.

J. Reinstatement of Student Status

If you lose your student status for any reason, such as for having stopped attending classes, you can ask for your status back if you act quickly. The first requirement is that you apply for reinstatement within five months of losing your status. If you want to try filing after five months, you'll have to show that you're filing late due to exceptional circumstances, and that you acted as quickly as possible given those circumstances. You won't get reinstatement if you've violated certain immigration rules, like having worked without permission or done something that makes you deportable.

You can ask to be reinstated only to the same school as issued your I-20. (You can't go out of status and ask for reinstatement as a means of changing schools.) The first thing you'll need to do, therefore, is get your school's DSO to give you permission to reenroll and give you a new I-20. Then you file Form I-539 with USCIS, along with that I-20, the filing fee (currently $370), and a good explanation, with documents, for what happened.

USCIS might reinstate you if you lost your status for a reason beyond your control, such as a serious injury or illness, the school having closed down, or a natural disaster, or if it was the DSO's fault. If a DSO could have done something to keep you in status even if you took too few classes, USCIS should reinstate you if not doing so would result in extreme hardship to you. USCIS won't reinstate you if you have a pattern of repeated immigration violations or if you purposely did something causing you to fall out of status.

If you get reinstated, USCIS will give you an I-20 indicating this, and your

SEVIS records will be updated. If USCIS decides not to reinstate you, unfortunately there is no way to appeal that decision. You'll have to return home or obtain some other legal status if you can.

K. Getting Permission to Work

When you have F-1 student status, you can work only under limited circumstances. M-1 students have almost no rights to work. In many cases, these work privileges do not come automatically with the visa. You are often expected to file a separate application. There are a number of different types of work situations recognized as permissible for those with F-1 student status, and different rules apply to each one. Each situation is described in this section.

1. On-Campus Employment

F-1 status permits students to work in an on-campus job for up to 20 hours per week when school is in session. During vacation periods, you can work on campus full time. No special permission or application is required, as long as the job does not displace U.S. residents. Students working on campus can be employed by the school itself or any independent companies serving the school's needs, such as at the school bookstore or cafeteria suppliers providing food on campus premises.

2. Employment as Part of a Scholarship

F-1 students may also be employed as part of the terms of a scholarship, fellowship, or assistantship. The job duties must be related to your field of study. No special work permission or application is required. This is true even when the actual location of the job is off campus.

3. Practical Training

Both F-1 and M-1 visas allow students to apply for permission to work on the basis of practical training. Practical training for F-1 students can be either curricular, pre-completion, or postcompletion ("optional" or "OPT"). Curricular practical training occurs before graduation as part of your study program, while postcompletion training takes place afterward.

Curricular practical training is available only to F-1 students who have been enrolled in school for at least nine months. The nine-month enrollment requirement can be waived for graduate students requiring immediate participation in curricular practical training. All requests for curricular practical training are approved by the designated school official (DSO), who notifies USCIS.

Only the following types of work situations qualify as curricular practical training:

- alternate work/study programs
- internships, whether required or not required by the curriculum
- cooperative education programs, and
- required practicums offered though cooperative agreements with the school.

Both F-1 and M-1 students can get permission to work in postcompletion (optional) practical training (OPT) after graduating.

Postcompletion practical training can be approved for up to one year for all F-1 students and six months for M-1 students.

In addition, certain F-1 students are eligible for an additional 24-month extension of OPT. These are students who receive degrees in science, technology, engineering, and mathematics (STEM), are employed by employers enrolled in E-Verify, and who have received an initial grant of postcompletion OPT related to such a degree. If you believe this may apply to you, check with your DSO for the "STEM Designated Degree Program List."

Time spent in curricular practical training will be deducted from the time available for postcompletion practical training.

Part-time practical training is deducted from the total period available at one-half the full-time rate. F-1 students are eligible for a new one-year period of post-completion optional practical training after every level of higher education they complete. For example, a student could do one year of OPT upon completing a bachelor's degree, an additional year after a Master's, and then, if the student newly enrolls in a doctoral program, a third year once the Ph.D. is completed. Both the designated school official and USCIS must approve all applications for postcompletion practical training. (Instructions are given in Section 6, below.)

4. How to Apply for OPT Work Permission Based on Optional Practical Training

Both F-1 and M-1 foreign students must apply to USCIS for work permission to accept OPT employment. Practical training employment is any position where the work is directly related to your course of studies.

a. OPT Work Permit Application Procedures for F-1 Students

As an F-1 student, you must apply for permission to take OPT before completion of your study program. You may not apply until you have been enrolled as a student for at least nine months. If you apply before your full course of study is completed, you may be granted permission to take practical training only if it is necessary to fulfill a specific requirement of your particular academic program or if the work will be scheduled exclusively during regular school vacations. If the practical training will begin after you graduate, you may work simply because you wish to do so.

If your initial postcompletion OPT is to start after your studies are completed, you can apply for work permission either before graduation or during your 60-day departure preparation period after graduation. OPT extensions may be applied for at any time before the expiration date. As an F-1 student, you can be granted permission to work in a practical training position for a total of 12 months, unless you qualify for the STEM program, in which case you may be granted permission to work for a total of 36 months. You must have an offer of employment.

To apply, assemble the items on the checklist below. Then ask your designated school official to review the paperwork. If you appear to qualify, the DSO will give you a recommendation for employment, endorsed on Form I-20 ID, which you must include with your application. The DSO will also enter the recommendation into the SEVIS database.

> ![caution icon] CAUTION
> **When filling out the work permit application, use your home address.** USCIS says that a lot of students just put their college address on the form and then USCIS doesn't know where to send the card—so it does nothing.

Submit the application to the USCIS Lockbox designated for the region where you are attending school. (The addresses are available on the USCIS website at www.uscis.gov/i-765.) Keep the fee receipt USCIS will give you so you can prove that the I-765 was filed in case USCIS loses it.

The law requires USCIS to make a decision on your employment authorization application within 90 days. If the decision is in your favor, you will receive a work authorization card.

Checklist for F-1 OPT Work Permit Application

☐ Form I-765, with filing fee (currently $410). The eligibility code is "(c)(3)(A)" for precompletion OPT, "(c)(3)(B)" for postcompletion OPT, and "(c)(3)(C)" for a 24-month extension for an applicant qualified under STEM.

☐ Photocopy of SEVIS Form I-20 ID.

☐ I-94 card.

☐ Job offer letter from prospective U.S. employer (for postcompletion training only). The letter should explain the details of the work you will perform and show clearly that the work is in the same field as your course of studies.

☐ If you are a STEM student requesting a 24-month extension, you must also submit a copy of your degree and, in Question #17, provide your employer's name as listed in E-Verify along with their E-Verify Client Company Identification Number. You will need to ask your employer's human resources or legal department for the E-Verify Client Company Identification Number.

b. OPT Work Permit Application Procedures for M-1 Students

As an M-1 student, you can apply for permission to take practical training only after you have completed your entire program of studies. Applications for work permission must be filed not more than 60 days before your graduation. M-1 students can be granted permission to work in a practical training position only for a period of one month for each four months of study, with a total overall maximum of six months.

While the time periods for getting practical training work permission for F-1 students differ from those for M-1 students, the procedures, forms, and documents are almost exactly the same. See Subsection a, immediately above. The one difference is that on Question 16, M-1 students will answer "(c)(6)."

5. Economic Necessity

Only F-1 students are eligible for work permission based on economic necessity. You will remember that in order to obtain a student visa, you were required to show that you had enough money on hand to cover all of your first-year costs. Therefore, work permission on the basis of economic necessity will never be granted during your first year of studies.

Special Rules for F-1 Students Who Take Practical Training as a Required Part of Their Studies

If, prior to graduation, you accept practical training employment that is a required part of your studies, as is frequently done by students on fellowships, only 50% of your employment time will be deducted from the allotted 12-month total. Practical training in this special situation is called curricular practical training and has the effect of allowing you to work for a total of 24 months prior to graduation instead of only 12.

If you work for six months in curricular practical training, you are required to deduct only three months from your allotment, meaning you may still accept nine months of additional practical training employment prior to graduation and the full 12 months after graduation. If, however, you work more than 20 hours per week, you lose the benefit of this special rule. Under these circumstances, once again you must deduct the whole amount of time you worked, meaning you are limited to a maximum of 12 months of practical training prior to graduation.

As an F-1 student, you can request work permission after the first year if an unforeseen change in your financial situation has occurred, and if you meet the following conditions:

- You have maintained F-1 student status for at least one academic year.
- You are in good standing at your school.
- You are a full-time student.
- You will continue to be a full-time student while working.
- You will not work for more than 20 hours per week while school is in session.
- You have tried but failed to find on-campus employment.

USCIS recognizes as unforeseen circumstances such things as losing a scholarship, unusually large devaluation of your home country's currency, unexpected new restrictions enacted by your government that prevent your family from sending money out of the country, large increases in your tuition or living expenses, unexpected changes in the ability of your family to support you, or other unanticipated expenses, such as medical bills, that are beyond your control. Work permission can be granted for one year at a time, and must be renewed each year.

> **CAUTION**
>
> **Request employment authorization based on economic necessity only if you have no other choice.** If USCIS denies the application, USCIS may also decide that you are not eligible to continue in your student status, since you are basically telling USCIS that you don't have sufficient funds to support yourself.

6. How to Apply for Work Permission Based on Economic Need

You'll start by filling out USCIS Form I-765 and assembling supporting paperwork. Then your DSO must review your paperwork to decide whether or not you meet all the requirements for work permission. If you appear to qualify, the DSO will certify a recommendation for employment by endorsing it on Form I-20 ID and entering it into the SEVIS database.

Next, you submit the application and endorsed form to the USCIS Lockbox serving the geographic area where you live. (The addresses are on the USCIS website at www.uscis.gov/i-765.) The fee is currently $410.

It is very important to keep the fee receipt USCIS will give you so you can prove that the I-765 was filed.

USCIS is required to make a decision on your employment authorization application within 90 days. If the decision is in your favor, you will receive a work authorization identification card.

The checklist below will help you prepare and assemble your work permit application.

Checklist for Economic-Necessity-Based Work Permit Application

☐ Form I-765, with filing fee (currently $410). Answer Question 16 of the form "(c)(3)(iii)."

☐ I-20 ID (student copy).

☐ Documents to support your claim that an unexpected change in circumstances is creating your economic need, such as:

  ☐ Letters from government officials of your home country stating that there has been an unusual devaluation of the national currency or that your country's laws have changed and prevent your family from sending money out of the country to help support you as they once did.

  ☐ Documents from your school showing a substantial tuition increase.

  ☐ Bills from hospitals and doctors evidencing a costly family illness or birth of a child.

  ☐ If someone who has been supporting you is no longer able to do so, a statement from a doctor or a death certificate showing that the person has become ill or died or documents demonstrating that the person is having financial problems and so is unable to continue with your support.

L. Transferring to a Different School

If you decide that your school is not right for you and you wish to transfer to another, you may be able to do so. Requirements for transfers are different for F-1 students and M-1 students.

1. Applications for Transfers of F-1 Students

As an F-1 student, you may transfer from one school to another by following a specific procedure. You must be a full-time student at the time—otherwise you will have to request reinstatement to student status.

First, you must notify your current school DSO of your transfer plans. The DSO will update your record in SEVIS as a "transfer out," indicate the school to which you intend to transfer, and indicate a release date. The release date will be the current semester or session completion date, or the date of expected transfer if earlier than the established academic cycle. The current school will retain control over your record in SEVIS until you complete the current term or reach the release date. If you request it, your current DSO may cancel the transfer request at any time prior to the release date.

Once you reach the release date, the transfer school will be granted full access to your SEVIS record and then becomes responsible for you. (Your old school will no longer have access to your SEVIS records.) Your new DSO must complete the transfer of your record in SEVIS and may issue a SEVIS Form I-20. You are then required to contact the DSO at the transfer school within 15 days of the program start date listed on the SEVIS Form I-20. Upon notification that you are enrolled in classes, the DSO of the transfer school must update SEVIS to reflect your registration and current address, thereby acknowledging that you have completed the transfer process. In the remarks section of the student's SEVIS Form I-20, the DSO must note that the transfer has been completed, including the date, and return the form to you. The transfer is complete when the transfer school notifies SEVIS that you have enrolled in classes. (See 8 C.F.R. § 214.2(f)(8)(ii).)

2. Applications for Transfers of M-1 Students

As an M-1 student, you can transfer from one school to another, but only during your first six months of study, unless the transfer is required by circumstances beyond your control (such as your school closing down). If you transfer schools without following these procedures, you are considered out of status.

You would apply to transfer by notifying your current school of your plans. Your school must then update the SEVIS database to show you are a "transfer out" and input the release date for transfer. Then your transfer school is permitted to generate a SEVIS Form I-20 (but will not gain access to your SEVIS record until the release date is reached).

Upon receipt of the SEVIS Form I-20 from the transfer school, you must submit USCIS Form I-539 (in accordance with 8 C.F.R. § 214.2(m)(11)) to the USCIS Lockbox with jurisdiction over your current school. You may enroll in the transfer school at the next available term or session. You must get in touch with the DSO of the transfer school as soon as you begin attending. The DSO must then update your registration record in SEVIS. (See 8 C.F.R. § 214.3(g)(3).) Upon approval of the transfer application, the USCIS officer will endorse the name of your new school on your SEVIS Form I-20 and return it to you.

If your request to transfer is denied, you will receive a written decision by mail explaining the reason. USCIS has discretion to deny your application to transfer for any legitimate reason. There is no way of making a formal appeal to USCIS if your request is turned down.

M. Changing Your Course of Studies

F-1 students can change their courses of studies within the same school as long as they remain in qualifying programs. No formal permission from USCIS is required to change major areas of studies.

M-1 students are never permitted to change their courses of studies. If an M-1 student wishes to make such a change, he or she will have to return to a consulate and apply for a completely new student visa.

Getting an Exchange Visitor (J-1) Visa

The exchange visitor visa (J-1) was created to promote educational and cultural exchanges between the U.S. and other countries. It is mostly available to people who have signed up with an approved program focused on teaching, receiving training, or conducting research. The J-1 visa is also used by U.S. employers that want to hire workers to receive on-the-job training or participate in an internship. (See I.N.A. § 101(a)(15)(J), 8 C.F.R. § 214.2(j).) There is no limit on the number of people who can receive J-1 visas; over 300,000 people use them each year.

SEE AN EXPERT

Do you need a lawyer? Applying for a J-1 visa may not require a lawyer's help if your school or exchange visitor organization provides you with help and advice with the application process. A lawyer can help determine whether you can use a J-1 to work or train with a U.S. employer. Also, if you've had trouble getting visas in the past, have ever overstayed a visa, or are from a country thought to sponsor terrorism, a lawyer's help can be well worth the investment. Finally, if you later decide to apply for a different nonimmigrant status or green card, but think you're subject to the two-year home residence requirement, you'll definitely need a lawyer's help.

Key Features of the J-1 Exchange Visitor Visa

Here are some of the advantages and disadvantages of the J-1 exchange visitor visa:

- Once you've been accepted as a participant in an approved exchange visitor program, the application process is reasonably quick and straightforward.
- Your spouse and children may receive visas to accompany you.
- You may work legally in the U.S. if work is part of your approved program or if you receive permission to work from the official program sponsor.
- Your spouse and children may apply to USCIS for permission to work, so long as they prove that the money is not needed to support you.
- You may travel in and out of the U.S. or remain here until the completion of your exchange visitor program.
- Participants in certain types of programs may be required to return to their home countries for at least two years before applying for a green card, before a change to another nonimmigrant status, or before an L or H visa petition is approved on their behalf.

A. Do You Qualify for a J-1 Exchange Visitor Visa?

You qualify for a J-1 exchange visitor visa if you are coming to the U.S. as a student, scholar, trainee, intern, teacher, professor, research assistant, medical graduate, or other international visitor and if you are participating in a program of studies, training, research, or cultural enrichment specifically designed for such individuals by the U.S. Department of State (DOS), through its Bureau of Educational and Cultural Affairs (ECA). You must already be accepted into the program before you can apply for the visa.

Some common programs for which J-1 visas are issued include the Fulbright Scholarship program, specialized training programs for foreign medical graduates, and programs for foreign university professors teaching or doing research in the United States.

You must have enough money to cover your expenses while you are in the U.S. as an exchange visitor. Only an insubstantial portion of those funds may come from personal resources. If your J-1 visa is based on work activities, the salary may be your means of support.

You must be able to speak, read, and write English well enough to participate effectively in the exchange program of your choice. In addition to all other qualifications, you are eligible for a J-1 visa only if you intend to return to your home country when the program is over.

To summarize, there are five requirements for getting a J-1 visa:

- You must be coming to the U.S. to work, study, teach, train, consult, or observe U.S. culture in a specific exchange visitor program approved by the DOS.
- You must already have been accepted into the program.
- You must have enough money to cover your expenses while in the United States.
- You must have sufficient knowledge of English to be able to participate effectively in the exchange visitor program you have chosen.
- You must intend to return home when your status expires.

1. An Exchange Visitor Program Approved by the DOS

J-1 visas allow you to study, teach, do research, or participate in cultural activities in the U.S. as part of any program specifically approved by the DOS. Sponsors of acceptable programs may be foreign or U.S. government agencies, private foreign and U.S. organizations, or U.S. educational institutions. Such groups wanting program approval must apply to the DOS. Those making successful applications will be authorized to issue what are known as

Certificates of Eligibility (Form DS-2019) to J-1 visa applicants. These can be produced only through the Student and Exchange Visitor Information System (SEVIS). They indicate that the applicant has been accepted into an approved program.

Each approved program appoints an administrator known as the Responsible Officer (RO). The RO plays a formal role in dealing with the immigration process for program applicants.

There are over 1,500 DOS-approved programs in existence. Current information about exchange visitor programs is available from the DOS at http://exchanges.state.gov.

2. Acceptance Into a Program

Before applying for a J-1 visa, you must first apply for acceptance into the DOS-approved program of your choice. Application is made directly to the program sponsor. The following are the basic categories of J-1 visas:

Au Pair (nannies)

Camp counselor

College or university student

Government visitor

Intern

International visitor

Physician

Professor or research scholar

Secondary school student

Short-term scholar

Specialist

Summer work travel

Teacher

Trainee

Each of these categories has its own eligibility requirements in addition to the general requirements discussed below. Any program you are interested in will work with you to make sure you are eligible.

3. Financial Support

You must establish that you have enough money to cover all expenses while in the United States. Since most exchange visitor programs involve either employment or scholarships, this particular requirement is usually easy to meet. You also must maintain health insurance for the whole time you'll be participating in the program.

4. Knowledge of English

To qualify for a J-1 visa, you must know English well enough to participate effectively in the exchange visitor program. If your program is for students, you should know that most U.S. colleges and universities will not admit people whose native language is not English unless they first pass an English proficiency test, such as the TOEFL. Tests can sometimes be arranged in your home country. The school will tell you if such a test is required and how to go about taking it.

Consular officials usually let each school decide for itself who is and is not qualified to study there. Still, the consulate may refuse to issue an exchange visitor visa based on its own judgment that you do not know enough English to function as a U.S. student.

5. Intent to Return to Your Home Country

Exchange visitor visas are meant to be temporary. At the time of applying, you must intend to return home when your program in the U.S. is completed. If you have it in mind to take up permanent residence in the U.S., you are legally ineligible for an exchange visitor visa.

The U.S. government knows it is difficult to read minds. Expect to be asked for evidence showing that when you go to the U.S. on a J-1 visa, you are leaving behind possessions, property, or family members that will serve as incentives for your eventual return. It is also helpful to show that you have a job waiting at home when your program is completed.

If you are studying or training to prepare yourself for an occupation in which no jobs are available in your home country, the immigration authorities may have trouble believing that you are planning to return there. To avoid trouble, it's best to choose a field of study that will give you career opportunities at home when you are finished.

6. Find Out Whether You Are Subject to the Two-Year Home Residence Requirement

One of the defining characteristics of the J-1 visa is its requirement that many J-1 visa holders return home for two years before applying for another U.S. visa or a green card. The reason for the home residence requirement is that the visa is intended for exchange programs where people learn something that is particular to the United States. Exchange students are then expected to go home and use their knowledge about the U.S. This is the "exchange" element of the visa.

Not all J-1 visa holders are subject to the two-year home residence requirement. It applies only to participants in the following types of exchange visitor programs:

- programs for foreign medical graduates who receive graduate medical training (residencies)
- programs in which the participant receives money from his or her foreign government, the U.S. government, or an international organization, and
- programs for teaching people certain skills that are in short supply in their home countries. The Department of State maintains a list of such skills and the countries where they are especially needed. The skills list can be accessed at www.travel.state.gov (click "U.S.

Visas," then "Study and Exchange," then "Exchange Visitor Skills List."

The Certificate of Eligibility, SEVIS Form DS-2019, which you receive from your program sponsor, has a space showing whether you are subject to the home residence requirement. Also, when you are issued a J-1 visa at a U.S. consulate, the visa will state whether or not you are so subject.

Neither the DS-2019 nor the J-1 visa designations are entirely authoritative, however. Ultimately, the DOS Visa Office has the final say on whether you are subject to the two-year home residence requirement. You may request an advisory opinion as to whether you are subject.

If you are subject to the two-year home residence requirement, then you are ineligible to apply for a green card, to change status to any other nonimmigrant status except A, G, T, or U, or to obtain an H or L visa; but see "Waivers of Two-Year Home Residency Requirements," later in this chapter.

7. Foreign Medical Graduates: Additional Qualifications

If you are coming to the U.S. as a foreign medical graduate for the purpose of continuing your medical training or education, there are some added requirements. First, you must have passed Parts I and II of the U.S. National Board of Medical Examiners

examination or its equivalent. Information on taking the exam is available from the Educational Commission for Foreign Medical Graduates in Philadelphia, at 215-386-5900, www.ecfmg.org.

Like all J-1 visa applicants, foreign medical graduates must prove they will return home when their status expires. However, your evidence must include a written guarantee from the government in your home country verifying that employment will be available to you when your U.S. medical training is completed.

Foreign medical graduates applying for J-1 visas should understand that they are legally required to return home for at least two years before becoming eligible to apply for green cards. However, they are exempt from this requirement if they participate in a so-called "Conrad 30 Waiver" program, by which they agree to work for three years in an underserved area of the U.S.—that is, an area recognized by the Secretary of Health and Human Services (HHS) as having a shortage of health care professionals.

8. Bringing Your Spouse and Children

When you qualify for a J-1 visa, your spouse and unmarried children under age 21 can get J-2 visas to accompany you. They will need to provide proof of their family relationship to you, such as marriage and birth certificates. Your exchange program will also need to provide each of them a SEVIS Form DS-2019 issued in their own name. J-2 visas authorize your accompanying relatives to stay with you in the U.S., but they may not accept employment unless they first obtain special permission from USCIS.

B. How Long the J-1 Status Will Last

How long you'll be allowed to stay in the U.S. on your J-1 visa depends on the type of program you'll be participating in (Sections 1 through 14, below) and the dates of your participation.

In seeking a J-1 visa, you will be asked to present a Certificate of Eligibility, SEVIS Form DS-2019. This form is provided to you by the sponsor of your exchange visitor program. The form will list the specific dates you are expected to be participating in the program. Upon entering the U.S. with a J-1 visa, you will be authorized (on Form I-94) to remain only up to the final date indicated on the Certificate of Eligibility.

The Certificate of Eligibility is usually issued for the period of time needed to complete the particular exchange visitor program for which your J-1 visa is approved. USCIS regulations, however, place some maximum time limits on J-1 visas according to the type of program.

Your RO can extend your participation in the program beyond the dates described below by sending the DOS good reasons for the extension and a $367 fee. The DOS must approve the extension.

1. Students

Most students may remain in the U.S. for the duration of their programs plus an additional 18 months of practical training employment. Practical training is any employment directly related to the subject matter of the student's major field of study. Remaining in the U.S. for the additional 18 months of practical training is at the student's discretion. Postdoctoral training is limited to 36 months minus any previously used practical training time.

However, students between the ages of 15 and 18½ who are participating in a high school exchange program (living with a U.S. host family or residing at an accredited U.S. boarding school) are limited to one year's stay. They cannot work, except at odd jobs such as babysitting or yard work.

2. Teachers, Professors, Research Scholars, and People With Specialized Skills

Exchange visitors who are teachers, professors, research scholars, or people with specialized skills may be given J-1 status for no more than five years, plus 30 days in which to prepare to depart the United States.

3. International Visitors

International visitors whose purpose is to promote cultural exchange, such as those working in the cultural/ethnic pavilions of Disney's Epcot Center, may be given J-1 status for no more than one year, plus 30 days in which to prepare to depart the United States. Persons qualifying under this category may also be eligible for Q visas.

4. Foreign Medical Graduate Students

Foreign medical graduates may be given J-1 status for the length of time necessary to complete their training programs, up to a usual maximum of seven years (with limited exceptions), plus 30 days in which to prepare to depart the United States.

5. Other Medically Related Programs

Participants in any medically related programs other than those for foreign medical graduates may be given J-1 status for the duration of their educational programs plus 18 months of practical training. However, the total time of both program participation and practical training may not be more than three years.

6. Business and Industrial Trainees

Business and industrial trainees may be given J-1 status for a maximum of 18 months.

7. Interns

Interns are eligible for up to 12 months of J-1 status to work with a U.S. employer while in the midst of a degree program in their home country or within one year of graduation.

8. Employees of the International Communications Agency

Participants in this particular exchange visitor program may be given J-1 status for up to ten years or even longer if the director of the International Communications Agency makes a special request to USCIS.

9. Research Assistants Sponsored by the National Institutes of Health

Participants in the NIH research assistants exchange visitor program may be given J-1 status for a period of up to five years.

10. Au Pairs

Au pairs who are between ages 18 and 26 may come to the U.S. on J-1 visas to live with and perform child care (but not do other housework) for U.S. families. Au pairs may work no more than ten hours per day, 45 hours per week, be paid at least the minimum wage, and must attend an institution of higher education to earn at least six hours of academic credit.

As of this writing, only 15 agencies have been approved to issue Certificates of Eligibility for bringing au pairs to the United States. Stays are limited to only one year and cannot be extended. If this program interests you, check the State Department website at http://j1visa.state.gov/programs/au-pair.

11. Government Visitors

Visitors may be invited by the U.S. government to participate in exchanges that strengthen professional and personal ties between key foreign nationals and the United States and U.S. institutions. They may be given J-1 status for the length of time necessary to complete the program, but no more than 18 months.

12. Camp Counselors

Youth workers over the age of 18 coming to serve as counselors in U.S. summer camps may be given J-1 status for no more than four months.

13. Summer Work Travel

Postsecondary students may use a J-1 visa to work and travel in the United States for a four-month period during their summer vacations, through programs conducted by DOS-designated sponsors.

14. Short-Term Scholars

Professors and other academics participating in short-term activities, such as seminars, workshops, conferences, study tours, or professional meetings, may be granted up to six months on a J-1 visa.

15. Exceptions to the General Rules

Any exchange visitor may be allowed to remain in the U.S. beyond the limitations stated above if exceptional circumstances arise that are beyond the exchange visitor's control, such as illness.

C. Students: Comparing J-1 Visas to F-1 and M-1 Visas

Students coming to the U.S. often have a choice between J-1 exchange visitor visas and M-1 or F-1 student visas. Student visas are discussed in Chapter 22. J-1 programs for students are very limited as to the level of education and types of subjects that can be studied. By contrast, F-1 and M-1 visas can be issued for almost any type of education program imaginable, including vocational, secondary, and high school programs as well as all courses of study at colleges and universities.

Assuming there is an exchange visitor program that will fit your needs as a student, there are certain advantages to holding a J-1 visa. It is much easier to get work permission as an exchange visitor than it is on a student visa. With a J-1 visa you may remain in the U.S. for up to 18 months after you graduate for the purpose of working in a practical training position. F-1 student visa holders are limited to 12 months of practical training employment (unless they're in a science, technology, engineering, or math program, in which case, it's 24 months or 36 months with an extension) and M-1 students are limited to only six months.

F-1 and M-1 student visas, however, are more flexible than exchange visitor visas in several ways. With an F-1 student visa, you may transfer from one school to another or change courses of study quite freely. After graduation, you may enroll in a new educational program without having to obtain a new visa. On a J-1 visa, you must remain in the exact program for which your visa was issued.

Most important, certain J-1 visa programs automatically make you subject to a two-year home residency requirement, which will cause problems should you later want to apply for a green card, change to another nonimmigrant status, or have a nonimmigrant worker L or H visa petition approved.

D. Business and Industrial Trainees: A Good Option for Work in the U.S.

J-1s are available for people coming to the U.S. to complete a paid or unpaid training program with a private company or nonprofit organization. The company or organization, or its attorneys, may work with an approved J-1 program sponsor to get J-1 visas for prospective trainees.

In order to qualify as a J-1 trainee, you must enter the U.S. to participate in a structured and guided work-based training program in your field of expertise and meet one of these requirements: (1) You must have a degree or professional certificate from a foreign postsecondary academic institution and at least one year of related work experience in your field acquired outside the U.S; or (2) you must have five years of related work experience outside the U.S. in your field.

If you wish to pursue a second training program, you must first spend two years outside the U.S. before you will qualify.

E. Internships as a Way for Foreign Students to Work in the U.S.

You may obtain a J-1 visa to participate in a work-based internship program in the U.S. that will build on your academic experience or develop practical skills in an academic or career field. In order to qualify as an intern, you must either:

- be currently enrolled in and pursuing studies at a degree- or certificate-granting postsecondary academic institution outside the U.S., or
- have graduated from an academic institution no more than 12 months prior to your internship program start date.

The maximum time you can stay in the U.S. on an internship program as a J-1 intern is 12 months. However, you can participate in an additional internship if it will help you develop more advanced skills or skills in a different field of expertise. If you no longer qualify for an internship because you no longer have student status abroad or are not within 12 months of graduation, you can apply for J-1 trainee status after a two-year residency period outside the United States.

F. Can You Apply for a Green Card From J-1 Status?

J-1 visas, like all nonimmigrant visas, are meant to be temporary. They are intended only for people who plan on returning home once the exchange program in the U.S. is completed. Should you decide to apply for a green card before your program is finished, the U.S. government will allow you to keep J-1 status while pursuing a green card, but only if you are able to convince it that you did not intend to get a green card when you originally applied for the J-1 visa and that you will return home if you are unable to secure a green card before your exchange visitor status expires. Proving these things can be difficult. If you do not succeed, your J-1 visa may be taken away. Some program sponsors have been known to withdraw J-1 privileges after an exchange visitor has applied for a green card.

The most serious drawback to applying for a green card from J-1 status is that many J-1 visas are granted subject to the two-year home residency requirement discussed above in Section A6. If you choose an exchange visitor program that carries this requirement, it means that you must return to your home country and remain there for at least two years before you are eligible to apply for a green card.

G. Quick View of the J-1 Visa Application Process

Getting a J-1 visa is a two- to three-step process:

- Your program sponsor sends you a DS-2019 Certificate of Eligibility.
- You apply for either a visa (from a U.S. consulate in another country) or, if you're already living legally in the U.S. and prefer not to travel, for a change of nonimmigrant status (from USCIS).
- If you are outside the U.S. and receive a visa, you enter the U.S. and claim your J-1 status.

(If you are Canadian, your application procedures will be different from those of other applicants. See Chapter 5.)

H. Step One: Your Sponsoring Organization Issues a Certificate of Eligibility

You can't start the visa application process until you have been admitted to an exchange program approved by the U.S. Department of State (DOS), through its Bureau of Educational and Cultural Affairs (ECA). This book does not discuss how to find the right U.S. school or program, or how to get accepted to it. However, the State Department provides a list of approved organizations, at www.j1visa. state.gov/programs. You'll probably need to get started well in advance.

Once a program has accepted you, it will issue you a SEVIS Form DS-2019. You do not fill out or sign any part of it. But carefully check the form for accuracy, then ask your sponsoring organization to correct any errors. You'll use the DS-2019 in the next steps of your application process.

I. Step Two for Applicants Outside the U.S.: Apply for a Visa at a U.S. Consulate

Anyone with a Certificate of Eligibility (SEVIS Form DS-2019) from an exchange visitor program sponsor can apply for a J-1 visa at a U.S. consulate in his or her home country. You must be physically present in order to apply there.

The exact steps to take to apply for your visa depend on the U.S. embassy or consulate where you're applying. You will probably need to:

- prepare and submit an online application
- schedule an interview at a U.S. embassy or consulate
- gather some personal documents
- pay the required fees, and
- meet with an official at the U.S. embassy or consulate.

For additional information on these application procedures, consult the website of the U.S. embassy or consulate where you're applying, and see the State Department website at www.travel.state.gov

Applying at a Consulate That's Not in Your Home Country

The law allows most people to apply for a J-1 visa at any U.S. consulate they choose— with one exception. If you have ever been present in the U.S. unlawfully, your visa will be automatically cancelled and you cannot apply as a third-country national (at a consulate outside your home country). Even if you overstayed your permitted stay in the U.S. by just one day, you must return to your home country and apply for the visa from that consulate. There is an exception. If you were admitted to the U.S. for the duration of your status (indicated by a "D/S" on your I-94) and you remained in the U.S. beyond the time for which your status was conferred, you will be barred from third-country national processing only if an immigration judge or USCIS (or INS, formerly) officer has determined that you were unlawfully present. You may find that your success in applying as a third-country national will depend on your country, the consulate, and the relative seriousness of your offense. Being unlawfully present is also a ground of inadmissibility if the period of unlawful presence is 180 days or more. (See Chapter 3.)

Even if you are eligible for third-country national processing, your case will be given the greatest consideration at the consulate in your home country. Applying in some other country creates suspicion in the minds of the consular officers there about your motives for choosing their consulate. Often, when an applicant expects trouble at a home consulate, he or she will seek a more lenient consular office in some other country. This practice of consulate shopping is frowned upon by officials in the system. Unless you have a very good reason for being elsewhere (such as a temporary job assignment in some other nation), it is often smarter to file your visa application in your home country.

(click "Study & Exchange" and then "Exchange Visitor Visa").

You can normally apply 120 days or less before your program begins. Because of processing delays, it's best to apply as soon as you can within that 120-day window.

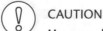 CAUTION

Have you been, or are you now, working or living illegally in the United States? If so, see Chapter 3 regarding whether you can still get a J-1 visa from a U.S. consulate. You may have become inadmissible or subject to a three-year or ten-year bar on reentry.

1. Preparing and Submitting Your Visa Application

Your visa application will consist of a government form and some documents that you collect yourself. The form, called a DS-160, can be completed only online. You will bring the supporting documents with you to your visa interview.

To access the DS-160, go to the State Department's Consular Electronic Application Center (CEAC) website at https://ceac.state.gov. If a question is marked "optional," you can leave the answer space blank. You can answer with "Does Not Apply" if the question does not fit your situation. Most questions require some answer—the system will not allow you to submit an application if you don't answer a mandatory question. Electronically sign your DS-160 by clicking the "Sign Application" button at the end of the form.

Because the DS-160 asks for a lot of information, it will help if you have the following documents nearby:

- your passport
- your travel itinerary, if you have already made travel arrangements, and
- your résumé or curriculum vitae (in case you are required to provide information about your current and previous education and work history).

Consult your travel records (or your memory!) before starting the application.

You'll need to provide the dates of your last five visits or trips to the U.S., if you have previously been there. You may also be asked for your international travel history for the past five years.

TIP

No need to complete the DS-160 in one sitting. It's a lengthy form. Fortunately, you can save your work and return to it later. When you begin a new DS-160, you will be issued a unique application identification (ID) number after selecting and answering a security question. Using that application ID, you can return to your application. The information you enter in your DS-160 is saved every time you click the "Next" button at the bottom of a page. However, an application is saved on CEAC for only 30 days. If you will want to access your application after 30 days, you must save it by selecting the "Save Application to File" button. Then, click the "Save" button on the File Download window.

You must also, as part of your application, upload a U.S. passport-style photo to CEAC. Information on how to provide a suitable photo is on the State Department's website, www.travel.state.gov. (Follow the links to "Study & Exchange," "Exchange Visitor Visas," and "Photograph Requirements.") If you have trouble getting the system to accept your photo, ask someone who's good with computers for help. As a last resort, you can just bring a photo to your interview at the consulate.

After submitting the DS-160 online, print and keep the barcode confirmation page. You'll need to bring it to your consular interview.

2. Schedule an Interview at a U.S. Embassy or Consulate

After your DS-160 has been accepted, it's up to you to schedule an interview at a U.S. embassy or consulate. While interviews are generally not required for applicants under 14 years old or over 80 years old, consular officers have the discretion to require an interview of any applicant, regardless of age.

The waiting time for an interview appointment varies from country to country. Check the Department of State's website at www.travel.state.gov for the current wait time at your consulate (click "U.S. Visas," then enter the city where your consulate is located in the "Plan Ahead" section).

3. Pay the Visa Application Fee

Most consulates require applicants to pay the visa application fee, currently $160 for J visas, before their interview. The consulate will give you instructions on how and when to make payment.

If you are in an exchange program sponsored by the U.S. government, you and your family may not have to pay visa application processing fees. Check your

DS-2019 for a program serial number beginning with G-1, G-2, G-3, or G-7. If you're participating in a Department of State, a U.S. Agency for International Development, or a federally funded educational and cultural exchange program with one of those serial numbers, you won't have to pay the visa application fee (or any visa issuance fee).

4. Pay the SEVIS Fee

Before your appointment, you'll need to pay a fee (currently $200) to support the U.S. student and exchange visitor tracking database called SEVIS. Your program sponsor may take care of processing this fee payment for you. If not, you'll need to do it yourself, either online or by mail. To submit the form online, go to www. FMJfee.com, complete the online Form I-901, and pay with a credit card.

To submit the form by mail, download it from the Immigration and Customs Enforcement (ICE) website at www.ice. gov/sevis/i901 and mail it, together with your check or money order drawn on a U.S. bank and payable in U.S. currency, to the address indicated on the form. SEVIS will not mail you a receipt for the paid fee. You'll have to print payment confirmation from the FMJFEE website (www.fmjfee. com). Click the "Check I-901 Status/Print Payment Confirmation" button. After entering your SEVIS ID, last name, and date of birth you will be able to print your payment confirmation. You'll need it for the interview at the consulate.

Don't wait too long to pay the SEVIS fee. Although you can't pay it before getting a DS-2019, and it doesn't have to be paid before you schedule your interview, it must be paid by the time of the actual interview. You can't get a visa or enter the U.S. without paying it.

5. Gather Supporting Documents

The consulate will likely tell you to come to the interview with documents that support your eligibility for a J visa. You'll definitely need to bring your passport, the DS-160 confirmation page, your fee payment confirmation (if advance payment was required), the DS-2019, and a photo if you weren't able to upload one successfully to CEAC, or perhaps even if you were. In addition, consulates like to see the following:

Evidence of intent to return. You will need documents establishing your intent to leave the U.S. when your visa expires. The consulate will want to see evidence that your ties to your home country are so strong that you will be highly motivated to return. Proof of such ties can include deeds verifying ownership of a house or other real property, written statements from you explaining that close relatives are staying behind, or letters from a company outside the U.S. showing that you have a job waiting when you return from the United States.

Evidence of sufficient funds. If neither employment nor a scholarship is part of your exchange visitor program, you must present evidence that you have sufficient funds available to cover all of your costs while you are in the U.S. on a J-1 visa. If your particular exchange visitor program provides you with a scholarship or employment, evidence of such support in the form of a letter from the program sponsor will satisfy this requirement.

If the exchange visitor program sponsor will not be furnishing you with financial support, you will have to show either that you can meet your own expenses without working or that a close relative is willing to guarantee your support. The best evidence of your ability to pay educational expenses is a bank statement or letter from a bank, either in the U.S. or abroad, showing an account in your name with a balance of at least one year's worth of expenses in it. Alternatively, you can submit a written guarantee of support signed by an immediate relative, preferably a parent, together with your relative's bank statements. Unless your relative can show enough assets to prove he or she is able to support you without additional income, you should also show that your relative is presently employed. You can document this by submitting a letter from the employer verifying your relative's work situation.

Although the guarantee of support may be in the form of a simple written statement in your relative's own words, we suggest you use USCIS Form I-134, called an Affidavit of Support, especially if the person who will support you lives in the United States. A fillable I-134 form is available on the USCIS website at www.uscis.gov/i-134. The questions on Form I-134 are self-explanatory. However, the form was designed to be filled out by someone living in the United States. Since it is quite likely that the person who will support you is living outside the U.S., any questions that apply to U.S. residents should be answered "N/A" (for "not applicable").

6. Attending Your Consular Interview

Most consulates will require an interview before issuing a J-1 exchange visitor visa. During the interview, a consular officer will examine the forms and documents for accuracy. The consular officer will verify your DS-2019 record electronically through the SEVIS system. Documents proving your ability to finance your study will be carefully checked, as will evidence of ties to your home country. During the interview, you will surely be asked how long you intend to remain in the United States. Any answer indicating uncertainty about plans to return home or an interest in applying for a green card is likely to result in a denial of your student visa.

Because of security requirements, you are unlikely to be approved for your visa on the same day as your interview. At some point in the application process, most likely at the interview, you will need to have ink-free, digital fingerprint scans taken. Based on these, the consular officer will initiate various security checks to make sure you haven't been involved in criminal or terrorist activity. This can add weeks or even months to the processing of your visa, particularly if you come from a country that the U.S. suspects of supporting terrorism.

To get your visa, you may have to pay a visa issuance fee (known as a "reciprocity fee") if you're from a country that charges similar fees for visas to U.S. citizens. Some J-1 exchange program participants are exempt from the visa issuance fee in any event. (See Section I3, above.)

J. Step Two for Some Applicants Inside the U.S.: You Apply to USCIS for a Change of Status

If you are physically present in the U.S., you may apply for a change to J-1 status without leaving the country on the following conditions:

- You have been accepted into an approved program, and the program has given you a Certificate of Eligibility, SEVIS Form DS-2019.

- You entered the U.S. legally and not under the Visa Waiver Program, nor using a C (alien in transit), TWOV (alien in transit without a visa), D (crewman), any K (fiancé), S (informant) visa, or M-1 (vocational student) visa.
- You have never worked in the U.S. illegally.
- The date on your I-94 has not passed.
- You are not inadmissible.

TIP
Eligibility to apply while you're in the U.S. has nothing to do with overall eligibility for a J-1 visa. Applicants who are barred from filing in the U.S. but otherwise qualify for student status can sometimes apply successfully for a J-1 visa at U.S. consulates abroad.

Overall, USCIS offices do not favor change of status applications. To approve a change of status, USCIS must believe that at the time you originally entered the U.S. as a visitor or with some other nonimmigrant visa, you did not intend to apply for a different status. If USCIS thinks you had a preconceived plan to use one visa to enter the U.S. with an eye to applying to change to a different status, it may deny your application. You can get around the preconceived intent issue by leaving the U.S. and applying for your visa at a U.S. consulate in another country. In fact, your visa application will stand a better chance of approval at most consulates than it will if filed in the United States. But understand the pitfalls involved in departing the U.S. (especially if you have lived here unlawfully) before making your decision. (See Chapter 3.)

If you decide to apply for a change of status within the U.S., realize that you still don't have the physical visa that you'll need to get back in if you ever leave the U.S.—a change of status gives you only J-1 status. Visas are never given inside the United States. They are issued exclusively by U.S. consulates in other countries. If you file in the U.S. and you are successful, you will get to remain in the U.S. with J-1 privileges until the status expires. But should you leave the country before that time, you will most likely have to apply for the visa itself at a U.S. consulate before returning to the United States. Moreover, the fact that your J-1 status has been approved in the U.S. does not guarantee that the consulate will also approve your visa. For these reasons, many people choose to leave the U.S. and apply through a consulate at the start.

1. Preparing Your U.S. Change of Status Application

Before submitting your application, you'll need to pay a fee to support the U.S. student and exchange visitor tracking database called SEVIS. Your school may take care

Checklist for J-1 Change of Status Application

- ☐ Form I-539, Application to Extend/Change Nonimmigrant Status, with accompanying fee (currently $370; if submitting by mail, send a check or money order, not cash). One Form I-539 and fee will cover you, your spouse, and all your children, if they are in the U.S. with you and in the same visa status or accompanying beneficiaries of your current visa status. But be sure to complete the I-539 Supplement for your spouse and children.

- ☐ Copy of Form SEVIS DS-2019, filled out by your school and signed by you.

- ☐ For participants in the J-1 trainee and intern categories, your training/internship placement plan, Form DS-7002.

- ☐ Copy of confirmation of having paid your SEVIS fee (currently $200).

- ☐ Copies of proof of your family members' relationship to you, such as marriage and birth certificates.

- ☐ Copies of Form I-94 (and those of your spouse and children, if they're applying with you) or other proof of your current lawful, unexpired immigration status (Canadians just visiting the U.S. are not expected to have I-94s).

- ☐ If either you or your spouse has ever been married before, copies of divorce and death certificates showing termination of all previous marriages.

- ☐ If your program involves studying at a school, copies of transcripts, diplomas, and results of any standardized tests required by the school you'll be attending, showing your previous education and your qualifications to pursue your chosen course of study.

- ☐ Copies of documents showing reasons that you'll return to your home country, such as ownership of real estate, relationships with close family members staying behind, or proof that a job will be waiting for you on your return.

- ☐ If your program doesn't include salaried employment, provide proof of sufficient funds, such as:
  - ☐ Form I-134, Affidavit of Support from a U.S. friend or relative, or a letter from a friend or relative promising support.
  - ☐ Bank statements.
  - ☐ Personal financial statements.
  - ☐ Evidence of your current sources of income.

of paying or processing this fee payment for you. If not, you'll need to do it yourself, either online or by mail. To submit the form online, go to www.FMJfee.com. There is an option now to pay by Western Union, which will allow speedy processing. To submit the form by mail, download it from the Immigration and Customs Enforcement (ICE) website at www.ice.gov, and mail it, together with your check or money order drawn on a U.S. bank and payable in U.S. currency, to the address indicated on the form. For more information on these requirements, see www.ice.gov/sevis/i901. SEVIS will not mail you a receipt for the fee payment. You'll have to print confirmation from the FMJFEE website (www.fmjfee.com). Click the "Check I-901 Status/Print Payment Confirmation" button. After entering your SEVIS ID, last name, and date of birth you will be able to print your payment confirmation, which you'll need for the adjustment interview.

The checklist below will help you assemble the necessary items for the change of status application.

For additional explanation of some of the items on this checklist, see Section I5, above.

2. Submitting the Change of Status Application

After assembling the change of status application, mail it to a USCIS Lockbox in Texas. You cannot visit Lockbox offices in person. The addresses for mailing (regular mail and express mail) are on the instructions to the I-539. (See www.uscis.gov/i-539.)

3. Awaiting a Decision on the Change of Status Application

Within a few weeks after mailing in the petition, you should get back a written confirmation that the papers are being processed, together with a receipt for the fee. This notice will also contain your immigration file number. If USCIS wants further information before acting on your case, it will send you a form known as a Request for Evidence (RFE). You should

supply the extra data requested and mail it back to USCIS or, if using ELIS, upload the additional evidence.

Change of status applications are normally approved (or denied) within two to three months. (At www.uscis.gov, follow the links to "Check Your Case Status" and "USCIS Processing Times.") USCIS will notify you using a Form I-797 Notice of Action. A new I-94 card will be attached to the bottom of the form.

K. Step Three: J-1 Visa Holders Enter the U.S.

If you're coming from abroad on a J-1 visa, you'll be allowed to enter the U.S. up to 30 days before the start of your classes or program, but no earlier. When you arrive in the U.S., the border officer will examine your paperwork, ask you some questions, and if all is in order, approve you for entry. An I-94 Arrival/Departure record will be created for you (if you enter by air or sea). If you enter at a land border, you will be given a small white I-94 card. Your I-94 shows how long you can stay in the U.S., either until a specific date or for the duration of your program ("D/S"). As a practical matter, however, you are permitted to remain up to the expiration date on your SEVIS Form DS-2019 Certificate of Eligibility. Each time you exit and reenter the U.S., you will get a new I-94.

L. Extending Your J-1 Stay in the U.S.

J-1 visas and status can be extended in the U.S. to enable you to complete your particular exchange visitor program. However, since J-1 status is usually granted for the period of time considered reasonable for the type of exchange visitor program in which you are participating, extensions are not easy to get. Also, certain J-1 categories have a limit on how long they last.

When you enter the U.S. on a J-1 visa, the CBP officer will most likely note on your I-94 that you can stay in the U.S. for the duration of your status (D/S), limited by the time period on your Certificate of Eligibility. However, if you come from a country where J-1 visa time privileges are especially limited, your visa may expire before your I-94 does. In such a situation, if you wish to leave the U.S. and then reenter to complete your exchange visitor program, you will have to extend your visa. To extend the visa that is stamped in your passport, you must apply at a U.S. consulate abroad.

Whether and how you can extend your J-1 stay depends on whether you were admitted for the duration of your status (with a "D/S" mark on your I-94) or until a specific date. It's easier with a D/S mark; in that case you can simply explain the situation to the RO at your school or program (most of them like you to give them at least 30 days' notice) and ask the RO to prepare a new Form DS-2019 showing the new expected completion date. The RO then notifies the State Department, and your extension becomes official.

Watch Out for Expedited Removal

The law empowers a Customs and Border Protection (CBP) inspector at the U.S. airport or border to summarily (without allowing judicial review) bar entry to someone requesting admission to the U.S. if either of the following is true:

- The inspector thinks you are lying about practically anything connected with entering the U.S., including your purpose in coming, intent to return home, and prior immigration history. This includes the use or suspected use of false documents.
- You do not have the proper documentation to support your entry to the U.S. in the category you are requesting.

If the inspector excludes you, you cannot be readmitted to the U.S. for five years, unless USCIS grants a special waiver. For this reason, it is extremely important to understand the terms of your requested status and to not make any misrepresentations. If you are found to be inadmissible, you may ask the CBP inspector to withdraw your application to enter the U.S. in order to prevent having the five-year deportation order on your record. The CBP may allow this in some exceptional cases.

If, however, you were admitted until a specific date, you must not only get a new Form DS-2019, but also seek actual approval from USCIS (if you don't want to leave the U.S.) or the State Department (if you're willing to leave and either reenter or reapply through a U.S. consulate).

To apply within the U.S., you would use Form I-539 (the form used for changing status, which you may have used once already—it's on the USCIS website). You'll also need to enclose the appropriate fee, your new Form DS-2019, copies of your old DS-2019 and your I-94 (and those of your family members, if any), and a letter from your program sponsor stating how long the extension is needed for, and explaining in as much detail as possible why you are unable to complete your program within the expected amount of time. Mail your package to the USCIS address indicated at www. uscis.gov/i-539. It may take several months to get an answer from USCIS, so plan ahead so that your permitted stay doesn't expire while the application is pending.

To apply from outside the U.S., your procedure depends on whether not only your I-94, but also your J-1 visa has run out. If only the I-94 has run out, but your visa is still good, you can simply arrive at the airport or port of entry with your existing J-1 visa, your new DS-2019, your old DS-2019, and, to be safe, all the supporting materials you used to get your J-1 visa in the first place. You will be given a new I-94 showing your new departure date.

Schools' Responsibilities to Track International Scholars

Schools must report to USCIS concerning scholars on J visas. When a program issues you a Certificate of Eligibility, it must tell the U.S. consulate in your home country. When that consulate approves your J visa, it must notify USCIS. During your time in the U.S., the school must keep USCIS up to date on your status and whereabouts, through the SEVIS database.

Schools must update SEVIS on your:

- name, date, and place of birth and country of citizenship
- current address
- visa classification, date of visa issuance, or classification granted
- academic or program status (full-time or part-time)
- certification for work authorization, and
- date that program was terminated, and the reason, if known.

On top of maintaining this database, the school must actually report news of changes in your status or activities to USCIS. Most importantly, the school has 21 days in which to advise USCIS that your address has changed—and you have only ten days after moving to tell your school.

If not only your I-94 but also your J-1 visa has run out, you'll need to reapply for everything through a U.S. consulate. In addition to your new DS-2019, you'll need to gather all the materials you used to apply for your original visa, as described in Section I, above.

Working While Your Extension Application Is Pending

If you file your application for extension of J-1 status before your authorized stay expires, you are automatically authorized to continue working for up to 240 days while waiting for a decision. If, however, your authorized stay expires after you have filed for an extension but before you receive an approval, and more than 240 days go by without getting a decision on your extension application, you must stop working.

M. Transfer to a New Sponsor

The Responsible Officers (ROs) of J-1 visa programs can allow you to transfer across programs in the same J-1 category, without you having to leave the United States. The RO of the program to which you're transferring must verify your visa status and eligibility, and then will issue a new Form DS-2019 reflecting the transfer. The RO of the program you're transferring out of releases you by completing and signing block

8 of the new Form DS-2019. You should start the process of transferring by talking with your current RO. Transfers are not permitted in all categories, and a transfer does not buy you any extra time in J-1 status.

N. Change of Category

You can request a change of J-1 category without leaving the U.S. if the change is clearly consistent with and closely related to your original exchange objective (such as research scholar to student), and the change is necessary due to unusual or exceptional circumstances. First, ask the Responsible Officer (RO) of your program. If the RO agrees, he or she will submit a written request with supporting justification for the change to the State Department on your behalf. You'll have to pay a nonrefundable change fee of $367 to the State Department.

If the State Department grants the request for a change of category, the RO will give you a new Form DS-2019 reflecting the change. If the request is denied, you'll need to return home within 30 days, unless you still have time left on your program.

O. Reinstatement

You might need to request reinstatement to valid program status if your participation in the exchange program has somehow been interrupted or has ended, or if you have remained in the U.S. beyond the program end date indicated on your DS-2019. If you fall out of J-1 status, your Responsible Officer (RO) might be able to reinstate you without State Department approval or might have to apply to the State Department to get you reinstated. There are situations in which reinstatement is impossible.

Your RO can easily remedy technical or minor infractions of the regulations. He or she will correct your records, and it will be as if the violation never happened. Examples of a technical or minor infraction would be:

- Failure to extend the Form DS-2019 in a timely manner due to inadvertence or neglect on your part or on the part of the RO.
- Your failure to complete a program transfer before the end date on the current Form DS-2019 due to administrative delay or oversight, inadvertence, or neglect on your part or on the part of the RO.
- Failure to receive the RO's prior approval and/or an amended Form DS-2019 before accepting an

Waivers of Two-Year Home Residency Requirements

You may be participating in the type of exchange visitor program that makes it mandatory for you to spend two years residing in your home country after completing your program before you are eligible to apply for a green card or other U.S. visa. This two-year period need not necessarily be an unbroken stretch of time. An aggregation of two years in your home country can also suffice.

If you wish to escape this obligation and apply for a green card immediately, you will first have to apply for a waiver of the home residency requirement. You cannot get around the requirement by spending two years in a third country or by switching to a different visa status within the United States.

To apply for a waiver, you'll have to show that you deserve it under one of the following five grounds:

- **No objection from your home government.** Unless you are a foreign medical graduate, the easiest way to obtain a waiver is by having your home government consent to it through a "no objection letter." In this letter, your government would assert that it doesn't mind your staying in the U.S. to apply for a green card—despite the fact that it may have helped finance your exchange program participation. Contact your home country's embassy in Washington, DC, to request such a letter. Be warned, however, that a no-objection letter may not be enough to secure you a waiver of the two-year home residence requirement. This is particularly true if you accepted scholarship funding to come to the U.S. in J-1 status.

Waivers of Two-Year Home Residency Requirements (continued)

- **Request by an interested U.S government agency.** If you're working on a project of interest to an agency of the U.S. government, and that agency decides that your continued stay is vital to one of its programs, it may support your request for a waiver. Foreign medical graduates most often qualify for an interested government agency waiver, through the Veterans Administration, the Appalachian Regional Commission, the Delta Regional Authority, or the Department of Health and Human Services.

- **Fear of persecution in your home country.** If you can show that you would be persecuted upon return to your home country based on your race, religion, or political opinion, you can apply for a waiver. Note that, unlike applicants for asylum, you cannot qualify if you fear persecution based only on your nationality or membership in a particular social group. Also, the standard is higher than in ordinary asylum cases, in which applicants need only prove a "reasonable fear" of persecution; you, by contrast, must show that you "would be" persecuted upon return.

- **Exceptional hardship to your U.S. citizen or permanent resident spouse or child.** If your spouse or any of your children are U.S. citizens or permanent residents, and you can show that your departure from the U.S. would cause them exceptional hardship, you may be granted a waiver. However, USCIS will demand a greater showing of hardship than the "mere" emotional pain of separation or economic or language difficulties. The classic exceptional hardship case is one in which your family member has a medical problem that would be worsened by your departure or by traveling with you to your home country; or where the family member would be persecuted if he or she departed with you.

- **Request by a state department of health.** If you're a foreign medical graduate with an offer of full-time employment at a health care facility in an area that's been designated as having a shortage of doctors, and you agree to begin working there in H-1B status within 90 days of receiving the waiver and to continue working there full-time for at least three years, you may be granted a waiver.

As you might guess, the waiver application process is complex and often depends on persuading reluctant government officials that you fit into a category whose boundaries are not clearly defined. We do not cover the waiver application process in this book, but strongly advise you to get help from an experienced immigration lawyer.

honorarium or other type of payment for engaging in a normally approvable and appropriate activity.

A substantive violation or infraction of the regulations requires the RO to apply for your reinstatement. Examples of a substantive violation would be failure to maintain valid program status for more than 120 days after the end date on the current Form DS-2019, or when a J-1 student fails to maintain a full course of study without prior consultation with the RO and the student's academic adviser. If the State Department approves the application for reinstatement, it will issue a new DS-2019.

The State Department won't even consider reinstatement if any of the following things have happened:

- You purposely failed to obtain or maintain the required health insurance at all times while in the U.S.
- You worked illegally in the U.S.
- You were suspended or terminated from your most recent exchange visitor program.
- You failed to maintain valid program status for more than 270 calendar days.
- You didn't pay the SEVIS fee.

Also, if you get the State Department's favorable recommendation when seeking a waiver of the two-year home residency requirement, the State Department will not then reinstate you to J-1 status.

P. Working as an Exchange Visitor

Special rules apply for you to be able to work while you're in the United States with a J-1 visa.

1. When You Can Work Without Special Permission

Exchange visitors are permitted to work in the U.S. if the job is part of the particular exchange program in which they are participating. Many J-1 programs, such as those for college and university professors or graduate medical students, are specifically created to engage the exchange visitor in employment. Others, like those for graduate students, often involve part-time employment in the form of teaching or research assistantships. The job may be located on or off the school premises. As long as the employment is part of the program, no special work permission is required.

2. When You Need Special Permission to Work

Working outside the bounds of your program often requires special permission, as described in the following subsections.

a. Practical Training

If your J-1 visa was issued for a study program, you may accept work that is not specifically part of the program but is related to the subject matter of your studies. This can include work that begins after your program is completed (but no more than 30 days after) with an 18-month aggregate limit. Such employment is called practical training. You must have written permission from the Responsible Officer of your exchange visitor program to accept a practical training position. USCIS plays no role in granting permission for practical training.

b. Economic Necessity

Remember that in order to get a J-1 visa, you must show that you have sufficient financial resources to support yourself while participating in an exchange visitor program. As we discussed earlier, such resources may be in the form of scholarships or salary earned for work that is part of or related to the program. However, if unforeseen financial problems arise after you arrive in the U.S., you may get work permission for employment that is unrelated to your exchange visitor program if the employment will not adversely affect your ability to be a full-time participant in the program. There is no special application, but you must have written approval from the Responsible Officer of your exchange visitor program.

3. Employment for Accompanying Relatives

Your accompanying spouse or minor children may apply to USCIS for permission to work. However, they cannot get work permission if the money earned helps to support you, or is needed to support you. They are expected to use the money for such things as recreational and cultural activities and related travel.

If your accompanying spouse or children want to work, they must file separate applications for employment authorization on Form I-765. This can be done by completing the items on the checklist below and filing them with USCIS (the appropriate address is on the USCIS website at www. uscis.gov/i-765-addresses; the instructions to the form are at www.uscis.gov/i-765).

It is very important to keep the fee receipt USCIS will send so your family members can prove that the I-765 was filed (in case USCIS loses it).

USCIS is required to make a decision on employment authorization applications within 90 days (See Chapter 4 for what to do if you haven't received a decision by then.) If the decision is in your accompanying relative's favor, he or she will receive a work authorization card.

Once approved, the work permit will be valid for the duration of your (the J-1 principal's) authorized stay as indicated on your Form I-94 or a period of four years, whichever is shorter.

Family Member Work Permit Application Checklist

- ☐ Form I-765 (answer Question 16 "(c)(5)").
- ☐ Copies of I-94s.
- ☐ Two photos.
- ☐ Filing fee (currently $410).
- ☐ Written statement explaining why the employment is for purposes other than supporting the J-1 visa holder, plus any supporting evidence regarding what's said in the statement.
- ☐ A monthly budget, detailing your sources of income and your expenses.

Q. Annual Reports for Foreign Medical Graduates

All foreign medical graduates training in the U.S. on J-1 visas are required to file annual reports with the USCIS local office having jurisdiction over their places of training. The reports are filed on Form I-644, which is self-explanatory. A copy of this form can be obtained from your program sponsor. Failure to file this report each year will result in the cancellation of your visa.

R. Traveling Outside the U.S. While on an Exchange Program

As long as your J visa is valid and has not expired, you may travel outside the U.S. for up to five months and then return to resume your program. (Make sure, however, that you haven't done anything to make yourself inadmissible, as discussed in Chapter 3.) Your passport must be valid at the time you reenter, and people from certain countries must have passports that are valid for at least six months after the time of reentry.

As a general rule, once your visa expires, you'll need to get a new one to reenter the U.S. if you leave for any reason. That means reapplying at a U.S. consulate using the same procedures discussed earlier in this chapter. An expired visa might never be a problem for some exchange visitors, since J-1 visas are typically issued for the expected length of your program.

If your visa does expire before your program ends, you might not necessarily have to get a new one if you want to travel. You can take short trips to Canada, Mexico, or certain Caribbean islands and return to the U.S. even if your visa has expired, as long as you get permission from your RO, have a valid DS-2019 endorsed for travel by your RO, and have a valid, unexpired I-94 (which usually just means that you're still in status). It's best if you don't apply for a new visa on such a trip, because if you do, you can't take advantage of this so-called "automatic visa revalidation," and you might get stuck outside the U.S. for longer than you want to be.

Make sure you travel with your DS-2019 (recertified within the last year by your RO) and I-94 so you can show them when you return. The CBP officer will be checking the SEVIS database as well. If there's a problem with your J status records, the CBP officer will let you in, but will give you a Form I-515A and notify your program sponsor. The I-515A tells you how to correct the problem, and gives you 30 days to do so. If the Student and Exchange Visitor Program (SEVP) doesn't hear from you in 30 days, it will send you and your sponsor a Notice of Intent to Terminate. You'll have 14 days to comply. If you don't, SEVP will terminate your J status.

Getting a Visa as a Temporary Worker in a Selected Occupation (O, P, or R Visa)

A few types of short-term work visas are available to people doing specialized work. These include O and P visas for certain outstanding workers in the sciences, arts, education, business, entertainment, and athletics and R visas for religious workers.

(See I.N.A. § 101(a)(15)(O), 8 U.S.C. § 1101(a)(15)(O), 8 C.F.R. § 214.2(o); I.N.A. § 101(a)(15)(P), 8 U.S.C. § 1101(a)(15)(P), 8 C.F.R. § 214.2(p); and I.N.A. § 101(a)(15)(R), 8 U.S.C. § 1101(a)(15)(R); 22 C.F.R. § 41.58; 8 C.F.R. § 214.2(r).)

A job offer from a U.S. employer is a basic requirement for all these visas. There is no annual limit on the number of people who can receive O, P, or R visas.

SEE AN EXPERT

Do you need a lawyer? You can't apply for an O, P, or R visa without having an employer first—and it's in your employer's interest to hire a lawyer to help. A lawyer can help make sure that your application gets done right the first time.

A. Do You Qualify for an O, P, or R Visa?

Pay close attention to the eligibility criteria for these visas: The O, P, and R visa categories are quite narrow in scope.

1. O-1 Visas: Persons of Extraordinary Ability in the Arts, Athletics, Science, Business, and Education

O-1 visas are available to persons of proven extraordinary ability in the sciences, arts, education, business, or athletics. To be considered a person of extraordinary ability, you must have sustained national or international acclaim in your field, or, if you work in motion pictures or television productions, you must have a demonstrated record of extraordinary achievement. O-1 visas can be given only on the basis of individual qualifications. Membership in a group or team is not by itself enough to get you the visa. In addition, you must be coming to work or perform at an event or a series of events in the area of your extraordinary ability. The term "event" is interpreted liberally outside the fields of athletics and arts and can include, for example, an ongoing research project for a private company.

a. Extraordinary Ability in Science, Education, Business, or Athletics

To meet O-1 standards, you must be able to show that you have extraordinary ability and that you have received sustained national or international acclaim. This can be demonstrated if you have gotten a major internationally recognized award, such as

Key Features of the O, P, and R Visas

Here are some of the advantages and disadvantages of these specialized work visas:

- You can work legally in the U.S. for your O, P, or R sponsor. If, however, you want to change jobs, you must apply to change your status or get a new visa.
- O, P, and R visas can be issued quickly.
- O visas will be granted for the length of time necessary for a particular event, up to a maximum of three years, with unlimited extensions in one-year increments.
- P visas will be granted for the length of time needed to complete a particular event, tour, or season, up to a maximum

of one year. However, P-1 athletes may be admitted for a period of up to five years with one extension of up to five years.

- R visas will be granted initially for up to three years, with extensions up to a maximum total of five years.
- You may travel in and out of the U.S. or stay continuously for as long as your visa stamp and status are valid.
- Your spouse and unmarried children under age 21 may accompany you, but they may not accept employment in the United States.

---

a Nobel Prize, or if you have accomplished at least three of the following:

- received a *nationally* or *internationally* recognized prize or award for excellence
- attained membership in associations that require outstanding achievements of their members in your field of expertise, as judged by recognized national or international experts
- been the subject of published material in professional or major trade publications or major media discussing you and your work
- participated, on a panel or individually, as a judge of the work of others in your field

- made an original scientific, scholarly, or business-related contribution that is of major significance in the field
- authored scholarly articles in professional journals or major media
- been previously employed in a critical or essential capacity for an organization with a distinguished reputation, or
- command or have commanded a high salary or other outstanding remuneration for your services.

If the above criteria do not readily apply to your occupation, the company petitioning for you may submit comparable evidence in order to show that you are "extraordinary." Be sure to explain why the above criteria do not apply.

TIP
Describe your field as narrowly as possible in order to demonstrate your national or international acclaim. If, for example, you are an environmental engineer whose specialty is hydrology, and many of your scholarly papers are in the area of predicting soil erosion from water runoff, then define the field as "soil erosion engineering" rather than "environment engineering." The reason for this is that O-1 visas are given to the big fish of the fields. If your field is as big as the Pacific Ocean then no fish will look particularly big. If your field is a fish tank, then you give yourself a good shot at looking like a major player.

b. Extraordinary Ability in the Arts

If you are applying as an O-1 alien of extraordinary ability in the arts, you should first make sure your work fits the definition of art. The category of arts is defined broadly in the USCIS regulations, to include:

… any field of creative activity or endeavor such as, but not limited to, fine arts, visual arts, culinary arts, and performing arts. Aliens engaged in the field of arts include not only the principal creators and performers but other essential persons such as, but not limited to, directors, set designers, lighting designers, sound designers, choreographers, choreologists, conductors, orchestrators, coaches, arrangers, musical supervisors, costume designers, makeup artists, flight masters, stage technicians, and animal trainers.

(See 8 C.F.R. § 214.2(o)(3)(ii).)

You must also be coming to the U.S. to perform in the area of extraordinary ability and must be recognized as prominent in your field of endeavor. You can demonstrate your recognition with documents showing that you have been nominated for or have received significant national or international awards or prizes in your particular field, such as an Oscar, an Emmy, a Grammy, or a Director's Guild Award. Alternately, you can supply (to your employer, for submission on your behalf) at least three of the following forms of documentation:

- evidence that you have performed, and will perform, services as a lead or starring participant in productions or events that have a distinguished reputation as evidenced by critical reviews, advertisements, publicity releases, publication contracts, or endorsements
- evidence that you have achieved national or international recognition for achievements evidenced by critical reviews or other published materials by or about you in major newspapers, trade journals, magazines, or other publications

- evidence that you have performed, and will perform, in a lead, starring, or critical role for organizations and establishments that have a distinguished reputation, as evidenced by articles in newspapers, trade journals, publications, or testimonials
- evidence that you have a record of major commercial or critically acclaimed successes (as evidenced by title, rating, standing in the field, box office receipts, motion pictures, or television ratings) and other occupational achievements reported in trade journals, major newspapers, or other publications
- evidence that you have received significant recognition for achievements from organizations, critics, government agencies or other recognized experts in the field. Such testimonials must be in a form that clearly indicates the author's authority, expertise, and knowledge of your achievements or,
- evidence that you have either commanded a high salary or will command a high salary or other substantial remuneration for services in relation to others in the field, as evidenced by contracts or other reliable evidence.

If the above criteria do not lend themselves to your situation, your petitioning employer may submit alternative but comparable evidence in order to establish your eligibility.

2. O-2 Visas: Support Staff for People With O-1 Visas

O-2 visas are available to people who work as essential support personnel of O-1 athletes and entertainers. O-2 visas are not available in the fields of science, business, or education. O-2 workers must be accompanying O-1 artists or athletes and be an integral part of the actual performance. The O-2 worker must also have critical skills, as well as experience with the particular O-1 worker, that are not general in nature and cannot be performed by a U.S. worker.

Special Rules for Workers on Television and Movie Productions

If you're an artist, an entertainer, a director, or technical or creative staffperson seeking a visa to work on a television or motion picture production, certain special rules apply to you. First, you must prove not merely a "high level of achievement," but a "very high level of accomplishment" in the motion picture and television industry. You'll need to show evidence that your skill and recognition is significantly higher than that ordinarily encountered. You'll need to show the same sorts of evidence as other artists, but you won't have the option of showing comparable evidence if you can't come up with anything on the USCIS's list.

In the case of motion picture or television productions, there must be a preexisting, long-standing working relationship between the O-2 applicant and the O-1 worker. If significant portions of the production will take place both in and out of the U.S., O-2 support personnel must be deemed necessary for the achievement of continuity and a smooth, successful production.

3. O-3 Visas: Accompanying Relatives of Those With O-1 and O-2 Visas

O-3 visas are available to accompanying spouses and unmarried children under age 21 of O-1 or O-2 visa holders. O-3 visas allow relatives to remain in the U.S., but they may not work.

4. P-1 Visas: Outstanding Athletes, Athletic Teams, and Entertainment Companies

P-1 visas are available to athletes or athletic teams that have been internationally recognized as outstanding for a long and continuous period of time. Entertainment companies that have been nationally recognized as outstanding for a long time also qualify. Unlike O visas, which always rest on the capabilities of individuals, P-1 visas can be issued based on the expertise of a group. However, don't be surprised to find a lot of overlap between uses and qualifications for O and P visas.

In the case of entertainment companies, each performer who wishes to qualify for a P-1 visa must have been an integral part of the group for at least one year, although up to 25% of them can be excused from the one-year requirement, if necessary. This requirement may also be waived in exceptional situations, where due to illness or other unanticipated circumstances, a critical performer is unable to travel. The one-year requirement is for performers only. It does not apply to support personnel. It also does not apply to anyone at all who works for a circus, including performers.

Like O-1 visas, P-1 visas are issued only for the time needed to complete a particular event, tour, or season. You may also be allowed some extra time for vacation, as well as promotional appearances and stopovers incidental and/or related to the event. Individual athletes, however, may remain in the U.S. for up to ten years.

a. Athletes

To qualify as a P-1 athlete, you or your team must have an internationally recognized reputation in the sport. Evidence of this must include a contract with a major U.S. sports league, team, or international sporting event, and at least two of the following:

- proof of your, or your team's, previous significant participation with a major U.S. sports league
- proof of your participation in an international competition with a national team
- proof of your previous significant participation with a U.S. college in intercollegiate competition
- written statement from an official of a major U.S. sports league or the governing body of the sport, detailing how you or your team is internationally recognized
- written statement from the sports media or a recognized expert regarding your international recognition
- evidence that you or your team is internationally ranked, or
- proof that you or your team has received a significant honor or award in the sport.

b. Entertainers

P-1 visas are not available to individual entertainers, but only to members of groups with international reputations. Your group must have been performing regularly for at least one year, and 75% of the members of your group must have been performing with that group for at least a year. When your employer files a petition on your behalf, the employer will have to supply proof of your group's sustained international recognition, as shown by either its nomination for, or receipt of, significant international awards or prizes, or at least three of the following:

- proof that your group has starred or will star or take a leading role in productions or events with distinguished reputations
- reviews or other published material showing that your group has achieved international recognition and acclaim for outstanding achievement in the field
- proof that your group has starred and will star or take a leading role in productions or events for organizations with distinguished reputations
- proof of large box office receipts or ratings showing your group has a record of major commercial or critically acclaimed successes
- proof that your group has received significant recognition for achievements from organizations, critics, government agencies, or other recognized experts, or
- proof that your group commands a high salary or other substantial remuneration.

c. Circuses

Circus performers and essential personnel do not need to have been part of the organization for one year to get a P-1 visa, provided the particular circus itself has a nationally recognized reputation as outstanding.

d. Waiver for Nationally Known Entertainment Groups

USCIS may waive the international recognition requirement for groups that have only outstanding national reputations, if special circumstances would make it difficult for your group to prove its international reputation. Such circumstances could include your group's having only limited access to news media or problems based on your group's geographical location.

e. Waiver of One-Year Group Membership

USCIS may waive the one-year group membership requirement for you if you are replacing an ill or otherwise unexpectedly absent but essential member of a P-1 entertainment group. This requirement may also be waived if you will be performing in any critical role of the group's operation.

5. P-2 Visas: Participants in Reciprocal Exchange Programs

P-2 visas are available to artists or entertainers, either individually or as part of a group, who come to the U.S. to perform under a reciprocal exchange program between the U.S. and one or more other countries. All essential support personnel are included. The legitimacy of the program must be evidenced by a formal, written exchange agreement. In addition, a labor union in the U.S. must have either been involved in the negotiation of the exchange or have agreed to it. The U.S. individual or group being exchanged must have skills and terms of employment comparable to the person or group coming to the U.S.

6. P-3 Visas: Culturally Unique Groups

P-3 visas are available to artists or entertainers who come to the U.S., either individually or as part of a group, to develop, interpret, represent, teach, or coach in a program that is considered culturally unique. The program may be of either a commercial or noncommercial nature.

You must be coming to the U.S. to participate in a cultural event or events that will further the understanding or development of your art form. In addition, your employer will have to submit on your behalf:

- statements from recognized experts showing the authenticity of your or your group's skills in performing, presenting, coaching, or teaching the unique or traditional art form and showing the basis of your knowledge of your or your group's skill, or
- evidence that your or your group's art form is culturally unique, as shown

by reviews in newspapers, journals, or other published materials, and that the performance will be culturally unique.

7. Support Personnel for P-1, P-2, and P-3 Visa Holders

Highly skilled, essential persons who are an integral part of the performance of a P-1, P-2, or P-3 visa holder may also be granted P visas (with the same visa designation as the primary visa holder). These persons must perform support services that cannot be readily performed by a U.S. worker and that are essential to the successful performance of services by the P-1, P-2, or P-3 visa holder. The support person must have appropriate qualifications to perform the services, critical knowledge of the specific services to be performed, and experience in providing such support to the P-1, P-2, or P-3 visa holder. (See 8 C.F.R. § 214.2(p)(3).)

8. P-4 Visas: Accompanying Relatives of People With P-1, P-2, and P-3 Visas

P-4 visas are issued to the spouses and unmarried children under age 21 of any P visa workers. The accompanying relatives are permitted to remain in the U.S., but they cannot work.

9. R-1 Visas: Religious Workers

An R-1 visa is available to a person who has been a member of a legitimate religious denomination for at least two years and has a job offer in the U.S. to work for an affiliate of that same religious organization. R-1 visas may be issued both to members of the clergy and to lay religious workers. The initial stay can be up to three years, and the maximum stay is five years.

The criteria for qualifying are the same as those for religious workers applying for special immigrant green cards discussed in Chapter 12 (see that chapter for the details), with one big difference. Unlike the green card category, it is not necessary that R-1 visa workers were employed by the religious organization before getting the visa. They need only have been members for two years.

Usually, people qualifying for R-1 visas also qualify for green cards as special immigrants and may prefer to apply directly for a green card.

10. R-2 Visas: Accompanying Relatives of Those With R-1 Visas

Spouses and unmarried children under age 21 of R-1 visa holders can get R-2 visas. This allows them to stay in the U.S., but not to accept employment.

B. Quick View of the O, P, and R Visa Application Process

Once you have been offered a job, getting the O, P, or R visa is a two- or three-step process:

- Your U.S. employer or agent files what's called a "visa petition" on USCIS Form I-129. If you're already in the U.S. in lawful status, this petition can simultaneously ask that your status be changed to O, P, or R, in which case, the process will successfully end here.
- If you're outside the U.S., then a visa petition must still be filed, but after approval, you take that approved visa petition to the U.S. consulate in your home country in order to obtain an O, a P, or an R visa.
- Finally, you use your visa (or if you are from Canada, a visa-exempt country, the notice of your approved visa petition) to enter the U.S. and claim your O, P, or R status.

> **TIP**
>
> **Nothing stops you from helping with the employer's or agent's tasks during this application process.** For example, you can fill out forms intended to be completed by your employer and simply ask the employer to check them over and sign them. The less your U.S. employer is inconvenienced, the more it may be willing to act as sponsor for your visa.

Possibilities for a Green Card From O, P, or R Status

Having an O, a P, or an R visa gives you no legal advantage in applying for a green card. Realistically, it is probably easier to get an employer to sponsor you for an O, a P, or an R visa than for a green card. Also, coming to the U.S. first with a temporary work visa gives you the opportunity to decide whether you really want to live in the U.S. permanently. Once you are in the U.S. with a work permit, it is also usually easier to find an employer willing to sponsor you for a green card.

O and P visa holders are not required to maintain a residence abroad. Though one is expected to work only temporarily in O or P visa status, there is no penalty for attempting to immigrate while working on these temporary visas.

By contrast, R visa holders must intend to return home once the visa or status expires and must demonstrate that they still maintain a residence in their home country to which they can return. Therefore, if you apply for a green card, it may be difficult to obtain or renew an R visa. Many religious workers qualify for green cards as special immigrants. If you are a religious worker and want to remain in the U.S. permanently, you should read Chapter 12 before applying for an R visa.

C. Step One: Your Employer or Agent Submits a Visa Petition

Your employer or agent begins the process by filing a visa petition with USCIS, on Form I-129. Employers or agents must be based in the United States. Agents typically file for artists and entertainers who are self-employed or who use agents to arrange short-term employment with multiple employers.

For O and P visas, that petition can be filed up to one year before a scheduled event, competition, or performance. The object of the petition is to prove four things:

- that you qualify for O, P, or R status
- that your future job is of a high enough level or appropriate nature to warrant someone with your advanced or specialized skills
- that you have the correct background and skills to match the job requirements, and
- in the case of O and P visas, that appropriate labor unions or similar organizations have been consulted concerning your eligibility.

1. Simultaneous Change of Status If You're Already in the U.S.

If you're already in the U.S. in lawful status, such as on a student or another temporary visa, the petition can be used to ask that your status be immediately changed to O, P, or R worker. (Part 2, Question 4, of Form I-129 offers choices addressing this issue.) You can't, however, take advantage of this option if you entered the U.S. on the Visa Waiver Program or if you entered using a C (alien in transit), TWOV (alien in transit without a visa), D (crewman), or any K (fiancé) visa. Certain J-1 (exchange visitor) visa holders are prohibited from changing status as well. Assuming none of these bars apply, you can change status to O, P, or R if you:

- entered the U.S. legally
- have never worked in the U.S. illegally, and
- have not remained in the U.S. beyond the expiration date on your I-94.

There is another problem that comes up only in U.S. filings. It is the issue of what is called preconceived intent. To approve a change of status, USCIS must believe that at the time you originally entered the U.S. as a visitor or with some other nonimmigrant visa, you did not intend to apply for a different status. If USCIS thinks you had a preconceived plan to use one visa to enter the U.S. with an eye toward applying for a different status after getting there, it may deny your application. (You can always avoid the preconceived intent issue by leaving the U.S. and applying for your O, P, or R visa at a U.S. consulate in another country.) Therefore, it is unwise to file a change of status application any sooner than 60 days from the date you entered the U.S. in some other visa category.

Your spouse and children, if they are also in the U.S. with you, can't change their status by being mentioned on your Form I-129. They must submit a separate Form I-539. They can submit this either at the same time as your employer submits Form I-129, or afterward. (If they submit it afterward, however, they will need to include either a copy of the USCIS receipt notice indicating that your petition is pending or a copy of the petition approval notice.)

> **TIP**
>
> **Your eligibility to apply in the U.S. has nothing to do with your overall eligibility for an O, a P, or an R visa.** Many applicants who are barred from filing in the U.S. but otherwise qualify for O, P, or R status may still apply successfully for an O, a P, or an R visa at a U.S. consulate in another country.

If you decide to apply for a change of status within the U.S., you will receive only O, P, or R status, not the O, P, or R visa itself. This is an important distinction. A visa is a physical stamp in your passport that you will need if you ever want to reenter the United States. (Note, however, that Canadian citizens are exempt from the need for a visa for most categories, including the O, P, or R categories.) Visas are never given inside the United States. They are issued exclusively by U.S. consulates in other countries. If you file in

the U.S. and you are successful, you will get to remain in the U.S. with O, P, or R privileges until the status expires. But should you leave the country for any reason before that time, you will have to apply for the visa itself at a U.S. consulate before returning to the United States. Therefore, whether you want to change your non-immigrant status to O, P, or R while in the U.S., or leave the U.S. to obtain the visa from a U.S. consulate abroad, is a decision you will want to seriously consider before making the application.

2. Assembling the Petition

The checklist below will help you and your employer assemble the necessary items for the visa petition.

A few items on this checklist require some extra explanation, provided in the subsections below.

a. Form I-129 and O, P, or R Supplement

The basic form for the visa petition is USCIS Form I-129 and its appropriate supplement form. The Form I-129 is used for many different nonimmigrant visas. In addition to the basic part of the form that applies to all types of visas, it comes with several supplements for each specific nonimmigrant category. Simply use the supplement that applies to you. Don't worry; the supplement form will clearly indicate on its face what visa it is to be used for.

Checklist for O, P, or R Petitions

☐ Form I-129, with O, P, or R Supplement.

☐ Filing fee (currently $460).

☐ If you will be applying in the United States and your family members are with you and need a change of status, Form I-539 with accompanying fee (currently $370) and copies of your family members' I-94s or other proof of lawful immigration status and of their relationship to you (such as marriage and birth certificates). One Form I-539 and fee will cover your spouse and all your children. This form is meant to be filled out and signed by your family members, not by your employer or agent.

☐ If you're in the U.S., a copy of your I-94 or other proof of your current lawful, unexpired immigration status (Canadians who are just visiting are not expected to have I-94s).

☐ If you're outside the U.S., a copy of your passport.

Additional documents for principal applicants (not support personnel):

☐ College and university diplomas, if needed to prove your qualifications.

Additional documents for O-1 visas:

☐ Consultation letter from a peer group or labor management organization with expertise in your field, stating that the group has no objection to the approval of your visa.

☐ Employer's written statement (or other evidence, e.g., employment contract) explaining the nature of the employment, the specific events or activities you will be participating in, the beginning and end dates of your participation, and why

your participation is needed. You may also want to supply a copy of your written employment contract, if you are not going to engage in regular full-time employment with a U.S. employer (if, for example, you are a musician or performer). USCIS needs to have some evidence that you actually have someone waiting to hire you!

☐ Either:

☐ Proof of your extraordinary ability in science, education, business, or athletics, as described in Section A1a, above, or

☐ Proof of your extraordinary ability in the arts, as described in Section A1b.

Additional documents for O-2 visas:

☐ Employer's written statement (or other evidence, e.g. employment contract) explaining the nature of the employment, the specific events or activities you will be participating in, the beginning and end dates of your participation, and why your participation is essential to the successful performance of an O-1 visa holder.

☐ Consultation letter from a labor and management organization with expertise in your field.

Additional documents for P-1 visas:

☐ Consultation report from a peer group or labor management organization with expertise in your field.

☐ For athletes, your employment contract with a U.S. league or team, or an individual contract.

☐ Proof of your or your group's international reputation, as described in Section A4, above.

Checklist for O, P, or R Visa Petitions (continued)

Additional documents for P-2 visas:

☐ Consultation letter from a peer group or labor management organization with expertise in your field.

☐ A copy of the formal reciprocal exchange agreement.

☐ A statement from the sponsoring organization explaining how the particular exchange relates to the underlying agreement.

☐ Evidence that your skills are comparable to those of the U.S. artist on the other side of the exchange.

☐ Evidence that an appropriate labor organization in the U.S. was involved in negotiating or approves of the exchange.

Additional documents for P-3 visas:

☐ An explanation of the event and itinerary.

☐ Documentation that all the performances or presentations will be culturally unique.

☐ Statements from recognized experts showing the authenticity of your or your group's skills in performing, presenting, coaching, or teaching the unique or traditional art form and showing the basis of the expert's knowledge of your or your group's skill, or

☐ Reviews in newspapers, journals, or other published materials, showing that your or your group's performance is culturally unique.

Additional documents for support personnel of P-1, P-2, and P-3 visas:

☐ A consultation from a labor organization with expertise in the area of your skill.

☐ A statement describing why the support person has been essential in the past, and his or her critical skills and experience with the principal P visa holder.

☐ Statements or affidavits from people with firsthand knowledge of your experience in performing the critical skills and essential support services needed by the principal P-1, P-2, or P-3 visa holder.

☐ A copy of the written contract or a summary of the terms of the oral agreement between you and your employer.

Additional documents for R visas:

☐ Diplomas and certificates showing your academic and professional qualifications.

☐ Detailed letter from the U.S. religious organization, fully describing the operation of the organization both in and out of the U.S., and explaining that the foreign organization belongs to the same denomination as the U.S. organization.

☐ Letter from the U.S. organization giving details of your U.S. job offer, including how you will be paid and the name and location of where you'll be providing services.

☐ Written verification that you have been a member of that same organization outside the U.S. for at least two years.

☐ Evidence that the religious organization in the U.S. qualifies as a tax-exempt organization under § 501(c) of the Internal Revenue Code or is affiliated with an organization that qualifies.

If requesting quick (premium) processing:

☐ Form I-907, with $1,225 filing fee.

The employer can choose to list more than one foreign employee on a single Form I-129 petition. This is done if the employer has more than one opening to be filled for the same type of job or if it is a group petition. Supplement 1, which is also part of Form I-129, should be completed for each additional employee.

b. Job Verification

Your employer must show that the job you have been offered really exists. To do this, the employer must describe the terms of your employment, including job duties, hours, salary, and other benefits, in a letter accompanying the Form I-129. If you will be going on tour, a tour schedule should be included.

For O and P visas, the employer should also submit a detailed written statement explaining the nature of your employment, the specific events or activities in which you will be participating, and why your participation is needed. P-2 petitions must also include a copy of the formal reciprocal exchange agreement, as well as a statement from the sponsoring organization that explains how the particular exchange relates to the underlying agreement.

The petitioning organization should provide as much material about itself as possible to demonstrate that it can credibly pay (or secure payment to) the O, P, or R workers being sponsored. Copies of financial records, such as an annual report for publicly traded companies, or a corporate tax return for privately held companies, will go a long way toward establishing that the petitioner is financially capable. A copy of the petitioner's payroll records may also be helpful.

c. Consultation Letter for O and P Visas

All O and P visa petitions must be accompanied by a consultation letter or written advisory opinion from an appropriate peer group, labor union, and/or management organization, concerning the nature of the work to be done and your qualifications. Alternatively, you may request that USCIS obtain an advisory opinion for you, but this will significantly delay your case.

For O-1 petitions, the opinion can simply be a letter stating that the organization has no objection to your getting an O-1 visa. In P-1 petitions, the opinion must explain the reputation of either you or your team and the nature of the event in the United States. The opinion in all O-2 cases and for P-1 visa support personnel must contain an explanation of why you are essential to the performance and the nature of your working relationship with the principal performer. It must also state whether or not U.S. workers are available or assert that significant production activities will take place both in and out of the U.S. and, therefore, that your presence is required for continuity.

P-2 advisory opinions must verify the existence of a viable exchange program. P-3 opinions must evaluate the cultural uniqueness of the performances, state that the events are mostly cultural in nature, and give the reason why the event or activity is appropriate for P-3 classification.

3. Mailing the Petition

After assembling a Form I-129 petition for O or P visa status, your U.S. employer or agent must mail it to the Vermont Service Center. If you're seeking R visa status, your Form I-129 petition must be filed at the California Service Center, regardless of the location of your work. If you'll be working in various locations across the U.S., your employer or agent must choose the Service Center with jurisdiction over the employer's or agent's place of business. If you'll be coming from outside the U.S., your employer must send duplicate versions of the form (two signed originals; copies are not acceptable).

The filing addresses can be found at www.uscis.gov/i-129-addresses.

4. Awaiting a Decision on the Petition

Within a few weeks after mailing in the petition, your employer should get back a written confirmation that the papers are being processed, together with a receipt notice (Form I-797) documenting payment of the filing fee. This receipt notice will also contain your petition receipt number (which will look something like this: "WAC-14-123-45678" or "EAC-14-123-45678"). Take note of this receipt number, as you will want to refer to it for any future correspondence with USCIS relating to the petition. To check the status of your pending petition, go to www.uscis. gov and click the link to "Check Your Case Status." If USCIS wants further information before acting on your case, it will send your employer or agent a form known as a Request for Evidence (RFE). Your employer or agent must supply the extra data requested and mail it back to the Service Center before the posted deadline. (Employers and agents are usually given 87 days to respond to a Request for Evidence.)

O, P, and R petitions are normally approved within two to four months. (Check current processing times online at www.uscis.gov; follow the links to "Check Your Case Status" and "USCIS Processing Times.") When the petition has been approved, USCIS will send your employer or agent a Form I-797 Notice of Action. If you plan to submit your visa application at a U.S. consulate abroad, USCIS will notify the Kentucky Consular Center, which will electronically send your file there. Only the employer or agent receives communications from USCIS about the petition, because technically it is the employer or agent who is seeking the visa on your behalf.

TIP

Faster processing—at a price. For $1,225 over and above the regular filing fees, USCIS promises premium processing of the visa petition, including a decision on the case within 15 days. To use this service, the employer must fill out an additional application (Form I-907) and submit the application to a special USCIS service center address. For complete instructions, see the USCIS website at www.uscis.gov/i-907. Premium processing for R-1 petitions is available only if the church has previously completed a successful on-site inspection at the location where you will be employed.

Unless you're changing status within the U.S., an approved petition does not by itself give you any immigration privileges. It is only a prerequisite to the next step, submitting your visa application.

D. Step Two: Applicants Outside the U.S. Apply to a U.S. Consulate

After the petition filed by your employer has been approved, USCIS will send a Form I-797B Notice of Action, with which you can apply for a visa at a U.S. consulate—normally in your home country. Check with your local U.S. consulate regarding its application procedures. All consulates insist on advance appointments. Just getting an appointment can take several days, or during certain times of year, weeks, so plan ahead.

TIP

If you're visa exempt, you can skip this step. Citizens of Canada and certain others need not apply to a U.S. consulate for O, P, or R visas, because they are exempt from the visa requirement for most visa categories. Instead, they can proceed directly to the U.S. with their Form I-797B petition approval notice, along with a copy of the Form I-129 petition, in order to request admission in O, P, or R status. (See 8 C.F.R. § 212.1.)

CAUTION

Have you been, or are you now, working or living illegally in the United States? If so, see Chapter 3 regarding whether you can still get an O, a P, or an R visa from a U.S. consulate. You may have become inadmissible or subject to a three-year or ten-year bar on reentry.

The checklist below will help you prepare your consular application.

As part of your application, the consulate will require you and your family members to pay an application fee and attend an interview. During the interview, a consular officer will examine the data in your application for accuracy. Evidence of ties to your home country will also be checked. During the interview, you will surely be asked how long you intend to remain in the United States. Any answer indicating uncertainty

O, P, and R Visa Application Checklist

☐ Form DS-160, Nonimmigrant Visa Application. This form must be prepared and submitted online at https://ceac.state.gov/genniv.

☐ Notice showing approval of the visa petition submitted by your employer or agent (Form I-797).

☐ Valid passport for you and each accompanying relative.

☐ If requested by the consulate or if you were unable to upload one with your DS-160 application, one U.S. passport-type photo of you and one of each accompanying relative. (This is best done by a professional photographer; the consulate can give you a list.)

☐ If your spouse and children will be accompanying you, original documents verifying their family relationship to you, such as marriage and birth certificates.

☐ If applying for an R visa, documents establishing your intent to leave the U.S. when your status expires, such as deeds

verifying ownership of a house or other real property, written statements from you explaining that close relatives are staying behind, or letters from a company showing that you have a job waiting when you return from the United States.

☐ Fee receipt showing that you have paid the relevant machine-readable visa (MRV) application fee (currently $190) according to the consulate's instructions. The financial institution at which you must pay depends on the country. Check the website of the U.S. consulate where you plan to apply for your visa to learn how to pay the fee. Most consulates will not allow you to pay the visa fee at the time of interview.

☐ Visa reciprocity fee. Before getting your visa, you may have to pay a visa issuance fee known as a "reciprocity fee" if you're from a country that charges similar fees for visas to U.S. citizens.

---

about plans to return or an interest in applying for a green card may result in a denial of your R-1 visa. Note that the rules for O and P visas are not so strict on this issue, but nevertheless you should consider the O and P visas to be temporary visas for temporary work assignments, and behave accordingly when applying for the visa.

RELATED TOPIC

See Chapter 4 for what else to expect during consular interviews, and what to do if your application is denied.

E. Step Three: Visa Holders Enter the U.S.

You have until the expiration date on your visa to enter the United States. The border officer will examine your paperwork, ask you some questions, and if all is in order, approve you for entry. He or she will stamp your passport and create an I-94 Arrival/Departure record for you (if you enter by air or sea). If you enter at a land border, the officer will give you a small white I-94 card. Your I-94 shows how long you can stay. Normally, you are permitted to remain up to the expiration date on your visa petition. Each time you exit and reenter the U.S., you will get a new I-94 authorizing your stay up to the final date indicated on the petition.

F. Extending Your U.S. Stay

Although an extension is usually easier to get than the O, P, or R visa itself, it is not automatic. USCIS has the right to reconsider your qualifications based on any changes in the facts or law. As always, however, good cases that are well prepared will be successful. In particular, explain why your period of stay will be temporary, even though you are asking to make it longer. USCIS is reluctant to grant extensions of O, P, and R status where indications are that the worker intends to work in the U.S. indefinitely. Therefore, present an itinerary explaining how a new project or performance has been scheduled. Do not simply assume an extension will be granted because the prior visa petition was approved.

To start the extension process, your employer will have to file a new visa petition on Form I-129. If you don't wish to leave the U.S., extending your status by means of this petition will be sufficient. However, if you leave the U.S. before the end of your overall stay, you will also need to visit a U.S. consulate outside the U.S., in order to get an O, a P, or an R visa stamp in your passport (to allow your reentry).

> ### Working While Your Extension Petition Is Pending
>
> If you file your petition for an extension of O, P, or R status before your authorized stay expires, you are automatically permitted to continue working for up to 240 days while you are waiting for a decision. If, however, your authorized stay expires after you have filed for an extension, but before you receive an approval, and more than 240 days go by without getting a decision on your extension petition, continued employment is not authorized and you must stop working.

1. Extension Petition

Extension procedures are identical to the procedures followed in getting the initial visa, except that less documentation is generally required. However, the best practice is to fully document the extension request with all of the documents submitted with the initial petition, as USCIS will probably not have the file on site.

2. Visa Revalidation

If you leave the U.S. after your extension has been approved, but the underlying visa has expired, you must get a new visa stamp issued at a consulate. Read Section D, above. The procedures for consular extensions are identical.

Introduction to Other Forms of Long-Term Legal Status in the U.S.

In this part of the book, we cover some ways to maintain status in the U.S. that don't neatly fit into the category of either "temporary" or "permanent." They are, for the most part, remedies meant to either protect the immigrant or protect U.S. society. Some of them can last for many years, or even lead to a green card.

Temporary Protected Status (TPS) and Deferred Enforced Departure (DED) (Chapter 25) are meant to protect people in the U.S. who would face difficult situations if they returned to their home countries, such as civil war or a natural disaster. Such people might not qualify individually for asylum. Those whose countries are designated for one of these types of protection may receive a right to remain in the U.S. with a work permit, a status which may be extended if the source of the difficulty continues.

Also in Chapter 25 is a discussion of humanitarian parole, which can provide a means of U.S. entry for people who have a compelling need to come here in emergency circumstances, but who have no way to get in under any visa category or are for some reason inadmissible to the United States.

Deferred Action for Childhood Arrivals (or "DACA," covered in Chapter 26) is a program created by the Obama Administration as a stopgap measure while waiting for Congress to act on possible future legislation. The DACA program assists undocumented young people whose parents brought them to the U.S. before they turned 16. It is limited to those who have successfully pursued or are pursuing an education in the United States.

The U visa is also covered in this portion of the book (Chapter 27). This provides temporary U.S. status to victims of crimes (including domestic violence) whose ongoing presence in the U.S. may be important to the law enforcement efforts of U.S. police and other authorities. A U visa may, depending on the course of the enforcement matters, eventually lead to a U.S. green card.

Humanitarian Remedies Allowing Stays in the U.S.

Whether the issue is an entire country in turmoil or an individual facing a personal emergency, U.S. immigration law may offer temporary protection in the United States. This chapter will discuss Temporary Protected Status (TPS), Deferred Enforced Departure (DED), and Humanitarian Parole.

TPS and DED are similar remedies. Both allow people who are already in the U.S. but whose countries are currently undergoing civil strife or in the midst of some sort of disaster to remain here until conditions in the home country improve. Recipients of TPS and DED are eligible for a work permit during this time.

Humanitarian parole is a more limited remedy, simply allowing for U.S. entry and a limited stay. It does not come with any other immigration benefits, though it can facilitate someone's ability to apply for a green card in cases where the person is otherwise eligible for this status.

A. Do You Qualify for TPS?

You cannot make an independent claim that your country is unsafe to return to. The U.S. government must act first, by putting your country on the TPS list. Countries in the midst of civil war, for example, or that have recently experienced a huge environmental disaster such as an earthquake or volcanic eruption may be put on the TPS list. (For the law on TPS, see I.N.A. § 244, 8 U.S.C. § 1254.)

In creating this list, however, the U.S. government always puts an expiration date on each country's TPS designation—as well as on the date by which would-be recipients must apply.

TPS does not help people currently living in the affected countries. You must be in the U.S. when TPS is established for your country in order to qualify, and you must submit an application to USCIS.

TPS status does not lead to a green card. When your country's TPS designation runs out, so does your right to stay in the United States. (The U.S. government may, however, if the disaster continues, renew your country's TPS designation, in which case you'll probably need to reregister.)

TPS also does not help people who have either been convicted of a felony or two or more misdemeanors committed in the U.S.; been found inadmissible on nonwaivable criminal- and security-related grounds; or are subject to any of the mandatory bars to asylum (such as for having participated in the persecution of others or having engaged in or incited terrorist activity).

Countries Currently Eligible for TPS

As of late 2016, TPS was available for citizens of El Salvador, Guinea, Haiti, Honduras, Liberia, Nepal, Nicaragua, Sierra Leone, Somalia, Sudan, South Sudan, Syria, and Yemen.

Whenever a new country is named, the government publishes a notice in the *Federal Register*, stating the time period for which the protection is granted (a minimum of six months and a maximum of 18 months) and the dates and procedures for registering. Also see the USCIS website (www.uscis. gov) for this information (under "Other Services," click "Humanitarian," then "Temporary Protected Status").

 CAUTION
TPS does not include travel rights.
If you leave the U.S., your TPS will probably be canceled unless you receive permission beforehand, by applying for Advance Parole on Form I-131 (see the USCIS website for the form and instructions).

B. TPS Application Process

Applying for Temporary Protected Status is a one-step process. You'll need to fill out two USCIS forms, Form I-821 (available at www.uscis.gov/i-821) and Form I-765 (available at www.uscis.gov/i-765).

The forms are simple and self-explanatory. The I-821 asks for your name, address, birth date, nationality, and the date you began living in the United States. The I-765 is an application for a work permit (EAD). You will mark Box (a)(11) in Question 16.

In addition to the above forms, you must also submit documents showing that you really come from the country that you say you do (such as a copy of your passport or birth certificate) and that you have lived

---

Checklist for Temporary Protected Status Application

Use this checklist to help organize your TPS application.

Forms

☐ Form I-821, with appropriate fee (currently $50 for the initial application; no fee for renewal or reregistration).

☐ Form I-765.

☐ Fee for Form I-765, if you'd like an EAD card in order to work (currently $410).

☐ Fee for fingerprints (biometrics) whether initial application, renewal, or reregistration

(currently $85). This fee is not required for applicants age 14 or younger. The fee is not required for persons age 66 or older if it's an initial registration and they are requesting an employment authorization document along with TPS.

Documents

☐ Evidence of when you entered the U.S.

☐ Evidence of your presence during the necessary time period in the U.S.

☐ Evidence of your identity and nationality (birth certificate, passport, etc.).

in the U.S. for the time required under the TPS rules for your particular country. Evidence of your stay in the U.S. could include copies of your passport and I-94, employment records, and school records.

Applicants must pay an initial application fee, plus separate fees for biometrics (fingerprinting and photographs) and for work authorization (see the checklist above). If you don't plan to work and thus don't need the EAD card, you need not pay the work authorization fee—but you still need to submit Form I-765. Check box 2.b. on the Form I-821 if you don't want an EAD.

TPS applicants are subject to the grounds of inadmissibility (see Chapter 3), though some of these can be waived.

You will need to submit your completed TPS application to a USCIS Lockbox. The address depends on which country you are from, so check the USCIS website instructions (the ones specific to your country) for this information.

After submitting your application, USCIS will send you an appointment to have your photos and fingerprints taken (biometrics). After that, you may receive your approval notice in the mail, as well as a work permit (if you paid the fee for one). If USCIS cannot tell from your paperwork that you are eligible for TPS, it will schedule you for an interview.

C. Are You Eligible for Deferred Enforced Departure?

If you're from a country in the midst of political or civil conflict, you may be eligible for DED. This temporary form of relief allows you to work and stay in the U.S. for a certain period of time. DED works much like TPS, except that a decision to grant it comes directly from the U.S. president, as a foreign relations consideration, rather than from the Department of Homeland Security. (For that reason, you won't find it written up within the U.S. Immigration and Nationality Act.)

Under present policy, only persons from Liberia are eligible for DED, and only if they have lived in the United States since October 1, 2002, and had TPS when it expired for Liberians on September 30, 2007. The period of DED is temporary and will expire on March 31, 2018 unless the president extends it, so check to make sure DED is still in effect.

DED protection does not extend to anyone:

- who has been convicted of an aggravated felony
- who is a persecutor of others
- whose removal, in the opinion of the U.S. attorney general, is in the interest of the U.S.

- whose presence or activities in the U.S. are found by the secretary of state to have potentially serious adverse foreign policy consequences for the U.S.
- who voluntarily returned or returns to his or her country of last habitual residence outside the U.S.
- who was deported, excluded, or removed before December 23, 1997, or
- who is subject to extradition.

For more information on DED, and on how to apply for a work permit if you qualify, go to the USCIS website (www. uscis.gov). Under "Other Services," click "Humanitarian," then in the links in the column on the left, click "Temporary Protected Status & Deferred Enforced Departure," then "Deferred Enforced Departure."

D. Humanitarian Parole

If you're faced with a compelling need to come to the U.S. in emergency circumstances, but you have no way to get in under any visa category or you're inadmissible for some reason, you can ask USCIS for "humanitarian parole." USCIS may grant this permission to be in the U.S. temporarily to anyone based on urgent humanitarian reasons or if there is a significant public benefit, for as long as the emergency or humanitarian situation lasts. Parole of children requires the consent of a parent or legal guardian.

Parole will not give you any immigration benefits other than the right to be in the U.S. for a limited time. It doesn't lead to work authorization, a green card, or citizenship. It does mean, however, that you have been legally admitted to the U.S., which can be important for some purposes, such as adjusting status.

> CAUTION
> **You cannot use humanitarian parole to avoid normal visa-issuing procedures or to bypass immigration procedures.** As noted above, there must be an urgent humanitarian reason or significant public benefit for the parole to be granted.

Anyone who can't get a visa to the U.S. can file an application for humanitarian parole. You will need to complete a Form I-131, Application for Travel Document, available on the USCIS website at www. uscis.gov/i-131. There is a $575 filing fee.

It's important that you include a detailed explanation and evidence of your circumstances. You're asking for a favor from USCIS, so be persuasive. Make USCIS understand the seriousness of your situation, or why it's necessary for you to be in the United States. Consider hiring a U.S. immigration attorney to help make your case.

USCIS will not want you to become a "public charge" if it lets you in—that is, it doesn't want U.S. government agencies to have to spend money for your care. You'll have to submit a Form I-134, Affidavit of Support, in order to demonstrate that someone in the U.S.—most likely a relative, although it could be anyone—will take care of you financially if necessary.

Parole for Medical Reasons

If you need humanitarian parole for medical reasons, you must submit the following, with documentation to support any assertions, if it's available:

- An explanation from a medical doctor stating the diagnosis and prognosis, and how long the treatment is expected to last.
- Information on why you cannot obtain treatment in your home country or in a neighboring country.
- The estimated cost of treatment and an explanation on how the treatment will be paid for.
- How you will pay to return to your country.

All requests for humanitarian parole are mailed to a USCIS Lockbox in Texas. A lockbox is just a mailing address—your application will be routed to a USCIS Service Center for decision.

If you are currently in U.S. removal (deportation) proceedings or have been previously removed from the U.S., you will need to submit your request to Immigration and Customs Enforcement (ICE) instead of USCIS. The addresses are on the USCIS website at www.uscis.gov/i-131. (Definitely get a lawyer's help in such circumstances.)

USCIS will send you a notice after it receives your application and another when it has made a decision on your case. If you do not receive a response within 120 business days, contact USCIS's Parole Branch in writing at:

Department of Homeland Security, USCIS
Attn: Chief, Humanitarian Affairs Branch
20 Massachusetts Avenue, NW Suite 3300
Washington, DC 20529-2100.

If you're granted humanitarian parole, you'll be given an "I-94" arrival/departure record, which tells you how long you can stay. You must leave the U.S. before the expiration date of your parole. However, you can submit a request for re-parole to USCIS. File this at least 90 days before the expiration date on your I-94. Send another I-131, filing fee ($575), I-134 affidavit of support, and a copy of your I-94 to the USCIS Dallas Lockbox (see www.uscis.gov/i-131 for the address), along with an explanation of why you need an extension of time.

If USCIS does not give you humanitarian parole, unfortunately there is no way to appeal. You can file another application, however, if something changes to make your case more compelling.

Deferred Action for Childhood Arrivals (DACA)

The Obama administration, via an executive order issued in 2012, created a new remedy for young immigrants who have no legal status. Called "Deferred Action for Childhood Arrivals" or "DACA," it allows noncitizens who were brought to the U.S. as children and who meet other legal requirements (described below) to apply for two years' protection from deportation (removal), as well as a work permit. Another benefit is that a DACA recipient stops accruing "unlawful presence" (relevant if you might ever apply for a visa or green card, as described in Chapter 4).

It's important to note what the DACA remedy is not. It does not confer amnesty, a green card, or U.S. citizenship. It simply means that U.S. immigration authorities are expected to exercise their discretion and decline to deport an otherwise removable person who meets the legal criteria.

Family members of the applicant cannot claim a work permit or any other derivative rights to deferred action status.

As with any new government policy, the road to implementation has been bumpy. Although DACA can be renewed after its expiration, it provides no protection against the possibility that a later administration or Congress will change or override the policy. Such a change could leave former applicants—especially those whose applications were denied—with a clear record of unlawful U.S. presence, which would pose a problem for their future green card eligibility.

In November 2014, President Obama signed an executive order that expanded DACA availability in certain ways. Several states sued, however, to prevent the order from coming into effect. As of the publication date of this book, their lawsuits were successful. If DACA is repealed or changed in any way in the years after President Obama leaves office, you can learn about the changes on the Nolo website, www.nolo.com.

A. Do You Qualify for DACA?

You may apply for DACA if you:
- had not yet turned age 16 when you came to the U.S. to live
- were, on June 15, 2012, under the age of 31 (that is, you were born after June 15, 1981)
- have continuously lived ("resided") in the U.S. since June 15, 2007, up to the time of your application (excluding any brief, casual, and innocent departures from the U.S.)
- were physically present in the U.S. on June 15, 2012, and are physically present in the U.S. on the day you file your application
- were unlawfully present in the U.S. on June 15, 2012
- are either in school now (unless absent for emergency reasons), have graduated

or earned a certificate of completion from an accredited high school, have obtained a general education development (GED) certificate, or are an honorably discharged veteran of the Coast Guard or Armed Forces of the U.S., and

- have not been convicted of a felony, significant misdemeanor, or three or more other misdemeanors; and do not otherwise present a threat to U.S. national security or public safety (such as by being a member of a gang).

You will, when it comes time to apply, need to supply proof of each item on the above list.

 TIP
You probably haven't missed the deadline. As of the time this book went to print, there was no set deadline to apply for DACA, nor any known end date to the program. Applications will be accepted on a rolling basis for as long as the program remains in existence (which it's likely to do at least through the conclusion of the Obama administration, or until Congress passes comprehensive immigration reform and hopefully replaces DACA with an actual long-term legal program).

B. Who Is Not Eligible for DACA

Eligibility depends on meeting each and every criterion listed above. If, for example, you fit nearly all the criteria but were already 17 when you came to

the U.S. to live, you will not qualify. The same goes if you haven't lived in the U.S. "continuously" for the required period but spent a few years in your home country. USCIS will also look closely at whether the schools from which you claim to have graduated are in fact recognized and accredited (in most cases, public) schools.

The criminal grounds of ineligibility are especially challenging for some applicants, especially because the term "significant misdemeanor" has not previously appeared in the immigration law, and thus has not yet been applied to many individual fact patterns by USCIS or the courts.

According to USCIS statements, significant misdemeanors include any that involved violence, threats, assault, burglary, domestic violence, sexual abuse or exploitation, larceny, fraud, unlawful possession or use of a firearm, driving under the influence of drugs or alcohol (DUI or DWI), obstruction of justice or bribery, drug possession, drug distribution or trafficking, fleeing from a lawful arrest or prosecution, or leaving the scene of an accident. The sentence imposed does not matter if you were convicted of one of those crimes.

Significant misdemeanors may also include any other misdemeanor for which the applicant was sentenced to more than 90 days in prison, not including suspended sentences, pretrial detention, or time held on an immigration detainer. (Again, three or more misdemeanors of any sort are a disqualifier for DACA.)

What "Currently in School" Means

If you are currently in school, or have graduated, you will need to make sure your school or program qualifies for DACA. USCIS has set forth narrow guidelines for those schools or programs that qualify.

You are "currently in school" if you are enrolled in one of the following.

1. **Elementary, junior high, or high school.** Applicants enrolled in a public or private elementary school, junior high school, or high school meet the "currently in school" requirement.

2. **ESL program.** An English as a second language program (ESL) can qualify you for DACA, but only if the program is a prerequisite for postsecondary education, job training, or employment and you are working toward one of these after completing the ESL program.

3. **Educational program; preparation for diploma or GED.** Other educational programs qualify if they are designed to help obtain a high school diploma or GED. The program must be funded by state or federal grants or, if privately operated, be of demonstrated effectiveness. Demonstrated effectiveness is measured by the success and quality of the program, including its length of operation and track record of success in placing participants in the workplace or in higher education. So, if you choose a privately run GED program, be selective and steer clear of ones that are recently opened or do not have a solid reputation. Programs run by local universities, adult schools, or community colleges are probably the best options.

4. **Education, literacy, vocational, or career training program.** One of these will meet the "currently in school" requirement if:

   - the program is funded by state or federal grants or the applicant can prove that the program is of demonstrated effectiveness (as described above)
   - the program is intended to place the applicant into postsecondary education, job training, or employment, and
   - the applicant is preparing for post-program placement.

If you are not now in school, you may still become DACA-eligible if you enroll in one of the programs described above. USCIS will look at whether you are enrolled in school at the time you submit your DACA application.

USCIS has also explained a "non-significant misdemeanor" as including a crime punishable by imprisonment of more than five days and less than a year and that is not on USCIS's list of significant misdemeanors.

C. Risks and Downsides to Applying for DACA

If you are considering applying for DACA but haven't yet done so, first consider your own personal, immigration, and criminal history and the risks of providing these details to the U.S. government, as described in this section.

1. DACA Offers No Long-Term Benefits

DACA is a discretionary, stopgap remedy that provides a stay of deportation from the U.S. for three years at a time and a work permit. It is not an amnesty, does not forgive past grounds of inadmissibility, and does not provide a pathway to U.S. legal residency or citizenship. And the longer you have already waited to apply, the less time you will likely have in which to enjoy DACA's benefits.

2. DACA Requires Sharing Personal Information That Could Later Lead to Deportation

USCIS has stated that DACA applicants' information will not be shared with Immigration and Customs Enforcement (ICE) unless applicants present national security, fraud, or public safety concerns. Nevertheless, the risk remains that a future event (such as a terrorist attack or a change in administration) could cause USCIS to interpret those categories more broadly.

Immigrants who have criminal records (including certain "significant misdemeanors," juvenile offenses, and expunged convictions), links to organizations flagged by the FBI, or past instances of committing immigration fraud are not only ineligible for DACA, but also risk being placed into removal proceedings if they submit a DACA application.

Similarly, USCIS may share the personal information of family members who are undocumented and listed on a DACA application with certain branches of the U.S. government if those family members are deemed a national security or public safety threat.

3. DACA's Travel Possibilities Create Risks of Being Stopped Upon Return to the U.S.

If you are granted DACA relief, you may not freely travel in and out of the U.S.—but you do gain the ability to apply for and obtain what's called "Advance Parole" (a travel document) for "humanitarian, work, or school purposes."

Even so, your travel will trigger the scrutiny of border agents upon your return. DACA is relatively new territory in immigration law, and questions remain as to how other agencies will treat its beneficiaries. Because U.S. Customs and Border Protection (CBP) is separate from USCIS and restricts U.S. entry to foreign travelers with valid visas, DACA recipients have no guarantee that they will not be detained when attempting to reenter the U.S., based on their past immigration offenses or criminal history.

D. Who Shouldn't Apply for DACA

If you face a significant risk that your case may be referred to Immigration and Customs Enforcement (ICE), which may lead to removal proceedings being instituted against you, DACA may not be an appropriate remedy for you.

1. Don't Apply If You Have an Incident of Fraud in Your Past

If you entered the U.S. by means of fraud or misrepresentation, you should not apply for DACA relief. Doing so would risk having your case referred to ICE. A common way in which entrants commit fraud or misrepresentation include using a counterfeit identity document such as a fake passport or a falsified birth certificate to obtain a visa or another immigration benefit.

Even if you entered the U.S. as a minor child or your parent or guardian used a false document on your behalf without your knowledge, until a law is passed that forgives misrepresentations that were committed unknowingly, USCIS will still consider it to be part of your immigration history.

2. Don't Apply If You Have Committed Serious Immigration Offenses

USCIS may disqualify applicants who have serious immigration violations in their history or have committed several offenses, such as multiple reentries, as well as immigrants who have been deported in the past.

If and when the DACA program ends, immigrants who have submitted such information may undergo scrutiny from immigration enforcement authorities.

3. Don't Apply If You Have a Criminal Record

You are ineligible for DACA if you have been convicted of a felony, one "significant" misdemeanor, or three or more misdemeanor offenses that do not arise from a single event. Minor traffic offenses will not count as a misdemeanor for purposes of DACA even if they were classified as a misdemeanor under state law.

Fortunately for DACA applicants, USCIS does not immediately disqualify people who have just one or two misdemeanors or juvenile convictions or expunged offenses. USCIS will look at applicants' juvenile or expunged records and decide on a case-by-case basis whether or not to grant DACA relief. But even after that, immigration officials might still deny your application.

If you have any doubt as to whether a criminal conviction could disqualify you from DACA relief and possibly lead to an ICE referral, consult an immigration attorney.

4. Don't Apply If You May Be Viewed as a Public Safety or National Security Threat

You may also be disqualified from receiving benefits under DACA and may be placed into removal proceedings if you are considered a threat to public safety or national security. USCIS may take into consideration any criminal activity that did not result in a conviction—even arrests and dismissed charges.

USCIS has stated that membership in a gang or an organization whose criminal activities threaten the U.S. public welfare would qualify as a public safety or national security threat. Again, since DACA is considered discretionary relief, any membership in a group that is flagged as having terrorist ties or anti-American views might lead to denial of your application and possible investigation by ICE.

E. How to Apply for DACA

The application process for DACA involves submitting two government forms along with supporting evidence showing that you qualify for this status, and paying a fee.

CAUTION
The procedures described here apply only to people who are not in removal (deportation) proceedings. You can submit a DACA application if you are in immigration court proceedings, but some procedures will be different—get an attorney's help.

1. DACA Application Forms

The forms to submit to apply for DACA include:

- Form I-821D, Consideration of Deferred Action for Childhood Arrivals, and
- Form I-765, Application for Employment Authorization, accompanied by a worksheet called Form I-765WS.

These are available as free downloads on the USCIS website, at www.uscis.gov/forms.

2. Preparing Documents in Support of DACA Application

In addition to filling out the forms, you will need to submit documents showing that you meet all the DACA criteria, including proof of your identity, age upon entry into the U.S., academic record, continuous physical presence in the United States since June 15, 2007, and unlawful presence is the U.S. on June 15, 2012. Such evidence might include:

- birth certificate
- copy of passport or other photo identity document
- copy of visa and Form I-94 (if you overstayed)
- past documents from immigration authorities, even if they showed you were stopped or ordered into removal proceedings
- travel receipts, for example showing plane tickets to the U.S.
- school records and correspondence, including acceptance letters, report cards, transcripts, progress reports, diplomas, and GED certificates, showing the name of the school and a description of the program, your dates of attendance, and degrees received
- copy of U.S. driver's license
- personal affidavits or statements by friends, teachers, employers, religious leaders, and others in authority
- tax records
- bank, credit card, and other financial records showing your activity in the U.S.
- store, restaurant, and online shopping receipts in your name and/or indicating items sent to your address
- Facebook check-ins or Tweets indicating presence in the U.S.
- medical and dental records indicating your presence at U.S. doctors' offices or hospitals
- records of working for U.S. employers, and
- U.S. military records.

These are simply examples, and you can present other documents unique to your situation. If, for example, you won a swimming contest at a U.S. summer camp, a copy of your certificate would be good evidence of your physical presence here. Some people have even submitted traffic or speeding tickets (though any more serious run-in with police might be problematic for your DACA eligibility—talk to a lawyer).

The fee for this application is $465, which includes the standard $85 biometrics (fingerprinting) fee for a background check and the $410 fee for an EAD (work permit). In limited circumstances, USCIS may grant a fee exemption to applicants who fall below the U.S. poverty line.

The USCIS website has additional information about how to apply, with suggestions for documentation. At www.uscis.gov, under "Other Services," click "Humanitarian," then "Consideration of Deferred Action for Childhood Arrivals Process."

3. Renewing Your DACA Status

An initial grant of DACA protects you for two years. To remain protected, you must apply to renew your DACA status, which you are eligible to do if you:

- have stayed in the U.S. since getting DACA (after Aug. 15, 2012), except if you left with advance parole
- have continuously resided in the U.S. since you submitted your most recent DACA request that was approved, and
- have not been convicted of a felony, a significant misdemeanor, or three or more misdemeanors, and do not otherwise pose a threat to national security or public safety.

Your request to USCIS for renewal should consist of:

- Form I-821D. Make sure you're using the most recent version, available at www.uscis.gov/i-821d.

- Form I-765, Application for Employment Authorization, and Form I-765WS Worksheet (both at www.uscis.gov/i-765)
- Filing fees: $410 for Form I-765 and $85 for biometric services (fingerprints and photo), for a total of $495.

You don't have to submit any additional documents at the time you file for renewal, except any new ones involving removal proceedings or a criminal history that you did not submit to USCIS in your previously approved DACA request. You might have to provide additional documents or statements to verify information on your renewal application, if USCIS asks for them.

TIP

Submit your renewal request well before your current period of deferred action will expire. Don't submit it any more than 150 days (five months) before your current period expires—USCIS will probably reject it and return it to you with instructions to resubmit it closer to the expiration date. By submitting your request at least 120 days before the expiration date, however, you improve your chances of being protected if USCIS gets delayed in processing renewals and your current two-year grant expires. In such a situation, USCIS may provide you deferred action and employment authorization for a short period of time until it finishes processing your request. Otherwise, until you get the renewal, you won't be able to work, and you will start accruing days of "unlawful presence" (important to avoid, as explained in Chapter 3).

Getting a U Visa as a Crime Victim Assisting Law Enforcement

The Victims of Trafficking and Violence Protection Act of 2000 authorized a new visa for immigrant victims of serious crimes, called the "U" visa. The legislation was a response to rising public safety concerns, with the idea that foreign victims of crimes in the U.S. should be allowed to remain here so as to provide law enforcement officials with information helpful in apprehending and prosecuting criminal offenders.

If approved for a U visa, you will be granted legal status in the U.S. for up to four years (which may be extended in "exceptional circumstances"). After holding U status for three years, you may be able to apply for a U.S. green card.

As with all U.S. visas, you will need to take several steps to prove that you qualify for it. In other words, it is not enough to simply claim that you have been a victim of a serious crime. Most notably, you will need to provide a "certificate of helpfulness" from a qualifying government agency and prove that you suffered mental or physical abuse by the U.S. criminal perpetrator.

Only applicants who come from outside the U.S. will, in literal terms, receive a U visa in their passport. (A visa is an entry document.) Applicants from within the U.S. will receive "U status," and will, if they leave the U.S., need to go to a U.S. consulate to get an actual visa stamp in their passport before returning.

Other Temporary Visas for Crime Victims and Informants

The "S" visa program was established to provide witnesses to crimes (and qualified family members) with an avenue through which to maintain nonimmigrant status in the United States in exchange for their cooperation in investigations and prosecutions.

There is also a "T" nonimmigrant visa for victims of severe human trafficking. The T visa allows victims to remain in the U.S. to assist federal authorities in the investigation and prosecution of human trafficking cases.

Because these visas are used far less commonly than the U visa, we don't cover them in this book.

A. Are You Eligible for a U Visa?

To qualify for a U visa or U status in the U.S., you must meet the following criteria:

- You must have been a victim of a "qualifying criminal activity," and this crime must have occurred in the U.S. or violated U.S. law. Indirect and bystander victims are also eligible to apply for U visas in certain circumstances. For example, a murder victim obviously cannot benefit from a U visa, but a person who witnessed the murder, or a close family member who was impacted by it, may have information that can help law enforcement.

- In the course of or as a result of this criminal activity, you must have suffered substantial physical or mental abuse.

- You are able to provide useful information about the criminal activity (or if under age 16, your parent, guardian, or "next friend" such as a counselor or social worker can provide this information for you).

- You (or your parent, guardian, or next friend) are cooperating with U.S. law enforcement in order to bring the perpetrator of the crime to justice.

- You are admissible to the U.S. or you are applying for a waiver. The public charge ground of inadmissibility has, however, been removed as an obstacle for U visa applicants. So you need not submit a waiver application if you are low-income and have received or might receive means-based government assistance. In line with this, the public charge ground of inadmissibility will not be considered if and when you apply for a green card (adjustment of status). This also applies to derivative family members of U visa applicants.

1. What Crimes Qualify Its Victims for a U Visa

In a typical U visa case, the crime occurred within the United States. In some cases, however, the crime might have violated U.S. laws overseas (such as a human trafficking or kidnapping crime).

Examples of qualifying crimes are:

- **Violent crimes:** murder, manslaughter, vehicular homicide, robbery, felonious assault (which usually involves the use of a deadly weapon, and can include statutory rape and other offenses), domestic violence, or stalking.

- **Enslavement crimes:** criminal restraint, kidnapping, abduction, being held hostage, forced labor, slavery, human trafficking, indentured or debt servitude, or false imprisonment.

- **Sex crimes:** rape, incest, sexual trafficking, sexual assault and abusive sexual contact, prostitution, sexual exploitation, or female genital mutilation.

- **Obstruction of justice crimes:** perjury, witness tampering, or withholding evidence.

- **Fraud in foreign labor contracting:** a later addition to the statute, made in 2014.

The crime need not have been "completed" to qualify its victims for a U visa. An attempt, solicitation, or conspiracy to commit one of the above-mentioned crimes is enough. For example, obviously a murder victim wouldn't be applying for a U visa. But the victim of attempted murder may qualify for a U visa.

2. When Indirect Victims May Be Eligible for U Status

USCIS may grant U status to noncitizen bystanders to crimes who suffered unusually severe harm as a result of having witnessed the criminal activity. The example most often used is that of a pregnant woman who suffers a miscarriage as a result of witnessing a criminal activity.

Also, certain family members can apply for U visas as indirect victims if the primary victim died due to murder or manslaughter or was rendered incompetent or incapacitated and therefore cannot help authorities with the criminal investigation. For crime victims who are age 21 or older, their spouse, as well as their children under 21 years of age, may be considered indirect victims. For victims under age 21, their parents and unmarried siblings under 18 can be considered indirect victims.

Indirect victims still need to establish that they meet the other eligibility requirements for U status, meaning that they:

- have been helpful, are being helpful, or will be helpful in the investigation of the crime
- suffered substantial harm as a result of the crime, and
- are either admissible to the U.S. or qualify for a waiver of inadmissibility.

EXAMPLE: Leticia's son Rodrigo was murdered in the U.S. at age 20. The mother, from Mexico, had a nervous breakdown soon after hearing the news. She helped the police investigation by providing information about her son and the events that happened on the day of the murder. Leticia would qualify as an indirect victim because she is the parent of a deceased victim under 21, she suffered harm as a result of the crime, and she helped in the investigation. She may still qualify even if several years have passed since the murder, because USCIS looks at the age of the victim when the murder took place to determine whether parents were indirect victims, and Rodrigo was 20.

USCIS generally considers minors to be "incapacitated," and therefore their family members often qualify as indirect victims.

EXAMPLE: Minjun, who overstayed a visa from Korea, has a four-year-old daughter, born in the United States. The daughter becomes the victim of child molestation by a nanny. As soon as Minjun realized his daughter was being abused, he reported the incident to the police, and assisted with the investigation. He suffered serious emotional harm because of what the daughter went through, especially because he was also the victim of abuse as a child. Because the daughter was born in the U.S., she does not need to apply for immigration relief. Minjun therefore could not be a derivative on her U status application. However, he may qualify for U status as an indirect victim, because his daughter was incapacitated (by definition, due to her young age), he helped the investigation, and he suffered harm as a result of the crime.

In both the above examples of indirect victims, the noncitizen would also have to meet the other requirements for eligibility for U status or a U visa, by showing admissibility to the U.S. or qualifying for a waiver of inadmissibility.

3. Requirement That You Suffered Substantial Abuse

It is not enough to merely be the victim of a qualifying crime. You must have also suffered "substantial" physical injury or mental anguish as a result of this criminal activity. In determining whether the harm was "substantial," USCIS will consider how severe the injury was, for how long the abuse occurred, and how likely it is to cause you lasting or permanent harm.

4. Requirement That You Are Helping Law Enforcement

One of the reasons Congress authorized U visas was concern that many U.S. immigrants refuse to provide information to U.S. police and other law enforcement authorities, due to cultural differences, language barriers, and fear of deportation. The unfortunate result is that many perpetrators of serious crime view immigrants as easy targets.

In order to further the public safety objectives of the U visa, your visa petition must be certified by a police officer or other law enforcement official. The official must attest that you were a victim of a qualifying crime and that you are likely to be helpful to an investigation or prosecution of the crime.

The chances of your getting a law enforcement official to cooperate with your U visa application are greatly improved if you are forthcoming with information that could lead to the identification, arrest, and conviction of a serious criminal. This could include (but is not limited to):

- Your identification of the criminals involved, such as their names and addresses, or choosing the correct person in a lineup.
- Information that helps apprehend the perpetrators, such as your tips as to where they may be "hiding out," names of their friends and family who might give information about where they are, or identifying details about their vehicle (make, color, license plate number).
- Descriptive details that help the prosecution convince a jury that the accused is guilty of the crime, rebut the accused's alibi, support a motive for committing the crime, or determine what penalty (or sentencing) it should request.

- Evidence that could help law enforcement classify the crime as more serious or charge the criminals with additional crimes. (This might be relevant if, for example, the officer is investigating a felony assault but you have evidence that could lead to an attempted murder charge, or that might lead to an additional charge of sexual assault.)
- Agreement to testify as a witness if the case goes to trial.

5. Available Waiver If You Are Inadmissible

To be eligible for a U visa, you must not be "inadmissible" to the United States. This means that you are not barred from U.S. entry due to factors such as multiple criminal convictions, immigration violations, certain medical conditions, or any of several other reasons (excluding the public charge ground of inadmissibility). (See Chapter 3.)

In order to apply for a waiver of inadmissibility, you must submit to USCIS Form I-192, Application for Advance Permission to Enter as a Nonimmigrant. Unlike many other immigration waivers, this one does not require a showing of extreme hardship to anyone if the waiver were denied. U visa waiver applications are reviewed on a case-by-case basis. You'll definitely want to get a lawyer's help, however, in order to identify and prove the reasons you deserve the waiver.

6. Qualifying Family Members May Receive Derivative U Visas

Certain family members may be eligible to become derivative U visa recipients if the principal petitioner's application is approved. These include:

- unmarried children under age 21
- spouse
- parents (if principal petitioner is under age 21), and
- unmarried siblings under 18 years old (if principal petitioner is under age 21).

Any derivative relatives must also be "admissible" to the U.S. (or apply for a waiver) and have good moral character.

B. How to Apply for a U Visa

Applying for a U visa involves the following steps:

- Prepare USCIS Form I-918, Petition for U Nonimmigrant Status.
- Have a qualifying agency provide certification of your helpfulness, to accompany this I-918 petition.
- Gather evidence to substantiate your eligibility and claim of substantial injury.
- If you have derivative family members, submit Form I-918, Supplement A, Petition for Qualifying Family Member of U Visa Recipient, either along with your own petition or after your U visa is approved. Also, if they're in the

U.S. and wish to work, prepare Form I-765 for a work permit.

- Submit your petition and supporting documents to USCIS.
- Attend an interview at a USCIS office or your local U.S. consulate, if required.

We'll explain each of these steps below.

1. Filling Out Form I-918 Petition for U Visa

Here are instructions for filling out the required U visa petition, on USCIS Form I-918 (the version expiring 1/31/2016). The form, its supplements, and further instructions are available on the USCIS website (www.uscis.gov/i-918).

Part 1, "Information about you." (Self-explanatory.)

Part 2, "Additional information." Your answers to these questions will determine whether or not you are eligible for a U visa or whether USCIS will require more information from you. If you answer "no" to any of questions 1 to 5, your application will be denied. Definitely see an attorney

---

Checklist for U Visa Application

Forms

- ☐ USCIS Form I-918. (No fee is required with this form.)
- ☐ Form I-918, Supplement A (if you want derivative status for a qualifying family member).
- ☐ Form I-918, Supplement B (completed and certified by a qualifying law enforcement agency).

Documents

- ☐ Personal narrative statement.
- ☐ Evidence that you are the victim of a qualifying criminal activity.
- ☐ Evidence that you have helpful information about the crime. Form I-918, Supplement B, should be sufficient, but if you have any further information about how you are being helpful to authorities in providing information about the crime, submit it.
- ☐ Evidence that the crime violated U.S. laws. Again, Form I-918, Supplement B, should

cover this, but if you have any additional information about the crime, especially if it occurred outside of the U.S. (but violated federal law), you should provide this.

- ☐ Evidence that you suffered substantial physical or mental abuse.
- ☐ Waiver of Grounds of Inadmissibility, if applicable. Submit Form I-192, Application for Advance Permission to Enter as a Nonimmigrant, with check or money order ($585 as of this book's print date), made payable to "U.S. Department of Homeland Security." If you cannot afford this amount, you may apply for a fee waiver.
- ☐ Information to prove relationship of derivative family members, (such as birth or marriage certificates). Foreign language documents must be accompanied by a full English translation.
- ☐ Form I-765, Application for Employment Authorization Document (EAD), with appropriate filing fees, for any derivative family members who wish to work and are in the United States.

if the true answer is "no"; lying on an application can get you into serious trouble.

Question 1. (Qualifying crime.) Answer "yes" if you are the victim of any crime involving one or more of the following or any similar activity in violation of federal, state, or local criminal law: rape; torture; trafficking; incest; domestic violence; sexual assault; abusive sexual contact; prostitution; sexual exploitation; stalking; female genital mutilation; being held hostage; peonage; involuntary servitude; slave trading; kidnapping; abduction; unlawful criminal restraint; false imprisonment; blackmail; extortion; manslaughter; murder; felonious assault; witness tampering; obstruction of justice; perjury; fraud in foreign labor contracting (as defined in Section 1351 of title 18, U.S. Code); or attempt, conspiracy, or solicitation to commit any of the above-mentioned crimes.

Question 2. (Substantial physical or mental abuse.) Answer "yes" to certify that you have been substantially injured as the result of the criminal activity.

Question 3. (Information about the crime.) Answer "yes" if you have information concerning the crime that you were a victim of.

Question 4. (Certification of helpfulness.) You'll definitely need to answer "yes," to show that a qualifying official will be providing a certification of helpfulness (Form I-918, Supplement B).

Question 5. (Place of the crime.) Answer "yes" if the qualifying crime took place in the U.S. or violated U.S. laws.

Question 6. If you are under age 16, answer "yes." Your parent, guardian, or "next friend" will need to cooperate with the agency and provide information on your behalf.

Question 7. (Employment Authorization Document.) If you want to apply for a work permit, answer "yes."

Question 8. (Immigration proceedings.) If you have ever been in U.S. removal (deportation) or exclusion proceedings, answer "yes" and provide dates.

Question 9. (Admissions to U.S.) List your date and place of entry to the U.S. and the status you held at the time, such as "F-1 student" or "B-2 visitor." Write the visa you entered with or "EWI" (entered without inspection) if you did not have legal status.

Question 10. (Application outside the U.S.) If you are applying for a U visa from abroad, complete this section. Otherwise, write "N/A."

Part 3, "Processing information." The questions that follow will determine whether you are "admissible" to the United States. If you answer "yes" to any, your application may be denied or you may have to file a waiver request. (By the time you read this, the question about whether you have ever received public assistance should have been removed from this form; if not, enter "N/A.") Consult an immigration attorney if you need to answer "yes" to any of these questions.

Part 4, "Information about your spouse or children." You will need to fill out personal information for your spouse and children (if applicable).

Part 5, "Filing on behalf of family members." If you are applying for U derivative status for a qualifying family member, check "Yes."

Part 6, "Attestation, release, and signature." Sign and date your application.

2. Obtaining a Certification of Helpfulness

As part of your application for a U visa, you will need to show USCIS that a law enforcement official has "vouched" for your petition. A judge, police officer, prosecutor, or other law enforcement official must complete a "certification of helpfulness" (I-918 Supplement B, U Nonimmigrant Status Certification) on your behalf. This document is a vital part of your application. It shows that you have been a victim of qualifying criminal activity, have information that will be useful to law enforcement, and are cooperating in order to bring the perpetrator to justice.

The agencies that will most commonly certify a U visa petition are local, state, and federal police departments and prosecutors. Even a judge may sign a U visa certification, although many will refuse to do so in order to avoid a showing of bias for the prosecution. However, any state or federal agency that has "responsibility for the investigation or prosecution of a qualifying crime or criminal activity" may complete the certification of helpfulness. For example, if you are the victim of a crime that requires the involvement of Child Protective Services (CPS), you could bypass the police and justice departments and instead have CPS help you with your application.

USCIS states that people who are in a supervisory role and have responsibility for issuing certificates of helpfulness must sign the petition, but it allows the agency to designate another certifying official if it chooses to do so.

Ultimately, it's up to the law enforcement authorities acting in your case to decide whether or not you are "helpful" to them and whether they should fill out the certification of helpfulness for you.

> ## TIP
> **Don't delay in obtaining the certification of helpfulness.** Not only is it a vital part of your application, but by showing interest and providing helpful evidence to authorities, you will show that you are eager to participate in the investigation. Also, if the criminals involved are arrested and plead guilty to the criminal charges before you contact police or answer a request for cooperation from law enforcement, your evidence and testimony may not be as useful, since the case will not go to trial.

3. Preparing Documents to Support Your U Visa Petition

Filling out the required forms will not be enough, by itself, to qualify you for a U visa. You will also need to prepare or gather various documents to support your claim, such as:

- Personal narrative statement, describing how you are a victim of criminal activity and the circumstances surrounding the crime. You can use this statement to show that you were not at fault in the criminal activity and that you were helpful (if you called the authorities to report the crime, for example). Also describe the extent of your injuries.
- Evidence that you are the victim of a qualifying criminal activity. This could include information in your personal statement as well as trial transcripts, newspaper articles, police reports, affidavits, or orders of protection (restraining orders) and affidavits from people who have personal knowledge of the criminal activity.
- Evidence that you suffered substantial physical or mental abuse. This could include affidavits from case or social workers, medical personnel, and police; and photographs of injuries.

An attorney can help you gather these documents, but you will still need to play a role in considering what the best sources might be, and in talking to friends, doctors, and others who might help.

How Long Does It Take to Get a U Visa?

It typically takes about a year for USCIS to fully process a U visa application, which includes taking biometrics (photographs and fingerprints), processing all forms and supporting information (such as the certification of helpfulness by a qualifying agency), and finally, issuing an approval notice and your work permit. Nevertheless, the amount of time USCIS actually takes to process your Form I-918 depends on its particulars.

For example, the USCIS officer assigned to your case might send you a Request for Evidence (RFE)—that is, a request for additional information. That will put a hold on your file until you respond.

---

4. Filling Out Form I-765 (If You Have Family Members Who Want to Work in the U.S.)

The principal petitioner does not need to worry about applying for a work permit (EAD). If the I-918 is approved, he or she will be sent an EAD automatically. Any derivative family members who want to work must, however, separately submit Form I-765 to request an EAD. They can do so either by including their form with the I-918 petition or by sending in a separate Form I-765 after USCIS has approved the I-918 petition.

Form I-765 is fairly short and self-explanatory. For Question 16, the eligibility category, derivative family members would fill in "(a)(20)." Your family members will also need to pay the Form I-765 fee ($410 as of this book's print date) or request a fee waiver.

5. Submitting Your U Visa Petition to USCIS

After you have completed the application, make a copy for your files. Then send the packet of forms and documents to the following USCIS address:

Vermont Service Center
75 Lower Welden Street
St. Albans, VT 05479

6. Attending a U Visa Interview

If you are applying from within the U.S., chances are you will not be required to attend an interview at a local USCIS office, which is why it is important to provide a strong statement with your I-918 application. However, it's possible that you may be required to attend an in-person interview at a local USCIS office. If you (or your family members) are applying from overseas, this interview would be held at the U.S. embassy or consulate in your home country.

The purpose of the interview will be for U.S. officials to review your file and talk with you personally about your eligibility for a U visa or your relationship with the principal applicant (if you are a family member applying for derivative status) and to make sure you are not inadmissible to the United States.

C. Will You Be Eligible for a Green Card After Your U Visa?

If you have received a U visa or U status as a victim of a serious crime assisting law enforcement, you may be able to adjust your status (receive a green card) after three years of continuous presence in the United States. If interested, you should apply as soon as possible. In order to qualify for a U.S. green card:

- You must continue to be eligible for U nonimmigrant status. This means that you must continue to assist law enforcement by providing helpful information used to investigate and prosecute the criminals who victimized you.
- You must not have abandoned this status (for example, by refusing to cooperate with government agencies or by living outside the U.S. for an extended period of time).

- You must have been physically present in the U.S. continuously for at least three years.
- You must not have unreasonably refused to cooperate with the law enforcement officials investigating and prosecuting the crime against you.
- Your continued presence in the U.S. must be justified either on humanitarian grounds, to ensure family unity, or because it is in the public interest.

These requirements are detailed below, along with suggestions for proving that you meet them when it comes time to apply for a green card.

1. Continuous U.S. Physical Presence of at Least Three Years

In order to successfully apply for U.S. permanent residence based on a U visa, you must show that you have lived in the U.S. continuously for three years. "Continuous" presence for immigration purposes means that you have not taken a trip outside the U.S. for 90 days or more or spent more than 180 days abroad during your time in U status.

You can demonstrate your continuous presence by documenting each trip outside the U.S. (to show that you were abroad only briefly) and providing proof that you now make your life in the United States. This can include pay stubs, tax transcripts, school records, and

affidavits from people who know you and can attest to your U.S. presence.

If you can't show continuous presence, you will need to provide a written explanation by a government official who is working on your case, stating that your presence outside the U.S. was necessary in order to assist the investigation or prosecution of the crime or that it was otherwise justified.

2. Continued Cooperation With Law Enforcement

In order to be eligible for a green card based on your U visa, you must continue to provide helpful information to law enforcement officials, and you cannot have "unreasonably refused" to provide requested assistance.

Ideally, you will submit another certification of helpfulness (Form I-918 Supplement B, U Nonimmigrant Status Certification) with your green card application. This will prove that you are a willing participant in the investigation and prosecution of the crime (or crimes) against you.

If you are unable to obtain another certification of helpfulness, contact an experienced immigration attorney to help, because you will need to instead submit an affidavit and other supporting evidence showing all of your contacts and meetings with law enforcement officials. You will also need to explain that you attempted to obtain this certification, but were unable to for good reason.

Additionally, if you ever refused an official request for cooperation, you must explain your reasons. USCIS will determine whether the request was "unreasonable" given the nature of the crime, your circumstances, and the extent of the assistance required. For example, if you are a rape victim and a police investigator asked you to meet with your attacker, USCIS would likely consider this to be an unreasonable request, and would excuse you for refusing it. However, if a police officer asked you to identify your attacker in a lineup where he would not see you and you refused, your denial might cost you a green card.

3. U.S. Residence Justified on Humanitarian, Family Unity, or Public Interest Grounds

Unlike many other types of green card applicants, U visa holders do not have to apply for a waiver of any applicable inadmissibility grounds. The only ground of inadmissibility that applies to U adjustment applicants concerns participants in Nazi persecution, genocide, or extrajudicial killings—and no waiver is available for these.

However, adjustment of status to permanent residence from a U visa is a discretionary benefit, which means it is completely up to the USCIS officer handling your case whether or not to grant it. Therefore, you should submit evidence with your application to show USCIS that you "deserve" a green card. Family ties in the U.S., achievements and accomplishments, and any reasons why you would experience hardship upon returning to your home country will all be relevant. This is especially important if there are any negative factors in your record (such as arrests or criminal convictions).

4. Immediate Relatives May Also Apply for Green Cards

If you have qualifying family members in the U.S. in derivative U status, the procedures to apply for adjustment of status are the same as for the principal U applicant.

However, if you have an immediate family member—spouse, child, or parents (if you are under age 21)—who has never received U derivative status, that person can also apply for adjustment of status or an immigrant visa at the same time you apply or after your approval. File Form I-929, Petition for Qualifying Family Member of U-1 Nonimmigrant, with USCIS.

You must show that you or your family member would be subjected to "extreme hardship" if not permitted to reside with you in the United States. This is no easy task, so we recommend consulting an attorney.

Checklist for Filing for U.S. Green Card From U Status

You (and each of your derivative family members) will need to assemble:

- ☐ Form I-485, Application to Register Permanent Residence or to Adjust Status.
- ☐ Filing fee or, or if you cannot afford it, a waiver request on Form I-912, Request for Fee Waiver.
- ☐ Form I-693, Report of Medical Examination and Vaccination Record.
- ☐ Form G-325A, Biographic Information Sheet (if you are between 14 and 79 years old).
- ☐ Form I-765, Application for Employment Authorization and supporting documentation.
- ☐ Form I-131, Application for Travel Document and supporting documentation.
- ☐ Copy of Form I-797, Notice of Action, showing that USCIS approved you for U nonimmigrant status.
- ☐ Copy of your I-94, Arrival/Departure Record. All arriving foreign visitors had this white card stapled into their passports until this form was automated in April 2013; subsequent visitors who did not receive a card can obtain a copy from https://i94.cbp.dhs.gov.
- ☐ If any of your family members has not yet obtained derivative status, Form I-929, Petition for Qualifying Family Member of U-1 Nonimmigrant.

- ☐ A copy of all pages of your passport, including the U nonimmigrant visa page. If you do not have a U visa, because you have not departed the U.S. since you were granted U status, make copies of all of your passport pages regardless. If you don't have a passport, provide an explanation as to why you do not have one, such as loss or theft.
- ☐ Copy of your birth certificate (with English translation).
- ☐ Two passport-style photos.
- ☐ Evidence that you have three years' continuous physical presence in the U.S., such as tax transcripts, pay stubs, leases, receipts, and utility bills for a U.S. residence, letter from your school or employer, and affidavits from people who can vouch for your U.S. presence.
- ☐ Evidence that you complied with requests for assistance from law enforcement officials, including new Form I-918, Supplement B, and your affidavit describing your attempts to contact law enforcement officials during your time in U status and reasons for any failure to comply with a request for cooperation.
- ☐ Evidence that you "deserve" permanent residence on humanitarian, public interest, or family unity grounds.

Keep in mind that these relatives (unlike you) WILL be subject to the inadmissibility grounds that prevent many noncitizens from entering the United States.

> ⚠ CAUTION
>
> **What if your U status will expire before you can apply for a green card?** As the principal applicant, your U status will likely last four years. However, due to consular processing delays, many derivative U visa holders are authorized to stay in the U.S. for three years or less. If your U status will expire before you are able to accrue the continuous presence needed, you may able to extend the time to no more than four years. Do so by filling out and submitting USCIS Form I-539. Provide the documents described on the USCIS instructions to the form (available at www.uscis.gov/i-539), and be prepared to describe how USCIS or consular processing delays slowed your entry into the U.S. or that you'd be unable to adjust to permanent residence if your U visa was not extended, through no fault of your own.

5. Submitting Adjustment of Status Application

After you compile all of the needed items for the green card application, make a copy for your files and send it to:

Vermont Service Center
Attn: CRU
75 Lower Welden Street
St. Alban's, VT 05479-0001

6. What Happens After Submitting Adjustment of Status Application

After you file, you should first receive a receipt notice. Later, you will be sent a biometrics appointment notice, requiring you to appear to have your photograph, fingerprints, and signature taken.

If USCIS has questions about your application, it may schedule you for an interview at a local USCIS office. Bring a copy of everything you sent and an interpreter if you are not fluent in English.

Glossary

Immigration law is full of words and terms whose meanings are not obvious. We've used many of these words in this book and you may encounter others as you use additional resources. For help in unpacking their meanings, see the plain-English definitions below.

Accompanying relative. In most cases, a person who is eligible to receive some type of visa or green card can also obtain green cards or similar visas for immediate family members who will be immigrating or coming to the U.S. at the same time or soon after. These family members are called accompanying relatives and may include only a spouse and unmarried children under the age of 21.

Advance Parole. Advance Parole may be granted to a person who is already in the U.S., but needs to leave temporarily and return without a visa. This is most common when someone has a green card application in process and wants to leave the U.S. for a trip.

Alien Registration Receipt Card. A name sometimes used in immigration law for a green card. USCIS calls this document the I-551.

Asylum status. See *Refugee and asylee,* below. Although the basis for eligibility is very similar, those applying for refugee status apply from outside the U.S., while potential asylees apply for asylum after having arrived in the United States (for example, on a tourist visa or after illegally crossing the U.S. border).

Attestation. Sworn statements that employers must make to the U.S. Department of Labor before they may petition to bring foreign workers to the U.S. on certain types of employment-based visas.

Beneficiary. If a relative or employer files a petition to start off your immigration process, you are a beneficiary. Almost all green cards as well as certain types of nonimmigrant visas require petitioners, and whenever there is a petitioner there is also a beneficiary. The word "beneficiary" comes from the fact that you benefit from the petition by becoming qualified to apply for a green card or visa.

Border Patrol. The informal name for an agency called Customs and Border Protection (CBP), which, like USCIS, is part of the Department of Homeland Security (DHS). Its primary functions include keeping the borders secure from illegal crossers and meeting legal entrants at airports and border posts to check their visas and to decide whether they should be allowed into the United States.

Citizen (U.S.). A person who owes allegiance to the U.S. government, is entitled to its protection, and enjoys the highest level of rights due to members of U.S. society. People become U.S. citizens through birth in the U.S. or its territories, through parents who are citizens, or through naturalization (after applying for citizenship and passing the exam). Citizens cannot have their status taken away except for certain extraordinary reasons.

Consular processing. The green card application process for immigrants whose final interview and visa decision will happen at a U.S. embassy or consulate in another country (outside the U.S.).

Consulate. An office of the U.S. Department of State located in a country other than the United States and affiliated with a U.S. embassy in that country's capital city. The consulate's responsibilities usually include processing visa applications.

Customs and Border Protection (CBP). See *Border Patrol*, above.

DACA. See *Deferred Action for Childhood Arrivals*, below.

DAPA. See *Deferred Action for Parental Accountability*, below.

Deferred action. A temporary status in which the U.S. government agrees to hold off placing a person in, or continuing with removal (deportation) proceedings or enforcement. May be accompanied by the right to apply for a work permit.

Deferred Action for Childhood Arrivals. Under an executive directive issued June 15, 2012, USCIS will consider (as a matter of discretion) granting deferred action status to foreign-born persons brought to the U.S. before the age of 16. (See Chapter 16.)

Deferred Action for Parental Accountability. A program created by Executive Order in late 2014, which would have allowed undocumented parents of a U.S. citizen or lawful permanent resident child of any age to apply for protection from deportation and a work permit, but was blocked after lawsuits.

Department of Homeland Security (DHS). A huge government agency created in 2003 to handle immigration and other security-related issues. Nearly all immigration-related departments and functions (including USCIS, CBP, and ICE) are under DHS control.

Department of Labor (DOL). A U.S. government agency involved with many types of job-related visas. It is the DOL that receives applications for labor certifications and decides whether or not there is a shortage of U.S. workers available to fill a particular position in a U.S. company.

Department of State (DOS). U.S. embassies and consulates are operated by this branch of the U.S. government. Generally, the DOS determines who is entitled to a visa or green card when the application is filed outside the U.S. at a U.S. embassy or consulate, while USCIS regulates immigration processing inside the United States.

Deportable. An immigrant who falls into one of the grounds listed at I.N.A. § 237, 8 U.S.C. § 1227, is said to be removable, or deportable. Such a person can be removed from the U.S., usually after a hearing in immigration court. Even a permanent resident can be removed or deported.

District office. A USCIS office in the U.S. that serves the public in a specific geographical area. District offices are where most USCIS field staff are located. They usually have an information desk, provide USCIS forms, and accept and make decisions on some types of applications for immigration benefits.

Diversity visa (the lottery). A green card lottery program held for persons born in certain countries. Every year (more or less), the Department of State determines which countries have sent the fewest number of immigrants to the U.S., relative to the size of the country's population. Persons from those countries are then permitted to apply. Lottery winners are selected at random from qualifying persons who register. To enter, you must meet certain minimum educational and other requirements.

EAD. See *Employment Authorization Document*, below.

Embassy. The chief U.S. consulate within a given country, usually located in a capital city. The embassy is where the ambassador stays. Most embassies handle applications for visas to the United States.

Employment Authorization Document (EAD). More commonly called a work permit, this is a card with a person's photo that indicates that he or she has the right to work in the United States. Green card holders no longer need to have an EAD.

Executive Office of Immigration Review (EOIR). See *Immigration Court,* below.

Expedited removal. The procedures by which officers at U.S. borders and ports of entry may decide that a person cannot enter the United States. (See I.N.A. § 235(b), 8 U.S.C. § 1225 (b).) The officer can refuse entry when he or she believes the person has used fraud or is carrying improper documents. People removed this way are barred from reentering the U.S. for five years.

Fraud interview. A specialized USCIS interview in which one or both members of an engaged or married couple are examined to see whether their marriage is real or just a sham to get the foreign-born person a green card.

Green card. Slang name for a Permanent Resident Card or I-551. The card is actually green in color.

This plastic photo identification card is given to individuals who successfully become U.S. legal permanent residents. It serves as a U.S. entry document, enabling permanent residents to return to the U.S.

after temporary absences. Unless you abandon your U.S. residence, commit certain types of crimes or immigration violations, or otherwise become deportable, your green card can never be taken away. Possession of a green card also allows you to work in the U.S. legally.

You can actually receive the green card only inside U.S. borders. If you apply for your green card outside the U.S., you will first be issued an immigrant visa. Only after you use that to enter the U.S. can you get a green card.

People who hold green cards for a certain length of time may apply to become U.S. citizens. Green cards have an expiration date of ten years from issuance. This does not mean that the permanent resident status itself expires, only that the resident must apply for a new card.

I-94. Formerly, a small green or white card given to all nonimmigrants when they enter the United States. (The green ones are given to people who enter on a visa waiver.) Now, however, an online database has replaced the cards for most types of entrants. The I-94 serves as evidence that a nonimmigrant has entered the country legally. The CBP officer enters a date indicating how long the nonimmigrant may stay for that particular trip. It is this date and not the expiration date of the visa that controls how long a nonimmigrant can remain in the United States. A nonimmigrant receives a new I-94 with a new date upon each legal U.S. entry. Canadian visitors are not normally issued I-94s.

Immediate relative. If you are an immediate relative of a U.S. citizen, you are eligible to receive a green card. The law does not limit the number of immediate relatives who may receive green cards. Here's who is an immediate relative:

- spouse of U.S. citizen. This also includes a widow or widower who applies for a green card within two years of the U.S. citizen spouse's death
- unmarried people under the age of 21 who have at least one U.S. citizen parent, and
- parents of U.S. citizens, if the U.S. citizen child is over the age of 21.

Immigrant. Though the general public usually calls any foreign-born newcomer to the United States an immigrant, the U.S. government prefers to think of immigrants as including only those people who have attained permanent residence or a green card. Nearly everyone else is called a nonimmigrant or alien, even if they are in the United States.

Immigrant visa. If you are approved for lawful permanent residence at a U.S. consulate or U.S. embassy, you will receive an immigrant visa. It enables you to enter the U.S., take up permanent residence, and receive a green card.

Immigration and Customs Enforcement (ICE). This agency of the Department of Homeland Security handles enforcement of the immigration laws within the U.S. borders.

Immigration and Naturalization Service (INS). The name of the former U.S. government agency that had primary responsibility for most immigration matters. In 2003, the INS was absorbed into the Department of Homeland Security.

Immigration Court. More formally known as the Executive Office for Immigration Review or EOIR, this is the first court that will hear your case if you're placed in immigration (removal) proceedings. Cases are heard by an immigration judge, who doesn't hear any other type of case. USCIS has its own crew of trial attorneys who represent the agency in court.

Inadmissible. Potential immigrants who are disqualified from obtaining visas or green cards because they are judged by the U.S. government to be in some way undesirable are called inadmissible (formerly, excludable). The grounds of inadmissibility are found at I.N.A. § 212, 8 U.S.C. § 1182. Green card holders who leave the U.S. for six months or more can also be found inadmissible upon attempting to return. Most people are found inadmissible because they have criminal records, have certain health problems, are thought to be subversives or terrorists, or are unable to support themselves financially. There are a few legal ways to overcome inadmissibility.

Labor certification. To get a green card through a job offer from a U.S. employer, the employer must first prove that there are no qualified U.S. workers available and willing to take the job. The U.S. agency to which the employer must prove this is the U.S. Department of Labor and the procedure for proving it is called labor certification.

Lawful permanent resident. See *Permanent resident,* below.

Lockbox. A USCIS facility that performs initial intake on applications submitted by mail, and then routes them to the appropriate USCIS service center or other office for further processing.

Lottery. See *Diversity visa,* above.

National Visa Center (NVC). Located in Portsmouth, New Hampshire, and run by a private company under contract with the DOS, the NVC receives approved green card petitions directly from USCIS or the DOS. In some cases, the NVC may hold onto these files for years, while the immigrant is on the waiting list for a visa. The NVC initiates the final green card application process by sending instructions to the applicant and forwarding the file to the appropriate U.S. consulate abroad.

Naturalization. When a foreign person takes legal action to become a U.S. citizen. Almost everyone who goes through naturalization must first have held a green card for several years before becoming eligible for U.S. citizenship. They must then submit an application and pass an exam. A naturalized U.S. citizen has almost all the same rights as a native-born U.S. citizen.

Nonimmigrant. A foreign-born person who comes to the U.S. temporarily for some particular purpose but does not remain permanently. There are many types of nonimmigrants. Students, temporary workers, and visitors are some of the most common.

Nonimmigrant visa. Nonimmigrants enter the U.S. by obtaining nonimmigrant visas. Each nonimmigrant visa comes with a different set of privileges, such as the right to work or study. In addition to a descriptive name, each type of nonimmigrant visa is identified by a letter of the alphabet and a number. Student visas, for example, are F-1, and treaty investors are E-2. Nonimmigrant visas also vary according to how long they enable you to stay in the United States. For example, on an investor visa, you can remain for many years, but on a visitor's visa, you can stay for only up to six months at a time.

Parole. This term has a special meaning in immigration law. It allows a person to enter the U.S. for humanitarian purposes, even when he or she does not meet the technical visa requirements. Those who are allowed to come to the U.S. without a visa in this manner are known as parolees.

Permanent resident. A non-U.S.-citizen who has been given permission to live permanently in the United States. If you acquire permanent residence, you will be issued a green card to prove it. The terms "permanent resident" and "green card holder" refer to exactly the same thing. As a permanent resident, you may travel as much as you like, but your place of residence must be the U.S.

Permanent Resident Card. A green card.

Petition. A petition is a formal request to USCIS that you be legally recognized as qualified for a green card or for some type of nonimmigrant visa. It is usually filed by an employer or a family member (on Form I-130 or on Form I-140) on behalf of an intending immigrant or visa applicant, to start off the application process. Paper proof that you do indeed qualify must always be submitted with the petition.

Petitioner. A U.S. person or business who makes the formal request that you be legally recognized as qualified for a green card or nonimmigrant visa. The petitioner must be your U.S. citizen relative, green card holder relative, or U.S. employer. A few categories of people may self-petition.

Preference categories. Certain groups of people who fall into categories known as "preferences" are eligible for green cards only as they become available year by year, subject to annual numerical limits. The preferences are broken into two broad groups: family preferences and employment preferences. The number of green cards available each year to the family preferences is around 480,000 and the number available in the employment preferences is 140,000. The categories are:

- **Family first preference.** Unmarried children (including divorced), any age, of U.S. citizens.
- **Family second preference. 2A:** Spouses and unmarried children under 21 years, of green card holders; and **2B:** unmarried sons and daughters (over 21 years) of green card holders.
- **Family third preference.** Married children, any age, of U.S. citizens.
- **Family fourth preference.** Brothers and sisters of U.S. citizens where the U.S. citizen is at least 21 years old.
- **Employment first preference.** Priority workers, including persons of extraordinary ability, outstanding professors and researchers, and multinational executives and managers.
- **Employment second preference.** Persons with advanced degrees and persons of exceptional ability coming to the U.S. to accept jobs with U.S. employers for which U.S. workers are in short supply or where it would serve the national interest.
- **Employment third preference.** Skilled and unskilled workers coming to the U.S. to accept jobs with U.S. employers for which U.S. workers are in short supply.
- **Employment fourth preference.** Religious workers and various miscellaneous categories.
- **Employment fifth preference.** Individual investors willing to invest $1,000,000 in a U.S. business (or $500,000 if the business is in an economically depressed area).

Preference relatives. A foreign relative of a U.S. citizen or green card holder as defined in the preference categories listed above.

Priority Date. If you are applying for a green card in a preference category through family or an employer, only a limited number of green cards are issued each year. You must wait your turn behind others who filed before you. The date on which you first entered the immigration application process is called the Priority Date, and marks your place in the waiting line. Each month, the U.S. Department of State makes green cards available to certain Priority Dates. You can get a green card only when your date or a later one comes up on the DOS list.

Public charge. Term used in immigration law for an immigrant who has insufficient financial resources or goes on welfare or other means-based government assistance. Immigrants who are likely to become public charges are inadmissible.

Qualifying relative. Any person whose familial relationship to a U.S. citizen or green card holder is legally close enough to qualify that person for a green card or another immigrant benefit, such as a waiver.

Refugee and asylee. Persons allowed to live in the U.S. indefinitely, to protect them from persecution in their home countries. Refugees receive their status before coming to the U.S., while asylees apply for their status after arriving in the U.S. by some other means. Both may eventually apply for green cards.

Removal proceeding. Formerly "deportation," carried on before an immigration judge to decide whether or not an immigrant will be allowed to enter or remain in the country. While, generally speaking, a person cannot be expelled without first going through a removal hearing, someone arriving at the border or a port of entry can be forced to leave without a hearing or ever seeing a judge. An immigrant who is found removable can be deported or forced to leave the United States.

Service Center. A USCIS office responsible for accepting and making decisions on particular applications from people in specified geographic areas. Unlike USCIS district offices, the service centers are not open to the public.

Special immigrant. Laws are occasionally passed directing that green cards be given to special groups of people. When it comes to visa allocation, special immigrants are considered a subcategory of employment-based visas, and receive 7.1% of the yearly allotment of 140,000 such visas. Common categories of special immigrants are workers for recognized religions, former U.S. government workers, and children dependent on the protection of a juvenile court.

Sponsor. For immigration purposes, usually means a petitioner. See *Petitioner*, above.

Status. The name of the group of privileges you are given when you receive immigration benefits, either as a permanent resident or a nonimmigrant. Nonimmigrant statuses have exactly the same names and privileges as the corresponding nonimmigrant visas. A green card holder has the status of permanent resident. Visas and green cards are things you can see. A status is not.

Temporary Protected Status (TPS). A temporary status for persons already in the U.S. who came from certain countries experiencing conditions of war or natural disaster. TPS allows someone to live and work in the U.S. for a specific time period, but it does not lead to a green card.

U.S. consulates. See *Consulate*, above.

U.S. embassies. See *Embassy*, above.

Visa. A stamp placed in your passport by a U.S. consulate or embassy. All visas serve as U.S. entry documents. Visas can be designated as either immigrant or nonimmigrant. Immigrant visas are issued to people who will live in the U.S. permanently and get green cards. Everyone else gets nonimmigrant visas. Except for a few types of visa renewals, visas cannot be issued inside U.S. borders, and so you must be outside the U.S. to get a visa.

Visa Waiver Program. Nationals from certain countries may come to the U.S. without visas as tourists for 90 days under what is known as the Visa Waiver Program. They are not permitted to extend their stays or change their statuses, with very limited exceptions.

Work permit. See *Employment Authorization Document*, above.

Index